HARVEY KURTZMAN:
THE MAN WHO CREATED *MAD*
AND REVOLUTIONIZED
HUMOR IN AMERICA

A BIOGRAPHY BY
BILL SCHELLY

Fantagraphics Books
7563 Lake City Way NE
Seattle, Washington 98115

Executive Editor: Gary Groth
Editor: Kristy Valenti
Editorial assistance: RJ Casey, Daniel Germain,
Daniel Johnson, Kim Rost Bridges
Designer: Keeli McCarthy
Production: Preston White
Associate Publisher: Eric Reynolds
Publisher: Gary Groth

Special thanks to the Kurtzman family, who permitted the use of
several images in this book.

To receive a catalog of comics, graphic novels, prose novels, and other fine
works of artistry, call 1-800-657-1100, or visit www.fantagraphics.com.
You may order books at our website or by phone.

ISBN: 978-1-60699-761-1

Library of Congress Control Number: 2014954774

First Fantagraphics printing: May 2015

Printed in Singapore

Front jacket photo: Kurtzman at the Playboy offices (1976), courtesy
of E. B. Boatner. Back jacket photo: from *Help!* #9 (April 1961).
Back flap: author photo courtesy of Adam Haney.

Endpapers: "Superduperman" and "Bat Boy and Rubin" were
written by Harvey Kurtzman and drawn by Wallace Wood; they ran
in *Mad* #4 (April–May 1953) and *Mad* #8 (December 1953–January
1954) respectively.

HARVEY KURTZMAN

THE MAN WHO CREATED

MAD

AND REVOLUTIONIZED

HUMOR

IN AMERICA

A BIOGRAPHY BY BILL SCHELLY

FANTAGRAPHICS

DEDICATION
To my daughter Tara

CONTENTS

FOREWORD
BY TERRY GILLIAM

In the beginning was the word
And the word was *Mad*
And Harvey Kurtzman was God
(or so it seemed to many of my generation).

He gave us the eyes to see the world anew, to relish all of its absurdities. He provided us with ammunition to attack and laugh at the system, at dumb authority, at fools. He taught us to recognize *Humbug* when it arose and, hopefully, *Trump* it with satire.

We worshipped Harvey.

He offered *Help!* to many, but he gave me a job. I was in heaven! I was his assistant!

Harvey was probably the most important teacher in my life and one of the most vital cultural forces in the second half of the twentieth century, yet most people have never heard of him. I think a part of Harvey would appreciate the irony. For such a seminal force, he was surprisingly humble and generous and small . . . a kind of unsung Mother Theresa for American comics artists, comedians, goofballs, outsiders, brainiacs and troublemakers. He inspired and nurtured so many who subsequently became successful and well known. His work still reverberates in those of us who were infected and we've passed it on . . . It's dangerously communicable. If you plot its flow you can argue that Harvey's influence was the hidden epidemic that changed much of our society for the better. Hopefully, science won't find a cure for it.

Kurtzman in 1973. Courtesy of Ben Asen.

"Truth is beautiful. What is false offends."
                    —*Harvey Kurtzman (1977)*

AUTHOR'S PREFACE

HARVEY KURTZMAN'S CREATION of *Mad*, in 1952, overshadows all of the other stellar accomplishments in his remarkable fifty-year career in the popular arts. His work as the editor, artist, designer and writer behind *Mad*, first as a comic book and then as a magazine, set the pattern for one of the greatest publishing success stories of the century.

Time magazine's Richard Corliss wrote, "Dreaming up and writing *Mad*, [Harvey] Kurtzman virtually invented what would become the era's dominant tone of irreverent self-reference: one form of pop culture mocking all other forms, and itself." In the *New Yorker*, Adam Gopnik stated, "Almost all American satire today follows a formula that Harvey Kurtzman thought up."

In the early 1950s, Holden Caulfield railed against the "phonies" of the world in *The Catcher in the Rye*. *Mad* exposed them. It questioned the status quo at a time of social conformity, creating a mindset that grew into what came to be called the "counterculture." Cartoonist and historian R. C. Harvey wrote, "Through all the years of *Mad*, Kurtzman's influence on the American public was incalculable. Who can say whether the Vietnam War protest among American youth was not in some way inspired by the satire in *Mad* . . .?"

Mad is a household name, yet the name of the man who invented it is known by relatively few, mainly those who study cartoons and comic books. That's because Harvey Kurtzman seldom blew his own horn, and after he left the magazine, the publishers of *Mad* omitted his name from reprints in those best-selling paperback books. In 1988, most of the students in Kurtzman's "Satirical Cartooning" class at New York's School of the Visual Arts didn't know that their soft-spoken instructor was a giant of American humor. At least, not until Art Spiegelman guest-lectured the class one day.

Harvey Kurtzman (1987): courtesy of Ben Asen Photography.

Kurtzman's original artwork for the cover of Glenn Bray's *Illustrated Harvey Kurtzman Index* (1976): courtesy of Glenn Bray. © the Harvey Kurtzman Estate.

The creator of the Pulitzer Prize-winning graphic novel *Maus* decided to enlighten them. Instead of bringing slides of his own projects to the class, he brought slides of Kurtzman's work over the years. Spiegelman later explained, "Seeing Harvey Kurtzman's work when I was a kid was what made me want to be a cartoonist in the first place. Harvey Kurtzman has been the single most significant influence on a couple of generations of comics artists."

By the end of Spiegelman's presentation, the students saw their teacher in a whole new light. They learned that not only had Kurtzman created *Mad*, he'd also created *Two-Fisted Tales* and *Frontline Combat*, two innovative, brilliant war comic books for the same publisher, EC Comics. They also found out that he edited three more humor magazines after leaving *Mad*: *Trump*, *Humbug* and *Help!*, and created *Little Annie Fanny*, the first fully painted comic strip, for *Playboy*.

Harvey Kurtzman—with the help of a handful of key colleagues—showed that comic book stories could be Art with a capital *a*. Newspaper comic strips had always garnered a modicum of respect, but comic books were disdained until this New York native showed otherwise. He elevated the medium, beginning a process of legitimization that's now, sixty-five years later, virtually complete. In an era when graphic novels win Pulitzer Prizes and reading comics is not only accepted but actually hip, we shouldn't forget the person who had the vision to get the ball rolling. Arthur Schopenhauer wrote, "Talent hits a target that no one else can hit; genius hits a target no one else can see."

Unquestionably, an artist of the brilliance and cultural consequence of Harvey Kurtzman deserves a full-bodied biography. Major figures in American popular culture such as D. W. Griffith, Walt Disney and Charles Schulz have all had more than one book written about their lives and careers. Why not Kurtzman? Science fiction (SF) and fantasy scribe Lin Carter once said (I'm paraphrasing) that he wrote the kind of books he most liked to read. As a longtime Kurtzman fan, I wanted an in-depth biography of the man and his work. That's why I wrote this book.

A fair amount has been written about Harvey Kurtzman, including the tragic dimensions of his later life, but it's scattered through hundreds of magazines and books, often in support of reprints of his work. What was needed was a single book that did Kurtzman justice by telling his story factually and completely. When I embarked on this endeavor four years ago, I knew one thing for certain: it had to do more than stitch together known facts and interview material. What was called for was a "back to square one" approach, requiring fresh interviews with Kurtzman's remaining colleagues, family and friends, and consulting archival documents and other resources that hadn't yet been plumbed. The subsequent journey of discovery far surpassed my expectations.

In this book's Acknowledgments, I thank the scores of people who helped make it possible. At the top of the list is the Kurtzman family—Adele, Meredith, Liz, Nellie and Adam—who generously gave their time and patiently answered all my questions. Kurtzman's colleagues Hugh Hefner, James Warren, Russ Heath, Al Feldstein, Jack Davis, Arnold Roth, Al Jaffee and Robert Crumb gave frank, revealing interviews—often conveying previously unknown facts and perspectives. Equally vital was the help of Denis Kitchen and John Benson, who opened up Kurtzman's archival papers, which included his correspondence to and from William M. Gaines, Hugh Hefner, Ian Ballantine, Harold Hayes, Stan Freberg and many others. (Kurtzman kept carbon copies of many of his outgoing letters.) Perhaps most important of all, I was allowed to quote freely from several previously unpublished interviews with the man himself. Therefore, it can accurately be said that Harvey Kurtzman speaks anew in these pages.

Was I really able to discover the complete truth about the origin of *Mad* and why Kurtzman left it so soon after its conversion from comic book to magazine? I believe I have, not only in terms of bringing every bit of known informa-

Kurtzman's idiosyncratic signature appeared on most of his self-drawn covers for *Mad*. He used it for the rest of his life.

tion to bear, but by introducing newfound facts, including heretofore unpublished statements by Kurtzman from his private correspondence, and taking into account a major revelation from Hugh Hefner from my recent interview. I don't mean to suggest these discoveries are earthshattering or terribly provocative. Some of them are, however, quite surprising.

I also discovered that Harvey Kurtzman is not an easy person to understand, in part because he was a man of many contradictions. He was a sublime humorist in print who wasn't a comedian in person. He was an iconoclast who sought the Establishment symbols of success. He was an intensely private man who gave many interviews. He was a man of great sensitivity who could be callous to others. He was a writer-artist with both a towering confidence and a deep insecurity about his work. Kurtzman never reconciled his contradictions. Indeed, they are one of the reasons why his life story is so fascinating.

—Bill Schelly
   Seattle, 2014

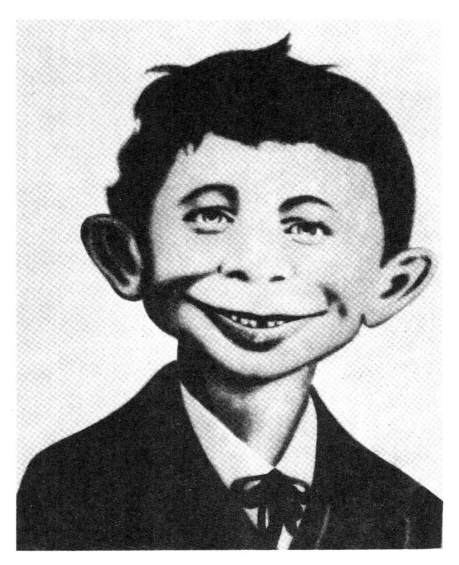

"What--me worry?"

Alfred E. Neuman as he appeared in *Mad* #27 (1956).

PART ONE:

CARTOONIST

"When I should have been doing other useful things like homework, I was cartooning. I had the call at a very early age."[1]

—*Harvey Kurtzman*

1.

A COMMUNITY IN CHALK

THE IMMENSE, CASTLE-LIKE building dwarfed the boy who stood before it. An activist government had dedicated the special school in the imposing structure to his artistic development. America's promise of opportunity through education was about to be fulfilled for young Harvey Kurtzman.

In the autumn of 1937, as the United States struggled to surmount the effects of the Great Depression, the New Deal embraced government sponsorship of the arts. The Works Progress Administration (WPA) employed artists to create murals and sculptures in public settings. Art was seen as a way to uplift the nation's morale. The City of New York showed its concurrence by subsidizing a public high school for talented young artists and musicians from its five boroughs, regardless of their economic, ethnic or racial status.

Both the boy and the building were twelve years old. Architect William H. Gompert chose the Gothic Revival style, inspiring the building's nickname, "the Castle on the Hill," although the structure Harvey approached for the first time that fall was properly known as the High School of Music and Art. He was determined to make the most of this grand opportunity.

SUCH AN OPPORTUNITY would not have been available to Harvey Kurtzman if his parents had stayed in Ukraine, in Odessa, where they grew up. Since the Russian Revolution, the once-vibrant Jewish culture in the city had been decimated. By 1937, its educational system had disappeared, and unemployment was at record highs. The city's Jewish populace had always received more than its fair share of hard knocks.

David Kurtzman, date unknown, and Edith Sherman, ca. 1914. All family photographs in this chapter are courtesy of Adam Kurtzman.

At the turn of the century, Odessa was a bustling tourist city on the north coast of the Black Sea. The fourth largest urban center in Ukraine had a rich cultural heritage, influenced by Greece, France, Turkey, Russia and various Asian countries. The climate was mild, and the beaches were sandy rather than pebbled. Jews had lived in Odessa and contributed to its culture since the eighth century. In 1920, they made up about 35 percent of the city's population.

Despite their numbers, and the fact that they were often better off and more literate than their rural brethren, the Jews of Odessa suffered for decades under the May Laws enacted by Alexander III of Russia, which imposed strict limits on the number of Jews permitted to obtain educations and enter certain professions. Periodic pogroms and other forms of anti-Semitism had caused more than two million Jews to flee Russia from 1880 to 1920. After the czar was deposed, and Ukraine became a founding member of the Soviet Union, Jews continued to flee. Most of them chose the United States as their destination. America offered a better life, including full citizenship.

David Kurtzman, Harvey's father, was one of those Jewish émigrés from Odessa who came to America after World War I. He was a slender, bespectacled man who was a jeweler by trade. Nothing is known of his family background except that he had no relatives waiting for him. He arrived in New York alone, but would soon be joined by his wife-to-be.[1]

David's fiancée was a petite brunette with an oval face named Edith Sherman. In later life, Edith seldom spoke of her early years except to say that her family was more prosperous than most. Of her numerous brothers and sisters, she was the only one to emigrate. The city was bombarded by the Turkish fleet and was occupied by the French and the Red Army after the Bolshevik Revolution. It was against this turbulent backdrop that David and Edith decided to seek a brighter future in America.

In later years, Edith told of "a desperate journey" involving a tense escape from the Soviet Union. "I was very brave," she said, describing how she hid under a truckload of hay, clutching the family candlesticks in her arms. This tale and the lovely jeweled pin that spelled her name (made by David) suggested that he was her great love, perhaps an unsanctioned one, given the risks she courted to be with him. Her fiancé was the only one waiting for Edith when she stepped off the boat from Ellis Island. The lovers were reunited and then joined in the eyes of the law in a civil ceremony, for neither were observant Jews. At first, their finances were such that they slept on the floor of their apartment. David and Edith were not, however, lovesick kids. A photograph of the two of them in each other's arms in front of a Brooklyn tenement, his thinning hair caught in the breeze and her thickening stomach giving evidence of pregnancy, was taken when he was about thirty years old and she was twenty-six.[2]

The Kurtzmans' first child, Zachary ("Zack"), was born on April 8, 1923. David made Edith a ring with a tiny diamond to mark the occasion. Their second son, Harvey, entered the world on October 3, 1924. The Kurtzmans lived in a tenement apartment at

David and Edith Kurtzman in Brooklyn, New York.

428 E. Ninety-Eighth St. in Brooklyn.³ David plied his trade, and for a time, all was well.

Then came heartbreak. On November 29, 1928, David Kurtzman died of a bleeding ulcer, which burst his stomach. He had become a Christian Scientist, which led him to believe that he could cure his illness with prayer. (It wasn't uncommon for Jews to become Christian Scientists at the time.) The secular Jewish man who Edith Sherman came to America to marry had "gotten religion" and, as at least a partial result, left her a widow. His remains were interred in Mount Lebanon Cemetery in Queens. She wore the pin that spelled her name for the rest of her life.

Edith Kurtzman found herself with two young children and no means of support. She had no relatives to ask for help. In desperation, she put her six- and four-year-old sons in an orphanage. Edith later claimed that she had no alternative. The family of three may have been homeless. In any case, it was only a temporary measure, while she found some form of livelihood.

Edith Kurtzman's decision likely had long-term emotional consequences for her sons, especially Harvey. He was the younger and more sensitive of the two. Four years old is too young to understand any reason for such abandonment, even if assured of its temporary nature. That kind of emotional trauma can affect a child's psyche: it can cause the child to develop poor self-esteem; or have difficulty expressing emotions because of an inability to trust; or to blame oneself. Perhaps it lurked somewhere behind Kurtzman's mild-but-suggestive statement years later, "I was always worried as a kid."⁴

The boys were in the orphanage for two or three months, and their care wasn't good. Edith later told relatives that she was upset when she saw how they were treated, and removed Zachary and Harvey from the place post haste. "It was horrible. The conditions were terrible," was how she described it years later, without providing specifics.⁵ By the time she made this discovery, she had secured employment as a milliner.

Edith's second husband was the man Harvey Kurtzman would con-

Abraham Perkes, ca. 1920.

Zachary and Harvey Kurtzman, ca. 1929.

sider his father. Abraham "Abe" Perkes was a Russian-Jewish immigrant two years Edith's senior.[6] He served in the US military in the World War. His official military photo shows a good-looking man with a cleft chin and wavy hair. Abraham Perkes was taller and more physically robust than David Kurtzman. He had been married before to the daughter of a Southern Baptist preacher, and, with the dissolution of that unlikely union, wanted to marry again. He had been acquainted with the Kurtzmans. Not long after Edith mourned the death of her first husband, she accepted Abraham's proposal of marriage.

Abraham Perkes worked as a brass engraver, a printing trade that had a certain creative component, and made a modest living. "Dad [was] part of the printing trades union," Kurtzman recounted.[7] "Mostly he made labels for jam and jelly jars, and he would engrave letters and designs onto the brass. The engraved plate would then be used to stamp impressions on gilt paper."[8] He was a kind, outgoing, affectionate man who was, in many ways, a good father to the boys. Edith took her husband's surname; the boys did not. The Perkes-Kurtzman family settled in an area of Brooklyn notable for its immigrant population: near Brownsville, the epicenter of the Jewish ghetto.

"I lived in kind of a strange neighborhood," Kurtzman said. "There was a lot of construction going on all around. Even though it was part of the city, and lots of buildings were being put up, it still had a country feeling to it."[9] They lived in the vicinity of Winthrop Street and East Ninety-Second Street. Some of Kurtzman's later memories of that neighborhood had a dreamlike quality. "One morning, when I walked out of my house to go to school, I saw a goat right in the middle of the street. It belonged to a group of people who lived in makeshift houses down at the far end of the block. I loved growing up in Brooklyn. It was like a big playground, filled with surprises."[10]

One of his earliest memories was going to the beach at Coney Island with his mother, and ending up in the ladies' steam room: "I didn't want to go with her but I . . . was too young to leave my mother's side, and she really wanted a steam bath. So there I was, surrounded by a group of big, flabby ladies wrapped in large white towels. Every now and then one would look down at me and smile, or say something that I didn't understand, and laugh."[11] Kurtzman's other pre-school experiences faded, but this Felliniesque image stayed with him.

Despite bad economic times, the family escaped real poverty. Abraham Perkes was a forceful, confident man who was an able provider for his new, ready-made family. "We weren't 'dirt poor,' but we never had all the things that we wanted," Kurtzman said. "I appreciated a buck. I was aware of the fact that making a living was hard work. Coming to terms with the world was not easy for me, which was why I drew."[12]

Kurtzman's shyness led him to begin expressing himself in cartoons rather than speech. As he learned to read and write, and gained a bit of awareness of the world around him, he was already a budding artist. "I had the call at a very early age," he remembered.[13] "Early as I could hold a pencil, I've always been cartooning."[14]

Even in kindergarten, his favorite period was art class, but not always because he was eager to draw. "The teacher would pass out art materials, and this always included a little dab of sweet-smelling, white library paste. Was it ever delicious! I can't remember what I drew, but I have fond memories of eating that paste."[15]

In grade school, Kurtzman entered poster contests and won some of them. They were things like "Healthy Teeth Are Happy Teeth." Some of the posters were cutouts, drawn in crayon, and some were on oak tag boards. The winning posters were usually pinned up in the halls around the school building. "I loved having my work up. It was the way I got attention and popularity. It was how I became visible."[16] His work in art class stood out more than his scores in other subjects. He later admitted, "When I should have been doing other useful things like homework, I was cartooning."[17]

NEWSPAPER COMIC STRIPS were wildly popular during Kurtzman's formative years. This was especially so with the immigrant population, whose grasp of the English language was often limited, but virtually everyone read them. In the 1930s, a new form developed: the adventure strip. In addition to the funny comics, Kurtzman thrilled to the adventures of the *Phantom, Dick Tracy, Buck Rogers, Flash Gordon, Jungle Jim, Tarzan,*

Mandrake the Magician, Terry and the Pirates and other "straight" story strips. He sometimes said, "I had no favorites in the sense that I loved 'em all. I had no single preference."[18] Other times, Kurtzman seemed to contradict this.

> My favorite days of the week were Sunday and Monday. On Sundays, my father got a newspaper called the *Telegram*. It had a full-color comics section, which I read from cover to cover. But it didn't have my favorite strips. Those I got to see on Monday morning, by doing a little trash collecting.
>
> Our neighbors read different Sunday papers. Each of these had a different selection of comics. So on Monday mornings, before the garbage trucks arrived, I'd go searching through the neighbors' garbage cans for the Sunday color comics I hadn't seen. I got to read all of my favorite strips, like *Tarzan*, Popeye [in *Thimble Theatre*] and *Dick Tracy . . .* And they were free.[19]

Kurtzman closely followed the announcements for a new strip called *Alley Oop*, by Vincent (V. T.) Hamlin. Alley Oop turned out to be a caveman, and Kurtzman became captivated by the prehistoric world where the hero anachronistically lived alongside dinosaurs. He would later cite it as a feature that particularly stimulated his imagination and inspired him to try his hand at his own strips. *Alley Oop* made its debut on December 5, 1932, when Kurtzman was eight years old. About that time, Edith devoted considerable time and energy getting Harvey into special art lessons. "My mother was always very supportive of my cartooning," he said. "I must give her credit."[20] On weekends, she packed him off to children's classes, some at the Pratt Institute and others at the Brooklyn Museum. Abraham appreciated art, and took the boys to museums to see painting and sculpture exhibitions.

Kurtzman was considered precocious enough to skip a year in grade school. It was an honor, but it came with a downside: he would always be the youngest and often the smallest boy in his class, for he was small for his age. Fortunately, the quiet boy's drawings spoke for him. His classmates laughed at his cartoons when they were passed around behind the teacher's back or on the playground. He had an identity. He was "the kid who drew funny stuff."

ABRAHAM PERKES WAS A COMMUNIST. Being Russian born, he may have felt a certain kinship with the working men who made the Russian revolution of 1919 possible. Though he appreciated American democracy, he was also aware of the negative aspects of the Capitalist system. Al Smith and the reformers in New York had made headway against the appalling labor conditions in the city, and unions had become a force for workers' rights, but the Depression was taking its greatest toll on the working class. Socialist and Communist remedies were openly espoused. There was great anger among the Jewish immigrant populace: many of them came to America for economic opportunity and were now out of work.

Kurtzman later spoke of his parents' political views. "They were politically left, took the *Daily Worker* newspaper and belonged to the International Workers Order. We were raised with a radical bent as regards things like race and labor unions."[21]

Edith claimed the Communist newspaper gave her a special perspective on the way news was reported in the mainstream American press. She had a native intelligence and always maintained that she could "read between the lines and get at the truth," detecting distortions and lies in the papers published by William Randolph Hearst and Joseph Pulitzer.[22] Harvey picked up his mother's propensity for looking "between the lines," and would use such observations as the basis for cartoons. This capacity for observing the disconnect between the stated and the real, learned from Edith, became an essential element in his later success as a satirist.

Jules Feiffer, cartoonist and contemporary of Kurtzman, observed, "A lot of what [the *Daily Worker*] said about the society was true, in terms of inequality, because they were in the forefront in terms of union organizing. And unions weren't corrupt in those days, and they were needed, and some of the most effective unions were Communist-led. The *Daily Worker* was about the first paper to ever suggest that Jackie Robinson should be on the Brooklyn Dodgers, and started that campaign about a year or two before anyone else was in on it. So, there were clear things that they did that were apt and accurate and appropriate."[23]

Kurtzman absorbed little of his parent's politics, and, in later years, would never become a Communist or Socialist. From a political standpoint, the main things he took from them were anti-rascist convictions and identification with the worker rather than management.

Abraham Perkes, like Edith, was a secular Jew. Kurtzman's parents occasionally spoke Yiddish, but the family didn't go to synagogue or temple on *Shabbos*, or eat kosher, or study the Talmud or observe the Jewish holidays. Abraham and Edith identified with the large mass of Jews who wanted to assimilate and who considered themselves Americans first. Whether by inculcation or his own sensibility, Kurtzman adopted this

view. "Like a lot of people my age, I didn't want to be identified with a minority group. I didn't want to go to *shul*, not to religious weddings or *bar
mitzvahs*."²⁴ By mutual consent or tacit assumption, none of the Kurtzman
brothers—who grew to a trio when the final sibling, half brother Daniel
"Danny" Perkes, was born February 17, 1931—became a bar mitzvah.

By the time Harvey turned ten years old, in the fall of 1934, his family
had outgrown its Brooklyn abode. His parents decided they had sufficient
wherewithal to leave Brooklyn for a more desirable area: the Bronx.²⁵ The
northernmost of the five boroughs of New York City had become a place
for new Americans who aspired to a middle-class life. It wasn't an urban
ghetto, a place for huddled masses, but a place for those who could claim
some sort of foothold on the American Dream. Though mainly a bedroom
community for the bustling center of commerce to the south, it had its
own central stroll of consumerism self-consciously named the Grand
Concourse.

The Perkes-Kurtzman family moved to 2166 Clinton Ave. in east
Tremont: a mainly Sicilian, Italian and Irish neighborhood, with Jews a
growing minority. Five- and six-story apartment buildings were the norm.
The Clinton Arms was a giant six-story apartment house with a courtyard in the center, two blocks east of the Bronx Zoo. Tenants in the interior apartments could watch the residents living in opposite units, as
in Alfred Hitchcock's *Rear Window*. Entry to the tan brick building was
through that courtyard, accessed by a breezeway from the street. It was
Kurtzman's home all through his teenage years.

Tremont, though in the "better" West Bronx, could still be a tough
neighborhood. Kurtzman learned to look out for trouble and avoid the bul-
lies on the walk to and from school. His status as an artist might impress
his teachers and schoolmates, but it wouldn't cut much ice if he ran afoul
of a gang of Sicilian toughs.

Kurtzman always considered himself a natural-born cartoonist.
"Artistic talent is genetic and you have it or you don't have it," he said
in later interviews.²⁶ He also believed that some brains were "wired" to
be picture-oriented, which went hand in hand with talent in the visual
arts.²⁷ Zachary also showed signs of artistic talent. The two of them competed with each other for a few years, but the older boy's work lacked the
spark that made Harvey's cartoons special. Zachary's real aptitude was in
math and science.

Kurtzman liked and admired his father (he never thought of Abraham
Perkes as a stepfather) and enjoyed watching him work. Like Edith,
Abraham was supportive. "Everybody encouraged me to become a pro-

fessional [cartoonist]," Kurtzman said.[28] No one, whether in his family, friends or schoolmates, was anything but positive about his cartoons. When he visited Abraham's print shop, his father gave him drawing problems to solve. "I don't think I actually finished more than one or two projects for him," Kurtzman said, "but I did love being asked to help."[29] It gave him his first taste of what it meant to be a professional artist. Abraham's occupation, with its creative quotient, further encouraged the notion of making a living as an artist.

At twelve, Kurtzman was already dreaming of such a career in the world outside Tremont: "When I was in junior high, I wanted to work for Walt Disney immediately." He sent for a job application, and received a drawing test by return mail. "I did these terrible drawings of Mickey Mouse which weren't acceptable. I'd send things to [Disney] which were dumb as hell. You know, your first efforts in trying to be professional at anything. You do all the obvious, wrong things. But then there were the times that I wouldn't be trying, and I'd make fun of . . . oh, some friends, or some controversial issue at school, and all of a sudden, boom!, I'd be doing very well. And that was my satirical stuff."[30]

One day, Kurtzman stumbled across some college humor magazines, along the lines of the *Yale Record* and the *Harvard Lampoon*. "I found them on a trash heap, or in somebody's cellar. They were the funniest things that I had ever seen. It was a major consciousness-raising moment where suddenly I became aware of a certain approach to humor. It was that quality of parody and satire that was so unique, and if I can point at any influence in my work, it was the random college magazines that I ran across. I think there were specifically one or two magazines—I forget the stories that I read—but they influenced me enormously."[31]

Kurtzman realized that a gift for satire was separate from the ability to create funny one-panel gag cartoons, the kind that appeared in the *New Yorker* and most other classy, slick magazines. He filled a whole notebook

Smokey Stover by Bill Holman was one of Harvey Kurtzman's favorite newspaper comics: this is the January 24, 1939 strip.

with them, but they didn't elicit the hoped-for laughs. "I was never very good at them. One [was] a picture of a guy on the ledge of a tall building. He's getting ready to commit suicide by jumping off. A cop is running across the rooftop toward the guy, waving his gun and yelling, 'Stop or I'll shoot!' It didn't get a laugh from anybody but me."[32]

Kurtzman's taste in humorous cartoons was all-inclusive, and he had a soft spot for what he called "dumb" humor. He became a fan of a Sunday newspaper strip that made its debut at roughly the same time as his family's Bronx relocation: Bill Holman's *Smokey Stover*.

> I remember Zack and I, sprawled on the Oriental rug in the living room, hashing over the comics section of the Sunday papers. Not that I could normally stand sharing the funnies. I would "hie" me away to a private place where I could peruse the gaudy sheets of newsprint without distraction or interruption. But the Holman feature inspired a rare camaraderie, you see, to experience the *full* pleasure of discovering the joke and then, the added pleasure of hearing brother Zack chortling at the same discovery.[33]

The Kurtzman brothers couldn't get enough of the adventures of Holman's wacky fireman, brimming with nonsense words and outrageous puns. "I remember reading the signs in . . . *Smokey Stover* . . . that said either 'notary sojac' or simply 'Foo.' As children, my brother Zack and I would faint with joy every time we saw 'Foo.'"[34] The strip, which also added a daily iteration three years later, had a marked influence on a certain humor magazine that he produced as an adult.

The recurring fact of his preadolescent years was that Kurtzman found his place in the schoolyard and his neighborhood by virtue of his art ability. "I was always the neighborhood cartoonist-clown. I used to do comic strips on the street in the Bronx . . . draw with chalk on the street. I had this community in chalk. Every day the kids would come around to see what was the latest. That was my first comic strip, called 'Ikey and Mikey.'"[35]

Kurtzman used either chalk or bits of plaster taken from local construction sites, which was just as good. "I knew I could get respect and attention with my street drawings. I would draw every afternoon after school. And the kids became interested in it."[36]

Ephemeral though the chalk drawings were, he was proud of them. "The cars would drive over the chalk and pick it up and then reprint it all the way down the street. By the next morning it would be gone, washed

Rube Goldberg's *Mike & Ike (They Look Alike)* ran in *Comic Monthly* Vol.1 #2 (February 1922).

away by a sanitation truck or by rain. Then all the kids would ask me what Ikey and Mikey were going to do next. Even the grown-ups on the block would ask, so I knew it was good. And that was my first comic strip."[37] Later he liked to say he got his start "in the gutter."[38]

No record exists of Kurtzman's "Ikey and Mikey," and no one in later years thought to ask him to draw what he remembered of it. He did later say it consisted of four panels an episode, like daily newspaper comic strips. The name was probably inspired by a comic strip by Rube Goldberg, *Mike and Ike (They Look Alike)*, featuring identical twin characters. It began in the *San Francisco Bulletin* on September 29, 1907. Though the strip's original Sunday formatted strips didn't last, comics historian Don Markstein wrote, "The concept hung around. For years afterward, Goldberg often slipped Mike and Ike panels, in which they played straight man and gag man, onto the ends of his daily comics, keeping them in the public eye. They were well enough known to have starred in the second issue of *Comic Monthly* (February 1922) a short-lived magazine that reprinted various King Features offerings."[39]

Alternatively, it's possible Kurtzman was inspired by the *Mike & Ike* comedy shorts which were on the bill of Saturday movie matinees. The comical antics of a Catholic and a Jewish man together would have played well to Kurtzman's audience.

Zachary Kurtzman was an extroverted, cocky youth. Harvey was reserved and non-athletic. "He was always drawing, always cartooning, and for me it was natural to see him doing it," Zachary recalled. Though he could be nasty to Harvey, he admired his younger brother's talent. "You could see that this guy was destined to become the top-notch humorist that he was. He was as stiff as a board as a person. He could hardly put two words together. I used to taunt him mercilessly with my glib pokes. And one day as I was practicing my art on his tender ears, he got behind me when I was sitting down and threw a handful of knuckles in my face. I said, 'What'd you do that for?' He said, 'Well, I can't say it, but this says it for me!'"[40] Zachary may have exaggerated when he related this anecdote, but its essence rings true.

Kurtzman spent a lot of time in the streets, talking baseball and playing marbles, but was hopeless at such typical street games as stickball. "I had bad reflexes and could hardly hit the ball. However, I did become a part of the game, and the gang, by keeping score. I'd use a piece of chalk and draw these beautiful, elaborate scoreboards on the street. The kids loved them."[41]

Kurtzman had plenty of curly hair and a complete lack of muscle. He recalled, "I was like two different people. One was the physical me—a wimpy kind of kid. But when I drew, I became a powerhouse."[42]

"Eat, skeleton!" his mother exhorted when she put a plate of food before him. Edith was a marvelous cook, much of it classic Ashkenazi Jewish cuisine: rugelach, babka, kasha varnishkas and kishkes. But, no matter how much the boy ate, he never put on weight.

Edith was never satisfied, never happy. Kurtzman described her as "just a nightmare of a nudge."[43] But she had another side. Edith went to night school. No job came of it, but she had a desire for self-improvement and aspired to a higher social standing.

Kurtzman might have welcomed summer camp to get away from his mother's nagging, but he hated Camp Kinderland, the Socialist camp where his parents sent him. "I didn't like Kinderland and I didn't like the *Daily Worker*. It seemed disagreeable, ideologically and visually. Other daily papers were more fun. And I had a terrible time at Camp Kinderland. I tried not to go, and I didn't make friends. I especially didn't like the Russian magazines and propaganda tracts that were distributed at the camp. I had the feeling they were taking cheap shots at America, and exaggerating about how wonderful life was in the Soviet Union. Without thinking, I reacted to the smell of the magazines from Russia. They smelled bad. There was something wrong with the paper, and the ink. It affected me emotionally. I enjoyed going with my family to places where we could swim and pick berries. But Kinderland seemed so goddammed programmed. There was something grim about the place."[44]

Kurtzman's creative impulses came from within, but the forms that would fascinate and influence him came from the vehicles of popular culture that flourished in the world around him: magazines, movies, radio and comics. He developed an abiding admiration for the great magazines of the day. Whenever he visited his favorite newsstands, they greeted him like gleaming icons of sophistication and success. *Collier's*, the *Saturday Evening Post*, *Liberty*, the *New Yorker* and others offered the finest journalism, short stories, illustrations and gag cartoons of the day. Kurtzman was mesmerized by their glossy, beautifully designed pages and their images of American life. For someone who had printer's ink in his veins, as Harvey clearly did, they represented at least one summit of the publishing world, one that he dreamed of reaching someday. A friend later affirmed, "Harvey told me how much he loved and admired the magazines and newspapers of his childhood. At a very young age, he decided to become a media mogul and started producing hand-assembled little periodicals complete with local news, illustrations and comics. He would then distribute them to friends and neighbors."[45]

When he was in eighth grade, Kurtzman received a gift from his parents that catered to another facet of his personality: a microscope. Zachary recalled, "He wanted to look at anything and everything that existed. He carried that microscope with him everywhere."[46] Looking at things close up, examining all their details, was an abiding personal trait that bordered on obsession.

IF THE JAZZ AGE of the 1920s was a time of good cheer and a certain innocence, exemplified by the great silent clowns—such as speedy Harold Lloyd and the unflappable Buster Keaton—the Depression was an era when the need for humor was deeper and more desperate, requiring a new type of popular comedian. As the economy and social stability seemed to be breaking down, the public developed a taste for movie clowns who brought an iconoclastic, absurd type of humor to the screen.

The chief purveyors of absurdist humor in the cinema were Harvey Kurtzman's all-time favorites, the Marx Brothers. Their Paramount films (*Coconuts*, *Animal Crackers*, *Monkey Business*, *Horse Feathers* and *Duck Soup*) coincided with Kurtzman's Brooklyn years. Their comedy was comprehensible to a child, but had other levels he understood later. Film critic

Roger Ebert wrote, "[Groucho] Marx and [W. C.] Fields were never just being funny. There was the sense that they were getting even for hurts so deep that all they could do was laugh about them."[47]

Groucho, Chico, Harpo and Zeppo poked fun at American history, Capitalism, foreign dictators, the immigrant experience and many other topics that especially appealed to the Jewish community. Not long after Harvey's family came up in the world with their move to the Bronx, the Marxes reached their zenith of popularity. They moved from Paramount to MGM, where Irving Thalberg guided them. *A Night at the Opera* was their masterpiece at the new studio, one that broadened their appeal in Middle America. It was Kurtzman's special favorite, because, he said, it had a good story along with the comedy. The spirit of anarchy embodied by the Marx Brothers was one of the three or four most important influences on Kurtzman's work as a humorist.

Radio broadcasting, one of the greatest sources of mass entertainment during the Great Depression, was going through its adolescence in the 1930s. At the start of the decade, it consisted largely of sponsored musical programs, but the success of comedic musical hosts and stars such as Eddie Cantor made radio comedy the coming thing. Ed Wynn and Joe Penner continued the trend. *Amos 'n' Andy* was hugely popular, much sharper and funnier than it was in its later years. Zachary, Harvey and Daniel grew up listening to the radio, like all their friends. As radio historian Elizabeth McLeod wrote, it was "an age when [Joe Penner's catchphrase] 'Wanna buy a duck?' echoed thru [*sic*] every schoolyard, and an entire nation wondered if Andy was going to have to marry Madame Queen."[48] Many of the comedians were Jewish. Ed Wynn was born Isaiah Edwin Leopold. Eddie Cantor's birth name was Edward Israel Iskowitz. Jack Benny, the greatest radio comedian of the 1940s, was born Benny Kubelsky.

Al Jaffee, Kurtzman's friend and colleague in the coming years, recalled, "Everyone in the Jewish community of the Bronx where I lived in the '30s and '40s was proud to hear Jewish success stories. In a period of severe economic depression and persistent anti-Semitism, it was encouraging to know Jews were becoming household names. Of course, the household names they had were not their original Jewish ones, but we knew who they were. When a Jew from the neighborhood got a job in the Gentile world, it spread like the proverbial wildfire. [The Jewish comedians] captivated large audiences who were glued to their radios, and in the case of the Marx and Ritz Brothers, into movie theaters all over the country."[49]

In the mid-1930s, newspaper comics became available in a new format called *comic books*. Calling them "books" was a bit of a misnomer, for, with their saddle-stitched binding, they more closely resembled magazines. Eastern Color's *Famous Funnies* #1 (July 1934) offered reprints of such strips as *Mutt and Jeff, the Bungle Family, Tailspin Tommy, Dixie Dugan* and *Toonerville Folks.* Comic books, usually sixty-eight pages for ten cents, were sold on newsstands and in corner candy stores. In 1936, they began featuring new material, though much of it, at first, looked like the reprints. Harvey Kurtzman was the prime age to latch onto this new medium of four-color humor and adventure, although with only a dime a week allowance, he found getting his fill problematic. Like most kids, he read as many as he could get away with in the store, bought a few and borrowed or traded for more. His good-natured father was often willing to buy him one or two, especially to keep Harvey amused while Abraham stepped into a local tavern for a beer, a frequent occurrence.

With his advancement through seventh and eighth grade, young Kurtzman was becoming more interested in the opposite sex. Suddenly he was looking at certain comics in a different way. One was Alex Raymond's *Flash Gordon.* "Every blessed line Raymond drew had sexuality, sensuality," he said in later years. "Everything moved in long, flowing lines. Rocket ships were penises; they were really blasting. The nude figure was always very close to the surface of the clothing. There was always that romantic interest. I never liked Raymond's stuff until I saw *Flash Gordon.* I remember him putting one of his women in a halter top which showed the bottom of her breasts, and he nearly drove me out of my mind. It was hot stuff."[50]

Writer Dave Schreiner interviewed Dan Barry, the artist of the *Flash Gordon* dailies beginning in 1951, who spoke of an encounter he had with Harvey Kurtzman, circa 1948: "Barry claims Kurtzman made a disparaging comment that nobody actually read *Flash Gordon*, but only took it to the bathroom to masturbate over."[51] Presumably Kurtzman spoke from personal experience.

Once he hit puberty, his pre-critical days were behind him. With *Flash Gordon*, he was not only seeing the flesh beneath Dale Arden's halter top, but began noticing the flaws in popular comics. He felt that *Flash Gordon* relied almost totally on the artwork and was devoid of good writing. For him, a comic strip ought to offer more than pretty drawings arranged in narrative order. There had to be good storytelling, both script and art. He had exercised both his writing and cartooning talents on "Ikey and Mikey," and later said that this was his strong suit: "Your ideas are the strength of your work. There are lots of people who can scribble a picture. But it is your insights into people that will set you apart."[52]

2.

THE CASTLE ON THE HILL

THE HIGH SCHOOL OF MUSIC AND ART was located at the intersection of 135th and Convent Street in upper Manhattan, on the crest of a hill by a well-maintained park. The grand, six-story structure was originally part of the City College of New York. When the Depression hit, the college students moved to other buildings on the campus to make room for both Public School 134 (an elementary school) and the Wadleigh High School for Girls.

In 1935, Mayor Fiorello LaGuardia noted that the school's facilities weren't being fully utilized. A dozen rooms were sitting empty. He decided they were sufficient to house the beginnings of a special school for talented children, something he had dreamed about for years. Soon students in the city were being tested for their art or music aptitude. A total of 250 students (half music, half art) were enrolled in the High School of Music and Art (M&A), beginning the first term on February 1, 1936. Teachers from around the city rushed to apply for positions at the exciting new educational institution, though initially the same teachers who instructed the Wadleigh girls taught the students' academic courses.[1]

LaGuardia proclaimed, "Music and arts were at one time the privilege of the wealthy. Now thousands upon thousands of talented poor will have their day."[2] He called the school "the most hopeful accomplishment of my administration."[3] M&A rumbled to life and proved to be an immediate success. Each year, a new crop of eighth grade students in city schools would be tested. Because teachers decided which pupils should take those tests, it was a foregone conclusion that Harvey Kurtzman, already recognized for his art ability, would get his shot.

The art aptitude test was made up of two parts. First, the candidates were given one class period to draw something of their choice. Kurtzman never described what he drew that day, but he was among the select group who progressed to the next step, a test consisting of several pages of multiple-choice questions. Al Jaffee recalled, "I clearly remember one question: 'Here are two lamps. Which do you think is the better designed?' One of the lamps had a very clean Art Deco design. The other was too fussy, too full of curlicues. I chose the simpler design, hoping that I wasn't going to be judged by some old-fashioned lady with a passion for the [overdone]."[4] Jaffee became a member of the first class in 1936.

Kurtzman was three years younger than Jaffee. Even though he had skipped a grade, he didn't take the test until spring 1937. Zachary hadn't made the cut the year before so he went to the School of Industrial Art, where many rejected M&A aspirants ended up. Harvey always said that when he learned he had passed the test, it was one of the most exciting days of his life. A letter on official Department of Education stationery informed his parents that their son had been accepted, and would begin at the High School of Music and Art in September. Kurtzman was still twelve years old when he entered the ninth grade. He turned thirteen a few weeks later.

Kurtzman's high school day started with a subway ride alongside regular business commuters. "It was a lonely trip. I was the only one from my neighborhood going to that high school."[5] He was luckier than many. His ride from the Bronx took under a half hour, allowing him to stay in bed later than students who had to endure rides up to ninety minutes (if they lived in the farthest parts of Brooklyn, Queens or Staten Island).

Just to reach the school's grand, arched doorway required a kind of physical workout. He had to climb the 137 steps of Nicholas Park (in a dozen sections), which wended their way upward through the grass and trees. As one mounted those stairs, the gothic edifice of the Castle on the Hill loomed ever-higher overhead. Sometimes the climb was accompanied by music. An M&A student later recalled, "As I walked to the school from the subway stop, I could hear the music. They were already practicing, and it was coming out of the school as I approached. The effect was absolutely beautiful."[6]

Students entered through large wooden doors into a vaulted lobby past a bust of Arturo Toscanini, the celebrated orchestra conductor. One wall was decorated with a WPA-like mural showing brown-clad men and women striving upward toward enlightenment, symbolized by a moun-

The High School of Music and Art: image from Benjamin M. Steigman's *Accent on Talent, New York's High School of Music and Art.* © 1964 Wayne State University Press.

tain peak.[7] Both the setting and the school's curriculum imparted a sense of importance to the arts, as did the mayor's periodic visits.

M&A pupils faced a longer school day than their peers in regular public schools, because they were required to take a full slate of college-preparatory academic classes (math, history, English, science) in addition to three art or music classes per day. Each was expected to become proficient in two foreign languages.

The art curriculum was wide-ranging. In the first year, students were required to take basic courses in contour drawing, painting, composition and art history. After that, they could choose among electives such as advanced painting, sculpture, ceramics, architecture, stage design, puppetry and textile design. Missing from the curriculum were courses in cartooning or illustration. Such commercial art wasn't considered a legitimate medium for a serious artist. Mayor LaGuardia did his best to make sure M&A was adequately funded, but it was difficult. Although public schools were expected to provide books, supplies and equipment, many of the art students augmented the school's meager supplies with their own brushes, paints and drawing implements. Kurtzman may have had help doing so, after winning one of the John Wanamaker childrens' drawing competitions, which awarded medals and small scholarships.

A ferryboat ride around Manhattan Island gave the members of the class of 1941 the chance to get to know their fellow freshmen. That's probably when Kurtzman met Harry Chester, a jaunty, easygoing boy who never grew much above five feet tall. Chester's father owned a filling station on Post Road in the Bronx. He quickly became one of Kurtzman's closest and most devoted friends. Another was Charles Stern, a handsome kid who was a bundle of energy—he became a class ringleader. The boat ride inspired Kurtzman to create a large, panoramic cartoon showing the students on deck in the midst of various comical situations. That drawing, which was pinned to a bulletin board by the gymnasium, served as Kurtzman's introduction to the student body in general. One of those students was Al Jaffee, a junior who was also known for his cartooning talent.

> Someone came to me and said, "You'd better look to your laurels because there's this new kid who came in who does cartoons that are fantastic." Even though the High School of Music and Art was primarily about classical music and fine art, some of us did cartoons to amuse our friends. I had a reputation for my humorous crowd scenes. The classmate said, "Wow, this kid is better than you are, he's got a thousand people in this boat ride drawing. It's hilarious." So I went to look at it and I was very impressed with it. I didn't meet him [at that time], but the signature, Harvey Kurtzman, was etched in my brain from that point on.[8]

Although Jaffee appeared to be another typical Jewish boy from the Bronx, few realized that he had been uprooted from the States and spent much of his childhood enduring the privations of life in a rural Lithuanian village. When he was finally able to return to the States, he had to effectively relearn English. Jaffee was then separated from his brothers and shunted from one distant relative to another, which he managed to take in stride.

Because of the boat ride cartoon, Kurtzman was quickly identified by his classmates as "one to watch." But, despite his auspicious introduction, he didn't become the center of attention. The diffident Kurtzman preferred to take in the school and his classmates from a distance, watching and analyzing everything going on around him. M&A was vastly different from his proletarian junior high in Tremont. Instead of the usual mix of Bronx youths, these schoolmates tended to be more intense, more individualistic and less traditional in outlook. "All the students were interesting, and each had a special talent," he remembered.[9] The ambiance at M&A was more freewheeling than standard high schools. M&A student John

Severin, who became one of Kurtzman's closest friends a couple of years later, described the atmosphere.

> It was very different for me. I had always gone to a parochial school where there was always a certain amount of discipline. I don't mean people standing in corners with whips and things like that, but . . . you wore a shirt and tie, your nails were clean, your hair was combed. When I went to the High School of Music and Art . . . the population was all these eccentrics. They're all artists, musicians, ballet dancers, etc. So these people are entirely different. Also the teachers, the faculty, were right out of the same mold. So it was a much looser, easier going, bohemian style of high school. Not that there weren't rules and regulations, and you'd have to abide by them, don't make any mistake about that. But at the same time, this was really freedom to me. Wow! I wasn't too sure I liked it. It grew on me.[10]

In the students' all-around art courses, they were taught why man created art, and how it developed over the ages. In his art survey class, Kurtzman received his only formal tutelage in its history. He was exposed to the work of Michelangelo, Leonardo, Rembrandt and Van Gogh, the context in which they created their art and why they were important and influential. The class went on field trips to the art museums in New York, which had extensive collections and often featured traveling exhibitions.

Similarly, in his English literature classes, Kurtzman was introduced to the works of Shakespeare, Charles Dickens, Jack London and Sinclair Lewis. He tended to neglect his homework—pushing his schoolbooks aside to get out a pen and India ink—but some of it sank in. He became a lifelong fan of Dickens and was particularly captivated by *A Christmas Carol*. It was Dickens's self-described "sledgehammer blow for the poor" that touched him, dovetailing nicely with the labor versus management ideas he'd picked up at home. But his spelling was uncertain (it would remain so all his life), and he put almost no energy into developing formal writing skills. At the time, history didn't interest him either: "I hated history. When I had to do schoolbook history and we'd get our assignments to read this and read that, it was the dullest, most boring exercise."[11] His focus on his artwork became total.

There could have been another factor: M&A had higher educational standards than his former school, and he may have been on unequal footing with other students. He later put it, "[I] moved, with difficulty, from a 'dumb' Catholic school [a Bronx junior high school] to a 'smart' Jewish school [meaning M&A, largely Jewish]. In my case, I combined the worst of all possible worlds in that I was Jewish and also dumb!"[12] His high grades in art classes balanced out mediocre marks in academic subjects.

Kurtzman's creative process grew more deliberate in high school. Earlier, he had been known for his speed, dashing out what he later called "very bad drawings" by the dozen. Working quickly was required when drawing in streets and gutters. At M&A, the quality of his work was important to maintain his social position and to get good grades. Actually, it was because his personal standards had risen. As he grew older and more critical, Kurtzman found it necessary to draw and redraw to produce work that satisfied him. "Speed . . . didn't matter when I worked on paper. I could start a cartoon in the morning and finish it in the afternoon. Or the next week, or even next month. Speed in drawing is not necessarily important."[13]

His experience at M&A was transformative in other ways. It provided a more positive educational atmosphere than regular high school, opened his mind to the world of art beyond cartooning, gave his aspirations a sense of importance and exalted the notion of making one's living in the arts.

ALTHOUGH HE FOUND the work in the art classes stimulating, he did have other things on his mind. "While I was getting educated and my interest in drawing was increasing, I was . . . more interested in girls than anything else. I can't remember when I wasn't secretly in love with one of the girls in my class. In every class! But I didn't get loved back. My being younger than everyone else had a lot to do with it. My social life was always torture to me. The social pressure of high school was rough."[14]

Not long into his freshman year, Kurtzman found himself noticing two boisterous upperclassmen. One was Jaffee. "Al was the

Harvey and Zachary Kurtzman (1938). Photograph courtesy of Adam Kurtzman.

BMOC [Big Man on Campus]," Kurtzman recalled. "I used to worship him from afar."[15] Kurtzman observed that many of Jaffee's antics included his

Al Jaffee and Will Elder goofing around in the cafeteria of Music & Art: courtesy of Al Jaffee.

pal, a scrawny teen with unruly hair and a rubbery face. Jaffee had originally met Wolf Eisenberg at Herman Ridder Junior High in the Bronx. Eisenberg became better known by the pen name he adopted after World War II: Will, Willy or Bill Elder. Born Wolf William Eisenberg in 1921, he was given the Yiddish nickname "Meshugganah Villy" (Crazy Willy) by his family. As the youngest sibling, he sought the spotlight by incessantly playing practical jokes. "Willy" also demonstrated remarkable art talent from an early age, with a special gift for portraiture. His drawing of a Dutch peasant gained him entry to M&A, where he was a poor student academically but a star artist. (For the sake of simplicity, this book refers to him as Will Elder throughout.)

"I remember seeing Will, originally, in the lunch room," Kurtzman said. "He used to have a routine with Al Jaffee. He was Costello to Jaffee's Abbott. Will was very physical back then. He was the Chaplin of that particular class. He moved very well. He was kind of a natural dancer, and he'd do all these physical things. One minute he'd be a ventriloquist's dummy. The next minute he'd be a fighter pilot in a telephone booth, with ketchup dribbling out of his mouth."[16] Elder's comic persona was akin to that of Jerry Lewis years later: moronic faces, physical humor and loud wisecracks. His pranks became legendary, even feared. "I was thrilled to be in that school and had so much mischievous fun that I nearly didn't make it through myself," Elder remembered.[17] Some of his practical jokes went to extremes. His biographer, Gary Vandenberg, recounted one of the cruelest:

> One of his teachers was prone to nervousness, and Will would always play on a person's vulnerability. Will enlisted the help of a classmate to properly execute one particular prank. As the teacher called attendance, Will didn't answer. His classmate informed him that Will had gone home early, not feeling well and apparently depressed. At the end of class the students and teacher went to the closet to collect their coats. The teacher opened the door first and to his astonishment, there was Will, hanging from a coat hook by the neck, his face ashen because he had whitened it with chalk. The teacher collapsed. Will took this opportunity to hop off the hook and disappear. When the teacher came to, the students assured him he had imagined the whole thing.[18]

Like Kurtzman, Elder took his art assignments seriously, something he never did with academic subjects. "The teachers . . . made you feel like you were part of a big, very important movement. I met some very interesting people [at M&A] and they inspired me. There's also a tremendous feeling of competition. Competition was good in a case like that. You want to be better than your friends, show them that you can do as good or better than they. It worked. It made me stand out in class. I was drawing cartoons on the blackboard, and the teacher would see my work and she thought I would be a good example for some of the other kids who refused to draw. She would display my work for the rest of the class to see. It was ego-building in the most positive way."[19] Because Elder and Jaffee were upperclassmen, they didn't befriend Kurtzman. They did, however, notice his entries in periodic student art shows.

Kurtzman's and Elder's personalities were almost diametrically opposed. Kurtzman wasn't a show-off, or a cutup, or even a Groucho-like wiseacre. He could make funny comments, but was the furthest thing from being an entertainer in person. There was a roiling world of imagination in his head and a hyperawareness of the world around him, but the only external indicator that the freshmen would one day become a notable humorist was in his cartoons. If there was a big event at school, stu-

Harvey Kurtzman's first published work was a runner-up in the Buffalo Bob contest in *Tip Top Comics* #36 (April 1939). "If I don't save Bob now, how the heck am I goin' to win this contest?"

dents often found Kurtzman's cartoon "take" pinned to a bulletin board or passed around the lunchroom. His satirical drawings "were making fun of something that was a truth about whoever I was drawing."[20] As he later put it, "I found out that to make somebody laugh, you draw a cartoon about him, make some joke about him, and that was satire."[21]

HARVEY KURTZMAN'S YEARS at the High School of Music and Art occurred against the sobering backdrop of impending war. Alarming newspaper headlines were inescapable. In March of 1938, the spring of Kurtzman's freshmen year, Germany annexed Austria, and soon would claim the Sudetenland in Czechoslovakia.

   A month later, a new hero appeared. *Action Comics* #1 featured Superman, a champion of the masses clad in patriotic colors. The appeal of Jerry Siegel's and Joe Shuster's super powered hero at this time in history is not difficult to understand. His instant popularity put comic books over as a unique type of entertainment, instead of an adjunct to newspaper comic strips. Before long, new titles featuring Man of Tomorrow imitations crowded the newsstands. Kurtzman was drawn to the proliferating comic books, but preferred those with reprints of newspaper comic strips. He thought Superman and the other original strips in *Action Comics* and elsewhere were crude in comparison. One of Kurtzman's favorite comic books was *Tip Top Comics*, which packaged reprints from United Feature

Syndicate, Inc., such as *Tarzan, Li'l Abner, Ella Cinders, Joe Jinks, Broncho Bill* and *Fritzi Ritz* (*Nancy*). Therefore, it's fitting that Harvey Kurtzman's first published work appeared in the pages of *Tip Top*.

Midway through the fall semester of his sophomore year, he submitted a cartoon to a Buffalo Bob contest in *Tip Top Comics*. Contest No. 15 asked for cartoon entries to show how Bob would avoid stepping in a bear trap, as depicted on the page. Kurtzman's solution was to draw himself coming from behind a nearby tree to push Bob out of the way, with the caption, "If I don't save Bob now, how the heck am I goin' to win this contest?" Although his cartoon was one of the four runners-up, rather than the winner, it was printed in *Tip Top Comics* Vol. 3 #12 (36) dated April 1939. It's striking and prophetic that even in his earliest extant cartoon, Kurtzman's gag involved bending the conventions of the form by breaking the "fourth wall."

"It's a great feeling, the first time you have your work printed," he later declared. "I could get the biggest spread in [a] magazine today and never get the thrill of the first time I was published. That crisp new dollar, when I was a kid living in the Bronx, was the biggest dollar that I ever owned in my life."[22] Shortly after his Buffalo Bob cartoon was published, he won a drawing contest for Sealtest Milk, and again had the delirious experience of seeing his work in print. By that time, Kurtzman was looking beyond the Sunday funnies for inspiration.

One of the outstanding features of M&A was its library, which had a substantial selection of art books and art-related magazines. Kurtzman haunted the place, becoming a well-known presence to school librarian Gertrude Loydon. Among the books on fine art and music, he found a few about the work of eminent cartoonists, and possibly copies of humor magazines such as *Judge* and *Punch*. This was probably where Kurtzman encountered the work of four artists that would become his personal favorites: Thomas Nast, Wilhelm Busch, Caran d'Ache and H. M. Bateman. Each made a substantial impact on his later outlook and work.

Kurtzman said, "I think if there is any kind of a satirical eye—a thing you can point to in an artist and say that's what makes him a satirist—it's when you can focus on something with a sharper-than-average eye, and you see something goofy." He realized that satire required the creator to be a critic. This was what drew Kurtzman to the work of Thomas Nast (1840–1902). "I did a lot of research on Nast. His criticism at a certain period was very useful. His most important years were . . . before and after Boss Tweed's period of power."[23] Nast's editorial cartoons were so powerful that they are credited with contributing to the politically corrupt Tweed's downfall. "If you ever followed his cartoons, you'd see that they had a marvelous continuity from day to day. He'd have a hundred side-gags going per drawing. You'd pick up all kinds of little things in the corners, much in the manner of Willy Elder. Nast . . . really got to me."[24]

Kurtzman also greatly admired the work of Wilhelm Busch (1832–1908), the German humorist and illustrator best known for his *Max und Moritz* stories and cartoons, which were the inspiration for Rudolph Dirks's *The Katzenjammer Kids*. His work satirized contemporary city life, including strict religious morality and bigotry, and some of it was banned by the authorities. "Oh, he was good," Kurtzman told an interviewer later. "He was a lot better than the finished engravings of his work led you to believe, because the engravings were, of course, done by a woodcutter. The Busch sketches for the engravings were *really* good."[25]

Another Kurtzman favorite was Caran d'Ache, the nineteenth-century French satirist and political cartoonist. "Caran d'Ache"—from the Russian word *karandash*, meaning pencil or writing instrument—was the pseudonym of Emmanuel Poire (1858–1909). He worked for the newspapers *Lundi du Figaro*, *La Vie Parisienne* and *La Rire* in the 1880s and 1890s, and created continuities that prefigured comic strips. He and cartoonist Jean-Louis Forain founded the magazine *Psst . . . !*, which lasted for eighty-five issues. It consisted entirely of cartoons by d'Ache and Forain, caricaturing French society and commenting on the issues of the day. D'Ache is documented as proposing a novel made up entirely of drawings and no words, i.e. a graphic novel, but was unable to find a publisher for it. (He did manage to get the shorter graphic novella *Maestro* published in 1899.)

Of the four, Kurtzman was especially enamored with the work of contemporary cartoonist H. M. Bateman (1887–1970). Bateman was an Englishman famous for his continuities, a series of sequential drawings on a page that told a story without words. "I just loved continuities, but he did them with such a heightened sense of movement, he affected a whole generation of *Punch* and *Judge* cartoonists. He's one of my really all-time favorites."[26] Bateman was best known for cartoons featuring comically exaggerated reactions to upper-class social gaffes, such as "The Boy Who Breathed on the Glass at the British Museum," which showed how a seemingly minor affront to decorum led to a life of degradation and abject failure. Bateman had a fair amount of his work published in America during his world travels, and passed through New York City in 1939 on his way back to Britain, just before the outbreak of war. Three of the four cartoonists worked outside America: in Germany, France and England.

Only Nast, though foreign born, worked and lived in the States. Kurtzman had an internationalist appreciation of cartoon art at an early age.

EVENTUALLY, HARVEY KURTZMAN developed a circle of friends. It was made up of Harry Chester, Ed Fisher, Frank Dorsey, Charles Stern and Harry Jaffee, Al's younger brother. Also in his orbit was African American Harold Van Riel, a natty dresser whose cartooning skills made him a friendly rival. "Harold was a lot better than me. We would both cartoon up a storm to consolidate our social positions. That was my motivation. I can't speak for him."[27]

Kurtzman began coming out of his shell. "My friends had a very good effect on me. There was a kind of cross-pollenization going on that I'm sure affected my thinking."[28] They found themselves satirizing popular culture instinctively. "I remember specifically sitting around in the lunch room doing . . . the 'airplane scene,' the German ace going down in the Fokker in flames, and the American ace waving goodbye as he watches the German go to his death. We picked scenes up out of the popular movies, like the Tarzan scenes, all the clichés, and we'd make them funny."[29]

Attending a school art show at M&A must have been an eye-opening experience, given the quality of the work produced by such precocious teenagers, each vying for "best in show." Will Elder's sensitively painted portraits, which showed the influence of the Impressionist and post-Impressionist painters, were unexpected and surprisingly accomplished. Other activities included fundraising parties in the gymnasium, when art students sketched portraits for a donation, followed by music students playing dance music. Hit albums in 1938 were Artie Shaw's *Begin the Beguine* and Benny Goodman's *From Spirituals to Swing*. Students danced to big band music just as their parents did. The school also had the usual clubs and a monthly newspaper called the *Overtone*. M&A pupils worked hard and played hard, as they enjoyed a more exciting and fulfilling high school experience than they would have had otherwise. But their experience was tempered by alarming world events.

On September 1, 1939, just as Kurtzman was about to start his junior year, Germany crossed the border into Poland. The resulting declarations of war on Germany by France and most of the countries of the British Empire and Commonwealth meant it was likely the US would eventually be at war. On the cusp of turning fifteen, Kurtzman became a fanatical news follower; he regularly tuned in to his favorite broadcasters while holed up in his room, doing his homework and drawing cartoons. He would closely follow the daily news for the rest of his life. The self-described "worried kid" found world events compelling and impossible to ignore.

Kurtzman's third year in high school marked the beginning of his friendship with John Severin, another promising illustrator and cartoonist. Kurtzman and Severin made an unlikely duo. Harvey was fifteen. John, a senior, was eighteen. Kurtzman hadn't reached his adult height (5'6"). Severin towered over him at 6'2". Kurtzman was Jewish. Severin was Catholic. Severin later recalled, "[In] my last year of high school, [Harvey] was following me around a lot. We got to be real friendly. Every time I turned around, we'd be talking about artwork. The kind of artwork he was doing—cartooning. I did cartooning, but that wasn't my main interest. He kind of liked my style, which was very, very loose."[30]

Severin had been selling cartoons to the *Hobo News* since he was fourteen. Kurtzman was impressed by the older boy, whose work was already much like his later art in comic books: strong on fundamentals, with nicely detailed inking. Here was a high school student who had achieved the status devoutly to be wished; he was a working professional. One frequent subject of conversation concerned Kurtzman's ideas for a newspaper strip. In June 1940, after Severin graduated, Kurtzman began sending him letters. Severin wrote back. "[Harvey and I] actually got closer through our correspondence than we had been in high school."[31]

Why write letters to someone who lives in the same city? "In order to see Harvey personally, it was a matter of getting on subways and making transfers and so on," according to Severin. "So we wrote letters."[32] Letters were more private than phone calls, and gave the graphically inclined the chance to decorate their envelopes and letters with doodles, even fairly elaborate drawings. Severin applied watercolor to some of the inked images on the envelopes he sent to Kurtzman in 1940 and 1941. This correspondence shows young Kurtzman's desire to find work as a cartoonist, and the connection between them. The correspondence lasted a couple of years, even after Severin enlisted in the military.

TWO YEARS AFTER SUPERMAN graced the cover of *Action Comics* #1, another important character in comics appeared. Will Eisner's *The Spirit* made its debut on June 2, 1940, just as Kurtzman was completing his third year of high school. The Spirit was masked crimefighter Denny Colt, whose weekly adventures were told in complete seven-page stories in a separately bound comic book inserted in Sunday newspapers. In New York City, the Newark *Star-Ledger* carried the insert. Kurtzman and all his friends loved Eisner's clever writing and evocative artwork. It had the

Senior yearbook photographs, L-R: Harvey Kurtzman, Charles Stern, Harry Chester and Harold Van Riel.

kind of sophisticated, even literary, stories that had never been seen before in comics. Kurtzman would write, "Within a year, *The Spirit* had become the standard by which other comic books would be measured. Eisner became a virtuoso cartoonist of a kind who had never been seen before."[33] *The Spirit* had an enormous influence on the medium and many of its future practitioners.

By the time Kurtzman reached his senior year at M&A, a sort of BMOC in his own right, some underclassmen were there who would become future colleagues. Joe Kubert had just entered M&A as a freshman, and Al Feldstein was a sophomore. The only encounter Kurtzman had with Feldstein in high school occurred when Harvey was smashing glass bottles on the cement floor between the tables in the lunchroom. Feldstein came up to him and said, "You'd better not do that. You'll get into trouble."[34]

In 1940, Charles Stern was elected Vice President of the student body. "Charlie was a character," Kurtzman recalled. "He burned his candle on both ends and used himself up much too early." His friends could see it coming by watching him in action. "Charlie was hyper, the most hyper guy I've ever known."[35]

The earliest known continuity by Harvey Kurtzman—a four-panel gag strip—appeared in the *Overtone*. "Many of my cartoons were published in the school newspaper," Kurtzman said. "It was my ability to say something that was both funny and true about a person that made me stand apart from other cartoonists."[36] A bit of his artwork was even published citywide: "One of my cartoons was reprinted in the *New York Times*, and I got invited into fancy homes—the outside world."[37] He didn't say how the invitations came about, but those early glimpses of life beyond Clinton Avenue showed him a kind of affluence that became the stuff of dreams.

Kurtzman did a series of charcoal nude studies. One is dated January 27, 1941, halfway through his senior year. While life drawing was a big part of the M&A curriculum, models were never entirely undraped. Therefore, he had to be taking classes on the side, perhaps at the Art Students League of New York. (They held ad hoc drawing classes in their building on West Fifty-Seventh Street.) These life study drawings show great confidence and considerable mastery of the charcoal medium. He gave the figures linear outlines, more typical of a cartoonist or illustrator than a fine artist.

Kurtzman took classes in the printing arts at M&A, which involved lettering, poster design, airbrush techniques and paste-up. The students were equipped to prepare layouts, title pages and illustrations for the school publications, such as its concert and art exhibition programs. According to Principal Benjamin Steigman, "They have stacks of magazine advertising pages in their studio, and they know where Madison Avenue is located. But they also know where exhibitions of the fine arts of printing are held."[38]

Two examples of Kurtzman's fine art from M&A have survived. Given all the gifted artists at the school, it was a signal honor that not one but two of Kurtzman's woodcuts are given special prominence in the 1941 yearbook, overshadowing several other engravings by his classmates.

Earliest surviving continuity by Kurtzman, from his high school newspaper the *Overtone*, date unknown.

He titled one "In the Groove with Solid Jive," and the other "In his mad rush for the paper, he never forgets to turn on the radio." Both are expertly composed and fairly well carved, with a highly sophisticated use of shapes and textures, and a sense of movement that's difficult to achieve in a woodcut engraving. It's the work of an A student.

In the yearbook, there is a rhyming couplet next to the photograph of each graduating senior. The poem for Kurtzman reads:

Draws his crazy cartoons all day,
He's even getting to look that way.

"When I was graduating—you know how everybody writes a dumb poem in the yearbook, and signs their autograph? I think I drew a picture in every single yearbook of my graduating class. Everyone wanted a little Kurtzman joke."[39] For example, in Harry Chester's annual, he drew a cartoon of "Chester's Garage Service," where his father says, "Oh that! That's my son Harry! Walks under the car without stooping even!" From under a car, where only his feet can be seen, Harry says, "Pass me the grease gun Pop!"[40] It was one of several jokes in Harry's annual alluding to his short stature.

In 1941, Harvey Kurtzman was one of 169 students who graduated from the High School of Music and Art, and certainly one of the youngest. At sixteen years old, he had gained an appreciation of art, by studying its history, and a hands-on education in a substantial number of artistic disciplines. His M&A experience did more than that. It cemented his desire for a career in art, and provided him with opportunities to develop his satirical bent. It gave him a group of talented friends with whom he hoped to work in the future, on projects that were already beginning to form in his mind.

THE ORIGIN OF THE SPIRIT

June 2, 1940

Will Eisner's *The Spirit* made its debut in the Newark *Star-Ledger*, Sunday, June 2, 1940, just as Kurtzman was completing his junior year in high school.

"In his mad rush for the paper, he never forgets to turn on the radio"

Kurtzman's woodcut, from the *High School of Music and Art* Vol. 4 (1941) yearbook. Right: second Kurtzman woodcut from the yearbook.

In the Groove with Solid Jive

3.

THE LITTLE SCHNOOK

THE CLASS OF 1941 matriculated into an economy still in recovery. Though the United States didn't officially enter the war until the Japanese attacked Pearl Harbor six months later, the Selective Service Act had been passed in the fall of 1940, the first case of a peacetime draft in the country's history. Young men were already being plucked out of jobs that were deemed nonessential, and it wouldn't be long before a full-employment economy became a reality, for reasons no one wanted.

Harvey Kurtzman wouldn't be required to register for Selective Service until the fall of 1942. With the standard six-month delay between registration and conscription, it looked like he had up to two years before he would have to face military service. Until then, the graduate needed a job. "My plan was to make money as quickly as possible," he said, "but there wasn't much money around. I also wanted to continue art school, so I did both."[1] Many of Kurtzman's classmates went on to college, but his parents couldn't afford to send him and his grades weren't good enough to make him a prime candidate for university scholarships. More to the point, he had no desire for further academic study. Had there been an art school for cartoonists, Kurtzman would have been interested, but such a place didn't exist. "Willy" Elder was already attending New York's Academy of Design. Another option was Cooper Union.

In 1859, American industrialist Peter Cooper created The Cooper Union for the Advancement of Science and Art. Abraham Lincoln gave a famous speech in the school's foundation building, an Italianate brownstone located in the East Village at Cooper Square and Astor Place. Cooper Union offered degrees in fine arts, and cost nothing to attend. One had to be judged worthy of a scholarship based on a portfolio submission. "I had graduated from high school with my good friend, Harry Chester," Kurtzman said. "Together, we applied for and received scholarships to Cooper Union art school. Because we planned to work during the day, we went to Cooper Union at night."[2]

Classes wouldn't begin until fall. Meanwhile, Kurtzman went to employment agencies for job leads. "I started my career handing out pamphlets for a guy who ran a CPA school. I would wait at the entrance to a place where they were giving examinations for CPA licenses and . . . would hand out pamphlets as the CPAs came out of the test room. The pamphlets would say, 'If you fail the test come to my school and learn how to pass.' This guy would stand in the background and whenever the crowds had come through and gone home, he would make us pick up the pamphlets that were tossed away and give them out again at the next testing.[3] I did all kinds of things. I got fired from a lot of jobs!"[4] He pushed clothing wagons in the Thirty-Fifth Street garment district.[5] He worked for a dry goods chain, adding up the daily receipts. "We'd have to record the receipts by hand in little notebooks. We'd sit around all day going 'one plus two plus three plus one . . .' It was the dumbest, most asinine work."[6]

Kurtzman continued to work on his cartooning at home: "During this time I always had a drawing board in my room. A drawing board and a smock. I used to feel good wearing that smock. It had a way of making you think you were an artist. Deep down inside, I was convinced I was a cartoonist. But nobody gave me [work in cartooning], so I kept going to the depressing employment agencies and picking up nondescript jobs."[7]

He wrote to John Severin often, needing someone to share his latest discovery of a new inking brush, or his infatuation with this or that cartoonist. Since Severin was older, military service was a frequent topic, but there was also pining over cute girls, and the sharing of family news. Brother Zack, who graduated from the School of Industrial Art in 1940, registered for military service when required, and soon would begin what turned out to be a career as a Lieutenant in the US Navy.

Kurtzman was trying to get any sort of job in commercial art. "My first break came from a neighbor whose daughter I was madly in love with. He knew a guy who knew a guy who worked at Schneider Press Printers, offset lithographers. He got me a job in the sign department. I became a letterer!"[8] He also worked on the presses, and got a sense of what it was like working in that environment. "When I was a printer's devil, I attended a couple of meetings where they were trying to start a union. I was very pro-union at the time."[9]

Cooper Union was a fair jaunt from the Bronx. Attending night classes probably meant staying downtown after work, meeting up with Harry, going to an automat for dinner or eating something his mother packed for him. Then it was on to class in the historic school building. "Cooper Union was a good school," Kurtzman said. "I'd been around art schools, and . . . I don't really believe in art school, in the sense that there are so many kids who are at art school who assume that the school will make them an artist, and that's like assuming a music school will make you a musician. Creative art and creative music talents are inborn, and no amount of schooling will give you the talent. But I think Cooper Union, as a school, for whatever a school does—and there is a value in that—if you are good it certainly puts you in contact with different mediums and forms. It had all the courses. It had good teachers."[10] He took classes in painting, sculpture and calligraphy.[11]

One memorable—if unpleasant—incident occurred about this time. It arose from an entry in Martin Sheridan's *Classic Comics and Their Creators* (1942), the first significant book about the newspaper comics, which were becoming American institutions. Naturally Kurtzman studied its inside information: the way comic strips were produced, the life of the cartoonists who drew them and (most tantalizing of all) the list of the syndicates and their addresses with instructions on exactly how submissions should be made. He was struck by the chapter by Alfred Andriola about the production of the *Charlie Chan* comic strip (which, as it turned out, was soon dropped, leaving the writer-artist free to create his own strip, *Kerry Drake*). Andriola wrote that he benefitted from the help of Milton Caniff and Noel Sickles, and had an open door policy himself. "I have found that in this business the established fellows always are ready to give a hand to the newcomers. I try to follow through, and I see anyone who so much as nibbles for an interview. If he has talent, he gets all the help I can give."[12]

Kurtzman made an appointment with Andriola and showed up one day at the man's studio with his portfolio. He recalled, "He looks at my stuff, goes through it very quickly, and tells me I shouldn't be a cartoonist. I should get out of the profession." Kurtzman surmised that Andriola, who was "kind of a slight guy, and very effeminate," was homosexual, and suspected there were ulterior motives behind his willingness to meet young cartoonists. But what bothered him was that Andriola had responded negatively to his work and potential.[13]

A major disaster befell the Perkes-Kurtzman family in the first half of 1942. Abraham Perkes, father and primary provider, was arrested, tried and convicted of the federal crimes of "Conspiracy" and "Counterfeiting US Defense maps" (according to sketchy, contemporary prison records). It's not clear exactly what occurred, but it had nothing to do with defense maps, per se. The version handed down in the family was that Abraham was involved in counterfeiting ration coupons. Many years later, Zachary boasted that he was the one who engraved the plates, having studied print-making in high school.[14] Abraham was also an engraver, and if Zachary's story was true, they were in it together. (By the time of the arrest, Zachary was in the military.) In later life, Edith would often describe Abraham as "a horse thief," her way of saying that his morals were questionable. In any case, the evidence was sufficiently compelling to convict Abraham Perkes of the charges in the Southern District Court of New York in New York City. He was sentenced to ten years in prison on June 11, 1942, and began serving his sentence a few days later.[15]

Perkes was incarcerated at Allenwood Federal Prison in Montgomery, Pennsylvania, near Bucknell University. Allenwood was (and still is) a prison for serious white-collar offenders. Kurtzman visited his father in the prison, and said only that it was depressing. However, it's on a farmlike campus and most of the inmates have a choice of various sports. Rarely were more than four guards present, and they were often nowhere to be seen. Allenwood Camp had no fences. Prisoners could go AWOL to the town motel for an unofficial conjugal visit. If you were a federal of-fender, you wanted to go there. It was "easy time."

This wrenching development—just months after Pearl Harbor—was accompanied by a practical problem. Edith Perkes suddenly had no in-come, and she still had Daniel, who was eleven, in her care. The effect his father's conviction had on Harvey Kurtzman from an emotional stand-point is unknown, but his incarceration put pressure on Harvey to support the family. (Zachary undoubtedly sent some of his military pay home, as well.) Until such time as Abraham returned, Harvey was tethered to the Clinton Arms and the "nightmare of a nudge"—who was increasingly em-bittered by the reverses that life dealt her.

WHEN ASKED HOW HE ENDED UP going into comic books, Kurtzman spec-ulated, "If I had been brought up in another time, in other circumstances, if I'd come from an affluent family, possibly I would have gone into mov-ies or something. We always try to flatter ourselves and tell ourselves we choose our direction in life, we're the stone flying through the void and we're thinking to ourselves we're . . . following our own course of our own free will, but we've really been thrown by an external force."[16] He had

The 1941–1942 Night Art School class at Cooper Union, from The 1942 *Cable* (yearbook). Harry Chester and Harvey Kurtzman are both in the first row, seated.

spent almost a year getting fired from job after job. His latest was working for a legal firm as a clerk, errand boy and telephone operator. "When they put me on the switchboard, I messed up mightily. I had those wires going every which way, a hopeless tangle of wrong connections."[17] After struggling with the job for three weeks, Kurtzman quit before they had a chance to fire him. He had gotten lucky. "I had a hot lead—a comic book offer," he said.[18] One of his instructors at Cooper Union told him that a friend (or friend of a friend) was looking for helpers to draw comic books.

It wasn't that Kurtzman was a fan of the super hero craze that had virtually taken over comic books—he wasn't, though he read some of them—or that he had given up his dreams of working in the slick magazines. Indeed, he disdained comic books' poor printing and shoddy paper. But the military draft was increasingly creating openings in the publishing world by the spring of 1942, and most of them were in the lower echelons of the business. "It was natural to grab a market that let you in," he later explained. "Comic books were one of the few places that I could sell my talent. I did some pretty gruesome things before I started doing comics, so cartooning seemed pretty exotic to me when I got into it, even though it was bottom-of-the-barrel stuff."[19]

Seventeen-year-old Harvey Kurtzman was referred to Louis Ferstadt. "He was a muralist and a portrait painter," he said. "He was considered a very good painter."[20] As part of the WPA program, Louis Goodman Ferstadt

Louis Ferstadt standing in front of a mural for WPA Federal Art Project, 1939: photograph courtesy of S. Horn.

had created murals at the RCA Building and the Eighth Street Subway for the 1939 World's Fair. Kurtzman recalled, "He used to have a system of painting that utilized pointillism [like] Seurat. He was a Communist. He did a comic strip for the *Daily Worker* [called *Li'l Lefty*]. It was so sad, because he had gone from all this idealism, from painting to comic books, and batting them out."

Ferstadt got his experience in the field working in comic book production shops run by Will Eisner, Jerry Iger and Emanuel Demby, operations that produced finished stories and art for various publishers. From 1942 to 1945, Ferstadt set himself up as a producer of comic books for All-American, Quality, Fox, Timely, Harvey and Ace. "Somebody would contract with him, and he would subcontract with all us little schnooks out of high school," Kurtzman said. "Louis was once upon a time a very active . . . left-winger, and here he was doing comics, and exploiting us in the most shameless way. He came off as the worst kind of Capitalist. I think his intentions were honorable. He just didn't know how to handle it."

In many respects, comic book publishers had a manufacturing mindset. They were selling paper and ink. The content of the books was of secondary consequence, especially during World War II when they sold 90 percent or more of their print runs due to restrictive paper allotments. With thousands of pages to fill each month, the industry was a major employer of aspiring and would-be artists in the greater New York City area, where nearly all of the editorial work on comic books was done. Shops were a way for immigrants with limited English skills, or those unwilling or unable to market themselves or for kids fresh out of high school, to work at a drawing board and be paid for it.

The basics of drawing comic books wasn't hard to master for anyone with a modicum of talent and some aptitude for storytelling in pictures. Original comic art was drawn on sheets of sturdy drawing paper twice as large as the pages in the eventual comic book. Working from a script, the artist first drew the action in pencil in rows of panels. Then the word balloons and captions were lettered and the artwork was gone over in India ink, sometimes by a different artist, to complete the page. Often a shop had an apprentice, someone who did the mundane work while he learned the ropes. That was Kurtzman's role when he began working for Louis Ferstadt in June 1942, the same month his father went to prison. "I got in at the bottom of the barrel, and I . . . swept up the studio," he said. "But I was into the business."[21]

All-American Comics's super hero The Flash was Ferstadt's big account. "He did these marvelous drawings of The Flash," Kurtzman recalled. "Nobody [in the shop] would touch The Flash except Ferstadt."[22] Harvey's first "artwork" involved assisting on Gilberton's *Classic Comics* #5 (September 1942), an adaptation of Herman Melville's *Moby-Dick*: it was pencilled by Louis Zanksy, who was just three years Kurtzman's senior, also from the Bronx and an ex-Cooper Union student. It was inked by Fred Eng. Kurtzman's task was to do what he later described as "bits and pieces" of the inking (probably finishing the backgrounds), fill in the areas that were to be solid black and erase the pencil lines that showed after the ink had dried.

"I was really not much of anything when I was an assistant," he recalled. "I was an inker, chief cook and bottle washer. I didn't graduate to pencilling for quite a while."[23] Eventually, Kurtzman did "Murphy's Mess Boy" (*Four Favorites* #8, December 1942), possibly his first published pencil work in comic books (after the Buffalo Bob cartoon in *Tip Top Comics*). It's a humorous one-pager signed by "Kurtzman with Looey," which suggests that Ferstadt did the inking. After that, it was on to super heroes, where Kurtzman would handle the complete art job.

The husband-and-wife team Aaron and Rose Wyn founded Ace Comics in 1940. They had been publishing pulp magazines for a dozen years and were able to carve out a modest niche in the comic book field with a small line of titles beginning with *Super-Mystery Comics* #1, dated

July 1940. The publisher of record was Periodical House Inc., one of their trade names. Their star character was Magno the Magnetic Man who, along with his sidekick Davey, occupied the lead feature in *Super-Mystery* for the majority of its forty-eight-issue run. *Super-Mystery* had been on hiatus since July 1942, but the Wyns engaged Ferstadt to produce the book for its return with Vol. 3 #3 (dated January 1943), as well as provide material for a companion title, *Four Favorites*. Kurtzman's job was to help fill those pages, starting with the cover of the first new *Super-Mystery* (which actually hit newsstands in October or early November of 1942). It depicted a giant robot towering over a chained Magno and Davey, dealing out fiery death and destruction. It is signed "H. Kurtzman."

Fortunately for comics historians, Ferstadt allowed the artists to sign or initial the work, because this early "straight" work by Kurtzman bears little resemblance to anything he did later. He was simply acquiescing to the imperatives of the job in the best way he knew how: approximating the approach of Joe Simon and Jack Kirby, co-creators of Captain America and the foremost action artists of the Golden Age of comics. By this time, they had moved to National to produce stories featuring their new creations, the Boy Commandos and the Newsboy Legion with the Guardian. "If there was anybody I followed beyond The Spirit, it was Simon and Kirby," he said. "They did these action drawings that were remarkable."[24] In the interior pages of that issue, after the opening Magno story drawn by Walter Davoren (an artist of middling ability), Kurtzman turned out an eight-page Mr. Risk story titled "The Race Against Death!" Again he signed it "H. Kurtzman," as he did with a second story in that same issue starring Paul Revere Jr. Next, his work appeared on Lash Lightning in *Four Favorites* #9 (February 1943), this time merely initialed "H. K."

This humble work inducted Harvey Kurtzman into the ranks of comic book professionals. It wasn't that he was unaware he was being exploited. He simply didn't care. He was getting published, and would later describe seeing his work in print at the time as "better than sex!"[25] (For a seventeen-year-old, that's saying something.) At that age, he had no compunctions about drawing panels featuring bloody knifings, people being thrown into pools of acid and other gory excesses typical of the day. The Clown, Magno's nemesis, was at least as psychotic as the Joker in *Batman*—unsurprising, since he was a bald-faced copy.

"[Louis Ferstadt] was a guy who was tense as a bowstring," Kurtzman said. "He would never yell. His voice was always under control. But you always felt that he wanted to yell. He'd practically whisper, and he had [a] nervous little whistle. He'd whistle between his teeth . . . He'd say [whispering], 'Harvey, here's what I want, the way you do this is . . . ' He'd always keep his voice down but you felt he was like a volcano underneath. He was probably a tortured man. It was very sad. His whole career seemed to go down, down. Every once in a while, he'd start painting a portrait of somebody or other. He was very hot with several well-to-do families."[26] Kurtzman worked for Ferstadt until he entered the army a year later, churning out forgettable stories starring the aforementioned Mr. Risk, Paul Revere Jr., Magno and Davey, Lash Lightning, Buckskin and The Unknown Soldier.

Somewhere along the line, Brooklynite Eli Katz, another Jewish boy, joined the operation. Katz was just six months older than Kurtzman, a lanky ghetto kid who was in love with comic books, and was doing everything possible to work in the field. He had recently left school in his junior year in order to pursue that calling. Later, Katz changed his name to Gil Kane and became an important comic book artist. At this point, he could barely draw. He was fired from MLJ for general incompetence and having a big mouth. After a stint in the Jack Binder studio, Kane found himself in a seedy downtown office shoulder-to-shoulder with Ferstadt, Davoren and Kurtzman.

Kane described Kurtzman's appearance: "When I saw him, he was absolutely a neighborhood boy . . . with those cloth, peaked caps that no one wears any more, with the sweater that came down to the knuckles. And the sweater tucked inside the trousers, over the shirt and inside the trousers, and with the belt drawn. He would always have lunch in a brown paper bag with butter stains on it." But when Kane watched Kurtzman at the drawing board, he was impressed. "I watched him work, and it was the most discouraging thing for me, because it was beautiful. It was all very influenced by Jack Kirby, and it was all storytelling. It was all natural. He would just go from one panel to another, just penciling and eating a sandwich. It was unnerving to watch him."[27]

Kurtzman disagreed with Kane's assessment. "[My] work . . . was really abominable. Really, it was terrible. Our beginnings were so crude. In those days, anything sold, I guess, because we turned out tons and tons of it. Very bad stuff. You'd spit on a page, and they'd publish it."[28] An examination of Kurtzman's super hero work confirms his personal appraisal. The work isn't good. Yet Gil Kane's more positive statements are understandable. The storytelling is reasonably clear, the figures have energy, and the covers and splash panels, where extra effort was expended, are better still. The splash of Mr. Risk for "The Race Against Death" in *Super-Mystery Comics* #3 has some good figure placement and nice crosshatch

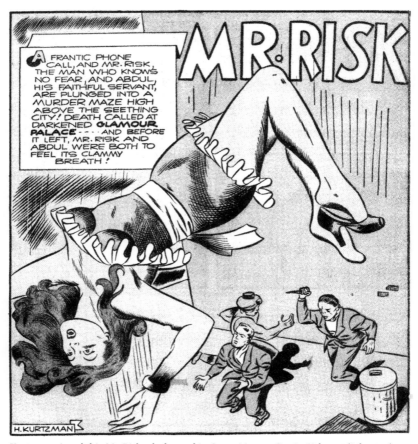

A FRANTIC PHONE CALL, AND MR. RISK, THE MAN WHO KNOWS NO FEAR, AND ABDUL, HIS FAITHFUL SERVANT, ARE PLUNGED INTO A MURDER MAZE HIGH ABOVE THE SEETHING CITY! DEATH CALLED AT DARKENED GLAMOUR PALACE - - - - AND BEFORE IT LEFT, MR. RISK AND ABDUL WERE BOTH TO FEEL ITS CLAMMY BREATH!

H.KURTZMAN

Kurtzman signed this *Mr. Risk* splash panel in *Super-Mystery Comics* Vol. 3 #5 (July 1943).

shading, as do the panels along the page's bottom. But the succeeding seven pages, each using a four-tier panel arrangement like Simon and Kirby at the time, are unremarkable, and appear to have been turned out quickly. The storytelling elements are sketchy, leaving a lot to the reader's imagination. The figures themselves are oddly stunted, making them look like short people running through rooms with low ceilings. (Kurtzman knew better, given his experience in figure-drawing classes.) The splash of Mr. Risk two issues later is dominated by a scantily clad woman displaying markedly better anatomical mastery—so good that it was probably a swipe—if not by Kurtzman, then by Ferstadt, who may have had a hand in certain splash panels. He was known to collaborate on some of the strips, either to instruct his staffers or simply to ensure the work would pass muster.

Toiling in junk comics paid as good or better than any other kind of employment available to Kurtzman. He never went back to Cooper Union after the first year. He was a working artist now. (Later, Kurtzman casually mentioned that he had been making $100 a week in comics when he was eighteen. That would have been toward the end of his prewar career when he pulled all-nighters to meet deadlines. Initially, he was probably paid in the $30 to $40 a week range, a substantial salary for a teenager in 1942.)

Ferstadt frequently relocated to get cheaper rent. They moved into a second studio, then a third. One was shared with a man who had a machine that filled little bottles with hair tonic. "He was an old guy, maybe in his sixties, and he was the most lecherous bastard I've ever met in my life," Kurtzman said. "He'd tell these stories, my first introduction to sex. How women would come in to have their hair washed . . . and he'd grab them from behind. He'd tell me stories . . . and I'd be sitting, listening, drawing."[29]

About the time Gil Kane moved on to something else, a new artist named L. B. Cole showed up. Leonard Brandt Cole was a New Yorker born in 1918. His father was in real estate and his mother was an illustrator for the *New York Journal American*. He got his start designing cigar box and liquor bottle labels for the Consolidated Lithographing Corporation in Brooklyn. Cole's first work in comics was on the Ace super heroes. He was a rank beginner, but improved rapidly. He proved particularly facile when inking with a brush. Kurtzman could have been referring to Cole when he later told an interviewer, "In that particular period, the technique of the brush, the #3 Winsor-Newton sable brush, was a world unto itself. The artist would actually, including myself, thrill to the manipulation of the brush, which had nothing to do with the idea of the cartoon, but had everything to do with technique. It was just a cosmetic part of the cartoon. Naturally the heart of the cartoon is the idea. But we were fascinated by the technique of the brush."[30]

On another occasion, he mused, "Working with a brush is practically indigenous to the comic book business because in syndicated cartooning they use pens. But in comics, lo and behold, the brush came into use. I don't know exactly why. I think it's just because it was speedier and because Lou Fine [the first star comic book artist] started using it very imaginatively. And the brush is a thing that really goes thick and thin. So these guys would be doing animated [i.e. funny animal, a.k.a. anthropomorphic] cartoons. Now, [inking] animated cartoons is purely an outline business and you don't need thick or thin lines. But these guys, particularly Chad Grothkopf, were masters of doing what should be a pen drawing with contour lines [using a brush]—thick and thin, and swirls and curves and swoops."[31] Sometime during this period, Kurtzman worked on funny animal pages for Grothkopf, perhaps doing a little inking. He did it because he had a crush on Chad's younger sister.

Of Kurtzman, L. B. Cole recalled, "Harvey was a doll. [He and I] used to eat our dinners in the Horn and Hardart [automat] on Forty-Fifth Street at three in the morning, because we really worked around the clock. We turned out tremendous amounts. To get paid, Louis would take a story into [the publisher], get a check, go to the bank and cash it and pay us in cash. [Kurtzman] was very, very organized, and [had] a sense of humor you could never forget. He was one of the geniuses."[32] Cole was speaking with the advantage of hindsight. No one was calling Kurtzman a genius in 1943.

War raged around the world, as Americans made do with various kinds of rationing at home. Big band music abounded, and uniformed men and women swarmed New York City. Kurtzman spent late 1942 and early 1943 shuttling between the Clinton Arms and the downtown offices where Louis Ferstadt was ensconced. In his free time, a common activity—now that he had a few dollars in his pocket—was spending time on the Grand Concourse with a pal or, perhaps, a date.

The Grand Concourse in the Bronx had the preeminent movie palace of the area, the Loew's Paradise Theatre. This theater, decorated in the baroque style that was popular in the 1920s, was a showplace in the neighborhood. Its famous starry ceiling loomed over marble and tapestries, transporting the patrons to a realm of fantasy and luxury. It was the perfect place to take a girl, and then afterward there was Krum's Ice Cream Parlor or other confectionary destinations.

Kurtzman became infatuated with certain young women (such as Grothkopf's sister), but he was shy and lacked confidence. Louis Ferstadt had women coming in and out of the studio, some of them working there for a time; most of them Kurtzman found unattractive. One was an exception. Kurtzman later told interviewer John Benson:

[Louis] had this very swift-looking girl. She looked like a hooker. And Lenny Cole would tease me, you know, he'd say, "Why don't you lay her?" And I had absolutely no experience. And one night, Lenny Cole said, "I'm going to fix you up." And he said, "You work late and . . . I'll give her the word." And sure enough, I worked late and this girl worked late. And I sat there frozen to my board—absolutely frozen to the board! I didn't know what to do. Here we were alone. I was alone with this girl, who had apparently been instructed by Leonard Cole. I was frozen, because I could never be sure . . . What's she thinking? You know, suppose I make a move, what if I do the wrong thing? And she finally got up and said, "Well, I've waited long enough." So she left, and I said, my God, it could have happened! It was genuine. Oh God, those were innocent days.[33]

Getting published had been exciting, but Ace Comics was low-rung. As the months in 1943 passed, however, with military service approaching, Harvey Kurtzman found himself taking a step up in the industry (through the auspices of Ferstadt) when he produced several dozen pages for Quality Comics. Quality was an A comic book publisher at this time, along with National (now DC), Timely, Fawcett and All-American. Quality had *Plastic Man* by the gifted Jack Cole, *Blackhawk* drawn by Reed Crandall, reprints of *The Spirit* by Will Eisner, and included above-average artwork by Ruben Moreira, Klaus Nordling, Alex Kotzky, Gill Fox, Paul Gustavson and Rudy Palais in popular titles such as *Police Comics* and *Hit Comics*. Kurtzman's *Flatfoot Burns* appeared in three issues of *Police*, and his work on *Bill the Magnificent* appeared in two issues of *Hit*.

Flatfoot Burns has the distinction of being Harvey Kurtzman's first humorous feature in comic books (apart from "Murphy's Mess-Boy"), and it fairly explodes with promise. The character was a comical Sherlock Holmes dressed in a deerstalker hat carrying a large magnifying glass, who had six pages to ferret out clues and solve a case. Kurtzman probably wrote the scripts.[34] The stories aren't especially funny, but they do provide situations where he could show his stuff. One can detect the influence of H. M. Bateman's exaggerated poses to heighten the action, and various design touches that hint at Kurtzman's mature style. It's the work of a cartoonist who is no longer a beginner, who knows how to tell a story and has a strong sense of composition, design and character.

Bill the Magnificent is a humorous "hero" strip featuring the adventures of a wimpy newspaper reporter who gains confidence and super strength when he utters the words "Jeepers Creepers!" A blow to the head changes him back to his regular self. In his super phase, he looks the same but becomes a stronger, bolder version of himself. This is worked for comic effect, as he tries to impress his girlfriend and his boss. Whereas Flatfoot Burns's stories are just six pages, the Bill the Magnificent tales stretch to eleven.

"I must say that I owe a debt of thanks to Ferstadt," Kurtzman stated years later. "He allowed me to go to work. He was the first step."[35] Though Kurtzman came to look down on this early work, at the time it was a source of substantial pride. Even though he was on the lowest rung of the ladder, he was now a working professional. However, just as he was pushing each assignment to a higher level, and he felt employment as a solo cartoonist was right around the corner, Kurtzman received his "Greetings" letter from Uncle Sam. The little schnook was going to war.

Kurtzman's earliest known comic book feature was *Murphy's Mess Boy* in *Four Favorites* #8 (December 1942). Special thanks to James Vadeboncoeur Jr.

Super-Mystery Comics Vol. 3 #3 (January 1943): Kurtzman art.

An example of Kurtzman's pre-war work: this Mr. Risk piece ran in *Super-Mystery Comics* Vol. 3 #5 (July 1943).

Flatfoot Burns in *Police Comics* #26 (January 1944). Kurtzman story and art.

4.

KURTZMAN IN UNIFORM

BY THE TIME HARVEY KURTZMAN entered the army, the tide of World War II was clearly turning against the Axis powers. Most of his classmates were already in uniform because they were older.

Al Jaffee had gone to US Air Force flight school but flunked due to motion sickness: "We tried to throw everything we could at the Nazis, but they didn't regard my parabolic vomit as an effective weapon."[1] He was transferred to a replacement center in Greensboro, North Carolina, then to the luxurious Miami Biltmore in Coral Gables, Florida, which had been converted into an army hospital. He led art therapy programs for shell-shocked soldiers.

Will Elder was living in New Brunswick, New Jersey, and was attending art school in Manhattan when he was inducted in 1942. Elder served in the 668th Topographical Engineers of the First Army, spending three years in Europe making maps. His biography reads, "Elder landed on the beaches of Normandy on D-Day plus six. He was among the troops that liberated Paris, went on with the shock troops and stormed Cologne, fought in the Battle of the Bulge, and was among the first American troops to cross the Rhine into Germany."[2]

John Severin volunteered in 1942, after working for A. C. Spark Plug Company, making 20 mm shells for the British and the French Air Force. He ended up in the Pacific theater working with military engineers in a non-combat role.

Harry Chester's diminutive stature was no obstacle at flight school. He served in the Philippines flying a Douglas C-47 and the Lockheed P-38 Lightning. Though he became an expert pilot, he laughingly told a story

Kurtzman was inducted into the US Army on June 23, 1943. Edith Kurtzman visited him at Fort Dix, New Jersey. Photographs courtesy of Adam Kurtzman.

about flying a planeload of Thanksgiving turkeys to Australia, but somehow missing the continent. After the war, he continued to work as a pilot.

On June 23, 1943, Harvey Kurtzman reported for duty at Fort Dix, New Jersey, where he would go through basic training. Though trained for the infantry, he was classified as a draftsman, and spent his twenty-eight months in uniform serving in a succession of stateside army bases. He looked grown-up in his crisp dress uniform. He is at his most handsome in the formal portrait taken by the military for the benefit of the recruit's family. Private Kurtzman's imperfect teeth don't show, nor does his still-plentiful hair. The eighteen-year-old may have known of his stateside posting when the photo was taken. If he did, he was smart enough to realize there was no guarantee he wouldn't eventually face combat. Storming Germany and Japan was going to take all the Allies' military might, and he was in for the duration, plus six months.

Edith made the trip to Fort Dix to visit Harvey before he was sent to his first post of duty. In a photograph taken that day, her face conveys two expressions: the right side shows an attempt to smile and look pleasant; the left, with its downturned mouth, is unhappy, remote. She must have hoped that her middle son, with his slight physique and mild demeanor, wouldn't have to go.

An unsettling event occurred not long after basic training began. Kurtzman was on a detail with a group of men ordered to demolish an old barracks. In the process, they discovered numerous rats' nests under the building. Kurtzman watched while the men gleefully chased after the rats, clubbing them to death. He recalled, "The cruelty of that moment where we [discovered] rats under that barracks . . . the little animals running in every direction, and there's this platoon of guys just having a wild old time smashing them . . . was to me an example of man's irreverence to . . . yes, even rats. I just had a very strong feeling that if mankind did have more of a reverence for life that possibly we'd have less killing."[3] It haunted him.

There were special duties at Fort Dix that required a certain amount of art ability, though it isn't known which ones Kurtzman performed, if any. The base had its own newspaper, the *Fort Dix Poster*, which regularly ran cartoons drawn by recruits. There was a sign shop where soldiers used their talents on such projects as painting the word "garbage" on metal cans, as well as creating posters and signs. At that time, Kurtzman may not have gotten more to do with his hands than hold a rifle and wash dishes. He was in the "Pearl Divers," i.e. the dishwashers' platoon. "I did a lot of KP [kitchen patrol]," he recalled.[4]

This changed when he was transferred to another camp in early 1944. Camp Sutton was located near the town of Monroe, North Carolina, in the rural, western part of the state. It was a twenty-minute drive to Charlotte, the nearest large town, which had a population in excess of one hundred thousand. Camp Sutton was built to house and train 18,750 soldiers, and was later expanded to handle more. It was the headquarters of the Engineer Unit Training Center, a training camp for army engineers. Kurtzman served in the Morale Services Branch of the Information-Education Division. A relatively small amount of his work for Morale Services has survived.

The period from ages eighteen to twenty-one years old is critical in the creative development of most artists, including cartoonists. Those are the years when the creative juices flow, when the imagination is at its most unfettered and when most successful cartoonists gain a handle on the requisite craftsmanship to produce professional work. It's a time when many first stand at their full creative height—perhaps wobbly, still green in many respects, but also when the artistic identity begins to jell. In Kurtzman's case, he spent those years in a military environment rubbing shoulders not with his usual group of creative New Yorkers, but with all manner of men who were under the typical stresses that come with war. His assignments addressed various aspects of combat: morale, readiness, equipment maintenance, and more. He saw how the soldier psychologically prepared himself for battle. It was a learning experience that had a profound effect on him.

Kurtzman was assigned to work on the *Carry All*, the Camp Sutton newspaper. It seems the men weren't paying enough attention to the bi-weekly publication. Kurtzman came up with a solution: he put a sexy woman on the front page of its April 15, 1944 edition. The cartoon artist stands in front of his huge drawing of a woman in a bathing suit, saying, "Howz's for a change, fellers?!!" The drawing is made to appear as if it's plastered over a regular front page, with bits of text showing at the corners where the drawing curls up. The idea that a soldier has "taken over" the paper has a clever, almost populist message. "Give the guys what they want!" it seems to say. As for the rendering itself, it's apparent that Kurtzman's love affair with the brush is complete. There's not a pen line in sight. A closer look reveals that along the contour of one curvaceous leg, Private First Class (PFC) Kurtzman has signed his name.

The Morale Services Branch had more serious items on its agenda than pictures of pin-up girls. They were responsible for producing items, such as posters, that visually drove home a slogan or training point. One poster Kurtzman drew was titled "Basic Training Counts!" It shows a soldier on a battlefield caught in an explosion over the words "He missed his basic in Booby Traps." He also created a fundraising poster titled "Army Emergency Relief," which uses a Salvadore Dalí-esque layout with over-sized coins in place of melting clocks, strewn across planks converging on a central point, where a soldier in shadow makes a gesture of supplication. The well-conceived poster showed that Kurtzman had the makings of an imaginative, effective propagandist.

Working in the department that produced artwork for training purposes meant he probably saw *Army Motors*, a preventive maintenance magazine which utilized cartoons and "how to" illustrations by Will Eisner. The creator of *The Spirit*, now in the military, helped develop the format of *Army Motors*. "I began doing cartoons and we began fashioning a magazine that had the ability to talk to the GI's in their language," Eisner said. "So I began to use comics as a teaching tool."[5] He created the comic strip character Joe Dope for the publication, which continued after the war. The army's use of cartoons as a teaching tool got Kurtzman thinking about working along similar lines.

He sent letters to his mother with funny drawings on the envelopes. Inside, along with his jottings, he sometimes enclosed photos and some of his pay. As a PFC, he received $50 a month. One snapshot shows him in sloppy army fatigues, with a word balloon added: "Podden my appearance! Getting ready for Sat. inspection."[6]

Being in the service gave Kurtzman a much wider view of the world, as it did for many of his comrades who had never been outside their neighborhoods or small towns. The majority of the approximately five million American Jews at that time lived in New York City, and had never ventured west. About 500,000 of them served in World War II, living side by side with Gentiles from all walks of life: Appalachians, Bible Belt Christians, cowboys, breadbasket flat-landers and so on. If he was the target of anti-Semitic incidents, as others were, he never mentioned them.

Kurtzman's comic book work was still appearing in print when he was at Camp Sutton. Quality's *Hit Comics* #32, with his last Bill the Magnificent story, came out after he had been there a few months, as did his final work for Ace Comics. The last of his prewar comics seems to have been the cover of *Four Favorites* #15, which appeared in May 1944. (It was done a year earlier.) He saw how much comics meant to his fellow recruits. The racks at the PX's [postal exchanges—an army base general store] in the States and around the world were jammed with such four-color fare, some 130 different titles in 1944, and they sold out as quickly as they came in. That year, *Captain Marvel Adventures* was the most popular comic book in the world, boasting an annual circulation of 14,067,535 copies. Sales of *Superman* weren't far behind.[7] The comics were a colorful diversion for bored, restless soldiers.

One type of comic book disturbed him: the war comics. Even before the United States had entered the war, Dell published *War Comics* and Fiction House put out *Wings*, an air-fighter book. In 1941, along came *Military* from Quality and *Rangers* from Fiction House. Three major war-themed character titles began during the war: *Boy Commandos* (Winter 1942–43), *Don Winslow* (1943) and *Blackhawk* (1944). Many of the super heroes fought "Krauts" and "Nips." Probably a third or more of the comics on newsstands featured war themes in one form or other. Kurtzman didn't object to comics depicting war, only the way they treated it. "[The] war comics . . . that came out during the war [showed] the American soldier killing little buck-toothed yellow men," he said. "I thought that was terrible."[8] He felt that dehumanizing the enemy was wrong. Perhaps because he was a Jewish man, he could understand what it was to be the "other."

Everyone was contributing to the war effort, even comic strip characters. Milton Caniff's Terry of *Terry and the Pirates*, one of the most popular and artistically influential strips of its day, became an Air Force pilot. Barney Google and Mickey Finn joined the navy. Joe Palooka served in the African campaign. Heroes in uniform enhanced identification and added relevance to the adventure strips. Those who wanted a simple laugh or escapism could still find it in *Alley Oop*, *Krazy Kat* and *Blondie*. In November 1943, Roy Crane launched *Buz Sawyer*, a more sophisticated strip than *Wash Tubbs*, his first big success. It was one of Kurtzman's favorites. In his new strip, Crane's artwork reached a highly accomplished level of storytelling and rendering. Kurtzman learned from Crane, observing the way he staged the unfolding action and story points, and his ability to lighten the material's serious tone by giving the character work a humorous tinge.

What could have been more natural than for Harvey Kurtzman to do his own original comic strip for the *Carry All*? His *Private Brown Knows* was a one-tier strip like a syndicated daily newspaper strip. There were about four months' worth of episodes beginning shortly after Kurtzman arrived on the base.[9] Often such strips offered an educational message along with a gag. The episode of *Private Brown Knows* titled "Rifle Inspection" includes an admonition to trainees about keeping one's weapon dust-free. Like his work in the super hero comics, PFC Kurtzman's figures appear stunted, as if they were between four and five feet tall. It's a curious affectation for art in the quasi-realistic world of super heroes and the military milieu. He seems to have been applying the conventions of humorous comic strips across the board. From a practical standpoint, shorter people were easier to fit into a panel. Anyway, Private Brown is at least half-humorous for most of its episodes.

After D-Day, the strip reflected the serious mood of the moment. On June 19, 1944, a final, full-page *Private Brown Knows* titled "Exodus" appeared on the cover of the *Carry All*, Vol. 1 #19. It's a tough, uncompromising "goodbye" message to the men from both Private Brown, who mouthed the words, and PFC Kurtzman, who created the strip. It reminds soldiers that they should focus their frustration and anger on the enemy, on "the job we've originally set out to do!" The "Give 'em hell!" in the final panel depicts a GI about to bayonet a German soldier, with the lettering large and without a balloon around it, as if being shouted.

Superficially, the conclusion of "Exodus" would seem to be at variance with Kurtzman's horror at the rat-clubbing incident. The thrust of the strip, however, was to deal with what was probably fairly low morale among the men, and to refocus their attention to the job at hand. Clearly

Kurtzman was tasked with doing something—it appeared on the front cover of the *Carry All*, not inside—to send off the exiting troops, many heading to combat, with a strong motivational message. Kurtzman had no illusions about the toughness of battle. The orchestration of the theatrics in "Exodus" is especially skillful, from a beginning so quiet that the first panel has no dialogue at all, to the final panel of all-out violence.

Besides honing his comic strip skills during his military stint, Kurtzman did freelance work for nearby businesses while he was at Camp Sutton. Kurtzman biographers Denis Kitchen and Paul Buhle wrote, "Among the now-brittle tear sheets he proudly saved were newspaper ads for the Plaza Airport and Union National Bank in Charlotte, and trade magazine ads for the Hatch Full Fashioned Hosiery Company in Belmont."[10]

In June, Kurtzman and the other remaining men at Camp Sutton were transferred because the Allies overseas needed it to house German prisoners of war. After D-Day, the number of such prisoners sharply increased. From 1942 through 1945, more than 400,000 Axis prisoners were shipped to the United States and detained in camps in rural areas, about 500 locations in all. At the same time, many American soldiers were being shipped overseas, to either close the deal in Europe or to face action in the Pacific.

FOR A TIME, KURTZMAN was with the US Army Engineering department in Louisiana. Being a Yankee from the liberal Northeast, he found Southern attitudes toward race differed from those he'd learned at home. The mainstream media—including comic strips and books—still portrayed black people in a grossly stereotypical manner, but the war sometimes brought the races together to work in proximity, and attitudes were beginning to change in some quarters. Kurtzman recalled:

> I remember being emotionally pro-Negro, anti-Southern, although we had no real contact with black people at home. When I was in the army down south and a large group of redneck soldiers and I were standing at a bus stop, a black officer from a black work battalion—something very unusual back then—came by, and the rednecks turned away instead of saluting. One could always claim ignorance by turning away, unless one was called to attention. So I called the group to attention, forcing them to salute. That was my outstanding blow against racism. It was a radical act at that time.[11]

Kurtzman received a Christmas furlough in 1944. It was good to be back in his old stomping grounds, but he had no intention of hanging around the apartment with his mother and Daniel (who was in junior high school). He had the perfect excuse: he would try to earn some extra money to help with Edith's household expenses. Kurtzman went into Manhattan, probably looking for Louis Ferstadt. He ended up picking up some quick cash not from Ferstadt, but from his old shop-mate, L. B. Cole.

Eighteen months had passed. By this time, Cole had advanced to the position of art editor for Continental Publications, elbowing aside the tired Charles Quinlan. He and Ray Hermann, Temerson's former editorial assistant, took over the operation and were soon producing comic books published under imprints such as Aviation Press. Aviation Press put out *Contact Comics*, which sport stunning aeronautic covers by Cole, who had developed into a masterful designer. Kurtzman worked on that title while on military leave. *Contact* offered aeronautically themed strips starring characters such as Golden Eagle (a Blackhawk imitator), Tommy Tomahawk (a Native American pilot), and Triggers (a Texan aviator). There's also Black Venus, a "modern Joan of Arc," who flies what looks like a Lockheed P-38 Lightning (like Harry Chester). She's really Mary Roche, a USO hostess in Burma, drawn in her early adventures by Rudy Palais and Nina Albright. The six-pager by Kurtzman in *Contact* #6 (May 1945), which dealt with Japanese POW atrocities, has his most mature work yet. He had obviously been reading *Terry and the Pirates*, because the faces show more than a little Caniff influence. Kurtzman later confirmed, "I went through a period of imitating Milton Caniff because that's what the market wanted. And that was the only way I could get work."[12] The heroine looks sleek and sexy in her form-fitting leather flying suit.

Kurtzman found that Cole's rise in fortunes brought out the worst in him: "[Cole] was very friendly. He was telling me about Louis Ferstadt. He said he'd given him a couple of jobs, and he'd deliberately given him a hard time just because he'd worked for the guy. He said, 'So I made him do things over.' He made *me* do things over, and I'm sure it was purely for the sadism of making me do it over." That sort of behavior repulsed Kurtzman; he later described Leonard Cole as "a snake, an absolute snake."[13] Louis Ferstadt died in 1954 while in his early fifties, an idealist of the 1930s who didn't live to see beyond the McCarthy Era.

NOT LONG AFTER THE ARDENNES offensive known as the Battle of the Bulge in late January 1945, Kurtzman was transferred to the Twenty-Fifth Infantry Regiment at Camp Maxey, near Paris, Texas. He began to think it was possible he would sit out the duration of the war in the middle of nowhere, almost one hundred miles from Dallas or any other sizable town.

That's where he mourned the death of President Roosevelt on April 12, and celebrated V-E Day less than a month later.

Kurtzman set about making himself useful in the art department. One of his early projects was illustrating a booklet called the *Guide to Camp Maxey Texas*. Its cover shows a GI looking befuddled as he arrives at the camp. Page two consists of a cartoon showing various stages of training, and text which begins, "As a member of the Infantry Replacement Training Center here at Camp Maxey, you will receive fifteen weeks of intensive training to enable you to take your place as a proficient infantryman replacement in either a rifle company or heavy weapons company. This is real basic training, during which time you will learn to take care of yourself and your equipment in battle."[14] The most notable piece of Kurtzman work in the booklet is an elaborate map, a two-page spread that shows the entire camp replete with little cartoon gags at various locations. The camp was enormous, covering an area of 36,683 acres, with billeting space for 2,022 officers, and 42,515 enlisted personnel.

Not all of Kurtzman's work was so elaborate. He also drew simple messages such as "What can you do?," a call for soldiers to take part in a big GI show, which were run off on a mimeograph machine.[15] For the May 25, 1945, edition of the *Maxey Times*, he added cartoon decorations to dress up the photo report "Yankee Ingenuity Deep in the Heart of Texas." He created cartoons for the paper celebrating the sporting achievements of certain officers and enlisted men. Plus, as he put it, "I did all kinds of training aids stuff: drawings and diagrams."[16]

Kurtzman had his buddies on the base, and when they had some time off, they sometimes made their way to Galveston. The seaside town was a party destination for military men from camps in Texas and Louisiana. Many a drunken revelry occurred in its bars, beaches and hotels. The straight-laced Kurtzman had at least one highly memorable night in Galveston. His brother Zachary later revealed, "[Harvey] was seduced, down in Galveston, by a couple of young ladies who admired his painting of the sunset on the beach and insisted on introducing him to the life of eros. I got a fourteen-page letter from him, profusely illustrated, with the opener, 'Dear Zack, now I know why people get married!'"[17]

THE END OF THE WAR was in sight, yet when Japan held firm against surrender, the path to victory was daunting. Kurtzman and many other soldiers on the base were set to ship out for the invasion of Japan when the Enola Gay dropped the "Little Boy" atomic bomb on Hiroshima on August 6, 1945. A second atomic bomb was dropped on Nagasaki on August 9. V-J

Day came, and the war was over. Despite the end of hostilities, demobilization was a huge undertaking, and Kurtzman was one of hundreds of thousands of men who were stuck waiting for a discharge and transport home. Camp Maxey was placed on inactive status on October 1, necessitating another move. Now Corporal Kurtzman (T-5) found a new billet at Fort Bragg, South Carolina.

In an effort to build up his portfolio, he submitted five cartoons to *Yank*, the weekly national military magazine. He received a letter dated October 10 from editor Sgt. Ray Duncan, stating that he wanted to use three of the five. One that saw print showed some enlisted men lingering in the mess hall after eating, something unheard of during wartime, with a fellow with a mop and bucket saying, "Awright, you guys, this ain't the officers' club!" Kurtzman was delighted when he received his copies of the over-sized magazine with his work inside.

His goal was to have as impressive a portfolio as possible when he returned to civilian life. In addition to items produced at M&A, the Art Students League and Cooper Union, as well as examples of his comic book pages, he was able to add printed copies and tear sheets of his work in army publications, advertising work from the *Charlotte Observer*, a sophisticated silk-screened Christmas card for 1945 (the only silk-screen work he ever did) and more.

Kurtzman summed up his time in the military as "pretty dreadful."[18] Nevertheless, it had an upside. After high school graduation, Kurtzman looked at the markets for cartoonists and wondered where he fit in. He

"AWRIGHT, YOU GUYS, THIS AIN'T THE OFFICERS' CLUB!"
—T-5 Harvey Kurtzman

Yank Vol.4 #23 (November 23, 1945): Kurtzman cartoon.

wasn't great at doing gag panels, breaking into newspaper syndication seemed almost impossible and working in comic books wasn't what he wanted. Not being an illustrator or gag cartoonist, what would he do for the slick magazines he so admired? Some other sort of humor features? Then came the war, which broadened him and gave him opportunities to do many kinds of artwork. It stretched him creatively and gave him experience in a variety of media and forms. His army work was the real beginning of his career, doing work he respected in a style that was becoming recognizably his own. And, as he was helping win the war with his creative abilities, he came away with a new idea: using cartoons to educate.

The work he did in those "wasted" twenty-eight months bolstered his confidence. He went in an uncertain eighteen-year-old boy, and emerged a more self-possessed young man. When twenty-one-year-old Harvey Kurtzman was discharged from the US Army in November 1945, he walked away with a respectable portfolio tucked under his arm, and a pent-up desire to get about the business of making good.

Kurtzman's final *Private Brown Knows* installment (June 10, 1944) eschewed humor for a grimly serious message, as many of the troops at Camp Sutton were being shipped overseas to the European and Pacific theaters of war.

5.

"WE OF A CERTAIN MILIEU"

HARVEY KURTZMAN HAD grown as an artist in the army, but projects had come to him like school assignments, with a paternalistic Uncle Sam giving him the work while taking care of his room and board. Now he was back in the world of business and commerce, and would have to find assignments himself. He had a certain amount of mustering-out pay and whatever he had been able to save—$300 or $400, at most—but was keen on getting to work as soon as possible.

Though his portfolio was stocked with items that could pass for commercial art, Kurtzman wasn't sure how he would fit in that highly competitive arena. Therefore, he returned to comic books. "Me, Will Elder, Al Jaffee . . . we of a certain geographic [and] economic milieu . . . all did exactly the same thing," he later observed. "We . . . went to exactly the same places, because we were in exactly the same fix. It's funny how people in common circumstances tend to do the same things."[1] Will Elder found his way to Ray Hermann, the only female owner of a comic book company. She started a firm called Orbit Publications in 1945, after working with Leonard Cole at Continental. She liked Elder's *Rufus De Bree*, his take on Mark Twain's *A Connecticut Yankee in King Arthur's Court*, and put it into *Toytown Comics*. Al Jaffee had gotten his foot in the door at Timely Comics before the war, drawing and writing all but the first episode of the humor strip *Squat Car Squad*, and creating, writing and drawing *Silly Seal and Ziggy Pig*. After his release from the military, he joined the publisher's in-house staff as a writer-artist.

Kurtzman's first port of call was Aviation Press, the domain of L. B. Cole. He didn't like Cole but had few contacts, so he found himself in Cole's office at 113 W. Forty-Second St. The editor welcomed him and quickly offered another *Black Venus* script. Super heroes were on the wane after the war, but a boomlet in super heroines kept *Venus* hanging on. The resulting six-pager in *Contact* #11 (March 1946) concerns wounded veterans being preyed upon by greedy racketeers. The result looks quite different from what Kurtzman turned out in his first *Venus* assignment, with oddly distorted faces and agitated, unattractive inking. It's almost as if his dislike of Cole came out in the work. He gave the man a wide berth after this, even during lean times in the coming years.[2]

Black Venus was probably drawn in Kurtzman's room in the Clinton Arms. His father was still in prison, serving the fourth of what would be six-plus years at Allenwood. For Harvey Kurtzman, that apartment was its own kind of a prison after being away for more than two years. Living with his mother meant enduring her nagging, her edicts about cleanliness and her criticism of other aspects of his life, which rankled more than ever now that he was a young man who had reached his majority. Despite this, he dutifully stayed to help support Edith and Daniel until Abe's release.

But Kurtzman didn't intend to work as well as live there. He needed a space solely dedicated to work, without the distractions of home life and in closer proximity to the multitude of publishers, both comic book and otherwise. Some cartoonists toiled at home, often after they had an established freelance arrangement with a publisher or two. To young up-and-comers, being "close to the action" meant an opportunity could be quickly seized, and helped build a network of contacts. Also, having a studio was a certain badge of professionalism that was especially important to young aspirants like Kurtzman, who sought to establish their credentials. To cut costs, artists banded together to share studio space. Usually one would lease the space, then sublet to others who supplied their own drawing board, lamp and taboret. Fred Ottenheimer, a young artist and designer, agreed to take Kurtzman in, probably for about $25 a month, so he carted his drawing board on the train into Manhattan, ready to start his career in earnest.

"There were comic book publishers hidden out in every loft in New York right about that time," Kurtzman later remembered. "There was a big boom in comics going on then."[3] Armed with a list of addresses, or following up on tips from fellow artists, cartoonists tramped from publisher to publisher, showing their samples until someone proffered a script. But Kurtzman seems to have gone directly to Timely Comics, because he never spoke of professional rebuffs at this time. Perhaps he got together with

Harry Jaffee shortly after his return, and Harry told him his brother Al was working there.

Timely publisher Martin Goodman hadn't let a fifth-grade education stop him from building one of the largest and most successful magazine and comic book publishing companies in the United States. The bespectacled, prematurely white-haired publisher liked having his offices in impressive buildings. Since before the war, the Timely office was located in the McGraw-Hill Building on Forty-Second Street, a landmark of Art Deco design. In mid-1943, Goodman moved his operation to the Empire State Building, then the tallest building in the world. Not long after 1946 arrived, Harvey Kurtzman found himself riding the elevator to its fourteenth floor to meet Goodman's editor, Stan Lee.

Stan Lee, born Stanley Martin Lieber in 1922, was a cousin of Martin Goodman's wife. In 1939, he began working at Timely as an office boy, and at eighteen years old, when Simon and Kirby went to National Comics, became temporary editor in chief of Goodman's entire comic book line. At the same time, he proved himself an enthusiastic and capable writer. Then Lee went into the military, officially classified as a "playwright" in the Signal Corps. A cartoonist named Vince Fago handled the editorial chores until Lee was discharged on September 29, 1945. Within a couple of days, Lee was back in harness, now officially editor in chief. He had been back about three months when he was shaking hands with Harvey Kurtzman and looking over his portfolio.

Kurtzman was ready to do anything Stan Lee offered. If Lee needed a penciller, he would be a penciller. Or he would be an inker, or a writer. "Finding work was the important thing. I wasn't too particular as to what kind of work it was."[4] Lee looked through Kurtzman's prewar *Flatfoot Burns* strips, and liked them. "So that's the way it all started, after the war. I started doing animated cartoons for Stan Lee."[5]

The feature was called *Pigtales*. Lee assigned Kurtzman to write and draw the first six-page story of its two porcine protagonists, Homer and Hickstaff. While funny animals weren't his

Stan Lee in the late 1940s.

favorite, Kurtzman was glad that he had a foot in the door at Timely, a firm that published dozens of titles. He later said it was the company for him because he got "the right vibrations" from Lee. Kurtzman was paid about $180 for the debut tale in *All Surprise Comics* #1 (Fall 1946), which introduced Homer, the big dumb one, and Hickstaff, the smart little guy, a familiar comedy-team formula. It begins, "Come with us, dear reader, and follow Homer Hog and Hickstaff through political intrigues and international scandals! See how justice triumphs and how clean living counts! See all kinds of stuff!" In panel two, Hickstaff announces, "Yep—We're all set, Homer, except for a minor thing! We need some money!"

Pigtales is fun, fast and has a number of Kurtzman touches, further confirmation that he was the writer. When a scene changes, a little character proclaims "now—let us shift scenes for a moment!," breaking the fourth wall. Actions are pushed to drastic extremes. When scientists trying to create life think their experiment has produced the doltish Homer, they throw him out the window of a skyscraper "for the good of humanity!"

All Surprise Comics #11 (Fall 1946).

When Hickstaff cracks a terrible joke, the enraged scientists again become murderous, screaming, "For such a phooey gag, they must die!" Homer and Hickstaff's goal to "make money" leads them to what they think is a counterfeiting den, an autobiographical echo of Abraham Perkes' transgressions. Lee was happy with Kurtzman's work and ordered five more *Pigtales*, though the second one ("Mountain Climbing") saw print first (in *Kid Movie Komics* #11, summer 1946).

Apart from his reservations about comic books' poor printing and paper, Kurtzman began feeling that he wasn't really cut out for working in that medium. In a non-commercial environment (like school), it might be true that "speed in drawing is not necessarily important," as he wrote years later.[6] In comic books, it mattered a great deal. Kurtzman had been able to churn out pages for Louis Ferstadt relatively quickly, but his standards were higher now. Reaching his true potential meant taking more time on the work, and he was constitutionally unable to turn in less than his best. Yet the rates were such in the comic book business that one had to be able to work quickly to make a decent living. Al Jaffee, who was able to produce at considerable speed, made more than $10,000 in his first year out of the army, a huge amount of money in 1946.[7] Kurtzman couldn't come close to that kind of pace. This was one of the reasons he wanted to move into slick magazines and other forms of commercial art. The pay was better, and quality was more important than quantity.

When the *Pigtales* work ended, Kurtzman was left with a filler strip that he had created, written and drawn concurrently with the adventures of Homer and Hickstaff. Filler pages, which helped complete the page count when the books were assembled for publication, were perfect for him. They fit easily between other projects and, because there were no deadlines, he could work at his own pace. Most fillers had continuing characters. When Lee saw Kurtzman's first untitled sample page, he liked it and gave it a name: "We'll call it 'Hey Look!'"[8] Because fillers were comparatively insignificant, and he recognized Kurtzman's talent, Lee gave the writer-artist *carte blanche*. "With *Hey Look!* I had a radical amount of control," Kurtzman said. "Stan Lee would buy pages from me sight unseen. I'd come in with a page and he'd take it. It was unlike anything I'd done before where people would say, 'Do this, do that, do the other thing.' I think the more freedom you have, the more power you have, the more creative you can be."[9]

Where did Kurtzman get the idea for *Hey Look!*? When French comics fan Jacques Dutrey interviewed him in 1980, and pointed out similarities between *Pigtales* and *Hey Look!*, Kurtzman responded, "In *Pigtales* there was a big fool and the little smart guy, and in *Hey Look!* I had again the big fool and the little smart guy. That's a very Freudian product of my imagination. The characters were something out of the subconscious. Perhaps I saw something in my childhood and that suggested the big fool and the little smart aleck."[10]

The first two *Hey Look!* pages appeared in *Joker* #23 (June 1946). They were sandwiched between such other items as *Tessie the Typist*, *Ruffy Ropes*, *Squat Car Squad*, *Little Vinegar*, *Snoopy and Dr. Nutzy* and *Powerhouse Pepper*. That issue carried a page called "Now YOU can be the Editor!," asking readers to fill out a coupon stating the best and worst features in the comic book, promising "If you send in one of the fifty neatest and most interesting coupons, the publishers of *Joker Comics* will send you a crisp new one dollar bill." This was one way Stan Lee and Martin Goodman could tell what readers liked, and weed out material that tested low.

In its early stages, *Hey Look!* is a cute, but not too remarkable, goofy page (or half page). A benefit of examining the *Hey Look!* strips in the order they were produced is that one can observe the growth of Kurtzman the cartoonist in the petri dish of total freedom. This wasn't possible at the time, since, as fillers, they were inserted into random titles (*Joker, Tessie the Typist, Willie, Kid Movie Komics, Gay Comics, Cindy,* etc.) and didn't run in chronological order. Only when they were finally published in one book in the proper order (*Hey Look!*, Kitchen Sink Press, 1992) has it been possible to closely trace the incremental development of Harvey Kurtzman's first important comic book work.[11]

Given that the initial episode begins with the little guy looking "fer de pot uv gold at de end uv de rainbow," Lee's choice of title *Hey Look!* was fitting. As for the world where Kurtzman's two protagonists live, there seems neither rhyme nor reason nor laws of physics. The big guy enters by walking down a vertical wall and then is kicked so high in the air that he's able to grab onto an airplane. In the final panel, the little guy threatens to shoot "de guy dat wrote dis gag!!" This initial page—the tryout page—didn't see print for more than a year. Instead, the first *Hey Look!* pages readers saw in *Joker* #23 showed the little guy making a jet-propelled back pack, and playing with boats in the bathtub. In each case, Kurtzman begins with a kernel of an idea then pushes it to absurd extremes. Characters fly in the air, carom off walls and fire real bullets with toy weapons.

Although nearly all of the pages go for some sort of funny twist in the last panel, they weren't constructed merely to build to a final gag (as was the norm for most comedy fillers). Its chief pleasures are in the way

The first *Hey Look!* page was promising, but crude compared to what came later. Timely didn't publish it until *Jeannie* #17 (January 1948), over a year after the feature made its debut.

Kurtzman develops each episode's premise from panel to panel. The wild behavior and heightened reactions of the characters are highly inventive and entertaining. When the big guy gets heartburn, flames shoot from his mouth. When a character is mad at himself, he punches himself in the face. The style is frenetic, alternating between violent gags and more subtle sequences, as the fellows deal with things such as hiccups, a police grilling under hot lights, pole-vaulting, eating corn on the cob or putting the laundry out to dry: ordinary things done in extraordinary ways. Even as the characters flip, spin and bounce through the panels, one notices Kurtzman gradually giving more visual unity to his pages. The solid black areas begin to be placed more effectively, and the action becomes more focused and easier to follow. The protagonists—it's usually just the two of them—seem more vivid and alive.

Though *Hey Look!* was just another filler to Stan Lee, to Harvey Kurtzman it was the equivalent of his own Sunday syndicated newspaper page. Whatever the scale, he had what he'd wanted since he was a kid cartoonist: his own ongoing professional canvas. If his audience wasn't the millions who read successful newspaper strips, it was still in the hundreds of thousands.

An especially appreciative reader worked right there in the Timely offices. As Adele Hasan proofread *Hey Look!* before publication, she was struck by its originality and panache. She later recalled, "I said to [Al] Jaffee, 'This is different stuff. This is funny.'"[12] Jaffee checked out the pages and agreed.

> [Harvey] was doing *Hey Look!*, and I was in a room with a bunch of other cartoonists—Mike Sekowsky, Ed Winiarski, Dave Gantz and a couple of others—and when we heard Harvey Kurtzman was delivering a *Hey Look!*, we all jumped up and ran in to look at it. That's how impressed we were with this young kid who was bringing these unusual things in because we were all locked into very standard comics. I was doing teenaged stuff, Mike Sekowsky was doing teenage as well as adventure, pencilling Captain America and what have you. We had a room full of pretty bright guys and, I think proof of it was we had an interest in what Harvey Kurtzman was bringing in. That was a very important element.[13]

Staffers wouldn't normally have paid much attention to a filler strip, but in the case of Kurtzman's page, they did.[14]

"He was nobody," Jaffee said. "He was doing this one page thing and you know, it wasn't as if he was another Ken Bald or one of those hot shot

Kurtzman's *Hey Look!*, with "the big fool and the little smart guy." From *Cindy* #17 (Fall 1947).

guys coming in from the outside. He was just this unassuming young guy delivering one page of nonsense." Not that there was much socializing in the Timely offices. That wasn't permitted. "We were all salaried and we didn't have a lot of freedom," he said. "We were pretty much expected to sit at our drawing tables and work."[15]

As Kurtzman put it, "I suddenly became a special character when I would go up to Stan Lee's office. I was the guy who did those strange fillers. This, to me was the first clue as to where I should put my energies. I knew I was better off being my own man than trying to be a part of the system."[16] When he brought in a new *Hey Look!* or two, Kurtzman paused briefly at the bullpen for a little comic book gossip—perhaps a lead on a possible job—and then was gone.

Jaffee later described Kurtzman's approach. "Harvey never created jokes. What Harvey created was these very, very, very outlandish and funny situations. Everything he did was satirical. I don't think Harvey could create a sitcom joke, but . . . he could take a sitcom and make it hilariously funny by taking off on it. He could have a sitcom situation that . . . so many people are howling at . . . and go a little step further and further until it is absolutely ridiculous, and then *he* starts laughing."[17]

ADELE HASAN, the appreciative proofreader, was a fish out of water in a comic book office. The diminutive twenty-year-old brunette (just 5'1" tall) had secured her post through subterfuge. She was looking for a job and answered a classified ad for a position as a proofreader. Not only could she not type but she had never proofread before. "A friend of mine typed the response to Timely," she said recently. "So that was a couple of lies, and that's how I got into the comics business."[18] She was born in the Bronx, and had one sister, Doris.

> My mother Betsy (or Bess) was a housewife and took in hundreds of family and borders. The beds never got cold in our house. Our parents were immigrants. My mother came over to this country when she was fourteen as a servant. My dad Joseph was a factory worker in a leather factory, finishing leather wallets and stuff.[19] I had great parents. If my mother would tend to give us a little swat, my father would stand in front of us and say, "Don't hit the children!"[20]

During her teenage years, Adele had been a bit of a wild child: "I was a horrible teenager. I went out with bad boys. When [my mother] said come home at ten, I came home at twelve. She used to call the police on me. But it didn't last that long."[21] Bess sent her to an all-girls high school to try to rein her in. It was a first-rate school, exposing Adele to great books (she described its library as "a terrific place") and art (through trips to local museums).

Adele was more dreamer than scholar, and often escaped into the darkness of the local movie houses like the Paradise Theatre in the Bronx. "I think growing up as a first generation American, you yearned for better things, and the movies affected you. You wanted to look like [the movie stars], you wanted to go places."[22] However, she didn't take advantage of classes that would help her find a place in the business world after graduation in 1944. Adele later quipped, "I thought I was going to be the Queen of England. I didn't take typing courses, or any kind of business courses."[23] Actually, she had higher education in mind: "I was going to be the first in my family to go to college. I thought about being an elementary school teacher."[24] But when it came to filling out applications, she put it off. "I was living with my parents [and] worked as a waitress [at Schrafft's], among other things."[25] Like Harvey, Adele came from a secular Jewish background. They shared the same birthday, October 3, though she was one year younger.

Adele joined Timely in late 1945, about the time Stan Lee returned from the Signal Corps. An assistant editor named Al Sulman hired her. "Al Sulman must have been impressed with my youth and my slenderness at the time, because I certainly didn't have any qualifications for the job

Adele Kurtzman, ca. 1948. Copyright © The Harvey Kurtzman Estate.

except that I could read English. He sent me in a room with tons of comic books, and he told me to read. I want to tell you, I hated comic books even before then. I don't have that kind of mind. I hate animals dressed up as people and talking."[26] At first, Sulman situated her in the bullpen area, where the other woman at the firm, an inker named Violet Barclay, was behind a drawing board. Occasionally, Adele got a glimpse of Martin Goodman when he walked by. "He floated," she said. "He looked like someone whose feet never touched the ground. He had white hair and an air of confidence. He was very impressive."[27] Then Sulman moved her into a room in the back, where Al Jaffee and Bob Lander were situated. Jaffee became her best friend in the place.

Adele Hasan reported to Stan Lee. During this period, by his own admission as well as accounts of some who worked there, Lee was a bit of a young autocrat who, while capable and generally upbeat, could also be arrogant and self-important. Adele thought he was "cute—good looking," but hated when he called her on the carpet.[28] She later told how he tested her on the names of some of the Timely funny animal characters, which to her was not only ridiculous, but humiliating. She wasn't a good proofreader. "I made so many mistakes. If I made a mistake I could tell by the tone of [Stan Lee's] voice. He'd go, 'Adellllle . . . ' That was Stan Lee, so that the whole office from Martin Goodman to Frank Torpey could hear that tone. And I knew I'd left out a period in this great work of art, and I'd have to get up and walk to that office."[29]

She didn't like working there. "I found it very depressing during the year or so I spent there. I hated it, the things that they did to the artists. Stan Lee would blow the whistle at nine o'clock in the morning and everybody was supposed to start drawing." She watched incredulously as Lee sent Frank Giacoia home and docked him a day's pay for reading the *Daily News* a few minutes past starting time. "Al Jaffee made the day bearable," she said. "He made me laugh all day long."[30]

Not long after Kurtzman started *Hey Look!*, Adele became his secret ally, though he didn't find out about it until later. She recalled, "They were running a contest, people would send in letters for their favorite comic book or comic whatever. Harvey wasn't getting many votes, and I [thought] his stuff was very funny, so I just put in lots of votes for his stuff. I lied. Let me just put it that way. I lied. I don't think it came to anything. I don't know what they were going to do with all that information, but I just put lots of checkmarks next to his stuff."[31] It wouldn't be unusual that readers didn't vote for *Hey Look!*, considering that it was a sporadic filler that had been going less than six months at that time.

Adele had dated some Timely artists, thinking they must lead glamorous lives. Although she found just the opposite, it didn't put her off when it came to Harvey. When she glimpsed him turning in finished work, she was intrigued. "I thought he was cute," she said, describing him as being "in his trench coat and pipe days."[32] He also noticed her. She was attractive, as a portrait photo taken around that time attests. (Later, she self-deprecated, "Well, you know, lighting is everything.")[33] Sometime in the autumn of 1946, Adele and Harvey spoke their first words to each other. She was on a date with Will Elder, who had been introduced to her by Al Jaffee. They were attending an M&A art show organized by another alumnus, Charles Stern. A Timely artist named Dave Gantz formally introduced Adele Hasan to Harvey Kurtzman. They hit it off immediately. She found him to be quiet—not a life-of-the-party jokester—but he had a smart, laid-back sense of humor, and a sensitive, gentle nature. Kurtzman discovered that Adele was bright and quick with a clever quip. Once they got together, others often remarked, "Adele is the funny one."

Yet Kurtzman's sense of humor, in person and in his work, was a big part of his appeal. "My parents were very funny, and I decided at some point that it just wasn't worth taking anything seriously," she said. "And everything *is* kind of funny. Well, Hitler isn't funny. Some things are not funny. But otherwise, what's the point? It's now or never. In our family, money was important, but funny was more so."[34] When she had first seen *Hey Look!*, Adele blurted to Al Jaffee, "There's the type of man I'd like to marry."[35]

Shortly before that art show, Harvey Kurtzman made a solid connection with someone else who would be of major importance in his life. It happened when Kurtzman was meeting Harry Jaffee for lunch. Jaffee showed up with Will Elder in tow. Kurtzman and Elder had only known each other from afar at M&A. Elder recalled, "I was oblivious to a lot of people [at M&A] because I was only interested in making them laugh. I'd seen [Harvey] but I never even spoke to him."[36] Kurtzman found Elder's zany sense of humor intact, and as they traded high school stories, the two established a quick rapport. Upon looking through Elder's portfolio, Kurtzman recognized the fellow's tremendous talent both as a fine artist and a cartoonist.[37] Will Elder later described this meeting. "We had a few laughs when we met in the streets of New York retelling stories about Music and Art, talking about teachers and episodes with some of our classmates who were kind of freakish. We thought it was fun and that we ought to get together more often and maybe as a team we could pick up some work."[38]

Kurtzman's original studio space with Ottenheimer was short lived, and so was his second Manhattan beachhead, a seedy room in Greenwich Village. He then rented space in the Fuller Building on Fifty-Seventh Street from Irving Geis, who would eventually become art director for *Scientific American.* Sharing this space was Ramon Gordon, one of Kurtzman's army buddies. Toward the end of 1946, Kurtzman and Geis had some sort of conflict (they would work together later), leaving Kurtzman looking for studiomates. Was Will Elder interested? He was, and when Charles Stern also expressed an interest, the Charles William Harvey Studio was born.

Financially speaking, 1946 turned out to be a fair year for Kurtzman. He had grossed about $2,500, the equivalent of about ten times as much today. Not a huge sum, but still significant money for a young man who was just getting started and still living at home. Nearly all of it went to his mother for household expenses. The main thing was that he was making his living as a cartoonist and saw his work getting better and better. He was growing both technically and creatively, discovering who he was artistically, and developing his style. For any artist, this type of self-discovery is nothing short of euphoric. Reuniting with Charles Stern and his newfound friendship with Will Elder gave him many things: camaraderie, people of like mind and background to bounce ideas off of and potential collaborators. To them, he wasn't a little schnook: he was that kid who had been a kind of star at M&A, a budding cartoonist with tremendous potential. They were not only impressed by his inroads at Timely, but they loved *Hey Look!*

The year 1946 also brought the beginnings of romance. Harvey and Adele began dating as the year drew to a close. "He didn't have any money," she recalled. Either that or "he was kind of cheap. Doubleday used to have a little booth where you could play records [and] listen to them for free. That's where he took me first."[39] There was an attraction and mutual enjoyment in each other's company. "He was a confident man," she recalled, "but desperate to get away from his family. He didn't get along with his brothers or his mother. It was a difficult atmosphere, and he was determined to get married."[40] But getting married wasn't high on Adele's agenda at that point. She had always viewed her period working for Stan Lee as a temporary stop before college. Adele was leaving, having enrolled in State Teachers College in Cortland, New York.

As the year ended, Kurtzman prepared to carry out a long distance relationship with the vivacious brunette. He was comfortable with writing letters. Indeed, putting ideas on paper brought out his more emotional, playful side. But the two weren't yet serious. Soon he would find himself in the midst of a second romance, one that would grow until it rivaled his affection for Adele.

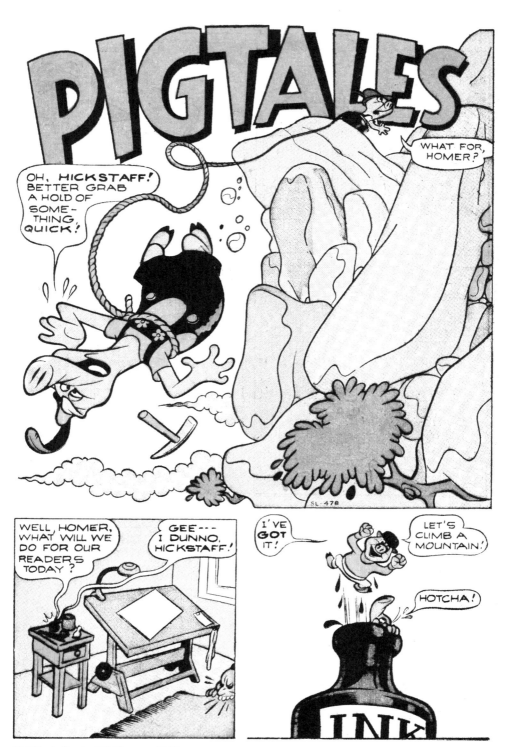

Kid Movie Komics #11 (Summer 1946).

From *Patsy Walker* #13 (November 1947).

6.

THE THREE MUSKETEERS

TEAMING UP WITH WILL ELDER and Charles Stern to form a studio not only made fiscal sense; it seemed like it would be a lot of fun. It was. They nicknamed themselves the Three Musketeers and adopted the slogan "all for one, one for all!" Rather than individually thrashing around, the M&A alums would work together to generate jobs, publicize the studio and collaborate on projects. It seemed like the ideal approach for types who didn't want to work in a production shop, a publisher's bullpen or at home. Harvey Kurtzman had no intention of working through middlemen like Louis Ferstadt again.

They found a space a couple of blocks south of Madison Square Park in the Flatiron District. The address was 24 E. Twenty-First Street. It was a "rat-hole" loft on the ninth floor. Will Elder recalled, "The loft had a skylight, one of those big, slanting skylights. I think that's what made it for us. We said, 'Hey a skylight, man, this is it, an artist's studio!'"[1] They managed to squeeze in a row of three drawing tables and not much else. "It was kind of a crammed place," Kurtzman said. "Occasionally we'd go out on this little flat roof that adjoined it. We played basketball out there."[2] To prove the Charles William Harvey Studio was a serious endeavor, they printed up stationery with their address and phone number. The trio envisioned it as a commercial art studio that would handle diverse art services: advertising, layout, paste-up, product design and illustration. But they hadn't a clue on how to make it work.

Kurtzman had learned nothing from his family about entrepreneurship or how to run a business. If a business management class was taught in high school, he didn't take it. His drive and determination to succeed turned out to be formidable, but a lack of business savvy and inability to comprehend the point of view of the businessman would be his Achilles heel.

Kurtzman said, "I got one of the classic lessons of business in working with Willy and Charlie. We never thought too much about the business of business, and three more unlikely businessmen you never saw in your life. To me it was the lesson of lessons. We spent the first month of our career doing up the sample book. Charlie was very good at that. This giant photo album. And after all was said and done with our sample book and our plans to pull in all kinds of work, we got our first major job through a relative of Willy, a distant relative. After all this lightning and thunder of studio and sample book and letterheads, how do we get work? Through relatives! It was a come-down. But nevertheless, it was our first big score, thanks to Will."[3]

They were engaged to design the press kit for a low-budget Paramount film starring Ernie Tubb, called *Hollywood Barn Dance* (1947). It was based on the west coast radio program of the same name, and starred Tubb, the Texas Troubadours, Lori Talbott and Helen Boyce. "So we sat down and said, 'Okay, how are we going to do this thing? We're the Three Musketeers,'" Kurtzman said. "We had to decide who would do what in this little booklet. The cover of the book was the plum, and the insides were more like hard-work production stuff. The three of us each secretly wanted to do the cover, so we sat around going, 'Uh, how're we going to do this thing?' And I said, 'Well, I think I should do the cover,' and Willy said, 'Well, I think I'd be best qualified to do the cover,' and of course Charlie thought he should do the cover. So I said, 'Well, let's vote on this thing.' So we took a vote and it came out one for each. Our system never held together."[4] He concluded, "The big lesson was that there's no such thing as a structureless organization without a pyramid. You have to have a boss." The idea of a collective—a term Kurtzman later used to describe the arrangement—sounded good, but it didn't work.[5]

The studio was also important as a social nexus, where tips were shared, cigarettes were cadged, flasks were passed around and invitations were extended. With Will Elder on the premises, there was no dearth of laughter. They "advertised" by making little paper planes with the studio name on it, and flying them into the street from the roof. "We would have parties up there," Will Elder recalled. "It was a place to go at night. After all, we were paying the rent, and it was only used half a day."[6] One of the key features of the small studio was a sofa bed along one wall. It came in handy if someone overindulged and was "unable" to make it home (they all still lived with their parents). It was also the site of innumerable sexual liaisons, as all of them were still free agents. Kurtzman said, "[Charlie] was the cocksman amongst us, and he took full advantage of . . . the bed."[7] However it seems likely they all had their innings. "I lived with Charlie Stern in his mother's west side apartment," Kurtzman said. "When she would go away, I would move in for a few days. Just spending time trailing after Charlie and his nightlife was an indescribable experience."[8]

This period was one of the few in his life that Kurtzman looked back on with nostalgia. "I used to do those [*Hey Look!* pages] out of the studio and I have a lot of fond memories. Those were good days. It was the first shot I got at having my own place. I'd lived with my folks in the Bronx all my life and I never had anything of my own."[9] By this time, it seems, Kurtzman had conquered much of his reticence and could be almost as voluble as Stern and Elder. There was the giddy thrill of "making it" in the real world, drawing next to others who had fantasized about their future careers as they worked on school projects together in high school.

During this time, Kurtzman continued taking life-drawing classes. On February 10, 1947, he wrote to Adele, "Last night, we went to a life class and I sat around all night looking at naked women. I did a couple of nice studies, which I would like you to see some day!'"[10] Harvey missed Adele and wrote frequent letters to her at college in Cortland. They were hand-written, addressed to "Ad Hasan," and most had little cartoons or other artistic embellishments. One envelope depicted Hickstaff (from *Pigtales*) riding Homer's back, exhorting, "Faster, Homer! We've got to de-liver this letter to Adele!" and Homer replying, "Ugh! But why the second highest point in New York?" Adele recalled, "He wrote me letters when I was in college that were hilarious. He made his own Valentine's [Day] cards and things like that. He was very good at that."[11] Many of his mis-sives urged her to write or call. Adele later admitted, "I was so dumb. When I was at college, for some reason I . . . played it cool, and wouldn't call."[12] There's a cute cartoon by Kurtzman showing him holding a phone receiver that has engulfed his head, with the caption: "Oops! That's what I get for trying to kiss you!!" Kurtzman took a bus to travel the 215 miles to upstate New York at least once. Still, Adele's "cool" left him uncertain about her feelings toward him.

At just this point, Kurtzman met another young woman who caught his fancy. Her name was Jo Ann Bergtold, a twenty-year-old model and aspiring actress from the small town of Wesby, Wisconsin. Sometime in the spring of 1947, Harry Chester was visiting his uncle, a garment maker. There he met Jo Ann, a petite, pixyish young woman who mod-

Chester introduced Kurtzman to Bergtold. Top: Family photo of
Irene and Harry Chester before the end of World War II. Bottom: Jo
Ann Bergtold, model and aspiring actress: courtesy of Jesse Drew.

eled junior-sized dresses. Bergtold's father owned three movie theaters in
Wisconsin, and she grew up on the movies. Between working as a model,
she was auditioning for stage plays. She was living in a womens' resi-
dence called the Rosemary House in the West Village. Chester introduced
Bergtold to Kurtzman. "The three of us would go out for dinner or to a
movie," she recalled in a later interview. But Harry was married. Soon
Harvey and Jo Ann were doing things on their own, and became smitten
with each other. The two of them went to the Village Vanguard club often,
just a couple of blocks from where she lived. They trod the famous fifteen
steps down to the intimate jazz club, which was legendary for all the great

talents who played and recorded there. "If Harvey was broke, we'd ride the ferry to Staten Island for a nickel, and there were also picnics at a gorgeous park in the Bronx," she recalled. "At that time it was completely safe to walk anywhere in the city. You could walk in Central Park. Once Harvey and I went horseback riding in Central Park. He was scared to death on a horse. It was so funny."[13] Kurtzman had an old car that he bought for $25 from Irving Geis so they could easily go on jaunts off the island. It was the first in a series of previously owned vehicles in Kurtzman's life.

DISSATISFACTION WITH the studio space on East Twenty-First Street set in early. In March, Harvey wrote to Adele, "The Charles William Harvey Studio is now attempting to move from this stinking-sky-lighted-cold-water-factory to another one. We have a lead on Broadway & Twenty-Sixth, also with a skylight. The renting agent is an American Veteran's Committee member, and the A.Y.D. [American Youth for Democracy] is located right downstairs in the building. It has an opening to the roof to escape through when the cops start clamping down on Jew Communists."[14] That particular location didn't pan out. They resolved to keep looking. The shabby surroundings didn't slow the steady stream of visitors. "All of our friends used to come up to the studio," Kurtzman said. "It was a hangout." Elder recalled, "From there we met a lot of people in the comic book business. At least, Kurtzman had a few accounts in the comic book business. And I had a few advertising accounts with some very strange characters."[15]

Sometimes Kurtzman dropped by Will Eisner's studio. Now that *The Spirit* had found its footing again after drifting into mediocrity during the war, everyone was talking about it. Kurtzman said, "We were all aware of Eisner, as being one of the real important people in the business. *The Spirit* was exciting."[16] He particularly admired Eisner's writing, feeling that he was one of the few in comics whose stories were both interesting and original. Therefore, he sought Eisner's opinion of his work.

An Eisner apprentice named Jules Feiffer recalled Kurtzman's visits. Feiffer was an eighteen-year-old Bronx native who assisted Eisner and would, in the next year, begin writing scripts for *The Spirit.* "If you worked for Eisner you met everybody, because they all came there," he said. "Harvey came by, and Eisner showed us his work, and I think I already knew *Hey Look!* [Harvey] was always above board, direct, loved to talk, very generous about other people, self-effacing. Took a compliment well, but it was clear that it embarrassed him."[17] The paths of Eisner and Kurtzman would cross at various junctures in the coming years, and eventually they became friendly colleagues. Eisner influenced Kurtzman in a number of ways, and at times it seemed there was a curious link between their careers.

The Musketeers continued to scout for a better studio space, spurred by a fire in their present location that apparently started on the premises of a chemical manufacturer in the building. In the fall, their hand was forced when the landlord decided he had had enough of them. Fortunately, a much more satisfactory accommodation turned up. In November 1947, the Charles William Harvey Studio moved to 1151 Broadway in midtown New York City. The four-story building, built about 1930, was sandwiched mid-block between similar structures, facing east. The studio space was above restaurateurs named Rosenblum who owned the building. Kurtzman signed the lease ($80 per month) and then sublet to Elder and Stern. Kurtzman also made sure the bills for the telephone, insurance and towel services were paid, then dunned his partners for their portions.

Kurtzman did his part on various commercial projects generated by his studiomates, but *Hey Look!* was his and his alone. (They didn't share monies earned for their individual jobs.) Kurtzman worked hard on *Hey Look!* "Doing a page was often sheer hell. I worked slowly, with intensity. I've always worked the hard way. It took so long for me to do each of those *Hey Look!* pages that the pay was never enough."[18] The most he made for a page was $37.50.[19] He later described his methods on the Timely filler in a lesson on creating comics:

"The first scribble," he wrote, "is the most important step of all. It is the birth of the idea. If it isn't good, nothing you do will save it. I also establish the story ending here.

"The thumbnail sketch is scribbled on anything that comes to hand. The purpose is to rough out the panels and dialogue at the same time. The thumbnail makes you aware of your space and your timing—how much room you need for lettering, how much for pictures.

"Next you write the text. What you have to do is flesh out what you've scribbled in step two. The text is neatly penciled onto the art board, which has been inked with ruled panel borders. I take special care to combine the art and lettering together, making the best use of space."

Then the final stage: "The artwork is inked. Where needed, I retouch with a good opaque white."[20] If, on the other hand, he decided not to take the layout to finalization, which must have been a fairly common occurrence given his selectivity, it was either tinker with the idea so that it worked better, or start over.

Kurtzman didn't know what readers thought of "Hey Look!" As a practical matter, he was doing it for Adele, the guys at Timely and his stu-

Kurtzman's favorite *Hey Look!* ran in *Joker* #33 (September 1948).

dio pals, in much the same way as he had drawn on the streets in chalk as a boy. He wanted to entertain and impress them, and their enthusiastic reactions emboldened him to push beyond surrealism into further realms of the absurd.

A page published in *Hedy De Vine* #25 (February 1948), drawn in the fall of 1947, was a key turning point for *Hey Look!* In that fifty-fourth episode, the characters acknowledge their relationship with us, the readers of the comic book. "See that character there?" the little guy asks, pointing to us. "Looks like a human being, only, it's just printed ink on comic book paper." He isn't admitting their existence as a cartoon but rather claiming that they are the readers and *the reader is the cartoon*. This began Kurtzman's push into satire of the sequential art medium itself. The riffs Kurtzman played on this theme led to the dizziest heights reached by *Hey Look!* over the next two years.

The first episode with a new, more stylistically suitable logo (*Margie* #40, April 1948) begins with the big guy brooding, "It's wet and gloomy and I am unhappy!" As he and his friend cross a bridge, he moans, "Deemed, destined and doomed to a comic book existence—nothing but a two dimensional caricature of a life. I want to die! I think I'll kill myself!" The use of repetition, rhythm and alliteration gives the dialogue a unique, almost poetic quality. Now Kurtzman's character has acknowledged his existence as a fictional cartoon entity.

The episode in *Gay Comics* #31 (Spring 1948), with the two characters making silly faces at the reader, throwing a pie and hitting themselves on the head in a series of twelve equal-sized panels, casts the protagonists as performers going through their competent paces to amuse, but it's all in a day's work. In the final panel, the little guy concludes, "Well—P! I think we've given our reader a page-full of entertainment! Let's knock off for lunch!" They are just entertainers who, it must be presumed, have a life apart from the page. In "Let's Go Diving" in *Comedy* #1 (May 1948), the two compete to see who can do the most flips in the air. The big guy spins in the air over a hundred times with no end in sight. Then a cartoon image of Kurtzman himself leans into the last panel, holding a brush inking the still flipping figure, saying, "—and if you go down to the swimming pool this very day, you'll find him there—still flipping!"

ONE CAN SURMISE that most pages appearing into mid-1948 were completed in the last months of 1947. Throughout that year, Harvey continued to write to Adele and date Jo Ann. Then, when Jo Ann went back to Wisconsin for a visit, he wrote to her, too. On December 16, 1947:

Hello Baby!

I miss you! At this very moment as I write, all hell is breaking loose in the studio. Three plumbers are at work installing a radiator next to my table. They are all banging three metal pipes with three heavy hammers. They can no doubt be heard by you in Wisconsin.

Back to Friday [after your plane took off], at 11:00 o'clock, I was home. There wasn't any liquor in the house—so there I was . . . poised beside the clock . . . a glass of water in my hand . . . . The radio was playing softly . . . . SUDDENLY the damn thing started playing that "ballerina" song— you know—your favorite. This was too much. I threw myself into my room and sobbed violently on the bed. 'Has it come to this?' I blubbered.

I am now sick with a stinken cold, which I contracted at [La Guardia] field. Write me, Jo—else I whither & die. No kidding, lemme get a long letter from you.

    Affectionately, Harvey

On December 26:

Hello Sweet:

How are you?

Christmas (sigh) is over!! Sitting here with my stomach full of turkey—I feel like I've been through a cement mixer. I don't think I'm happy. Yesterday, everyone made merry. I went to 3 parties—had 3 dull times and wonder of wonders—I didn't get drunk. Didn't even get high. This amazes me no end. I think it is significant. Do you think it is significant?? After all the yelling & shouting died away, I got to thinking, amidst the stained glasses & crushed cigarette butts. You know—you're nice. It kills me to have to see your trunks & typewriter standing there in the corner every day. My eyes blur—my head reels—SUDDENLY—I see a vision!! It's JO ANN!!! GAD!! When I come to, I am embracing the trunk, & have my nose caught in the typewriter! I can't go ON like this!!

This evening, more than ever, I wish it was summer & I was moved down town. I am tard [*sic*] of being tangled up with home and stuff. It doesn't work out at all—this is becoming so so clear. Brother Zachary came home for X-mas. Consequently, I have had to eat home a couple of times &, gee—I'm just not happy.

It's colderin hell & it snows every now and then! COLD is like DEATH! Think of me for about 5 seconds on new years eve—willya? And—have a nice time.

    Love, Harvey

The cold Kurtzman felt as he wrote this note presaged an enormous snowfall. The next day, one of the biggest storms in the city's history dumped over two feet of snow onto Gotham. The letter's reference to "summer" may have to do with the family's expectation that Abraham would be paroled by then, which would free Harvey from his obligation to live at home.

IN THE NEW YEAR, Kurtzman looked for work in New York newspapers. An opportunity arose when Harold Straubing, formerly of Timely and a fan of *Hey Look!*, became cartoon editor of the *New York Herald Tribune*. The newspaper ran weekly one-tier tryout strips by some of New York's most talented young cartoonists, such as Irv Spector's *Coogie* and Gill Fox and Selma Diamond's *Jeannie*. If they were popular, the New York Herald Tribune Syndicate would attempt to enlist other papers to run them.

In early 1948, at Straubing's invitation, Kurtzman created a feature called *Silver Linings*. He produced nine of them, which began appearing in the *Herald Tribune* on March 7, 1948. By this time, Kurtzman's work had progressed via *Hey Look!*, and the graphics of *Silver Linings* are reminiscent of the remarkable Timely filler. Just as *Hey Look!* was a sort of equivalent for a Sunday newspaper strip for Kurtzman, *Silver Linings* was his daily strip, albeit in color. It was the closest he ever got to syndication. They saw print in Sunday sections from March to June along with the other regular color comics. It was a great opportunity, and the type of thing that impressed friends, family and colleagues. Unfortunately, as graphically attractive as they are, a reading of *Silver Linings* reveals their weakness: the writing. The format of a daily humor strip requires a satisfactory gag at its conclusion. Kurtzman was a satirist, not a gag-man, and the gags he came up with for *Silver Linings* don't deliver the requisite laugh at the end. They're cute and clever, but not especially funny. The final gags hadn't been his strength on *Hey Look!* either, but a full page gave him room to score with readers with his characters' offbeat antics along the way. At least at this point, Kurtzman needed a writer to succeed with the gag-strip format. In the coming months, he worked harder on the ending gags in *Hey Look!* and achieved better results. In terms of the art itself, *Silver Linings* is "prime Kurtzman" from this period: confident, dynamic, eye-catching.

Kurtzman tried another newspaper. In autumn 1948, he took his portfolio to the *New York Star*. A young cartoonist named Walt Kelly, whose strip *Pogo* had just made its debut in its pages, was working as a political cartoonist and art director for the paper. "Kelly was [the] editor who interviewed aspiring young cartoonists," Kurtzman said. "He wasn't impressed with my work. As a matter of fact, he gave me the bum's rush."[21] Kelly's rejection letter of November 2 is—while brief—civil, even complimentary in part. He wrote, "We believe that your material is still too specialized for syndication. However, it's actually 'funny' and we hope that some time you will work out a strip that we can use."[22] Nevertheless, Kurtzman always resented Kelly for the rejection, despite admiring his work on *Pogo*.

In spring of 1948, John Severin joined the Charles William Harvey studio. "I had decided to exhibit some paintings of mine in a High School of Music and Art exhibition for the alumni," he recalled. "Charlie Stern was in charge of it, so I went to see him at his studio. They asked me if I'd like to rent space with them there. I did, and started working with them. When Charlie left . . . I became the third man, but they didn't want to change it to the John William Harvey Studio, so they left the name. Harvey was doing comics, but Willy and Charlie were doing advertising stuff, and I just joined in. It [was] design work, logos for toy boxes, logos for candy boxes, cards to be included in the candy boxes, everything but the candy itself."[23]

Severin became interested in what Kurtzman was doing. He described how he got into doing comic book work to interviewer James Vadeboncoeur Jr. in 1980.

> Harvey had been turning out the *Hey Look!*'s for Stan Lee. One day I asked him how much he got per page and how many he could do a day, and when I found out how much he got paid . . . I said, "That's for me. Now what do you call this stuff?" I sat down and did some samples . . . for myself. I figured if I got something halfway decent, I'd go out and try to sell it, having no idea what the hell I was getting into. In the meanwhile, Harvey took a look at my work and said, "Why don't you have Bill ink your stuff?" So we turned out a bunch of pages where I pencilled and Willy inked, and took them to every comic company on the planet. I got my first comics job. It was me drawing a story for the first time, and Willy inking for the first time, and it was atrocious.[24]

Severin's first story was "The Clue of the Horoscope" for *Headline* #32 (October–November 1948). It's hardly atrocious compared to much that was being published at the time. He was obviously a "natural" for comics. Eventually Severin ended up selling work to Crestwood where Joe Simon and Jack Kirby were packaging comics under the Prize banner. John Severin was just one of a number of young artists who rented studio space at the Charles William Harvey Studio at different times, including Robert Q. Sale, Dave Berg, Frank Dorsey and Rita Gerstein. There was also Leon Gehorson, who later designed buildings at Fairleigh Dickson University. Providing workspace for others helped pay the rent.

So many people tramped up and down the steps to the studio that Mr. Rosenblum, the landlord, complained. "All kinds of characters used to come through," Kurtzman said. "There was a little guy who used to hang around. He was a friend of Charlie's and a PR man. He had a particular trick where one day he invited us all to what we assumed was a free client lunch at his latest client, a restaurant. So we all went down and at the end of the meal, we were given bills. We had to *pay!* What this guy would do is he'd invite bunches of us to what we thought was a free lunch and his boss would be very happy with the increase in business. Well, this guy turned out to be Lester Persky. He produced *Equus*, he produced the movie version of *Hair*. He became a very big man in Hollywood."[25] On Persky's behalf, Kurtzman called Jo Ann Bergtold. "Harvey asked me if I wanted to go to plays and premieres with Lester, who was gay and needed a date for those occasions," she said. "It was the most fun I had in New York, because Lester took me to all these plays, and we'd go to Sardi's, and [he] wined and dined me. One night Adolph Green [who had cowritten the Broadway musical *On The Town*] was at our table. It didn't bother me at all that Lester was gay."[26]

Meanwhile, Adele had her fill of State Teachers College in Cortland, and returned to New York with the idea she would attend Hunter College at its Bronx Campus. Harvey's romance with Adele heated up, and they saw a lot of each other over the summer. His relations with the Gentile from Wisconsin became platonic. He and Jo Ann remained friends, and she met Adele. Kurtzman put Bergtold in an episode of *Hey Look!*[27] She worked in children's theater and other off-off Broadway productions. In 1949, Jo Ann married actor Robert Drew and moved to Queens. She exchanged Christmas cards with Harvey for years thereafter.

Severin created a memorable cartoon titled "A 'Normal' Day at the Chas - Wm - Harvey Studio!!!" It includes Dorsey, Persky, Elder, Stern, Severin and Sale. Kurtzman is shown at his drawing board, exchanging gunfire with Severin, shouting "Goodbye old friend!" Kurtzman praised Severin's drawing as an example of his excellent inking with a pen (rather than a brush). As a reminder of the days at CWH, it hung in Kurtzman's living room in the latter part of his life.

Roughly 500,000 ex-service men returned to civilian life in New York City in 1946.[28] Kurtzman was one of a flood of young, aspiring artists in the city, many of them attending art school on the GI Bill. To fill an obvious need, syndicated *Tarzan* artist Burne Hogarth and Silas Rhodes co-founded the Cartoonists and Illustrators School in 1947, opening its doors to a first class of thirty-five students.[29] C&I offered a two-year course to prepare students for a career in cartooning and commercial art. Its first instructors were Hogarth, Marvin Stein and Harry Fisk. Some members of the first graduating class went on to considerable success, such as Dick Cavalli (*Winthrop*), Jerry Marcus (*Trudy*) and Bob Weber (*Moose*). One of its early students was a precocious, skinny chain smoker named Wallace Wood.

Arriving in New York City after his military discharge in July 1948, the twenty-one-year-old Wood attended C&I for a semester, then dropped out to earn a living. After lugging his portfolio all over town looking for work, he was becoming discouraged. Then Wallace Wood met John Severin in a publisher's waiting room, and showed him his work. Severin recognized Wood's talent and invited him to visit the Charles William Harvey Studio. Wood recalled, "In the studio were Harvey Kurtzman, Willy Elder and Charlie Stern. I was really impressed with John and how nice he was to me. Harvey was kind of nasty—'Why are you letting a kid hang around here?' But they each did me an original and wished me luck and gave me a couple of lessons."[30] Kurtzman and the others saw the potential in Wood's artwork, and told him that Will Eisner was looking for a background artist for *The Spirit*. Wood hustled over to Eisner's studio and landed the job. Thus began the career of one of the most celebrated comic book artists of all time.

AFTER WORLD WAR II, American popular culture—comics, movies, books—took a decided shift toward reality-based material. The colorful, often patriotic super hero comics gave way to other genres, largely geared to the tastes of ex-soldiers who had the comic habit but wanted grittier, more mature fare. In 1948, one of the hottest trends was crime comic books supposedly based on true stories. The form's leader was Charles Biro's *Crime Does Not Pay*, begun in 1942 but not hitting its stride until the postwar period when its sales reportedly soared to a million copies per issue. Kurtzman picked up on them right away. "I remember how Biro's stories affected me," he said. "I felt the same excitement about them that I felt about the underground comic books of twenty years later. In both cases, it was something of a shock to be brought nose to nose with reality. A lot of young readers, sated with super hero make-believe, were not so much shocked as delighted, and they were quick to lay down their dimes for this exciting new kind of entertainment."[31] Reality-based comics struck a chord with Kurtzman, one that would have reverberations throughout the rest of his career. He talked about how, in the realm of popular entertainment, there was the reality-based and the fantasy-based, and he preferred the former: "This feeling for reality is a quality that apparently I was born with. I'm a fantasy idiot, but with reality I'm good."[32] This isn't surprising for someone with a talent for satire, since it has its roots in exposing the reality beneath the surface of its subject.

Crime Does Not Pay #42 (November 1945).

After demobilization, Kurtzman had attempted to use his experience educating soldiers with reality-based graphics to generate work. He recalled, "I was trying to get somebody interested in—not comics, really, but educational graphics."[33] Painted examples of his efforts to "explain the ulcer graphically" have survived, though they appear to be unpublished samples. This came together with another interest, related to his morale-boosting role in the service. One of the hot topics during and immediately after the war was psychiatry, as the need to treat military veterans suffering from the post-traumatic effects of battle came to the fore. It was reflected in films such as Alfred Hitchcock's *Spellbound* (1945), a story of a young psychiatrist (Ingrid Bergman) who falls in love with a traumatized man (Gregory Peck) who is impersonating her new supervisor. Kurtzman's admiration for Hitchcock may have begun with this motion picture.[34] Although the details aren't clear, in September 1946, Kurtzman wrote to Dr. Karl Menninger, founder of the Menninger School of Psychiatry in Topeka, Kansas, who was working with the Veterans Administration to help fill the postwar demand for psychiatrists. It seems Kurtzman thought "pictorial graphics" could be used to explain how the mind affected other parts of the body (such as ulcers), and asked the psychiatrist to become his adviser on the topic. Menninger wrote, "I am glad you are thinking along these lines of pictorial education. I believe it is a very useful technique in education and I think something along this line is valuable."[35] However, he declined to advise Kurtzman further, writing, "I am already doing three men's jobs, so I feel a little inclined to duck any such additional responsibility. I think you can inform yourself well enough in regard to psychiatry if you pursue a course of reading such as is indicated in the appendix to the revised edition of *The Human Mind*."[36] Although Kurtzman didn't read many books, preferring newspapers and magazines, his interest in psychology motivated him to consult Menninger's *The Human Mind* and delve into books on psychoanalysis by Freud and others.

Kurtzman's attempt to explain psychological matters in visual terms didn't go anywhere, but he did come up with a couple of paying assignments in the "educational graphics" field. In 1947, he created a program manual for the Upholsterer's International Union to explain Social Security to its members through cartoons. In 1948, he was employed by Timely to provide the artwork for a booklet called "Survey," subtitled, "A Comic Magazine for the Juvenile Market." The booklet was designed to sell advertisements in Goodman's comic books. It presented the results of a survey of 1,940 children regarding their reading habits. Will Eisner was already moving in that direction, having formed an enterprise called American Visuals in 1948 to pursue projects that involved the production of promotional, commercial and educational comics. Eisner's long-running *P*S: The Preventive Maintenance Monthly*, a sort of continuation of *Army Motors*, was just such a project.

Kurtzman felt the viability of educational graphics was partly proven by the success of the "all true" *Crime Does Not Pay*. He had the opportunity to express this idea on March 19, 1948, when he attended a symposium on comic books held by Dr. Fredric Wertham, a German-born psychiatrist whose crusade against violence in comics was gaining steam. The symposium, titled "The Psychopathology of Comic Books," was held at the New York Academy of Medicine. Wertham and several other self-appointed experts on the subject revealed the findings of their research, all condemning crime comic books. A transcript and a summary of the discussion that followed was subsequently published in the *American Journal of Psychotherapy*. Several members of the comics industry were present at the symposium, although they were allotted little time to make remarks. Kurtzman's editor on *Silver Linings* was the only pro-comics attendee who was quoted at any length in the report. Harold Straubing said, "Whether the responsibility for delinquency rests with the comic book influences is doubtful, because we are exposed to so much crime, violence, conflict-

ing ideas and social problems in life and other mediums of expression."
Charles Biro "stated vigorously that comic books are getting better." Alden
Getz and Harvey Kurtzman (representing Timely comics) "suggested that
comic books should be improved and made educational."[37]

HEY LOOK! ISN'T "OF A PIECE." Kurtzman experimented ceaselessly. It
often looks substantially different from page to page. *Cindy Comics* #31
(October 1948) had "a comment on radio programs that keep billions of us
in a state of nervous prostration by giving away thousands of dollars to the
party that answers the telephone!" There are no less than twenty-five panels on the page, some so small as to defy reading, others large with black
backgrounds and drawings in white "ink." The page has an overall unity,
yet there is no clear path for the eye to follow. Some are story panels, some
illustrate the opening caption, and others, while they carry action, are so
small that they are more decorative than narrative.

The Often, Kurtzman let his characters' emotions erupt. In one of the most
outstanding episodes (*Gay Comics* #34, October 1948), the big guy—now
notably slimmer, even with a sort of resemblance to Kurtzman himself—
was frustrated by his attempt to crack the shell on a hard-boiled egg. Soon
placid calm is replaced by perplexity, then full-blown anger ("I'm getting
SORE!" he yells, shooting a gun at the egg) and finally unmitigated rage
("BREAK, EGG!" as he fires a machine gun at it). Finally, unwilling to
admit defeat, he swallows the egg whole.

The last twenty-five episodes of *Hey Look!* carry on this high level of
creativity and craftsmanship while (marginally) conforming more closely
to the conventional comic strip filler. Kurtzman was then applying his
heightened skills toward a more disciplined approach. Some have speculated that Stan Lee asked him to pull back from the experimentation. A
page or two, such as one where Kurtzman used photographs in the background, didn't run at all. Adele recalled, "Stan was always saying 'More
whites, Harvey! Too many blacks!' It would make Harvey cringe."[38] In any
case, the filler couldn't continue its trajectory toward deconstruction or
it would become virtually incomprehensible to the average reader. The
last group of *Hey Look!* pages achieves a near-perfect marriage of inventive craft and humor strip construction. The page in *Margie* #43 (October
1948) gives some rein to the anger that he had portrayed earlier, yet within
the context of a logically developed narrative sequence leading to an effective punch line. A noisy movie patron who claims it's his democratic
right to crackle his peanut brittle loudly is physically crackled by the disgruntled fellow sitting behind him. ("In a democracy, I too can crackle!!")

In his introduction to a later *Hey Look!* reprint book, comics historian John Benson wrote, "If Kurtzman's shop work [before World War II] showed promise mainly in hindsight, this is not so for [*Hey Look!*]. Had he left comics in 1950, his name would still be highly regarded among the cognoscenti for this small, but original body of work. Even compared to his later more famous achievements, the best of these strips represent some of the high points of his career."[39] Though most comics can be discussed in terms of their apparent influences, *Hey Look!* is utterly original. It's like nothing that came before, a truly radical comic strip. Kurtzman proved himself an innovator, and he was just getting started.

Why, then, did *Hey Look!* stop? This was how Kurtzman explained it: "I continued to do *Hey Look!* until it suddenly went out of style. What that means, is that Stan Lee's boss had decided that one-page fillers were no longer needed."[40] The page count of Timely comics shrank from sixty-eight in the first half of the 1940s to thirty-six pages toward the decade's end, a result of postwar inflation. With fewer pages, there apparently weren't as many places requiring filler. Lee used the last in his *Hey Look!* inventory in *Willie* #19 (May 1949).

Unfortunately, Kurtzman wasn't allowed to keep his original art. He would have had nothing but the published comic books (with their poor printing) to refer to this work in the future if he hadn't had the later ones photostatted. (Original artwork, at that time, was photographed, using a large camera—a.k.a. photostat machine—that generated a film negative that could be used for print-quality reproduction.) Kurtzman had watched, aghast, as Stan Lee drew large black X's with a grease pencil on a couple of *Hey Look!* originals after they had been photographed. He was told this was done "to prevent them from being re-used by other comics companies."[41] This made no sense, since such pages were routinely destroyed. Despite knowing the pages were destined for the incinerator, Kurtzman never forgot the violence of Lee's grease pencil.

THE BURST OF CREATIVE ENERGY and ideas in the latter days of *Hey Look!* led up to Harvey Kurtzman's marriage to Adele Hasan in the summer of 1948. As September arrived, he asked her if she was going back to college. "No, I'm not," she responded, having decided higher education wasn't for her. Later she said, "I don't remember a formal proposal. I just think he kind of took it for granted that we were going to get married."[42]

By this time, Kurtzman had finally moved out of the Clinton Arms. It seems Harvey went ahead and got an apartment in anticipation of his father's release from prison. Adele later said that Kurtzman was already situated in a place on Manhattan's Upper West side when they got married. "[It was] near Columbia University on 114th Street, an old brownstone-type house," she said. "It had been converted. It was a storage room originally and it had like one window on the ground level. It was one long room. It had a bathroom and a kitchen, barely. Harvey built a table on hinges that you could fold down so that you could get to the bathroom in the other room."[43]

Kurtzman made the wedding plans. Their nuptials, on September 7, 1948, had a comical side. Adele recalled, "We went up to Connecticut and were married by a Justice of the Peace in his little garden. We looked around and suddenly saw little gravestones for all his dogs. It was a dog cemetery!"[44] Despite the fact that Adele's parents liked Harvey, and his mother approved of Adele, no parents were invited to the civil ceremony. Just three others were present: Doris, Adele's sister and maid of honor, and Harry Chester, best man. Also present was Harry's wife Irene. (The Chesters had been married in the Bronx two years earlier and were living in an apartment in Mount Vernon.)

L-R: Abraham Perkes, Edith Perkes, Daniel Perkes (kneeling), Zachary Kurtzman and Harvey Kurtzman. Photograph courtesy of Adam Kurtzman.

Adele and Harvey honeymooned at the historic Captain Jack's Wharf in Provincetown. Harry drove them as far as Rhode Island and they took a bus to Cape Cod from there. The Wharf had been built as storage for fishermen at the turn of the century, and then was converted into summer housing. During Prohibition, it was the site of a famous speakeasy known as the Circus Bar. The place wasn't especially fancy but the rambling rooms stretched out over the water and had an extraordinary, romantic view of the tidal flats and the harbor. "I'd never been there before," Adele remembered. "It was really very pretty. We were there in September so it was kind of empty."[45] This was the same time period when Tennessee Williams famously partied all night at Captain Jack's, but there's no record of the Kurtzmans' repose being disturbed by the playwright or his entourage. The only real record of their Cape Cod idyll are some drawings of the wharf that Kurtzman uncharacteristically went over in watercolor to complement his line art.

Abraham Perkes was paroled on October 25. His release may have been the occasion for a photo of the immediate Perkes-Kurtzman family. Though Dad was home, and all appeared well, the fact is that the stress fractures in the family would never heal. Indeed, they would widen over time. The most problematic relationship for everyone was with Edith. The brothers weren't close, either. Perhaps the combination of his mother's negative personality, overbearing treatment from his older brother, his father's criminal behavior and underlying resentment over being abandoned as a four-year-old, caused Harvey to distance himself from all of them. Whatever the cause, Kurtzman would always be a dutiful son and brother, but no more than that.

"A 'Normal' Day at the Chas-Wm-Harvey Studio!!!" by John Severin. Reprinted from *Squa Tront* #9 (1983).

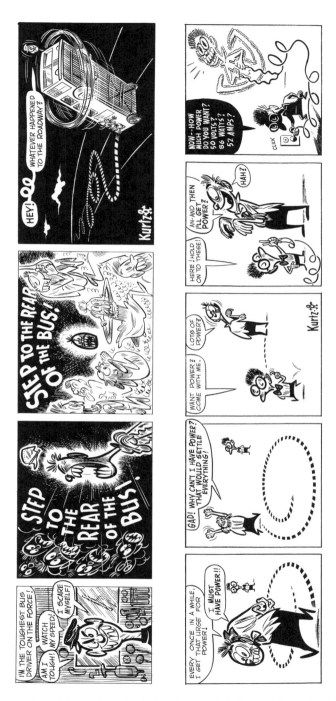

Two of the nine *Silver Linings* strips published in the New York *Herald Tribune*, dated May 9, 1948 and June 6, 1948, respectively.

Kurtzman showed he could imitate other popular comics artists in this *Hey Look!* from *Lana* #2 (October 1948). In order, he emulated Will Eisner, Al Capp, Chester Gould and Chic Young. (The last panel is Kurtzman being Kurtzman.)

7.

DESPERATION

RETURNING FROM HIS HONEYMOON, Harvey Kurtzman was unprepared for what he discovered when he unlocked the door to the Charles William Harvey studio. "The place [was] like a shipwreck, with papers on the floor," he recalled.[1] "The whole thing had collapsed. Charlie [Stern] had gone to Europe, and he left me holding the bag. The place was a wreck . . . and nobody was there."[2]

On top of that, he had "no job, no work, no money, no income."[3] His main source of revenue from 1946 through 1948 was *Hey Look!*, and now it was over. Kurtzman spent weeks doing very little. He pressed Stan Lee for something new, but at first nothing was offered. Then he met Elliot Caplin, the younger brother of Al Capp (born Caplin), when Capp's satirical comic strip *Li'l Abner* was at its peak of popularity. Although he had a college degree (unlike Al), Elliot followed his brother into the newspaper syndication field, beginning in 1937 as a writer for King Features Syndicate. By 1940, he was also employed by the Parents Magazine Institute, editing their comics line (*True Comics*) and *Parents* magazine. In 1948, he went to work editing a comic book line for his brother's new company, Al Capp Enterprises Inc. Elliot named it Toby Press after his son. Caplin also took over as writer of *Abbie an' Slats*, Capp's other newspaper strip, in 1945. (Ray Van Buren drew it.) Soon he would originate his own syndicated strips in collaboration with other artists.

When Harvey Kurtzman met him, Elliot Caplin was in the process of setting up Toby Press, which would begin by bringing *Li'l Abner* into the fold (from Harvey Comics). Though he was impressed with *Hey Look!* and immediately became a Kurtzman booster, it was too early for Caplin to give him comic book assignments. Instead, before he relinquished his duties at the Parents Magazine Institute, he gave Kurtzman some projects for another of the publisher's magazines. "The guy that stands out in that period is Elliot Caplin, who came in with work, just gave me work, on the basis of knowing I was desperate," Kurtzman said. "I'll never forget that man for that."[4]

Varsity, "The Young Man's Magazine," was started in mid-1947 with Elliot Caplin as editor. Though Caplin departed, it became a semi-regular venue for Kurtzman's work over the next couple of years. He also did some illustrations for the well-regarded *Parents*

Varsity magazine (March 1949).

magazine. (Well regarded, that is, by parents; kids hated it for telling parents which books and movies weren't suitable for children.) The amount of work for *Varsity* wasn't large, but it turned out to be an important developmental step for Kurtzman, because he was producing material for a somewhat older audience: the college male of 1949. The March 1949 issue carried his piece, "The Secret Thoughts of an Undergraduate, Case History #1—at the dance." It's Kurtzman's cartoon version of the inner workings of a college male's head. The four scenes deal with the student's delusions of being a great dancer, his resentment of guys who always cut in, his attempts to work up his courage to ask an especially attractive young woman to dance, and his sexual excitement at dancing "with that little blonde" only to have his pants fall down, revealing his boxer shorts. The caption, which identified the writer-artist as Harvey Harmon (a rare case of Kurtzman using a pen name), describes the piece as a "stroll down the subconscious of a typical undergraduate." A sequel of sorts appeared in the June issue, titled "The Secret Thoughts of an Undergraduate—The night before exams." This time, inside the cutaway profile of the student's head, readers saw eight images representing temptations and distractions from studying.

Having passed muster, Kurtzman received additional assignments. He appreciated the pay rates, higher than those available in the comic book trade. Apart from that, *Varsity* represented something else that was important to him: breaking into magazines. True, it wasn't a "slick" magazine (the paper wasn't glossy), but it was undeniably a large newsstand magazine as opposed to a pulp or comic book. This was a significant step toward realizing his childhood dream.

Meanwhile, the Charles William Harvey Studio showed signs of life. The reasons for the state of the place when Kurtzman returned from his honeymoon aren't clear. It may have been no more complicated than his partners choosing to take a break at the same time as Kurtzman. In any case, Will Elder and John Severin were back at their drawing boards turning out artwork for the comic book *Prize Comics Western*. Being a student of the Old West, Severin's pencils have an unusual authenticity for such comics, and Elder's inking provides the appropriate enhancement. Their creative partnership jelled in the fall of 1948, and became one of the better art teams to grace a comic book. Some of their later American Eagle stories are minor classics of the form. That Severin and Elder came together at Kurtzman's suggestion indicates their respect for his opinion. He was already thinking like an editor.

Around this time, Kurtzman helped Elder ink a Western story, his first serious comic book work since before the war. It was on the entirely undistinguished "Prairie Schooner Ahoy!," an entry in the Black Bull series

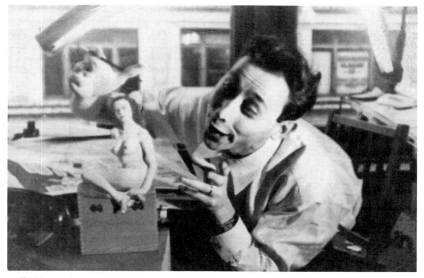

Will Elder in the Charles William Harvey Studio, ca. 1949. Courtesy of the Will Elder Estate.

in *Prize Comics Western* #74. Here and there one can detect a Kurtzman touch. It was commonplace for others to help finish projects to meet tight deadlines.

Sometimes studio hijinks got out of hand—literally. Elder was fooling around one day and discovered that if he covered a finger with rubber cement, he could light it and it would look like his finger was on fire. The effect got him a laugh from his studiomates, but then the fire burned through the rubber cement. Panicking, Elder shook his hand, sending little fireballs around the studio, igniting the rug and the curtains. The flames got out of control and they had to call the fire department. This didn't endear them to their landlord, but Kurtzman—who often had a calming influence on others—managed to convince the Rosenblums to renew their lease anyway.[5]

Publisher David McKay had dedicated *King Comics* and *Ace Comics* to the characters from King Features Syndicate. But McKay was getting out of comic books in 1949, which left the licenses for King's properties up for bid. Among them were *Little Orphan Annie*, *Henry*, *The Katzenjammer Kids*, *The Phantom*, *Dick Tracy* and *Blondie*. Timely's Martin Goodman watched from the sidelines as his competitor Alfred Harvey bid and won the rights to publish *Dick Tracy* and *Blondie* in comic books. Both were popular properties in films and radio as well as their newspaper strips. By 1949, Harvey Comics' output was large, some thirty to forty-five books a month. *Dick Tracy* and *Blondie Comics Monthly* became two of its most successful and long-running titles, both lasting through the 1950s.

Licensing newspaper characters wasn't Goodman's style. The last license Goodman had was with Terrytoons, and he let that go in 1947. Instead, the publisher preferred to copy a popular character as closely as possible without crossing the line into actual copyright infringement. In order to make Georgie, his Archie imitation, closer to the mark, he instructed his artists to put Archie-like crosshatching on the back of Georgie's head. Now Goodman ordered Stan Lee to produce a clone of Chic Young's *Blondie*.

Since 1947, Timely had published eight issues of *Rusty Comics* with comedic tales of the eponymous protagonist, her husband Johnny and their two children. Instead of creating a new set of characters, Lee decided to convert *Rusty* to fit the Blondie mold. He worked up some scripts and began looking for an artist. In *Lana* #2 (October 1948), a page of *Hey Look!* showed that Kurtzman was able to emulate the styles of other cartoonists. It made fun of the recent spate of newspaper strips doing takeoffs of other popular comics. On that single page, Kurtzman copied the styles of Will

Hedy Devine #35 (October 1949).

Eisner, Al Capp, Chester Gould and Chic Young. This may be why Lee gave
Kurtzman the "new *Rusty*" assignment.

Kurtzman was conflicted. The idea of outright imitating another strip
repulsed him. He called it "counterfeiting." But his work for *Varsity* was
finished for the time being, and, while he would continue to look for work
elsewhere, he had to do something to pay the bills. Reluctantly, he took
the job, but felt having to copy Chic Young's *Blondie* was "the lowest point
in my life."[6] Maybe Lee, like Walt Kelly, considered Kurtzman's work "too
specialized" and thought he was doing Kurtzman a favor. But, after the
artistic freedom of *Hey Look!*, it was especially hard to take. Even in the
Ferstadt shop, he hadn't been expected to imitate someone else's work.

Kurtzman's first *Rusty* story was "Her Peaceful Night Out," a five-
pager that appeared in *Rusty* #20 (May 1949). He was working on it about
the time he and Adele rang in the New Year. Kurtzman adopted the typical panel layouts of the *Blondie* newspaper strip but only approximated
Young's drawing style. His character designs are much like those of the
earlier *Rusty* stories. It's a waste of his talent, but the story is readable and
somewhat amusing. Apparently it was close enough to satisfy Lee. He accepted it and gave Kurtzman more *Rusty* scripts.

IN EARLY 1949, KURTZMAN also found work with a small outfit putting
out children's books called Kunen Publishing. He designed three jigsaw
puzzle books, which sold for twenty-five cents each. They were *Playtime
Reader*, *Let's Take a Ride* and *The Paper Doll*. The artwork was done in
multicolor tempera paint with inked outlines. The back cover blurb on
Let's Take a Ride reads, "Little Willy and Jilly go to school by horse and
wagon, motorcycle, and train. The jigsaw pieces of Willy and Jilly fit into
all the puzzle subjects when they are removed from the book." Kurtzman's

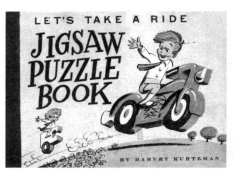

Harvey Kurtzman collaborated with René Goscinny, co-creator of *Asterix*, on *Let's Take a Ride* from Kunen Publishing. L-R: Kurtzman, Severin and Goscinny, ca. 1949. Courtesy of Kurtzman estate.

writing and art in these little books is just right: light, energetic, visually appealing and fun.

More Kunen children's books would be done in collaboration with a new friend and studiomate. René Goscinny was a couple of years younger than Kurtzman, and just beginning his career as a writer and artist. Later, he became a major figure in European comics when he founded *Pilote* magazine and co-created *Astérix* (with illustrator Albert Uderzo), one of the most popular Franco-Belgian comic book characters of all time. Goscinny was born in Paris in 1926, and grew up in a French enclave in Buenos Aires, Argentina. When his father died in 1945, he and his mother moved to New York City to live with his uncle. After a stint in the French military, Goscinny returned to the city in 1947. He spent much of the following year jobless, then came into contact with the Charles William Harvey Studio. "I was lucky enough to meet a typographer who was working for young comic book artists who welcomed me in their group," Goscinny remembered. By early 1949, he was a regular presence in the studio and the Kurtzmans' lives.[7]

Both Harvey and Adele Kurtzman enjoyed the Frenchman's company enormously. "[René] was around a lot, and we had a lot of fun," Adele said. "He lived in Manhattan with his mother, and his mother was charming. She was a wonderful cook, and we went there to dinner a lot, and they came to our apartment. René was very funny, and very charming."[8] Goscinny had an elfin quality and a way of raising an eyebrow that spoke volumes. He was a writer who never typed with more than two fingers.

Not long after Goscinny joined the group, a Belgian artist named Maurice de Bevere began visiting the studio. Under the pen name Morris, he also became an important figure in European comics. He was the cartoonist and first author of the hugely popular comic book series *Lucky*

Luke. Another Belgian cartoonist named Joseph Gillain, better known as Jijé, was also in the group. He became best known for his artwork on the *Spirou et Fantasio* strip. Kurtzman's growing circle of artist-friends from the Continent wasn't surprising, considering his appreciation of European cartoonists such as Wilhelm Busch and Caran d'Ache.

Even though Kurtzman wasn't making much money, his wife had a difficult time controlling her spending. "They were tough times [and] I had a terrible attitude," Adele admitted. "My mother used to say, 'Adele, live like you've got it,' so, of course, I lived like I had it—as much as I could."[9] This would be a source of conflict between her and her husband in the coming years.

Kurtzman poured much of his energy in the first half of 1949 into *Rusty.* He produced about sixty *Rusty* pages, which, if added to eight pages of miscellaneous material in Timely's *Little Aspirin* title at this same time, probably paid him a total of about $1,700. He made no more than $2,000 in the first three quarters of 1949 (amounting to about $20,000 in current dollars), just enough to get by. Working on *Rusty* was as depressing as *Hey Look!* had been exhilarating. The work wasn't good. Kurtzman recalled, "Stan Lee would take it to Martin Goodman, who didn't know beans about art, and between Stan Lee, Martin Goodman and myself, I kept running back and forth trying to imitate *Blondie.* I was like a counterfeiter, trying to do plates of a dollar bill, and being run by a couple of bosses who didn't know about counterfeiting too well, any more than the counterfeiter. It was just a kind of madness. And I was desperate for the money! I really needed the dough! It was such a rotten experience."[10]

With *Rusty* #22 (September 1949), the title was canceled. "Martin Goodman came through one day and said, 'That's not like *Blondie and Dagwood,*' threw me out of the job and I was just newly married at the time—oh, God! So I associate personal horror with the business of following techniques and I just never had a slick technique going for me."[11] "At Home with the Rumples," a ten-pager that was his last *Rusty* story, is claustrophobic and uninspired—a cry for help. It was delayed almost a year, then shunted into the back of *My Friend Irma* #4 (August 1950). By then, the feature was dead. "That was the lowest period of my life, not because of Stan, but because of the Martin Goodman mentality," Kurtzman said. "Goodman treated artists like chairs and tables. I mean, you were just a piece of equipment."[12]

Kurtzman felt like a failure, even when he was fired for doing something he thought was beneath him. Later, he expressed some of those feelings: "I was never successful at standard comics. I was a lousy comic book man. It was only when I created my own form that I was successful at comics. I wasn't successful doing someone else's form. I couldn't do Superman. I couldn't do super heroes. I couldn't do any of that stuff. I couldn't even do the funny stuff. I was bad at all of it."[13] Even *Pigtales* was idiosyncratic, not standard funny animal fare. Plus, as he had already realized, he was a slower worker than others in the field. "I never do anything right the first time," he said. "I have to do it twice, three times. And it's always been that way."[14] To compensate, he was willing to work longer hours, but he needed the right opportunity.

THUS BEGAN A NIGHTMARISH interlude in Harvey Kurtzman's life. In July and August, the height of New York's most uncomfortable season, its luckier denizens fled to cooler climes. In downtown Manhattan, amid the sweltering heat, Kurtzman shopped for work. "It was one of the very few times I went around hustling," he remembered. "I was a beggar. I'd grab a morsel here, a tidbit there. You just went from door to door and I never really had anything to sell."[15]

Work for Will Eisner? Jules Feiffer was there, and so was Wallace Wood, handling whatever part of *The Spirit* that Will himself didn't do.

Get a job with one of the remaining shop operations? Jerry Iger still had his shop in 1949. But for Kurtzman, returning to the Ferstadt days was worse than nothing.

What next? Go back to L. B. Cole, who was getting his new, low-rent Star Publications comics line off the ground?

At his lowest ebb, Kurtzman came back to the idea of using cartoons to educate. He discovered the writings of Dr. Harvey Zorbaugh, a fifty-two-year-old Professor of Educational Sociology at New York University. Educated at the University of Chicago, Zorbaugh came east to NYU and edited the *Journal of Educational Sociology.* In 1944, he began publishing articles that were generally sympathetic to the comics industry and recognized the potential of the comic art medium. He joined the editorial advisory boards of Fawcett Publications and a publisher named Educational Comics.[16] What probably caught Kurtzman's eye was an article by Harvey Zorbaugh and Mildred Gilman called, "What can YOU do about Comic Books?" in *Family Circle* magazine (February 1949). The opening photograph showed children perusing comics at a newsstand, with the most prominent boy reading a copy of *Rusty.*

The article said, in part, "You may take your choice in the current controversy, but one thing you must reconcile yourself to—the comics are here to stay. The bewildered parent . . . finds among authorities complete disagreement concerning the comics." He quoted Dr. Lauretta Bender, a professor of psychiatry at the New York University Medical School, who also served on advisory boards of comic book publishers. She asserted that some comics "like the folklore of other times, serve as a means to stimulate the child's fantasy life and so help him solve the individual and sociological problems inherent in his living."

Zorbaugh then paraphrased Sidonie Matsner Gruenberg, director of the Child Study Association, who "points out that the comics have become a medium for the promotion of socially useful attitudes, that during the war they sold war stamps, collected salvage, enlisted volunteers for the various services and for essential war work, and in many ways furthered the war effort. Certain comics help to foster understanding between races and to combat prejudices among people. Others educate about the prevention of tuberculosis." While Zorbaugh mentioned Dr. Fredric Wertham's anti-comics views, he maintained there were plenty of good comics, and that comics themselves hadn't been shown to directly cause harm to children. He concluded they could be an appropriate form of "entertainment, release, or aid to education."[17]

Kurtzman called on Dr. Zorbaugh at NYU. They discussed the educational potential of comic books. At some point, Zorbaugh told Kurtzman that he had worked for a firm called Educational Comics, and suggested he contact them. The address was 225 Lafayette St., in lower Manhattan, several blocks south of Zorbaugh's office.

When he found the building, rode its elevator to the seventh floor, and walked through the door with the EC placard, Harvey Kurtzman entered the domain of the one man in comics who would give him the creative freedom he needed. His fortunes were about to change.

Kurtzman was hired to draw *Rusty*, a *Blondie* imitation: from *Hedy Devine* #35 (October 1949).

8.

SON OF GAINES

UNLIKE HARVEY KURTZMAN, William "Bill" Maxwell Gaines grew up wanting nothing to do with cartoons or the world of publishing in any form. This was probably because his father, Maxwell Charles (M. C., "Charlie") Gaines, was in the comic book business, and he had a love-hate relationship with the man—mostly hate. Today M. C. Gaines's treatment of his son would be considered verbally and physically abusive: constant berating, telling him that he "would never amount to anything," hitting and kicking him in the presence of others and generally spewing anger at his son.[1]

M. C. Gaines was a better father of the American comic book than he was to his beleaguered son. Scratching for a living as a novelties salesman during the Great Depression, he came up with the idea of creating giveaway comic books to sell products. Then Gaines realized people liked those colorful little magazines enough that they would probably pay for them. He tested the idea by placing a number of them on local newsstands, and when they quickly sold out, he knew he was onto something. Soon others were printing comic books strictly for commercial sale, and in 1938, M. C. Gaines formed All-American Publications to publish such comic books on a regular basis. The venture was an immediate success. His first book was *All-American Comics* #1 (April 1939), followed by titles introducing such heroes as The Flash, Green Lantern, Hawkman and Wonder Woman. His paper allotments during World War II meant he virtually had a license to print money. Suddenly Gaines was on his way to making a fortune.

William Gaines, M. C.'s only son, was born in 1922. The younger Gaines was a chubby, awkward youth with an abhorrence of sports, an inability to do anything that required physical prowess and a mediocre school record. His father's treatment severely undermined his self-confidence. He sequestered himself with his radio and pulp magazines, and tried to stay out of his father's way. Bill Gaines recalled, "As a child, I had two great loves. One was horror pulps—*Horror Stories* and *Terror Tales*—and the other was science fiction pulps—*Astounding, Amazing* and *Wonder Stories*."[2] He spent his weekends in the darkness of local movie houses watching *Flash Gordon* and other serials.

When Bill reached high school age, his father demanded that he help in the All-American offices during the summer. He worked in the stock room, hating every minute of it. After graduation, Bill entered the Brooklyn Polytechnic Institute to study chemistry. By the time the United States was at war, he was struggling in school, flunking out according to one source.[3] Gaines decided he'd rather face an Axis attack than his father's wrath. After being rejected by the US Army, Coast Guard and Navy, he ended up in the Army Air Corps where he trained to be a photographer. He spent most of his time doing KP duty on bases in Oklahoma, Louisiana, Kansas and on Governors Island in New York. In 1944, Bill married Hazel Grieb, his second cousin, a union largely engineered by his formidable mother, Jessie Gaines. After the war, Bill Gaines returned to school, switching from Brooklyn Polytech to New York University, with the revised goal of becoming a chemistry teacher. This sat well enough with M.C., who believed in education and had experimented with factual and educational comic books.

M. C. Gaines's *Picture Stories From the Bible* was published to considerable success in 1942, encouraging him to produce more in the series. But, by 1945, his relationship with his partner Jack Liebowitz (who was forced on him by his investor, Harry Donenfeld of National Comics) had soured, and he asked Donenfeld to buy him out. National Comics paid Gaines $500,000 in after-tax money for his paper allocations and nearly all of the creative properties of All-American. Gaines retained the rights to *Picture Stories From the Bible*, and started a new company called Educational Comics (EC) to publish more of them and their ilk. The new company was operating in the red when he was killed in a boating accident on Lake Placid in the summer of 1947.

Despite their difficult relationship, the death of his father devastated Bill Gaines.[4] His divorce from Hazel came shortly thereafter. Jessie Gaines was now a widow who owned a failing comic book company. For partly sentimental reasons, she wanted the company to continue and asked Bill to take the helm. Gaines reportedly responded, "How the hell can I run a business when I couldn't even make it as the old man's stockroom boy?"[5] Eventually, he complied with her request. At some point after M. C.'s death, Jessie gave Bill half of the stock in the corporations making up EC. She became president and treasurer. Bill was vice president, and his sister Elaine was secretary. The EC staff consisted of editor Sol Cohen and business manager Frank Lee. Freelancers did the creative work.

At first, Bill Gaines visited the office infrequently, mainly when Frank Lee told him there were checks to be signed. He replaced the poorly selling educational titles with books in genres then popular: Western, romance, crime. Gaines changed the title of his father's *International Comics* to *International Crime Patrol* with #6 (Spring 1948), and started *War Against Crime!* (Spring 1948). The losses were stemmed, although following the marketplace is hardly a recipe for great success. It didn't help that he was saddled with a distribution contract with Leader News, one of the worst of the firms that transported comics from printers to wholesalers around the country.

Just as he learned about the vicissitudes of comic book distribution, Bill Gaines received tutelage—from Sol Cohen, Frank Lee and from EC's attorney, Dave Alterbaum—on "how to run a comic book company the Maxwell Gaines way." That involved how much writers and artists were paid, and the fact that the one-time payment covered any and all rights (including reprints). That meant creative personnel gave up ownership of the titles or characters that they invented. The arrangement, known as "work for hire," was a much different system from the one artists and writers faced when working for magazines and the book trade. This pernicious policy was accepted mainly because there was an abundance of hungry writers and artists, and most of them intended to move on to other, more respectable work. No one thought comic books would have enduring value. This was the way the comic book publishers operated in the 1940s, and Bill Gaines accepted it.

In other respects, Gaines became an enlightened comic book publisher. During the process of looking for artists for his new titles, he quickly developed an appreciation for comic art. Rather than seeking to establish a "house style," Gaines liked artists who demonstrated individuality (along with the other requisite skills). Not only did he encourage such individuality, he adopted a relaxed supervisory style, which gave the artists a great deal of creative freedom. He let artists sign their work and even published one-page biographies of many of them. Gaines paid a bit more than most of his competitors because he wanted the best young talent available. Over time, he demonstrated a great deal of loyalty to his freelancers. Yet when it

came to the basic exploitive practices in the industry, he was about the same as others. While the original art wasn't destroyed, he kept it in a vault rather than return it to the artists.

Early in 1948, Albert Feldstein arrived at the EC office. The graduate of M&A was now twenty-three years old. Apart from his substantial art ability, Al Feldstein was a go-getter with a burning desire for financial success. As a freelancer, he found himself working for Victor Fox, one of the sleaziest purveyors of comic books in the postwar era, but used the opportunity to develop his craft, learning that he could write comics as well as draw them. He did humor and "good girl art" (the latter means well-drawn pin-up-style art) comics for Fox, but the firm was rumored to be on the verge of bankruptcy so Feldstein looked for assignments elsewhere. The teenage humor comic he was initially going to do for EC was scuttled, but Gaines and Cohen were quick to see his value, and gave him work in their ongoing titles.

In the eighteen months from the time Feldstein started working for Gaines to the time Kurtzman showed up, a lot happened in the world of EC. Although titles such as *Gunfighter*, *Saddle Justice*, *Crime Patrol*, *War Against Crime* and *Modern Love* were unremarkable, Gaines began to enjoy the business and gradually pulled together what became the most impressive group of artists ever assembled at a comic book company. Artist Johnny Craig came into his own during this period, turning out a series of beautifully composed, striking covers for the crime titles. Al Feldstein further developed his emphatic, solid style. Within a short time, Wallace Wood and his partner Harry Harrison offered themselves as an art team, producing work that showed promise. Gaines was a good judge of talent, although some credit goes to Feldstein, whose opinion carried considerable weight. He filled the editorial vacuum created when Sol Cohen left the company to edit comic books for Avon.

Meanwhile, American Comics Group published *Adventures into the Unknown* in the fall of 1948, the first ongoing horror comic book. Feldstein did a freelance assignment titled "The Creekmore Curse" for its third issue (February–March 1949). Gaines and Feldstein decided to try their hand at horror and see what happened. Their early efforts, which introduced the horror hosts the Vault-Keeper and Crypt-Keeper, were scheduled for *War against Crime!* #10 (December 1949–January 1950) and *Crime Patrol* #15 (January–February 1950), under "Vault of Horror" and "Crypt of Terror" banners, respectively. These stories were written and drawn around August or September 1949, but hadn't appeared in print when Kurtzman came calling.

NEITHER KURTZMAN NOR GAINES knew that EC may have already published a bit of Kurtzman's work. When he was laboring in Louis Ferstadt's studio before the war, Kurtzman had worked on—maybe created—a funny animal strip called "Kangy Roo." All he ever said about it was, "Ferstadt sold this animated cartoon for me, which I wrote and drew. [It was] some kind of animal thing: a kangaroo and a panda. It was . . . 'Kangy Kangaroo.'"[6] Louis Ferstadt's client was Charlie Gaines. EC's *Animated Comics* #1 (effectively a one-shot in 1947) in-

PR photo of EC editor-writer-artist Al Feldstein. (Shown: *Weird Fantasy* #10.)

cluded a four-page Kangy Roo story, the only documented appearance of the character. That comic book hit newsstands in November 1947, three months after the elder Gaines's demise. It doesn't show much evidence of Kurtzman's style, but the same is often true of his prewar work. In any case, Kurtzman and Gaines had never met.[7]

Harvey Kurtzman entered Bill Gaines's office, introduced himself, and said he was interested in creating educational comics. He discovered that Educational Comics was no longer publishing them, and, indeed, its initials now stood for Entertaining Comics. Gaines recalled,

> Harvey walked in, and we rapidly advised him that we were not the proper outfit for that. However, as long as he was there, he showed us his *Hey Look!*s. And I remember I was sitting at my desk, and Al Feldstein was looking over my shoulder, and we were going through one of these after another, and, you know, it was building. We chuckled at the first few, and by the end of this mess we were . . . just dying, our stomachs ached with laughter. So we agreed that we had to get this talent. But how—he didn't fit at all into what we were doing. But we tried to make him fit.[8]

Kurtzman recalled, "[Gaines and Feldstein] were modern, intelligent, they were a breath of fresh air."⁹ They "got" him, and that alone was a relief. Of course, he and Feldstein had the brief encounter over the bottle-breaking incident way back at the High School of Music and Art, so they probably recognized each other.

"[Gaines] didn't give me any work immediately," he said, "but his uncle [David Gaines], who happened to be on the scene that day, gave me an assignment to do a cartoon pamphlet for Columbia University, a cowboy strip about the lucky cowboy who contracts syphilis. In subsequent pages we showed what you should do . . . and shouldn't do. How you should take care of it. It was a government-grant thing, [and] a pretty radical thing to do at the time."¹⁰ This was "Lucky Fights it Through," subtitled, "The Story of That Ignorant, Ignorant Cowboy." It was a use of comics to warm Harvey Zorbaugh's heart.

The sixteen-page comic strip paid just $10 a page, a fraction of what he had been getting at Timely, but Kurtzman saw it as an opportunity. With little else in the offing, and liking Gaines, he vowed to make something of this new contact. If he showed that he could handle a "straight" comic book story, then maybe Gaines would give him work at EC. Since EC was publishing *Gunfighter*, the fact that "Lucky" was a Western (if set in the modern West) made it a fitting tryout. Even a job paying only $160 would provide a welcome paycheck. Excited, script in hand, Kurtzman headed uptown to his studio and got to work, determined to show what he could do.¹¹

He had done serious comic art before the war, but the quality of the work published at the decade's end had to be more sophisticated than the rudimentary comics he had drawn for Ace. Kurtzman had inked two Severin-pencilled stories in *Prize Comics Western*, which helped prepare him for "Lucky Fights it Through." The stories were "Timberline Showdown" and "The Stranger of Benton Bowl," standard Western melodramas that benefited from Kurtzman's punchy inking style. He had learned to use his brush aggressively on *Hey Look!,* and now applied it to straight stories with good results. Looking at the finished "Lucky Fights it Through," it's also clear that the Milton Caniff influence, apparent in his *Black Venus* work for L. B. Cole, was still in evidence. Lucky doesn't quite look like Steve Canyon's brother, but he could have been a cousin. Stiff and awkward in certain places, the artwork is nevertheless executed with real panache. Gone are the scrunched figures of his early work. The narrative on the dangers of syphilis (and its cure) is clearly told, and there's real beauty in some of the design and composition work. The strongest points are Kurtzman's placement of the black areas and his powerful brush strokes. "I killed myself doing this commercial strip," Kurtzman said, though "educational" would be a better descriptor than "commercial."[12] Gaines and Feldstein were suitably impressed, as was David Gaines. It was printed some time before the end of the year.

LEAN AS WORK HAD BEEN in 1949, Kurtzman had other things on his drawing board. He had continued to submit

Panel from "Lucky Fights it Through" (1949). Kurtzman turned an educational comic book assignment on the diagnosis and treatment of syphilis into an audition for EC comics.

ideas to *Varsity* magazine, which led to a two-pager in late summer called "Follow That Girl." He would do more for the magazine periodically over the next couple of years, including the continuity strip "Girls with whom you wouldn't like to be stranded on a desert island," and the large double-page spread "Spring comes to the campus" in the March 1950 issue. It's a panorama with dozens of figures, with visual gags woven throughout. It roots could be traced back to the big drawing of the freshman boat ride at M&A. The last Kurtzman piece in *Varsity* appeared in the December 1951 issue, "An exposé of fraternity initiations." What did Kurtzman know about college life? Not a thing, although he lived across the street from Columbia University.

Kurtzman worked up a new humor filler called *Pot-Shot Pete*, which he said was inspired by his entry in the "Buffalo Bob" contest as a youth.[13] It was a Western burlesque that allowed him to indulge in exaggerated cowboy vernacular, something he enjoyed enormously. He sold a couple of them to editor Julius Schwartz at National, and they appeared in *All-American Western* #112 (February–March 1950) and *Jimmy Wakely* #4 (March–April 1950). They were the only pages he ever sold to the publisher of Superman and Batman. When he showed them to Elliot Caplin at Toby Press, Caplin asked for some longer Pete stories, and Kurtzman eventually complied. Three five-pagers appeared in Western titles from Toby Press, beginning the following year. Kurtzman also adapted *Pot-Shot Pete*, possibly at Caplin's suggestion, to daily newspaper strip form. At least three of them have survived. It apparently engendered no interest among the syndicates. Drawn in his evolved, post-*Hey Look!* style, they are Kurtzman at his brilliant best. By this time, the twenty-five-year-old's humorous cartooning had essentially reached its maturity.

Elliot Caplin also published Kurtzman's new filler page *Genius* that same autumn. Toby Press editor Mell Lazarus described Caplin's admiration for Kurtzman's work when he told interviewer Jim Amash that it "was not Harvey's title. Elliot Caplin named his character because he considered Harvey a genius, and so insisted, 'That's the name of the character.'"[14] *Genius* is the nickname of a mischievous, rather nasty little boy. With his unruly blond hair, he resembled Hank Ketcham's Dennis the Menace, who came along a year later. The difference was that Dennis caused chaos by accident; Genius did it deliberately. One wishes that Kurtzman had done more than nine of them. *Genius* first appeared in *Al Capp's Li'l Abner* #75 (March 1950).

A low-paying educational strip, a few pages for *Varsity*, some initial pages of *Pot-Shot Pete* and *Genius* wouldn't alleviate Kurtzman's immediate financial crunch. Nor would several more children's books for Kunen, done in collaboration with René Goscinny.

There were four of the new Kunen books. Kurtzman drew the covers (uncredited); Goscinny did the interior art and assisted Elliot Liebow with the scripts. They were all published in 1950 in the Bright Book series: *'Round the World*, *Hello Jimmy*, *The Little Red Car* and *The Jolly Jungle*. The books were die-cut in various shapes, about three inches square. "Harvey had a lot of pride in what he did," Adele recalled. "René and Harvey knocked themselves out doing something very different." The elephant's trunk on *The Jolly Jungle* is a cylindrical appendage attached to the front of the book. Goscinny was named art director for Kunen, which didn't mean much in an outfit so small. "Kunen didn't pay them," Adele added, "so Danny Cunningham and René went up to Kunen's office and kind of threatened him, so he paid them, but Harvey never got paid. He wasn't in on the threat."[15] That fall, there was another reason to hope EC would give him work. Adele announced she was pregnant.

KURTZMAN'S PLAN TO IMPRESS with "Lucky Fights it Through" worked. After looking it over, Al Feldstein became intrigued and gave him a horror script. It was "House of Horror," a tale that Kurtzman assumed was written by Feldstein, but was (according to Gaines) authored by someone else, possibly Ivan Klapper, a writer who had been selling scripts to EC before they tried horror. "I spent weeks with a pen doing pen work [on "House

of Horrors"]," Kurtzman later revealed. "After that, I was on my way with
EC. Because I did that job like engraving a dollar bill. It couldn't miss."[16]
Indeed, if "Lucky Fights it Through" was a hit to first or second base,
"House of Horror" sailed over the bleachers for a home run.

The story, like many early EC horror scripts by Gaines and Feldstein,
was suggested by a published source. Sometimes they simply stole an entire story, changing little more than the characters' names. More often,
they took the kernel of an idea and spun it out into something relatively
original. Such "swiping" was often done in comics, the creators figuring
that "it's only a comic book and no one will care." When readers (and
authors) began pointing out the more egregious instances of plagiarism,
Gaines stopped basing entire stories on the work of others. "House of
Horror" originated from one of the old chestnuts—the horror equivalent
of urban legends—recounted in the "Trail of the Tingling Spine" chapter
of Bennett Cerf's book, *Try and Stop Me* (Random House, 1944). It was the
source of quite a few EC plots.

The story involves members of a fraternity who haze three pledges
by forcing them to enter a so-called haunted house. Kurtzman's artwork
makes it special; it creates tremendous spooky atmosphere and tension
as, one by one, the boys enter the dark Palmer house and then fail to signal with their flashlights from the attic window as agreed. The house itself, in the splash panel, is detailed with all sorts of little features that
"sell" it to the reader. Somewhat prefiguring the famous house from
Hitchcock's *Psycho* in appearance, the Palmer house is a character in the
story. Kurtzman seems to etch every bit of flaked paint in its wooden clap-
board siding, every spiderweb, every bit of cracked glass, and does it with
impressive technical virtuosity. The characters in the story are similarly
well realized. Considerable attention is paid to the way the expressions
on their young, callow faces are revealed in light and shadow, not an easy
task. Largely eschewing "stock" facial expressions, there's unusual subtlety in a lot of the character work. It enhanced the point of the story,
which was the psychological effect the events had on the young men.

"House of Horror" is an altogether outstanding achievement. The only
flaw, and it isn't Kurtzman's, is that the script was forced into just six
pages. The conclusion is rushed. Had there been another page, the ending
might have been more satisfying. Some might say the panels have too
much detail; that Kurtzman is trying too hard. That may be true, and he
did gradually simplify the art in subsequent assignments, but the story
more than accomplishes its purpose. As he said, "It couldn't miss," and
it didn't.

By the time Harvey Kurtzman turned in the story, big things were afoot at EC. Bill Gaines had decided to launch five new comic books (each one continuing the numbering of a former, discontinued title): *Vault of Horror*, *The Crypt of Terror*, *Haunt of Fear*, *Weird Science* and *Weird Fantasy*. EC's renowned New Trend line was about to begin. Once Gaines got a look at "House of Horror," he invited Kurtzman to play a part in his bold experiment in comic book horror and science fiction. Comic books would never be the same.

Pot-Shot Pete from *John Wayne Adventure Comics* #5 (October 1950). Harvey Kurtzman story and art.

This *Genius* installment ran in *John Wayne Adventure Comics* #6 (November 1950).

"House of Horror" in *Haunt of Fear* #15 (May–June 1950) was Harvey Kurtzman's first assignment for EC comics.

9.

FROM ZERO TO SIXTY

ACCORDING TO ITS COVER BLURB, *Vault of Horror* #12 began "a new trend in magazines." Four men who became stars in the EC universe drew the stories: Johnny Craig, Wallace Wood, Al Feldstein and Harvey Kurtzman. It hit the stands in mid-February 1950.[1]

Harvey Kurtzman's contribution to this seminal comic book isn't the superb "House of Horror" but "Horror in the Night," working from another script of uncertain authorship (though, again, possibly by Ivan Klapper, because Feldstein later disavowed it). Kurtzman's process of illustrating "House of Horror" had been painstaking. The second story appears to have been produced more quickly, which got it into the publisher's hands not long after the first one. Why Gaines ran it first is anyone's guess. Kurtzman's interpretation of the script (a man whose horrific dreams come true) is looser but no less assured than his first story. "House of Horror" was held for the debut issue of *Haunt of Fear*, which wasn't published until the first week of May. Gaines loved "House of Horror" so much that he reprinted it a few months later, one of very few cases of such reprinting at EC.

A problem arose. Kurtzman didn't like working on horror stories. The fantasy aspects of horror—werewolves, ghosts, walking corpses—didn't interest him. If he was going to work in a horror comic book, he preferred psychological horror, something along the lines of Klapper's script for "Madness at Manderville," his assignment for *The Crypt of Terror* #18. (The comic was soon retitled *Tales from the Crypt*.) It asks the reader to guess which member of a troubled marriage is the insane one.

Harvey Kurtzman continued to be favorably impressed with Bill Gaines. He later assessed the publisher: "First and foremost . . . very bright! . . . An intellectual of sorts. He has an extremely brilliant methodical mind, what I regard as a mathematical mind. He was unusual in the comic field, relative to comics and EC, in that he was able to apply democratic principles to the people he gathered and let them, in

The Kurtzman-drawn "Horror in the Night!" appeared in the first New Trend comic book published by EC: *Vault of Horror* #12 (April–May 1950).

the vernacular, do their thing!"[2] Gaines recognized Kurtzman's talent and clearly felt lucky to have him. After seeing how well Kurtzman handled his initial jobs, he wanted to have as much of the artist's work as possible in his magazines. This meant that Kurtzman had found a creative home, if he wanted it. He did, and would have continued working for Gaines even if EC only published horror comics—at least, until he had righted his financial ship and found other work. But EC was also set to introduce two science fiction titles, giving Kurtzman another avenue. He snapped up scripts for the first issues of *Weird Science* and *Weird Fantasy*. Thus, Harvey and Adele bade farewell to 1949, their year from hell, and welcomed the New Year with open arms. Nineteen-fifty looked like it was going to bring all the work Kurtzman could handle, in the employ of a simpatico boss and alongside congenial colleagues. By the time the Kurtzmans' first child arrived, they figured to be doing much better financially.

"I LIKE SCIENCE FICTION very much," Kurtzman said.[3] "I was never a science fiction reader. In fact, I'm not a reader—period. But I do recognize H. G. Wells [and] Ray Bradbury."[4] In saying he wasn't a reader, Kurtzman was referring mainly to fiction, especially fantasy-oriented fiction. He did read nonfiction books, such as the psychology books that he delved into from time to time. But he recognized that science fiction often had a basis in fact, which, from his point of view, added to its appeal.

At first, Kurtzman worked from scripts written by another new SF convert, Al Feldstein. "Bill [Gaines] introduced me to science fiction, which I had never read," Feldstein recalled. "He said, 'Here, take these home,' and I read the *Astounding Science Fiction* books edited by John Campbell."[5] Campbell's reign was characterized by an emphasis on stories that extrapolated from scientific facts, including a propensity for stories about atomic power and nuclear disasters. *Astounding* eschewed ray guns and "space opera," and so did EC. (Meanwhile, the aging *Planet Comics* from Fiction House continued featuring covers and stories reminiscent of the old SF pulps, which were passé in 1950.)

Evidence of Kurtzman going from "zero to sixty" when he arrived at EC—while making the transition from humor to serious work—can be found by looking at "Lost in the Microcosm," the lead story in EC's first science fiction comic book, *Weird Science* #12. The plot came from Gaines's memory of the story "He Who Shrank" by Henry Hasse, which had appeared in *Amazing Stories* (August 1936). The gimmick: a shrinking man discovers that "The tiny atom . . . is actually . . . an astronomic solar system!" As he continues to shrink, he keeps finding solar systems within solar systems. In the end, the scientist friend of the protagonist wonders, "Can it be that this earth is just a puny world within a world all somewhere within an atom in the flesh of some professor's palm? And is this country . . . this United States . . . still a crude civilization compared to what exists in the infinite cosmos?"[6]

In his first foray into SF, the Kurtzman-drawn entry is artistically superior to the other stories in the issue drawn by Wallace Wood, Jack Kamen and Al Feldstein. Its design elements, its storytelling, its orchestration of dramatic beats, and the imagination (and execution) of the "outer space" panels, are like the work of a veteran comics pro, not a virtual neophyte who had done a mere handful of "straight" stories in his postwar career. Kurtzman's understanding and mastery of all the elements involved in creating mature, serious comic art—and so quickly—is no less than astonishing. Perhaps it was because his competitive instincts were aroused. A friendly competition existed among artists at EC, with each one vying for more "ooohs" and "aaahhs" from Bill Gaines as he looked over the completed pages. Though only a few years older than most of his artists, Gaines took a quasi-paternal interest in them. He would point out the things he especially liked, offering praise as well as a paycheck. The competition among the artists fostered constant improvement in the artwork in EC's New Trend titles.

After proving he could draw both horror and SF stories (having produced a respectable thirty-three pages in two-and-a-half months), Kurtzman asked if he could write his next script: "Since Bill and Al were hard up for writers, they let me take a crack at it."[7] As he was still doing assignments for the horror comics, this one would be for *Vault of Horror*. Gaines was open to it, merely wanting to approve the story idea first.

What Gaines didn't know was that Kurtzman was far from confident in his writing ability. He learned little about it in high school English, partly because he hadn't felt an affinity for it. "Writing is an abstract exercise that some people are geniuses at, but I am terrible at," he said in an interview thirty years later. "I don't work well with that particular talent of manipulating words. Oh, I can make up for it, I make do, but I know writers who write and what they're good at is, they can put together these abstractions we call letters and words. After all, what is writing? It's just one of many ways to communicate and it's very abstract—it's not sound and it's not objects that you see. You read. It's like mathematics. And it's not what I'm good at! What I do is visual. I do timing, I do rhythm, I do sequence, I create movement by arranging panels."[8] Then why did he want to write his scripts, beyond making the extra money? Certainly, on a superficial level, writing the stories would allow him to express his own ideas and write about things he wanted or liked to draw. Also, "Writing gave me the power to initiate projects."[9] And it was a point of pride. But, the reasons were considerably more complicated than that.

"My writing and drawing are totally integrated," he explained. "I can't work on one without working on the other."[10] In order to do what he did best—rhythm, sequence, movement—he had to conceive the stories as well as draw them. For him, the artwork not only grew out of the narrative, but its dramatic flow suggested changes in the script. Each bled into the other. "Once I have my pictures, then I know what the characters have to say," he said.[11] Also, a story's visual requirements had to be taken into account when the lettering was placed on the pages to achieve the optimum flow. In that way, Kurtzman's story and art were perfectly unified. "The more closely integrated the good text and the good art is," he said, "the greater the opportunity is to create the capital *a* Art."[12]

Kurtzman later told Michael Barrier, "Gaines and Feldstein started working with the short story form, as I did, and it was the first time I became aware of writing structure. Bill Gaines inspired me with much of my respect for short stories."[13] When Barrier suggested that the EC approach was highly formulaic in its adherence to the use of surprise endings, Kurtzman agreed. "Yes, as was mine. I looked for the O. Henry twist, very deliberately."[14] Toward that end, he read short stories by O. Henry and Guy de Maupassant, both known for their twist endings. Kurtzman also studied the short story form in literature, consulting books on fiction writing to gain insight. He learned the other tenets of good short stories:

only a few characters, unity of time and place and making the first and last lines the strongest in the story (often planting the seeds of the ending in the beginning). The six, seven and eight-page stories published by EC were the comic book equivalent of literary short stories.

For him, structure was the key that demystified the writing process: "I have always respected story structure. A good story is like a good joke, or like the bursting of a balloon. You invest the story with tension, you invest it and invest it and then you release it with great suddenness and a certain amount of surprise. That kind of resolution seems to satisfy something deep down inside." But it doesn't have to be like blowing up a balloon until it explodes. "In a short story, it's gentler than a joke," he said. "You don't have the same need for abruptness, although the best short stories do end very quickly and with great surprise. Of course, [if] you are working with a reality situation . . . sometimes the reality carries the story and takes it out of your hands."[15]

Kurtzman said, "My system for writing was to start with a point I wanted to make." This took the form of written notes indicating all the primary beats of the story. "When I had that settled in my head, I'd shape the story to the point."[16] Then he began breaking it down into pages and panels: "Once I'm clear on the theme, content and ending . . . I create a picture structure with thumbnail sketches along those lines of force determined by my verbal story. In other words, you start with abstract ideas. Your system starts with the statement you have to make."[17] He discovered how to dramatize his initial ideas by creating increasingly elaborate thumbnail sketches, essentially the same method he used for *Hey Look!* Then he worked on the final script, which could require changes in the way the action unfolded. The action and text evolved together. He didn't start working on the final drawing paper until he knew how each of the panels would look.

Kurtzman couldn't work directly on the art boards. He made many revisions before the transfer was made. "My roughs are very rough," he said. "There is a forest of lines. There doesn't seem to be a shortcut to a good piece of work." He was seldom satisfied with his first attempt at a drawing: "Certain things come easier than others. For instance, if you're drawing a sequence and you have a lot of figures crowded into the page, obviously it takes a long time. You have one figure in the panel and you can get to it quickly."[18] If he went to the final paper too soon, numerous erasures would compromise the integrity of paper's surface, and it might not take India ink smoothly and crisply. When the text was written, the captions and balloons were placed, and the layouts were set, Kurtzman transferred the layouts to the big sheets. Only then did he refine the layouts into finished pencil drawings, and do the inking. Few writers and artists in comics put this amount of thought into the work, or were willing to expend the amount of energy Kurtzman did, in his quest for an optimum result.

Over the next year, Harvey Kurtzman produced thirteen science fiction stories (totaling ninety pages) for *Weird Science* and *Weird Fantasy*. They make up a significant body of work, yet have been given short shrift by those who have studied Kurtzman's work and career. His science fiction work is some of his best, and is especially precious because in future years he worked mainly with collaborators who finished the artwork from his layouts.

Describing the way Gaines and Feldstein generated their stories, Kurtzman said, "They picked up on the classics. Gaines would read everything he could lay his hands on, then he'd make a little outline. He and Feldstein would then make it into a horror story."[19] As a fledgling writer, Kurtzman did the same. "I did a certain amount of plagiarism, particularly at the beginning, when I was trying to fall into the Gaines system. But slowly I developed my own system and I wrote [original] stories."[20] His first writer-artist job (only his sixth assignment at EC) was "Island of Death," which he loosely based on Richard Connell's famous story, "The Most Dangerous Game." It appeared in *Vault of Horror* #13 (June–July 1950). Despite the skeleton with an arrow through its skull on p. 1, it isn't really a horror story. It's an adventure story.

The inexperienced wordsmith's opening caption was rather overheated: "Little did we realize, looking down on a tiny island lying beneath us on the surface of the ocean, that this little jungle island . . . this lonely speck of dirt, would, in the following moments, bring us as close to Hades as mortal man might come!" His handling of the shorter captions and dialogue is better. Kurtzman attacked the pages aggressively with his brush, producing powerful visuals that eschewed nonessential details.

In 1950, newspapers headlined that the USSR had an atomic bomb, and everyone was fascinated with America's own A-bomb testing in the Pacific. Kurtzman often looked to current events for ideas, which allowed him to make a comment on such things while telling an entertaining story. This led to "Atom Bomb Thief!" in *Weird Fantasy* #14, a tale that doesn't really belong in a science fiction comic book, despite dealing with atomic energy. Kurtzman decided to experiment with the first page of the story, varying the number of panels and how they are arranged. Most EC stories begin with a large splash panel: sometimes full page, other times accompanied by smaller panels along the bottom. P. 1 of "Atomic Bomb

Thief!" has no large panel at all. Instead, Kurtzman arranges six panels (three rows of two panels) against a field of black, leaving space for the title in large white letters to their left. In those panels, and in the one stretched the width of the page along the bottom, he teases the reader with partial shots of a man leaving some sort of secure manufacturing facility, a tactic to incite curiosity. Kurtzman used a similar approach in the opening of " . . . The Man Who Raced Time," a seven-pager in the second issue of *Weird Science*. Instead of splitting the splash panel into sixths, he made it a three-panel triptych, this time with action that foreshadowed the story. Kurtzman didn't continue with those sorts of lively, provocative openings. They are an example of one of his key creative traits: the desire to try something new, to constantly experiment.

Kurtzman also looked to current events for the best true horror script that he produced. In 1950, the widespread acceptance of television was as exciting as the emergence of the Internet in the mid-1990s. He wouldn't own a TV for some time, but some of his friends did. One of the popular social activities was getting together to watch a program such as *Your Show of Shows* on Saturday nights. His "Television Terror!" in *Haunt of Fear* #17 capitalizes on the television craze. It's essentially a rewrite of "House of Horror," with a television crew (instead of fraternity boys) taking the viewer into a supposed haunted house on "live" TV. After the splash page, Kurtzman divides the pages into a strict six-panel grid, each one the same

Panel from "Television Terror!" in *Haunt of Fear* #17 (September–October 1950). Kurtzman story and art.

size, each with rounded corners like TV screens of the day. The television host Al Hunt, preparing to follow Professor John Poltergeist of the "London Society of Psychic Research" into the house, addresses the camera with light-hearted banter. The professor warns him, "If there are evil spirits here, you may be engulfed by a terrible depression!" After some preliminaries inside, Hunt becomes unsettled, then frightened as he mounts the stairs to the second floor looking for the professor. Upon entering the door at the top of the stairs, Hunt is confronted with something so horrific (off panel) that he loses all reason, and seems to converse with a supernatural entity. "Hee-hee! Put this around my neck? Hee-hee-hee! Why not! Hee-hee! Ya-ha! Ha . . . uk!" All that's visible to the television viewers watching the live broadcast are Hunt's dangling legs after he hangs himself. What could have caused Hunt to commit suicide? "Televison Terror!" takes the reader, like the imaginary television viewers, from reason to insanity. The "live" TV element gives the story its special frisson.[21]

"In vain, Gaines and Feldstein tried to edit me," Kurtzman said, "but we never really saw eye to eye, and I used to drive Gaines up the wall with the things I wanted to do. He took to leaving me alone."[22] Gaines even stopped asking Kurtzman to submit plots in advance. The publisher liked what Kurtzman was doing and respected him as a creator. Besides, Gaines was consumed with his working relationship with Feldstein on the horror and science fiction titles, as well as other duties. With a total of nine stories for EC under his belt, Kurtzman had a proven track record and had become a trusted associate. He became his own de facto editor.

HARVEY AND ADELE were elated that he had found steady work. Now they had money to find something better than their storage-room apartment. In the spring of 1950, Harvey's high school friend Frank Dorsey was moving to France to take a teaching position. The Kurtzmans sublet his two-bedroom apartment in Washington Heights, which had a panoramic view of the Hudson River. It was a four-floor walkup.

Now they had a place where there was room to start their family and they could entertain friends. True, it was a climb to get up there, but guests were rewarded with the view and Adele's wonderful cooking, especially her desserts. She wasn't the type of cook who invented her own recipes, or improvised by combining this dish and that. She considered cooking akin to a laboratory project, and followed the specific directions to put all the "chemicals" together properly. Her advancing pregnancy didn't deter her culinary efforts, and the results were heartily enjoyed by their guests, most often Harry and Irene Chester, and Will and Jean Elder.

While anticipation built for the birth of their child, Kurtzman worked long days at the Charles William Harvey Studio (where his work on final EC pages was done). Somehow he managed to squeeze in more *Genius* and *Pot-Shot Pete* pages for Toby Press, and a few more pages for *Varsity* magazine. He also created a new single-page filler for Timely called *Egghead Doodle*, the humorous doings of a much nicer little boy than Genius. This was all the humor work Kurtzman was able to manage that year. Almost all his time was devoted to the EC stories.

Kurtzman produced a prodigious 153 pages for Gaines in approximately nine months. That was about the number of all the *Hey Look!* pages he wrote and drew over a three-year period. The total was made up of twenty-two stories, of which he wrote seventeen. The EC crew were all laboring mightily, none more than Kurtzman. Al Feldstein was a much faster worker and was able to write almost all the firm's other stories.

As both writer and artist, Kurtzman's work fell into a rough routine: one week to write a story and lay it out, a second week to finish it. That meant he could finish two stories a month and often start on a third. Given work on a few side assignments and interruptions of various kinds, it probably amounted to four, not five days a week on the EC story. Even when he wasn't at the drawing board—in the evenings, while doing other things with Adele and his friends, on weekends when he was relaxing—he was always thinking and jotting down ideas.

Kurtzman wasn't complaining. He was in his prime, just twenty-six years old, and didn't mind working long hours. He was young enough to have energy, old enough to have mastered his craft. While he had been sidetracked from his dream of working in magazines, he was excited and a little surprised at what he was turning out. By heading in this unexpected direction, one he wouldn't have taken if he had other opportunities in the humor field, hidden creativity surfaced. Readers discovered unexpected sides to his talent almost as he was discovering them himself. EC was his institute of higher learning. This stretch into serious material and unexpected genres helped him expand his horizons and develop his writing ability. The ideas came easier than the execution, but this was a hurdle he surmounted so that his career could progress. Relieved to have what amounted to a steady paycheck, Kurtzman was happy to work this side trip for all it was worth. The nightmare of 1949 was still fresh in his mind, and there remained room to grow at EC.

Kurtzman was fully occupied and so was his studiomate John Severin, which meant Will Elder was also busy with his pen and brush. Severin was turning out stories for *Prize Comics Western* (Lazo Kid, Black Bull), as well as *Real West Romances*, *Western Love*, *Young Love* and *Young Romance*, most of which Elder inked. Severin and Elder saw the exciting material Kurtzman was doing for Gaines and heard all about EC, but they had their hands full.

On July 28, 1950, the Kurtzmans welcomed a daughter into the world at New York Doctors' Hospital on the Upper East Side. Adele suggested naming her Meredith, after the author of a book she was reading. George Meredith was the British novelist and poet of whom Oscar Wilde wrote, "Ah Meredith! Who can define him? His style is chaos illuminated by flashes of lightning." Adele recalled, "Harvey was a very good father. He changed his share of diapers."[23] Despite accepting the traditional roles of men and women typical of the day, Harvey didn't want to be a remote presence in his child's life. He had looked forward to fatherhood. He was now a married man with a daughter, a nice apartment and rewarding work. His life was beginning to fall into place.

FOR HIS SCIENCE FICTION stories, Kurtzman steered clear of tales of interplanetary exploration and alien beings, focusing instead on earthbound stories of the sort that were later the specialty of Rod Serling's *The Twilight Zone*. One of Kurtzman's scripts was based on a story in the *New Yorker* probably given to him by Gaines. "The Sounds from Another World!" in *Weird Science* #14 (September–October 1950) was patterned after Roald Dahl's short story "The Sound Machine."[24] It was about a man who claims to have invented a machine that allows him to hear sounds beyond the normal human range, including screams from plants when they are cut or trimmed. In the end, the reader discovers that he is telling his story to a gardener on the grounds of a mental hospital. Did the apparatus actually allow him to hear the screams of plants? Or did the device trigger (or perhaps uncover) lunacy? Although plagiaristic, it represents a sort of collaboration between Dahl and Kurtzman. The result is exceptional.

Sometimes his science fiction stories didn't fit well alongside the general run of stories in those EC titles, or they seemed as if he had something else in mind. Such was the case of one of Kurtzman's best scripts of 1950, "The Radioactive Child!" in *Weird Science* #15. True, the idea that a child who was exposed to radiation while still in the womb would develop a

premature and advanced scientific intellect was a science fictional concept, but the setting, characters and action of the story dominate. Its portrait of a greedy South American dictator who uses the child as the way to
realize his dreams of brutal conquest is vivid and frightening to behold.
The images of the dictator's military actions as he attacks other countries
have a power that had never been seen in comic books before. Kurtzman
responded strongly to this subject matter, and returned to it in the next
issue. "The Last War on Earth" explores the causes of warfare, as a history
professor futilely tries to come up with a way to end war for all time.

Years later, Kurtzman was asked to comment on his science fiction
work at EC. After recounting some disparate memories and observations,
he said, "I don't think there was an antiwar message in 'The Radioactive
Child' and 'The Last War on Earth.' But, sometimes I'm embarrassed to
say that I was overconcerned with morality where I should have been
admitting that my best work was entertainment. However . . . if I have any
consistent morality in my work, it has been my concern with truth, as I see
it. Truth is beautiful. What is false offends."[25]

Despite the high level of his EC stories, Kurtzman was capable of
less-than-stellar results. Of "The Giggling Killer," the last of his *Crime
SuspenStories* entries, crime writer Max Allan Collins opined, "[It's] a
beautifully told story, unfortunately not particularly worth telling. The
lame 'ironic' ending, and Kurtzman's calling his salesman Mr. Loman
(death of a salesman? Get it?) reveals his attitude: he's slumming, here,
and knows it. Nevertheless, the opening sequence in the park is textbook
graphic storytelling, and its subjective camera psychopath not only predates John Carpenter's *Halloween*, it practically predates John Carpenter."[26]

"The Giggling Killer" did show one positive change to Kurtzman's
stories produced in July and after: the use of hand-lettering in the captions
and word balloons. One of the practices Bill Gaines continued from his
father was the use of Leroy lettering, which was mechanically produced
with stencils, making all the letters uniform. Gaines felt that the Leroy
lettering worked better on Feldstein's copy-heavy stories, allowing for
more words than could be hand-lettered in the same space. The uniform
lettering gave EC comics a unique look, which is part of the nostalgia that
fans have for those classic stories, but Kurtzman hated it. Gaines came to
understand why: "Harvey was really using the comics format in the way
it should be used. When Harvey conceived a story, he conceived it pictori-
ally. That was why to him the lettering was part of the picture, and he insisted on hand lettering. To Al and me the lettering was nothing, it could
have been typography. What the hell, we were working with words."[27]

In contrast to Feldstein's text-heavy stories, Kurtzman's stories have light copy, including panels with no words at all. In July, Ben Oda was hired to letter Harvey Kurtzman's EC stories. Oda was a Japanese American who fought in World War II as a paratrooper, and was lettering in the Simon and Kirby studio. He would often take his lettering pens and visit offices around the city to work "on site" on an assignment. Kurtzman may have met him when he showed up at the Charles William Harvey Studio to letter a Severin-Elder story. Oda became a dean among letterers, working on many leading comic strips and comic books over the next forty years.

While Kurtzman's "The Giggling Killer" may not have been top form because he didn't like doing horror stories, no such attitude dragged his science fiction work down. The seven-story run in *Weird Science*—all but one written by Kurtzman—is especially strong, and finishes with two of his best.

The seven-page "Man and Superman!" in *Weird Science* #6 (March–April 1951) has a number of humorous elements, though its basic story is serious. A scientist named Niels has a brother-in-law named Charlemagne who is a competitor in the Mr. America physique contest. Niels demonstrates that he has invented a way to harness cosmic rays, and by training the ray on a piece of paper, causes it to toughen to the point that it can't be torn. Thinking it will make him stronger, Charlemagne exposes himself to the ray. Instead, it greatly increases his mass. He breaks the sidewalk when he walks, falls through the floor of an elevator, and deflects bullets with his chest. ("Look at me, Niels! Bullets bouncing off me! I'm a real comic book character!") Finally, so much energy is required to sustain his mass that he burns up, consumed in a burst of energy. Kurtzman later told interviewer S. C. Ringgenberg that this is one of his favorites among his SF stories.[28]

The other is " . . . Gregory Had a Model-T!" in the next issue. Bill Gaines called this story, Kurtzman's last for the science fiction titles, one of "EC's classics of science fiction." In some ways, it was reminiscent of the kind of story Will Eisner occasionally did in *The Spirit*. (Eisner, as always, is a creative touchstone for anyone studying comics of this era.) Kurtzman's story bears some stylistic resemblance to Eisner's short fable, "The Story of Gerhard Shnobble," which appeared in his newspaper section of September 9, 1948. Like the Eisner story, " . . . Gregory Had a Model-T!" has a narrator; in this case a Will Rogers-type named Clem. It's set in a small town in 1920, telling the story—"just the facts as I seen 'em and heard 'em"—of Gregory Gearshift, who lives in the narrator's boarding house. Gregory has no family or friends. All he has is his "true love," his car. Gregory is a fastidious fellow who keeps his Model-T immaculate and running smoothly, so it's still in perfect condition when the story shifts to 1951. When Clem remarks, "The way you're allus payin' attention to that car . . . a body'd think it wuz human!" Gregory replies, "Why Clem! Don't you know? My Model-T *is* human!"

An elderly Gregory takes his car to a gas station, and then falls ill. After the attendant phones for help, he goes back outside to find the car and its passenger gone. At the boarding house, Clem sees the Model-T pull up outside with an unconscious Gregory in the front seat. He doesn't realize Gregory's car has taken him home. Gregory's illness becomes extended, and, while being tended by a greedy sibling, he watches helplessly as his beloved Model-T is sold to a callow youth. Clem: "If'n anything killed Gregory, it was his dang-fool sister!" But the Model-T abandons its new owner, and speeds home just as Gregory's body is being taken out in a casket and put into the back of a hearse. Townspeople watch with jaws agape as the driverless Model-T joins the funeral procession. The last witness to the unlikely event watches the car heading down a road toward Suicide Bluff. The final panel shows the Model-T crumpled at the bottom of the bluff, a sad wreck that has joined its friend in death. Clem concludes, "If you ask me, old Gregory made that machine live! And when he died, the machine couldn't bear to go on livin'! But you figger it out your own way! Them's the facts as I seen 'em and heard 'em!"

This story may have a folksy ambience, but it leaves the reader with a downbeat, bitter feeling. If taken as an allegory, its ending shows the power of true love to lead to destruction. Writer Douglas Menville described it as "not really science fiction, it is a quiet and sad fantasy. Kurtzman blunted the usually sharp edge of his satirical saber in this story, but that edge still bites now and then as human greed and stupidity unthinkingly destroy the lives of two close friends. This original story . . . with its gentle humor and sensitivity, stands as a high point in Kurtzman's career."[29] " . . . Gregory Had a Model-T!" has stylistic traits that became Kurtzman trademarks: the use of textual repetition; the use of the three equal-sized panels at the start of the story, all from the same distance and height, showing the different sides of the car (instead of making one a close-up, for example); the simple, direct way the story unfolds; the lack of sentimentality and the seemingly detached narrator, not begging for emotion from the reader.

It's a creative achievement that was a fitting end to this neglected period of Kurtzman's career. The only conceivable reason why this body of work hasn't received more comment and recognition among the cognoscenti—if not more casual readers—is that he went on to create even better work. Wonderful as they are, these stories fall into shadow when compared to what came next, stories that cemented Harvey Kurtzman's reputation as one of the masters of comic art.

Out of the horror and SF tales, an idea for another kind of comic book had gradually come to Kurtzman, one that would provide him with a platform for even more profound thoughts about the human experience. To do that, he would need a raise in status at EC so that he could edit not only his own work, but that of a group of talented collaborators.

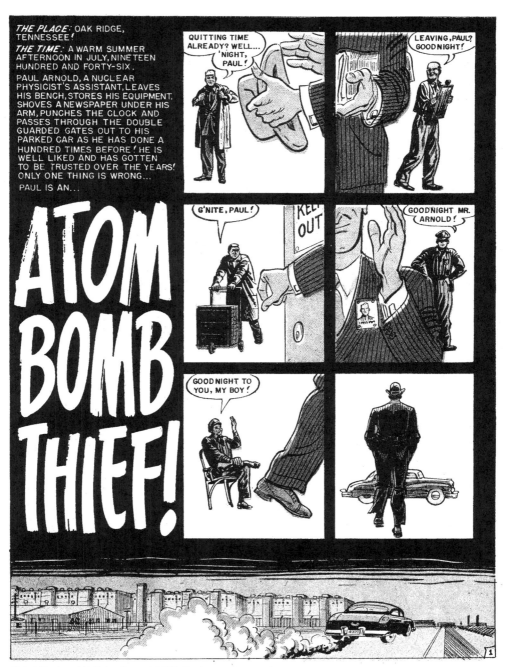

Weird Fantasy #14 (July–August 1950). Kurtzman story and art.

Top: from *Weird Science* #13 (July–August 1950). Bottom: from "The Radioactive Child!" in *Weird Science* #15 (November–December 1950).

NOW MIND YOU! YOU DON'T HAVE TO BELIEVE THIS STORY I'M GOING TO TELL YOU! I'LL JUST GIVE YOU THE FACTS AS I SEEN 'EM AND HEARD 'EM! YOU CAN TAKE IT OR LEAVE IT, ONE WAY OR T'OTHER! THESE ARE THE *FACTS!* IT WAS BACK IN... OH... 1920... THEREABOUTS! GREGORY GEARSHIFT RENTED A ROOM IN MY BOARDIN' HOUSE! NEVER DID HAVE SUCH A GOOD BOARDER.. NEAT.. CLEAN... QUIET! GREGORY DIDN'T HAVE MANY FRIENDS OR RELATIVES! HE DIDN'T HAVE A WIFE OR CHILDREN! ONLY *ONE THING* GREGORY HAD!

...GREGORY HAD A MODEL-T!

THAT CAR WAS GREGORY'S TRUE LOVE! THAT'S THE WAY IT IS WITH SOME PEOPLE!

THEY DON'T HAVE ANYONE TO LOVE, AND SO THEY CHOOSE SOME-THIN', AN ANIMAL OR A MACHINE...

AND THEY GIVE THEIR LOVE *TO IT,* 'CAUSE PEOPLE *HAVE* TO LOVE! THAT'S THE WAY IT WAS WITH GREGORY!

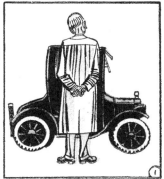

Weird Science #7 (May–June 1951). Kurtzman story and art.

PART TWO:

EDITOR

"When I initially entered the business, my goals hadn't yet been worked out. I didn't know where I was going. All I wanted was to see my work in print. That was my guiding passion. After I got a foothold in the business, then I started getting ambitions to do strange and new and wonderful things."[1]

—*Harvey Kurtzman*

10.

A WAR COMIC WITH A CONSCIENCE

THE EC HORROR COMIC BOOKS, which have gone on to legendary status in the history of the medium, were nearly nipped in the bud by wary wholesalers. Already under fire for the violent crime comics that had proliferated in 1948 and 1949, wholesalers didn't want to stir up more trouble.

Bill Gaines and Al Feldstein were excited about what they were doing in the pages of *Crypt of Terror*, *Vault of Horror* and *Haunt of Fear*, which had generated mail from readers and seemed to be catching on. However, in the spring of 1950, before he knew how they were selling, Gaines began receiving phone calls from agitated wholesalers expressing concern about the EC horror titles coming through the pipeline. (He once estimated that there were eight hundred to nine hundred wholesalers in the early 1950s.)[1] Gaines later theorized, "In those days [wholesalers] were as a rule not college [educated], they were people that had brought themselves up by their bootstraps and gotten nice businesses, but they were unsophisticated, and unsophisticated people are [usually] appalled by things more easily than more sophisticated people."[2] They objected to the word "terror" in a title, so Gaines changed *Crypt of Terror* to *Tales from the Crypt*, with the word "Tales" almost three times as big as the word "Crypt" on the cover. The calls kept coming, and it seems he concluded that horror, as much as he liked it, wasn't going to fly. Without the wholesalers, comics couldn't get on newsstands. Reluctantly, Gaines decided that *Vault of Horror* would change its format and title to *Crime SuspenStories* with its fourth issue (#15). Something also had to be done with *Haunt of Fear*—but what?[3]

Harvey Kurtzman had a dilemma of his own, though one by no means as urgent. His writing and art earned him a berth at EC, but the kind of stories he wanted to write didn't fit into the established titles. A new Kurtzman story for *Vault of Horror* wasn't really horror. "High Tide!" is about four men leaving a prison island by boat, then discovering that one of them is an escaped killer. His earthbound approach to SF was likewise different than the other stories in *Weird Science* and *Weird Fantasy*. As a writer-artist, Kurtzman wasn't on the same wavelength as Gaines and Feldstein, and constitutionally wasn't able to write the kind of horror or science fiction that fit the EC mold. Also, he didn't think horror comics of the gorier variety were appropriate in a medium that was largely the province of young readers.

Then Kurtzman heard that Gaines was looking for a new type of title to replace *Haunt of Fear*. Recognizing opportunity staring him in a face, Kurtzman pitched the idea of doing a new book called *Two-Fisted Tales*. He envisioned it as "a slam-bang high adventure book," one with "blood and thunder tales and rip-roaring adventure."[4] He had already done stories that would fit into that sort of book.

"I recall when Harvey made the suggestion that he do an adventure book," Gaines said. "Now, adventure is something that I never had any feel for. I had a feel for science fiction, of course, and for horror and suspense, but I didn't know what the hell he meant by adventure."[5] Such a comic book genre didn't exist, though a couple of books came close. One was Timely's *Men's Adventures* ("stories for men, by men, about men!") that carried a mix of boxing, aviation, jungle and crime stories. Another was Famous Funnies's wholesome *New Heroic Comics*, dedicated to sanitized tales of firemen, soldiers, aviation heroes and so on. Kurtzman later explained, "The adventure I had in mind can best be summed up by recalling the old *Captain Easy* and *Wash Tubbs* strips by Roy Crane, and I'm sure it goes back to John Ford movies."[6] It's not hard to see why Kurtzman was drawn to Crane and Ford, for his work, though in a different medium, shared their clarity and strong visual composition within the frame, and seamlessly melded touches of humor with predominantly serious stories.

Two-Fisted Tales would consist of adventure stories with a true-to-life basis. "I think that's essentially what it was that I could get excited about and Bill couldn't," Kurtzman said. "It had something to do with history and historical dates and places, and processes. *Moby-Dick*—how you flense a whale. I had this vague idea of adventure which greatly excited me, which wasn't on [Bill's] wavelength at all."[7] Kurtzman was thinking in terms of tales of pirates, soldiers of fortune, the American West, explorers and perhaps a certain number of war stories.

Of course, he hoped to edit *Two-Fisted Tales*. Kurtzman had always wanted to edit a magazine, and while this would be merely a comic book, the same impetus applied. It would be a book where he set the tone, hired the artists, and assigned them stories that catered to their talents. In later years, Kurtzman gave the impression that he was editor from the start of *Two-Fisted Tales*, but the facts show otherwise. Even as he accepted Kurtzman's suggestion, Bill Gaines wasn't initially prepared to make Kurtzman editor. He green-lit the title, and work began in the spring of 1950. When *Two-Fisted Tales* #18 (the debut issue) appeared in September, its indicia carried the credit line, "William M. Gaines, Editor. Albert B. Feldstein, Associate Editor," just like Gaines's other comics. Moreover, all of the artists who drew the stories (Craig, Wood, Feldstein) also wrote them, probably because of a short deadline.

Two-Fisted Tales #18 (November–December 1950) featured Harvey Kurtzman's first cover for an EC comic book, a scene from the inside story by Johnny Craig. It broke from the cover design used on the other EC titles, which set the logo in a separate box. Kurtzman wanted the cover image to "breathe," so he extended the artwork behind the title logo to the top of the page. The horror and SF covers were "busy," with little blank space. Kurtzman's emphatically delineated cover image has substantial areas with nothing in them but color. Another difference could be seen in the coloring choices. EC's coloring wasn't yet done in-house, but it's clear that Kurtzman provided a guide that was followed by the engraver's colorist. Yellow and orange would almost always be prominent colors on Kurtzman's EC covers. The banner down the left side reading "He-Man Adventure" was also new. Kurtzman instinctively knew how to create covers with visual impact.

When the reader opened the book, he found a cannon barrel staring him in the face. This was "Conquest" by Kurtzman, a tale of predatory Spanish conquistadors arriving on the coast

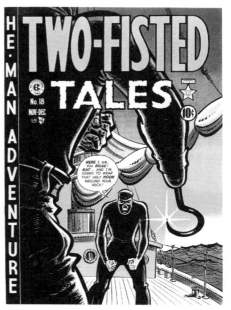

Two-Fisted Tales #18 (November–December 1950).

of Mexico in search of gold. The arrogant Capt. Juan Alvorado leads a crew—little more than pirates—in an attempt to take over the city of the indigenous people so that it could be looted. In the violent, hard-hitting ending, the European invaders discover they have underestimated the natives. "Conquest" is Kurtzman in fine form: bold, history-based and exciting.

"Revolution!" by Wood and "Mutiny" by Craig are serviceable. The Gaines-Feldstein entry was not. Of "Hong Kong Intrigue," Gaines admitted, "The first and only adventure story that Al and I ever wrote . . . was the most dreadful, horrible, stupid story. It was my attempt to plot what I thought Harvey meant by adventure. And I hated it! From then on Harvey handled his books by himself simply because I didn't have the faintest idea what the hell he was getting at."[8]

While the indicia in the next issue reads "William M. Gaines, Editor. Harvey Kurtzman and Albert B. Feldstein, Associate Editors," the contents make it clear that Kurtzman was taking over. There were also indications that the original concept of the book was changing.

"WHEN THE KOREAN WAR broke out, I naturally turned to the war for material," Kurtzman recalled.[9] As the new decade began, tensions escalated between Communist North Korea and Democratic South Korea. When North Korean forces crossed the Thirty-Eighth parallel into South Korea on June 25, 1950, President Harry Truman felt he had no choice but to "stand up to the Communists" by sending US troops to Korea. The war would have a major impact on the home front, including the American comics industry. Shortly after work on *Two-Fisted Tales* began (a matter of weeks), troops were being called up, including Kurtzman's eighteen-year-old brother Daniel Perkes, who entered the Air Force. The United States was once again at war.

When converting *Two-Fisted Tales* into a full-fledged war comic, it made sense for Kurtzman to invite the Severin-Elder team to EC. He asked John Severin due to his interest and expertise in drawing the weapons and accoutrements of warfare, and Will Elder to ink Severin's pencils. Bringing them to EC proved to be one of the wisest and most far-reaching decisions Kurtzman made as editor. "When John and Willy used to draw these things together, I just loved the results that we'd get," Kurtzman said. "John was just about the best there was in drawing World War II. [Severin] never really appreciated Willy because Willy would really hurt John's authenticity. John would draw four buttons and Willy would turn them into three and a half and that would *kill* John. And yet Willy would ink his stuff with great clarity. And Willy . . . had been through that scene, [had] been right in the thick of the Ardennes offensive, I think. He knew all about World War II. He got the flavor and he got the look."[10]

Two-Fisted Tales #19 opened with "War Story!," a seven-pager co-written by Severin and Kurtzman. Though it opens and closes in Korea as a sergeant tells a green recruit a story about his outfit during World War II, most of the action is set on a jungle island in the Pacific. It recounts a tale of twins in his unit, one a good guy and one a killer, and how the killer's bloodlust leads him to accidentally kill his brother. The sergeant concludes his story, "You see . . . there's a moral! War's a tough deal! We kill men not because we wanna, but because we gotta! It's a dirty job we have to do . . . but doesn't mean we have to enjoy doing it!" This isn't a message one would expect to find in a comic book in 1950.

"War Story!" was originally slotted to be the last of the four in the book, but was moved to the front when the change in format was either contemplated or decided. We know, because its last caption invites readers to send letters on "how you enjoyed this book." Such requests for letters, with the publisher's address, generally appeared on the last story of an issue. Kurtzman's cover depicted a scene from this story. (He did finished art on all the covers for the next two years.)

The title of virtually every Kurtzman script from this point forward was brief—often one or two words—and ended with an exclamation point. The exclamation points seem to have originated simply because each story began with a brief text introduction ending with the story title. Sentences in comic books were routinely punctuated by exclamation points for added clarity and impact.

The other three stories in *Two-Fisted Tales* #19 remained in the adventure formula. Jack London's "Lost Face" inspired Kurtzman's excellent "Jivaro Death!" (The shrunken head plot also appears in Bennett Cerf's *Try and Stop Me*.) Kurtzman wrote and laid out Wallace Wood's "Brutal Capt. Bill!" Only Johnny Craig's self-written and drawn "Flight from Danger!," which still uses the hated Leroy lettering, had no Kurtzman involvement. Kurtzman said,

> When I thought of doing a war book, the business of what to say about war was very important to me and was uppermost in my mind, because I did then feel very strongly about not wanting to say anything glamorous about war. Everything that went before *Two-Fisted Tales* had glamorized war.[11]

His mind went back to the types of war comics that crowded the newsstands during World War II, which portrayed the enemy as less than human.

> I was absolutely appalled by the lies in the war books that publishers were putting out. What they did when they produced a war book is they focused on what they thought the reader would like to read, which was, "Americans are good guys and anybody against us is the bad guys. We're human. They're not. And God is always on our side." This trash had nothing to do with the reality of life.[12]

Kurtzman aspired to something better. "I was preoccupied with giving the reader something insightful. After [coming to] EC, I started asking myself, 'What am I trying to do? What does my work mean?' I concluded that what I was trying to tell my reader was what I perceived as being true. I didn't want to be a preacher, but I did want to tell the truth about things."[13] Later, he put it succinctly: "I wanted to do a war comic with a conscience."[14]   For Kurtzman, everything started with reality. He wanted to portray the costs exacted by war so as not to give young people false notions. He told interviewer Jeffrey K. Wasserman, "To make war into something glamorous and wonderful is a terrible immorality."[15] This was the beginning of his self-identification as a "truth teller," a descriptor he would use for the rest of his life. He felt this played to his strengths as a writer: "I'm fast and observant and I can outdo the average guy in [that] particular field."[16]

Kurtzman wasn't a pacifist. If war was inevitable, if a nation was being attacked or its security was being directly threatened, then he acknowledged the need to fight. "There are certain times you don't particularly want to be a pacifist, and you don't want to take a negative attitude. Although war is horrible, I feel that there are times when we have to fight. You know, if you're in a fistfight, when you're getting pounded on the head, or something like that, it's no time to feel negative. When you're really at grips with it and you have to win, you'd better not be antiwar because you'll get killed! I mean, you'll cancel yourself out."[17] As a man of Jewish heritage, if not religious conviction, Kurtzman certainly felt the battle against the Axis powers in World War II was justified. On the question of whether he was a crusader, Kurtzman expressed contradictory thoughts. He told an audience in 1972, "I don't regard myself as a man who pushes specific opinions or strong points of view."[18] Yet in an interview four years later, he said, "I used to regard myself as an advocate of sorts. I had opinions and I tried to assert them to a certain extent."[19] Typical among those of his generation, Kurtzman accepted the necessity of the Korean War.

WITH *TWO-FISTED TALES* #20, Kurtzman was fully in charge at last. It was "announced" in the issue's indicia, which now read, "William M. Gaines, Editor. Harvey Kurtzman, Associate Editor." This made him a peer of Al Feldstein, who received the same credit, even though he was the true editor of the other EC books. (Gaines was a Managing Editor at most, and less so of *Two-Fisted Tales* than the other titles.) Kurtzman's move into an official editorial position was an important validation and a major turning point in his career. The editorial prerogatives brought him much of the creative control he craved. Now he increased his writing output and, on top of that, began collecting a fee as a freelance editor (not an employee of EC) for each issue. It also had a downside: it began a process that led to him working less and less on finished art.

Kurtzman had a vision of the comic book he wanted to produce and needed the right artists to make it so. His ability to select and gather talent turned out to be one of his strongest suits as editor. He had already recruited John Severin and Bill Elder and he would keep Wallace Wood, who had been there from #18. Though Kurtzman supposedly wasn't all that friendly when they first met—"Why are you letting a kid hang around here?"—he loved Wood's artwork. Wood recalled, "It seemed that overnight I was working for EC and there was Harvey and he was my editor."[20] Since Kurtzman kept one foot in the science fiction books until he knew if this new venture was a success, he would illustrate only one story per issue of *Two-Fisted Tales* himself, plus the cover. That meant he needed another regular artist. His choice for the slot was inspired.

Jack Davis was born in Atlanta, Georgia, and was just two months younger than Kurtzman. Like Kurtzman, he had a cartoon published in *Tip Top Comics* as a boy, drew for his high school paper, and (it turned out) was particularly gifted at humorous cartooning.[21] In 1949, he decided to move to New York and worked briefly as an inker on Leslie Charteris's *The Saint* comic strip. Then he collected rejections from various publishers before trying EC. In a *Wall Street Journal* profile years later, Davis recalled, "I was about ready to give up, go home to Georgia and be either a forest ranger or a farmer. But I went down to Canal Street and Lafayette, up in an old rickety elevator and through a glass door to Entertaining Comics where Al Feldstein and Bill Gaines were putting out horror [comic] books. They looked at my work and it was horrible and they gave me a job right away!"[22] Davis had only done a few stories for EC when Kurtzman pulled him into his orbit, later saying, "His talents are as a craftsman, a stylist and a humorist all combined. He's one of those people who has a great facility with his tools and he creates swift and pleasant effects—as opposed to a guy like Graham Ingels, whose effects are effective but they're not pleasant necessarily. They're gruesome."[23]

"[Artists] didn't go to Harvey," Gaines said. "Harvey would go to them. Harvey would only use the artists he wanted to use, which was not a lot of the artists. For example, he'd use Wood and he'd use Davis, but he wouldn't use [Joe] Orlando and he wouldn't use [Jack] Kamen."[24]

Like Feldstein on the other books, Kurtzman wrote all the stories in *Two-Fisted Tales*. Word usage, grammar and spelling weren't his strengths, but he had gained confidence in his ability to concoct effective six-, seven- and eight-page stories. Because he wanted historical accuracy, he began studying the history of combat through the ages. Just as his latent writing ability was awakened at EC, his interest in history was similarly stimulated. "School history was just pale, dumb and unbelievable," he said. "When I did the . . . war books and I had to find out about things, suddenly history became a fascinating subject. I could stay in the library forever and just read and read."[25]

Kurtzman's approach to editing *Two-Fisted Tales* was very different than Feldstein's on the horror and SF books. He required that artists take an unprecedented amount of direction from him. They were given the art boards with the lettering and panel borders already in place. A sheet of tracing paper with Kurtzman's rough layouts in pencil was taped on top of each page. Somewhat akin to a film director, Kurtzman determined where a long shot was needed, where the close-ups would be, and how the characters would move within the frames. Alfred Hitchcock planned key sequences in his films in a similar way: the visions in his head were so specific that he was able to create storyboards to plan the action, camera angles and cuts. Hitchcock's actors, who he once joked "should be treated like cattle," were free to create their own performances, as long as they adhered to the script and moved within the frame as prescribed by the director. Kurtzman never referred to his artists as cattle, but was adamant that they follow his layouts. They weren't expected to draw like him, just follow the basic visuals created as he wrote the stories. On his horror and SF stories, Kurtzman himself had taken those layouts (some have called them "breakdowns") to final form. On the war stories, others tightened the layouts and finished the artwork.

This particular division of labor initially took the artists by surprise. Comic book artists didn't expect to be required to follow another artist's layouts. That might be done for neophytes (in a comic shop or bullpen) who were beginning to learn how to tell stories in comics form, but was considered part of the job for those who knew the ropes. Severin, Wood and Davis had already shown that they could tell an effective story in visual terms, yet they acceded to Kurtzman's methods. They were willing because they were young, they needed the work and because they respected his talent. Also, Kurtzman had a very real personal charisma, a Pied Piper quality that made it seem like they were going on an exciting adventure together.

The purpose of Kurtzman's methods was explained in a letter he wrote to an artist he was inviting to participate in one of his EC books:

> Before you take a look at the job, allow me to explain the obnoxious system I foist upon the artists. First, I write all the . . . stories! I also rough each panel out. I do all this, full well knowing that that I am squelching the artist's opportunity to work free and uninhibited. I do this, knowing that an artist's *best* work is done when he is left *completely* alone, unbothered by rules and regulations. Let me explain why I work in such a conservative fashion. All the elements in [this book] are details of a large compact unit. While each detail—writing, lettering, drawing—is important in itself, the whole thing should fit together smoothly as a uniform *unit*. In order to get this uniformity and tightness, the stories are visualized in toto . . . text and art together, and so I write the stories right on the Strathmore board with accompanying layouts.[26]

Kurtzman envisioned a book with the kind of cohesion in its themes and its storytelling that could only be achieved if it essentially came from one mind. His enormous belief in his vision perhaps reflected an oversized ego, but it was in service of substance. He was unapologetic about the restrictions because he was convinced they would produce a better overall result.

Kurtzman was also demanding in terms of the accuracy of the uniforms and weapons of war, and provided the necessary reference material. His research had another purpose. Accessing original source material gave him ideas and helped him avoid hackneyed story tropes and clichés. "I would do research and tell the reader about something he had never been aware of particularly," he explained. "It's very time-consuming working that way, but it's the only way that I could get the pleasure of feeling that I was being original and creative."[27]

As editor, Kurtzman stopped trying to please others and began expecting others to please him. In a sense, he had crossed the line from worker to management. He knew he was asking a lot. "I think that one of the things that you do as an editor is, if you really know what you want, you can give your people a terrible time. Because in knowing what you want—and in comics I always knew exactly what I wanted—it can be pretty tough on people. Because knowing what you want necessarily makes you demanding, I think, and I'm sure I was demanding and always asked the guys to give their very best effort. I never regretted it then, and to this day I think it was good for everybody concerned. I think the guys did good work."[28]

The lineup in *Two-Fisted Tales* #20 (cover dated March–April 1951) included two adventure stories: a Western called "Army Revolver!" drawn by Jack Davis, and "Pirate Gold!" drawn by Kurtzman. According to Davis, Kurtzman wrote "Army Revolver!" because "I think he knew that I liked to do cowboys."[29] It adopted the story device from the film *Winchester '73* of a gun passing from hand to hand.

Those stories are well done, but mixing genres was a remnant of the past. The eight-page war story "Massacred!" by Severin-Elder leads off, a tale of North Korean Colonel Yun who gives orders that all prisoners are to be shot. "This is the way I want all prisoners treated in my command!" In the end, when he and his men are masquerading in uniforms of the United Nations forces, they are caught by North Korean troops and given the treatment that he himself had ordered.

The second war story is "Devils in Baggy Pants!," set in World War II, about paratroopers of the Eighty-Second Airborne being dropped in France on the eve of D-Day. Kurtzman personalized the situation, focusing on a squad of men who attempt to dynamite a bridge to block Nazi reinforcements. The theme is set on p. 1, when the lone survivor is found, muttering, "One man can be a mild little gink while another can be a loud-mouthed tough guy! But which is really the coward! You can't tell!" As the story is told in flashback, we learn that the so-called "tough guy" who has bullied a "mild little gink" turned coward when the chips were down. Being true-to-life, to Kurtzman, meant showing the types of real human dramas that happen in the midst of battle when ordinary men face life-and-death situations.

OTHERS CONTRIBUTED IMPORTANT aspects of the finished stories. Ben Oda, who lettered Kurtzman's SF stories, continued on the war title, and Marie Severin was brought on board as in-house colorist. (It seems certain she began on #19 and colored all of #20. There is no exact record.) Up till then, Chemical Color Engraving in Bridgeport, Connecticut, colored all EC comics. The firm's work in that area was, at best, mediocre. Kurtzman knew the importance of coloring and wanted it under his editorial control. When he spoke to Gaines about it, he found out Gaines and Feldstein were also dissatisfied by the color work by Chemical Color. Apparently, Kurtzman asked John Severin if he knew a good colorist. Severin suggested his younger sister, although he couldn't vouch for her coloring aptitude because he was color-blind.

The Severin household had been an artistic one, and Marie had always been fascinated by color. "As a kid in church, I'd just sit and watch the colors [of the stained glass windows] change," she recalled.[30] She read her brother's Western comics, then became a fan of Superman and Batman. When she graduated from high school, Marie attended the Cartoonists and Illustrators School briefly, but didn't really know what she wanted to do. She accepted the opportunity to color for EC and discovered she liked the work. "It wasn't really nepotism because they would have fired me at the drop of a hat if I wasn't any good. [After] the first story I did, my brother came home and said, 'Harvey liked your stuff. You're the first person who didn't color the moon yellow.' It was little things like that. I was a little more thoughtful. The subject matter was fun to work with . . . and I learned a lot."[31] Her job was to provide a guide for the employees at Chemical Color to follow, by coloring the comic book-size brown-and-white sheets (provided by the printer) called Silverprints. Kurtzman did his own guides for the covers, creating color roughs that Severin reinterpreted on Silverprints. He allowed her to color the inside stories as she saw fit. Once it was clear that she could handle the job, Marie was given the entire EC line to color. (This meant that she was there to color the last of Kurtzman's SF stories, including "Man and Superman!" and " . . . Gregory had a Model-T!")

THE EC SUITE ON the seventh floor at 225 Lafayette had white walls with elegant heavy mahogany wood panels that divided up the workspace. Those panels' upper halves were blue, translucent, frosted glass panes. Only Bill Gaines had an entirely enclosed office. His room was also the only one with a carpeted floor. All the rest of the place had linoleum flooring. As an editor, Harvey Kurtzman rated an office. When Marie came on board and began coloring all EC comics, she shared it with him. He was out a fair amount of the time, since he continued to do his writing and artwork in his midtown studio where he could concentrate better. His EC office began filling up with items gathered in his research: books, magazines, military publications (some of them classified), clippings and other reference material. His list of contacts grew to encompass various experts, historians and soldiers who had served in World War II and Korea.

Marie Severin described the atmosphere in the EC office as professional but relaxed. "They were very polite, shirt-and-tie guys. At that time in the '50s, women went to work with heels on, which is why most of us ended up with bad feet. It was a regular business office. You could have been downtown or uptown. It was just an office."[32] Nevertheless there was a friendly, almost familial, feeling among those who worked there and the freelancers when they dropped by. Most of them saw each other after work. Kurtzman recalled, "We not only enjoyed working together—I don't mean to imply that we were without problems—but we enjoyed each other's talent and we enjoyed each other's presence. The guys that I worked with—I'm talking mainly about Will Elder, Jack Davis, John Severin and Wally Wood—we worked together and we played together. We were close professionally and socially. We were all about the same age, same circumstances. We'd all gotten out of the army or navy, we all got married during the same period. We would picnic together, have outings together, have parties together and like that."[33]

Each had his own distinct personality. John Severin was the house conservative in the midst of a group of mostly liberals. Jack Davis has been described as "a Southern Jimmy Stewart" and was liked by all. Will Elder had calmed down from his days as a class clown but his zany sense of humor was still in evidence. Kurtzman liked Gaines. "Gaines was unusual," he later affirmed. "He was a publisher who was accessible. It was a unique situation. We were friends. We'd pal around. He'd argue. He was . . . open to influence. And that's what made the war books . . . possible."[34]

Of Wallace Wood, Kurtzman said, "He had this enormous talent and his curse was that he was introverted. Everything was bottled up. The dominating thing in Wally's life was this bottled up quality which eventually did great harm to him and destroyed much of him."[35] Will Elder saw another side of Wood: "There was a very quiet warmth about Wally that I liked. Wally was very unpretentious. He actually projected himself through his work. I felt that Wally could only exemplify himself through his art. There was a need of showing his sensitivity through his work since I don't think Wally had the personality to show it any other way. He [was] a tremendous talent . . . a very gifted guy."[36]

Of Kurtzman, Elder said, "Harvey has always seen the delightful side of people. He would extract the better part of people . . . without them being aware of it."[37] One of the ways Kurtzman elicited the best from his artists was to act out the stories for them. Marie witnessed it and was enchanted. "When he would be telling you a cartoon, or tell you what he's going to do in a story, he would suddenly turn from a serious gnomelike figure into this elf, and he'd be dancing around, and funny. Harvey would act out these things and he looked like his drawings. And you were just charmed by the whole thing, you couldn't help but like him, even if he was so autocratic with how he wanted the work done. You didn't mind because he was just as nutty as you were!"[38]

The catalyst for the launch of *Two-Fisted Tales* had been the wholesalers' resistance to EC's horror books. Then things changed. Sales for the titles were greater than expected, so profits overrode their concerns. Bill Gaines was able to keep all three of his horror titles going after all. As Frank Jacobs later put it in his biography of Gaines, "Even the wholesalers, who at first took a dim view of such sensational fare, showed grudging interest as they saw the EC sales figures zoom."[39] The three horror titles had print runs of about 450,000 copies of each issue, with a high sales percentage, from 80 to 85 percent. Others noticed, such as Martin Goodman, who quickly began adding horror titles to his roster, a sure sign EC had found a hot new genre. Goodman's horror books (there were a slew of them) were profitable though they sold considerably less than EC, around 60 to 65 percent of print runs in the 250,000 to 300,000 range.[40] Harvey Comics' first horror title, *Witches Tales,* appeared in the fall of 1950 (nine months after the debut of *Vault of Horror*), and was joined by three similar books that bore marked resemblances to those of EC.

Two-Fisted Tales #18 had a print order of 350,000 copies and sold in the 70 percent range (or perhaps a little higher). That was a solid (if not great) sale for a comic book at the time. Its sales held at that level during the Korean War. By the beginning of 1951, Kurtzman knew he had a viable book on his hands.[41] With *Two-Fisted Tales* #21 (May–June 1951), it completed its metamorphosis into an all-war comic.

The issue opened with "Ambush!," drawn by Jack Davis, the story of eight American soldiers traveling in jeeps through hills swarming with North Korean guerillas. Pinned down by rifle fire, they are picked off one by one as they attempt to extricate themselves from the situation. "Ambush!" has a number of ideas that would appear in subsequent stories: the suddenness of death, the way soldiers deal with the deaths of their buddies, how men react under great stress. In swift strokes, the personalities of most of the men are sketched, making them more than mere cardboard characters. Kurtzman and Davis create a wordless sequence when a live grenade lands near the men. A soldier manages to throw it away in time but is riddled with bullets in the act. The dialogue approximates realistic patterns, where men talk across each other and the language is colloquial. John Benson wrote:

> "Ambush!" was the first of a series of powerful gutsy stories about the Korean conflict written by Kurtzman and illustrated by Davis. Emphasizing small incidents involving just a few soldiers, skirmishes too small to be reported in the papers or history books, these stories were told with great skill and economy. These [stories] don't show Kurtzman's passion for historical detail. The "moral" is often only a tagline; for the most part any comment Kurtzman might be making is only implicitly stated. But these are the stories that originally drew readers to Kurtzman's war comics, and many still consider them the finest part of *Two-Fisted Tales.*"[42]

They must have been especially sobering reading for young soldiers on their way to the war zone.

In Kurtzman's self-written and drawn "Search!" in that same issue, he introduces one of the persistent devices he used in his stories: the new recruit being taught by an experienced soldier, allowing readers to discover the realities of war through the eyes of a neophyte. In the midst of combat, a grizzled Italian American soldier in Italy watches out for the newbie while looking for his brother who never came to America. In the end, they abandon a foxhole just before a mortar shell hits it. The explosion throws a half-buried corpse to the surface, the body of the sought-after brother. (Though they are mostly associated with EC's horror and SF stories, Kurtzman sometimes used the O. Henry-style ending in his war comics, too.)

The issue also includes "Pigs of the Roman Empire," a historical story illustrated by Severin-Elder, about a wine-guzzling Roman commander who recklessly leads his troops into battle. After a devastating defeat, he is stranded in a desert and dies of thirst, becoming food for vultures. It's an example of the arrogance and decadence of the Roman Empire, which brought about its demise. The other story is "The Murmansk Run!," a cautionary sea story about an American fuel tanker attempting to cross the north Atlantic Ocean in 1940. One careless man makes a mistake that gives away its location to a German U-boat, with disastrous results. Kurtzman wrote it for Wood, who had been in the Merchant Marine and had heard stories about the Murmansk Run.

Because *Two-Fisted Tales* was selling well, Gaines and Kurtzman decided to add a second war title. Kurtzman named it *Frontline Combat*.
The news was announced to the readers in the "Cosmic Correspondence"
letter column in *Weird Science* #8, which hit the stands in May.

> [We have] a very painful announcement . . . painful for you SF fans, that
> is! With the birth of the newest addition to the EC family . . . *Frontline
> Combat* . . . Harvey Kurtzman will no longer grace the pages of *Weird
> Science* and *Weird Fantasy* with his wonderful work. All of his time will
> now be taken up with editing, writing and drawing for EC's war mags,
> *Two-Fisted Tales* and *Frontline Combat!* And he's doing an incredibly
> fine job, too!

Gaines had a hands-off policy when it came to Kurtzman's war books.
"I couldn't help him, but I recognized that what he was doing was fantastically good," Gaines said. "Harvey . . . had a great love for what he was
doing, and this love showed through."[43] Kurtzman and his talented team
were just getting started.

IN ORDER TO MAINTAIN the high level of authenticity in two war books,
Kurtzman hired an editorial assistant named Jerry De Fuccio. De Fuccio
was a twenty-six-year-old native New Yorker who was a rabid comics
fan, and an aspiring cartoonist and writer. He wrote, "My first encounter
with Harvey was not at EC on Lafayette Street, but at the Charles William
Harvey Studios . . . . As I recall, Billy [Elder] and Harvey took me to their
everyday restaurant in that area, the Raven, and Harvey touted me on the
good dishes and exhorted me to have whatever I wanted."[44] De Fuccio was
immediately enamored with Kurtzman.

> My initial feelings about Harvey, which have been immutable, were that
> he was attentive, solicitous, precise and sedately amicable. One of his
> most endearing traits became readily apparent. He always looked back
> over his shoulder when leaving a store or restaurant, to ascertain whether
> he left anything after him. It seemed Harvey had a complete filing system
> under each arm: all shapes and conditions of folios, packages and enve-
> lopes, slipping and sliding as he went along. Despite his constantly en-
> cumbered state, Harv was the greatest door-holder and turnstile threader
> I ever met.[45]

One of De Fuccio's first contributions was writing the text story "Hero" in *Two-Fisted Tales* #21. Due to postal regulations, comic books were required to carry two pages of text to qualify for Second Class mailing privileges. This was a thankless chore, especially because it was known that few people bothered to read them. His main function, however, was to assist Kurtzman with the research. De Fuccio found that he enjoyed spending hours in the American History room of the Forty-Second Street branch of the New York Public Library, telling Bill Kieffer in *Comics Interview*, "Harvey and I . . . would always go to the American History room which was headed by one Mr. Vigilante. I always loved his name. Harvey and I would get involved with one phase of the research and we'd get so involved that Harvey would remind me that we weren't there to have fun, we were there to do research. Harvey was a very good tutor, I guess you could say."[46]

Kurtzman was a stickler for accuracy. He told his artists never to draw a weapon based on someone else's drawing. At one point, he got his hands on a cast iron replica of a German Mauser, a gun being used by the Koreans. He told De Fuccio to deliver it to Wallace Wood so he could use it for reference. "I put it in a paper bag and ran down to the train station right at rush hour," De Fuccio recalled. "As I was standing on the train, holding the strap, the damn thing fell out of the bag and onto the floor. Everybody on the train turned into statues. I just scooped it up and put it back into the paper bag."[47] De Fuccio enjoyed the job a great deal, though it wasn't always fun. He balked when being sent on a mission to an air force base or naval depot when it was pouring down rain. On one such occasion, Jerry tried to beg off. Kurtzman pointed to the door, and said (in mock command), "Go, Jerome!"

De Fuccio turned to Gaines, hoping for a reprieve. Gaines responded, "Why, with a good-sized man's umbrella, you can fend off a monsoon, Jerry."[48]

With the addition of De Fuccio, Kurtzman had all the members of his team in place. Now he was ready to embark on a journey that would prove exciting for both the creators and the readers. His goal was nothing less than producing comic books of the highest possible quality, books that weren't only among the best written and drawn in the business, but actually elevated the medium itself.

Clockwise: PR photo of Elder (sitting) and John Severin (standing); Marie Severin photo courtesy of Marie Severin; R–L: Kurtzman and Bill Gaines, courtesy of Grant Geissman; PR photo of Kurtzman.

Harvey Kurtzman cover for *Two-Fisted Tales* #21.

Top: "War Story" splash panel from *Two-Fisted Tales* #19. Art by John Severin and Will Elder.
Bottom: Harvey Kurtzman cover for *Two-Fisted Tales* #20.

11.

A NEW KIND OF COMIC BOOK

WHEN AN INTERVIEWER asked Harvey Kurtzman whether he conceived his war stories as a series of images or as a narrative that had to be put into pictures, Kurtzman responded, "I always started with a statement. The technique follows. There are some writers who work as very highly paid professionals and they are very competent. Their technique is gorgeous. They are total professionals. They don't have a fucking idea in their head. But they say their non-ideas beautifully. The woods are full of that, artists with beautiful techniques that have evolved from other people's work. True technique comes from when you have something to say and you decide how to say it best."[1]

In *Two-Fisted Tales* #22 (July–August 1951), the credits were finally straightened out, showing "William M. Gaines, Managing Editor" and "Harvey Kurtzman, Editor." Each of the stories has an idea at the center. "Enemy Contact!" is a Korean War story drawn by Jack Davis. A medic risks his life to get to a patrol pinned down by rifle fire in order to perform an emergency appendectomy. Although the operation is a success, the patient is killed by mortar fire. Kurtzman's final caption, which runs in segments over the last three panels, reads, " . . . And so, men marched off to kill men! And isn't it strange! While one instinct makes man move heaven and earth to save a life . . . Makes man give his all to his fellow man . . . Another, less noble instinct makes man a cold, brutal, dispassionate monster . . . Lets him tear other men to bits without mercy! This paradox, this puzzle marches on forever."

In "Dying City!," pencilled by Alex Toth and inked by Kurtzman, a young Korean man leaves home to become a soldier, telling his grandfa-

ther, "You are old! Times are changing! Today, the youth of Korea is join-
ing the march of Russia and China to stamp out the enemies of the people!
If blood must be shed, so be it! What are a thousand lives now compared
to the millions of years of future happiness!" When the soldier returned
to his village, after all his family except his grandfather was killed by
combat around them, the grandfather asked, "What does the future mean
when everything you love is dead? What is left? What good is your revolution? What good?"

In "Massacre at Agincourt!," drawn by Wallace Wood, Henry V leads
his troops back to Calais, but finds the French army in the way. The French
commander decides to attack, despite a warning that "the English have . . .
new weapons that will revolutionize warfare!" The English, armed with
the longbow designed to cover distance with more power than a crossbow,
decimate the French Army. The story ends with the death of the French
commander "who believed that the art of war had gone as far as it could
go! But he was wrong!"

The last story in the issue is "Chicken!," with art by John Severin and
Will Elder. On Okinawa in 1945, pompous army officer Captain Harold
Black makes a bad decision and effectively orders men to their death. His
lieutenant goes back to get another squad and finds out that the Marines
plan to blast the area with big guns. When the lieutenant returns to warn
the captain, Black won't listen, and orders the lieutenant to certain death
like his comrades. The lieutenant refuses, telling him, "There's one thing
you don't know." After Black shoots him ("I was within my rights! He
didn't follow orders!"), the captain is killed by the American artillery
attack. The final caption reads, "Chicken Captain Harold Black was so
completely blasted to bits, he will be listed as 'missing in action.' What
is it he didn't know? Very simple! He knew his infantry regulations front
and back . . . He knew the articles of war inside out . . . But what he didn't
know was that soldiers are human beings like you and me! . . . That's all!"
These thought-provoking stories were all the more remarkable when one
considers they appeared in a single issue, and it was just Kurtzman's third
in charge of *Two-Fisted Tales*. They stand in stark contrast to stories of
heroic war action being published by EC's competitors.

Kurtzman avoided the plagiarism of some of his non-war EC stories, yet sometimes a movie or magazine article inspired the kernel of an
idea. *All Quiet on the Western Front* was never far from his mind. When
Kurtzman was making the decision to change the book's format, Universal
rereleased *All Quiet on the Western Front* (1930), the acclaimed film adaptation of Erich Maria Remarque's novel. The movie's realistic, harrowing

portrayal of savage warfare in World War I created a sensation upon its initial release, winning the Academy Award for Best Picture in 1930 as well as Best Director for Lewis Milestone. While the version released in 1950 had about forty minutes cut from its original 132-minute running time, its impact (and antiwar message) remained. The *New York Herald Tribune* noted the "curious timing in its re-release at this moment," and went on to say, "There is nothing equivocal about the message of *All Quiet on the Western Front*: it argues the horror and futility of war both in words and in action. It points up the tremendous gulf between cause and effect, between considerations of international policy and the individual suffering that is their result."[2] After the novel was published in 1929, the author explained, "my work . . . was not political, neither pacifist nor militarist, in intention, but human simply. It presents the war as seen within the small compass of the front-line soldier, pieced together out of many separate situations, out of minutes and hours, out of struggle, fear, dirt, bravery, dire necessity, death and comradeship."[3] Kurtzman acknowledged that Remarque's message and movie made a deep impression on him. He was inspired by a couple of its sequences when he wrote "Enemy Assault!" for *Frontline Combat* #1 (July–August 1951), one of his most thematically important, emblematic tales of the Korean War.

Kurtzman tells his story from the point of view of an American soldier sitting in a trench, awaiting an enemy attack. The only text on the first two pages is in first person captions: "My heart was pounding like a trip hammer! They were visible now! Tiny figures moving slowly toward our position! Chinese Communists! Hundreds of them! The inside of my mouth was bone dry! Soon they'd be within rifle range!" Page two shows the Chinese coming closer and the American firing at them like targets in a shooting gallery. This scene echoes shots of the enemy soldiers in Milestone's film, running en masse toward the protagonist's trench and being picked off by gunfire. In the comic book, some break through and get close enough to pose a more immediate threat.

In the ensuing battle, the American loses consciousness. When he awakes, he finds a wounded Communist soldier in his trench. This sequence is unmistakably suggested by *All Quiet on the Western Front*, though in the film the American was responsible for wounding the enemy soldier, who never spoke. In Kurtzman's story, each claims the other as his prisoner, and trains a gun on the other. On p. 5, while they wait to see which one's troops arrive first, they talk. The Chinese man can speak English, having learned it while working as a houseboy for an American in Hong Kong. He tells how he accompanied his boss to New York, and

MY HEART WAS POUNDING LIKE A TRIP HAMMER! THEY WERE VISIBLE NOW! TINY FIGURES MOVING SLOWLY TOWARD OUR POSITION! CHINESE COMMUNISTS! HUNDREDS OF THEM! WE WERE SOUTHEAST OF SEOUL, IN THE 'OLD WORLD WAR TYPE' TRENCHES! I PRESSED A CLIP OF AMMUNITION INTO MY M1, SLAMMED HOME THE BREECH, AND WAITED FOR THE...

ENEMY ASSAULT!

THE SKY WAS OVERCAST, AND WE DIDN'T HAVE ANY AIR SUPPORT! HIGH OVERHEAD, ARTILLERY SHELLS HURTLED THROUGH THE AIR WITH A SOUND LIKE TEARING PAPER, AND THEN EXPLODED FAR AHEAD IN LITTLE PUFFS OF SMOKE!

BUT STILL THEY CAME ON! CREEPING OVER THE FROZEN KOREAN GROUND! IF YOU WANT TO KNOW IF A MAN IS SCARED, ASK HIM TO SPIT! THE INSIDE OF MY MOUTH WAS BONE DRY! SOON THEY'D BE WITHIN RIFLE RANGE!

MANY SUMMERS I HAVE BEEN IN NEW YORK AS HOUSEBOY!

NEW YORK? NO KIDDING! I LIVED THERE! I WENT TO COLLEGE IN NEW YORK!

I STILL REMEMBER...RADIO CITY... EMPIRE STATE BUILDING... FIFTH AVENUE ...

WHATAYA KNOW! ...WHERE'D YOU WORK IN NEW YORK?

MY BOSS LIVED ON RIVERSIDE DRIVE, NEAR, 110TH STREET! HAD NICE HOUSE ...

NO KIDDING! I WENT TO COLUMBIA UNIVERSITY... 116TH STREET...ONE BLOCK FROM RIVERSIDE DRIVE!

"Enemy Assault!" from *Frontline Combat* #1 (July–August 1952), by Harvey Kurtzman and Jack Davis, shows the influence of Lewis Milestone's film *All Quiet on the Western Front* (1930). It acknowledged the humanity of enemy soldiers, even as the protagonist is obliged to kill them.

saw Radio City, the Empire State Building and Fifth Avenue. They discover he had stayed just a few blocks from the American's apartment (which, like Kurtzman's place, was on the Upper West side). Suddenly they are human beings to each other. The Chinese soldier shows photos of his family to the other.

Abruptly, the nearby battle resumes. When another American leaps into the trench, the Chinese shoots him. The American then kills the Chinese soldier, whose photos flutter onto his dead body. The American is shocked by the realization that the person he killed was a man much like himself. "I had to choose sides!" He thinks. "I had to! You can't fight a war by comparing baby snapshots!" The final caption returns to the tale's beginning, a common structural device of the short story writer, which Kurtzman used fairly often: "Tiny figures were moving across the frozen Korean fields toward our position! I rammed another clip into the breech of my M-1, and waited for the next enemy assault!" Kurtzman's humanization of the enemy soldier was an enlightened, if not radical, approach during wartime. (Even Remarque's book didn't see print until a decade after World War I.)

Unsurprisingly, the mainstream media in America offered little that was sympathetic to the ordeal of the soldiers of North Korea. In October 1950, the Chinese began their Phase One attack. Kurtzman's "Enemy Assault!" hit the stands just as the Korean War had reached its peak of ferocity. To write about the humanity of a Communist soldier took a certain fortitude. Kurtzman later stated there were no accusations of anti-Americanism from the readers. A few complained about the stories' downbeat endings, but judging by the print runs and sales, it seemed the majority of the readers appreciated a realistic look at war.

SOME SECTORS OF THE POPULACE felt any kind of war comic book was inappropriate, even for teenagers. The Committee on Evaluation of Comic Books in Cincinnati, formed in June 1948, periodically rated all comic books. Their ratings, which consisted of "no objection," "some objection," "objectionable" and "very objectionable," were published in *Parents* magazine. *Two-Fisted Tales* and *Frontline Combat*, and other war comics from other publishers, were consistently rated "objectionable," primarily for their violence. (The EC titles showed little or no blood, but there were plenty of whizzing bullets and people dying.) Comics were also branded "objectionable" for "propaganda against or belittling traditional American institutions." But then, those ratings were ridiculously strict. For example, no comic book that portrayed any sort of criminal activity, even if the criminals were brought to justice, could receive a "no objection" rating.[4]

Kurtzman's war comics were not only new, they were ahead of their time. There was simply nothing else like them in comic books. Those who didn't want anything like reality could choose other war comics on the newsstands in 1951. Some of EC's competitors starred larger-than-life characters such as G. I. Joe (Ziff-Davis). That kind of vainglorious heroism was anathema to Kurtzman. Only one other publisher, inspired by EC, put out thoughtful, mature war comics: Martin Goodman's Timely, which became known as Atlas beginning in 1951. Early in 1952, Atlas war comics dramatically improved. Hank Chapman, one of the publisher's most talented writers, was clearly influenced by Kurtzman's war books. Chapman was a prolific scripter who brought his experience experience as a military photographer and gunner in the Air Force to the page. He wrote many fine, memorable war stories, often dealing with catastrophic injury, shell shock and the death of American soldiers. This period of high quality, realistic stories from Atlas lasted through the end of the Korean War. It isn't known whether Kurtzman saw or read any of these comics, though he generally ignored the competition.

The way Harvey Kurtzman treated his choice of subject matter was new, and the artistic skill of his gifted artists on *Two-Fisted Tales* and *Frontline Combat* matched the other EC titles in setting a new standard for comic book visuals. But these were just the starting points of his innovations as a sequential art storyteller.

In order to appreciate Kurtzman's innovations, one must consider them against the way comic book stories were told in the years before. Comic books began as reprints of newspaper comic strips, and when original material was introduced, it attempted to emulate the comic strips. Then, as time passed, basic changes in page design were adopted to take advantage of the virtues of the sixty-eight-page comic book. One was the splash panel, a large panel on the first page of each story, sometimes a full page, because there was plenty of space. Another was panel arrangement that allowed for variation in the shape and size of the illustrations, even more than the full-page Sunday comics that had already broken the tight grids of their predecessors. Jack Kirby popularized action panels with flailing limbs breaking through the panel borders, and, later, huge, double-page panels. Sound effects were lettered much larger than in the newspaper strips, sometimes becoming an important part of the graphics. However, through the end of the 1940s, relatively little development had occurred in the syntax of comic book stories. The tales were told with the most basic visual components: long shots, medium shots and close-ups. Stories moved forward in predictable fashion, and story structures were numbingly repetitive. Changes of scene accomplished by captions reading "Meanwhile . . . " were used so often that they became a cliché.

The lack of creative innovation in the comic books was largely due to the sheer speed that they were produced, and to the view that the storytelling should be as simple as possible so as not to confuse the readers. Moreover, it was thought that additional effort—finer points—would be wasted on the mostly young customers. Commerce and condescension ruled out subtlety. Even as comics aimed at older teens and adults were produced after the war (such as crime and romance books), few showed significant attempts to tell stories in new ways, or plumb the possibilities of the graphic story medium.

If there were occasional and scattered innovations in comic books of the 1940s, Kurtzman was unaware of them. He stopped reading comics when he left the military (and maybe before that). Apart from the crime comic books, he wasn't aware of trends. "That would have just cluttered my mind," he said. "I would just do what had to be done. My story technique was all very logical to me. It had little to do with the kind of stories you're supposed to write."[5] *Hey Look!* showed that he was already predisposed to experiment with different ways of telling comics stories.

Kurtzman said he didn't think Eisner was an influence, but he followed *The Spirit* and recognized it as an exemplar of the creative heights possible in a short, seven-page story. Eisner's inventive tales, produced week after week, set a standard that few have matched, let alone exceeded. But Eisner's variations on the traditional way narrative comics stories unfolded—the ways he arranged the panels on the page—were principally used to heighten melodramatic moments. Kurtzman had less use for melodrama. *The Spirit* influenced Kurtzman mainly by inspiring him to work on his writing.

When Kurtzman began educating himself on short story structure, he discovered that their relative brevity made them more akin to poems than novels. He found some aspects of poetry appealing and realized such elements as rhythm, repetition and personification, as well as poetic language, could be used to enhance and even shape the way a story was told.

"Rubble!," a six-page story in *Two-Fisted Tales* #24, is a good example. First came the idea. "I would start with a plot first, and then I would go out and do my research," Kurtzman said.[6] "With 'Rubble!' the plot was [determined] well in advance; someone who spends his life building something, and whoof, it goes up in an instant, just like that." His story would be about a Korean man building a house for his wife and son. "I went to the Korean Consulate for information, to get authentic Korean dialogue. I asked what houses were like, what this family was like, how they conducted their day-to-day life. And the Consul General would sit and talk to me for hours." Out of the research came details of the action.

Then came the organizing process, when poetic structure came into play. "You need some kind of structure to hang it on," he said. He chose the elegant idea of devoting each of the interior pages to a distinct segment of time in a stanza-like progression, as the construction of the house moves through various stages: the foundation on p. 2, the walls and roof on p. 3, and the stone fence and gate on p. 4. The completion of each stage is shown in a single, wide panel at the bottom of each page like the refrain of a ballad. These flashback pages are then sandwiched between pages showing an American Long Tom gun on p. 1, and the finished house "disintegrated in a moment from a single artillery blast," leaving only rubble—and under it, the dead family—on p. 6.

Once the structure was established, Kurtzman wrote the words, and they too reflect a poetic sensibility. The introductory page's caption ends with, "If the rubble could talk, it would tell a story . . . A story that started five years ago!," using both repetition and personification (the notion that rubble itself could tell a story). Page six brings more repetition in the captions, and the symmetry of ending the story as it begins, on "the torn, naked earth."

Despite the research, Kurtzman didn't claim the story was truly realistic. "It was my interpretation of reality. I'm sure that somebody right then and there in Korea would say this isn't the way it really was." "Rubble!" stands as one of his most powerful stories due to the overall concept, its poetic elements and the finished artwork by Kurtzman himself. He met the challenge of finding a way to tell an effective story in a mere six pages.

KURTZMAN ALSO WORKED on improving his artwork. As his aesthetics progressed, Kurtzman's own art became simpler than in his science fiction stories. In a later interview, he discussed the story "Air Burst!" from *Frontline Combat* #4 (January–February 1952), and his art at that stage in his career. He considered it "my work at its very best."[7]

He began, "I love action, and I think of things in terms of lumps, so I never draw straight lines. It's almost like Einstein's theory that everything eventually curves in on itself. For me, the horizon isn't straight; it's part of that great lump of the earth. And my perspectives are always like lumps."[8] His inking became more forceful, with thicker outlines as he pulled the

By the time Kurtzman did "Air Burst!," his artwork was stripped down to the essentials.

brush stroke toward himself. With regard to the increasingly spare quality of his artwork, he explained,

> The torture was in the planning. The lines look casual, because they were indeed. The strokes themselves were very swift, but there's preparation for the stroke, you know, like twenty strokes. I was primitive in a sense. Yet, you know, my *Hey Look!*s were very primitive, and yet they're good because they said all they have to say. A good drawing, not only in comics, is where you say the most with the least. So you try to reduce your thinking to try to compound it into simplicities. That's not saying that you say little, but everything you do is meaningful. You don't waste any lines or space. A bad drawing, conversely, uses a lot of lines and a lot of technique and doesn't say much.[9]

Bill Mason later wrote about Kurtzman's self-drawn "Air Burst!" in *Frontline Combat* #4: "By concentrating on essentials . . . Kurtzman imparts a blunt expressive power to every panel of the story and achieves a kind of realism that is entirely his own."[10]

Some don't like this trend in Kurtzman's artwork. Like artists in any field, he has his detractors. Probably the majority of rank-and-file comics fans consider the stories with finished art by Kurtzman less attractive than EC stories drawn by Wallace Wood, Al Williamson and even a horror specialist like Graham Ingels. Simplicity doesn't appeal to everybody. Often, superficial complexity is perceived as more impressive. Those who prefer the illustrative realism of Harold Foster on *Prince Valiant* wouldn't care for Kurtzman's stripped-down style.

Kurtzman's contemporary, comics artist Howard Nostrand, complained, "Kurtzman's art . . . left something to be desired. Especially when you put Kurtzman up against . . . those sharp-shooters he was working with up there. It suffered by comparison."[11] Among other things, Nostrand felt that Kurtzman didn't properly articulate human anatomy in his work. Artist and Kurtzman admirer Landon Chesney later responded to Nostrand's criticism of Kurtzman. "It takes an artist," he wrote, "and not a strict realist, to appreciate that the spirit of Kurtzman's loose depictions of weaponry, for instance, was sometimes truer than the most uncompromisingly accurate drawing. Especially if the weapon is firing. Kurtzman would draw the gun in terms of its kinetic energy, which for his purposes was truer than the way it would look if you just copied it sitting on a table and then drew flames spewing from the barrel. It's these little touches that you would logically expect Nostrand as a pro, and particularly as an EC fan, to appreciate."[12] Kurtzman's work on this and all the subsequent stories he drew in finished form for EC was so strong in terms of portraying the essentials that it had a subjective reality more effective than that of artists whose work had more detail. He came from a background of humorous cartooning, where the emphasis was on gesture, exaggerated movement and quick communication. Therefore, it wasn't surprising that his serious work was a bit of a hybrid, retaining certain elements of his humor work such as a non-slavish (or literal) way of articulating human anatomy.

IN *TWO-FISTED TALES* #25 (January–February 1952) came "Corpse on the Imjin!," one of probably the two best stories he wrote and drew for the EC war comics. "Imjin!" is particularly notable for its sophisticated use of the syntax of comics. It was one of Kurtzman's favorites.

The opening caption reads, "Lightning flickers in the South Korean hills, and a storm wind roars over the Imjin River! Out in the middle of the rain swollen Imjin, a lonely corpse floats with the rubble down to the sea! For this is what our story is about!" The splash panel illustrates the image described in these opening lines, with the hills in the distance, the river flowing left to right, and the riverbank in the foreground littered with shell casings. On the bottom of p. 1, Kurtzman uses the first triptych, a three-panel sequence dividing a single panorama twice in order to show the progress of the corpse as it drifts with the river's current. The division allows each panel to depict a subsequent moment in time, each with its own caption. The third caption reads,

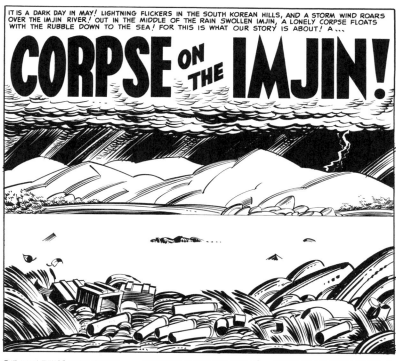

IT IS A DARK DAY IN MAY! LIGHTNING FLICKERS IN THE SOUTH KOREAN HILLS, AND A STORM WIND ROARS OVER THE IMJIN RIVER! OUT IN THE MIDDLE OF THE RAIN SWOLLEN IMJIN, A LONELY CORPSE FLOATS WITH THE RUBBLE DOWN TO THE SEA! FOR THIS IS WHAT OUR STORY IS ABOUT! A ...

CORPSE ON THE IMJIN!

BUT MANY THINGS FLOAT ON THE IMJIN! DRIFTWOOD, AMMUNITION BOXES, RATION CASES, SHELL TUBES!

...WE IGNORE THE FLOATING RUBBLE! WHY THEN, DO WE FASTEN OUR EYES ON A LIFELESS CORPSE?

...THOUGH WE SOMETIMES FORGET IT, LIFE *IS* PRECIOUS, AND DEATH IS UGLY AND *NEVER* PASSES UNNOTICED!

HIS HANDS HAVE STOPPED CLAWING AT THE AIR...HIS FEET HAVE STOPPED THRASHING...

...BLOOD AND BUBBLES ARE COM-ING TO THE SURFACE AND THE MAN YOU ARE HOLDING RELAXES!

IT SEEMS LIKE HOURS HAVE GONE BY! THE BUBBLES ARE BARELY TRICKLING UP AND ALL IS STILL!

Top: From *Two-Fisted Tales* #25 (January–February 1952). In the triptych along the bottom, the background panorama stretches the width of the page. The corpse's progress down the river in each panel shows the passage of time. Bottom: Kurtzman uses a triptych again in the same story, to bring the reader into the "real time" action of drowning an enemy soldier.

"Though we sometimes forget it, life is precious, and death is ugly and never passes unnoticed." On the far bank, an American soldier has noticed the floating corpse.

On p. 2, the point of view shifts to that of the American. The thought balloons reveal that he's wondering just how that person met his death. On the bottom of the page, as he muses that it probably wasn't the result of hand-to-hand combat, an enemy soldier lurks in nearby foliage. Pages three and four show the American and a North Korean soldier desperately fighting in close quarters, ending with them tumbling into the shallow water at the river's edge.

Then comes an expansion of the triptych to four panels across the page. Each panel shows the American struggling to hold the enemy under water, each one from the same distance and angle. This unchanging point of view emphasizes the increments of the action as it progresses from panel to panel, creating the illusion of movement like flip-cards. A triptych below continues to show the progression of time, each panel now moving closer to the American, until all that is visible are his arms continuing to hold the enemy under the surface. Kurtzman keeps the reader's attention fixed as the action calms, the bubbles subside, and the Korean soldier stops struggling. In so doing, the reader is brought into identification with the American, and the extended sequence, closer to real time, allows for more contemplation of the nature of the act than a quick panel or two.

The story ends after the American runs away, and the Korean's corpse floats out on the Imjin. "And now the current, weak near the shore, slowly turns the body around and around. And it is as if nature is taking back what it has given! Have pity! Have pity for a dead man! For he is now not rich or poor, right or wrong, bad or good! Don't hate him! Have pity." Then, over a panorama panel at the bottom of the last page that echoes the image from the splash panel, "for he has lost that most precious possession that we all treasure above everything . . . He has lost his life." And, as a coda, along the bottom of that panel showing the corpse from a distance, Kurtzman concludes, "Lightning flashes in the Korean hills, and on the rain swollen Imjin, a corpse floats out to sea."

"I thought it was a real tear-jerker," he said later. "You know, I wanted it to be poetic, and I wanted it to be neat. It was a lot of work. It was a real exercise in editing my type, my narration so that everything fit. Even in the balloons on p. 2, I worked to keep a rhythm going so that they'd be four lines deep. I loved the rhythm. Some people would criticize. They'd say 'You're repeating. What are you repeating for?' To me the repetition was very important, because you get a flow, you get a movement, you get a sense of time as well as space."[13]

Kurtzman's use of triptychs and polyptichs has been described as cinematic, but he pointed out, "They're not really movie devices. I mean, you're working with a system of graphic continuities . . . that don't really move. Movies do move. But in cartoon continuities, you can create the effect of movement very often by using movie techniques, or one step away from movie techniques, and they're related. Graphic continuities and motion pictures are cousins."[14] A sense of movement can occur in comics, especially when the reader is truly immersed in the story, and his or her mind automatically fills in the action between the panels. Kurtzman's triptychs, which he used frequently, aid the reader's impression of movement, as well as more tightly control the amount of time presumed to occur between each action. Triptychs are also quasi-cinematic when the artist holds constant the way a sequence is framed and the size of the objects in a series of panels. This is similar to a film director's (and/or film editor's) decision to let a shot taken by a locked-down camera run without cutting.

KURTZMAN HAD CONFLICTING feelings about his work, expressing the contradiction between a healthy ego and an insecurity that would never leave him. He later admitted, "I have a high opinion of my work. And at the same time a low opinion. I really like my stuff, but I'm very dissatisfied with it in the sense that I wish it could be a lot better. I think my stuff is great, but I'm completely convinced that I'm the only one who thinks so. At the same time, I can't stand to see my stuff after I've done it because I'm always embarrassed at what could have been better. I think that's very necessary thinking to improve your work, because if you're not critical of your stuff . . . and I don't do this deliberately, but I think that's part of the game. [It's] constantly working . . . and feeling a need to make your stuff better, that makes it better, if anything makes it better."[15] This striving resulted in possibly his finest self-drawn story for the EC war comics. It was also his last.

Kurtzman said "Big 'If'!" in *Frontline* #5 (March–April 1952) was inspired by a photograph of a crying soldier in *Life* magazine, which was taken by David Douglas Duncan, the preeminent photojournalist of the Korean War.[16] However, the most famous "crying soldier" photo in *Life* shows the subject's head in profile, which doesn't correspond to the image in "Big 'If'!" Kurtzman was actually referring to another Duncan photo of a crying soldier, which appeared in the photographer's book *This is*

War!: A Photo-Narrative of the Korean War (June 1951). The book, which consists of 192 pages of searing images, was undoubtedly in Kurtzman's library. (It has many memorable images of the massive retreat from the Changjin Reservoir. It would be an invaluable reference for Kurtzman, who was preparing the special issue of *Two-Fisted* featuring the action at that reservoir at the same time as "Big 'If'!" in *Frontline*.)

The image in *This is War!* is unforgettable. It's a shot of a Marine weeping after his jeep hit a mine around the Nakdong River in August 1950, resulting in the death of a friend. The close-up of the youthful soldier shows the anguished facial expression that Kurtzman adapted in a key panel in "Big 'If'!" Kurtzman said, "I built the character around that one picture that was so impressive to me. The crying face was the visual strong point of the whole story."[17] Rather than literally copying the photograph, Kurtzman rendered his impression of it.

In the splash panel of "Big 'If'!," a soldier sits before five ancient Korean totems called "devil posts." Such posts were usually placed at the approach to a village to frighten away evil spirits, although there is no village in sight. In the first panel at the bottom of the page, the soldier named Paul Maynard says, "'If!' . . . 'If!' Not much of a word! A little word! But lots of meaning!" His mind flashes back twenty-seven minutes, when his squad was sent on a reconnaissance mission. Maynard volunteers to stay behind with the .50 caliber machine gun. He becomes restless, abandons the position and, on the way to rejoining the squad, stops near the devil posts to buckle his boot. An exploding shell bursts nearby, tossing him into the air.

Page seven brings the reader back to the present, with Maynard contemplating the word "if" in successive close-ups of his face, a triptych of him alternately looking haggard, then crying (echoing the Duncan photo), then breaking down farther. Speaking aloud of himself in the third person, he says, "If Paul Maynard hadn't stopped to buckle the combat boot! . . . Could've walked fifty more feet in the time it took to buckle that boot!" Contemplating how all kinds of "ifs" would have changed his fate, a shaking Paul says, "It was only a stray mortar shell! It could have landed anywhere! If only that shell splinter had gone five more inches to the right . . ." Next panel, "Or if Paul Maynard's heart had only been five more inches to the left . . . or if Paul Maynard hadn't even been born!" Then, "If . . . if . . . if . . . (sob) . . . if . . . if . . . " as he falls over, dead.

Kurtzman was rightfully pleased with this story. "That was a real clean idea. It was a very simple premise that I started with, that, 'What if we were two feet to the left of where we were at some particular time,

The crying soldier panels in "Big 'If'!" in *Frontline Combat* #5 were inspired by these Korean War images. Photographs from *This is War!* (1951) © 2015 David Douglas Duncan: used with permission.

how might our lives have been affected?' I wish I'd done more of this kind of thing. I think the story was successful because it concentrates on one personality. It humanizes the story, and I've never done enough of that. When a story makes you feel the humanity of someone, it really works. There's nothing you can do more strongly than touch the reader with the humanity of your characters. Usually I had crowds of characters, but this concentrates on [one] guy."[18]

Thematically, there's a deeper level to Kurtzman's war stories. In his article titled "Kurtzman's Legacy" in *Crimmer's* magazine, Tom Durwood encapsulated it: "Kurtzman's naturalistic conviction, brought out by the absurdity of the war milieu, leads to an existentialism implicit in his work. Kurtzman is tied neither to an ideal of heroicism nor to a perspective of taking sides, and as he follows each situation while it plays itself out, he inexorably approaches the stoic honesty of early existentialism. These people exist, these events happen. The only element Kurtzman adds to shape the events is drama, which serves to tease out the absurdity skulking just below the romantic surface."[19] Kurtzman was saying there's no reason why certain things happen in war, and they only have the meaning man attributes to them.

HARVEY KURTZMAN'S WORKAHOLIC period began when he dropped science fiction and dedicated himself solely to war stories. He didn't know the toll those stories would take on him. He had already been working hard. Now, he was laying out and writing four stories a month, doing the finished art on one, and a cover each month. This amounted to about 50 percent more work than he had done during his suspense and science fiction phase. While less than the approximately fourteen stories a month Feldstein was writing, it was a stressful period. Even so, he could have managed it except for his perfectionism and his obsession with research.

Keeping up with present-day weaponry and equipment would have been daunting enough, but getting accurate elements into the historical stories was more difficult and time-consuming. John Severin had some highly informative books that helped a lot, and Kurtzman managed to find local experts to consult. "I read an awful lot of World War I stuff," Kurtzman recalled.

> Every regiment had its regiment book. I don't know if they did it in World War II, but in World War I apparently there was a lot of camaraderie and every regiment left a regimental history. They're personal histories. I remember that I picked up one regimental history from John

Severin with illustrations by then-Private Percy Crosby who went on to do *Skippy*. You'd get very personalized descriptions of traveling through the Ardennes, the Argonne forest motifs and what happened on the way to relieve the sentries. I picked up on that stuff like crazy.[20]

Kurtzman assembled an enormous library of photographs of equipment and combat, and used every opportunity to actually use the equipment, or see it used. He found soldiers back from Korea and talked to them. "The army would send me to veterans who were still there, in the army. There was no formula. [Adele] had a cousin who was in Iwo Jima. He was my reference. [Comics artist] Dave Berg was also a reference for Iwo Jima."[21] Kurtzman's story "442nd Combat Team," about a squad of Americans of Japanese descent in Europe, was based on material from Ben Oda, who served in the unit.[22]

Adele remembers the content of the stories affecting him. "Harvey would interview people for the war stories. They were authentic, and it was devastating, of course. He talked about how terrible World War I was, with the trenches, the mud and the rain, and then the Civil War. I had Civil War books, and he'd look at the faces of these photographs. They looked like teenaged boys, many of them."[23] His own experience in the military haunted Kurtzman. "He had nightmares from being in the army, about having to go back," she said.[24]

Time and time again, Kurtzman found himself gathering far more material than he could ever use. Even as he was advising Jerry De Fuccio not to get drawn into reading historical reference books when they were on specific information-gathering missions, he found himself unable to stop digging beyond all necessity. As had been the case of his younger self with the microscope, discovering the details in his search for the truth was the doorway to deeper understanding.

Although Kurtzman and Feldstein got along personally, they had different ideas about what made a good comic book story. Feldstein said, "I recall long knock-down drag-out discussions with Harvey on a theoretical, philosophical level as to what were the elements that were important to the work we were doing. Harvey wanted to do something that was uplifting. He would bog down on the minutest detailed investigations of his story background material. We had great arguments in this area since I felt the plot and the character developments were the most important aspects of a story."[25]

Part of Marie Severin's job was helping with research. "Harvey used to send me to armories with a knapsack to do research," she recalled. "In the 1950s, if a girl had a knapsack, there was something radically wrong. He used to send me there all day, with my camera to take pictures of a bazooka or some such thing. He [sent] me to all sorts of crazy places and I would wear out a pair of shoes in a week. He was interesting to work for because you never knew where you were going to end up."[26] Kurtzman insisted that his artists follow the information that he provided. In re-searching ["Combat Medic" in *Frontline* #4], he got a standard medical kit with all the tools and gave it to Jack Davis for reference, reminding him that the suture had to be in one specific place and the gauze pad in another.[27] Davis later said, "Harvey was always making sure that every-thing was just right. He was always very meticulous with his work and is a very talented guy. He's a fantastic artist, but he's a perfectionist. I think he should back off and loosen up a bit."[28]

Harvey Kurtzman imposed himself on every aspect of the books. No one could argue with the result, but there were tensions due to his need for control. Al Feldstein commented, "I was totally opposed to . . . Harvey's way of working. He would supply the artists with tracing paper overlays of exactly the layout that he wanted in each panel. To me, it was apparent that he frustrated, distracted and limited the artists' own abilities which may have surpassed Harvey's . . . as I believed the artists' abilities sur-passed mine."[29]

Wallace Wood didn't like Kurtzman's editorial style. "I quit working for Harvey twice," he recalled. "I wasn't exactly going to quit, but I had a fight with Harvey once and Bill [Gaines] had to be the peacemaker and talk Harvey and me back together again. Harvey had a very annoying way of criticizing your work. He would never pick on anything specific, he'd just say, 'Gee, it seems like you really didn't feel this one.' . . . vague stuff like that. How do you respond to that? I responded by quitting. I like Harvey and I admire him and respect him, but he's a hard man . . . he's a tyrant. He's gotta have everything his way, which I suppose I admire in a way too."[30]

Will Elder was less annoyed. "Harvey's picky attitude irritated me at one time, but after I realized why he was like that I didn't have any regrets. I think he has always been ahead of a lot of us and was demanding. I think most people resent anyone being demanding, especially when you're an artist and you want to give expression to your own thoughts and your own talents. Naturally, there was some resentment on my part, but it was overcome by the fact that it made me work harder."[31]

Severin had his fights with Kurtzman, but later conceded, "Some of the best work the guys did in their careers was done for Harvey under those, what do you call it? Restrictions. They're not restrictions. Directions, I guess. Sometimes it's very difficult to work with a man like that, because the guy was fantastic! Working for him was delightful, it was terrible. He brought out the best in all of us, and sometimes you'd like to break his damn neck. But by God, he was good."[32]

Even Alex Toth, who often had problems with editors (due to his greater understanding of the medium than most, and to his temper), was surprisingly philosophical about Kurtzman's methods. "[Kurtzman] wasn't easy to satisfy. He knew graphics, though, and I could accept his methods. In a way it's offensive to be told exactly that you have to do something this way or that way, but it was just a matter of respecting the man who'd written the story and laid it out. You usually agreed with him."[33]

While Kurtzman micro-managed his artists, he gave a lot of latitude to colorist Marie Severin. Naturally there were discussions about the kind of coloring he liked, but he was impressed with her approach from the beginning. The coloring in the war comics was excellent not because more time was spent on it, or because of its complexity. It was simple, yet artful. As was common in comics of the 1950s, panels would often have just two or three colors, and figures were frequently colored with a single hue. It was a timesaving device, but also had the virtue, if used correctly, of adding emotion to the scene and helped differentiate the foreground from the background. In the splash panel of "Contact!" (*Frontline Combat* #2, September–October 1951), the Chinese sniper and tree branches in the foreground are colored green (a "cool" color) and the background is orange (a "hot" color). Not only does it establish that the soldier was hidden in shadow and the American soldiers are out in the sunlight, but it differentiates the two main visual planes by juxtaposing the cool and hot colors. Severin intuitively knew that color could enhance the storytelling. "I would take a story and read it, and try to color it [according to] the mood they are trying to project in the story line and in the art. Sometimes you would try to add to it as if it was a painting."[34]

Chemical Coloring sent proofs of the color work, both covers and interiors, and Kurtzman reviewed them. Despite all the hours he was working, he found time to mark the tiniest flaws on interior stories, and even the advertisements, many that wouldn't be noticed when the comic book was printed. As with the time he spent on research, Kurtzman's nature drove him to go beyond what anyone else would do, or even care about. The truth was that he was producing work that was too good for comic books, over and above what was needed, expected or cost-effective, because he wasn't able to work any other way. "I may be kidding myself, you know, but I like to have this illusion of a grand *raison d'être*," he later offered in partial explanation. "I have to feel that I'm not hacking for money."[35] Kurtzman's personality compelled him to put in the kind of effort he did, which was more appropriate for slick magazines than comics as they existed at the time. By the autumn of 1951, he was simply unable to keep up. "Big 'If'!" is his last self-drawn story for the war titles. That bought him a week each month. Other than the covers that he continued to do himself, he became a "behind the scenes" artist.[36]

ALSO IN MID-TO-LATE JULY 1951, roughly when he wrote "Rubble!," the story of house-building in Korea, he and Adele became real estate owners. Adele recalled, "Frank [Dorsey] was coming back from Paris and we had to leave. That's when we bought a real old house."[37] They might have found another apartment, but wanted more children and buying real estate would be an investment into their future. Work was steady, so they could make the mortgage payments although Adele was jittery about it: "Harvey would always say, 'don't worry, things will be okay,' and I believed him."[38]

The "real old house" was located at 11 Audrey Ave. in Mount Vernon, a couple of blocks west of North Columbus Avenue, on a short, dead-end road. The Audrey Avenue house was a Victorian with dark red shingles. "It was tall and narrow," Adele said. "It had a cellar and a sub-cellar. I don't think I ever went into the sub-cellar because there were creepy old things down there, like patent nostrum bottles with peeling labels." Both residents and visitors variously described the three-bedroom house as "funny" and "spooky." ("When we first moved in, there were noises at night that scared the hell out of me," Adele remembered.)[39] The neighborhood was predominantly Italian working- and middle-class families. The Kurtzmans' neighbors were a policeman, a shoe-store salesman and a furniture-store owner. Commuter trains in the New Haven line passed just a block away.

One thing that made this purchase feasible was an attic suitable for a studio. That meant Kurtzman wouldn't have to continue paying for space at 1151 Broadway and could put that money toward the house payment. By pulling out, he ended the five-year saga of the Charles William Harvey studio. After that, Elder and Severin worked from home, Elder in Englewood, New Jersey, and Severin in Brooklyn.

Though Kurtzman was happy to see Frank Dorsey again, he was reminded how much he missed his close friend René Goscinny, who had boarded a ship for France earlier in the year. All Goscinny's friends went with him to the pier to wave goodbye. John Severin drew an elaborate cartoon commemorating the moment, with Kurtzman in his trench coat, and the rest of the EC gang crowded around. Kurtzman understood Goscinny's reasons: "It seemed that everything we touched [in collaboration] failed and René didn't do well in New York at all. I'm sure he left in disgust."[40] It was precipitated by an offer from the chief of the World Press agency, who convinced Goscinny to return to Paris and head the agency's Paris office. Despite visiting New York City on three occasions in the mid-1950s, it was in France that Goscinny found success. Referring to his time in America with Kurtzman and his crowd, he later commented, "On a professional level I can say that it's what I learned there which enabled me to work here."[41]

In the fall of 1951, Bill Gaines threw a party in the EC offices, when he gave out movie cameras as gifts. "We had just started doing well, so I had a party," Gaines recalled. "Everybody got cameras except certain individuals who already had [one]. Graham [Ingels] wanted an outboard motor badly. Feldstein . . . wanted a lawnmower."[42] Photos of this party show the smiling faces of Johnny Craig, Jack Davis, Wallace Wood and Harvey Kurtzman as they received their cameras. Gaines's paternalism, represented by Christmas gifts to the staff, meant little to Kurtzman. Later, Kurtzman revealed his true feelings: "Gaines was a very paternalistic guy. Paternalism has its good and its bad sides. It gives you a certain kind of security, but at the same time you always have to go to Papa."[43] He felt he didn't need a father, or a movie camera. He needed more money. Adele confirmed, "Bill gave us a movie camera and a projector . . . and it was nice, but Harvey's point of view was, 'We should be paid.'"[44] While he was making a little over $8,000 a year at the time, what most would consider a good salary in 1951, he was having difficulty making ends meet.[45]

WHY DIDN'T BILL GAINES pay Kurtzman for the layouts, since the artists didn't have to do them? When queried about this, Gaines responded, "I think the artists would have been very aggrieved had I done it, because their position would have been, 'Who asked for [it?]' Most of them really didn't want to work that way. Some of them enjoyed it, some of them liked it, some of them recognized that probably what Harvey wanted was better than what they would have done. Nevertheless, it was an imposition on their freedom of action."[46] Besides, paying Kurtzman for the layouts would have meant deducting that amount from the artists' page rates, which wouldn't have gone down well.

Kurtzman began looking for ways to supplement his income that wasn't as time-intensive as his EC war stories. In late 1951 or early 1952, he heard that artist Dan Barry was looking for a writer to help with the *Flash Gordon* daily newspaper strip. Barry was working in a building owned by the American Bible Society across from Cooper Union, where freelance artists could rent a low-cost space. Kurtzman and Barry first met in 1948 (when Barry was drawing the *Tarzan* daily strip) at a meeting of cartoonists who were discussing forming a union. Now Kurtzman pitched himself as ghostwriter for *Flash Gordon*.

Although fantasy wasn't his strong suit, he could work in that milieu. Barry recalled, "Here was Harvey, a guy with a wild, way-out imagination, and here I was, someone who could make it all look a little more convincing because the buttons and bows on the rocket ships I did looked real." Times had changed, and syndicates would no longer accept the type of artistic eroticism in the strip that had inflamed Kurtzman as a youth. Barry's work was far more prosaic and sterile than that of Alex Raymond. The wild Kurtzman and the staid Barry seemed to balance each other out. Barry only had one concern: "I always had a problem with Harvey's taste, and I told him that at the beginning. 'Your books are clever, the palate is obvious, but the taste!' It was not for me. It was a little bit raw. It certainly wasn't for a syndicated strip that went out to families and Baptist ministers. Now, I like action and ballsy, violent stuff, but somehow I try to keep a thread of logic in my story, and that didn't matter to Harvey. He's really a Bronx boy whose tastes are very broad, and — I'm just different from that."[47] For his part, Kurtzman saw Barry as a "colorful John Garfield-type, a real tough guy. I don't say that in a pejorative sense, because I liked him. He had sort of a reputation for having a short fuse, but I never saw that."[48]

Kurtzman wrote the strip as he did with the war comics: coming up with a basic story, working up rough layouts to determine the basic flow of each daily episode, and then finishing the captions and dialogue. The first Kurtzman-Barry *Flash Gordon*, dated April 7, 1952, introduced a rhinoceros-like ice monster. At first, Barry found Kurtzman's layouts too broad to follow closely, but eventually one can detect Kurtzman's lively panel designs beneath the buttoned-down art in the finished strips.

Barry recalled, "He'd call me and say, 'Why couldn't you get more action into that strip? Why couldn't you exaggerate that more? Why aren't you understanding what I'm trying to tell you?' I said 'Harvey, I understand perfectly well what you're trying to tell me. The real problem is, you don't understand what I'm trying to tell you.'"[49] Kurtzman had to accept that Barry was in the driver's seat. He wrote *Flash Gordon* for one year.

(His last strip was probably the April 20, 1953, episode.) Kurtzman left the *Flash Gordon* dailies to work with Mac Raboy on the *Flash Gordon* Sunday strips, but that proved to be a non-starter. Raboy was insulted when presented with Kurtzman's layouts. By the spring of 1953, however, Kurtzman had a new project that was taking all his time and energy.

AFTER EIGHTEEN MONTHS, the bloody Korean War had bogged down. Despite the stalemate and unpopularity of the war by this time, war comics became even more popular in 1952. Atlas, Harvey Comics and St. John also published them. Conservative National entered the field in mid-1952 with *Our Army at War* (#1, August 1952) and the reformatting of *Star Spangled Comics* and *All-American Western* to *Star Spangled War Stories* and *All-American War Stories*. Semi-realistic war comics like these were unthinkable during World War II, but now GIs and the public ate them up. The genre became a hardy mainstay of the industry for the next twenty-five years. Meanwhile, the EC war comics had come under the scrutiny of the United States government. When confidential documents were declassified in the 1990s, it was discovered that an FBI investigation into Kurtzman's comics had been conducted.

J. Edgar Hoover, Director of the Federal Bureau of Investigation, was contacted by an officer in the G-2 Intelligence division of the US Army to find out if EC and Harvey Kurtzman could be prosecuted for Sedition (Internal Security) under the Smith Act. In 1940, the Alien Registration Act (commonly known as the Smith Act) was passed, making it a federal crime to advocate or teach the desirability of overthrowing the United States Government, or to be a member of any organization that did the same. Beginning in 1949, some 140 leaders of the Communist Party in the US were put on trial under the Act. By 1957, court rulings began to reverse the convictions, and the law—still on the books—has been moribund since 1961. However, the US Supreme Court upheld it in 1951 in the case of Dennis v. United States.

According to an April 20, 1952, report to Hoover, the Pentagon "has received comic books from various commands throughout the United States and overseas." The report continued, "G-2 has advised that a review of the contents of these comic books reveals that some of the material is detrimental to the morale of combat soldiers and emphasizes the horrors, hardships and futility of war. These comic books portray the seemingly needless sacrifices due to blunders on the part of officers and demonstrate the lack of protection of the United States forces against the trickery of the enemy. G-2 considers these publications subversive because they tend to discredit the army and undermine troop morale by presenting a picture of the inevitability of personal disaster in combat." G-2 cited *Two-Fisted Tales* and *Frontline Combat* as titles that warranted investigation.[50]

Hoover immediately contacted a special agent in New York City, writing, "Harvey Kurtzman is listed as the editor of both of these publications and . . . William M. Gaines [is] also mentioned as affiliated with those publications. It is requested that you institute an immediate investigation [of the officers of EC comics] and the persons directly responsible for the publication and distributions of the comic books together with background information which might be of assistance in determining the true purposes of the publications." Hoover wanted to know the methods of distribution, and "whether an effort is made to reach any certain class of persons by this dissemination such as those having obligations under the Universal Military Training and Service Act or members of the Armed Forces."[51] The Bureau's confidential agent interviewed someone at Leader News about the distribution and circulation of *Two-Fisted* and *Frontline*, investigated the backgrounds of Gaines and Kurtzman, examined the firm's Second Class mailing permits, and looked into the origins of EC.

The agent sent his report to Washington, DC on May 12, including copies of *Two-Fisted* #28 and *Frontline* #7, the latest issues. (They would seem to be poor choices if one was looking for potential sedition, with just one Korean War story between them, and not one that could be seen as inflammatory.) The report itself disclosed some basic information, all of it innocuous. While the agent continued digging, the FBI Director sent the initial material and a copy of each of the comic books on June 18 to Assistant Attorney General James M. McInerney at the US Department of Justice, as evidence in a charge of "Sedition—Internal Security" if warranted. It wasn't until September 16 that Hoover forwarded the rest of the investigation, which found that none of the subjects had a criminal record with the New York Police Department, and that "Confidential informants . . . of known reliability, who are familiar with Communist activities in the New York City area, advised that the subjects were unknown to them."[52] The fact that Kurtzman's father bore a different last name may have worked in his favor because it was very possible his parents were (or had been) members of some Communist organizations. (Indeed, Kurtzman's own fleeting involvement with union organizing before and after World War II meant his name might have surfaced on the roster of a supposed "Red" organization, if anyone kept attendance records.) While the Department of Justice considered whether the facts constituted a violation of the Sedition statutes, copies of *Frontline* #10 and *Two-Fisted Tales* #29 were also forwarded to the department. (There were two Korea-based stories in the two titles, which did show the brutality of war, one carrying the "subversive" notion that "each and every life on this earth is important.")

Finally, according to an FBI document, "The Department stated that this review has failed to disclose any evidence that the subjects of the investigation had the required specific intent toward the acts proscribed by Section 2387 and 2388 of Title 18, USC." According to a later FBI report, the Department decided that while the stories "appeared to be unnecessarily graphic in depicting battle scenes and the horrors of war, they could not be construed as advising, counseling or urging insubordination, disloyalty, mutiny or refusal of duty by any member of the military or naval forces of the US."[53] Thus ended a "shadow event" in Kurtzman's career. It was ironic that Kurtzman was being helped by the US military to research his war comics while being investigated for subversive activity at the request of the Pentagon.[54] The FBI would have occasion to add another report to Kurtzman's file some fifteen years later.

DESPITE HIS CENTRAL ROLE in determining what and how the stories in the EC war comics were told, Harvey Kurtzman was far from the whole show. John Severin, Will Elder, Jack Davis and Wallace Wood all did exceptional artwork in those comic books, reaching early pinnacles of their careers. Davis and Wood were also turning out superb work for EC's other books. Years later, Kurtzman was interviewed on a television show by Harold Hayes, the editor of *Esquire*. Midway through the discussion of the EC period, Hayes commented, "It's astounding there was this much effort going into what was then seen really only as a comic book form." Kurtzman answered, "We worked with great pride and competitiveness. I think this was unique to our little operation. We took a pride in our work. The comic book business was really a hack business. You were encouraged to turn out volume. And we went against that tide. We wanted to do good drawings. I don't know why. It was some kind of an insane compulsion. Everybody competed with each other, and they did some of their best work back in that time."[55]

John Severin both pencilled and inked a second story to make up for the slot Kurtzman could no longer fill. A highlight in *Frontline* #6 (March–April 1952) was Severin's fine solo effort, "Ace!," which especially pleased Kurtzman: "He worked with a pen . . . and the design problems were at a minimum. He knew airplanes, and he knew movement. John has the talent of an actor. And he also understands movement in space, which is essential in making World War I airplanes move through the sky.

This, to me, was one of his absolutely best stories."[56] Severin did another fine aviation tale, "Red Knight," the story of the Red Baron, Manfred von *Richthofen*, in *Two-Fisted Tales* #29.

Wallace Wood's art shone in "Custer's Last Stand" in *Two-Fisted* #27. In 1952, the popular view of General George Custer was probably based on Errol Flynn's portrayal in the highly inaccurate *They Died with Their Boots On*, a 1941 Warner Bros. film directed by Raoul Walsh. The movie ended with Custer meeting his end while trying to prevent a massacre. Kurtzman's research revealed a different story. "Custer was a fool. He wanted to be president. He was vindictive about not being chosen as a political candidate. Actually, I'm convinced he was suicidal. Because he attacked this enormous concentration of Indians without even pausing to think, and it was a hopeless thing that he did. It was like a mouse running into a volcano. And he was very vain, not a likeable person."[57] School textbooks at this time also accorded Custer the death of a hero. This story is a prime example of Kurtzman attempting to educate the youth of America.

Kurtzman introduced special historical issues: for example, *Frontline* #7 focused on Iwo Jima. All four stories revealed aspects of the Pacific island battle. On the cover, Kurtzman has a soldier declaring, "If there ever was a true hell on earth, it was here . . . here on Iwo Jima!" Dealing with the intricacies of that issue was hell for Kurtzman. "Those jigsaw puzzles that I used to have to do, they took the life out of me. Getting the stories to fit all the conditions. Fit the plot together, fit the picture elements together, fit them into the number of pages, fit the cartoonist's style, fit the schedule, balance the issue. It was pure blood—bloody work."[58]

One of the most visually extraordinary EC war stories was "Thunderjet!" in *Frontline* #8. Coincidentally, it hit newsstands shortly after an article called "The Forgotten Heroes of Korea" by James Michener appeared in the *Saturday Evening Post* (May 10, 1952), about American pilots in Korea who were heroic not just for their exploits, but also because they risked their lives without sufficient support from the home front. Kurtzman's story of an air battle between the American jet and Russian MiG jet fighters has a similar theme.

"Thunderjet!" was the second of three stories drawn by Alex Toth for EC. "I wanted to use Toth very badly, but there were always problems," Kurtzman recalled. "I finally found a gimmick, a way to reach him. Toth was going into the service, and he was thinking of getting into the Air Force, so I gave him a proposition: 'Why don't you do some air stories, and maybe this will give you entrée into some part of the Air Force.' He went for it."[59] Toth appreciated Kurtzman's concise scripts. "Too rarely have I come across scripts where the writer really thought in terms of picture continuity," he said. "Kurtzman of course was one who did. It is a visual medium, after all. But too many writers use top-heavy dialogue and captions."[60] The low word count in Kurtzman's scripts put greater emphasis on the visuals to carry the narrative and themes. The middle six pages of the eight-page "Thunderjet!" have no captions. Pages 3 and 4 each have four panels with no text at all. The story's progression relies on the skills of the Kurtzman-Toth team.

Toth was a master designer. While he follows Kurtzman's layouts, the panels have his stamp on them. The airplanes are expertly choreographed and the blacks are carefully placed. The panels have a kind of dynamic perfection, making the artist's handling of a complicated narrative look easy. The word balloon pointers shoot across the panels like jagged lightning, adding visual excitement. Kurtzman was thrilled by Toth's visuals. "[Toth] knocked himself out and did this beautiful story 'Thunderjet!,' and it was the best story he ever did for me."[61] It was complemented by one of Kurtzman's finest covers.

Kurtzman's war comic books were special in many ways. There was the choice of subject matter, the sophistication of story structure, the lit-

Frontline Combat #8 (September–October 1952).

erary qualities (poetic elements) and the degree of authenticity. There was also the well-considered balance of text and visuals to tell the stories, the artistic clarity, the sensitive coloring and the cohesion that came from having one writer-artist at the helm. The result was nothing less than a new kind of comic book, one with extraordinary dramatic power in the early 1950s, and with a potency that remains undiminished by the passage of time.

In "Front Lines" in the "Thunderjet!" issue, a letter writer felt each new *Frontline Combat* was better than the last, and wondered, "How long can this go on?" An exasperated Kurtzman replied, "'*How long can this go on?*' This is your editor's nightmare! Very often, in the middle of the night, we wake with a start, shrieking those very words!"

An emblematic page from "Dying City!" in *Two-Fisted Tales* #22 (July–August 1951). Alex Toth pencilled and Harvey Kurtzman inked.

Two-Fisted Tales #24 (November–December 1951). Story and art by Kurtzman.

John Severin handled the aerial combat story "Ace!" in *Frontline Combat* #6 (May–June 1952). Wallace Wood drew "Custer's Last Stand" in *Two-Fisted Tales* #27 (May–June 1952).

BEFORE THE TOWN OF X — IN KOREA, A G. I. SITS THINKING IN FRONT OF A ROW OF ANCIENT KOREAN DEVIL POSTS! AND, AS IF TO MOCK HIS THOUGHTS, THE DEVIL POSTS GRIN DOWN AT HIM... JAGGED WOODEN GRINS FROM EAR TO EAR... AS IF THEY KNOW HE'S THINKING OF THE BIG...

BIG 'IF'!

YEAH...'IF'!...'IF'! NOT MUCH OF A WORD! A LITTLE WORD! BUT LOTS OF MEANING!

LIKE...IF THOSE DEVIL POSTS HAD ONLY BEEN A LITTLE FURTHER DOWN THE ROAD!

OR...IF THAT SHELL CRATER WAS ONLY A HUNDRED FEET FURTHER AWAY! YEAH...

Frontline Combat #5 (March–April 1952). Story and art by Kurtzman.

12.

MAD BEGINNINGS

COMIC BOOK SERIES come and go. In most cases, when a new one is born, it's no big deal, and when it dies, it slips into oblivion with little notice. Publishers routinely launch new comic books all the time. Relatively few of them—individually or in series— make much impact or last very long. Change is part and parcel of the business.

When EC added a comic book called *Mad* to its roster in 1952, the publisher hoped it would do well, but the odds were stacked against it. That's because 1952 was the biggest year in comics history up to that point (and would remain so for many years to come), in terms of the number of individual issues published. That year, roughly 3,250 different comic books appeared on newsstands. An average of sixty different books a week jostled for browsers' attention.

Bill Gaines okayed the new comic book by Harvey Kurtzman without expecting great success. He had a gut feeling that *Vault of Horror* and *Crypt of Terror* would catch on, but no such feeling about Kurtzman's *Mad*. Neither did Kurtzman. *Mad* was initiated not because anybody thought it had tremendous potential, or because it was the right time for a satirical comic book, but for more obscure, complicated reasons.

Throughout 1950 and 1951, Kurtzman had worked feverishly writing and drawing comic books of the highest quality, yet was struggling financially. Gaines agreed *Two-Fisted Tales* and *Frontline Combat* were outstanding comic books, even that they were qualitatively better than the horror titles, but was adamant that Feldstein and Kurtzman be paid the same editorial rate per book, and the same rate per page of script.[1] Kurtzman became fixated on the idea that he deserved more. He later explained, "I idealized my role and my purpose as a writer, and I used to work very hard at it. We were working on a piece-work basis, and Feldstein would be turning the sausage machine, and cranking them out, you know, and the thinking was, 'Well, it's perfectly fair. The horror stuff makes lots of money, and you get the same per-page rates.' And I couldn't accept that emotionally for obvious reasons. I'd be piss-poor all the time, and Al would be raking in the dough. I bashed a lot of plaster off of the walls trying to cope with that one."[2] Constitutionally unable to work faster, Kurtzman felt he should be paid more because of the amount of time he put into each page and the quality of the result.

Bill Gaines, like all viable publishers, was ever mindful of the bottom line, and in his case, had more reason than most. Not all of the EC books were as profitable as the horror titles. The war comics sold moderately well, but the science fiction titles, by 1952, were drifting toward the loss column. He was also handicapped by the terms of his contract with Leader News. EC received one-fourth of a cent less per copy than publishers like National or Atlas, who had their own distribution networks, or most other publishers with distribution contracts. If a book's sales were 300,000, EC got $750 less than most of its competitors. When multiplied by the number of books in the EC lineup, the one-fourth cent disadvantage added up to $3,000 or more a month, a significant sum for a small publishing operation. "That's why, in addition to everything else, we had to try a little harder because we were getting a little bit less," Gaines recalled. "Those quarter of a cents hurt."[3] If Bill Gaines paid Harvey Kurtzman a higher rate, then he felt he had to give Al Feldstein the same raise, or he risked losing the editor and writer of his most profitable books, and he claimed he couldn't afford it.

When Gaines stood firm, Kurtzman did work outside EC, the kind that didn't require time-consuming research. He had already been doing occasional humor fillers on the side, such as *Egghead Doodle* for Stan Lee. He did more *Genius* pages for Elliot Caplin, as well as more of *Pot-Shot Pete*. Kurtzman would have preferred to do more humor work, but took the job writing *Flash Gordon* because it paid regularly, week after week, and also didn't require research.

Kurtzman had dreamed since childhood of publishing and editing his own magazine. After his time at M&A, evidence indicates that he began thinking in terms of some sort of humor publication to be filled with the work of his cartooning buddies, although he was scarcely in a position to make it happen at the time.[4] Given the many hours Kurtzman and Gaines spent together at work and socially in the two-and-a-half years they had known each other, it seems certain Kurtzman would have told Gaines of this dream. Gaines clearly knew Kurtzman's financial crunch was real enough that he had resorted to doing "easier" humor and straight work for other publishers. The Kurtzman-scripted *Flash Gordon* newspaper strips began appearing on Monday, April 7, 1952, about the same time Gaines and Kurtzman had a discussion that led to the creation of *Mad*.

According to Kurtzman, he suddenly got the idea of doing an all-humor book for EC. Adele Kurtzman recalled, "Al and Bill had come to dinner. They talked about doing something different. Harvey said, 'Let's do something funny. That's what comics are, let's do something funny.' And that to me seems to be the beginning. I remember what we served, everything."[5]

When later asked about the origin of *Mad*, Kurtzman's response was unequivocal. "I invented the whole thing from the word go," he said. "It was started very simply. I suggested a humor magazine because I wouldn't have to do the research. I could just go into a room and write it. So [Bill Gaines] said, 'Okay, see what you can come up with.'"[6] On matters of a creative nature, this fits the established pattern between the two men: Kurtzman made a request (to become a writer, to replace the Leroy lettering, to start an adventure book, to become an editor) and Gaines said, "Yes."

However, Bill Gaines's version of this discussion differed. According to a later interview, he recalled, "I said, 'Look, for God's sake, it takes you a month to research *Frontline Combat* and a month to research *Two-Fisted Tales.* But you can stick *Mad* in there. It will take you a week to write it'—it wasn't *Mad* yet, but it became *Mad*—'and your income will go up fifty percent,' and that's why *Mad* was born." Gaines added, "Harvey remembers that he suggested to me that he put out a humor book, but that's not what happened. I suggested to him that he put out a humor book because . . . I remembered what I had first seen him doing, which was that stuff he brought in that had me rolling on the floor." (He was referring to *Hey Look!*)[7]

Kurtzman and Gaines also differed on how the comic book got its name. Kurtzman said, "I went home and came up with the title *M-A-D*. Then I went back to the office and said, 'How about *Mad*?' [Gaines] said 'Great!' So I drew up a cover, I wrote four stories, and I laid them out. I took them back to him and he said, 'Great!' That's the way we did *Mad*."[8]

But Gaines said, "When Al and I would write the letter pages, we referred to our magazines as 'EC's mad-mags,'" pointing to issues as early as 1950 (such as *Vault of Horror* #14). He then described an editorial meeting. "Johnny Craig, Al Feldstein, Harvey and myself sat around [and] we said, 'we're going to do a humor magazine,' and the title proposed by Feldstein was *EC's Mad-Mag*. It was an expression we'd been using right along. Johnny Craig came up with the side strip, 'Humor in a Jugular Vein,' and then Harvey, in a stroke of genius, either then or later, took off '*EC's*' and '*Mag*' and just made it *Mad*, which is a brilliant title. But he didn't just sit down and think up the title *Mad*. He got the title from *EC's Mad-Mag*."[9] Feldstein confirmed Gaines's much-repeated version of events.[10]

In 1962, Kurtzman stated, "I have no recollection that Feldstein so definitely suggested the title *EC's Mad-Mag*."[11] This doesn't deny that the name was mentioned, only that if it was, it wasn't necessarily put forward as a usable idea for the title, or may have been referenced *after* Kurtzman proposed the name *Mad*. Adele said, "I can remember Harvey trying to think of a name. We went through a whole bunch of names."[12] Kurtzman pointed out, "There was practically no creation done in committee between me and Gaines. His and his group's influence was generally exercised negatively, in that I would bring up ideas that were accepted or rejected. I rarely create 'in committee,' preferring to work in deep solitude, at home."[13] In the soup of the various titles that he considered, one simple idea surfaced. *Mad*—just one short word—suggested infinite possibilities. It was Kurtzman-like in its conciseness. *EC's Mad-Mag* would have been unworkable. *Mad* was inspired.

Consider the seven definitions of the word in *Webster's New World Dictionary of the English Language*:

> **mad** (mad) *adj.* **mad'der**, **mad'dest 1.** mentally ill; insane **2.** wildly excited or disorderly; frenzied; frantic [*mad* with fear] **3.** showing or resulting from lack of reason; foolish and rash; unwise [a mad scheme] **4.** blindly and foolishly enthusiastic or fond; infatuated [to be mad about clothes] **5.** wildly amusing or gay; hilarious [a mad comedy] **6.** having rabies [a mad dog] **7.** a) angry or provoked (often with *at*) b) showing or expressing anger—vt., vi. **mad'ded**, **mad'ding** [Archaic] to madden—n. an angry or sullen mood or fit—**have a mad on** [Colloq.] to be angry—mad **as a hatter** (or **March hare**) completely crazy [14]

In its multiple meanings, the word made a title that was intriguing, even a little mysterious.

The cover rough of *Mad* #1 has survived. It has the title *Mad* in large, yellow letters at the top, in the design that was ultimately used. If Johnny Craig came up with "Humor in a Jugular Vein" for the side strip, it would

Left: Kurtzman's cover "rough" for *Mad* #1. Right: Final cover of *Mad* #1 (October–November 1952).

logically have come when he saw Kurtzman's horror-themed rough for that cover. "A Funny Funny Book," Kurtzman's side strip on that rough cover drawing, reflected the original conversation that Adele remembered. ("Let's do something funny. That's what comics are.") Therefore, by the time of the group editorial meeting described by Gaines (with Craig present), when he says *Mad-Mag* was proposed, Kurtzman had already settled on the title *Mad*, unless there were two such meetings, which Gaines never claimed.

Putting the pieces together, the creation of *Mad* appears to have occurred in three stages: 1) dinner with the Kurtzmans, when the idea of a humor comic book was broached, 2) a follow-up discussion with Gaines when Kurtzman said he wanted to call it *Mad*, after considering other names, and 3) a somewhat more formal editorial meeting that included Gaines, Feldstein and Craig, when Kurtzman showed the group a rough presentation for *Mad* #1. Short of discovering heretofore-unknown documentation (doubtful, since Gaines and his editors didn't communicate by memo, and all the principals are deceased), this is the most probable, complete account of the way one of the great publishing success stories of the century was born.

Considering what *Mad* became, and that neither Bill Gaines nor Al Feldstein contributed to it for its first four years, it's understandable they wanted credit for what they believed was their part in founding the peri-odical.[15] Ultimately, it was a case of both Kurtzman and Gaines agreeing that a humor comic book—presumably easier and quicker to produce—would help Kurtzman make more money at EC. When asked about these matters in later years, Kurtzman would wearily sigh, and respond with the aphorism, "Success has many fathers, failure is an orphan."[16]

These questions aside, Bill Gaines deserves enormous credit for his willingness to gamble on a comic book that was unlike anything else on newsstands. He did it because he wanted to help Harvey Kurtzman. He acted as Kurtzman's patron. Kurtzman didn't have the business savvy or track record to elicit such support elsewhere. Gaines, by that time a Kurtzman believer, was the only publisher who would have put out *Mad* and allowed Kurtzman to have total creative control. In so doing, Gaines gave Kurtzman what he needed to produce something extraordinary. Had *Mad* been diluted by the work and/or sensibilities of others, it would have been just another comic book. Without Kurtzman's vision and policies to achieve creative cohesion, it wouldn't have been special enough to catch on in a big way.

WHATEVER THE COMIC BOOK was called, it would be its contents that really mattered. As Kurtzman worked at his drawing board in his attic studio, he put aside the reference books and again worked unfettered as the humor cartoonist that he was born to be. He had spent endless hours writing grim stories of death and destruction. Now, he could once again be the guy whose cartoons made people laugh. But what kind of humor would he go for? Kurtzman's original inspiration for doing such a maga-zine came from the college humor magazines that he found as a youth. "These magazines were outrageous in their approach to humor, and I wanted to be outrageous," he said. "[There was] an attitude that I picked up on. Not ideas—a mood, an attitude, bigger than detailed ideas."[17] At first, he wasn't focused on satire.

> I didn't really know what the hell I was doing. All I was doing was "fun-ny." Funny. Gotta make it funny, gotta make me laugh, gotta tickle myself. And so, while influences were shaping me, I wasn't necessarily aware of what the influences were, except my own brain.[18] I'd read the usual . . . [S J.] Perelman, [Max] Schulman, but I hadn't thought much about satire. As a matter of fact, I didn't regard this thing as satirical when I first started. *Mad* was kind of a natural step for me from what . . . came easily to me, *Hey Look!*[19]

He added the prefix *Tales Calculated to Drive You* over the title on the cover. It was inspired by the *Suspense* radio program, which began each week with the opening, "Tales well calculated to keep you in . . . Suspense!"

Kurtzman's only finished art for *Mad* was on the covers (other than a few reprints that appeared in the comic book later, and headers for text features). For the first one, Kurtzman drew a scary scene in an old, dark house. A terrified man and woman cringe from a monster indicated to the reader only by its approaching shadow, and gasp, "That thing! That slithering blob coming toward us! What is it?" Their little boy, finger in his nose, informs them, "It's Melvin!" The name "Melvin" amused Kurtzman, and may have come to mind because Jerry Lewis played a character by that name in *Sailor Beware*, a film still playing in local theaters. He gave the name to a different character in each of the stories. "Melvin" wasn't developed into a continuing character, although it almost happened later when a name was needed for a certain moronic mascot.

The inside front cover carried "Mad Mumblings," an editorial introduction with a fanciful account of the origin of *Mad*. Kurtzman wrote:

Greetings, you MAD readers! You're now holding in your MAD hands the very first MAD issue of MAD!

For us, the editors, this is a great occasion . . . for in the next few moments, you will be one of the many who are deciding the fate of MAD all over the country.

Many months ago, we had a meeting in the New York offices of Entertaining Comics. We decided we wanted to add another mag to our line . . . so we met behind locked doors to figure out what our new book would be. Well, we looked through our mail for a lead . . . we thumbed through our idea files . . . we paced the floor, beat our heads against the wall, and bit off all our fingernails! Should we do another war mag? No! Plenty of them on the stands already! Another science-fiction book? Nah! Market is filled to capacity! A horror book? Nyeh! Far too many of them around. Romance? Adventure? Western? Nope . . . nope . . . nope! We were tired of the war, ragged from the science-fiction, weary of the horror. Then it hit us! Why not do a complete about-face? A change of pace! A comic book! Not a serious comic book . . . but a COMIC comic book! Not a floppity rabbit, giggly girl, anarchist teenage type comic book . . . but a comic mag based on the short story type of wild adventure that you seem to like so well. THAT WAS IT! Immediately we leaped to our typewriters, our drawing boards, and our India ink . . . we worked like a crew of inspired demons! In no time at all, MAD was born.

You are holding our dream child in your hands. We had a swell time creating MAD . . . and we hope that MAD will have a long successful life. But you, the reader, will decide that!

This type of greeting became typical of the first issues of all Kurtzman's magazines. Of course, it was pure blather. Any relation to the real genesis of *Mad* was coincidental, although he did characterize its original concept as "a COMIC comic book," echoing his "funny funny book" idea. His mention of the "anarchist teenage type comic book" was a reference to Archie comics and their ilk. A pitch for subscriptions at the bottom of the page revealed that *Mad*, like the other EC comics, would be published six times a year.

Kurtzman began with parody, imitating stories with a humorous bent. "My intention in the early *Mad*s was primarily moods and storytelling, and it was a little later that satire became dominant."[20] "Hoohah!," the first story in the issue, begins with a caption reading, "Terror Dept.! Please! We warn you! Do not read this story! Throw this comic book away before it is too late! . . . Very well, rash fool! Read on! But remember! We warned you! There are many things not meant for the eyes of man!"

The premise of "Hoohah!," a horror-story parody, seems inspired by the opening scenes of James Whale's Universal film *The Old Dark House* (1932), based on J. B. Priestley's novel *Benighted.* "I saw the horror mystery movies [that] everybody else saw," Kurtzman acknowledged, although he didn't name the Whale movie specifically.[21] He was eight years old when it was initially released and a teenager when it was rereleased in 1937. The film begins on a stormy night, when a couple (Raymond Massey and Gloria Stuart) and a friend (Melvyn Douglas) are stranded in the Welsh countryside, and forced to take refuge in a spooky house owned by the eccentric Femm family. Boris Karloff plays their grotesque butler.

Kurtzman put *Mad* together using the template that he had established with the war comics (which he was still doing). The opening page of "Hoohah!" (and the other stories in *Mad* #1) begins with a three-line caption, leading to a one-word title ending with an exclamation point.

Below the two-thirds-page splash panel is a row of three panels to start the story, often employing the same sort of verbal repetition found in his other EC work. His creative process also stayed the same: establish a plot, rough in his ideas with small thumbnail drawings of each page, then complete the script as he did larger page layouts on vellum overlays to guide the artist. The surviving tiny thumbnails reveal that the title to the first story was originally "G-G-Ghosts!"[22] "Hoohah!" is an expression that is thought to have originated from the Yiddish "hu-ha," which means a to-do, an uproar or an exclamation. Yiddish words, which seemed quite exotic to readers in Middle America, became a staple of the book.

For *Mad*, Kurtzman used his war comics artists, all of whom were gifted humor cartoonists, were on his wavelength and were accustomed to his working methods. As elsewhere, he shaped the stories to fit each artist's strengths. He selected Jack Davis to draw the first story, possibly because he handled horror so well in *Tales from the Crypt*. Also, Kurtzman may have figured Davis's work was the most accessible and ingratiating.

Most of "Hoohah!" consists of gags involving a young couple named Galusha and Daphne who became gradually more terrified as they approach and enter the spooky house, meet the old man who lives there and decide there really aren't any ghosts or monsters on the premises. Kurtzman constructed his story in four- , five- and six-panel sequences, each one building to a humorous climax. Along the way, there are lots of sound effects, a gag where Galusha grabs the gutter between two story panels for support and even a triptych. Its most EC-like characteristic is the twist ending. The old man is revealed to be a ghost after all. "Hoohah!" is a frenzied, "in your face" story that quickly establishes the wild, unbridled kind of humor that readers could expect in *Mad.*

Next came "Blobs!," drawn by Wallace Wood, a science fiction story based on E. M. Forster's "The Machine Stops." It uses Jonathan Swiftian humor in its portrayal of life in the far-flung future when humans are totally dependent on machines to do everything. For example, there are vending machines with "disposable prefabricated robot women," allowing Wood to draw the only sexy woman in *Mad* #1. A man's tongue hangs out as he watches, bug-eyed, as a nubile pseudogirl is dispensed from the machine. Male characters drooling over shapely women became a fixture of the publication, because Kurtzman's sense of humor always had an adolescent streak.

The most providential decision Harvey Kurtzman made when determining the art assignments for *Mad* was giving Will Elder a chance to both pencil and ink. This opportunity for Elder had been a long time coming. He would prove to be the funniest cartoonist of the bunch, and the most influential on the comic book *Mad*. It's almost as if *Mad* was created for Elder, and Elder was born to draw *Mad*.

One day, Kurtzman told Elder that he had just come up with the idea of a comic book called *Mad*. "I think it's up your alley," Elder recalled Kurtzman saying. He told him that he would have a considerable amount of freedom, but "It's got to be funny. And you can do it!" Kurtzman "encouraged me like a football coach," Elder said.[23] Kurtzman made Elder understand that this was a chance for him to realize his potential, because humor was such an integral part of his personality. Elder agreed: "I felt that if I could expose this . . . bottled-up zaniness in me, in some kind of medium, I would really burst forth, you know. Explode. War stories weren't my cup of tea. I did it because it was a living, it was a chance to get into the business and work at it, and develop techniques. But *Mad* gave me a tremendous amount of license."[24] However, he acknowledged that he needed an editor. "I [needed] Harvey's control. He harnessed whatever energies I had into the proper channeling. I felt that all my wild energies had to be harnessed into saying something important, something [that] needed to be said."[25] Even Kurtzman was surprised by Elder's explosion of creativity in *Mad*.

Inking John Severin's pencils was a valuable experience for Will Elder. Now there were no technical deficiencies holding him back. His humor work bursts forth in *Mad* #1 with "Ganefs!" Kurtzman's opening caption sets the tone: "Come away from your fresh paint homes on tree-lined streets! . . . Away from your clean linen, your Grade-A milk! Come to the garbage-canned, broken windowed land of the Underworld! Come to the home of gangsters, gorillas and . . . Ganefs!" ("Ganef" or "gonif" was another Yiddish word, in this case from the Hebrew *gannabh* meaning a thief, scoundrel or rascal.) The story had originally been titled "Goons!"

"Ganefs!" ostensibly tells the story of an extortion attempt by Melvin, a short, rat-faced gangster, and Bumble, his huge, dim-witted assistant. Most of the humor comes from their interactions, as Melvin continually slaps Bumble, vowing, "This time, we're gonna pull this big job without fumbling!" Elder's commitment to the work—the gags, the settings, the action—is apparent in every panel. "They were more or less influenced by the early comedians' [type] of physical humor," Elder later commented. "Buster Keaton . . . Harold Lloyd . . . Charlie Chaplin. You can see that in the little guy who uses violence in his humor. Always slapping the big dumbbell."[26] Although Kurtzman's script is outstanding, it's Elder's artwork and fertile imagination that make it extraordinary.

Elder's background details in the panels aren't yet as elaborate or as attention-getting as they would become, but they are there in incipient form: a mink coat hanging out of a garbage can in an alley, a dartboard with a cop's picture as the bull's-eye, barbed wire protecting Melvin's secret hideout. These details draw the reader deeper into the panels. Kurtzman's script sets up the dynamic between the two characters, but Elder's artwork is so good that one almost feels like it's entirely his conception. "Willy was our number one cartoonist," Kurtzman later maintained. "Willy was not our best artist, but he was our best *Mad* artist."[27] "Ganefs!" bespoke a rare creative chemistry between the two men. It marked the real beginning of their thirty-six-year collaboration.

"Hoohah!," "Blobs!" and especially "Ganefs!" were hard acts to follow. The issue's last story, the Western spoof "Varmint!"—first titled "Owlhoot!"—demonstrates John Severin's knack for humorous cartooning. In the coming years, that sort of work would represent a major portion of his creative output. That it wasn't in the same league as Davis's, Wood's and Elder's only meant that those men were extraordinarily gifted in the field. Kurtzman had particularly liked Severin's "A 'Normal' Day at the Chas-Wm-Harvey Studio!!!" cartoon. "John had a good sense of humor," Kurtzman said. "He was an actor. He could make his figures move and act very precisely. And he was not an unfunny guy. We'd joke, we'd kid around."[28]

In "Varmint!," the gunslinger's catchphrase ("when I makes up muh mind to do somethin', I don't change easy!") is overworked in the story, but Kurtzman's delight in creating exaggerated Western colloquial speech (as in *Pot-Shot Pete*) is contagious. It's a more-than-competent story to end the first issue of *Mad.* All in all, the inaugural issue was amazingly well realized, something highly unusual for a new comic book with no precedent. It happened because it was masterminded by Kurtzman, and because the artists all had experience in working with him. They were already a well-integrated team. *Mad* #1 was produced quickly and instinctively, in an inspired frenzy of pent-up creative energy.

The first reference to *Mad* in an EC comic book occurred in *Haunt of Fear* #14 (July–August 1952), which meant that Gaines had seen enough of a presentation that he had given the green light to the book.[29] In "The Old Witch's Niche," the horror host says, "There's a big secret up at the office! They're working on a new EC baby, a new mag, another addition to the EC line. 'Course, I can't tell you the title, they've got the first cover locked up in a safe! And I can't tell ya what the book's about, they've got the new artists locked up there, too! But at least I've broken the news!" Actual house ads for *Mad* appear in the October–November issues of EC titles such as *Tales from the Crypt* #32, carrying the tagline, "Undoubtedly the zaniest 10¢ worth of idiotic nonsense you could ever hope to buy! Try it . . . just for laughs!"

Bill Gaines loved *Mad* #1 as did everyone at EC. The next house ad shows a cartoon version of Kurtzman holding the first issue, and Bill Gaines nearby, saying, "We at EC proudly present our latest baby . . . a 'comic' comic book! This is undoubtedly the zaniest 10¢ worth of idiotic nonsense you could ever hope to buy! Get a copy of *Mad* . . . on sale now! We think you'll enjoy it!" The first issue, which had an October–November 1952 cover date, hit the overcrowded newsstands the first week in August 1952.[30]

WITH *MAD* #2, Kurtzman began using the same storytelling approach as the first issue in the opening story "Hex!," a tale of a baseball player who comes to believe he is hexed by an old crone in the stands (EC's Old Witch in a supporting role). The rest of the issue shows Kurtzman settling down and thinking a bit more about what he was doing.

> That [storytelling] form didn't intrigue me too much and that's one reason why *Mad* evolved into something different. It's a very easy form to follow because . . . it leans on clichés. An artist is respected more for inventing or creating something of his own, whereas an entertainer can create moods without inventing. For satire you must create.[31]

Kurtzman recalled how he'd gotten laughs in his school days. "I was just trying to capture something I had developed in high school that was very effective," he explained. "[At M&A] I found through trial and error that I had the strongest effect when I said something about the person I was drawing. It came easy and had the maximum effect because it had that little bit of truth."[32] For the purposes of a mass market magazine, this move toward specificity translated into satirizing familiar popular culture icons. "Melvin!," Kurtzman's Tarzan satire in *Mad* #2, was the breakthrough. Instead of a generic jungle movie satire, the Severin-drawn tale "tells the truth" about Edgar Rice Burroughs's iconic character—who happens to be a seminaked man swinging on vines through a jungle. It makes fun of Tarzan's yell ("HOOO HAAA!"), his pseudodomesticity with Jane, his relations with native tribes and so on. In a way, it harkened back to the days when Kurtzman and his buddies satirized Tarzan in the M&A lunchroom. Kurtzman began thinking along similar lines as he worked on the second and third issues of *Mad*. (The book used the same template of the other EC comics. There were four stories, of lengths in the following strict order: eight, seven, six, seven.)[33]

"Gookum!" is another satire of SF stories that benefits immensely from Wallace Wood's deft, highly detailed humor artwork. Kurtzman commented, "'Gookum!' [was] something that was near and dear to the horror and science fiction writers' hearts, the mysterious alien blob that absorbs everything in its path." In the punch ending, the escaping astronaut is served a dessert of Jello—or, as it was called on his home planet, "Dormant Gookum!" Kurtzman liked this story better than "Blobs!" in the first issue.[34]

Despite the breakthrough of "Melvin!" and the charm of "Gookum!," an Elder-drawn story is (again) the highlight of the issue. In 1941, Chester Gould introduced a villain named the Mole in the *Dick Tracy* newspaper strip. "Mole!," based on Elder's idiosyncratic version of that villain, is about a small, mole-faced crook whose shtick is digging tunnels to commit crimes. The Mole could tunnel himself out of any prison with any sort of implement, even—in the end—a nose hair. The protagonist is so demented, and the story construction and execution so splendid, that it ranks as one of the top Kurtzman-Elder collaborations in all of *Mad*. "Harvey gave me a lot of freedom to do whatever I wanted on the *Mad* stuff," Elder recalled, including using an Elder suggestion for a story occasionally (as with "Mole!").[35] "Harvey would give me a basic story and say, 'Take it home and go crazy. Throw everything in. Be really 'Elder.'"[36] As a boy, Kurtzman loved the subgags in *Smokey Stover*, and encouraged Will Elder to elaborate on what Bill Holman was doing. "Willy would take my work and add twenty additional situations into the background," he said. "He was much funnier than I, certainly for that sort of thing. He would carry my stuff forward and enrich it by a multiple of five."[37]

In the third bimonthly issue—the first to hit the stands after Dwight D. Eisenhower was elected president—Kurtzman continued working in a satiric mode. It offers a comedic version of *Dragnet* ("Dragged Net!") with Elder art, apparently based on the radio rather than the TV show. (Elder's version of Detective Joe Friday resembles Sherlock Holmes rather than actor Jack Webb.) The other pop culture target is The Lone Ranger ("Lone Stranger!"), who also had both a radio and TV show. In *Mad* #3, however, it's the generic horror story that is the most distinctive. "V-Vampires!" is best known for its atmospheric splash panel with an attractive young woman walking alone through a London fog, the only sound being her high heels on the sidewalk. ("Klek klek klek klek klek klek klek klek klek.")

Will she be attacked by a vampire? Wallace Wood's talent for drawing sexy women and bratty kids is perfect for the well-conceived, character-driven romp, which is funny and even a little frightening.

Kurtzman said that before the sales figures were available, letters of praise began. The mail was his first indication that *Mad* might be a big success. *Mad* #3 carried "Mad Mumblings," its first letter column, with excerpts from thirty-two such letters, all but five praising the debut issue. M. C. Sinald of Canton, Ohio, wrote, "Please inform how to get one disposable, prefabricated robot woman."

At the column's end, after the five negative comments, Kurtzman wrote, "We hope the critics are wrong! In any case, as long as we have a drop of India ink left in our veins, *Mad* will go marching on!"

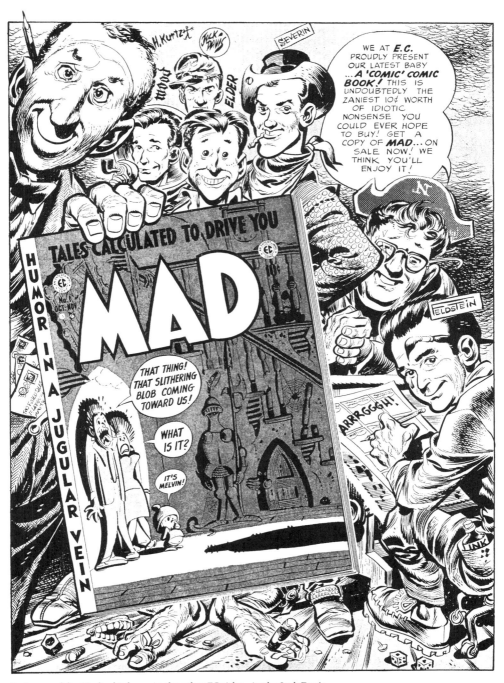

In-house ad for *Mad*, which ran in the other EC titles. Art by Jack Davis.

"Hoohah!" and "Ganefs!" from *Mad* #1. "Melvin!" from *Mad* #2. "V-Vampires!" from *Mad* #3.

Mad began as a comic book in 1952. Art by Harvey Kurtzman.

Kurtzman drew eight of *Mad*'s first ten covers.

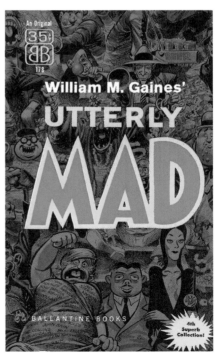

The first four *Mad* paperback books, published from 1954 to 1956, are entirely made up of reprints from the Kurtzman-written *Mad* comic books.

In "Mickey Rodent!" in *Mad* #19 (1954), Will Elder perfectly mimicked the look of the Walt Disney characters. Story by Kurtzman.

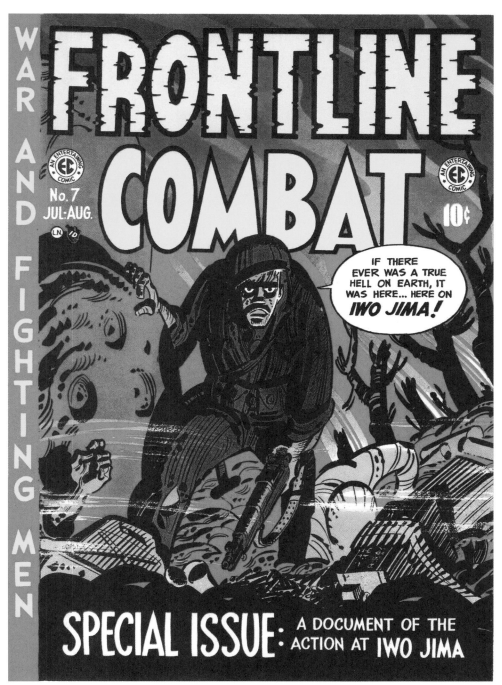

Harvey Kurtzman's *Frontline Combat* #7 (July–August 1952) cover uses bold color and emphatic brushwork to convey the savagery of war.

Hey Look!, Kurtzman's first opportunity to show what he could do in comic books, was a series of one-page fillers that ran in Timely Comics from 1946 to 1949: from *Margie* #43 (October 1948).

R. Crumb (left side of the newspaper) and Gilbert Shelton (right), both fans of Kurtzman, assisted on *Little Annie Fanny*: from the July 1970 *Playboy*.

From the March 29, 1993 *New Yorker*: Will Elder's tribute to Harvey Kurtzman upon his passing. They worked together for nearly forty years. Courtesy of the Will Elder Estate.

13.

FROM GI TO GENERAL

MAD HAD BEEN CONCEIVED as a way for Harvey Kurtzman to make more money by producing a comic book for EC that required no research. But for Kurtzman, *Mad* was the fulfillment of a longtime dream. Once he had the opportunity, he wanted to put everything he had into it. Something had to give. His first move was to stop drawing the covers of *Two-Fisted* and *Frontline*, assigning those to Wallace Wood and Jack Davis. Kurtzman's last covers appeared on the first two "theme issues" of a series that had been brewing for the past year.

Kurtzman's fascination with the Civil War probably began while doing research for "Gettysburg!," his first story about that war. It appeared in *Frontline* #2, drawn by Wood. Next came "Stonewall Jackson!" in *Frontline* #5, handled by Davis. Then Kurtzman encountered the writings of Fletcher Pratt, a science fiction writer and historical scholar specializing in the War Between the States. He was a charter member of the Civil War Round Table of New York, and had written *Ordeal by Fire: an Informal History of the Civil War* (1935) and *The Monitor and the Merrimac* (1951). The idea for *Mad* and for a major series about the Civil War came about the same time.

Kurtzman called on Pratt in his New York apartment and found him to be gnomelike, with a pet marmoset on his shoulder. Kurtzman asked if Pratt would help with research for more Civil War stories. The enthusiasm of Pratt's response may have led to the conception of a grand series on that conflict, just as other stories were inspired by the availability of the research material. He was a "one stop" source. "We were going to do the whole Civil War," Kurtzman recalled. "I would go up to his . . . apartment, and with his help I'd break down the war into stories, plot them out and check them for authenticity. Specifically, I asked him to help me lay out the whole Civil War and break it down into [parts]." It came to seven parts, or twenty-eight stories. "I had the whole Civil War sectioned off and I knew what parts of the [war] I'd treat in each issue, and then we would divide the issue into four parts," he said. "I would write four stories, and then I'd come back to Pratt to authenticate the details—speech and customs."[1]

After one more lone story—"Chickamauga!" in *Frontline* #8—the series was officially launched in *Frontline* #9 (November–December 1952). On the inside front cover, surrounded by an elaborate border of historical drawings, Kurtzman wrote an introduction welcoming the reader to the first of seven issues about the Civil War, a conflict with "all the tragedy and disaster that goes with war."

As with his other war stories, Kurtzman brought the Civil War to life by focusing on an individual or a few people in each story. In "Abe Lincoln!," the story is told through anecdotes—some of them comedic, others recounting formative moments in Lincoln's life—as related by a slave on the eve of war. It culminates with an authentic account of President Lincoln giving his famous inaugural address, which incorporates an incident from Margaret Leech's book *Reveille in Washington*. While listening to the speech, an onlooker falls off a tree branch. Scenes of the soldiers sleeping in doorways in "Bull Run!" in that same issue were also gleaned from Leech's book.

Kurtzman's skillful use of language enhances the period stories in the war books, especially in this series. "I worked at it," he said. "In the Civil War books particularly. How do you pick up language? How do you know how people spoke one hundred years ago? Well, a lot of the litera-

From the story "Abe Lincoln!" in *Frontline Combat* #9 (November–December 1952). Art by Jack Davis.

ture that's passed along gives you clues. The songs of the times give you idiom, the vernacular."[2] The second all-Civil War issue was *Two-Fisted* #31 (January 1953), with its outstanding story "Grant!" by Kurtzman and Severin. Wallace Wood and Jack Davis also did some of their best work on the stories "Blockade!," about the battle between the *Monitor* and the *Merrimac*, and "Donelson!," with more ironclad naval action on the Cumberland River.

Readers from the South wrote letters complaining there were too few stories from the point of view of the Confederate soldiers. Kurtzman responded, "As we mentioned once before, we are trying to take a neutral path between the North and South. We find ourselves in a situation that cannot help but give our books a 'Northern' tinge. For some reason, while the South turned out much colorful story material on the war, the North seems to have documented the actual history of the war a lot more completely."[3] His main sets of reference, universally accepted as the most accurate and authoritative, were *The Picture History of the Civil War* (ten volumes), and *Battles and Leaders* (four volumes), both containing a larger proportion of history from the Northern viewpoint.

The third (and, as it turned out, the last) Civil War issue, in *Two-Fisted* #35 (October 1953), is more Southern focused, beginning with "Robert E. Lee!" set in Fredricksburg, "New Orleans!," "Memphis!" (Reed Crandall's war book debut) and "Chancellorsville!," with the death of Stonewall Jackson. Unfortunately, the Civil War issues didn't prove as popular as those centered on the Korean War and World War II. "It wasn't enough," Kurtzman said. "All the stuff that I put into the Civil War stories— it just wasn't all that popular. They essentially were subtle by comic book standards. A little too quiet. It was like asking a kid to read the *New York Times*."[4]

JUST AS *MAD* TOOK A CHUNK of Kurtzman's time, it was additional work for his cadre of artists. Davis was fast and continued to appear in every issue of the war comics, but Wood was occasionally absent, as was Severin. There were openings for others in *Two-Fisted* and *Frontline*. "We tried people like Gene Colan, Dave Berg, Joe Kubert, even the house people like Johnny Craig [and] Reed Crandall, and they didn't work out," Kurtzman said. "Bernie Krigstein, George Evans, they weren't quite right. God knows what the alchemy was."[5] Instead of using Krigstein in the war comics, Kurtzman recommended him to Gaines for the other titles. "I could see that Harvey's recommendation had great force with Gaines," Krigstein said, "and it was strictly on that basis that I came to EC."[6]

Kurtzman only wanted artists who would work from his script and blueprints, and was loathe to try anyone with what he considered insufficient experience: "The artists that I used were all very good and the stories that I wrote were all very elaborately written and I couldn't bring myself to throw away a story on a guy who was developing, if you know what I mean."[7] Kurtzman would get frustrated when artists weren't on his wavelength. It wasn't uncommon for him to tell even his star artists that their work on a particular job had fallen short, yet he wasn't good at giving clear criticism. He had higher standards than any other editor in the business, and they were standards that he alone fully understood. Kurtzman had his likes and dislikes, which sometimes mystified others. This element of unknowability added to the development of what Gaines and others began to refer to as "the Kurtzman mystique."

One of the new artists was Joe Kubert. He was a Jewish ghetto kid who went to the High School of Music and Art a couple of years after Kurtzman, and had established himself at National with his work on Hawkman in *Flash Comics* and on the Justice Society of America in *All-Star Comics*. After his first meeting with Kurtzman, he emerged with the already laid out and prelettered pages for a story called "Tide!" for *Two-Fisted Tales* #32 (March–April 1953). He did two more stories for EC, then became busy at St. John Publishing and did no more.

Kurtzman was reasonably satisfied with Kubert's work. He felt it was competent, but left something to be desired in the area of absolute authenticity: "Kubert was almost good. I mean, Kubert in his own right was terrific, but he tended to work too fast. Kubert is a speed artist and there is a conflict between speed and doing something that's authentic and true, because you can't do both at the same time. Kubert tended to go in that direction."[8] Kubert later said, "Harvey's books looked beautiful. He was getting the best color, best reproduction, and that's why I went up there. Harvey was always the sweetest guy in the world, except my stuff never really worked for him. I found it really difficult to work with [him] because I felt so goddamn inhibited and lacked the freedom I had had up to that time. Harvey didn't seem too excited about giving me additional work."[9] He was right.

Cuban-born Ric Estrada also drew EC war stories. In the winter of 1947, Estrada left Havana, Cuba, and moved to New York City to break into comics. He rented cheap studio space at the Bible House in Greenwich Village, where he met Dan Barry, Mort Meskin, Alex Toth, Frank Frazetta and others. Eventually, he assisted Dan Barry on the *Flash Gordon* daily strip. Through Barry, Estrada met Kurtzman, who subsequently gave him two scripts: "Bunker!" (*Two-Fisted Tales* #30) and "Rough Riders!" (*Frontline Combat* #11). "Bunker!," a tale of two platoons—one of white soldiers, the other black—taking the same hill, is the EC war story in which African American soldiers in the US Army figure most prominently. "[Estrada] had a Cuban background," Kurtzman said, "so he was very excited about doing ['Rough Riders!'])," a story about Teddy Roosevelt leading the charge up San Juan Hill in 1898. Kurtzman was unimpressed. "At the time Ric wasn't as good as I would have liked him to have been and so we didn't use him again."[10]

Another artist whom Kurtzman tried out was Gene Colan. He was a former Timely staff artist who had become friends with John Severin. Severin gave Colan pointers, and recommended reference material that helped the younger artist make sure the weaponry in his strips was accurate. Colan began a campaign to break into the highly respected EC war comics. He told John Benson in April 1999: "I nagged him so much to work for him, because I felt I could do it. I nagged the life out of him, and he finally gave me a chance to work. And it was this war story about Wake Island. I knew I had to produce in order to work for him, so I killed myself, I really killed myself on it."[11] Colan invited Kurtzman to his home for dinner, and to hear Kurtzman's assessment of the work.

"I lived in Bronxville, and he was going to come up to my house and give me the lowdown as to whether I'll be working for him or not, based on how that story turned out. After dinner . . . he said he didn't like it. And I just didn't feel that his opinion was justified. I was hurt by it."[12] Some EC readers and fans feel that "Wake!," which saw print in *Two-Fisted Tales* #30, was one of the great stories in the whole run of the war titles. Colan continued doing above-average artwork in the Atlas war books, but when later asked, Kurtzman said,

Gene Colan art from "Wake!"

"I tried Gene Colan for something, but he was very young and very inexperienced."[13] Kurtzman may have felt Colan had overworked the art in "Wake!" Although Kurtzman himself started at EC with the busy "House of Horrors!," by this time he was a firm believer in the virtue of simplicity. Kurtzman was so used to rebuffing artists that he seems not to have realized how graceless it was to reject Colan's work while accepting his hospitality.

George Evans also had difficulty with Kurtzman's editorial methods. Evans got his start in comics after the war as a staff artist at Fiction House, and then did a great deal of work for Fawcett before coming to EC. He drew some of the most celebrated horror stories, but his real love was aviation stories, especially those set in World War I. However, Evans didn't care for working from Kurtzman's layouts. "He had put all this time and effort and so on into his meticulous layouts, and we would go over them and he would explain what he had in mind," Evans recalled.[14] "You were allowed to do it in your own style, but he did not want one facet of his pictures changed. So what did the artist contribute, then? You were really just a hand for Harvey's mind. You were . . . nothing more than a renderer and not a thinker. And that I didn't like."[15] Sometimes, Evans departed ever so slightly from Kurtzman's layouts. "I drew it the way Harvey wanted . . . for the most part. But every now and again Harvey looked distressed."[16]

Bill Gaines said, "Harvey, like a conductor of an orchestra, made a pencil sketch, pretty tight pencil sketch, of every single panel of every single story, and God help the artist who tried to change it! What would happen is, Harvey was very timid, and he didn't really like to fight with people. And so with Evans more than anybody—I think Evans deliberately did these things—he made a change that he knew would drive Harvey crazy, he knew that Harvey would not have the nerve to say anything about it, and so it would go through, and then after it was over, Harvey would say, 'You ruined my story.'"[17] Evidence suggests Gaines was wrong when he stated that Kurtzman's layouts on the vellum were "pretty tight." Alex Toth once referred to the "very rough stick figures" on the overlays.[18] A rare surviving example of vellum overlays from the story "Lost Battalion!" (in *Two-Fisted Tales* #32) reveals Kurtzman's guiding layouts were loose, with only the placement of figures in the panels and rough facial expressions indicated.[19] (It's possible the specificity of his layouts varied.)

Evans remained equivocal in his estimation of Kurtzman. On one hand, he respected Kurtzman's talent. "In listening to him explain what he was doing, it was an education in how to lay out this sort of stuff, to tell a story, what the key points are," he said in an interview with John Garcia in 1979.[20] On the other hand, he felt Kurtzman's war stories (in this case, the Civil War story "Choose Sides!" from *Frontline Combat* #9) were too relentlessly downbeat, too often without any characters to admire. Evans, who was from the small Pennsylvania town of Harwood, attributed it to Kurtzman's New York background.

> Harvey had that downbeat, savage kind of approach. One story that I did not like at all, that he had Wally Wood do, had a totally downbeat ending about bad people, rotten doings, and no uplifting thing in the end. It was downbeat from panel one to the final panel. I came from out of central Pennsylvania, with people much more naive than city people. Harvey had a city boy's point of view on many of these things. And this is fine for cynical old people, but for young people reading this stuff I felt that, in its way, [it] might be more objectionable than the tongue and cheek horror stuff.[21]

Though Kurtzman later said of Evans, "He takes criticism very badly," he appreciated the artist for the authenticity of his airplane drawings.[22] Their differences didn't prevent Evans from later saying, at a 1972 panel discussion, "We got on pretty well."[23]

John Severin wasn't always happy with Elder's inks on his pencils, and now he had the chance to show what he could do on his own (working from Kurtzman layouts, as always). When Severin inked in pen, Kurtzman was satisfied, but he didn't like Severin's brushwork: "What was nice about his stuff was his honest pen line. It wasn't imitative of anything; it was just pure John Severin. And in its honesty and purity, it was just good cartooning. He lost that."[24] Kurtzman's relationship with Severin began deteriorating in 1953. Severin found it more difficult to produce work that satisfied Kurtzman, especially when he both pencilled and inked.

Another artist whom Harvey Kurtzman ultimately came into conflict with was Alex Toth. Kurtzman had been pleased with Toth's very complete pencils on "Dying City!," and the artwork on "Thunderjet!," but there had been a problem on the latter story. "I had a fight with Toth," Kurtzman later remembered. "Toth threw patriotism into it. I don't think he changed the words. I think what he did was, he shot all the bad guys down, and it wasn't supposed to happen that way."[25] They would only work together one more time. The story appeared toward the end of the war comics' run.

"F-86 Sabre Jet!" is another dramatization of Air Force action over Korea, a sort of sequel to "Thunderjet!" It deals with America's answer to the enemy's MiG-15 fighters in the closing panels of the earlier story. This time, the problem is the artwork. Kurtzman said, "The trick with

Toth was to keep him away from that runamuck shadow technique of his, which he swore up and down was God's gift to art. Essentially, he'd blank out large areas of drawing with black shadow. He would carry this to outrageous lengths, protesting all the time that what he was doing was art."[26] That technique had been present in "Thunderjet!," putting whole shapes in the panels into all-black shadow rather than providing outlines for the colorist to fill in, but it was fairly minimal and worked well. In "F-86 Sabre Jet!," Toth relies much more heavily on this technique. It's most pronounced on p. 6, when a pilot's head is totally blacked out in five of the six panels where it's shown. Kurtzman recalled, "It was so bad that I had to come in and break the shadow into detail myself [in certain panels]."[27] This was the last time Toth worked for Kurtzman, though Toth spoke respectfully of him when interviewed in later years.

Kurtzman briefly considered using artist Al Williamson. Williamson was a star artist in *Weird Science* and *Weird Fantasy*, drawing the kind of science fiction stories that were his personal preference. Williamson's favorite artists at EC, though he liked them all, were Kurtzman, Wood and Craig. One day, Williamson delivered his latest art job to Gaines, which the publisher liked. Hearing this, Kurtzman picked up the pages, took them into his office and closed the door. Marie Severin, who shared the office, came out and whispered to Williamson, "I think Harvey's going to give you a strip." Eventually Kurtzman emerged from his office, handed the six pages back to Gaines, and returned to his office without saying a word. He never used Williamson.

SINCE HARVEY KURTZMAN wasn't a pacifist, were his war comics truly antiwar? In his first war story back in *Two-Fisted* #19, an American sergeant says, "We kill men not because we wanna, but because we gotta! It's a dirty job we have to do, but it doesn't mean we have to enjoy doing it!" The combat stories most prevalent in the war comics' first year, written from the point of view of foot soldiers in the war zone, showed the costs exacted by war in terms of human pain, trauma and death, not just on the American side but also the side of the enemy. This was antiwar enough to be investigated for sedition by the FBI and the US Department of Justice. War militants have traditionally avoided considering the effects of war on the individual, some would say because it could deter their rush to war. In this regard, one can consider *Two-Fisted Tales* and *Frontline Combat* legitimately antiwar, at least for their first year to eighteen months.

Then something changed. Kurtzman was increasingly interested in military operations, evident in *Two-Fisted Tales* #26 ("A Document of the

Action at the Changjin Reservoir"). The issue was based on recent events in the Korean War where the UN troops had been surprised by an influx of Chinese troops, and had to make a tactical retreat and escape by sea, as recounted through the four stories. The interlocking tales have incidents on the ground, but are really about military strategy. It was a turning point in terms of the types of stories Kurtzman would tell. John Benson wrote, "It gradually became apparent that Kurtzman was no longer content merely to tell combat incidents. His research, probably entered into at first to ensure authenticity of minor details, had begun to exert its own fascination. The issues that came after [*Two-Fisted Tales* #26] are recognizably different in outlook from those that came before. The viewpoint was no longer that of the GI but of the general."[28]

Kurtzman considered the strategy-and-equipment stories truthful in their own way, but there's no denying they are less emotional and more didactic than his earlier efforts. He admitted, "After a while you'd be desperate for a plot and you'd cast about for just a plot. Sometimes you came upon a little bit of thinking that didn't necessarily say that war was hell."[29] His penchant for producing educational comics came to the fore. Working with the military when gathering research contributed to the shift, which reached its apogee in *Frontline Combat* #12 (May–June 1953), the "Air Force Issue." It opens: "Our Air Force is doing a fine job all over the world! We owe them a debt of gratitude!" One of its four stories, "B-26 Invader!," is about a "routine" bombing run undertaken with an "all in a day's work" attitude. Nevertheless, the quality of the writing, art and coloring remains high, and the new stories are engrossing in their own way.

Kurtzman sent his editorial assistant Jerry De Fuccio on missions to gather material and get firsthand experience to bolster later stories. De Fuccio, on one memorable sojourn:

> I was sent up to New London, Connecticut, to ride on the submarine. The officer of the day on the training submarine said we were going to go forty miles out on Long Island Sound and we're going to submerge. I told him my editor never mentioned that to me and that I was to come up and listen to the AAAAOOOGA, AAAAOOOGA,and all the bells and claxons. I had no idea I was going to make a dive. The officer had me sign a release and I'm signing my life away. It turned out to be a great experience. When we were under water it was so placid. It was wonderful.[30]

Kurtzman reportedly said, "I know you have a lot of books on the subject so don't lie about going up there. I already made an appointment with the officer of the day." He told De Fuccio to call him from New London when he was finished. Instead, De Fuccio sent him a telegram that read, "Many brave hearts are asleep in the deep, glub, glub."[31] Kurtzman allowed De Fuccio to work from his layouts to write the captions and dialogue for the resulting story, "Silent Service," which was drawn by Jack Davis.

To research "Albatross!" (*Frontline* #14), Kurtzman made arrangements with the US Air Force to fly in one of Grumman's amphibious rescue planes known as a "dumbo." When he arrived at the airfield, a parachute was strapped on his back. "We took off in a sea plane. It was very thrilling. And I kept saying, 'Why the parachute?' We were well over the water by that time, and they said, 'Well, this actually isn't an ordinary flight. We're test-flying the plane, because every time we sell an airplane we have to test it out. So we put a parachute on you in case things happen.' They shut off one engine. Then they shut off the second engine. And like that."[32]

One of the reasons why there were so many airplane stories in the war comics as time went on, especially in *Frontline*, was because Kurtzman was fascinated with aviation and its trappings. "I love airports, airplanes, flying," he told an interviewer in 1982. "It has a magic for me that I can't really understand. I used to go to the airport . . . just for the fun of being at an airport. Airports, for me, are the frontiers. There are so many mechanical firsts at an airport . . . that it became an exciting place just because of the newness of invention, and of what human beings are doing. It's like the Wild West before it was tamed, at least that's the emotion I feel. I always wanted to be a pilot, secretly."[33]

Kurtzman's last World War II story was both the most horrific and the most hopeful of all. For "Atom Bomb!" in *Two-Fisted* #33 (May–June 1953), Kurtzman and Wood teamed up to show the effect of the atomic bomb explosion on the people of Nagasaki, Japan. Again, Kurtzman's focus is on the humanity of the "enemy" as they go about their daily lives, particularly one family in which a grandmother pines for her son in the military while she cares for his three children. The three-page sequence of the bomb's detonation doesn't pull back for the obvious shot of a mushroom cloud. Instead, the explosion is depicted three times for three characters: the flash (a black and white panel), the impact (overlaid with waves of color) and the heat (an all-red panel). One of the children is killed in a blazing building, another by radiation poisoning. But the third, then an infant in the grandmother's arms, lives—and is shown happily running off to school a few years later. The final caption reads, "On August 9, 1945, the A-bomb killed 29,793 people and destroyed 18,409 homes! But *hope* was not destroyed in Nagasaki! And life nurtured by *hope* blooms again! Plants, buildings, children grow in Nagasaki, for there is hope in Nagasaki! There is *hope* in the whole world!" This is Kurtzman and Wood at their best, another of the true classic stories of any kind from EC.[34]

With the end of the Korean War on July 27, 1953, sales began dropping on the EC war comics. Gaines had watched them soften from 70 percent of 350,000—eventually he described them as "slipping badly"—and this finally brought about their demise. *Frontline Combat* was dropped after issue #15 (January 1954).

It's worth noting that National and Atlas, two other major producers of war comics in 1953, continued to publish them all through the 1950s, though there was a period toward the end of the war when Atlas drastically cut back the number of such titles. But Atlas was back to eight different war titles with February 1955 cover dates, a year after EC dropped the genre. It seems clear that the educational direction of Kurtzman's books doomed them. Sequential art could still have successful applications in the educational arena, but was a hard sell in comic books. (By late 1953, Kurtzman was concentrating on *Mad*, a more financially profitable enterprise.)

Kurtzman began delivering his scripts to the artists late. John Severin recalled, "Harvey used to take a lot of time writing the stories. He just couldn't make the deadlines getting scripts to the guys. Everybody was having trouble getting in scripts, and Bill [Gaines] was giving him a hard time."[35] Kurtzman had been pulling out of *Frontline* since #13 when he brought in other writers. An announcement appeared in *Two-Fisted* #35 (October) that the book was going to a quarterly schedule. What it didn't say is that much of the editorial work on the *New Two-Fisted Tales* would be done by Severin. "[Kurtzman] asked me if I would handle *Two-Fisted Tales*," he said. "I didn't know whether I should do it or not. Then I decided, what the hell, maybe I could have some fun with it. I liked all kinds of adventure stories. We changed the format slightly. It looked all right. Some of the covers were fairly good." Severin recruited his friend Colin Dawkins to write the stories.[36]

Despite John Severin' editorial work on the *New Two-Fisted Tales*, the stories continued to pass through Harvey Kurtzman's hands. Kurtzman remained the sole editor of record, and wrote the full-page announcement ("In Memoriam") that appeared on p. 1 of #41, the last issue. On that page, he said, in part, "as many of you have probably noticed, our efforts to sustain what we felt was a quality magazine have floundered and finally collapsed under the pressure of having to compete with the more 'stimu-lating' type of comic book."

In all, Kurtzman edited thirty-three issues of *Two-Fisted Tales* and *Frontline Combat* (combined), not counting the six *New Two-Fisted Tales*. Out of a total of 132 stories, Kurtzman wrote 115. That meant that he wrote over 800 pages in the two titles over three years. He did the finished art-work on eleven stories, eight of them war stories. Kurtzman also did twen-ty-two of the thirty-three covers. Of the war stories, forty-four were set in the Korean War (36 percent), twenty-four in World War II, ten in World War I and eighteen in the Civil War. The Korean stories were mainly pub-lished from mid-1951 to mid-1952, although only six issues had no Korean War story at all.

Editing and writing these high quality war stories, so many of them innovative both in their stories and their art, was an achievement that Kurtzman himself sometimes tended to gloss over in later interviews looking back on his career. But when asked about them specifically in 1965, he made it clear he felt good about what he had been able to achieve.

> I'm very proud of the stuff I did, and I'm happy I did it, and I wouldn't have done it any other way. And with the war books, with *Two-Fisted Tales* and *Frontline Combat*, I really sent out a lot of information, I really did, and I get a lot of satisfaction out of that, that when I was telling my stories the kids were getting the gospel.[37]

Yet, with Harvey Kurtzman, there was always ambivalence. On an-other occasion, he said, "When [those war comics] were good, they were good. But I was reading them the other day, and I got sick. I was saying, 'Oh, God, how could I be so corny?'"[38] While probably referring to the occasions where the stories speak of the sanctity of human life, which can sound "preachy," his ambivalence was to be a kind of curse. It kept Kurtzman striving to improve, which led him to create work that was the best in the field. It also made it harder for him to bask in the satisfaction of a job well done.

Finished Johnny Craig art on "The Lost Battalion" in *Two-Fisted Tales* #32 is based on Harvey Kurtzman's rough layouts. Kurtzman determined the panel arrangement and placement of characters within them. The rest was up to Craig, or the other artists who worked with Kurtzman at EC. Layout drawing is © the Harvey Kurtzman Estate.

Two-Fisted Tales #33 (May–June 1953). Story by Kurtzman, art by Wood.

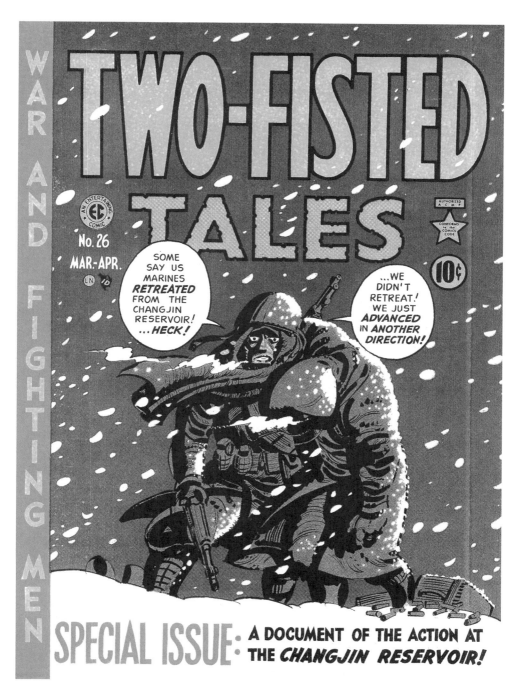

After *Two-Fisted Tales* #26 (March–April 1952), with all four stories documenting the retreat of the United Nations forces from the Changjin Reservoir, the tenor of Kurtzman's war comics changed.

14.

MAD TAKES OFF

BILL GAINES HAD SENT a print order of 400,000 copies of *Mad* #1 to Clement Company, EC's printer in Buffalo, New York. While Harvey Kurtzman was dividing his time between the war comics and finishing up *Mad* #3, the staff at Leader News was busily compiling data to determine how many of copies of those issues actually sold.

Gaines, who later described himself as "a born pessimist," feared *Mad* would flop.[1] Kurtzman was, by nature, more optimistic. His instincts told him *Mad* had struck a nerve. "Something was in the air with the first issues," he later recalled. "We got an avalanche of mail. When the mail started coming in, I knew that we had something hot."[2]

When the reports arrived, Gaines's fears were confirmed. Although details haven't survived, *Mad* #1 lost money, which meant it couldn't have sold much more than half of its print run, or even less. Kurtzman was understandably glum when he heard the news. From Gaines's point of view, losses from *Mad* not only meant lost capital, but the potential failure of the plan to bolster Kurtzman's income. The publisher was willing to give *Mad* a chance to build a readership, but for how long if it continued to lose money? Kurtzman would live with uncertainty for the next year. As it turned out, sales numbers for *Mad* #2 (already on the stands) and #3 were also disappointing.

In the course of those first three issues, *Mad* found itself. Satirizing comic book characters such as Tarzan and The Lone Ranger was a natural step. Kurtzman said, "We made fun of the business we were in—comic books. No one had thought to do that before, and I think the time was right for it."[3] For *Mad* #4, Kurtzman set his sights on the most popular comic book hero of all.[4]

The splash panel of "Superduperman!"—the first thing the reader sees when opening the book—is a highly detailed splash page depicting the muscle-bound, grinning hero as he punches an old man in the stomach.

Mad #4 (April–May 1953).

Kurtzman has busted Clark Kent from star reporter to pathetic spittoon wrangler, who admires the pulchritudinous Lois Pain from afar. On p. 3, Lois disdainfully responds to his interest, sneering, "Whataya want, you incredibly wretched ol' creep?"

Most of the tale centers on a battle between Superduperman and his doppelganger, Captain Marbles. Billy Spafon, boy reporter, says his magic word "Shazoom!" and transforms into a crimson-clad bruiser. When Superduperman wonders aloud, "Vas ist das Shazoom?" Readers find out the letters of the magic word stand for, "Strength, Health, Aptitude, Zeal, Ox, power of, Ox, power of another, and Money."

Eventually, Superduperman tricks Marbles into punching himself in the head, exalting "Captain Marbles has been destroyed by the only force as strong as he . . . HE!" Despite his victory, Lois fends off Superduperman's advances in the final page: "So you're Superduperman instead of Clark Bent! . . . Big deal! Yer still a creep!" Thus ends what turned out to be the first great comic book parody in *Mad*.

Superduperman strikes out with Lois Pain: art by Wallace Wood.

The initial, tiny thumbnail layouts of the pages of "Superduperman!" still exist, revealing that Wood's finished art follows them in almost every panel. Regrettably, none of Kurtzman's second-stage, full-sized layouts for *Mad* have survived (except for a couple of panels of a later story). But it's obvious that Kurtzman knew what he wanted from the start, and Wood's art never looked as supple and dynamic as when he was working over Kurtzman's lively underpinnings.

With the Superman satire, Harvey Kurtzman finally had a firm grip on the kind of story that was right for *Mad*. One didn't need to know about the National vs. Fawcett lawsuit to get a kick out of the two comic book rivals going head-to-head. "Superduperman!" is the archetypical *Mad* story. Kurtzman zeroed in on what everyone knew about the character simply from being exposed to American pop culture. He was writing for the widest possible audience, not for the readers of Superman comic books. His

Superman satire followed the narrative structure of the Max Fleischer Studios animated cartoons of the 1940s, which were seen by millions in movie theaters, adults and children alike. It parodied a popular character, and it was Kurtzman's funniest yet. Everyone, it seems, was laughing—except the owners of National, who threatened to sue EC over it.

When Bill Gaines received a letter from Dave Alterbaum, his attorney, he was startled to discover that Alterbaum was writing on behalf of his other client, National Comics. The letter informed the EC publisher that satirizing Superman or other National characters constituted copyright infringement. "That's really all there was to it," Gaines recounted, "a letter from a lawyer, but it evolved into an interesting story."[5] Initially, Gaines believed Alterbaum. He immediately wrote a letter of contrition, promising not to do that sort of thing again. Kurtzman was incensed. Finally *Mad* was creatively on course, and Gaines was telling him he couldn't make fun of copyrighted characters. He felt the magazine would be unnecessarily hamstrung, and began researching the subject.

Kurtzman found a book by a lawyer who said satire of the "Superduperman!" sort was legal. When Gaines and Kurtzman met with that attorney/author (name unknown), the man insisted on addressing the matter in written form. After paying him $500, Gaines and Kurtzman were shocked to discover that the lawyer had reversed his position. Then Bill Gaines's recent acquaintance Lyle Stuart—publisher of *Exposé*, a monthly muckraking tabloid—introduced them to his lawyer, Martin Scheiman. Scheiman listened to the story, and, according to Gaines, said, "I don't think there's any law on this. I don't think anybody knows whether you can do it or not do it, but I would tell them to go to hell." Based on Scheiman's opinion, Gaines told Kurtzman he could go ahead with such parodies.[6] (Eventually, case law would establish that satire wasn't a violation of copyright unless it could reasonably be mistaken for the original.)

Not only is "Superduperman!" one of the best-known and most highly regarded stories in the comic book *Mad*, but it's often given credit for propelling *Mad* into profitability. Gaines recalled, "The first three issues [of *Mad*] lost money, but then the fourth made it, and from then on it just took off."[7] On another occasion, he stated, "*Mad* was a loser until 'Superduperman' came out."[8]

Of the three other stories in *Mad* #4, two more satirized popular characters: "Robin Hood!" (art by Severin) and "Shadow!" (art by Elder). The latter was another inspired Kurtzman-Elder effort. Kurtzman gives the character the full name "Shadowskeedeeboomboom." He later said, "There was a comedian who did a record that went something like 'Bim-bede-bim-bim,

boom-bede-boom-boom, bim-bede-boom-bede-haskede-boom-boom.' I
don't remember who he was. It might have been a guy by the name of
Aaron Lebedeff, who did some unusual Yiddish records. I remember he
did a 'Roumania' record. And 'Haskede-boom-boom' sounds like I picked
it up off his record. It had a nice sound, a nice lilt. I did that often. I would
pick something up, I didn't know why, it just sounded or looked good."[9]
Most of the action involves Margo, the Shadow's girlfriend, the first of
Elder's nubile, surprisingly sexy women.

While Will Elder had begun throwing in a lot of verbal and visual
background jokes in "Dragged Net!," he pulled out the stops this time.
The panels are crammed with funny signs. The restaurant "Cafeteria
Bacteria" is labeled, "The only restaurant where you can eat dirt cheap!,"
"Our eggs can't be beat!" and "Don't laugh at our coffee. You too may grow
old and weak someday." Kurtzman came to call these subgags "chotchkes"
or "eyeball kicks," but Elder's term for them has stuck. He called them
"chicken fat," explaining, "Chicken fat is the part of the soup that is bad
for you, yet gives the soup its delicious flavor."[10] At least ten subgags appear in the splash panel alone, although the way the panel is designed and
colored, they don't distract from the main action. Kurtzman loved Elder's
additions. "He never said a word, because he figured whatever I did would
only enhance the humor of what he did," Elder recalled.[11] From this point
on, the "chicken fat" was a popular feature of Elder's stories.

By its fourth issue, *Mad* had well and truly become a satirical comic
book. Kurtzman later gave his definition of satire.

Satire is a form of criticism. Suppression of satire establishes a status
quo, while its encouragement fosters change. The gadflies are vital to
an improving life. It goes without saying that criticism isn't necessarily
right, and those who are criticized aren't necessarily happy. That's why
satire always provokes resentment and controversy. But a world without
criticism would be a world without improvement.[12]

It wasn't that he was on a crusade for change, or felt the objects of
satire needed to be momentous or especially meaningful. Later, he would
aim at some weightier targets in *Mad*.

ALTHOUGH *MAD* #4, with "Superduperman!," would be pivotal in igniting
the popularity of *Mad*, sales reports for that issue were months away as
it was being prepared around Christmastime. Then, while working on
Two-Fisted #34, Kurtzman's exhaustion turned into real illness. He expe-

rienced flu-like symptoms, including headaches, nausea, muscle and joint aches and malaise. His skin took on a yellow cast. He was diagnosed with acute (short term) hepatitis. "The doctors said they thought he might have gotten it from eating bad clams," Adele said. "They really didn't know."[13] Stress was a contributing factor, if not the actual cause. Hepatitis is a serious matter. Doctors couldn't do much except conduct tests to monitor liver function. Drugs could help with the itching that accompanied jaundice. Otherwise, Kurtzman was put on a low-fat diet, told to drink lots of water and no alcohol, and wait for the condition to subside. It usually does, though it can take two or three months, depending on underlying factors. He checked into Mount Vernon Hospital for what turned out to be an extended stay. In the letter column in *Two-Fisted Tales* #34, Gaines wrote, "A few words about the unique and unprecedented circumstances surrounding the production of this issue! Harvey Kurtzman . . . *Two-Fisted's* brilliant writer-artist-editor, who generally masterminds the mag from cover to cover . . . suddenly developed a serious case of yellow jaundice and was quickly retired to a hospital bed! Harvey managed to write the Guynemer story for Evans while the nurse wasn't looking . . . ." Jack Davis, Wallace Wood and Jerry De Fuccio wrote the other scripts in that issue.

Meanwhile, with Kurtzman sidelined, Gaines and Feldstein conceived an item for *Mad* #5 that went horribly wrong. Not only did it threaten the future of Kurtzman's brainchild, it briefly looked as if it might bring down all of EC. "Kurtzman was sick with jaundice, and Feldstein and I and everybody was trying to help him get *Mad* #5 out," Gaines recalled. "We wrote a lampoon tongue-in-cheek biography of me. We'd done legitimate biographies of everybody else, so we did this thing, and this was supposed to be funny."[14] When the wholesalers got a look at it, they were outraged.

Gaines felt that the negative reaction was mainly due to a line in the piece suggesting that he got his start by selling pornographic magazines. This was an allusion to early softcore porn published by Harry Donenfeld, who went on to own National. "These wholesalers, who I didn't think would catch on, got it, and they were angry because they were very friendly with this publisher. That *started* the problem."[15] This may be true, but the reference to Donenfeld was obscure, merely stating that Gaines "began selling 'cartoon books' (you know the kind) on dark street corners outside burlesque houses." More likely, wholesalers objected to other elements in the piece.

It begins, "William M. (for 'Mad') Gaines, twisted publisher of the perverted EC line, was born on Feb. 30, 1922, in an abandoned cattle-car on a siding outside the Chicago stock-yards. His father was an International

Communist Banker." It went on to say, "He turned to peddling dope near nursery schools . . . and finally, seeking the ultimate in depravity and debasement, quite naturally turned to the comic magazine industry. Here he found a home!" Wholesalers took this as an insult to the industry. The piece then reports Gaines's insistence that all his stories include sadism, masochism, pyromania, fetishes, necrophilia and phallic symbols. This sort of talk, even in a parody, was beyond the pale for an American comic book in 1953. "We thought it would be a funny lark to surprise Harvey with this biography of me," Gaines recalled. "Of course, with characteristic bad taste, we offended Harvey, and also offended . . . a lot of the wholesalers." Indeed, when he saw the page, Kurtzman was livid. "I wanted to kill," he remembered, adding with mock seriousness, "They were trying to drive me over the edge."[16] (He could laugh about it later.)

The Gaines pseudo-biography, which appeared on the inside of the front cover of *Mad* #5, wasn't the only thing in the issue that caused the furor among wholesalers, as Gaines explained.

> The second problem was that face to face with this was the first page of "Outer Sanctum," and you know crazy Bill Elder who put all this junk in his stuff back in those days, and he had something like "Fat Errand Boy Wanted." Of course as any horror person would know, what would a ghoul want a fat errand boy for? It would be to *eat* him! But not these wholesalers, they had something much worse in mind. They had sexual perversion in mind, and they accused us of putting this thing in there, meaning that they wanted a fat errand boy to screw or whatever you do with fat errand boys. And it almost put us out of business. It was another one of these insane things where the combination of that biography and p. 1 of "Outer Sanctum" was more than these old-style wholesalers could absorb.[17]

This crisis occurred in early April, when *Mad* #5 was moving through the wholesaler pipelines to newsstands. By then, Kurtzman was out of the hospital and improving. (He worked from his bed at home after his hospital release, with De Fuccio delivering research material to his home. Kurtzman's complete recovery took months.) Bill Gaines's distributor rousted him from bed on a weekend morning. The call, possibly from Mike Estrow, president of Leader News, told Gaines about the criticisms leveled at EC over *Mad* #5 at the meeting of the Bureau of Independent Publishers and Distributors (BIPAD), which just happened to be in progress in Manhattan. Something, he told Gaines, had to be done right away in order to avoid a wholesalers' boycott of *Mad* and the entire EC line.

Gaines immediately corralled Kurtzman, Feldstein and others for an emergency meeting to devise a course of action. Within hours, eight copies of an elaborate apology with various attachments were prepared. It had a color cover by Kurtzman with the EC staff—Gaines front and center— with their heads bowed, begging forgiveness. The apology package was rushed to each of the eight members of the powerful BIPAD Committee 29, who were considering the matter.

Titled a "humble apology and explanation" for "the representatives of *the most important link in the chain between our readers and ourselves— namely, Committee 29, of BIPAD,*" it begins, "Our purpose in presenting this brochure . . . is to state genuinely and sincerely, via its pages, that we now realize we have been wrong . . . but that we have been wrong NOT in our MOTIVES, but in our METHODS!" They explained that the "biography" was meant to be funny, that it "was intended, by the obviously unfavorable and absurd picture it painted of Mr. Gaines, to demonstrate that the comic magazine publisher is NOT any of the things mentioned therein, and that the comic magazine publisher does NOT conduct his business in any of the ways suggested therein. But we missed the boat. We stand with heads bowed and hats in hand. We are sorry."[18] This is followed by a sober biography of Gaines, a listing of numerous examples of highly moral and educational EC stories (such as the Kurtzman war comics), and a promise "that there will be no future errors in judgement [*sic*], and that our magazines . . . insofar as the inherent subject-matter permits . . . will contain only such material as is considered within the bounds of good taste!" It ends with attachments such as "a sampling of the reader reaction to the EC line . . . from your geographical area, wherever possible."[19] No reference is made to the "fat errand boy" phrase in "Outer Sanctum!" EC's apology did the trick. The committee members were mollified, and the flow of EC comics continued unabated. However, this flap wasn't easily forgotten, and contributed to mounting resentment toward Gaines and his horror comics.[20]

From a creative standpoint, *Mad* #5 is another outstanding issue, all the more remarkable for being generated when Kurtzman was ill. Kurtzman and Elder's spoof of the "Inner Sanctum" radio show ("Outer Sanctum!") is among their most memorable, and Kurtzman and Wood's satire of the Blackhawks (then being published by Quality Comics) has possibly the most assured, well-conceived story construction among the comic book satires, and is one of the funniest. Their enemy in the story is another of Wood's typical ultra-sexy vamps, this time clad in a form-fitting red satin outfit that left little to the imagination.

Just weeks after the wholesaler dustup, about the time Kurtzman was starting work on *Mad* #7 (May), Gaines told Kurtzman that sales of *Mad* #4 had jumped. The book was now profitable! Kurtzman had established a creative and financial beachhead apart from the war comics. *Mad* was on its way.

The book was Kurtzman's baby, but *Mad* could never have made it without Gaines's backing. Most publishers would have read the sales reports on the first issue, or perhaps the second issue, and canceled the book. Not Gaines. He used the profits of the horror comics to subsidize *Mad* for a full year before it was known that sales had picked up. Not only did he go out on a limb to let Kurtzman create an unusual comic book, he supported it beyond what any other publisher would have done. Such was Gaines's commitment to the plan devised to help Kurtzman make more money. In a certain respect, Kurtzman was now indebted to Gaines.

However, Bill Gaines's notion that a humor book would be easy and quick for Harvey Kurtzman to produce was unrealistic. Kurtzman hadn't disabused Gaines of this notion partly because, in a way, humor work was easier because he had a special gift for it. But quick? The *Hey Look!* pages had required a great deal of effort, often taking more than a day to write a single page. As he said, "It took so long for me to do each of those *Hey Look!* pages that the pay was never enough. That's the problem with working so slowly."[21] *Mad* didn't involve research, but in terms of the thinking, the writing and laying out the pages—the only way Kurtzman could work—*Mad* stories took nearly as much time as the war stories.

KURTZMAN'S *MAD* SATIRES were constructed differently than the war tales. They were made up of short sequences, several panels (or more) in length. Each built to a moment of tension, reached a climax and "the balloon popped," releasing the tension: then, on to the next sequence. The structure of the individual sequences was like that of a joke, with a setup that built to a punch line.

"Ping Pong!," the Kurtzman-Elder satire of the movie *King Kong* (1933) in *Mad* #6, consists of six distinct sequences. The rerelease of the film created a sensation in 1952. (It grossed four million that year, then a staggering sum.) Elder's rendition of the monstrous Ping Pong in the splash panel doesn't match Kong in the film, but it's appropriately powerful. Among the panicking populace in the splash panel is a helicopter with a rear rotor chewing up the panel border, a baby (carried by a stork) firing a machine gun at the beast, someone holding a sign reading, "This is not a 3-D movie! This is definitely it!," a cannon firing puffed rice, a guy on a pogo stick, and perhaps a dozen other subgags.

Sequence #1 began with a panel showing a knife cutting through an impenetrable fog. Tension: "We'll never find the island of the ferocious Ookabola-ponga!" Revelation: when the fog lifts, the explorers discovered their paddleboat (a river steamboat) is on dry land. Sequence #2 introduces the characters such as director Cecil B. V. D. Mills and actress Lana Lynn; the latter wonders, "why you all look this-a way when landmarks are all that-a way!" The third sequence, the longest, shows the crew meeting the natives on the island. The ship's captain tries talking to them in their native tongue, but the tribe's chief responds, "I say! You fellows speak English? Why didn't you say so in the first place? For a moment I thought you only spoke that filthy Ookabolaponganese! Horrible language!" After the director excitedly trades Lana Lynn for a set of Brooklyn Dodger baseball cards, the giant Pong makes his entrance.

Sequence #4 shows the crew frantically fleeing. The captain stops them and decides Lana Lynn must be rescued from Pong. But how to find the beast? Kurtzman pulls back and reveals the clueless crew standing in one of Pong's giant footprints. (This panel provided the basis for the issue's cover.) In Sequence #5, the crew finds Pong, only to discover Lana Lynn is battering him. The final sequence ends with their return to New York City.

Like the other early *Mad* satires, "Ping Pong!" deals with the broad, best-known aspects of its subject. Kurtzman may have missed the film's rerelease and was relying on his memory, but that wasn't important. One can "hear" the sound of actor Robert Armstrong's voice when Kurtzman writes of the film crew "riding to its destiny . . . with *death* . . . with PONG!," even though the image of Cecil B. V. D. Mills looks and behaves nothing like Armstrong.

Often Elder's "chicken fat" involved inside jokes, and Kurtzman added his own. In-jokes became an expected part of *Mad*. Kurtzman used them sometimes only for the amusement of himself and the EC crew, but mostly in ways that made regular readers feel they were members of the club. On p. 2 of "Superduperman!," Wood added background graffiti that reads, "Al loves words," "Bill loves EC" and "Harvey loves Harvey." Other kinds of in-jokes involve the running "Melvin" gags, non sequiturs such as "How's your Mom, Ed?," Jewish or Yiddish words like "furshlugginer" and "veeblefetzer," and odd words like "potrzebie" (pronounced "por-

CHYEB-ya" in Polish). According to Kurtzman, those words also contributed a certain "air of mystery."[22]

Kurtzman spotted the word "Potrzebie" in the multilanguaged
"Instructions for Use" sheet accompanying a bottle of aspirin. It first
surfaced in the letter column of *Mad* #10, as Kurtzman's one-word answer when a fan asked, "Please tell me what in the world 'Furshlugginer'
means." Readers adopted it and the other odd words, as well as expressions such as "hoohah." Later, in an introduction for a *Smokey Stover* reprint comic book, Kurtzman cited Bill Holman's use of "nonsense words
that appeared in no particular place for no particular reason" as the probable source for the practice in *Mad*, and for the subgags: "'Foo!,' 'Notary
Sojac.' Could it be that that's what inspired me to 'Potrzebie' and 'furshlugginer'? Was it Holman's technique [of] putting those 'tchochkas' in all
corners of the panels? Could that have been what inspired us to fill our
Mad . . . panels with those nonsensical details? Could that have been it? I
think so, Bill Holman. I think that you stamped my young, impressionable
brain with your indelible ink."[23] Recently, college professor and pop culture writer M. Thomas Inge wrote, "Reading *Mad* made the reader feel
part of a special group, a select society, if one recognized the targets of the
humor and the parodic references. This is one reason why Kurtzman is
remembered as such a powerful influence on the perceptions of readers.
He opened their eyes to the absurdities and inadequacies of their own
childhood culture and did it in such a way that made them feel smarter,
if not superior. One needs to know a lot to read *Mad* informatively, and it
confirms one's sense of intelligence."[24]

Along with running gags, another type of continuity occurred when
elements of the last story in *Mad* #6 ("Ping Pong!") were brought into the
first page of the lead story in *Mad* #7, "Shermlock Shomes!" Another thick
fog was torn open, again with B. V. D. Mills peering through, this time
asking Doctor Whatsit, "Could you direct us to Ping-Pong Island?"

Mad #7 and #8 each reprinted six pages of *Hey Look!* That gave the
writer, who was still getting up to speed after his illness, a bit of a respite.
These were among a handful of items with finished Kurtzman artwork inside the comic book. As an explanation, he (in the guise of Gaines) wrote
in the opening panel of the first *Hey Look!*, "Collector's Item Dept.: On the
following six pages are reprinted what your managing editor feels are some
of the best examples of the early zany creations of that master of nonsense,
Harvey Kurtzman! We know you'll go *Mad* over . . . *Hey Look!*" Kurtzman
contacted Martin Goodman and arranged a payment in exchange for their
use. He made sure to use his personal favorite, the *Hey Look!* where a

nature lover dives into a mountain lake with a mirrorlike surface, only to smash a hole in it, exclaiming, "Hey! This really is a mirror!"

Another Kurtzman-Elder story harkened back to their experience as kids at the movies in the 1930s. "Frank N. Stein!" in *Mad* #8 showed off Kurtzman's gift for writing comical, foreign accents, in this case Dr. Stein's German-influenced dialogue. This sort of thing was reminiscent of Sid Caesar's dialect work on *Your Show of Shows*, the television program that had become a national sensation in the early 1950s. Kurtzman later said it was a case of Jewish men from the same background who had many of the same experiences (and were exposed to a great deal of Jewish humor) coming up with similar approaches—and even specific ideas and routines.[25]

The Jack Davis-drawn "Lone Stranger Rides Again!" appeared in *Mad* #8 (December–January 1954), which hit the stands in October. However, the issue's highlight was "Bat Boy and Rubin!," a satire of National's Batman and Robin with art by Wallace Wood, in defiance of National. This time, Kurtzman and Wood make the "this is only a satire" theme ubiquitous throughout, starting with the opening caption: "Hero worship dept.: You have heard of those two masked, bat-like, crime-fighters of Gotham City . . . You have heard of their exciting deeds, of their constant war against the underworld! . . . This story, then . . . has *absolutely nothing* to do with *them!* . . . This story is about two *different* people." Also, to drive the point home further, another caption at the beginning reads, "Notice! This story is a *lampoon!* If you want to spend your dime on cheap, rotten lampoons like this instead of the ever-lovin' genuine, real thing . . . Go right ahead, boy!"

When the reports came in on *Mad* #6 and *Mad* #7, in the second half of 1953, Gaines and Kurtzman discovered they had a book that wasn't merely profitable, but one that was taking off like a rocket. *Mad*'s print run was increased. By the end of the year, Gaines wrote, "Today, the print order on *Mad* is 750,000 and on the way to a million. The monthly is selling eighty-six percent."[26] This meant that sales of *Mad* left Gaines's horror titles (with print orders of 400,000 to 450,000) in the dust. Obviously, the rapid sales surge was due to strong word-of-mouth. Other than EC's in-house publicity, there were no other advertisements. Those who found it and liked it were telling their friends. That sort of reader support meant there was nowhere to go but up.

To put *Mad*'s enormous sales in perspective, it's important to note that a comic book selling anything approaching one million copies was rare. Kurtzman's comic book was becoming one of the most successful comic books ever published, like *Superman* and *Captain Marvel Adventures* during World War II. *Walt Disney's Comics and Stories* and *Donald Duck* managed the feat at Dell in the 1950s, benefitting from the baby boom. Two other postwar titles that are said to have reached that level were the seminal crime and romance titles, *Crime Does Not Pay* and *Young Romance*, products of Charles Biro and the Simon and Kirby team, respectively. They too struck gold by creating an original title in a new genre that proved explosively popular.

To reach sales figures of those proportions often required comic books to be read and enjoyed by those who didn't normally read them. During World War II, sales skyrocketed because GI's were bored and needed diverting reading matter; after the war, sales of nearly all of those "hit" comics plummeted. *Mad*'s enormous circulation growth was because it was selling to people who didn't normally buy comic books, but heard about it from friends. Hip adults were being turned on to *Mad*. Arnold Roth, a cartoonist who would later become a colleague of Kurtzman, recounted, "I [was] a great fan of *Mad*, because everyone was, and because we all felt it was something being done by soul mates. I was very friendly with the Dave Brubeck Quartet people, and particularly Paul Desmond. Paul gave me a copy of *Mad* #2, and that's how I'd learned about it. I made sure I always got it, every issue. Harvey's name was well known to me. Everybody would be talking about *Mad* and Harvey."[27] While it's difficult to quantify, there's anecdotal evidence that suggests that a great deal of its circulation was due to its appeal to non-comic book readers.[28] This helps explain how *Mad*'s influence could spread relatively quickly, because it had plenty of older readers who worked (or would soon work) in various creative capacities in popular media.

Kurtzman recalled his and his colleagues' ebullience over its sales. "*Mad* had the excitement of a winner. There was a feeling in the air that we were onto something very hot and things started happening that were very exciting."[29] He turned twenty-nine on October 3, 1953.

BY VIRTUE OF RUNNING letter columns in all its titles, EC emphasized the importance of its readers. The publisher and his editors encouraged honest feedback, creating a mutually respectful relationship with those readers, further fostered by the humor, the informality and the candor in those columns. When combined with the biographical pages on each of the EC artists and writers, readers felt they knew the EC crew. Some of them wanted to know more, and Gaines was friendly and receptive to their requests.

Robert Stewart of Kirbyville, Texas, (a.k.a. "Bhob" Stewart—who added the "h" to his first name to differentiate himself from another "Bob Stewart" in fandom), began contributing to science fiction fanzines at the age of fifteen. This led him to consider doing a publication devoted to EC comics. He recalled, "One day it hit me like a flash that I should be doing a fanzine—not about science fiction, since there were hundreds of them—but about the thing I was most interested in, EC comics."[30] The first issue of the *EC Fan Bulletin* was published in the summer of 1953, after the announcement in *Weird Science* #20 (July–August 1953) brought about eighty orders to Stewart's mailbox.

Kurtzman welcomed this development. "I think fans are great," he said. "To me, they're life—they're your supporters."[31] He always read the incoming letters, and believed they legitimately gauged how certain stories were received. In an effort to answer the letters, Kurtzman prevailed on Gaines to buy him a Dictaphone. He attempted to use it on the train to and from the office. "I tried to answer all the letters," he recalled. "It was crazy!"[32] From this point on, Kurtzman's contacts with fans became an ongoing aspect of his life and career.

Gaines and Kurtzman discussed dropping one of the war comic books to make it possible for *Mad* to go to a monthly schedule. Before long, *Frontline Combat* and *Two-Fisted Tales* were canceled, after periods when Kurtzman was less involved. Gaines and Kurtzman hammered out a deal that gave Harvey $9,600 a year to edit twelve books annually, as he'd been doing before *Mad*, presumably taking into account the enormous profits being generated by the humor comic book. Now he could give *Mad* his full attention.

The completed *Mad* #9 (cover dated February–March 1954), the last bimonthly issue, offers a comic strip satire of *Little Orphan Annie* ("Little Orphan Melvin!") with Wood art, a comical adaptation of Edgar Allan Poe's poem "The Raven" drawn by Elder, and a collection of various jokes Kurtzman had collected from readers called "Bop Jokes!," illustrated by Severin. Its highlight is the Davis-drawn "Hah! Noon!," the first time *Mad* satirized a new movie, the Fred Zinnemann-directed film *High Noon*. Kurtzman wrote the story from notes taken after having seen it. That allowed for a freshness and precision that makes it quite different than the stories "from memory." Its protagonist resembles Gary Cooper, the sheriff in the movie. It parodies the movie's ballad, "Do not forsake me, oh my darlin'," as "Dyew not for-sake me, oh mah dollink!" This story set the pattern for future parodies of new movies in *Mad*.[33]

Decades later, at a comics convention panel, a fan said that reading *Mad* made him wonder if Kurtzman was high when he wrote the *Mad* stories. "What were you on?" asked the fan. After audience laughter died down, Kurtzman responded, "I was on . . . the joy of life. When I do good work, it's a high in itself. When you do a good piece of work and you can lean back and it looks good, makes you laugh and sing and dance, it's its own reward. You don't try to get high to do the thing, you do the thing and it makes you high."[34]

THE FALL OF 1953 was a halcyon period in Harvey Kurtzman's life. Ebullience over the success of *Mad* minimized cracks that were beginning to form in the Kurtzman-Gaines relationship. One year earlier, they had received word that *Mad* #1 had lost money. Now a huge print order for *Mad* #9 was about to be sent to the printer, roughly double that of the first issue. It was a time of high spirits and camaraderie among the participants. Kurtzman was healthy again. The only change in his appearance from younger days was his receding hairline.

Bill Gaines was a frequent presence in the Kurtzman's home, as were the others. Adele recalled, "It was a family. Bill made no bones about dropping in whenever he felt like it, you know. He had a car and he drove up . . . and it was never unwelcome, because Bill was shy and awkward and I think he felt okay because there were no pressures with us. It was easy, it was easy."[35] Gaines was dating his secretary, Nancy Siegel. Harvey and Adele chaperoned them on a trip through Pennsylvania Dutch country. The Kurtzmans also organized a trip to Cape Cod with Jack Davis and Will Elder, and their wives, showing them Captain Jack's Wharf where they had honeymooned. Alcohol was imbibed and the 8mm movie cameras came out. Kurtzman's home movies captured glimpses of Elder clowning around at the beach. He remarked, "One thing I've always felt that the world missed out on . . . if Willy could have been a performer. I've got little bits of film of Willy that I took on Cape Cod. We were out there once with Jack Davis when we were all young, with our wives. And Will was always so funny on film! So funny! It's a shame he could have never been a stand-up performer. Of course, he was much too self-conscious to have been a performer. When he knows someone is watching him special, he collapses."[36]

An expansive Kurtzman threw what Gaines later called a "great Halloween party" with many of the EC staff (and their spouses) invited, as well as other friends in the business. Dena Davis, Jack's wife, helped Adele with decorations and refreshments. Jack dressed as a hillbilly. Will Elder came as a headless man (with the shoulders of his suit up over his head). Jean Elder dressed as a mummy, wrapped in gauze. ("I don't know how she sat in the car," Adele quipped.) The Audrey Avenue house was jammed with guests. René Goscinny, who happened to be back in the States buying stories for Georges Troisfontaines's World Press agency, came dressed as a detective. A masked Maurice de Bevere was also there. He had to lie down after overindulging in food and drink. The movie cameras whirred, capturing Bill Gaines dressed as the devil, and the other colorfully clad revelers. Davis led the roisterers in an old Boy Scout game called "Thar's a Bear!"

On that Halloween, there was another reason to celebrate: Adele was pregnant again. Meredith would have a sister or brother some time the following June. The future looked bright. *Mad* #8 was on the stands and good cheer flowed.

THE 🄴🄲 "PUBLISHER OF THE ISSUE" • WILLIAM M. GAINES
ALIAS MELVIN

William M. (for "Mad") Gaines, twisted publisher of the perverted E.C. line, was born on Feb. 30, 1922, in an abandoned cattle-car on a siding outside the Chicago stock-yards. His father was an International Communist Banker of Persian, Iranian, Egyptian and Danish stock, and his mother came from the Bronx. His early childhood was relatively uneventful, having been spent in picking pockets, stealing government checks from mail-boxes, running errands for bookies, counterfeiting lead nickels, and playing with Teddy-bears. Bill's formal education consisted of four years in first grade, followed by nine years in reform school. Upon breaking out, he took the alias of "Melvin" Gaines and began selling "cartoon books" (you know the kind!) on dark street corners outside burlesque houses. When he had read them all, he turned to peddling dope near nursery schools . . . took the cure . . . opened an establishment in a district of scarlet illumination . . . took the cure . . . and finally, seeking the ultimate in depravity and debasement, quite naturally turned to the comic magazine industry. Here he found a home! Utilizing his vast background of worldly and literary experiences, coupled with the tidy fortune he had accumulated from same, Bill introduced to the American public the notorious E.C. line . . . E.C. standing for Evil Comics. His editorial policy is a reflection of his highly developed sense of immoral obligation. As he was heard to remark at his last bi-annual editorial conference: "I don' care if it don't gotta plot! I don' care if it don't got grammar! I don' care if the pitchers ain't from talent! All I care is get inta every story *sadism, snakes, masochism, pyromania, snakes, fetishes, snakes, necrophilia, phallic symbols, snakes,* and all the rest of that *esoterica* what I can't think of this minute." Today, Bill lives in a sixty-nine room mansion in wholesome Westchester County, N. Y. He owns a grey Cadillac for grey days, a blue Cadillac for blue days, a green Cadillac for bilious days, and a pogo-stick for hopped-up days. Bill's hobbies include selling "cartoon books" (you know the kind!), peddling dope, running his scarlet-illuminated establishment, and collecting snakes. At this writing, he is single . . . having been married and divorced 69 times. Don't send fan-mail . . . he can't read!

Mad #5 (June–July 1953).

Mad #4 (April–May 1953). "Shadow!" by Kurtzman and Elder.

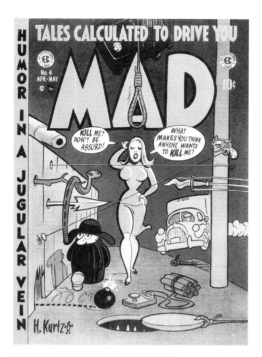
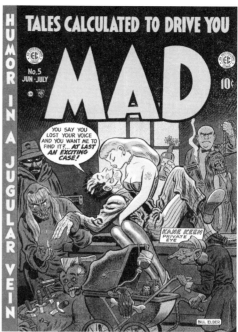
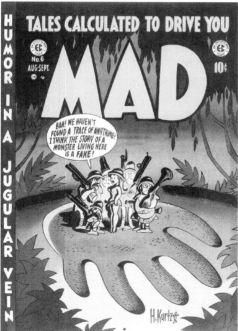

The covers of *Mad* #4 through #7: Kurtzman drew all but #5. He had hepatitis when #5 was being prepared, so Will Elder handled that one. When the sales reports for *Mad* #6 and #7 came in, it was clear that *Mad* was a hit of major proportions.

Top: *Mad* #6 (August–September 1953). Bottom: Kurtzman left no doubt that the satirical Bat Boy and Rubin were not to be confused with characters owned by National Comics.

15.

MAD GOES MONTHLY

FREE SPEECH WAS UNDER ATTACK in the United States in the late 1940s and early 1950s. The US Congress investigated the so-called infiltration of Communists and their sympathizers into the American film and television industries. The Hollywood Ten had gone to prison for contempt of Congress, and now many more were vilified. Hundreds more screenwriters, directors and actors discovered their names were on a Hollywood blacklist and could no longer find work.

A large number of *Mad*'s readership consisted of teenagers born before the United States entered World War II. They were the young people (mostly boys) who populated the junior and senior high schools across the country. As is typical of all adolescents, awareness of parental and societal hypocrisy was hitting them hard, and the world around them was cooperating by presenting a society obsessed with outward appearances and apparent morality, while underneath, injustice, racism, fear of the atomic bomb and political paranoia seethed.

The world of the teenager was regulated by parents—many who read hand-wringing articles about the "juvenile delinquent problem" and feared youth was getting out of control. Watchdog groups screened books for "appropriateness" before they were added to libraries. Teenagers chafed at such restrictions. It's no wonder that Holden Caulfield's rants against a world of "phonies" in J. D. Salinger's novel *The Catcher in the Rye* (1951) resonated with young readers. School boards immediately banned the book.

Voices outside the mainstream may have been heard on some college campuses or in literary magazines, but were rarely available to the average teenager, especially those outside urban areas. (The writings of the "beat" novelists and poets such as Jack Kerouac and Allen Ginsberg didn't surface until the second half of the decade.) Radio shows were entertaining but generally bland, and the Production Code sanitized movies to the extent that married couples could only be shown sleeping in twin beds. There were science fiction books and digests for those with that inclination, and many flocked to them as a harbor for unconventional ideas. The "approved" mass media was largely stultifying and boring.

One area remained unregulated and uncensored: comic books. Due to their status as junk literature, comic books had fallen under the radar of the most powerful arbiters of public taste. Protests against crime and horror comics were on the upswing, but if a wholesaler took a comic book, it would find its way into the hands of readers in virtually every town and neighborhood in the land. A great deal of the rise of the wild and woolly EC horror titles was because they crossed the line beyond what was considered good taste in other media. Gaines struck a nerve precisely because teenagers hungered for something that wasn't "good for you." *Mad* was an irreverent beacon to youth that made fun of relentless consumerism (starting with all those Burma Shave gags by Elder) and offered satire that challenged the status quo with an anarchy antithetical to the country's political and social atmosphere. Kurtzman's comic book came as a bolt from the blue. Published alongside mainstream material, *Mad* was so unusual that it seemed like a cult publication.

"There was nothing to compare it to," Kurtzman later acknowledged. "*Mad* was satirical, and satire was not very strong in that period when [it] came into being. Oh, you could find satire if you burrowed and looked real carefully, you could see that Jack Benny had been satire all along and Fred Allen had been satire all along, but it wasn't strong satire, it wasn't irreverent sledgehammer satire. That kind of satire didn't exist much except in college magazines, where I discovered it for myself [as a youth]."[1] But publications such as the *Yale Record*, the *Columbia Jester*, the *Harvard Lampoon* and the *Stanford Chaparral* weren't for sale on national newsstands.

Yet *Mad* wasn't created to fill a gap in the marketplace, or because of a perceived need for satire. Kurtzman didn't look around and decide to make a statement against societal repression. He didn't think that way. *Mad* came from the inside, not the outside. Its humor reflected everything that had shaped Kurtzman's creative sensibilities, from his experience as a boy cartoonist, his time at the High School of Music and Art and beyond. In a 1976 interview, Kurtzman stated, "When we did *Mad*, I didn't particularly think about what I was doing. I did what I thought was funny. Over the years, I've been forced to think about why I did what I did, and now I've got certain conclusions." Popular entertainment, he said, could be divided into the type that entertained "through telling the reader about the world as he'd like it to be," i.e., fantasy, and "its counter-area" which was "the world of reality."

> When it's the way you would like it to be, it usually takes care of your problems, your frustrations. It's the trouble-free concept, because that's the place you get rid of your troubles. The other kind isn't a world where you get rid of your troubles, but you define, you express what your troubles are. In the make-believe world, the fantasy world of Andy Hardy, of the early MGM movies, it's almost like taking dope or tranquilizers. It makes you feel good. It doesn't make you more aware of anything. So in a sense, it has a decadence about it—which is why I think reality stuff is so enjoyable after you have had a belly full of make-believe. I think that's why the wave washed over us, over the country so violently—because for years, we had been living with make-believe humor, make-believe radio, make-believe movies. Suddenly came the age of reality art, of consciousness-raising.[2]

As he had discovered with Biro's *Crime Does Not Pay*, the postwar era found the public ready for a shift toward more realistic entertainment. In *Mad*, Kurtzman brought his readers back to the reality of real life. Today, it may be difficult to understand just how startling Kurtzman's satires of pop culture characters were in 1953. *Mad* was the first regularly published comic book dedicated to satirizing the likes of Superman, Batman and Tarzan. In the case of the comics parodies, the fact that *Mad* was drawn by artists as good (or better) as those who drew the original strips made it doubly effective.

Mad's print order of 750,000 copies "on the way to a million" as 1954 arrived (and selling 86 percent of those copies) meant it was about twice as profitable as any of the EC horror titles. With its tenth issue, it became EC's first monthly comic book. Kurtzman went from being writer-editor of twelve sinking war comics a year to the man in charge of twelve issues of EC's hottest seller.

A REINVIGORATED HARVEY KURTZMAN began work on *Mad* #10 around the time of his and Adele's celebratory Halloween bash. While much would remain the same, the book's next year brought a number of changes. One was new kinds of features and subject matter. Another involved some shifts in creative personnel.

"Sane!," a satire of the 1954 Alan Ladd movie *Shane*, is the last collaboration between Harvey Kurtzman and John Severin in *Mad*—or anywhere else. Their conflict had nothing to do with Severin's capability of doing funny material: "We disagreed on technique. [John] would want to do brush technique, and I'd tell him to leave the brush alone. He always wanted to be that which he was not. And he wasn't Jack Davis, but he wanted to do those swooping brush strokes, which he had no talent for. And when he did *Mad* stuff, then he really went to town with the brush. Those Tarzan stories . . . drove me crazy. So I tried to make him stay with the pen technique. But he'd get angry."[3] Severin later confirmed that he and Kurtzman had "blow-out" arguments over art technique: "It got to be personal on his part, and I didn't care for that."[4] By the time "Sane!" appeared, Severin had left *Mad* to edit the *New Two-Fisted Tales*, where he continued to have difficulties with Kurtzman. Severin discovered that he didn't have editorial autonomy, and was required to have his work reviewed by Kurtzman. This led to unspecified disagreements. They were able to share the editorial duties, then Severin was sufficiently incensed to write a letter to Bill Gaines (with a copy sent to Kurtzman) dated August 14, 1954, which read in full:

> Dear Mr. Gaines:
> Due to operating methods of Harvey Kurtzman I find it necessary to resign from any book edited by him.
> > Sincerely, John Severin

It was written as the final issues of *Two-Fisted* were being prepared, about nine months after the two collaborated on "Sane!" In later years, they both had good things to say about their time together at EC, but in the short term, Severin's only subsequent work for EC appeared in a short-lived book edited by Johnny Craig in 1955 called *Extra*. Other publishers recognized his talent for humorous cartooning, and he became chief artist of *Cracked*, the hardy *Mad* imitator. For the rest of his career, Severin was known for inking with a pen, not a brush.

In the same issue as Severin's last work in *Mad*, another artist showed up for the first time, if only in a minor way. Basil Wolverton was a cartoonist and illustrator who had worked in comic books since the late 1930s. His work had appeared in some of the same Timely comics as *Hey Look!* Wolverton's Powerhouse Pepper had been in *Joker Comics*, *Gay Comics* and

Tessie the Typist, and even had his own title for five issues from 1943 to 1948. Kurtzman also knew Wolverton from a famous episode of Al Capp's *Li'l Abner*. In 1946, the artist won a contest to draw "Lena the Hyena," the world's ugliest woman, a running gag in the strip. "I enjoyed Wolverton's work," Kurtzman recalled. "It was—and this is, believe it or not, high praise—real *dumb*."[5] Wolverton's humor, Kurtzman said, was silly like that of Bill Holman, and his grotesque drawing style was completely original. He was a perfect choice for a special assignment: create the final image in the *Mad* version of H. Antoine d'Arcy's poem "The Face Upon the Floor!," otherwise drawn by Jack Davis. At first, Kurtzman wanted to use "Lena the Hyena" as the face on the floor, but after encountering difficulty getting permission from the United Features Syndicate (who handled *Li'l Abner*), he offered Wolverton $25 for a new drawing of a grotesque female face. This was speedily done, and the drawing was inserted into the last panel of the story.

Mad #11 (May 1954): art by Basil Wolverton.

Wolverton also figured into a new style of covers for *Mad*. Kurtzman and others had drawn the first ten, but for the monthly issues, he switched to conceptual covers. The humor would arise from the idea and overall design, rather than from a cartoon situation. The change made *Mad* resemble a magazine, albeit one that was comic book size. For "The Face Upon the Floor!," Wolverton had submitted two drawings. Kurtzman decided to use the alternate version on the cover of *Mad* #11, making it part of a parody of *Life* magazine's covers, which often had head shots of glamorous celebrities. The photographic cityscape along the bottom of that cover was taken through the window of the men's room at 225 Lafayette St.

The *Life* parody cover brought another brush with potential legal action. On the back of the Wolverton cover was a page titled "Beware of Imitations," created in an attempt to stave off a lawsuit from the real *Life* magazine. It backfired because Kurtzman used an actual *Life* cover in the humorous ad. However, the threatened lawsuit for copyright infringement came to naught.

The cover of *Mad* #12 was designed to look like the front of *Atlantic* magazine, which consisted of a list of the contents sans artwork. At the bottom was an explanation: "This special issue is designed for people ashamed to read this comic book in subways and like that! Merely hold cover in front of face making sure it's not upside down. *Mad* cover design makes people think you are reading high-class intellectual stuff instead of miserable junk."

The Mona Lisa cover of #14 created quite a stir. It slyly answered the question, "Why is she smiling?" by showing her holding a copy of *Mad*. Years later, Adele remembered the controversy. "He got tons of mail about that one," she recalled. "People thought it was a religious picture!"[6] Kurtzman printed one of the letters, and mildly responded: "*Mad*'s #14 cover is the famous Mona Lisa by Leonardo Da Vinci and has no connection with any religious figure whatever."

Harvey Kurtzman also tapped Wolverton for a new type of interior item in *Mad* #11, a series of comical portraits in a six-page "Mad Reader!" gallery. Kurtzman sent the Strathmore drawing pages with his vellum overlays to the artist's studio in Vancouver, Washington. It was accompanied by a letter explaining his system of doing layouts for the artists to follow, in order to achieve an overall visual unity to the book. However, in reference to the sketches he did for each portrait, he wrote, "I can't be too emphatic! Please . . . please . . . do not restrict yourself line for line to the layouts! For God's sake, don't allow the layouts to inhibit you, short of getting across the central idea!"[7] Wolverton took Kurtzman at his word.

His drawings were gleefully uninhibited, even for him. Six months later, Wolverton returned with a similar pin-up parade, "Meet Miss Potgold!"

With Severin gone, Kurtzman filled the empty slot in #11 with a satire of a three-page "EC Quickie" story named "Murder the Husband!," which had seen print in *Crime SuspenStories* #12 (August–September 1952). Gaines and Feldstein allowed him to reprint it along with a relettered new version called "Murder the Story!" Kurtzman likened the concept to what Woody Allen did in the movie *What's Up, Tiger Lily?* (1966), turning a weak spy movie into a comedy by redubbing all the dialogue. "Murder the Story!" is notable for another reason. It's the first time "potrzebie" appears in a story. Among some of the newspaper cutouts used to put foreign languages in the word balloons, one of them contains the Polish word.

Mad #13 offered "Book! Movie!," showing how movie versions of books cleaned up and distorted the source material. This time, just one "typical" book is its subject, a generic domestic-strife-and-murder tale laid out in the first four pages, contrasted with the movie version in the next three. The next issue's "Movie . . . Ads!" shows how movie posters distorted elements from films to make them seem more tantalizing. Over time, comparison pieces became a regular part of *Mad*.

Trying new things was more than a response to a staffing change. Kurtzman was always creatively restless. To stay interested, he needed to challenge himself, experiment, mix things up. To what end, he couldn't have said, because he wasn't working toward a predetermined goal. It was just that he could never be satisfied with repeating a successful formula. He did continue to satirize comic book and strip characters, sometimes rivaling the excellence of "Superduperman!" *Mad* #10 has "Woman Wonder!," another comic book satire drawn by Will Elder. Elder's artwork has by this time become more focused on the main action, with the "chicken fat" pared back. William Moulton Marston's Wonder Woman, an instant hit since her debut in *All Star Comics* #8 (December 1941), provides plenty of fodder: her magic lasso, her see-through robot plane, her bullet-repelling bracelets and the gender politics involved when a woman is strong enough to be a super hero. In the end, Diana Banana marries Steve Adore and becomes a household drudge.

The opener of *Mad* #12 was "Starchie!," a parody of the teenage denizens of Riverdale. In probably the second-most celebrated story in all of *Mad*'s comic book run, Kurtzman and Elder savage the fantasy of wholesome high school life in America. Archie is a hoodlum (threatening Betty with a broken bottle until she falls out a window), Jughead carries a switchblade, Mr. Weatherbee is a drooling lecher, Betty has a syringe in

Panels from "Woman Wonder!" by Kurtzman and Elder, in *Mad* #10 (March–April 1954).

her purse, Reggie is an abusive bully who cavorts nude through several panels and Archie's parents are white trash. In the end, Starchie ends up a bitter old man in a prison cell. All this is drawn in a manner that expertly mimics the look of the real Archie comics.

That kind of visual mimicry—the essence of parody—didn't come easily, according to Elder: "Many people comment on my ability to imitate the style without realizing what I really put into it. I wouldn't expect them to know, but I always had the impression that the fans thought I was up in my studio with a rubber stamp or something, and I was just able to punch this stuff out, but I put in a tremendous amount of time, research and effort in every story I did. I don't see how I could have done it any other way."[8] Despite the extreme nature of "Starchie!," EC heard nothing from Archie Comics's owner John Goldwater, though Goldwater and Gaines were soon to lock horns over the issue of comic book censorship.

In that same issue, "Mark Trade!," the Jack Davis-drawn spoof of the *Mark Trail* syndicated strip, makes much of a Girl Scout camp named "Camp Nit-Ge-Die-Get." This is a reference to a Communist-run New York state camp called Camp Nitgedaiget (Yiddish for "carefree"), presumably inspired by Kurtzman's own experience as a teenager at Camp Kinderland. (Some twenty-seven such camps existed in New York State alone in the 1930s and 1940s.)

Other comics parodies from Kurtzman and his team include "Flesh Gordon!," "Prince Violent!," "Manduck the Magician" and "Plastic Sam!" The Plastic Man spoof in *Mad* #14 is Russ Heath's only art assignment for the book. "I liked what he did," Kurtzman said. "In fact, that story was the most agreeable thing that ever happened between me and Russ Heath. It was very strange, because nobody had ever reacted to my technique before. I did the layouts, and they had a certain technique, but everybody would then draw with their own techniques, except Russ. He held on to my technique very faithfully."⁹ "Plastic Sam!" is the closest thing to a new Kurtzman-pencilled strip in *Mad*.

"3-Dimensions!" in *Mad* #12 parodies not a character but a new variation of the comics form itself. It deconstructs 3-D comics, a fad that required special glasses to perceive the illusion of multiple layers of action on the flat page. St. John Publishing's *Three Dimension Comics* #1 (September 1953), starring Mighty Mouse, introduced the 3-D comic book and became a million-plus seller (at twenty-five cents). Kurtzman-Wood make fun of the very idea that a flat comic book page could have more than two dimensions, claim the process causes eye strain, and point out that when it was working, it means that the pages lacked color. (The last three pages of "3-Dimensions!," except for one panel, are monochromatic.) On p. 5, the characters—supposedly living in a world of three dimensions—actually fall from one panel to another, and finally off the page. The last page of the story is completely blank, the ultimate deconstruction.

EC was a latecomer to the 3-D comics craze. Its books in the format arrived on newsstands when the fad had cooled considerably. Gaines published just two issues of *Three Dimensional EC Classics*, both dated spring 1954. Each has four redrawn versions of earlier EC stories from the same scripts (with a few minor changes). Harvey Kurtzman and George Evans produced a new version of "Frank Luke!" (*Frontline* #17) which runs eight rather than seven pages, interpolating panels to extend the action and make it more spectacular. The new Kurtzman-Wood "V-Vampires!" (*Mad* #3) expanded from six to eight pages: they enlarged the original splash panel to a full page, and extended the opening sequence (a woman being stalked in the London fog) by several panels. The reworked version is even better than the original.

IF IMITATION IS THE SINCEREST form of flattery, then Kurtzman had every reason to feel exceedingly flattered by the number of *Mad* imitations that began popping up on newsstands. In Bill Gaines's article in *Writer's Digest* announcing the 750,000 print run of *Mad*, he wrote, "Already there are eleven imitations of *Mad* on the newsstand. We're publishing one ourselves; it's called *Panic*."

The first out of the gate was by Joe Kubert and Norman Maurer, who started the 3-D comics fad. *Whack* #1, a 3-D book, was dated October 1953. This meant it was prepared months earlier, before the extent of *Mad*'s success became known. Kubert and Maurer, who were creating their own raft of comic books for St. John Publishing, loved *Mad* and were inspired to do something similar. Their first issue offered a parody of the *Dick Tracy* strip, a farcical story about the 3-D craze itself, a funny animal parody and a send-up of romance comics. The work is professional but unremarkable, and quite tepid compared to *Mad. Whack* continued as a regular, non-3-D book for just two more issues.

Other *Mad* imitators piled up: *Crazy, Wild* and *Riot* (Atlas), *Eh!* and *From Here To Insanity* (Charlton), *Get Lost* (MikeRoss), *Nuts!* (Premier), *Madhouse* and *Bughouse* (both from Ajax/Farrell) and *Unsane!* (Star). One of the best was *Flip* from Harvey Comics. Its most attractive aspect is the artwork by Howard Nostrand, who could draw like Jack Davis or Wallace Wood to fit the occasion. EC ran ads warning readers not to confuse the imitations with the real thing, at one point identifying the copycats by name. Kurtzman was philosophical about the imitations: "When someone breaks new ground, the crowd quickly rushes through the break. But that's good, that's okay. That's the way things evolve and change, and that's life. Imitation is flattery and I never resented it that much. But I guess we always all felt that there were a lot of greenbacks slipping away." He also said of the imitators, "They didn't have the profound understanding that you do have when you start something and have a real reason for starting it." Gaines was less sanguine: "I always resented people stealing our stuff and imitating. There was nothing you could do about it." But Gaines had no problem publishing EC's own imitation of *Mad.*[10]

Mad #9 carried an ad for *Panic* #1, and also touted it in the letter column: "Not bad! Not as funny as *Mad*, but not bad. Try one! Why not?!" (The EC horror hosts often denigrated each other's books, so this notice wasn't unusual.)

Kurtzman was angry. "*Panic* was [a] sore point. Gaines, by some convoluted reasoning, decided to double the profit of *Mad* by doing a Feldstein version of *Mad*, and he just plundered all of my techniques and artists. For me, there was a real conflict of interest."[11] Finding material for the pages of the monthly *Mad* was more difficult when Gaines launched *Panic.* Although it was published bimonthly, it would be covering the same ground as *Mad*: parodies of television shows, comic strips, books and movies—essentially taking possibilities away from Kurtzman. Both magazines couldn't satirize the same subjects.

Kurtzman's claim that *Panic* plundered his artists showed a certain insensitivity to the artists' needs. With the demise of the war comics, he was in a position to offer Will Elder no more than one story a month. This left Elder relying on inking Severin's Western stories at Prize, which was not his favorite thing. While it's true that fans of Elder's humor work could find it in *Panic*, it's hard to imagine anyone foregoing *Mad* for the Feldstein-edited variation. (Elder drew fourteen stories for *Panic* over its twelve-issue run.) What really galled Kurtzman was how closely *Panic* was able to resemble *Mad* due to its in-house status. The splash pages were set up the same way, with an opening caption beginning "Sex and Sadism Dept.," "Grim Fairy Tale Dept.," and ending with the title of the story. The running expressions and non sequiturs (Melvin, potrzebie, furshlugginer) were carried over, and Basil Wolverton was again brought in as a guest artist (his "face on the floor" headshot was used to end another story), and so on. Al Feldstein aped superficial aspects of *Mad* with impunity. He even imitated Kurtzman's signature, using a little beer stein at the end, in exactly the way Kurtzman's idiosyncratic signature ended with a little figure of a man.

Panic has its amusing moments, such as Will Elder's parody of Clement Clarke Moore's classic poem "The Night Before Christmas," and was generally superior to the other imitators, but couldn't hold a candle to *Mad*. Feldstein's word-heavy scripts piled gag after gag, and lacked carefully constructed comedic sequences. The difference between *Mad* and *Panic* was the difference between art and craft, between inspiration and perspiration, between Kurtzman and Feldstein. The merely moderate sales of *Panic* helped cement Kurtzman's irreplaceable status in Gaines's mind. Kurtzman had created a blockbuster of humor, and Feldstein (and Jack Mendelsohn, who wrote nearly all of the last six issues of *Panic*) could barely muster a credible imitation.

ABOUT THE TIME *Mad* #14 hit the stands, the Kurtzmans added another member to their family. Peter "Pete" Kurtzman was born on June 29, 1954. Adele recalled, "I think I read somewhere that 'Peter' meant not 'made of stone,' but related to being strong."[12] Other family news included Kurtzman's parents' move from the Clinton Avenue "*Rear Window* apartments" in the Bronx to an apartment in a new co-op building on the Lower East Side, overlooking the East River and the Brooklyn Naval Yard. Their finances had recovered since Abraham's incarceration, and they wanted a nicer place. By the end of the decade, Edith agitated for a move to Florida, where they lived until Abraham's passing.

Zachary Kurtzman married. His wife Sonia, who everyone called Sunny, was ten years younger. Harvey's older brother was a frustrated painter who ended up studying engineering—the "responsible" thing to do—and was unhappily employed as an electrical engineer for the rest of his working life. Zachary and Sonia would have two sons: David, born in 1956, and Adam, a year later. Zachary worked for Kearfott Guidance and Navigation for most of his career, designing inertial guidance systems for aeronautics, and they lived in Wantagh, Long Island, not far from Jones Beach.

Dan Perkes had never gone overseas while in the military and when he was discharged, stayed in Texas where he married and became a journalist. He spent many years working at various bureaus of the Associated Press in small Midwestern towns, and eventually moved back to the New York area.

Abraham and Edith Perkes in 1954: courtesy of Adam Kurtzman.

The Perkes-Kurtzman family got together occasionally, but Harvey's relationship with his mother remained problematic. "[Edith] was just an unhappy, bitter woman," Adele recalled. "I never saw the funny side or good side."[13] He also wasn't close to his brothers, though in truth he wasn't especially close to many people. Besides Adele, his closest friends were Will Elder and Harry Chester. Harry and Irene Chester both adored Harvey. "He was so interesting and so clever and funny," Irene recalled. "He was perfect. We would go to their house and visit, just sit around and talk. No matter what he discussed, it was always interesting."[14] Will was off in New Jersey and his own life, but the Chesters lived in an apartment in Mount Vernon not far from the Kurtzman home on Audrey Avenue.

Harvey and Adele enjoyed socializing, though Adele was essentially a homebody. Having small children had a lot to do with it. Meredith turned four shortly after Peter's birth. Adele's confidantes were her sister Doris and Irene Chester. She liked having Harvey at home a lot of the time, although he was mostly sequestered in his studio during the day. "He was always willing to help, to watch the kids if I needed to go to the store or whatever," she said. One of Kurtzman's genuine pleasures was working in the yard. Meredith later said, "Dad was a city boy, and I think he really liked the new things in the suburbs like gardening. On the side of the house, there was a little garden where we grew fruits and vegetables. He had a peach tree he'd grown from a pit."[15] The Kurtzmans now owned a television, a business necessity for someone making his living partly by writing satires of popular TV programs. One of the comedians he and Adele came to admire was Ernie Kovacs. "Adele would rave about this guy in the morning, and I watched him one morning, and he was dreadful," he recalled. "That was my first impression of him. He was putting a show together daily and it was full of junk. But then after you watched the guy for a while you began to realize he was a genius of sorts."[16]

The 1950s saw the advent of a new era of comedy, and Kovacs was one of the most innovative with his blackout skits and camera tricks. Mort Sahl had created a sensation at the hungry i in San Francisco, and then brought his brand of political comedy to New York's Bitter End, inspiring many more "rebel comedians." Stan Freberg was another popular new comedian. He recorded his own *Dragnet* satire record, as well as a spoof of radio soap operas called "John and Marsha." Clearly, the times were ready for smart new comedians and humorists. Eventually, Kurtzman would publish work by a number of them in *Mad.*

Kurtzman split his time between home and the office. EC's midtown office mainly served as a central point to meet with the artists. Jack Davis came into Manhattan from Scarsdale just long enough to drop off a story and pick up another. Then he was out the door, working hard to keep up with the cost of living in one of New York's most upscale suburbs. Gaines may not have participated creatively in *Mad*, but he always enjoyed going through the material as it came in, laughing long and hard as he read the pages. He loved *Mad* and was, along with everyone else at EC, a fan of Kurtzman and his artists.

The quality of the work in *Mad* maintained the same high level. For the cover of *Mad* #15 (September 1954), Kurtzman used an illustration by John Tenniel of the Mad Tea Party from Lewis Carroll's *Alice's Adventures in Wonderland.* Inside, it seems Carroll's novel inspired a key element of Kurtzman's *Gasoline Alley* satire. Like Alice, who shape-shifts after reaching the bottom of the rabbit hole, Wilt's son Skizziks ages from an infant to a grandfather in the space of eight pages. One of the most distinctive aspects of King's comic strip was the fact that his characters aged. Picking up on that, Kurtzman has Skizziks willing himself from childhood to lanky adolescence in just three panels in order to flirt with the older Nin. Will Elder's emulation of Frank King's artwork is uncannily close to the original. It's yet another stellar work by Kurtzman and Elder. As Elder recalled, "Harvey and I were alter egos at work. There was a very magical chemistry that was formulated by the two of us. Everything we did seemed to jell."[17]

IF 1953 AT EC is best characterized by the rise of *Mad* and the continued health of its horror titles, 1954 was about the fall of its New Trend comic books, and not because they were no longer profitable. Bill Gaines's sales reports on *Tales from the Crypt* and the other horror books continued to look good. True, Gaines had hired other writers, partly because he and Al Feldstein had exhausted their plot ideas. The new writers' scripts were generally less inspired than Feldstein at his best, and the stories became formulaic and gorier (they became desensitized to horror and needed to top their previous stories), but the readers stayed loyal. About 23,500 joined the EC Fan-Addict Club. Still, Gaines's horror titles were under attack. The *Hartford Courant* began running a series of anti-comics articles titled "Depravity for Children—10 Cents a Copy" in February. When such articles appeared in newspapers in increasing numbers, the future of horror and crime comics was seriously in doubt. Dr. Fredric Wertham's book about the effect of violent comics on America's youth fanned the flames of the anti-comics hysteria.

On April 19, 1954, Rinehart and Company, Inc. published *Seduction of the Innocent*. Its author Fredric Wertham pulled together material he had written for various journals and magazines on the detrimental effects of comic books, based not on scientific studies, but on anecdotal evidence and questionable notions of cause-and-effect. Other experts had testified before the Senate Committee in 1950 that comics, even violent comics, were a harmless release for young readers, but the fact was that a significant number of comics—like those of EC—carried material that many parents felt was unsuitable for young readers. That these books were aimed at teenage and older readers meant nothing, because they were displayed and sold alongside *Walt Disney's Comics and Stories*, *Looney Tunes* and other child-oriented fare.

Seduction of the Innocent, a shockingly poorly written book, was widely reviewed in newspapers and national magazines, and received largely favorable coverage. Many of the reviews played up its most sensational aspects, further fueling the public's outrage. The book's release was orchestrated to occur just days before a new round of US Senate hearings on comics began in New York City. The Senate select committee was soliciting testimony to help its members decide what sort of government action, if any, was warranted. (Although Senator Joseph McCarthy was also conducting his infamous televised hearings at the time, they had nothing to do with comic books.) The pressure on Bill Gaines was enormous. On April 21, 1954, he appeared before the Senate committee to speak on behalf of comic books and to defend the type of books published by EC. It was a disaster, mainly because he had difficulty defending some of the gory covers (held up for the TV audience to see) as well as certain stories in his books. As a result, Gaines and the other comics publishers were left scrambling to figure out what to do to satisfy the committee and quell public furor. Ultimately, Gaines had no choice but to drop his New Trend horror and crime books, and come up with replacements that would offend no one. This effort consumed much of Gaines's energy and attention through the rest of the year.

Looking back in 1985, Kurtzman remembered, "Censorship is highly undesirable, particularly in creative areas. It was my feeling that creative comics were going to suffer, and creative comics were my bag. I was personally very depressed about the [comic book] witch hunts." But, he added, "I can understand how they were generated."[18] While *Mad* had material that was open to criticism by the crusaders and moralists of the day—mainly its shapely women and unfettered comic violence, as well as its antiestablishment tone—it escaped mention at the hearings. However, simply being a comic book brought increased scrutiny. An attack could come from any quarter at any time. When it came, however, it was against *Panic*, not *Mad*.

In Feldstein's *Panic* #1, Will Elder's comic version of "The Night Before Christmas" was vociferously lambasted by a wholesaler, reported the *Springfield Daily News*. Under a headline reading "Santa Claus Comic Draws Holyoke Ban," the Massachusetts newspaper article read, "A comic book described by Atty. Gen. George Fingold has been dropped from sale by the Holyoke News Co., local distributing agency, reported Martin Zanger, owner, today." The principal objection was to a "Just Divorced"

Panel by Will Elder in *Panic* #1 (February–March 1954). The "Just Divorced" sign on Santa's sled caused problems for EC.

sign on the back of Santa's sleigh. Another article in the same paper announced "the Governor's council requested the book be banned."[19]

HARVEY KURTZMAN approached Bill Gaines with an idea. As Gaines later
put it, "Somewhere along the line Harvey, who, as you know now, was
ashamed of doing comics, broached the idea to me of turning [*Mad*] into
something other than a comic. And I was having none of it because I was
a comic publisher. I didn't want to be anything but a comic publisher, and
I said 'No.'" Kurtzman had suggested that *Mad* be converted from a comic
book to a magazine.

Despite the comic book controversy, *Mad* received positive publicity after its meteoric rise became known outside industry circles. The EC
crew was invited to appear on *The Steve Allen Show*, a late-night, forty-
minute local television program (on what is now WNBC-TV). Allen was
another example of a non-comics reading adult who read and championed
Mad. The show aired in early 1954, probably before the Senate hearings.
Mad was discussed, and other EC comics too. According to Feldstein, they
all wore prop glasses in imitation of the bespectacled host. Kurtzman was
there, and at one point Steve Allen was shown examining a copy of *Mad*
#6. It's no surprise that Allen, a comedian who often used non sequiturs
in his comic banter, appreciated *Mad*.

More publicity came when Kurtzman got a call from a national magazine. He recalled, "There was a guy by the name of Harris Shevelson. He
was a very unusual editor of the times. He decided to have an article about
us in *Pageant*. And we were very impressed. He sent Harold Hayes over to
do the article."[20] Hayes was a twenty-eight-year-old up-and-coming magazine editor with a nose for interesting material, a literary bent and a quick
mind. Born in North Carolina, he graduated from high school in Winston-
Salem and attended a small, in-state college where he edited the college
magazine, became a jazz fanatic and aspired to a career in journalism.
Author Carol Polsgrove described Hayes as "a tall, lanky southerner, son
of a Southern Baptist minister [who] enjoyed life, gunning his motorcycle
through the late-night New York streets after a party. In a conversation, he
listened intently, laughed appreciatively. He gave the impression he really
cared—really wanted to know what people were doing and thinking."[21]
Kurtzman and Hayes hit it off at once. Hayes loved *Mad*, and Kurtzman
admired slick magazines such as *Pageant*. Their meeting would prove pivotal in Kurtzman's career.

The article titled "Now Comics Have Gone Mad" appeared in the June
1954 issue of *Pageant*, along with sample pages from four *Mad* stories.

It was accompanied by an elaborate new piece of artwork done by Elder especially for the occasion. "To fans, this was the first 'official' recognition that *Mad* was as great as they believed," John Benson later wrote. "This article stood alone among the countless others denouncing comics as the cause of juvenile delinquency that were appearing simultaneously in all kinds of periodicals. With this article, we knew that *Mad* had it made."[22] Hayes wrote, "In the comic book business, where 350 titles are published monthly and everybody follows trends, a very unusual comic book—called *Mad*—has emerged as the leader of the latest trend. *Mad* is satirical and it's funny."[23]

MAD #16 (OCTOBER 1954)—which hit newsstands in mid-summer—dealt directly with the comic book controversy. Its cover simulates a newspaper's front page. Under a fake "photo" (painted by Elder) of a "Comic Book Raid" is the caption:

> As a result of charges that certain comic books are contributing to crime, these comic book artists were rounded up today at their hideout where they had stored a sizeable cache of brushes, drawing paper and ink. From right to left, they are a "crime" cartoonist, a "science-fiction" cartoonist, and a "lampoon" cartoonist.

Another simulated photo shows a comic book being surreptitiously sold as if it was a pornographic magazine, over the headline, "Comics go Underground." Inside, the corresponding feature begins with a caption reading, "Youth! Even as we speak, grown-ups of America battle tirelessly to destroy evil reading material that is corrupting youth! . . . However, behind their backs loomed unchallenged, evil reading matter that is corrupting grown-ups! . . . Youth! . . . Save our grown-ups! . . . Save them from the bad influences of . . . Newspapers!" The first page shows an adult so shocked by what he saw in a comic book that he rips it up. The caption reads, "While grown-up destroys youth's reading matter . . . no one destroys grown-up's reading matter!" On the next six pages, Kurtzman and Davis present their version of a contemporary tabloid newspaper (this one called *The Daily Poop*) full of sensational articles and lurid pictures loaded with sex, violence and other sordid material, in both the news and the advertisements.

The other standout item in *Mad* #16 is "Restaurant!," in what Kurtzman called "The American Scene Dept.," which lampoons the typical experience of a family going out for a Sunday afternoon meal. (The restaurant is overcrowded, the staff is rude, the food is unsanitary, etc.) "Newspapers!" and "Restaurant!" are two more examples of Kurtzman expanding the comic's horizons, and laying more of the groundwork for what *Mad* would become.

Since his humor was reality-based, it's not too surprising that Harvey Kurtzman was a news junkie. He had been since his teenage years. He once told an interviewer, "I'm fascinated with the news—have a fetish with it— and I love to read it, watch it, hear it."[24] He shaved and got dressed in the morning listening to the news on the radio, regularly read the newspaper, and watched the evening news on TV (only fifteen minutes long in 1954). He saw a great deal of the televised McCarthy hearings, which inspired "What's My Shine!" in *Mad* #17. It proposed jazzing up the staid hearings broadcasts by changing them to a game show format. Based on the popular *What's My Line?* TV program, where a celebrity panel asked questions in order to determine what the guest did for a living, Kurtzman's story postulates a panel with senators (including Senator Joseph McCartaway) and a few pretty women to give it the "proper balance." When McCartaway accuses the "guest" of being a "redskin," chaos breaks out and the "friendly quiz game" ends in a wrestling melee. Thus, Kurtzman managed to satirize not only the Senate hearings, but televised wrestling and game shows in one story. Satirizing Senator McCarthy at that juncture wasn't as perilous as it might have been at the beginning of the year. The senator's popularity plunged after the American public reacted negatively to his interrogation tactics on television.

Bernard Krigstein was a guest artist in *Mad* #17. It was his second outing in the comic. The first instance had been for "From Eternity Back to Here!" in #12. Now Kurtzman used his art as a contrast to Will Elder's pages in "Bringing Back Father!" Elder drew lighthearted "comic strip pages" and Krigstein's interspersed pages show what the physical humor in *Bringing Up Father* (Maggie throwing dishes at Jiggs) would be like if it happened in real life. Elder's approximation of George McManus's artwork is fine, but Kurtzman wasn't happy with Krigstein's portion. "The worst relationship I had was probably with Bernie Krigstein. I respected Bernie, I thought he was a very fine cartoonist of sorts. There was probably more fine art in Bernie's work than in anyone's. But he just didn't understand the essence of the story. And I think I have a perfect right to say what the essence was, since I created it, and I knew where it was supposed to be heading, I knew what I wanted. But Bernie would take off on a tangent. And he did *not* have a great sense of humor."[25] The cover of that issue consisted of a message reading, "Attention! This issue is going to change your whole viewpoint of *Mad*." The inside pages were bound into the cover upside down. One had to turn it over to read it, making it appear that you were reading it the wrong way up.

Mad #18 was the last issue (other than #22, a special case) to be wholly made up of narrative stories. The subsequent comic book issues of *Mad* have only one or two such stories, as it continued to evolve. Even within the narrative story, there was innovation of form. In "Alice in Wonderland!," Jack Davis was first called upon to approximate the John Tenniel drawings from the books, mix in his own drawing style, and then imitate the animated look of Bugs Bunny, who took over for the Tenniel White Rabbit. Alice's landing after falling in the rabbit's hole ends with an unceremonious "SPLAT," and the caption, "What a mess!"

"Howdy Dooit!" in that same issue continues Elder's trend of minimizing the subgags, perhaps because the panels are often filled with the pint-sized members of the "Peewee Gallery." After Howdy Dooit spends a great deal of time huckstering for various products, Buffalo Bill asks one child what he wants to be when he grows up. The kid responds, "Of course . . . advertising and entertainment are lucrative fields if one hits the top brackets . . . much like Howdy Dooit has! In other words . . . what I want to do when I grow up, is to be a hustler like Howdy Dooit!" Buffalo Bill points out that Howdy Dooit was merely a wooden marionette with strings, "no mercenary, money-grubbing hustler," adding, "I, Buffalo Bill, am the mercenary, money grubbing hustler!" In the end, Bill is revealed to be a puppet himself. Presumably, his strings are manipulated by corporate puppeteers.

Mad #19 and #20 continue the almost unbroken string of superb comic strip or comic book parodies by Kurtzman and Elder. Being denizens of that milieu and fans of the medium all their lives, they had a special feel for them. Merely satirizing the comics in the pages of another comic book made it more possible to imitate the original in a way that the movie and TV satires could not. Having someone as talented and dedicated as Will Elder doing the art in the style of the original creator made these comics almost indistinguishable from the original at first glance.

In "Mickey Rodent!," the team has a lot of fun pointing out certain aspects of the Walt Disney comics: the characters inexplicably wear white gloves, Darnold Duck doesn't wear pants, all the animals talk except Pluto, and so on. Not that Kurtzman felt any of it was of great importance. To him, it wasn't a big deal that Mickey only had three fingers on each hand: "It's a flaw in the sense that the public is accepting a three-fingered thing with white gloves. After all, let's not forget that Mickey is a huge,

Mad #19 (January 1955).

upright, talking mouse . . . bigger than a giant rat. All I'm doing is trying to entertain people and remind them how the world really is. It's not a terrible disaster that Disney draws three fingers, it's just a comment. If there's anything there, it's that you're bringing your audience back to the reality of what life is alongside of what Disney is making it into."[26]

Kurtzman felt that his "Katchandhammer Kids!" was one of his best-constructed parodies, but what's most remarkable about it is his use of language in the story. He had already amply shown a facility with comic accents and slang, but with this satire of the *Katzenjammer Kids* (originated by Rudolph Dirks in 1897), he took it to a new level. Hans and Fleetz, portrayed as cigarette-smoking juvenile delinquents, begin speaking in German that's not understandable to those who don't speak the language, but on p. 5, that changes. As the two incorrigible urchins torture "der Captain," their "German" suddenly becomes penetrable. "Ven ich ist gefinished mit eim, der kapitan ist *kaput!*" The way Kurtzman plays with the language is entertaining in itself, though the visuals by Elder are first rate, too. The kids are tied to a railroad track after having been flogged by the Captain. In a universe filled with the kind of over-the-top comical violence in the earlier pages, it almost seems justified.

The front cover of *Mad* #20 was famously designed to look like a school composition book, something that was blasted by the *Hartford Courant*, and didn't endear the publication to teachers when students playfully tried to read it in class. (Most teachers hated *Mad* anyway.) Also in that issue: the inventive "Sound Effects!" drawn by Wallace Wood. It gave Wood an assignment with an innovative script that was heavily dependent on his ability to put it across. "Sound Effects!" has no dialogue, except for a few grunts and groans. Kurtzman begins, "You know . . . in a comic book, there's plenty going on you sometimes don't notice! Take for instance, when the villain is getting stabbed he goes 'gnnngg!' Do you appreciate what goes into writing the 'gnnngg'? So for this whole story, we gave it to write to our man who writes the 'gnnngg' and all the rest of the comic book sound effects!" Here are Kurtzman and Wood at the top of their form, working without any words other than "Thud!," "Klomp klomp klomp," "Smak," "Aarrgh?" and the like. The story of a murder, a detective, a femme fatale, a villain and three cops is told with perfect clarity, with humor (not only in the exaggerated sound effects, but the events in the story) and a final panel that tops a running gag begun on p. 1. It's a virtuoso example of pure comics.

Top: "Starchie" by Kurtzman and Elder. Bottom: "Concept covers" from *Mad* #12 and #14.

16.

MAD AT EACH OTHER

IN 1954, THE *MAD* JUGGERNAUT rolled on, delivering brilliant satire issue after issue, and selling better than ever. Harvey Kurtzman was producing comics that constitute the creative peak of his career. His work was never more inspired or better realized than in the title's monthly issues, even more remarkable because they were produced against a background of acrimony and rising dissatisfaction.

In the beginning, things went smoothly between Kurtzman and Gaines. In 1949, Kurtzman was desperate for work, and Bill Gaines provided a safe harbor for the struggling cartoonist. Kurtzman was grateful, and worked with great intensity to earn the paychecks (at good rates for the industry), to prove his worth to the publisher, and to advance his art. Very quickly, Gaines recognized Kurtzman's talent as both a writer and artist, and before long, gave Kurtzman carte blanche as editor on first one, then two, comic book titles.

Gaines and Kurtzman also developed a personal relationship and saw each other outside the office. On weekends, Bill Gaines's Cadillac convertible was a familiar sight to the residents of Audrey Avenue. Often it would pull up in front of the dark red Kurtzman house around dinnertime. Gaines never failed to bring wine and a prodigious appetite. When the doorbell rang, from his attic, Harvey would look outside, spot the vehicle and head downstairs to greet his publisher. "I was very fond of him as a friend," Gaines recalled. "Some of the most pleasant nights of my life were spent sitting in front of Harvey's roaring fire in that old haunted house. We'd . . . drink Cherry Heering and chew the fat and have a wonderful time."[1] After dinner, dessert and coffee, they would have rambling discussions on current events, the arts and undoubtedly some aspects of work.

"It was fun," Gaines said, "although all we did was argue, because we could never see eye-to-eye on anything."[2] One of the topics of contention, which intensified over time, revolved around Kurtzman's objection to the EC horror comics. Kurtzman felt it was immoral to publish gory comics in a medium readily available to children. Over time, he also blamed those comics (and others like them) for bringing down the wrath of parents and the government on all comic books. Gaines felt that anyone interested in an EC horror book wasn't going to be harmed by it, and therefore the hue and cry against those comics was misguided. He felt no responsibility for the ravings of people he regarded as totally off base.

As the anti-comics furor built in 1953, Gaines was concerned that his livelihood was in jeopardy and was upset that one of his key men opposed those comics. After all, the horror and crime comics paid for other books that were less profitable or even losing money: "What Harvey never could grasp . . . is that the only reason there were his war books and the only reason there was a *Mad* was from the money we made on the horror books, and it doesn't seem fair . . . that Harvey has these bad feelings toward those very magazines—whatever he may have thought of them—which provided the money that the magazines he edited were published with, because his magazines didn't make money then."[3] This issue in its various facets became a sore point between the two men. Gaines continued to visit the Kurtzmans.

Al Jaffee, who knew both men well, is of the opinion that those visits weren't always as welcomed by Harvey as they were by Adele. "[Bill] would . . . take them to a big restaurant and feed them and spend the whole weekend, *every* weekend, with Harvey. And Harvey was not an easy person to get too close to. Harvey always had a hand out . . . pushing you away. He wanted to have . . . intellectual interchanges, but he was comfortable in his own skin and in his own house and in his own things, and he didn't want to have anybody move in too close. So there had to come a time where he would, in my view not consciously, test Bill Gaines's love."[4]

Other disagreements cropped up. Kurtzman had been angered by the publication of *Panic* and the Gaines parody-profile in *Mad* #5. Many of their quarrels were over financial matters. Gaines thought like a businessman and Kurtzman was an artist and an idealist. Neither understood the other's point of view, but Gaines signed the checks. What Kurtzman later called "one of the bitterest quarrels between me and Gaines" was over the twelve *Hey Look!* pages reprinted in *Mad* #7 and #8.

> I had contacted [Martin Goodman's] Magazine Management, and they had offered to let me have the pages for $25 per, for reprint rights. I naive-ly accepted the offer, which Gaines issued an EC check for. I had assumed that since Gaines, through me, had made a bargain for material at nearly half the price of what he paid for pages, my residual would be the dif-ference. Gaines refused to pay me anything since EC had paid [Martin] Goodman for the rights and if I was to get a cut, it would have to come from Goodman. Naturally, at that point, I couldn't go back to Goodman. I was too pressed by my deadline to lose the pages. I had been too naive to buy the rights myself, from Goodman and resell them to Gaines.[5]

As a result, Kurtzman lost a substantial amount of anticipated in-come. When he wanted to reprint *Pot-Shot Pete* in *Mad*, he knew to handle it differently.

Roughly coinciding with that disagreement and the deteriorating re-lationship between Gaines and Kurtzman was the appearance of a new player on the scene: Lyle Stuart, publisher of *Exposé*. It was *Mad* that drew Stuart to Gaines, as Stuart recounted.

> I accidentally picked up a copy of *Mad* #4 at my local ice cream/candy store in North Bergen, New Jersey. I was so intrigued by the quality of its humor that I sent a seventy-five cent check to Bill for the three back is-sues. Bill returned the check together with about two-and-a-half pounds of his magazines because he wanted to let me know that I had been one of his heroes. *Exposé* had inspired him to include at least one story against racism in every one of his books. I returned the check, and he returned the check, and the check went back and forth for several weeks until he finally realized I insisted on paying for those three back issues.[6]

Both *Mad* and *Exposé* were antiestablishment and broke taboos. Stuart also worked in comics, earning most of his living by writing scripts for *John Wayne Adventure Comics*, *Billy the Kid* and other titles. He said, "I didn't happen to be an EC reader at all. *Mad* #4 was the first EC I recall seeing."[7]

If Gaines and Stuart had their first contact when that issue of *Mad* hit the stands, it would have been in February or March of 1953. They met in person over dinner at the Art Students League. Gaines was nothing less than enthralled by Stuart. When his business manager Frank Lee decided to retire, Gaines offered Stuart the job even though he had no accounting background. Lyle Stuart was a high school dropout. His publishing résumé wasn't especially impressive. But Gaines was convinced that Stuart was street-smart and trustworthy, especially after Stuart went through EC's ledgers and showed him how he could cut expenses. Feldstein and Kurtzman discovered that Gaines was relying heavily on Stuart's advice. Part of Stuart's appeal for Gaines was that the latter wanted a friend who understood a publisher's point of view, but there was something deeper in the attachment. Possibly Gaines, whose self-esteem had been severely battered as a youth, was drawn to Stuart's aura of supreme self-confidence. Before long, Stuart moved his offices to 225 Lafayette St. (on another floor than EC), where he spent about half his time as publisher of *Exposé*, then renamed the *Independent*, and the rest of his time handling the business affairs of EC.

Stuart created friction almost from the start. Feldstein said, "Lyle and I were like oil and water. I didn't particularly care for him. Nobody liked Lyle. He was a manipulator and a controller. I had been like Bill's partner. He wouldn't admit it, but we would consult all the time on . . . everything. But Lyle drove a wedge between Bill and me. He talked Bill into not plotting stories with me anymore. He told Bill he was a publisher, and Al could hire writers, which I had to do.

"When the Senate hearings came along, I was totally against Bill testifying. So many people involved in those hearings had different agendas. But Lyle built it up, and suddenly Bill decided he would demand to be brought publicly before the committee. That was how Bill got pilloried on national television. He got crucified."[8] Stuart was also the instigator of the "Are You a Red Dupe?" editorial page that ran in all the EC comics, which essentially branded the anti-comics crusaders as Communists or their patsies. It enraged the members of the Senate committee, who felt it was aimed at them. Kurtzman shared Feldstein's dislike of Stuart. "Lyle Stuart was a freaky guy who . . . met Bill because he was my fan. I couldn't stand Lyle. It was one of those visceral reactions that I had. Did you ever run into a person where your flesh crawls?" He continued, "Lyle Stuart [was] obnoxious. He came to my house one night with Bill. And I have fairly traditional attitudes about conduct around the house. He's sitting in the middle of the living room yelling, 'Prick! Fuck!' at the top of his voice, apropos of something he was saying. And I kept saying, 'Look, my kids are in the house.' But he was without a sense of anything traditional. He was bad news."[9] Adele seconded Harvey's opinion of Stuart. She later said,

"Gaines had advice from a man who I don't mind saying I find very nasty, Lyle Stuart. He's coarse and crude. And he was Bill's best friend."[10] As Nancy Siegel, who would soon become Gaines's fiancée, put it, "[Stuart] was a horrible man. He was truly evil."[11]

Of Kurtzman, Stuart—who had contacted Gaines because he enjoyed *Mad*—said, "Harvey was a prima donna who really didn't have a popular touch. [He] was like one of those crazy Hollywood directors who thinks the more money spent, the more positively it reflects on them."[12] Although the serious problems didn't begin until Stuart officially became EC's business manager in the second half of 1953, Gaines was consulting with Stuart shortly after they met. His response to Harvey's position vis-à-vis the payments for the *Hey Look!* reprints was more Stuart's style than that of Gaines. The fact that the EC publisher was (by his own admission) taking Dexedrine as a diet aid didn't help. Dexedrine was a stimulant that acted similarly to methamphetamine (which was developed later) with its attendant mood swings, from tremendous highs when one is bursting with self-confidence to terrible lows (which can present as paranoia) when the drug wears off.

Gaines and Kurtzman's relationship deterioration mostly centered on financial matters. When Gaines gave expensive gifts and picked up large dinner tabs, Kurtzman was reminded that Gaines was making a lot more from *Mad* than he was. As Bill Gaines saw it, he was paying Harvey Kurtzman a good salary for *Mad*, one that had been adjusted to take into account the comic book's profitability. Beyond that, he felt Kurtzman was owed little more than token raises, even as EC's coffers were filling up with those profits. It wasn't really that different than the situation that Siegel and Shuster found themselves in after creating Superman while working for National Comics. Millions were made off the Man of Steel, but the creators were simply among the better-paid employees. Bill Gaines felt Harvey Kurtzman was a highly talented man who was also a pain in the ass, that he was a "nudge" who seemed perpetually dissatisfied.

"There was a growing unhappiness between me and the publisher," Kurtzman recalled. "I resented him and he resented me. [Gaines] and I got into a series of ever-increasing arguments going around in ever diminishing circles."[13] At a company like National, cowed creative personnel hardly dared question management decisions. At EC, Gaines was always willing to listen when Feldstein or Kurtzman had a problem or idea, and there were times he got an earful. Despite a pronounced distaste for confrontation, Kurtzman didn't hesitate to assert his views and try to push Gaines in certain directions. As with Dan Barry on *Flash Gordon*, occasionally

Harvey seemed to forget who had the final say. "Sometimes Harvey [lost] sight of the fact that this was my business," Gaines said. "Harvey could never realize that *Mad* was mine. He thought it was his."[14] Apparently, Gaines couldn't understand why Kurtzman was upset with the inequity of the work-for-hire system.

"Bill . . . always had a very strong intellectual understanding of democratic processes, up to a certain point," Kurtzman remarked. Then, he said (only partly tongue-in-cheek) Gaines "turns into a monster."[15] Of course, a business—unless it's a cooperative—isn't a democracy. An owner, whose capital is at risk, must exercise fiscal prudence and caution, and make decisions based on factors that often aren't apparent to those in his employ.

Sometimes Kurtzman's questioning of Gaines led to things highly beneficial to EC. Kurtzman was the one who insisted that Gaines made a mistake by quickly capitulating when National said they couldn't legally satirize its copyrighted characters. Had Gaines's position been allowed to stand, and especially if it was extended to the characters of other comic book companies as well, *Mad* would have been unduly constrained. (Gaines later called Kurtzman a "hero" for getting him to reverse the ill-considered position.)[16]

Secondly, it would soon become clear that Kurtzman's idea to convert *Mad* to a magazine ensured that it not only dodged the Comics Code, but that it became the kind of cash cow that no single comic book could ever be. Kurtzman felt all along that he and his artists weren't paid well enough for their work, and knew that magazines were able to pay much higher rates than comic books. Thus, a *Mad* magazine would potentially have the resources to better reward the creative staff which, in turn, would help retain top talent. Eventually, that's exactly what happened.

Another instance when Kurtzman pushed for something that proved to be immensely profitable for EC occurred in the summer of 1954. The paperback book industry was exploding in the 1950s, because paperbacks were a more attractive and streamlined product than pulp magazines. Paperbacks were proliferating in most of the old pulp genres: Western, romance, crime, science fiction, mystery and so forth. Fawcett's Gold Medal originals were so profitable that the firm scarcely missed the revenues lost when they closed their comic book division. Ballantine Books was another up-and-coming paperback publisher. In response to the meteoric rise of *Mad*, Ian Ballantine met with Bill Gaines to propose paperback reprints of *Mad*. Gaines was interested until he found out the kind of royalty Ballantine was offering. However, Kurtzman stepped in and urged Gaines to accept the deal: "Bill Gaines didn't want to do it. He didn't think the terms were good enough. So [Ballantine] kept coming back, and he kept turning them down. And I wanted it bad! I wanted the paperback very bad."[17] Kurtzman understood that getting comics material published in paperback form was a good idea even if the terms weren't as rewarding as they wished. Paperbacks were a much higher form than comic books, and such reprints hadn't happened before. For the material in *Mad* to be considered important enough to actually be reprinted in a book, even a paperback book, would be a coup in the world of publishing, and a real validation of what they were doing. "I finally wore Bill down, or at least that was my impression," Kurtzman said years later. "We went back to Ballantine and did the first [book]. I think I chose the material . . . in collusion with Bernie Shir-Cliff [Ballantine's editor]. There was a lot of back and forth. Bernie was very bright."[18]

Gaines verbally agreed that Kurtzman would be paid 25 percent of all royalties from the reprint books. The artists would split another 25 percent, and EC would get 50 percent.[19] Kurtzman stated, "I put four times the work into a story than [most creators in comic books] normally would. I deliberately used techniques that would have a residual value. Our approach was unconventional and with unconventional understandings."[20] Gaines apparently bought into that theory by agreeing to share the roy-

alties, although he had no legal obligation to do so. Other publishers routinely reprinted work with no additional payment to the writers or artists, although not in paperback books at this time.

The Mad Reader deal inadvertently provided a source of inspiration that would have another far-reaching effect for *Mad*. When he was visiting Bernard Shir-Cliff's office, Kurtzman noticed a postcard (pinned up on the editor's wall) with the image of a grinning, moronic face. The words "What, Me Worry?" were printed underneath. He remembered seeing a drawing of that face somewhere before: "What interested me about this Ballantine version was that of all the reproduc-

The Mad Reader (November 1954).

tions I remembered, this one looked like the authentic, original-source portrait—the real goods. While everything I'd seen before was a cartoon, this seemed to be a photograph of the actual face! So I pocketed the card and rushed back to the workshop where I inserted the 'What, Me Worry?' face on and in subsequent issues of *Mad* magazine."[21] It also appeared on the cover of *The Mad Reader*. Ultimately named Alfred E. Neuman, that character's face would become the visual trademark of *Mad*, originally appearing in the comic book before the magazine. Had *The Mad Reader* deal not happened, not only would Gaines have lost the financial returns for the books which racked up staggering sales, but Alfred E. Neuman—at least with that unforgettable face—would never have existed.

Ballantine published *The Mad Reader* in November 1954. Kurtzman designed the cover and the book's format. It reprinted "Superduperman!," "Newspapers!," "Starchie," "Flesh Garden!," "Dragged Net!," "What's My Shine!," "The Face Upon the Floor," "Gasoline Valley!" and "Lone Stranger," as well as several ad parodies. Although having to hold the book sideways to read the stories was a bit awkward, the artwork looked dazzling in black and white. Some of the tiny details that had been colored over by Marie Severin were more easily discernible. Roger Price, who was well known for his *Droodles* newspaper comic strip, wrote the introduction to *The Mad Reader* gratis, presumably because he was a fan of *Mad*, and because the association could help publicize his other books (which were published by Ballantine). In his introduction, he wrote these much-quoted lines about Harvey Kurtzman: "He is 5 feet 6 inches tall and has a physique that is just barely noticeable and a long expression. In fact—Harvey looks like a Beagle who is too polite to mention that someone is standing on his tail."[22] The paperback sold so well that Ballantine went back to press six times in the following year. *The Mad Reader* remained continuously in print for two decades. As soon as the initial sales reports were in, a sequel (*Mad Strikes Back*) and a whole series of follow-up books were set into motion. Over the years, EC made a fortune on the paperbacks.

In any case, the Gaines-Kurtzman relationship was seriously damaged by late 1954, and with Lyle Stuart getting between Gaines and his editors, opportunities for rapprochements were more difficult to find. The visits to the Kurtzman home tapered off once Gaines had a new best friend.

WHILE KURTZMAN DISLIKED aspects of the comic book field—notably that writers and artists were paid so little for their effort, the cheap printing and the low regard comics had in the literary world—he felt grand things could be done in the sequential art form, as he told an interviewer in 1974:

"There have been genuine artisans, hard at work, doing stuff that has given me a genuine thrill."[23] In 1954, Kurtzman began work on an ambitious story that, had it found a publisher, would have been what is now called a graphic novel.

Kurtzman, a fan of Charles Dickens, was especially enamored of *A Christmas Carol*. He thought a comics adaptation of the story published in book form could sell very well during the holiday season. Thus, while keeping up the demanding schedule of *Mad*, he invested a great deal of time and energy producing a presentation for such a book. The project was an early example of his bent for exploring new formats and frameworks for comic art.

Kurtzman created thumbnail guides for about seventy pages of "Marley's Ghost," although his adaptation would ultimately run in excess of one hundred pages. Then he took eight of them to final form, using ink, watercolor and tempera paint. The dark, moody pages were executed in the lean, expressionistic style of his self-drawn war stories. Kurtzman's extraordinary interpretation perfectly suited the story of Ebenezer Scrooge's harrowing encounters with supernatural forces. However, to provide an alternative to his "extreme" style of art, Kurtzman had Jack Davis work up a sample page in his own, more mainstream, style—impressive in its own way, though less evocative. In his cover letter to Simon & Schuster, Harvey pitched it as a large coffee table book. Not surprisingly, Kurtzman's proposal garnered no interest. No one, certainly not editor Dorothy Bennett or her editorial assistant at the publishing house, had the vision to see the potential of such a graphic novel. Kurtzman might have pursued it farther with the help of a literary agent who believed in the project, but it would have taken a publisher with the instincts of a gambler to invest in such an uncertain proposition at the time.

Kurtzman's belief in the sophisticated use of the graphic story medium was far ahead of its time. Graphic novels wouldn't find acceptance for decades. Nevertheless, "Marley's Ghost" was concrete proof that he saw great potential in telling extended stories in illustrated form. His response in August 1954 to a column by the respected journalist Dorothy Thompson in the *Ladies' Home Journal* related to this subject, and is worth quoting at length.

> Dear Miss Thompson:
> Being a comic book writer editor artist, I was attracted to your *Ladies' Home Journal* article on comic books. Reading the article, an accusing finger took shape pointing out of the pages at me, and suddenly I could

not refrain from writing you. Two ideas your article dealt with interested me especially . . . the first being the Freedom of the Press issue, and the second being the evils of reading pictures.

Being a writer has, I am sure, made you more sensitive to the meaning and purpose of freedom of the press, and you expressed its relation to children very well. I think I agree with you in that I believe that since children are not legally responsible for their acts (their parents are), they are therefore in a legal caste that should allow their relation to Free Press to be restricted. There is certainly a legal basis with which to deal with comic books.

Now as to your attitude towards pictures, I can't help feeling it is a "holier than thou" attitude that you have. Towards the end of your article you expressed the idea that reading pictures tends "to make the bright dull, the dull feeble minded." From our own rather large picture-reading experience, we find it very hard to go along with you there. We have a very active correspondence with our readers and from the mountains of letters we have received, patterns have taken shape . . . none indicating that we with our pictures have lured children away from their intelligence.

Let me explain. We have discovered that our product consists of two elements . . . the picture and the text. We know, from a thousand experiences, that we can roughly divide our readers into three groups . . . the reader who has a mind for the text, the reader who has a mind for the picture, and the reader who has a mind for both. Very often, an artist will do an especially fine job on the pictures . . . however, the accompanying text will be badly written. Such a story will get letters of praise usually from would-be cartoonists, kids going to art school and generally readers with a mind for the picture. And of course, the critical letters will come from the readers with the literary bent. It never ceases to amaze me that the one type reader doesn't see the well drawn picture and the other type of reader doesn't see the well written text.

Here's the point.

The reader who is attracted by pictures is not necessarily a truant from the classics. He is rather one with a talent for receiving a picture image. It is usually the person who finds no interest in pictures who is seemingly deficient in that particular ability or sensitivity towards absorbing a picture. I wonder if amongst your own friends, the ones that read and enjoy *Life* magazine, whether that is any measure of their intellect.

This is no rationalization for the vulgar comic book. It just grieves me to see people treat the "picture," whether it be printed, projected or televised, as an indecent medium.

Gutenberg invented moveable type and marked a high-point in the advance of communication. However, the science of mediums of communication did not end with "type." Because of developments and discoveries in the last one-hundred years, we can reproduce pictures as never before. To say that "in the 'comic' or picture-book, nothing is left to the imagination of the child" is simply untrue and reflects a short acquaintance and understanding of pictures. It will do no good to treat pictures as the poor illegitimate substitute for type. Type and pictures are relatives with different properties and potentials.

Pictures . . . comic book pictures are put to good and bad use just like radios, telephones, and "slick" magazines. There is a lot of good to be said for comics. If either you or the *Ladies' Home Journal* are at all curious, I would be glad to forward to you some comic book work I feel sure can lay a slight claim to distinction . . . ethical, aesthetic, and intellectual."

Sincerely,

Harvey Kurtzman

The letter made it clear that, while Kurtzman felt the physical package of the comic book was vulgar, he believed in the legitimacy of the sequential art medium and was an advocate for it.

Harold Hayes's article on *Mad* in the June 1954 issue of *Pageant* magazine had seemed a pleasant but relatively inconsequential occurrence. What came from it, however, proved to be the most important event in Harvey Kurtzman's career since he entered Bill Gaines's office five years earlier. Alex L. Hillman, publisher of *Pageant*, had founded his publishing house in the late 1930s with magazines such as *Real Confessions* and *Crime Detective*, then branched out into comic books. Airboy and The Heap were Hillman's best-known comic book characters. In 1944, he began publishing the digest-sized, slick *Pageant* as a competitor to the popular *Coronet*. Ten years later, it was selling in the 400,000 range. Hillman—a right-wing Republican who one might expect to look askance at *Mad*—was intrigued by the Hayes article and the excerpts from the Kurtzman comic book in his magazine's pages.

Several months later, Harvey Kurtzman received a lucrative job offer from Hillman periodicals. Kurtzman's memory of the timing, the exact position and salary offered was hazy in interviews done decades later. He said merely that he would have become Harris Shevelson's assistant

Bill Gaines (1954). AP-Wide World wire service photograph.

editor. Gaines, who claimed he had a good memory for such things, said, "Harvey got an offer from Shevelson to come to *Pageant* and edit a section of the magazine."[24] The offer, Gaines said, was for $12,000 a year. He didn't remember the exact date of the offer, only that it came "some time later, as a result of the *Pageant* article."[25] Kurtzman recalled that the offer was tendered at a "crossroads," when "the comic *Mad* was in trouble. There was the pressure of the Comic Code."[26] However, since Gaines at that time intended to publish his comics without joining the Code (something he was soon forced to do), the decision to change *Mad* to the magazine format was purely a result of the *Pageant* offer. It occurred sometime in December 1954.[27]

Gaines recalled, "Harvey was getting something in the neighborhood of $800 an issue [at EC]. And twelve issues times eight was nowhere near $12,000."[28] Remembering that Kurtzman had broached the idea of converting *Mad* to a magazine, Gaines asked his mother (who owned half of the EC stock) if she would support such a change in order to keep Kurtzman. It would be a risk. They would essentially be betting their company on its success. Would enough readers be willing to pay twenty-five cents for a satire magazine? Jessie Gaines approved the plan. "I countered Shevelson's offer with $10,000, but offered to let Harvey change *Mad* into a slick," Gaines said. "Harvey accepted."[29]

Kurtzman's acceptance of Gaines's counter-offer signaled three things. First, money wasn't his top priority (although he did anticipate royalties from the *Mad Reader* and follow-up paperbacks). Second, being editor of *Mad* magazine was better than being an assistant editor of *Pageant*. Third, Kurtzman wanted to do a satire magazine, and had little interest—and probably little confidence—in doing general editing work.[30] One remembers his insecurity with grammar, spelling and as a writer in general. It seems doubtful he would have accepted the job, but it made a good bargaining chip to get what he wanted at EC.

The format change couldn't happen overnight. Gaines needed time to crunch the numbers, discuss the matter with his distributor, and generally get ready to enter a new publishing arena. Plus he was in the middle of coordinating the production of a new raft of "clean, clean" comic books, after having realized he had no choice but to drop all his horror and crime titles. Likewise, Kurtzman needed time to plan for the changeover. Meanwhile, the comic book *Mad* was going strong, and the monthly deadlines kept coming.

Kurtzman continued to experiment with the covers of the monthly *Mad*. After the *Life* magazine parody on #11, he never returned to the comic-art approach of the earlier issues. Some of the conceptual covers worked better than others. The joke of the "racing form" cover of #19 (that the comic book was "educational") wasn't particularly funny, whereas the "composition book" cover of #20 ("designed to sneak into class") went over big with readers. The cover of *Mad* #21 (March 1955), an elaborate satire of comic book ads for arcane products and novelties, was undoubtedly the most time-consuming to create. The satirical ads offered such novelties as a live crocodile for seventy-five cents ("this seven foot animal will provide hours of fun"), "Sure Win Dice" ("anyone who wants a pair is a dirty no-good bum thief") and a genuine Gatling Gun ("especially useful in case you happen to be going to India up around that Rudyard Kipling neighborhood and that Gunga Din territory"). Kurtzman got a huge kick out of that cover, commenting, "You have to read it with a microscope . . . and every sentence is funny. About a year's worth of writing went into that cover."[31] It was the first time the "What, Me Worry" face appeared on a cover of *Mad*, albeit quite small. More than once, Gaines said this was his favorite cover of the comic book issues.

In the issues before the changeover, *Mad* carried more excellent comic strip parodies. "Poopeye!" drawn by Elder in #21 expertly emulated E. C.

Segar's work and went several steps farther by including cameos by Li'l Abner, Tarzan and Superman, each drawn in the style of their original artists. *Mad* #22 was entirely devoted to a biography of Will Elder in comics form.

The satire of Walt Kelly's *Pogo* in "Gopo Gossum!" in #23 was even better than "Poopeye!" Kurtzman and Wood focused on the political component of Kelly's strip, with animals resembling certain well-known public figures. In this take-off, the political squabbling ended up taking over the strip, capped by an atomic bomb explosion in "Okeekeefoonie Swamp." In the course of the story, an interloper named "McCarthy" appeared, and, though he has the face of Charlie McCarthy, ventriloquist Edgar Bergen's famous dummy, he clearly represented Senator Joseph McCarthy. He echoed the now-censured Senator's "Don't get cute with me!" refrain and accused his critics of being Democrats. The story concluded with the Disney characters looking on, wondering why any cartoon character would want to learn politics. Wallace Wood's imitation of Kelly's art was so close that he could have ghosted the actual strip, and Kurtzman's parody of the writing in *Pogo* was another example of his facility for creating comical dialogue in dialect, while also lampooning the work of a specific writer. These last issues of the *Mad* comic book ran features that would be carried over in the upcoming magazine, such as, "Scenes we'd . . . like to see!," "Believe it or Don't!," and "Slow Motion!" (a sports satire), as well as movie parodies such as "Under the Waterfront!" and "The Barefoot Nocountessa!"

Then came the announcement of the upcoming change: Page 1 of *Mad* #23 (May 1955) was emblazoned with these words in large print:

very very
very very
very very
important
announcement
in the back
of the book!

In the back of the comic book, Kurtzman wrote:

Though it may come as a shock (or a pleasant surprise) to you, with this issue, #23, we are discontinuing *Mad* comic book. But don't go away.

We're expanding *Mad* into a regular big 25 cent magazine with pictures, printed lettering, covers, and everything, gang. Boy, what exciting plans. Are we excited. Mainly since this may put us out of business,
we're sick to our stomachs with excitement. For the past two years now,
Mad has been dulling the senses of the country's youth. Now we get to
work on the adults.

As yet, we haven't determined our publication date, but the new *Mad*
should be on the stands within three months. Now if each one of you
good-old loyal *Mad* readers gets your parents to go out and buy 150 copies
of the new *Mad* when it appears, we are bound to be a success. We know
you'll do this little favor for us, eh, loyal readers?

Indeed, the announcement came as a shock to *Mad*'s readers, especially
those who were more than casual followers. Bhob Stewart was one of the
comic's loyal readers. "I became fascinated by the subjects Kurtzman satirized, and in that sense, *Mad* was educational. For instance, after 'From
Eternity Back to Here!' appeared in issue #12 (June 1954), I read the James
Jones novel. Later, inspired by *Mad*, I experimented with satirical writing
and soon completed a twelve-page parody of my high school newspaper."
When the big announcement appeared in *Mad* #23, Stewart feared the
worst. "I was disappointed to read the announcement of the switch from
comic book to magazine. It seemed too perfect to change."[32]

Wallace Wood signed this Pogo satire "Copied Right 1954 by Walt Wood." From *Mad* #23 (May 1955), the last issue of *Mad* in comic book form.

17.

MAD GOES "LEGIT"

WHEN BILL GAINES agreed to convert *Mad* to a magazine, it was an electrifying moment for Harvey Kurtzman. The thirty-year-old writer-artist was more than ready to make the transition. "I'd always dreamed of getting into the slick magazines," he said. "I wanted to go legit. The difference between slick and newsprint and comic books was like the difference between champagne and mud water. That was my dream."[1]

The change in format immediately raised dozens of questions. Kurtzman recalled, "The next day was one of the most exciting times in my life. I ran down to the newsstand and bought a bunch of slick magazines to see what other people were doing."[2] Though familiar with the basic format used by most magazines, Kurtzman saw them from a new perspective. He examined them with an eye for specifics, much like his boyhood self had studied the details of natural objects under a microscope. Unlike most comic books, magazines had contents pages, which could be set up in various ways, and the letters sections were organized differently. Most ran advertising on the inside of the front cover, which Kurtzman realized would be a perfect place to satirize popular ads. "I designed a format based on what was being done in magazines that year, and on the basis of what our production man George Daugherty told us that Gaines could afford," he said. "I chose the printer, the process, the package, and we were in business."[3]

Through the holiday season, visions of magazine pages danced in his head. "Eventually, I decided on a format that would departmentalize day-to-day events. It was a big experiment. I was scared to death when we abandoned the comic format, and I couldn't sleep wondering whether

Mad would succeed in its new format."[4] When he said in the back of the final comic book issue, "We're sick to our stomachs with excitement," he wasn't kidding.

The twenty-five-cent price was the first thing that was decided. Kurtzman worked backward from there. Ten-cent comic books in 1955 consisted of thirty-two pages plus covers. Page dimensions were seven by ten inches. The new *Mad* would measure 8" by 10 ¾", the size of *Time* and many other magazines. After the type of paper was selected and the cost of printing was taken into account, Kurtzman and Gaines determined that a length of sixty-four pages plus covers was feasible. Since each issue would be twice as long as the comic book, they decided *Mad* magazine would be published bimonthly. Gaines and Kurtzman also agreed that the magazine would contain no ads, at least for the present time. One of the big changes was printing the inside pages in black and white. Kurtzman explained why this was necessary:

> We went into another world. The comic book presses were very specifically made to do comic books—to do a certain size, to do a certain quality of printing. We graduated to good paper using a totally different kind of fine screen press. The comic book press was essentially a newspaper press used for coarse work, and whatever they did came out coarse. And we needed certain refinements. We wanted to upgrade the stock, we wanted to use halftones [to reproduce photographs and paintings], so it was an entirely different package with an entirely different set of figures. There was nobody who was printing anything comparable. We were reproducing strip cartoons in a large magazine format with 120-screen halftones. Our package was truly unique. The offset press couldn't handle a cheap color system and besides that, we didn't want a comic book. We wanted to get away from comic books.[5]

Avoiding the appearance of a comic book would put the new *Mad* firmly outside the purview of the newly minted Comics Code. "We didn't want to abandon our audience, but we wanted to get out from under the censor's thumb. We didn't change our readers, we changed our format."[6] While the paper was better quality than the cheap pulp of comic books, it was not the glossy, high quality slick paper of the top magazines. Therefore, it isn't technically correct to call *Mad* magazine a "slick" as did Gaines and Kurtzman. A better descriptor would be "a standard-sized magazine."

Another change that came with the conversion was the way the original pages were prepared. Kurtzman decided that instead of hand-lettering, all the text would be typeset. This meant sending it all out to a typesetter who would return the titles and text printed in uniform lettering fonts on little pieces of paper. All those pieces (and often parts of the artwork) had to be meticulously pasted-up on art board in such a way that everything was absolutely lined-up and straight. For the production work, Kurtzman selected John Putnam, a fan of the EC war comics who had assisted a bit on the research. Putnam knew nothing about pasting up a magazine. He was hired because he needed a job and Kurtzman liked him: "I decided one day that we needed a production man and Gaines agreed. And there's a lot to that, a lot of work. Above all, it needs order and organization and neatness. I always sensed that John could conceivably have those qualities."[7] Kurtzman gave Putnam detailed layout drawings, and patiently taught him how to translate them to the final pages. Putnam, initially insecure about it, ended up as the production man on *Mad* for decades.

Kurtzman planned on using Wallace Wood, Jack Davis and Will Elder as his main artists. While he intended to do most of the writing himself, he began looking for other writers. This was partly for variety, and partly because he wanted help filling the pages with high quality material. Fortunately, the *Mad* comic book had generated interest from a number of talented writers. Television comedian Ernie Kovacs had gotten in touch with Kurtzman. At one point, Kurtzman visited Kovacs at his Central Park West apartment. Fan letters arrived from Stan Freberg and Doodles Weaver. Kurtzman was a big fan of the comedy team Bob and Ray, and wanted them to write something for the magazine. Roger Price and Bernard Shir-Cliff, who had been involved in the *Mad* paperbacks, would be likely candidates. "We started using text, so we went to the popular funny writers, people like Roger Price and Ernie Kovacs," he said. "We used reprint stuff because we really didn't know how to contact funny writers for original material. We were in a totally new field, so we did what we could understand. We picked up stuff out of books and out of files."[8] This was necessary because the rate EC paid freelance writers was $25 a page, well below the going rates at other magazines. (Kurtzman called it a "schlock rate.") Rates for outside writers would became a bone of contention between Kurtzman and Gaines.

When the comic book *Mad* went monthly, Kurtzman's art no longer appeared on the covers or inside pages. That held true for *Mad*'s new incarnation, except for one important item, arguably the best known piece of artwork Kurtzman ever produced: the *Mad* magazine logo. From both a design and marketing point of view, the most important thing on a magazine cover is the title logo. The style of the logo must express something about the periodical itself, be distinctive enough to stand out on newsstands, and be instantly recognizable. Once designed, the same logo is used on every issue. It comes to represent the magazine in the reader's mind.

The comic book *Mad* sported the same yellow logo on its first ten issues. Then, Kurtzman began playing around with it, customizing it to fit with the concept of the cover. That worked for a comic book, but in magazines of that era, a logo was so important that once set, it never varied (until and if it was redesigned). Kurtzman wanted something different and more impressive than his former yellow logo. What he came up with was a variation of the red logo on the cover of *Mad* #12, which had the three italicized capitals connected by the serifs at the base of each letter. He removed the italics, broadened the letters to make them fatter and wider, and used curved rather than straight serifs. He also added a black shadow to make it stand out on the page. Then, inside the letters, Kurtzman drew little cartoon figures performing various actions. Upon close examination, they appeared to be part of a festival of Dionysus, the Greek god of wine and revelry, whose gamboling figures contrasted with the semi-stuffy look of the sculpted serifs. *Mad* would, it seemed to suggest, threaten staid repression with wild abandon. The red, ornate logo became an indelible

Top: Kurtzman's original logo for *Mad* magazine. Bottom: With issue #27, he revised the interior cartoons slightly. This version was used through *Mad* #86 (April 1964). After that, the interior cartoons were dropped, but the basic outlines of the logo remain on *Mad* to the present day, making it the best known piece of artwork of Kurtzman's career.

symbol of the magazine, though the figures were eventually removed. By then, some might say the anarchistic spirit of Kurtzman's *Mad* was gone, anyway.

The other key part of Kurtzman's cover design was an ornate, filigreed frame that wrapped around all four sides, with images of famous people and aspects of life woven throughout. The historical and cultural figures depicted were Socrates, Napoleon, Freud, Marilyn Monroe, Alexander the Great, Rembrandt, Galileo, Lassie, Tom Swift, Columbus, Caesar, Buffalo Bill, Copernicus, Pasteur, Beethoven and, at the top in the center, Alfred E. Neuman (although he hadn't been given that name yet). All the famous figures (including Lassie) were reading *Mad* except for Marilyn. Also, on the bottom left, there was a somewhat inconspicuous EC symbol. The thick border served several purposes. First, it was another way to make the magazine look distinctive on the newsstand, since it would be used on every issue. Second, by using revered cultural figures, many of who wouldn't be recognized by young readers, it indicated that the magazine had some sort of content for adult readers. Third, having vaunted cultural figures reading *Mad* reinforced the fact that it was a humor magazine, for those who missed the subtitle "Humor in a Jugular Vein," which was carried over.

A message in large letters (with words divided as shown below) filled the picture area of the cover of *Mad* #24. They read:

> This new magazine
> is vital for you
> to read and in-
> side you will find
> an extremely im-
> portant message
> from the editors

When one opened the cover, the first interior page showed the "editors" on their knees with their hands folded in attitudes of supplication, begging in unison,

> Please buy this magazine!

This cartoon was the only other bit of Kurtzman's finished art in that issue, other than the pointer—a six-fingered hand—on the contents page.[9]

Other than the *Mad* logo, the six-fingered hand and cartoon with the creators of *Mad* on their knees are the only pieces of finished Kurtzman art to appear inside *Mad* #24 (July 1955).

The magazine version of *Mad* was a much-anticipated event for regular readers, but none could have been as anxious as Bill Gaines or Harvey Kurtzman. *Mad* was Gaines's only big moneymaker in the midst of the ill-fated New Direction books (and a few New Trend titles that were carried over), and his hopes were pinned on a vessel that was sailing into uncharted waters. As for Kurtzman, both his creative vision and his commercial instincts were on trial, and there was no going back to a comic book format without facing emasculation by the Comics Code. They felt the first issue was a good product, but would it sell? Kurtzman and his staff made a special trip to the Brooklyn printing plant to inspect the pages as they came off the presses, and were heartened when they saw men at the plant laughing as they examined the pages.

Amazingly, the first magazine issue of *Mad* reached newsstands on time, given its new bimonthly schedule: just two months after *Mad* #23. This was quite an achievement for a publication that was reconceived and designed from the ground up. *Mad* #24 was cover dated July 1955, but reached newsstands in mid-May.[10]

With regard to Kurtzman's statement, "now we get to work on the adults," a look at the first magazine issue reveals that it was more the format than the maturity of the subject matter and humor that made it seem to cater to older readers. The contents page was the type found in adult magazines, with photographs of some of the writers. In the letter column, which immediately followed, Kurtzman took the opportunity to reproduce the cover and a couple of panels from *Mad* #23, visual reminders of the magazine's "notorious" past. He also brought forward "potrzebie" in a mock-erudite letter addressing its pronunciation.

Wallace Wood rendered busty movie star Jane Russell in a faux advertisement for her latest film, *Underwater*, renamed *Gluggle*. ("She Wanted to Drown her Troubles.") Wood was able to achieve a great deal of subtlety by using a wash-tone technique (painting with watered-down India ink to create shades of gray), though the crowd of men swimming behind her was drawn with typical cartoon outlines. Wood had used the wash-tone technique in the comic book, but the result was much better in the magazine due to the improved printing and paper.

This wash-tone art technique, widely used in other adult magazines, also helped create a look that was familiar to older readers. The other *Mad* artists employed it, too, enabling them to produce images that approximated the appearance of photographs and paintings. Just as much of the humor of "Mickey Rodent!" had been derived from Will Elder's ability to imitate the cartooning style of the Disney artists, so the effectiveness of movie and advertising parodies in the black and white magazine would be greatly enhanced by wash-tones. The ability to "counterfeit" was a key factor in the success of *Mad* parodies such as the fake ads for "Bofforin," "Bind-Aig Plastic Strips" and "Jell-Y" on the two color back cover, all painted by Elder.

Wallace Wood's value to the magazine was amply apparent in "Is A Trip To The Moon Possible?," the issue's stunning nine-page opener. His handling of rocket ships, moonscapes and space suits demonstrated why many consider Wood the greatest science fiction cartoonist of all time. This comical look at the "realities" of a trip to the moon was Kurtzman at his best, and must have enticed many browsers to plunk down their quarter without looking farther. Two ten-pagers drawn by Jack Davis (one on professional wrestling,

Mad #24 (July 1955). First magazine issue of *Mad*.

the other a satire of the movie *Vera Cruz*) were also top flight, as was the shorter "Anyone can build this Coffee Table" by Kurtzman and Davis. Will Elder contributed the art to Kurtzman's parodies of a number of daily newspaper strips, as well as a nine-page burlesque of the *This is Your Life* television program. Most of the magazine wasn't too different than later issues of the comic book, but it did include items for the college and adult customers. Kurtzman ran a Hemingway parody in the "Literature Dept.," a crime story satire, "Who put the Strichnine in Mrs. Murphy's Husband?," and a guide for college graduates looking for a job. The first issue of *Mad* magazine was excellent in almost every respect, including the most important: it was funny all the way through. Kurtzman and crew were determined to produce an irresistible magazine, and they succeeded. It set the bar high for future issues.

When the sales reports on *Mad* magazine came in, Gaines and Kurtzman found that it didn't simply sell well—it sold out. Copies flew off newsstands so fast, and so many wholesalers received requests for more copies, that the distributor asked for a second printing. A 100 percent sell-through was almost unheard of in the magazine business, and publishers rarely went back to press with an issue. Gaines did. (He estimated that 400,000 copies were initially printed, and then 50,000 more.)[11]

Kurtzman was ecstatic. For him, going "legit" had two parts: adopting a more respectable format, i.e. a magazine, and then being *successful* in that format. "We always had danger two steps behind us," he explained. "I didn't know that [a satire magazine] would sell. I didn't know what I was doing, at the time, as far as success goes. It was just another stab in the dark, and it worked. And then, after it worked, then it felt good, then I felt legit, but before I knew the sales figures, I didn't feel legitimacy."[12] The gamble had paid off: Kurtzman's concept for a satirical magazine worked on all levels.

Shortly after the success of *Mad* magazine was known, there was a party to celebrate the engagement of Bill Gaines to Nancy Siegel at New York's Plaza Hotel. Adele, who was standing next to her husband, recalled, "Al Feldstein was a little tipsy, and he came up to Harvey and said, 'You saved us,' because *Mad* was doing well. It was embarrassing. Harvey said, 'Oh gosh,' you know, didn't say much. But it's true. It happened."[13]

BILL GAINES DESPERATELY needed the good news about *Mad*. The reports from Leader News regarding the new line of comic books launched at the beginning of the year showed sales almost unbelievably bad.

To his credit, Gaines didn't play it safe when considering ideas for EC's New Direction books. That would have meant falling back on proven genres: one or two Westerns, a couple of romance books, maybe a new war or funny animal title. It would have been a sad follow-up to the glory of the New Trend. Instead, he and Feldstein made a brave attempt to produce another innovative line of comics, a line that was worthy of support from their readers, and one that they themselves would enjoy. To *Panic, Piracy* and a revamped *Weird Science-Fantasy* called *Incredible Science Fiction*, the only survivors of the New Trend, Gaines added six books: *Impact* (a sort of watered-down horror title), *Valor* (stories of knights in armor), *Aces High* (a book about World War I air battles), *Extra* (tales of globe-trotting reporters), *Psychoanalysis* ("people searching for peace of mind") and *MD* (doctor and hospital stories). If none of them seem like propitious ideas for four-color thrills and excitement, at least they were different. In the final analysis, their subject matter made no difference. They were fated to fail.

Many wholesalers refused EC's books outright. One reason was because they didn't carry the Comics Code Authority seal of approval. "I put out the six first issues, six bi-monthlies, and they sold 10, 15 percent," Gaines said. "You can't believe how horrendous the sales were. And I later found out that it was because the word was passed by the wholesalers, 'Get 'em!' So they got me." As soon as he heard that, he submitted his books to the CCA. "My sales figures went up from ten to twenty, but it was still disastrous," he recounted. "I kept it up for as long as I could, and then I dropped all the comics and went into Picto-Fiction."[14]

EC's four Picto-Fiction magazines consisted of text stories with illustrations that somewhat resembled comic books. They were Feldstein's idea. He and Gaines hoped the magazine format would succeed like it had for *Mad*, while avoiding the Comics Code because they weren't comic books. Unfortunately, *Shock Illustrated* and three other titles sold even worse than the New Direction comics, despite featuring art by many of the EC stars. News dealers didn't know whether to put them with the comics or the magazines. If there were any readers who were interested, few of them were able to find them. By the end of 1955, all the New Direction and Picto-Fiction titles were gone. The EC Christmas party that year was more like a wake than a celebration. Gaines could only afford to give out $4.95 salt-and-pepper shaker sets as bonuses. After the holidays, he had the unpleasant task of informing the regular freelancers (apart from those working with Kurtzman) that he had no assignments for them. He also had to let Al Feldstein go.

Damaged by the anti-comics drumbeat of the past few years, comic books were in serious trouble. Some new titles were released, but there was a big drop in the total number of books published. According to Mike Benton in *The Comic Book in America*, "From an all-time industry high of six hundred fifty titles in 1954, there were now barely more than three hundred titles—a 50 percent-plus drop. Artists and writers left the field, publishers closed their doors, and circulation fell."[15]

Mad #25 arrived in July looking a little leaner, having dropped eight pages. Its sixty pages (counting covers) held steady through Kurtzman's tenure. The most notable Kurtzman-written pieces were "The Jack E. Glisten Story" and "They Built Their Dream House," both drawn by Wood, "The Stark Club" drawn by Davis, and ad parodies of "Ol' Craw" whiskey, "Kennt" cigarettes and "Ipuna" toothpaste illustrated by Elder. Kurtzman had written nearly all of issue #24. This time, about a third of the issue came from other writers. Stan Freberg contributed a parody of movie magazine articles, Doodles Weaver wrote a "critique" of Lincoln's Gettysburg Address, Steve Allen contributed some goofy square dance lyrics, Ernie Kovacs authored "Was Snow White Really Snow White?" and Roger Price offered "Advice to Young Men on How to get into the Army" (one of his funniest pieces). That issue also carried Al Jaffee's first work in *Mad*.

Kurtzman contacted Jaffee. "I knew Harvey's *Mad* and I thought it was terrific," Jaffee recalled. "But I went along doing my thing with *Patsy Walker* [for Stan Lee at Atlas comics]. You never feel your path is going to cross with someone who's gone off into a totally different thing. So Harvey calls me up, and he's saying, 'Yeah, you can do it, you can do it.' So I wrote a baseball story for *Mad* that Jack Davis illustrated. That was my first."[16] In "Baseball . . . Science or Skill?," Jaffee proved himself a writer whose work was clever, compact and droll.

Another important "first" occurred in *Mad* #25: the first linking of the "What, Me Worry?" boy with the name Alfred E. Neuman. On p. 30, an article titled "*Mad* Awards" showed an Oscar-like statuette bearing that grinning face. It was called "The Alfred E. Neuman Award." However, since the face also appeared over the name Mel Haney in #25 and subsequent issues, the permanent pairing of face and name began with Kurtzman's editorial successor (who also made Neuman a mascot, with a prominent presence on the covers). Kurtzman later said that readers had insisted on calling the boy "Alfred E. Neuman" and that this was what he had settled on. The name was inspired by the use of the name Alfred Newman on *The Henry Morgan Show*, a radio program in the late 1940s and 1950s. The acerbic Morgan named his bland everyman after composer and music arranger Alfred Newman because it was his idea of the ultimate colorless name. Kurtzman added the middle initial and altered the spelling because he thought it looked and sounded better that way.

In his years editing EC comic books, Harvey Kurtzman managed to meet the publishing deadlines and get the comics out on time. Now that he was editing a bona fide magazine, he found himself slipping behind schedule. *Mad* #26 met its deadline, but the next issue was very late. All the admonitions and imprecations from Bill Gaines seemed to make no difference. Kurtzman discovered that running a magazine brought many ancillary duties and distractions.

The new *Mad* generated much more correspondence than had the comic book. While he no longer tried to answer all the fan mail, there were letters from high-profile supporters that required responses, as well as letters and phone calls to outside contributors. He had no secretary and was more of a hunt-and-peck than touch typist. For every specially written piece from other writers, there were queries, approvals, suggestions and other communications exchanged. In addition, there were promotional activities to be pursued, and appearances at social

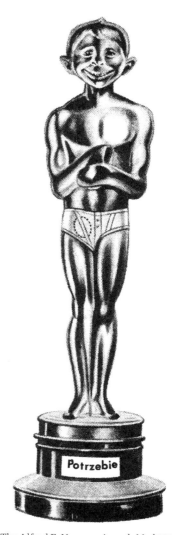

The Alfred E. Neuman Award, *Mad* #25.

occasions where a certain amount of promo and useful networking could be done. Plus, Kurtzman laid out every page of the magazine, reviewed all the artwork, signed all the pay vouchers and so on.

While working on the periodical, Kurtzman was also responsible for producing the *Mad* paperbacks: designing the covers, selecting the stories to be reprinted and writing the required editorial matter. He also arranged for special introductions by various writers. In December 1955, *Inside Mad* became the third in the series, following *Mad Strikes Back*. The introduction to *Inside* became a "Backword" by Stan Freberg (at the end of the book, of course). Its predictably laudatory text described *Mad* as "a first-rate humor magazine" which was "an example of pure and honest satire, written brilliantly by my friend Harvey Kurtzman, and drawn hysterically by Jack Davis, Will Elder and Wallace Wood."

Kurtzman was determined to keep the quality of the magazine up, and wouldn't send an issue to the printer until it met his perfectionist standards. His propensity for making changes and minor improvements became more pronounced. Every text correction had to be sent back to the typesetter, causing delay after delay. He later admitted, "I got too involved on the detail level, which I shouldn't have."[17] Plus, the adrenaline rush and excitement that came with the conversion to magazine form couldn't last forever, and the hours of overtime caught up to him. Another factor had an effect: Kurtzman knew how valuable he was to EC, and was no longer as fearful of dire consequences if he was late.

In an attempt to speed things up, Gaines approved Kurtzman's request to hire an assistant after the completion of *Mad* #26. Kurtzman brought his old friend and classmate Harry Chester on board as managing editor. The timing was perfect for Chester. "Harvey saved our lives," Irene Chester declared. "Harry worked for his Uncle Herman, who was a son of a bitch. He owned a Cessna airplane and insisted that Harry, who was an experienced pilot, work for him as a traveling salesman. Herman lived in Scarsdale and wanted Harry near him. He knew someone who owned an apartment building in Mount Vernon, where he got us this apartment which was lovely except it was on the fourth floor, with no elevator." Once they had two kids, getting up and down those stairs became difficult, and because they had no dryer, she had to hang the laundry on rooftop clotheslines. "So I had to tie David to the line when I was hanging the clothes. He hated being tied up and carried on like crazy. I had terrible nightmares of David going off the roof." Finally, she had enough. Irene told Harry she was leaving and using their savings to buy a house in Queens near her sister and mother. She said, "You can come with me, or you can stay with your uncle Herman." Then Harry got the job offer from Kurtzman. "Harvey saved our lives, because I was really leaving," she said. "Harvey asked Harry to work with him at *Mad* magazine, so Harry left his Uncle Herman and moved with me."[18]

Harry Chester loved the magazine *Mad*. He thought the initial issues were "very exciting" and was eager to work with his friend on it. His duties were wide-ranging, acting in any capacity necessary to assist Kurtzman in putting together the magazine. That took some of the pressure off Kurtzman, though, inexplicably, it didn't speed up production.

All along, Kurtzman considered Lyle Stuart a thorn in his side. The magazine's lateness increased the friction between them. When Chester came on the scene, he also didn't like Stuart's manner. Chester characterized Stuart as a "mean person." He recalled, "[Stuart] scared the hell out of me. Because I was on unsure ground. I was brand new."[19] By December, Kurtzman had had enough: "The thing that really tore it for me . . . was a jealousy factor between [Lyle Stuart] and Harry and me. There was a real conflict because Lyle was of no use to me. I couldn't work with the man, and I needed an assistant. And Lyle was, of course, resentful that I chose Harry rather than Lyle Stuart."[20] Stuart would play games, trying to embarrass or make Chester uncomfortable. He wouldn't, for example, give Chester a key to the office, and he watched every nickel Harry spent on supplies.

"It was a personality clash," Kurtzman said. "It was like torture going into that office. Finally I decided one day, is the rest of my life going to be tied up with this? And that was what I was faced with. It's like a bad marriage, you suddenly decide you've got to quit."[21] Kurtzman offered Gaines a choice: unless Stuart resigned, Kurtzman would leave. A weakened Gaines, desperate to hang onto Kurtzman, reluctantly asked for the business manager's resignation. (Gaines continued to consult informally with Stuart; they remained friends.)

The arguments and disagreements between Kurtzman and Gaines continued, with one becoming preeminent as 1956 arrived: the rates that he could pay outside writers. In 1983, Gaines recalled, "When I got into comics and the prevailing rate for script was six bucks a page—I never paid that little, but that's what it was—and art was about $25 [a page] at that time. I said, 'This is craziness! The artist has nothing to draw if he's got no script!' And . . . I said, 'I'm bringing it up to parity as soon as I can.' Back in 1956 I'd already gotten script to twenty-five and art to seventy-five and that was basic. And then I started working it up until a long time ago I had script up to art. And absolutely that's the way it should be."[22]

Kurtzman recognized that he couldn't write all of *Mad* magazine. Yet, when very talented people indicated they were interested in writing for it, he found himself embarrassed to be able to offer no more than $25 a page. He was not only embarrassed, but often out of luck. Why should writers work for *Mad* when they could get two or three times as much elsewhere? He couldn't go on apologizing and asking for favors, or using reprints, or scavenging for public domain material. In his mind, the quality of the magazine was at stake. Apparently, he began making certain financial commitments without Bill Gaines's authorization.

Gaines was furious. Money was tight. "[Kurtzman] was spending a lot of money on artists and writers," he recalled. "And I said, 'Harvey, I can't afford it. You just can't keep spending money like this. It's impossible.'" Then Kurtzman made a surprising request. His salary had increased after the magazine became successful. He offered to reduce his salary by $50 a week and use that amount to pay artists and writers more money. "He really did that," Gaines later recounted, adding, "Very unusual. I mean, who would do that? But of course it [wouldn't] help too much because $2,500 [a year] was a drop in the bucket compared to what he was spending."[23] This occurred, according to Gaines, in January 1956. A patch had been put on the problem, but Kurtzman wasn't happy. Gaines assured him that if the circulation of *Mad* continued to grow, and after more issues were published, there would eventually be more money for writers. Kurtzman had difficulty accepting that, because his faith in Gaines had eroded. "With Bill," he said, "it was always promises, promises."[24]

Kurtzman didn't seem to understand the seriousness of EC's financial position at the time, until Gaines informed him, probably in early February, "I'm trying to work out a deal to pay off my printing bill, but until I do, we're going to have to stop *Mad*."[25] He explained that the failure of the New Direction comics and Picto-Fiction books had not only eaten up the last of the horror profits, but had run him seriously into the red. Kurtzman became even more alarmed when he heard rumors that the suspension was really a prelude to the magazine's end. He later wrote, "Gaines . . . was about to divert his remaining capital to safer ground (a camera store, I heard). I told him my feelings, that it was a pity because *Mad* had a tremendous future."[26]

Gaines realized that suspending *Mad* meant delaying future profits that he desperately needed.[27] He may have considered other options, but what he really wanted was to stick with *Mad* and Kurtzman. He decided that he would put more of his savings into EC if his mother would do the same, but didn't relish making the request. Bill and Jessie Gaines had a quarrelsome relationship that hadn't improved when they lived together in the years leading up to his second marriage. Now that he and Nancy had their own place, the tensions had scarcely subsided because of all the business troubles at EC. Because Bill's mother owned 50 percent of the firm's equity, she shared the losses from the ill-fated New Direction comic books and Picto-Fiction magazines equally with her son.

Gaines and Kurtzman met with Jessie in her uptown apartment to make their case. One of Kurtzman's strengths was his ability to convince others that he knew what he was doing, but needed their help to succeed.

The excitement and sales generated from *Mad* gave Kurtzman every reason to feel confident. He was at his most persuasive that day. Jessie Gaines saw the logic in their argument. She agreed to put up the money, which, combined with Bill's portion, totaled one hundred thousand. Kurtzman said, "When I spoke to Gaines's mother, I [told] her I wanted to dedicate my energies to *Mad*."[28] According to Frank Jacobs's *The Mad World of William M. Gaines* (and never contradicted by Kurtzman), Kurtzman entered into an employment agreement to edit *Mad* at least through the end of 1956.[29]

MAD #27, DATED APRIL 1956, hit newsstands in early March. That meant it was published three months past its deadline. It's not possible to know how much of the delay was due to Kurtzman, and how much was attributable to EC's cash crunch. The publishing frequency cited in the magazine was now quarterly, though Gaines wanted it to return to bimonthly as soon as possible.

Kurtzman made a couple of subtle changes to the cover iconography with that issue. He drew a new *Mad* logo with some minor alterations, and redid the frame on the cover. Having had second thoughts about the cultural figures shown in the border, he had Will Elder replace them with images of the various subjects that would be parodied in *Mad*, such as literature, drama, music, politics, etc. Also, the EC logo on the lower left corner of the frame was omitted.

The standout feature of *Mad* #27 was the Kurtzman-Elder send-up of *The Ed Sullivan Show*, which so pleased Sullivan that he requested the original art. Another was "Ulysses," a Wood-drawn satire of Hollywood movies that bowdlerized literary classics like Homer's epic poem. New contributors in the issue were Abe Burrows and Russ Heath ("A Sea Chanty") and cartoonist Phil Interlandi ("Scenes We'd Like to See"). Stan Freberg was on hand again (with "Uninterrupted Melody," a piece on ice cream truck music). Kurtzman filled a couple of pages with a cartoon sequence by one of his idols from his teenage years: French cartoonist Caran d'Ache. To explain its inclusion, he created a department called "Rare Old Cartoons." (He had used a Thomas Nast "Boss Tweed" cartoon as the cover to #25, not as a filler or homage, but as a gag.) On the inside of the back cover, Kurtzman ran a full-page pin-up of Alfred E. Neuman, an acknowledgment of how popular the "What, Me Worry?" kid had become (see p. 13). Despite the five-month gap between Mad #26 and #27, sales increased. *Mad* was a phenomenon, and nothing could stop it.

Just as the *Mad* comic book inspired imitations, so did *Mad* magazine. Mandated by Martin Goodman to follow every hot new trend, Stan

Lee put out *Snafu*, a twenty-five cent magazine billed as "The Funniest Magazine in the World!" Its cover and grinning mascot blatantly copied the look of *Mad*. Its first issue, dated November 1955, contained artwork by John Severin, Joe Maneely and other Atlas regulars. It lasted three issues. Then came *Lunatickle* #1, dated February 1956, from Whitestone Publications, Inc., edited by Myron Fass. Although Fass was a bottom-of-the-barrel publisher, he managed to put together a magazine with work by talented folks such as Joe Kubert, Russ Heath, Lee Elias, Arthur Peddy and Jack Mendelsohn. The result was uninspired except for a burlesque of the *Mad* offices, with a Bill Gaines look-alike at its center, in its second and final issue. A long-lasting imitation of *Mad* magazine didn't take root until *Cracked* came along in 1958.

A new tide of pointed satire and edgy comedy was rising in the second half of the decade. Did Kurtzman realize that *Mad* influenced the humor of the times? "No," he said later.

> I didn't have the long view yet as to what place we held in history. History was too close to us for us to recognize what we were doing compared to . . . to what? Who would know that the humor of the country would change, and in our direction? I tended to think and I still do, that it was the times that determined what people decided to do, the times and the leaders that came out of the times, and we were one of the leaders, in the sense that we were an influence.[30]
>
> I don't think these things happen by themselves. I don't think movements come about without people. I think there are leaders who come forward and break new ground and create the environment behind them as they go for other people to rush in. There's always somebody with a vision who starts a trend or discovers a way to the West Indies. There's always somebody.[31]

Kurtzman was one of those leaders "with a vision who starts a trend," though the full effect of a trend only becomes known with the passage of time. "We weren't aware that [we were an influence] when it was happening," he said. "There was nothing to compare it to."[32] Even with the advantage of hindsight, his modesty prevented him from making that claim.

HARVEY KURTZMAN had no sooner begun working on *Mad* #28 than Bill Gaines found his firm in yet another financial crisis. Toward the end of February, payments from Leader News stopped. The distributor declared bankruptcy, partly a result of lost income when EC's New Trend horror and suspense comic books were dropped. Though it couldn't have been entirely unexpected, it came as a body blow to Gaines. According to *Quest*, John Redmond Kelly's weekly media newsletter, "Leader News owes about $400,000. It has assets of $30,000, perhaps $100,000 or so to come in, and less than $3,900 in cash in the bank. Hardest hit is publisher William Gaines of EC Publications. He stands to lose up to $191,861."[33] When the dust settled, EC lost roughly one hundred thousand in the Leader News bankruptcy.[34] It's not clear what sort of legal and financial maneuvering took place, but somehow *Mad* was able to go forward. At least the magazine's healthy sales figures meant finding a new distributor wasn't a problem. Gaines made a deal with American News, the largest and most powerful distributor of periodicals in the nation. As long as *Mad* continued racking up stellar sales, EC would be able to climb out of its financial hole—eventually.

Kurtzman went back to work, but something still nagged at him. Though he was editing a magazine, its package wasn't all that impressive. While he felt it was a big step up from comic books, it was still printed on relatively cheap paper rather than the pure white of the slicks, and had no interior color. "I used to go around with *Mad* magazine hidden," he said. When people asked him what he did for a living, he would say, "Umm well . . ."[35]

At just this juncture, Harvey Kurtzman got a phone call from a young hotshot magazine publisher named Hugh Hefner. Hefner later wrote of discovering *Mad*: "From the beginning, in 1954, it was obvious that the editors of *Playboy* and the editors of *Mad* were kindred spirits. In those early days, *Playboy*'s original four-man staff traveled to the printing plant each month to put their new men's magazine to bed, an all-night ritual that included a predawn breakfast break at a local drugstore. During one such session, while perusing the drugstore's magazine display to see how *Playboy* was doing, and to check on the competition, we discovered *Mad* . . . and the delighted roar of our laughter rivaled the roar of the presses."[36] *Playboy* was an even more phenomenal success story than *Mad*. Its print run had more than doubled in its first year, and as it passed its second anniversary in business, topped 500,000. It was a true slick magazine with interior color, and sold for fifty cents a copy. Unlike *Mad*, *Playboy* generated additional income from advertising.

Hefner recalled meeting Kurtzman. "My awareness of Harvey began with *Mad*. I liked the comic parodies . . . because I was a frustrated cartoonist myself. I grew up on the funny papers and comics, so parodies of comics were delicious for me."[37] Kurtzman told his troubles to Hefner, who suggested they talk in person. "I met with Harvey because he was talking about leaving [*Mad*]. He was not happy in his relationship with Bill Gaines. He wanted a piece of the action. I was sympathetic with that, and indicated before the fact that if he left Gaines, I would support a *Mad*-type publication. When he jumped ship, he knew what he was going to be jumping to."[38] Kurtzman recalled,

> I felt I had developed something really hot with *Mad*. I felt that there was a great future in the idea. I felt I had built it, but I had built it for some-body else. Professionally, I was completely unhappy. I was feeling pretty low. Hefner was in town—this was early in his own career, too—and we went out to lunch together. I was impressed with him. He came on with all that gusto and optimism he was putting into his own book, and we just talked back and forth. His high opinion of my work did much for my ego at that lunch, and put me into just the right mood to go ask my publisher for a substantial piece of the magazine as an alternative to my leaving.[39]

As Kurtzman mulled this over, work on *Mad* #28 was completed. One of the things addressed in its pages was an article that had just seen print. In its February 1956 issue, *Readers' Digest* published T. E. Murphy's article, "Progress in Cleaning up the Comics." Murphy was the reporter who wrote a series of front-page articles in the *Hartford Courant*, which helped put Hartford in the forefront of the push to ban comic books. He wrote, "William Gaines, a publisher of comics largely devoted to mur-der and mayhem, recently submitted material to the association which Administrator [Charles] Murphy ruled unacceptable. Gaines withdrew from the association. Since then, by altering the price and format of his magazines, he has been able to put similar stuff into two new thrillers named *Mad* and *Shock*, which are not classified as comic books. The first edition of *Mad* to be published without the seal of approval carries a crime story titled, 'Who Put the Strychnine in Mrs. Murphy's Husband?'" The article not only mischaracterized the content of *Mad*, but suggested that some of its issues had been Code-approved before EC dropped out of the association. (No issues of *Mad* were ever submitted for Code approval.) It looks like Murphy was intentionally disingenuous, trying to "get" Gaines by attacking his most successful publication. He didn't get away with it. So many people wrote in objecting to the false information about *Mad* that DeWitt Wallace, the editor and publisher of *Readers' Digest*, wrote a letter of apology that was published in *Mad* #28: "You will be glad to know that we have heard in the past week or so from quite a number of loyal readers of your magazine. And some of us on the staff have for the first time become acquainted with your particular brand of 'humor in a jugular vein.' The experience has been rewarding: the copies of *Mad* that I have seen are not only inoffensive, but positively entertaining. I am sorry indeed that the *Digest* reference to the publication gave a misleading impression."

As a result of the lateness of *Mad* #27, the next issue—Kurtzman's last—was the "spring issue" (as stated on the cover, which had a painting of a bedspring by Wallace Wood) even though it was dated July 1956.[40] The contents page in #28 read in part,

> Here we are again, dear readers, with another twenty-five cents worth of happy happy happiness. Where are you now? Curled up on your living room sofa with your freshly bought copy of *Mad*? Riding home on the commuter train with your newly purchased *Mad*? Hanging around the paper-store magazine rack reading *Mad* for free? You no-good cheapskate bums reading *Mad* for free—PAY MONEY OR PUT IT BACK! All other readers please keeping reading. Man alive, gang, what stuff we got in this issue!

Two things were missing from *Mad* #28: the "humor in a jugular vein" subtitle, and Lyle Stuart's name on the masthead. It maintained the quality of its predecessors, though some of its pages were filled with a reprint of the Blackhawks satire from issue #5. There were movie and TV satires, plus items on stamp-collecting, tooth decay, guided missiles, children's primers, young men's spring fashions, the income tax, horseracing and more. All in all, another sizable chunk of American life was superbly satirized.

When *Mad* #28 was completed, the final act of the *Mad* drama unfolded. Kurtzman felt boxed in at EC. He didn't think he could continue without a sufficient budget to pay outside writers enough to produce a consistently first-rate satire magazine. "I wanted control of the editorial package. I didn't have it really. Bill gave me the freedom to write what I wanted, but there were larger questions, like the design of the magazine and how much we could spend on it. I had no power in this area. I tried experiments with new kinds of material and talent, but the rates I wanted to pay were more than what Bill wanted to pay. There's some value in trying new things."[41] Kurtzman doubted whether Gaines really sympathized with his desire to improve the magazine when it was already selling well, or that Gaines understood that Kurtzman himself could not write it all himself as he did with the comic book *Mad*. Kurtzman later wrote, "Gaines and I separated at the climax of years of arguments due to editorial differences. I felt then, as I do now, that he was ever pushing me to do crap."[42]

One day, out of the blue, Harvey asked Adele, "How would you feel if I left *Mad*?" She replied, "It's okay by me. Do what you have to do."[43]

In April of 1956, Kurtzman informed Gaines that he wanted an ownership position in EC, something Jacobs called "a chunk of EC stock." Gaines offered 10 percent and said it was his last and best offer. A few days later, Gaines received a phone call from Harry Chester, telling him that Kurtzman wanted 51 percent ownership of *Mad* or he would walk. Gaines could hardly believe his ears and immediately phoned Kurtzman. Gaines related the conversation to Frank Jacobs:

"Hello, Harvey. Harry tells me you want 51 percent of the business."
"That's right, Bill."
"Harvey! You want 51 percent of my business?"
"Yes, Bill."
"Goodbye, Harvey."
"What do you mean?"
"Goodbye, Harvey."
"You'll be sorry, Bill."
"Goodbye, Harvey."[44]

Gaines asked his attorney Martin Scheiman to call Kurtzman to confirm the conversation, which he did.

Gaines was stunned. Did this mean EC was dead? "I was there the night Bill [Gaines] was given the ultimatum by Kurtzman," EC artist Joe Orlando recalled. "He came home and was holding his head in a state of shock. I actually heard him say that he would be willing to give Kurtzman 49 percent, but not 51 percent. Bill was . . . saying he was going back to teaching."[45] Perhaps Gaines made no counter offer (as far as is known) because he realized this was Kurtzman's way of quitting. Others have speculated that it was a ploy to make Gaines the bad guy and Kurtzman, who was fired, the victim.

There may have been another dimension to what Kurtzman would refer to as his supposed "great stock grab." As would be the case with the arrangement behind one of Kurtzman's later magazines, stock ownership can be divided into two classes: voting stock (a class of common stock), which would give its majority owner editorial control, and dividend stock, which determined how the profits from the business were to be divided.

In later correspondence, Kurtzman maintained, "I was resolved to leave EC, Gaines and *Mad*. I'd made up my mind. My decision was firm but with the one possible long-shot reservation, and a highly improbable reservation. I would stay if I could have legal control of the magazine, which was the only way to have real editorial control that I knew of. Let there be no mistake in my motives, which Bill [Gaines] knew. I wanted control and not the profits."[46] He seemed to be saying that he demanded fifty-one of only the voting stock, which would allow him to determine the budget of the magazine. Yet Gaines's initial 10 percent offer was certainly about sharing the profits, and it's questionable whether Kurtzman understood the existence of the two types of stock at that time. Certainly, spending more money on the editorial content would have a direct effect on profits. In any case, he knew the chance of Gaines acceding to the demand was virtually nil. He had decided to go with Hefner. (He told interviewers that Hefner made no specific offer before he left *Mad*, but according to Hefner, an offer for a new magazine was definitely on the table.)[47] By essentially forcing Gaines to fire him by demanding something Gaines wouldn't give, Kurtzman could assuage any guilt he felt about leaving shortly after convincing Gaines and his mother to sink $100,000 into EC. More to the point, being fired would release him from the employment contract.

Kurtzman later claimed that he had done no harm to Gaines by leaving so soon after the cash injection because *Mad* went on to great success. But both Gaines and Kurtzman believed that the magazine was doomed without Kurtzman at the helm. ("You'll be sorry, Bill.") In desperation, Gaines telephoned Lyle Stuart who was vacationing in Florida.

> "Lyle, I've got a problem. Harvey and Harry want fifty-one percent of the business. What should I do?"
> "Throw them out the window," Stuart said.
> Gaines did not welcome the levity of the reply. "Lyle, I'm serious. *What should I do?*"
> "I repeat—*throw them out the window*."
> "Well, I guess that's the end of *Mad*."
> "Get Feldstein."
> "I'm not sure he can do it."
> "Of course he can. He did *Panic*."[48]

Gaines entreated Feldstein to return to EC: "Harvey's left and I'd like you to come back. I don't know if we'll continue with *Mad*, but we'll do something."[49]

As for Kurtzman, when his new magazine with Hefner was being prepared, *Time* magazine stated (obviously echoing language in a Hefner press release), "[Hefner] has hired the whole staff of *Mad*, a short-lived satirical pulp [and] will launch a still unnamed new magazine this winter."[50] One Feldstein-edited issue of *Mad* (#29, September 1955) had come out before the September 24 issue of *Time* was published, but, knowing his record as editor of *Panic*, Kurtzman probably felt secure in assuming *Mad* would be "short-lived" without him. It seems clear that when Kurtzman walked, it was with the assumption that it would finish Gaines in publishing. From the Gaines point of view, this was cold treatment considering he had given Kurtzman work when he was desperate in 1949 and supported *Mad* through its first unprofitable year. He felt betrayed, and would not forgive Kurtzman for many years. Even Kurtzman sympathizers who feel Gaines had profited inordinately from Kurtzman's *Mad*, and had brought many of his financial problems on himself, have difficulty justifying Kurtzman's departure so soon after the large cash injection. The decision to leave *Mad* would haunt Harvey Kurtzman for the rest of his life, and be second-guessed by virtually everyone who has assessed his career.

On the surface, the future couldn't have looked brighter: *Mad*'s sales figures were steadily rising, Lyle Stuart was out of the picture, Kurtzman's best friend was working at his side, he had no one telling him what he could or couldn't put in the magazine, and his phone was incessantly ringing with calls from people who wanted to get on the *Mad* bandwagon. Gaines had promised that freelancer rates would eventually be raised. All this, and Gaines had offered 10 percent ownership. *How could he throw it all away?*

This question, of course, is posed with the advantage of hindsight. Moreover, had Kurtzman stayed, *Mad* would have evolved into something different than it did under Feldstein.

The situation was more complicated than it appears at first or even second glance. Other factors played into Kurtzman's decision. One was that he had lost confidence in Bill Gaines as a businessman. Kurtzman put the blame for what he called EC's "total business failure" squarely on Gaines's shoulders.[51] Gaines's horror comics, which Kurtzman considered immoral, had brought down the wrath of the public and government on comic books. Gaines had brought in a man as business manager—Lyle Stuart—whose tactics only exacerbated Gaines's problems with the Senate Subcommittee and with other comics publishers and who alienated Feldstein and Kurtzman, Gaines's chief editors and writers. Gaines had poured money down the drain on the New Direction and Picto-Fiction books, which adversely affected not only the editorial budget of *Mad*, but the magazine's very existence.[52] Given what he had seen, Kurtzman had no guarantee that Gaines wouldn't again put *Mad* in jeopardy as a result of other ill-considered decisions and ventures.

Kurtzman thrived on creativity, experimentation and change. Even when he got much of what he wanted with *Mad*, the weight of his dissatisfaction didn't lessen, because he felt he was saddled with the status quo for an indefinite period of time: "I didn't see any working future for me with things the way they were. I felt that if I couldn't get a better arrangement, there was no point in continuing."[53] Feeling stuck, he would have to struggle to stay interested. Kurtzman was an innovator, and without that possibility, everything was ashes. Will Elder said of his friend, in the period after the Hefner meeting, "I felt emotionally he was probably disappointed. He was kind of blue and he wasn't sure of anything."[54] He and Gaines had been fighting for the past two years, and Kurtzman was tired of it. Adele put it succinctly: "He felt it was time for a change."[55] Going with Hefner offered relief and a chance to invent something new.

But the main reason, the reason that trumped them all, came down to one thing. Hugh Hefner's offer represented the fulfillment of a dream Harvey Kurtzman had nurtured as long as he could remember: the chance to edit a high-class slick satire magazine with color both inside and out. To say this was alluring to Kurtzman is a gross understatement. He simply couldn't let such an opportunity pass him by. Given the state of his relationship with Gaines, a better question than "How could he throw it all away?" is "How could he resist Hefner's offer?"

AL FELDSTEIN OVERSAW the final assembly of *Mad* #28, then got to work on his first credited issue. A small amount of material generated under Kurtzman's editorial reign appeared in *Mad* #29 and #30. In #29, the most significant items written by Kurtzman were the two-page "Hot Weather Photos" and the five-page "The Underground Around Us (The Epic Case History of Early Men)," a piece about the development of cave men. Also, the "Gringo" game, edited by Kurtzman and illustrated by Elder, was Ernie Kovacs's funniest contribution to *Mad*. In the next issue, "What Happened to Pulp Magazines," a four-page item, was the only significant item by Kurtzman. After that, all material originated under Al Feldstein, though much of what appeared in the immediate aftermath of Kurtzman's departure was deliberately done in a Kurtzman-esque style. One of Kurtzman's comedic constructs, using the word "mainly" to reveal the reality of a situation, would be repeated ad infinitum in the text of *Mad* stories for decades.

Given what he accomplished with *Mad*, some have speculated on where Kurtzman would have taken the magazine had he stayed. He offered this thought: "If I had stayed with *Mad* I would have pushed and pushed and pushed for advertising. I think we would have eventually developed as an advertising vehicle. I wanted to investigate the advertising possibilities, and at the time I was involved with *Mad* we were playing around with a few potential advertisers."[56] Advertising revenue, in turn, might have paid for an upgraded package with interior color. Other than that, it seems certain that Kurtzman would have continued to gear the magazine toward the older-teenager-and-adult audience, rather than shift toward younger readers as Feldstein did. In turn, this probably meant that the magazine wouldn't have been as successful sales-wise as the Feldstein product over the years.

When Harvey Kurtzman was "rescued" by Bill Gaines in 1949, the office door on the seventh floor of 225 Lafayette had an EC symbol on it. When he cleared out his office and left for the last time, a little over six years later, that same door bore a new identifier for the name of the business inside, just one word: *Mad*.[57]

MAD

NO. 24 ✱ HUMOR IN A JUGULAR VEIN ✱ JULY 1955

WILLIAM M. GAINES, PUBLISHER.

STAFF

Editor **HARVEY KURTZMAN**
Production **JOHN PUTNAM**

CONTENTS

CONTRIBUTORS

PRICE SHIR-CLIFF KOVACS WALLACH

Amongst our contributors in this issue are: **Roger Price** the man who has made "Droodles" a by-word on the American scene. As well as contributing an article, Roger has been very helpful in advising us on scatalogical avoidism and like that. So watch out. **Bernard Shir-Cliff,** (see pages 32-34) as well as being an author, is night cable editor at Ballantine Books, publishers of the MAD Reader, (35c at your neighborhood newsstand, cheap. [the whole MAD operation is one complex insidious cartel.]) **Ernie Kovacs,** author of our Tom Swiffft piece has conducted various zany east coast television shows which we have watched faithfully in the interests of enjoyment and mainly to steal material. Readers of **Ira Wallach** parody will be happy to note that we're running an article of his and all we have to say is...Don't be so happy, readers, the article is a reprint and you've probably read it already. However, if you haven't seen any of **Wallach's** work yet, by all means turn to *Out of the Frying Pan and into the Soup.* (Pages 17-19)

Mad, July, 1955. Vol. 1, No. 24. Published Bi-Monthly by Educational Comics, Inc., at 225 Lafay-ette Street, New York 12, N. Y. Entered as second-class matter at the Post Office, New York, N. Y. Subscription, 8 issues for $2.00 in the U.S. Else-where, $2.50. Entire contents Copyrighted 1955 by Educational Comics, Inc. Unsolicited manuscripts will not be returned unless accompanied by stamped return envelope. No similarity between any of the characters, names or persons appearing in this mag-azine of those living or dead is intended, and any such similarity is coincidental. Printed in U.S.A.

As a comic book, *Mad*—like most comic books—never had a contents page. Magazines did have them, and so would *Mad* from this point forward. Ample credit is given to outside contributors such as Roger Price and Ernie Kovacs, perhaps to to make up for the small amount they were paid.

Is A Trip To The Moon Possible?

DR. X. FLINE SAUCER CAPT. BUCK ROGER MELVIN COZNOWSKI COMMDR. ZORK ARGH

SCIENTISTS ANSWER IN LIGHT OF POSITIVE PROOF OF MAN'S CONQUEST OF FLIGHT AND EVIDENCE OF MAN'S ABILITY TO EXPLORE OUTER SPACE: IN OTHER WORDS...NO!

SHIP ABOUT TO BLAST OFF NOTE SLOW BURNING FUSE

No, not right this minute a trip to the moon is not possible, but sometime in the future, it is quite possible. In exploring this interesting question, MAD has brought together four of the leading authorities on space travel; authorities because they are the presidents of the largest science-fiction fan-clubs in the country. This article then, is a digest of a round table discussion they had. Naturally, a trip to the moon is quite possible, the panel of experts agreed; *not* (as we mentioned before) *right now*. The experts are not such dreamers. They realize such a stupendous feat is no simple matter, but is a slow and fantastically complex undertaking that needs incredible amounts of testing...lengthy amounts of time. A week from now would be more like it. Our experts were asked what a trip to the moon might look like. Although they could not agree whether the course would be through the 4th dimension or not, the following picture story is the way they decided a moon trip might look like. On the left is a cutaway diagram of a rocket that might take us to the moon. On the right is the rocket, about to blast off. Turn the page, dear reader, and blast off with us.

Above, right: Wallace Wood artwork in *Mad* #24. Text by Harvey Kurtzman.

The space station. All kidding aside...the rocket has now freed itself of the earth's gravitational pull and is drifting in space. But the trip is halted at the half-way mark.

Since the rocket, packed as it is with instruments will have no room for luxuries, it is with understandable joy that the crewmen scramble towards the welcome space station.

The trip resumes. A note now on a phenomenon you will experience. As you leave gravity, you see objects rising.

You know the reason is because without gravity, everything floats. So you hasten to unfasten your safety belts.

Your reason why objects rise is all wrong. Real reason is mainly because rocket ship is flying upside-down!

However, once you do get away from gravity, a warning. Don't have a sloppy rocket-ship with left-out tools floating all over the place, not put away. What's more, don't take baths!

If you take a bath, the water will, in all probability, float out of the bath-tub in a great big glob, and you'll float with it. And if you can't swim out, you'll drown!

The covers of Harvey Kurtzman's last four issues of *Mad*. Top: *Mad* #25, art by Thomas Nast. *Mad* #26, art by Wallace Wood. Bottom: *Mad* #27, art by Jack Davis. *Mad* #28, art by Wallace Wood.

18.

NINE GLORIOUS MONTHS

HUGH HEFNER'S AND HARVEY KURTZMAN'S backgrounds and personalities couldn't have been more different, yet on the surface they had quite a bit in common. They were close to the same age (Hefner was eighteen months younger). Both were cartoonists who had grown up on the same comic strips, radio shows and movie serials. Both were heavily involved in print media and had cast their lot in the publishing world. Both were highly knowledgeable about what it took to put a magazine together, and produce creative material. Each was a charismatic leader who inculcated a sense of embarking on "a great adventure" in his collaborators. Both were workaholics. Both were married, and both had two children, first a daughter and then a son. Both were mainly interested in popular culture rather than the high arts, and both were visionary thinkers who had invented new kinds of magazines. Both of their magazines squarely targeted hypocrisy.

Their differences were equally notable. Hefner's marriage was unhappy, he was distant from his kids, he had a better grasp of business matters than Kurtzman and he was a man with a mission as a cultural reformer. Kurtzman's marriage was solid, he was an involved parent, his workaholic tendencies were largely kept in check and his goal was mainly to reveal the way things were rather than change them. Hefner had gained most of his experience in the slicks. Kurtzman had spent nearly all of his career in comic books.

Started on a shoestring budget of $8,000 on a card table in Hefner's living room, *Playboy* made its debut in November 1953 with a printing of 70,000 copies. Featuring the famous nude calendar photograph of Marilyn

Monroe (whose career was catching fire), it sold 80 percent of its print run. *Playboy* was an instant hit, and suddenly Hugh Hefner was on a dizzying ascent to a level of success that he had never dreamed possible. His "pleasure-primer styled to the masculine taste" was a publishing sensation—soaring past sales of 500,000 by the time he met Harvey Kurtzman.[1]

In early 1956, Hefner's HMH Publishing Co., Inc. was in a period of rapid expansion. A four-story office building at 232 E. Ohio St. was completely remodeled at a cost of $325,000 in order to make space for several important additions to his staff. One was A. C. Spectorsky, a distinguished New York journalist and literary figure who became Hefner's second in command. Plans were afoot for moves into television, book publishing and other areas.

Entering the world of the high-class slicks was an intoxicating moment in Harvey Kurtzman's life. With a portfolio that included preliminary ideas, proposals, sketches and notes tucked under his arm, Kurtzman (with Chester) boarded a plane to Chicago in May 1956. There were no more depressing days in the contentious atmosphere at 225 Lafayette St. It was a fresh start and a step up. At the age of thirty-one, he had finally hit the big time. Coming off the success of *Mad*, he fell easily into Hefner's mood of contagious optimism.

They discussed their vision for the magazine and reached a meeting of the minds. Following the *Playboy* model, the magazine—dubbed *X* until the name *Trump* was chosen—would be printed on high quality paper with many (but not all) interior pages in color. It would have about the same number of pages as *Mad*, but like *Playboy*, it would sell for fifty cents. Publishing frequency was to be bimonthly, also like *Mad*. (Had Hefner noticed the lateness of *Mad* #27? If so, Kurtzman was able to reassure him on that score.) *X* would publish irreverent satire with a contemporary feel that was aimed more or less at the readers of *Playboy*. Kurtzman later said they wanted to do "an upgraded *Mad*."[2] It would contain comic strip satires (which Hefner particularly loved) and other art-heavy content, but also have text pieces accompanied by cartoons and illustrations by top cartoonists in the business. As editor, Kurtzman would have a free hand, though Hefner naturally wanted to see each issue before it went to press. Hefner recalled, "I gave him pretty much complete control. It was not like *Playboy* [where] I was hands on. *Trump* was his baby."[3]

On the matter of whether or not to carry advertising, "Hef" (as everyone called him, never Hugh) later explained, "I think the concept of advertising was kind of inconsistent with the satire or parody aspect that Harvey wanted to create. He wanted it to be pure."[4] Actually, Kurtzman was in favor of running ads, though he wouldn't have pressed the point if Hefner was against it. This was an important decision, because eliminating advertising income had major financial ramifications. Nearly all magazines needed ads in order to be profitable. And, since Hefner agreed that Kurtzman could have a small ownership position in the magazine, it would in theory have some effect on Kurtzman's potential income.[5]

Would Kurtzman be able to bring his *Mad* cartoonists to *X*? This didn't appear to be a problem, since the future of *Mad* without Kurtzman was doubtful. It was a key point, because he couldn't envision the project without Elder, Davis and Wood. Hefner wanted an exclusive arrangement with the artists, or at least exclusive to the extent that they wouldn't work for a competing magazine like *Mad*. Kurtzman indicated that he would have to discuss it with them. What sort of pay could he offer? Determining how much to pay the artists led him to ask about the budget. Hefner's answer proved especially fateful, though it was well received at the time. "I asked Hefner for some kind of budget, and his attitude was that we didn't have any budget. We'd spend whatever we had to make a magazine, which is as it should have been."[6] It was acknowledged that there would be some initial, one-time expenses generated while the operation was set up. Therefore, no budget for *X* was established.

Finally, Kurtzman and Chester would have a chance to do their ultimate magazine without tight budgetary constraints. What a difference from dealing with Gaines's cheap ways and hand-wringing. The magazine looked to be a "go" though Kurtzman still had to secure the services of his key artists. In this, he met with near total success. Within a day or two, Kurtzman offered Wallace Wood, Jack Davis, Will Elder and Al Jaffee jobs with *X*. Though each of them had various degrees of regret about leaving *Mad*, all wanted to be a part of this.

Al Jaffee had only done a few items for *Mad* magazine. Kurtzman wanted him to do more, but Jaffee had a good thing going elsewhere. "I was very nervous with the whole operation . . . but finally Harvey convinced me that I should really come in, get more involved, because this was my kind of stuff." Jaffee quit one of the Patsy Walker comic books he was doing for Timely. "I called Harvey that night and I said, 'Harvey, I'm coming with you!' Harvey says, 'Now, wait a minute, Al. I just quit *Mad*.' And I said, 'I just quit Stan Lee. To go with you who just quit *Mad*.' And Harvey said, 'Listen, I can't tell you what I'm up to, Al, but can you hold on for like two weeks? I think something good is going to come up.'" Shortly thereafter, Kurtzman invited Jaffee aboard *X*. Then, Jaffee dropped all of his Timely work. He had been making about $15,000 a year at that time. "I

went with Harvey for $10,000, which I think showed some kind of intesti-
nal fortitude on my part. It was a turning point in my life."[7]

Will Elder recalled, "I was sorry to hear that [Harvey] was going, but
he happened to be going into something a little more lucrative. He said,
'Will, here's your chance of becoming one of the artists at [X]. You couldn't
work for a better outfit.' So I jumped at it."[8] Jack Davis struggled with the
decision: "I knew how upset I'd be if I left Bill, but Harvey started *Mad*
and was a close friend. I had a choice and I went with Harvey."[9] However,
he said that if it was to be exclusive, he wanted a contract guaranteeing a
certain amount of work from Hefner. He was the only one who got such a
contract. While the details were being worked out, Davis continued with
the Feldstein *Mad* for three issues.

Wallace Wood wanted to work on the new magazine, but he also wanted to continue with *Mad*. Wood's close friend Joe Orlando remembered, "I
was calling Wood repeatedly saying 'don't go with Kurtzman. You don't
want to be chained to his layouts.'"[10] Kurtzman and Hefner visited Wood
and his wife Tatjana at their apartment on West Seventy-Fourth Street and
urged him to sign an exclusive agreement with them. Wood demurred.
While Kurtzman convinced Hefner that they should still use him in their
first issue, Wood never agreed to leave *Mad* and consequently did nothing
more for the magazine.

When Kurtzman "raided" his art staff—the most gifted cartoonists
around for that sort of material—Gaines was infuriated, but he didn't
blame the artists. They had standing invitations to return. He attributed
it to "the Kurtzman mystique." In a letter to Kurtzman, Gaines spelled it
out: "For many years I listened to you expounding morals and scruples in
business, but what you've done transcends business. What you've done is
traded on your friendship for Willy and Jack to gain what you believed
would be a business advantage for yourself. You've hypnotized both of
them into accepting less money from *Trump* with no contracts over more
money from *Mad* with personally guaranteed contracts."[11]

Kurtzman responded: "After five years of mutual friendship, you now
sit back there figuring what a rat I actually am and what jerks Willy and
Jack are and how it's all because of hypnotism. We have both done well
by each other and I want nothing that rightfully belongs to you. What do
you want from my life?"[12] The loss of Davis and Elder made the prospects
of *Mad* magazine under Feldstein seem even dimmer. It also deepened
Gaines's enmity toward his erstwhile editor and friend.

THAT THE EDITORIAL OFFICES of Kurtzman's new magazine would be located in New York City was a foregone conclusion. Space was found on the first floor of a brownstone on E. Thirty-Seventh St. facing the Morgan Library block. Since *Playboy* also needed a promotions office in Manhattan, the two operations were co-located and split the cost. Soon Kurtzman and Chester set up headquarters in the midtown office, and work on the new magazine began in earnest. Because arriving at a final name was postponed, stationery was printed bearing the working title *X*.

Kurtzman's first order of business was announcing his new project to the rest of his former colleagues and collaborators, and soliciting their participation in the magazine. Among them, Ed Fisher, Roger Price, Phil Interlandi, Bernard Shir-Cliff, Doodles Weaver and Russ Heath came aboard, and Irving Geis, who had helped with the layouts for the last issue or two of *Mad*, was made art director. Chester had the title managing editor, as before, and John Mastro was hired to do paste-ups. Kurtzman had certain ideas regarding the artists and writers he felt were right for *X*. When word got out about the magazine, a steady stream of freelancers came looking for work, some very experienced. Few were accepted. Kurtzman personally invited nearly all who made it into its pages. One was cartoonist R. O. Blechman, who was working in the Storyboard animation studio. Blechman went on to become an important artist for the *New Yorker* and other top magazines.

Kurtzman had more confidence in himself than ever. He already had a long list of ideas for the new magazine. Gearing his approach to a slightly more adult reader didn't seem to present a problem. But, while he had the same editorial freedom that he'd had at *Mad*, the truth was "what Hefner might think" could never have been far from his mind. Bill Gaines had always been an appreciative, non-critical audience for his work, freeing Kurtzman from worrying about how the latest issue would be received at the top. Now, he had a new boss who, while clearly a fan, wasn't going to be a uncritical one. Hefner had given him a free hand, but was the "elephant in the room" (as Al Jaffee later put it) and hard to put out of mind.[13]

Kurtzman floated the idea of calling the magazine *Profusely Illustrated*, a play on *Sports Illustrated*. He also liked the name *Humbug*, which he may have become enamored with while working on his aborted adaptation of Dickens's *A Christmas Carol*. Significantly, it was Hefner, not Kurtzman, who named the magazine. He wanted to call it *Trump* and that's what it became. Hef was particularly devoted to competitive tabletop games, with contract bridge high on the list. Bill Gaines probably didn't miss the fact that the word "trump" suggested surpassing or triumphing over a competitor. To go with the title, Kurtzman invented a little trumpet-playing mascot wearing a sandwich board made of playing cards.

Kurtzman's memories of this period were uniformly positive. "We had a particularly good time turning out *Trump*. We enjoyed the magazine. We enjoyed each other. And it was a very good period of my life."[14] He called it "a glorious experience."[15] Adele announced that she was pregnant not long after work began on the first issue, so the gestation of Kurtzman's creative "baby" (as Hefner called it) and the prenatal period of the Kurtzmans' third child, ran parallel.

While Kurtzman entertained pitches from writers for proposed text pieces, he concentrated on producing material for Elder, Davis and Wood for the first issue. June, July and August passed as its contents were prepared. If Hefner thought it was coming together too slowly, he apparently didn't express serious concerns. Harry Chester later said, "[We saw Hefner] maybe once a month, maybe not even that. We made occasional trips to Chicago, and he'd come in [to New York]. Whenever he came in it was always upbeat, you know, to get us up. He was good at that, really good."[16]

Kurtzman's perfectionism, which had slowed down *Mad*, was in evidence. Even when pages were completely pasted up, he would ask for changes. "Harvey would come in and would look at the page all pasted up with the artwork and the type and everything," Jaffee recalled. "He would read a caption and he would say, 'no, let's take that word out and put another word in.'" That meant the caption needed to be sent out to be reset. Kurtzman was perpetually honing, improving, fiddling. Sometimes he tabled a piece when he saw it put together, or asked for it to be largely redone.

Kurtzman's cover for *Trump* #1, like the one on *Mad* #24, consists of a prose appeal to newsstand browsers. In this case, it's even bolder, dominated with the word HELP! in bright red letters three inches high, against an all-white background. The full message reads, "A new magazine which would like to say . . . mainly HELP! Never mind other magazines—Buy us." Again there's an indirect reference to *Mad*, one of those "other magazines." Inside, on p. 1, a "Prospectus" for "an important new publication" proclaimed:

This Prospectus shall set forth our purpose.
Trump proposes to be a magazine with ideals.
Trump proposes to be a magazine that will hew to its ideals with a steadfastness of purpose.

Trump #1 (January 1957). Kurtzman art.

Trump will not be distracted nor frightened.
Trump will work toward our goals, unbiased.
This, then, shall be the purpose of *Trump*.
Making money.
You have money.
You give money to us.
This is our Prospectus. We invite you to stand at the magazine rack and examine our product.

 —the editors

Under this is a P.S.:

If you are standing at the magazine rack examining our product, let us call your attention to certain pages. Let us call your attention to those pages which are bent and soiled with your fingerprints from examining! The man that runs the newsstand will be only too happy to change a five dollar bill!

Opposite (on the inside of the front cover) is a comical color photo of Kurtzman, Davis, Wood and Elder, part of a fake Smirnoff vodka ad. The text has another oblique reference to *Mad*. After listing the full names of all four, it reads,

That's the way the liquor ads might introduce distinguished gentlemen. However, this isn't a liquor ad and those aren't distinguished gentlemen. Nevertheless, they can numb your mind with their artwork and writing as they have in other magazines in the past. For now they have gotten together to produce this newer, finer, blended-to-perfection magazine that you can start the social evening with—and remember—*Trump*, a new magazine for brihgt people. [*sic*]

To start things off, Kurtzman went to his ace artist Will Elder for a parody of the Glenn Ford movie *The Fastest Gun Alive* called "The Fastest Gun There Is." This is followed by Ed Fisher's feature on "sexed up" covers of paperback versions of literary classics, and the Elder-drawn "L'l Ab'r" comic strip parody in full color. Then comes Al Jaffee's bit about "realistic" toys for kids like the "Playtime Flamethrower," and Ira Wallach's parody of Erskine Caldwell's Depression era novel *God's Little Acre*. Jack Davis's first appearance in the issue is a collaboration with Kurtzman on a comical look at hunting (mainly duck hunting), just a warm-up for their six-page spoof of the *Adventures of Rin Tin Tin* ABC television series. "Tin Rin Rin Tin Rin" is one of the finest, funniest Kurtzman-Davis collaborations ever. Jack's rendering of the ridiculously intelligent dog is incredibly deft. The story's apex is a sequence in which the dog gets his owner to follow him by using charades ("two words" . . . "sounds like").

Like *Playboy*, *Trump* had a full-color foldout, titled "Our Own Epic of Man," an elaborate painted tableau showing how people in the far-flung future, conceivably after a nuclear holocaust, would reconstruct what life was like in 1956 based on a few remaining artifacts. They decide men wore army helmets as regular hats, people lived in subway kiosks, others bowed down in worship of the RCA Victor dog, etc. Alfred E. Neuman is there, wearing a bikini top on his head. The left third of the foldout has a photo of a typical *Playboy* "Playmate," with a note scribbled on it that says, "Hey! Wrong foldout! This foldout goes in a different magazine!"

Trump #1 featured a six-page spoof of the *Adventures of Rin Tin Tin* ABC television series. "Tin Rin Rin Tin Rin" is one of the finest, funniest Kurtzman-Davis collaborations. Davis's rendering of the ridiculously intelligent dog is deft.

Wallace Wood's first work doesn't appear until page forty-three, a projected version of an upcoming "Walt Dinsey" animated film version of Hansel and Gretel, written by Ed Fisher. Wood painted the artwork on clear acetate over painted backdrops (like animation cells), with only the foreground figures outlined in black, to simulate the look of a Disney animated film. Wood also drew an "Elvis Pretzel" page (Presley had broken into mainstream stardom in 1956) and a two-page parody of Allen Funt's *Candid Camera* TV show. Single-page continuities and cartoon items by Howard A. Schneider, R. O. Blechman, Al Jaffee and Phil Interlandi fill out the rest of the issue. The inside back cover is a subscription ad with a fantastic Jack Davis drawing of King Kong pausing to read *Trump* while in the midst of ravaging New York City. The back cover is a "Liptone Tea" ad with color art by Elder.

   Trump #1, dated January 1957, went on sale in early December. Meanwhile, Kurtzman and his crew were busily working on the second issue, and lining up material for future issues. Congratulatory letters arrived, including one from Bill Gaines. According to Jacobs, Gaines wrote, "Saw *Trump*. Some very nice art. Beautiful print job. I wish you great success. But frankly, I doubt it! Not at half a buck! I'm not that impressed. In fact, we were all relieved around here."[17] On January 10, Gaines wrote a follow-up note, after watching Hefner on a television show:

Dear ole Harv,
Caught Hugh on TV last night.
Gee, Harv, you're out of the immoral
frying pan into the smutty fire,
aren't you boy?
Love and kisses,
    Bill[18]

Trump #1 is a credible effort that yielded mixed results. The anarchy of *Mad* is somewhat subdued. It was going to take some time for Kurtzman to figure out what worked in the upscale format. "Our Own Epic of Man" is hard to scan and confusing. "The Fastest Gun There Is" is just so-so. Selecting a more commercially successful film like *The Searchers* starring John Wayne (a hit that made its debut in March) would seem to have been a better choice than *The Fastest Gun Alive*, a relatively unremarkable Western. While Kurtzman was fascinated with the psychology of the Glenn Ford character in *Fastest Gun*, he strangely chose to focus only on its generic Western elements. He would satirize the film again, two years later, with better results. The standouts in the issue are the Rin Tin Tin piece drawn by Davis, the paperback book covers by Fisher, and the *Li'l Abner* parody drawn by Elder. All are top drawer, funny and as good or better than anything in *Mad*. On the other hand, a few items fall completely flat, such as "God's Littered Acre" by Wallach, reprinted from one of his recent books. Reprinting classic work by Caran d'Ache—nice work, but essentially filler—is also odd. That might have worked in the twenty-five-cent *Mad*, but wasn't a good idea in the fifty-cent *Trump*. With the Hefner "elephant in the room," Kurtzman might have been overthinking. Producing a more sophisticated magazine for adults was turning out to be tricky.

AFTER THE ASSIGNMENTS for the first issue of *Trump* were given out, a promising new freelancer arrived at the brownstone. Arnold Roth was a gifted writer-cartoonist who would become one of Kurtzman's key collaborators over the next decade. The twenty-seven-year-old was born in Philadelphia and graduated from the Philadelphia Museum School of Industrial Art (now the University of the Arts) in 1950. He was selling

drawings regularly to *TV Guide*, as well as *Holiday* and the *Saturday Evening Post*, and was a regular reader of the Kurtzman *Mad*. A chance meeting with his friend Ed Fisher brought Roth and Kurtzman together. Roth explained, "Ed told me 'there's this magazine, I'm going to be doing some work for them, and it's Hefner. It's just starting now, and you would be the perfect guy for this bunch.' So I went over to their offices and introduced myself. It wasn't a very large place. And there was Harvey. He looked through my portfolio, and offered me a retainer to work for them. I agreed immediately."[19]

Roth contributed some key pieces to *Trump* #2, including the "Russian Inventions We Invented First," "Movie Scenes You Must Have Seen," and a piece showing "how the use of ballet dancers as commercial demonstrators on TV is having a startling effect on the public." That issue includes a ten-page parody of *Sports Illustrated*, a satire of the movie *Giant*, "Death to a Salesman" (a parody of the Arthur Miller play) by Mel Brooks, Al Jaffee's article on planned obsolence in consumer products titled "Engineering for Prosperity," and so on. This time, there isn't a centerfold or any work by Wallace Wood.[20]

Above and below: The *Trump* staff appeared on page one of the second issue. L-R: Jack Davis, Harvey Kurtzman, Harry Chester, Al Jaffee, Irving Geis (art director), Arnold Roth (sitting). Next to Kurtzman: Arnie Lewis (assistant art director). Bottom of page: Will Elder.

In most respects, it's about on a par with the first issue. *Trump* #1 has an all-white cover with a text message; *Trump* #2 has an all-black cover with another text message. It's a tiny text box in the middle that one had to squint to read: "If you're reading this, you're interested, and you should look inside where it's more interesting because the printing is better for your eye-sight which will soon be gone if you're still reading this and . . . " At that point, the lettering grows smaller, then fades away. The issue also has a photo of the creative team on the inside front cover: Davis, Kurtzman and Elder, along with Arnie Lewis (assistant art director), Chester, Jaffee and Roth. A "warm personal message from the editor" states, "When *Trump* #1 went on sale, with hundreds of titles to choose from, you went to your newsstands . . . you went and picked up our magazine . . . and then you put it down again . . . Now that's not the right idea. You must not do this." Although sales of the first issue weren't known when it was written, the message is curiously downbeat.

THE SCENE TOOK PLACE in a waiting room at Doctors Hospital, located at 170 East End Ave. in Manhattan. On January 21, 1957, the day of President Dwight D. Eisenhower's second inauguration, Adele was about to give birth while her husband paced the floor in a waiting area. Having been working long days to get *Trump* out on schedule, Kurtzman was stressed out and exhausted.

Through bleary eyes, he recognized a familiar figure in the hallway. It was Bill Gaines. (Nancy was in the hospital for an ulcer operation.) Gaines, representing Kurtzman's past, walked by without noticing his former editor. Kurtzman thought, "My eyes are going. I'm going crazy."[21] The scene took on an even more surreal quality when he spied Hugh Hefner, who represented his future, making his way toward him. At first Kurtzman thought Hefner was there to wish them well. Then Hefner revealed the real reason for his appearance: to tell Kurtzman in person that publication of *Trump* was being suspended. The second issue would be published, and then there would be no more until some future date.

"I don't think I have to go into detail beyond saying it was the blackest day of my life," Kurtzman later said.[22] Apart from everything else, the discontinuation of the magazine sullied an otherwise happy occasion, the birth of his second daughter, Elizabeth ("Liz").

Like the reasons why Kurtzman left *Mad*, the reasons for the demise of *Trump* have been murky. Subsequently, Kurtzman described the situation as he understood it, revealing that the shocking demise of mighty *Collier's* magazine, on January 4, 1957, had been the catalyst:

Hefner was going through a period of heady expansion, as he should have, and he, as many businessmen, depended on loans to expand, and at the time he was operating on bank loans. You don't have the cash in your pocket, but you assume you're going to make the cash, so you borrow from a bank, and on the basis of the bank loan you expand. And Hefner was expanding as fast as he could. He was really expanding recklessly. He expanded his advertising and editorial departments, and started *Trump*.

And then *Collier's* folded. And the bank suddenly decided magazines were a risky investment. Hefner was then faced with a serious crisis. He had to cut back in every department. He cut *Trump* out. That was the easiest expendable to cut. He cut everybody's salaries at *Playboy* drastically . . . and he cut back his advertising staff. And that's what happened, as I understand it. *Trump* was an expensive magazine. We would have had to go a long way to break even. Our break-even point was high, but we hadn't considered break even, so I don't know what the statistics for our break-even point were. Hefner's whole attitude was, "Let's set up an operation here. What does break-even have to do with setting up an operation?"

We intended to put out *Trump* again. Hefner fully intended to come back with *Trump*, but as time passed, he and his people talked themselves out of it. They finally decided, and rightly so, that everything they did should be sort of an offshoot of *Playboy*.[23]

Years later, regarding the situation at *Playboy*, he quipped, "Everybody took pay cuts, and I got my throat cut."[24]

It's unquestionably true that HMH Publishing Company, Inc. was going through a financial crisis much as Kurtzman described in late 1956 and through 1957. According to Steven Watts in *Mr. Playboy*, his biography of Hugh Hefner, "Hefner had invested a large amount of funds in the new offices on Ohio Street when his banker unexpectedly pulled his line of credit. With no working capital, a financial crisis ensued. Hefner took strong measures: cutting 25 percent from all executive salaries, giving up his salary entirely, discontinuing *Trump*, and temporarily giving up 25 percent of his company's stock to help secure a bank loan for $250,000. As [Hefner] confessed in July 1957, 'This has been a rough six months—months of difficult decision and of payment for some wrong decisions in the past.'"[25] Probably all of Hefner's advisers were telling him *Trump* had to go.

Trump's demise wasn't due to poor sales. After the fact, Kurtzman investigated to find out just how the magazine had done on newsstands. He wanted to know for sure, partly to ascertain the chances of the magazine's return. The print run was 200,000. He visited the distributor in Chicago, and found that *Trump* sold 65 percent of the copies printed. While not the eighty percent of the first *Playboy*, or the even higher percentage of sales garnered by *Mad* after its first year, this was still a respectable figure that would not have been cause to axe the magazine.

Indeed, sales couldn't have been a decisive factor at all. *Trump* #1 may have first appeared on newsstands in December 1956, but its cover date of January 1957 meant that it would remain on sale through the end of that month. Therefore, when Hefner pulled the plug on or slightly before January 21, he couldn't have known the sell-through percentage. Those figures would have been expected weeks later. (If there were preliminary reports, they would have indicated good if not spectacular sales.) One key issue was the amount of money HMH had sunk into the magazine up to that point. The exact amount isn't known, but is generally understood to be about $100,000 (according to a later letter from Hefner to Kurtzman).[26] It was a sum he couldn't possibly recoup in the short term, given how expensive the magazine was to produce. Costly photo sessions had run up the bills, and because the first issue took seven months to produce, monies going out while nothing was coming in mounted up. Hefner had known he had to spend money to set up the operation, but he may have expected the first issue to be ready earlier than it was.

Al Jaffee had a pertinent conversation about *Trump* at a party thrown by *Playboy* in New York some time later. In the course of a conversation with Robert Preuss, who had become Hefner's chief financial officer, Jaffee said he missed working on *Trump*, and it was "too bad that Hef ran into deep financial straits . . . and had to fold our magazine." Preuss replied that the financial crisis wasn't the reason the magazine folded. "That magazine folded because with Harvey it was never going to come out on time." Such delays added to printing costs and other expenses, and also made it difficult to sell advertising, according to Preuss. When Jaffee expressed surprise, stating that he understood Hefner would have continued the magazine except for financial pressures, Preuss said, "Well, what is he going to tell you?"[27]

This view is supported by an account in *The Mad World of William M. Gaines* when Jacobs quotes an unnamed "Playboy Executive" (maybe Preuss) as saying in a letter to Lyle Stuart after *Trump* was discontinued, "What we didn't recognize at the time . . . was Bill Gaines's own considerable part in the non-creative end of *Mad*'s growth and success. And when Kurtzman was left to his own devices, without this very necessary control, chaos resulted."[28] Hefner himself caused delays in the publication of *Playboy* in its early years due to his perfectionism, but he was highly aware of costs, and those occasions were rare. Later, he would memorably say, "I gave Harvey Kurtzman an unlimited budget and he exceeded it."[29] Would Hefner have spared *Trump* the axe if the first issue had come out in October instead of December?

Apparently not. In a recent interview for this book, Hugh Hefner discussed *Trump* and why it was discontinued. Rather than blame its demise on financial factors, he said the decision had to do with the magazine itself. Hefner described his reaction to *Trump* as "mixed."

> I think [Harvey] was feeling his way, and I don't think the magazine really found itself. The magazine didn't seem to be coming together. I thought the concept for *Trump* was beyond the earlier *Mad*, but it wasn't conceptually as successful. I was more impressed with the early *Mad*. The point is that I did not see it coming together in a way that looked as if it would be successful.
>
> Sometimes it's like a baseball game. When the bat hits the ball, you know it's going over the fence, you know it's a home run. I knew that from the very first issue with *Playboy* magazine. It was not there with *Trump*. The things that are naturals just somehow resonate in a unique way.[30]

Hefner implied that if he thought *Trump* had hit a creative home run, he might have fought to keep it going, or brought it back after he got past the financial crisis. A few years later, he had a similar experience when he tried publishing another magazine. Like *Trump*, his *Show Business Illustrated* in 1962 was short-lived. After that, Hefner decided not to undertake magazines unrelated to *Playboy*. At any rate, after the severe cost cutting, *Playboy* weathered its financial emergency in 1957, and scaled ever more impressive heights in sales and influence in the coming years.

This sudden reversal of fortune was humbling for Kurtzman. He was able to save face with friends by truthfully explaining that *Trump* had sold well and was a victim of short-term money problems at *Playboy*. Ironically, Kurtzman left *Mad* partly because he lost faith in Gaines's business judgment, yet it was "reckless" expansion (according to Kurtzman) and "wrong decisions" (admitted by Hefner) that greatly contributed to (if not entirely caused) the end of *Trump*.

"We tried to do a magazine with a professional look," Kurtzman said. "It looked like a magazine, not a kid book. *Mad* was still a kid book and still is, but with *Trump* we were trying to do something adult. We were using coated stock and four-color process. We went all the way—using the same talent and the same point of view." He ruefully added, "One of the reasons I hated to quit *Trump* was because of all the marvelous things we were going to do and never got to do."[31] Kurtzman had planned to work with a number of people for the first time in future issues, such as Shel Silverstein and Jean Shepherd, as well as bring Ernie Kovacs and Stan Freberg into the magazine. Kurtzman himself had spent hours working on a "hexaflexagon," an elaborate, long strip of paper printed on both sides that could be folded into a hexagonal shape in various ways to display a variety of different images. It was to have been a foldout in *Trump* #3. A parody of a Norman Rockwell painting had been completed by Elder for a *Saturday Evening Post* take-off, and other items for the interior were finished or well on their way to completion. In 1981, Kurtzman said, "*National Lampoon* came along many years later and did something in between what [*Trump* was] doing and what *Mad* was doing, with a lot of text, and it worked out very well for the *Lampoon*."[32]

Hugh Hefner's regard for Kurtzman's talent was undiminished. *Trump* would never return, but Hefner's door remained open to the humorist. Perhaps in the future there would be an opportunity for him in the pages of *Playboy*.

Elder didn't tell Kurtzman, but he felt his friend and collaborator had overreached. He admitted his candid thoughts in a late-in-life interview. "I thought [Harvey] moved too fast. He might have moved a little better a couple of years from that particular period. But he moved too fast and he wanted too much. I think that was a mistake. Harvey deserved a lot of credit, but that's no way to seek it."[33]

According to Adele, Harvey was "matter of fact" when he told her the news, and assured her everything would be okay. In truth, he was shattered. He had a wife, three kids, a mortgage and no job. "[Those days were] the closest I ever came to being a boozer," he said. "Harry and I . . . used to pace the streets of Manhattan [and] I'd say, 'Let's go in for a drink.' Because all the worry mechanism would be going. And if I ever loved booze it was in one of those sessions where, all of a sudden, all the anxieties go bye-bye. You have a couple of drinks, and you don't worry."[34]

As it turned out, a decision made "in the bottom of a bottle of Scotch" led to his next satire magazine, and his first venture as both publisher and editor.

19.

HUMBUG

HAVING EXPERIENCED *magazine interruptus*, Kurtzman and his collaborators on *Trump* gathered in the brownstone to commiserate. The termination of the magazine had come with no warning. The others wanted to hear the details of Kurtzman's conversation with Hefner. The news was still sinking in. "After we finished with *Trump*, we all sat around . . . and we were very unhappy that we were about to break up," Kurtzman recalled. "And Arnold Roth, who is a dear, sweet fellow . . . was the only one who came up with an optimistic attitude."[1] He also came up with a large bottle of Scotch.

As they passed around the bottle, the mood lightened. They knew they could produce a terrific magazine if only they had a fair shot at it. They were proud of *Trump* and confident it would have done well. (This was before Kurtzman had the actual sales figures in hand.) Given the talent in the room—each of Kurtzman's crew was destined to have a successful career—how could they fail, if only a publisher had the good sense to back them solidly? If *Mad* magazine became a publishing phenomenon, there was no good reason why they couldn't produce a magazine that would sell as well or better.

"Quality will sell" was the refrain, but after getting burned by Hefner, seeking another publisher met with little enthusiasm. One can imagine a still-resilient Kurtzman saying, "All we need to do is get a magazine on the stands next to *Mad*, and we could all make a fortune." As the supply of Scotch dwindled, someone said: "Let's publish it ourselves!"

Outrageous as it sounded, publishing their own magazine would have many benefits. The group of six—Kurtzman, Elder, Davis, Jaffee, Roth and Chester—had gotten along well in their nine months together. They would have creative control, own the rights to their own work in the magazine and split all the profits. That meant they would benefit if the material was reprinted, possibly in the paperback format that was doing so well for *Mad*. They would also be able to keep their own original art. (Gaines had never returned the original pages.)

A publishing cooperative, with each participant owning part of the enterprise, had never been tried in comics. Some creators had owned their own companies, like Simon and Kirby with their short-lived Mainline Comics, but the writers and artists who worked for them received none of the benefits of ownership. With the formation of Humbug Publishing Co., Inc., the workers were rising up to take group ownership of an enterprise. It was agreed that the "six musketeers" would create the magazine and split the profits equally, even though the setup differed from being a purely cooperative effort. The individual members wouldn't simply "do their own thing." The operation was predicated on Harvey Kurtzman being the editor and guiding force. The others wouldn't have entertained the idea except for their confidence in their charismatic leader's talent and vision. (Kurtzman had learned at the Charles William Harvey Studio that someone needed to be at the top.) As John Benson once put it, *Humbug* could be more accurately called a "commune" than a "co-op."

However one describes it, the idea of artists putting out their own magazine was new in the world of mainstream professional publishing, just as the comic book and magazine versions of *Mad* and the Kurtzman-produced war comics had been new concepts. Those ideas had opened vistas of creativity and met with commercial success, emboldening the *Humbug* crew to try this innovative twist on the standard publishing model. "We all ended on a happy note where we somehow talked ourselves into [becoming] a union of artists to turn out [our] own magazine," Kurtzman said. "That was *Humbug*."[2]

But could they come up with enough money to get started? Yes, barely. According to surviving documents, Humbug Publishing Co., Inc. was funded with a mere $6,500 in capital. The largest investor was Arnold Roth, with $2,500; he had been doing well in the past couple of years. Al Jaffee ponied up all his savings: $1,500. Elder came up with $1,000 as did Kurtzman. Harry Chester kicked in $500. Only Jack Davis became a stockholder without helping fund the magazine. Even as the others would forgo payment until profits came rolling in, Davis asked for and got a guaranteed monthly salary of $125. Everyone agreed that Davis was invaluable, and there was no resentment toward him. Indeed, whatever the amount invested, all were issued the same number of shares. (The variances were probably considered inconsequential and could be equalized out of expected profits. The actual stock certificates were issued on May 17, 1957.)

A contrite Hugh Hefner played a part in helping them get started. He allowed them to operate out of the brownstone office for the time being, and soon offered *Humbug* space in Playboy's advertising offices at 598 Madison Ave. For that, he charged them a mere $150 a month. Given the expense of office space in Manhattan, this was an enormous boon, even a de facto subsidy of sorts.

While dealing with a severe bout of chicken pox (in these years, he had one childhood disease after another), Kurtzman began looking for a printer and distributor who would work with them on a credit basis. No record exists of his travails in this regard, but the going was tough. In the aftermath of *Collier's* failure, the mighty American News Corporation closed its wholesale periodical division. Many of the top magazines—*Time*, *Life*, *Look*, the *New Yorker* and *Vogue*, as well as *Mad*—were obliged to find new distributors. Amid the resulting turmoil, who in the industry wanted to bother helping one little magazine get started? Door after door was figuratively slammed in Kurtzman's face until there was just one option left.

Charlton Publications, in Derby, Connecticut, was owned by two men who met in prison. John Santangelo, Sr., a Sicilian immigrant, was a former bricklayer whose first publishing endeavors resulted in a conviction for copyright infringement. While serving a year in the County of New Haven jail, he met Ed Levy, a disbarred lawyer, and the two of them decided to start a new publishing company. They called it Charlton after their two sons, both named Charles. It was to be an above-board organization, though a whiff of Mafia seemed to pervade Santangelo's demeanor. (Many of the people behind the distribution and trucking of periodicals are said to have had ties to organized crime.)

Located on the Naugatuck River, Derby was and remains the smallest municipality in the state, covering a mere five square miles. The massive Charlton building stretched over seven-and-a-half acres, on land between a marsh and the railroad tracks. It housed a unique, all-in-one publishing facility that included front offices, editorial space, an engraving department, printing presses, a bindery and a distribution warehouse. The firm even had its own fleet of trucks. It made the bulk of its income by putting out all manner of cheap newsprint magazines, from puzzle books to coloring books to song-lyric books. (The long-running magazines *Song Hits* and *Hit Parader* were its most successful publications.) Undeterred by the coming of the Comics Code, Charlton pumped out a dizzying array of comic book titles, and was notorious for paying the lowest rates and having the worst printing in the business.

Desperate times make for exceedingly strange bedfellows. Since Charlton owned both its own printing plant and distribution company (Capital Distributing Company, or CDC), it could give Kurtzman what he needed. On the strength of the success of *Mad*, he was invited to Derby to meet with Santangelo and Levy. In mid-April, he and Harry Chester made the seventy-mile drive. After getting a gander at the mammoth presses, the editorial area (Charlton had an in-house staff of editors, writers and artists), and the cavernous distribution warehouse, Kurtzman was ushered into an office for the meeting. John Santangelo had already published an inconsequential imitation of the comic book *Mad* called *Eh!* Now he wanted to do a knockoff of *Mad* magazine. The Charlton mogul, who had an intimidating presence despite his broken English, wanted to hire the creator of *Mad* and his crew on a freelance basis.

When it became clear Kurtzman was looking for a printer and distributor for a creator-owned magazine, and that he was asking Charlton to perform those functions on a credit basis, Santangelo wasn't happy, but he agreed to give Kurtzman what he wanted. If the new magazine could match the sales of *Mad*, Charlton stood to make a lot of money. Santangelo asked Levy to send Kurtzman an assignment agreement. The costs would be secured by the assets of Humbug Publishing Co., Inc., a not unusual arrangement. In better days for the industry, any number of new, undercapitalized comic book publishers started that way. (The only asset *Humbug* had, at this stage, was its name, but it would soon be generating editorial material that would be worth something.)

When Kurtzman left, he had mixed feelings. On the one hand, the magazine was now a go. On the other, he was nervous about working with Santangelo, and well aware of the poor quality of Charlton's printing. He knew that Gaines tried having Charlton print *Impact* #1, the first New Direction comic book, and was so appalled by the poor printing job that he had all the copies pulped, and paid to have the book printed elsewhere. Of course, everyone was clear that this would be a magazine, not a comic book, but still . . .

Naming the new magazine came easily, since *Humbug* had been one of Kurtzman's title ideas for *X*. As for the format, he decided it would be different size than any other magazine on the stands in 1957: a 6 ½" x 9 ½" booklet. Beneath full-color covers, it would be printed in black and white with single color accents, mostly light blue or yellow (one color per issue). The magazine would have thirty-two pages plus covers, the same as comic books, and sell for fifteen cents. True, it would cost 50 percent more than the standard comic book, but Kurtzman felt *Humbug* should be priced in comparison to magazines, not comic books. It would have two-thirds as many pages as the twenty-five cent *Mad*, so it was priced accordingly. A monthly schedule was declared.

Why not make it the same size, price and frequency as *Mad* magazine? That was doubtless what Santangelo wanted, and logically it would seem to be the safest route, but Kurtzman wanted to try something new. He would never be an imitator, not even of himself. *Trump* had been highly conscious of its competitive stance vis-à-vis *Mad*. Although this wouldn't be expressed overtly in *Humbug*, it's probable that its format was an attempt to show that Kurtzman could be equally successful in a whole new way.

The new format had several virtues. In contrast to the black and white *Mad*, *Humbug* would have some interior color, have a lower cover price, and, as a monthly, deliver about one hundred pages more per year than the forty-eight page, bimonthly *Mad*. The use of limited color would minimize the matter of color registration (one of Charlton's perennial problems). Two-color printing was simple enough that it wouldn't require a separate colorist. Kurtzman probably felt the unusual size would help *Humbug* stand out from everything else. (Even smaller magazines, like *Pageant* and *Reader's Digest*, worked on newsstands.) Once Kurtzman determined *Humbug*'s format, he announced it to his partners. As Al Jaffee put it, "He was not a great consulter. Harvey had visions."[3]

As for the contents, *Humbug* wasn't to be a continuation of *Trump*. Kurtzman now had to shift from a classy, slick high-end magazine with interior color to a humble two-color magazine printed on cheap pulp paper. No longer would he be trying to produce something geared to the *Playboy* reader. Instead, *Humbug* would be a sort of sophisticated college humor magazine. It would be geared to a slightly older readership than had Kurtzman's *Mad*. While being limited technically, *Humbug* would be freer than *Trump* and smarter than *Mad*.

As soon as the stockholders of *Humbug* signed the agreement with CDC, work on the new magazine began. On April 2, Kurtzman wrote Hefner, "Together with Jack, Willy, Harry, Al and Arnold, I'm plunging ahead into our new venture and God knows where it will all end." In that letter, Kurtzman itemized six items left over from *Trump* that would fit the new magazine. They included a four-page series of drawings by Davis of "little television screens showing TV boners," pieces on model airplane and boat making, medicine in the US, a Du Maurier cigarette ad satire, a piece about the verbiage on cereal boxes and a one-page idea showing pictures of money that the reader could cut out and use. On April 17, Hefner responded:

> The very best wishes to you and those strange ones you have gathered around you in your new venture. May [it] prove most prosperous and if things don't work out for me here in Chicago, I may drop in on you in a year or two with an idea for a new magazine. Hoo ha!
>
> I've affixed my official mark on your note regarding the material listed. We can work out the details on the matter when I next get to New York, but my thinking on the matter runs something like this—you will purchase the material from HMH for whatever it cost us to produce it in the first place. What we will have to work out when I see you is the method of payment. Some sort of part now, part later arrangement should be able to be worked out. I hope to be in New York the very early part of May and should have some time for talking and such.[4]

The ideas left over from *Trump* jump-started the creative process of *Humbug*. One thing would become clear: unlike *Mad* and *Trump*, *Humbug* would have almost no comment on, parody of or reference to comic books or strips, even in passing. Comic book publishers were closing their doors left and right in the aftermath of the Senate hearings and the establishment of the Comics Code. Since comics were in a tailspin, maybe even dying, satirizing them was pointless. Also, *Humbug* would have a sharper focus than its predecessor at EC. While *Mad* was about the '50s as well as popular culture in general, *Humbug* would in most ways be specifically about 1957 (and, then, 1958).

Harry Chester handled the practical aspects of the start-up, and had a long list of things to tackle. He organized the bookkeeping system and ordered stationery. Harry contacted Wally Howarth at *Playboy* for advice on how to handle subscription fulfillment. He created a list of people and organizations to receive promotional and complimentary copies of the magazine, such as Steve Allen, Jack Paar and Ernie Kovacs. Chester was the one who arranged for the engraving to be done at Chemical Color, the company used by EC, rather than in-house at Charlton, ensuring a better result. "Harry was a very aggressive, hard-working guy," Al Jaffee recalled. "He had a kind of entrepreneurial spirit, which is why Harvey chose him as our business manager. He was somebody that Harvey could always turn to and say, 'Harry, while I'm dealing with the artists, you take care of the printing and production.' It was a big job."[5] When all the elements for an issue of the magazine came in, Chester would put it all together based on Kurtzman's layouts.

As before, Kurtzman often absented himself from the office, retreating to his home studio where he generated ideas, wrote and laid out stories, typed letters, and communicated by phone with Roth (in Philadelphia), Elder (in Englewood), Jaffee (on Long Island) and Davis (in Scarsdale), as well as others who did a little or a lot for the magazine, like Wallace Wood and Ed Fisher. Since there were limited funds to pay for outside work, most of *Humbug* was produced by its core group of stockholders. The monthly schedule forced Kurtzman to rely heavily on the talent and judgment of the group. Jaffee and Roth were listed as editors on the masthead. The do-overs and changes were kept to a minimum. That pleased Roth, who disliked Kurtzman's proclivity for requesting changes in the work. "When I would have these conversations with Harvey, I would say, 'If I do it over, it's going to lose something. It'll be tighter. I'll correct certain things. Some things will be a little better, but it will kill the soul of the thing.' It's just the way I feel. It's like playing in a jazz band. You know, if a guy's going to take a jazz solo and the leader says, 'I don't want one false note,' well, how free can you feel to just improvise?'" In this case, due to the time constraints, "[Harvey] really had to accept a lot of stuff and go with it even though he really wished it could be done three more times."[6]

It wasn't as if Kurtzman's willingness to change things at the last minute never made a significant improvement. One instance involved the cover of *Humbug* #1 (August 1957). The proofs had been made for a cover that originally said, "ANOTHER NEW MAGAZINE" in red, with some text in the bottom corner to balance it out. When someone laughingly suggested it should be "THE END OF THE WORLD IS COMING," Kurtzman liked it so much he had the cover changed. (He also took the opportunity to have Jack Davis design a new, more impressive title logo.) The final result was far more inspired and striking.

Under the masthead on p. 1, the headline announces, "Here we go again." In response to an admiring letter from John C. Roberts of Wheatridge, Colorado, a typically downbeat Kurtzman wrote:

> We don't believe in standing still and letting the grass grow under our feet! Oh no! We're going to spring into action, Mr. Roberts! We're going to hustle on down to that Unemployment Insurance office for money. After that, we're going to hustle back to work on our latest magazine, *Humbug*.

> *Humbug* will be a responsible magazine. We won't write for morons. We won't do anything just to get laughs. We won't be dirty. We won't be grotesque. We won't be in bad taste. We won't sell any magazines.

The issue starts off with a parody of the movie *Baby Doll*. Tennessee Williams' somewhat scandalous story of two Southern rivals for the affections of a sensuous nineteen-year-old virgin provided the basis for the first movie ever to be approved by Hollywood's Production Code Authority while being given a "C" (condemned) rating by the Catholic Legion of Decency. "Doll-Baby" is Kurtzman and Davis at their best, with Davis's likenesses of Carroll Baker, Karl Malden and Eli Wallach on target. A sequence with Baker and Wallach tiptoeing in and out of doorways in a hallway reached dizzying heights of absurdity when Walt Disney's Goofy and other cartoon characters also tip-toe through the same doors and hallway.

Unlike *Trump*, *Humbug* would have a fair amount of political satire. For satire to work at its best, one must necessarily be familiar with the subjects in question. Many of the politically oriented items in *Humbug*, which depict public figures and events of 1957, tend to be obscure to readers decades later. That's not to say that one can't enjoy Arnold Roth's "Bird Watchers Guide for Humbugians," with its quasi-editorial cartoon drawings depicting Dwight D. Eisenhower, Gamal Abdel Nasser, Fulgencio Batista and others in bird form, simply for its graphic appeal, and the sly wording of the captions. The same is true of the "Pin-Up of the Month" showing portly labor leader Dave Beck reclining coyly at poolside. This pin-up, obviously inspired by Hefner's

Humbug #1 (August 1957).

"Doll-Baby" in *Humbug* #1. A sequence with the characters tiptoeing in and out of doorways reached the height of absurdity when Walt Disney's Goofy and other cartoon characters joined them.

Playboy centerfolds, is definitely grotesque—*Humbug*'s avowed editorial statement notwithstanding.

For his part, Al Jaffee contributed two of his most ingenious features in *Humbug* #1. The first is a cereal box opened and flattened out to show all printed surfaces, revealing an endless array of gimmicks, prizes, coupons, text fields and disclaimers. Next, his "Model Making" presents an incredible and yet seemingly feasible method of building models with a kit, in which all the pieces are connected by a piece of heavy string. "With this cleverly constructed kit the young craftsman need only give one good yank and all parts fly into place."

Elder's main bit in the issue is "Twenty-Win," a Kurtzman-written parody of the popular *Twenty-One* television show, which would, a year later, be at the center of a giant scandal concerning rigged TV quiz programs. When *Humbug* #1 was published, the show's star contestant Charles Van

Doren, a college professor, was a household name, and the program was at its zenith. Elder is in top form, though rather constricted by the amount of dialogue, since the strip satirizes the complexity of the show's rules. Work by Jack Davis, screenwriter Ken Englund, Ira Wallach, R.O. Blechman and even a bit by Wallace Wood make up the rest of *Humbug*'s first issue. The back cover is a subscription ad next to a fake five-dollar bill "as a subscription bonus" that appears to have been cut out of the page (with a simulated version of the interior page below "showing"). All in all, the first issue is nearly perfect. Everything works. It's a propitious beginning that set the pattern for the issues that followed.

KURTZMAN AND CHESTER visited the plant to see the first printed copies of *Humbug* #1 come out of the bindery. As they beheld the first issue with its "THE END OF THE WORLD IS COMING" cover, they were confident it would grab the attention of browsers. When they got back to the city, copies were passed out to the participants who also reacted favorably. The size met with approval. As Arnold Roth said later, "I kind of liked the size, personally. I thought it was good. It was perfect."[7]

Humbug received a bill from Charlton for the first issue on June 13, 1957. Some 297,055 copies were printed for a total cost of $5,049.94. The bill was marked "paid in full by Capital Distr. Co. per assignment agreement." Now all that remained was for the magazine to take off. Kurtzman calculated that the book needed to sell about 50 percent of the copies to break even. If they could match the 65 percent sales of *Trump*, they would be in "deep clover." As usual, there was nothing to do but wait until sales reports arrived.

Kurtzman met with the team monthly to hand out assignments and discuss pertinent matters. He would have the structure of the next issue in mind, with major pieces designed to relate to things like upcoming holidays, the sports seasons and political events. "He would block out what the people would be responsible for," Roth recalled. "Where there were gaps, he would say, 'We'll have to fill this. We'll have to do that.' Those decisions came very quickly. Sometimes he would call me and ask me to do something overnight."[8]

Despite having little to pay for outside talent, one new writer turned up who became one of the magazine's best. He wasn't really an outsider. Larry Siegel met Kurtzman while manning the HMH promotions office that shared space with *Trump* in the Thirty-Seventh Street brownstone. Siegel had been editor of *Shaft*, the University of Illinois satire magazine that had once, in the late 1940s, been edited by Hefner. While he continued doing the promotional work, Siegel asked Kurtzman if he could write for the new magazine. With "Something of Mau Mau," a satire of Robert Roark's violent *Something of Value*, Siegel immediately showed himself to be a clever satirist and became a regular contributor to *Humbug*. "I never got into one of those group things that they used to have with Jaffee, Elder, Jack Davis and the rest of them," Siegel recalled. "I would get together with [Harvey], and I would make some suggestions, or he might say, 'Why don't you do something on *Peyton Place*?' He was a very easy guy for me to work with. He was an absolute doll, that's all I can say."[9]

Along with Siegel's piece, *Humbug* #2 offers the Kurtzman-Elder film parody "Around the Days in 80 Worlds," as well as a cartoon of Groucho Marx accompanying a piece by British novelist and playwright Alex Atkinson (reprinted from *Punch*) which expertly captures Groucho's comic persona. Jack Davis teams up with Kurtzman to satirize the smash Broadway show *My Fair Lady* ("My Fair Sadie") and "Television Bugs," a look at typical goofs made during live TV broadcasts of drama programs. A new ongoing feature by Arnold Roth called "The Humbug Award" appears ("Dedicated to outstanding people who have made extremely unimportant contributions to society"), given in this issue to Robert Harrison, editor of sleazy *Confidential* magazine. By the time the first two issues were finished, Kurtzman and company were settled in their new offices on Madison Avenue.

Humbug #3 is the first issue with a letter column. There are missives from Bhob Stewart and George Metzger, the future underground comix artist. ("Underground comix," spelled with an *x* to distinguish them from the Comics Code-approved comic books of the time, were 1960s–70s self- or small press-published comics that defied taboos and were mainly distributed through tabloids, head shops and the mail.) *Humbug* quickly became a *cause célèbre* among readers who had followed Kurtzman from *Mad* to *Trump* and then to the new magazine, and recognized that something extraordinary was happening: Kurtzman and crew were producing a more evolved, more intelligent satire magazine than *Mad*. A trickle of letters at the start quickly became a flood, with dozens arriving on some days. As with the early days of *Mad* in 1952, the letters convinced Kurtzman that they had struck a nerve.

AT HOME, all was not well. A tragedy of proportions that would only be fully understood with the passage of time was unfolding in the Kurtzman household. Peter Kurtzman, who turned three years old in June 1957, was diagnosed with autism. Adele recently explained, "Peter was a beautiful, normal-looking baby, and he walked early, but in his second year, we began to feel something was wrong. When he wouldn't speak, at first we thought he was deaf. He didn't like to be held or touched. It creeps up on you, little signs, and of course you deny it to yourself. Eventually we went to doctors. Some of the doctors told us crazy things like 'he'll grow out of it.' But eventually it was clear that Pete wasn't a normal child. Harvey was very good. He'd always say, 'it'll be okay. We'll deal with it.'"[10]

When Adele had difficulty caring for the three children, Harvey always emerged from his studio to lend a hand. Having her husband often working from home made it possible for her to handle the challenges involved in raising a child with autism, particularly low-functioning autism as in Peter's case. (It was common to put such children in institutions, but the Kurtzmans were determined to keep Peter home with them.) At times, they despaired, but they got through it. Laughter helped a lot. Adele once said, "Life is a cruel joke if we don't laugh."[11]

About this time, Kurtzman discovered the *Okeh Laughing Record*, a 78 rpm record released in 1922. It begins with the sound of a mournful trumpet playing, then the sound of a woman's laughter, who is then joined by a man who is also laughing uncontrollably, and so goes on for almost three minutes. Kurtzman loved to play it for friends and visitors. Its laughter was always contagious. On a few occasions, Arnold Roth slept on their couch after late-night sessions finishing an issue of *Humbug*. In the morning, Kurtzman would wake him up with the laughing record, turned up full volume. The second or third time it happened, Roth said, "Why are you playing it for me again? I've already heard it." Kurtzman replied, "It gets better."[12]

JUST AS THE COVER of *Mad* #11 parodies *Life* magazine, Will Elder's cover of *Humbug* #4 (November), featuring Queen Victoria, parodies *Time*. In the opening editorial, Kurtzman wrote, "Mail is rustling into the office at an accelerating rate of one-hundred plus letters a week. We've inked a pact for a *Humbug* paper-bound book which will appear in November." A letter on that same page from Ray Russell of *Playboy* magazine reads, "Of the four leading American humorists (you, me, S. J. Perelman and Louella Parsons) none better deserves the acclaim and recognition of the masses than me. You're next though. And I say this from a heart filled with sincerity, warmth, regard, esteem and professional jealousy. Viva Kurtzman! Long live *Humbug*!" The quality of the material in *Humbug* was consistently high, and the issues were on time. The movie and television parodies continued to be drawn by Davis and Elder, with Roth doing most of the politically oriented material. Larry Siegel branched out into humorous poems and song parodies, as well as book and magazine satires ("Consumer Retorts"), and Al Jaffee zeroed in on absurd aspects of the American scene.

Jaffee later discussed his working method for *Humbug*. "I never felt that my proposing an idea for an article was ever going to be really successful. I decided . . . that I would invest in speculating and draw out my entire article. But I [did] it on lots of pieces of paper, and Harvey would assemble it into an article. Because I had an opening, and then I had a dozen ideas to go with it. He would put it together and arrange it, and it worked very well that way."[13]

Meanwhile, no one would be paid for their efforts until and if the magazine was profitable. Each of the players handled the situation in his own way. Kurtzman could collect New York State unemployment benefits for twenty-six weeks, but was counting on royalties for the *Mad* paperback books to get him through. When he was still at *Mad*, and Gaines ran into financial difficulties, Kurtzman agreed to temporarily forego payment. According to his estimate, Gaines owed him about $2,000 for paperbacks sold when he was still at EC, and probably a similar amount in the months after he left.[14] (Those sales would only accelerate in the coming years, ultimately bringing Kurtzman's collaborations—which dominated the early paperbacks—to millions who hadn't seen them in the original comic books.) He wrote to Gaines, reminding him of the debt and asking to be paid. The only monies *Humbug* was generating for the stockholders were advance payments on royalties for *The Humbug Digest* ($2,500, received in April 1957, probably used for ongoing production expense), and whatever orders for magazine subscriptions arrived in the mail.

Arnold Roth and Jack Davis worked on assignments for other publications in order to pay the bills (or, in Davis's case, to augment what he was getting from *Humbug*). Al Jaffee did not, and was strangely serene about making no money on *Humbug* for months on end. "I was at a party and I remember someone saying to me, 'You're working on this magazine *Humbug*. How long have you been on it?' At that time I think it was six or seven months. 'And you don't get a salary?' So I said, 'No, I don't.' For so many years I was grinding stuff out, the comic book stuff. I said, 'I've never felt so at peace and so relaxed and so unworried as I am in this situation.'"[15] Deep down, he had faith that Kurtzman would pull them through and the magazine would become successful. In the meantime, having invested all his savings in *Humbug*, he was borrowing against a personal insurance policy.

The process of producing the magazine itself was a good experience for all concerned. The creative work was stimulating and satisfying. They knew they were generating something good, and enjoyed each other's work immensely. Kurtzman and Chester were closer than ever. "We used to have great times going [to Derby]," Kurtzman said. "Harry and I would take the trip regularly to see our book go to press."[16] The *Humbug* editorial meetings were rife with laughter, though Kurtzman was mainly the audience for the jests of others. A master of satiric humor on paper, he was never a teller of jokes. Roth recalled,

> Once when things were getting a bit depressing after a few issues of *Humbug*, Harvey was giving us all a sort of pep talk. Harvey's back was to the windows. About eighty feet away there was another building at least as high as ours. We were looking at Harvey and he waved his arm to the window and said, "Remember, they're all out there." Like in a movie all our eyes went to the end of his hand and out the window. Right across in the window of the other building there was a guy screwing a woman on a couch. We all leapt to the window. He didn't know what the hell we were doing.[17]

Kurtzman kept former contributors to *Mad* such as Doodles Weaver abreast of the status of the new magazine. In October, he wrote, "Right now, we're barely eking out a living. I'm trying to publish *Humbug* with my own shoestring. We've got a great system for handling the writing. A little midget is chained to a desk and if he doesn't write funny, I beat him till he does, and he works very cheap. He pays me."[18]

All were frustrated by the lack of sales reports. Based on scattered information, Capital Distributors estimated that *Humbug* #1 sold roughly 45 percent (about 135,000 copies) of its print run. If true, this was disappointing, but it did mean they weren't too far from being a going concern. It was the final sales report that really mattered. When it arrived, in mid-October, it documented sales of only 35 percent, which would normally be cause for immediate cancellation. But Capital Distributing informed Kurtzman that issues #2, 3 and 4 were seeing a consecutively steady rise in sales. Also, the sale on #1 was eccentric from town to town, which wasn't typical of a flop magazine. It suggested to Kurtzman that there were problems on the distribution rather than the buyer level. "It's all very mysterious," he wrote Ed Fisher, "but our distributor . . . seems to see enough [potential] to give us an assist through issue #8."[19] In a follow-up letter to Fisher a few weeks later, he wrote, "The world is upside down. We're God-knows how many thousand dollars in debt and *Mad* continues to grow like some horrible Frankenstein monster. But there is still hope. *Playboy* has printed a lovely twelve-page article on us. Ballantine has printed a *Humbug* pocket book. If we can hold out for another half year, I think we'll be in! The publishing world is an astonishing place!"[20] It didn't help that the nation's economic climate was far from robust. The United States economy had slipped into an officially declared recession that would last a year or more, the worst since 1947. The *Humbug* paperback went back to press, and a contract was signed for a second *Humbug* collection on December 2, about the only bright spots in a consistently downbeat financial picture.

"The Little World of Harvey Kurtzman" in *Playboy* (December 1957) was the kind of publicity money couldn't buy. The article by Rolf Malcolm couldn't have been more complimentary of the work of Kurtzman and his *Humbug* collaborators.[21] Kurtzman is described as "a star of the first magnitude," and the text is accompanied by material from *Mad* and *Trump*, mostly in full color. At one point, the piece describes how *Humbug* was put together:

Behind the intricate excellences of the artists' pens is Kurtzman, who writes most of the scripts and personally sketches detailed layouts and breakdowns to guide the artists in doing the finishes. Ideas are fed into the hopper by all members of the group, however, when they periodically come in to Manhattan from Scarsdale, Long Island, Westchester, Philadelphia and other outlands for editorial meetings, of which the following extract is typical:

KURTZMAN: Actually, there's not too much to talk about . . .

JAFFEE: We came from fifty miles around to hear that.

KURTZMAN: But there are a few spots here maybe you can help me out on. For the Christmas cover, I've been trying to think about something with Ebenezer Scrooge on it. And about the closest I got to an idea that satisfied me was—you know that old poster of Uncle Sam saying "I want you"? I was just wondering how Scrooge would look pointing out from the cover like that and just saying "Humbug!" to the world out there.

JAFFEE: And maybe we could put our title, *Humbug*, in a balloon.

ROTH: Why don't we run a message from Manischewitz wine on the cover?

EVERYBODY: For Christmas??!!

ROTH: Sure, and we'd have What's-His-Name, Commander What's-His-Name . . .

KURTZMAN: Whitehead?

ROTH: Yeah, only we'd change his name; you know, he says, "Hello theah, this is Monty Schewitz . . . " Well, he *looks* like Santa Claus, that guy!

JAFFEE: But it would be too long to say, "Manischewervescence."

KURTZMAN (in *desperation*): I'm not getting ANY HELP HERE!!

Hefner showed more support for Kurtzman by sending him 500 gratis copies of the issue, so that he had plenty of tear sheets for promotional purposes. That issue of *Playboy* appeared on newsstands about the same time as *Humbug* #6 (January, 1958), the Christmas issue, which introduces the new, "cleaner" title logo. The issue has the Ebenezer Scrooge cover discussed in the *Playboy* article. Kurtzman selected Davis to draw a wizened Scrooge holding a newspaper full of depressing headlines, responding, "Humbug!" to Bob Cratchit's "A Very Merry Christmas Uncle!" Roth was just as big a fan of Charles Dickens as Kurtzman. He contributed a masthead illustration of Scrooge throwing a snowball at Santa Claus and a six-page parody of "A Christmas Carol." At one point Scrooge's legacy is described as " . . . a tombstone . . . a magazine title."

The Humbug Award is given to Fake Santa Clauses "who stimulate the spirit of giving by taking." Larry Siegel provides versions of "A Night before Christmas" as Joe Friday, Paddy Chayefsky, Cecil B. DeMille and others might tell them. Also notable is Al Jaffee's two-page spread featuring an elaborate drawing of a neighborhood over-decorated with Christmas lights, etc. ("Of course," he wrote, "some can afford to spend more on this than others, and this does create a certain amount of bitterness.") The TV show satire ("Why Tell the Truth") and a brief movie spoof ("The Man of 1000 Faces, 500 Bodies, and 348 Voices, Growls and Shrieks") are the work of the Kurtzman-Elder team. The issue wraps up with a message of holiday cheer on the back cover by Roth, with caricatures of the staff toasting the readers. Standing with them is one Seymour Mednick, whose name appeared as a non sequitur gag through a number of issues. (Mednick was actually Arnold Roth's next-door neighbor in Philadelphia.)

Despite producing a superb magazine issue after issue, they still hadn't received so much as a dime from their distributor. In mid-December, a meeting with John Santangelo to discuss the fate of *Humbug* was held at Charlton's Derby headquarters. Jack Davis chauffeured the entire crew of six to the event, slipping and sliding on the snow-covered highway. Instead of the usual kibitzing, the atmosphere in the car was charged with apprehension. They took turns predicting the outcome of the meeting. Some were cautiously optimistic, while others were pessimistic. Only

Davis kept his thoughts to himself, concentrating on maneuvering around cars that had skidded into grotesque positions all over the road.

"It was a pre-Christmas luncheon with Charlton's execs," Al Jaffee recalled, which was attended by John Santangelo, his son Charles, Ed Levy and his cousin Burton Levy, and general manager Allan Adams. "Santangelo's Christmas gift to us," Jaffee said, "was that Charlton would take over ownership of *Humbug* and pay us the way freelance comic artists and writers were paid, by the page."[22] Roth said, "He was trying to coerce us into doing what he wanted. This is a gentleman of Sicilian origins and he had hands like hams and fingers like salamis. And on each finger he had a ring. He held up his hands and said, 'You listen to me, you get a ring on every finger. You don't listen to me . . . ' and he made a huge fist."

After some back-and-forth discussion, Santangelo said, "You gotta have $6,000 to go on. You can't do this thing unless you get $6,000."

"Can't your company advance the $6,000?" Kurtzman asked.

"Where am I gonna get it?" He seemed to be suggesting that all his money was tied up. Then Santangelo made more noises about Charlton taking over the magazine, and paying them as freelancers.

Kurtzman had heard enough, and finally declared, "If we don't own our own magazine, there's no reason why we [would] want to do it anymore!"

Santangelo thought about it a moment, then told one of his minions, "Give 'em the money." The group drove home in the midst of a blizzard, stopping along the way to celebrate their independence in a funky mountaintop restaurant (The Red Barn), as a grim Christmas approached.

Kurtzman held out hope that *Humbug* could be saved, even as the magazine slipped more into debt to Charlton. Based on escalating numbers of subscriptions and the volume of letters, he was convinced that their contents weren't the problem. Although he relayed reports to the publisher from frustrated readers who had difficulty finding *Humbug* on the stands, he could do nothing to improve CDC's distribution. He began thinking in terms of converting it to a full-size, twenty-five cent magazine, to bring in more money and stop it from getting lost behind the bigger magazines and comic books. To do that, he needed an outside investor or two.

Christmas was a subdued affair for the *Humbug* crew, though they did have a small office party. Kurtzman invited some friends and associates and brought a bottle of whiskey. Arnold Roth recalled, "A Jewish guy who doesn't drink was in charge of doing the provisions. So he buys whiskey, and he doesn't buy glasses of any kind, plastic or whatever. He buys those pleated, paper Dixie cups. When you poured the whiskey in, it would soak up the whiskey and elongate. They didn't break, they just kept getting longer. And they looked like used condoms."[23] Their cups and their spirits drooped as 1957 drew to a close.

HUMBUG #7 (FEBRUARY 1958)—the first issue to appear in the New Year— was completed before the pre-Christmas conference in Derby. Its cover addresses one of the most electrifying events of 1957, the Soviet Union's successful launch of the Sputnik satellite on October 4. The fact that mankind's first object to reach beyond the earth's atmosphere had been put there by "Commies" shocked the American government and public. The news was splashed across the headlines and covers of virtually every publication in the country, and the world for that matter. Kurtzman decided to show the Commie "spy satellite" spying on the nude of Paul Chabas's *September Morn*, a famous pre–World War I painting. (Though the woman's hands did their best to cover her nudity, anti-vice crusader Anthony Comstock had charged that it was obscene.) The "arf arf" sound effect coming from the superimposed satellite refers to a subsequent Soviet launch with a canine passenger, less than a month after Sputnik.

One of the highlights in the issue is the Kurtzman-Elder parody of James Whale's *Frankenstein* (1931), a cinematic classic brought to late-night television in October 1957 as the lead-off film in a package of movies under the heading "Shock!" With the title spelling changed oh-so-slightly, this "Frankenstien" is one of the funniest movie parodies in all *Humbug*. (Hans, assistant to Dr. Frankenstien, regarding the monster: "He's ugly! How can you stand him?" Frankenstien to Hans: "If I can stand you—I can stand him. Come to think of it I can't stand you." It was Kurtzman à la Groucho Marx.) Fortunately, Kurtzman's roughs for this story—developed from small thumbnail drawings of each page—have survived, and are quite revealing.

The surviving tracing paper overlays for "Frankenstien" provided all the important storytelling elements: facial expressions in many variations, background characters and design, and placement of black or dark areas on the page. Not only that, but the script was written on the tracing paper pages, in balloons that show where they should be positioned in the panels. These layout pages are a thing of beauty in themselves, and show Kurtzman in total command of the strip in all but the finest details. The way the gags are framed, how the figures work in tandem with the balloon placement, the forceful shading and the characters' gestures are all highly accomplished. True, Dr. Frankenstien wasn't made to resemble Colin

Clive. That was Elder's job. But it's clear that Kurtzman's contributions to the story—presumably similar to what he did on all the movie and TV parodies in *Humbug*—were more elaborate than those done for artists at EC. That may explain why those sorts of features were fewer in number and shorter in *Humbug* than *Mad*. Kurtzman, the master planner, was more deeply involved than ever in his collaborations with Will Elder and Jack Davis.

Although *Humbug* #8 offers a parody of Elvis titled "Jailbreak Rock" and Larry Siegel's parody of automotive magazines, and some fine cartoon work by Jaffee, Roth and Davis, it's the first issue that falls somewhat flat. Perhaps this was a reflection of the crew's sinking spirits. In an effort to bring in some cash, a *Humbug* bound edition, with the first six issues, was offered for $2.50.

After #8 was printed, and sales on earlier issues hadn't risen as hoped, the magazine's end was near. Was Charlton "cooking" the sales reports in an effort to force them to work on a freelance basis? If so, nothing in the realm of practicality could be done about it. The documents clearly indicated that *Humbug* was in debt to Capital for thousands of dollars, and the distributor was ready to reject any further advances. It was especially galling that *Humbug* was on the ropes when they got the word that *Mad*'s press run passed one million. Instead of collapsing without Kurtzman, *Mad* was a bigger hit than ever. However, Al Feldstein believed that *Humbug* would also be successful if brought back into the EC fold.

Feldstein came up with an idea and somehow managed to convince a reluctant Bill Gaines to go along with it: offer Harvey Kurtzman the chance to take *Humbug* to EC, and publish *Mad* and *Humbug* bimonthly on alternate months. "Bill wasn't keen on it because he was antagonistic toward Harvey," Feldstein recently recalled. "But I thought it would be a great idea to bring Harvey back under our auspices and our kibitzing."[24] The idea was that *Humbug* would appeal to the older readers, and *Mad* would go for the younger crowd. Al Feldstein got in touch with Harry Chester and floated the idea. An incredulous Harvey Kurtzman dispatched Chester to meet with them, perversely curious what would be offered. No details are known, only that when Chester returned, Kurtzman summarily rejected the concept on principle. He had no desire to work with Gaines again under any circumstances. Besides, it was highly unlikely Gaines would have allowed Kurtzman and the others to retain ownership of their material, or the *Humbug* name. Kurtzman chose not to tell his partners about Gaines's offer, which he ought to have done, from an ethical standpoint. Whatever the terms offered, Al Jaffee later felt they should have been discussed with the *Humbug* stockholders. "No money was coming in, and I think Harvey should have at least discussed it with us. But at the same time, I'm pretty sure they would only take us on if Harvey came with it, so voting wouldn't mean anything if Harvey didn't want to go back.'"[25] Arnold Roth recently concurred. "Harvey should have mentioned the offer, but I think his decision not to tell us is understandable since he'd made up his mind not to entertain it. He was our peerless leader and if he didn't want to take *Humbug* to Gaines, then I wouldn't have been in favor of it, and I can't imagine that the other guys would have, either."[26]

Instead, Kurtzman and Chester worked up a prospectus for a plan to convert *Humbug* to a full-size twenty-five cent magazine. Arnold Roth had turned up a potential investor in Yellow Springs, Ohio: his father-in-law. On January 10, Kurtzman wrote to Dr. P. B. Wingfield, "We propose to put out a [twenty-five cent] magazine identical in size to *Mad* and with the original *Mad* talent (which is in our opinion superior to *Mad*'s present talent). We are willing to sell stock for work capital up to the point of a controlling interest in *Humbug*." In the end, the doctor chose not to invest.

Wanting to recoup its investment, Capital finally agreed to advance sufficient funds for Kurtzman and company to implement the change. But when one Charlton executive saw the cover for this first full-size issue, he was dismayed. On March 10, 1958, Allan Adams, general manager of CDC, wrote:

> Dear Harvey,
> I have just received an advance copy of the June issue of *Humbug* and I feel that you have an extremely bad cover on this issue. I believe you are going to see a great deal of confusion among readers as to just what you are offering. I had hoped that on your initial kickoff into the larger format et al., that you would have pulled all the stops and particularly a cover at which you are past master. To say the least, I am really extremely fearful that this one won't get off the ground. Internally, the book looks very good to me and I am hoping that it is sound and solid enough to overcome my feelings about the cover.[27]

Kurtzman's cover of *Humbug* #10 (June) consisted of a photo of a labor riot (the Memorial Day Massacre in Chicago, 1938) with a fashion model pasted in the center, under the slogan, "Today's fashion photos have smartest settings." From a conceptual point of view, the politically themed cover was terrific, but its humor—not really dependent on knowledge of the specific labor riot—flew over the head of Adams, as it would with many newsstand browsers.

In the spring of 1958, Crown Books published *Mad for Keeps*, a $2.95 hardback book made up entirely of Kurtzman-produced material from *Mad* without crediting him anywhere in its pages. Kurtzman was outraged. Between that (which paid him nothing) and the outstanding paperback royalties, Kurtzman decided to seek legal recourse. On May 14, he sent relevant materials to Charles Rembar of the Levine Rembar and Zolotar legal firm, and the process began. Gaines would not capitulate. He took the position that any obligation he had to pay Kurtzman royalties on the paperback books ended when Kurtzman left EC. Kurtzman's hope for a quick cash infusion was dashed, a major blow at a time when he was in dire financial straits (which Gaines knew). Gaines took the matter to his attorney Martin Scheiman. It wouldn't be resolved for years.

Meanwhile, the *Humbug* gang did what it could to publicize the change in format. About the time their tenth issue hit newsstands, the group appeared on the Long John Knebel radio program, a popular late night show, to promote the magazine. It seems to have occurred on the brink of the magazine's cancellation.

On June 18, 1958, Kurtzman met with fans Larry Ivie and John Benson for an interview in a coffee shop near the *Pageant* offices. The key revelation was that *Humbug* would end with #11. Kurtzman elaborated briefly: "There aren't any magazines doing well except for the specialty magazines, you know, like the hot rod ones, or *Popular Electronics*. And *Playboy*. And *Mad*. Damn it. There's a real feud between us now. I'm suing Gaines for using my work in *Mad for Keeps*. Since I left, he's been using my work like crazy.[28]

THE DECISION TO DISCONTINUE *Humbug* occurred in mid-to-late May. Its failure couldn't entirely be attributed to a depressed magazine market. Clearly, the small format and price had been a big part of the problem. Converting it to a format similar to *Mad* would seem to almost guarantee a better sales response. Why, then, didn't the format change turn things around for *Humbug*?

In his prospectus, Kurtzman estimated that it would take at least three issues to see if the new format worked. There were only two. *Humbug* #10 was the larger size, but had no more pages than the original format. *Humbug* #11 swelled to forty-eight pages by using reprints from *Trump*, but didn't appear until August (though it carried an October cover date, in order to have the longest display period possible). What seems to have happened is that Charlton held out hope of getting its way, but finally realized that Kurtzman and crew would never agree to transfer complete ownership of *Humbug* to them and work as freelancers. At the very end, Kurtzman did say (in a letter to Ed Levy that is, unfortunately, not dated) that his group would consider a 50-50 partnership in the magazine if a budget could be agreed upon, but this was rejected. Santangelo and Levy were done with them. Kurtzman had failed to secure outside investors and had no choice but to bow to the inevitable.

Given the May termination, it's unclear why *Humbug* #11 was published at all. The issue's bright crimson cover was certainly apropos, given the financial red ink that engulfed the magazine. The readership of *Humbug* at large received the news on p. 1. In an editorial titled "Man— We're Beat!," Kurtzman laid out a frank description of the course of events:

> 1953—We started *Mad* magazine for a comic book publisher and we did some pretty good satire and it sold very well.
>
> 1956—We started *Trump* magazine . . . and we worked much harder and we did much better satire and we sold much worse.
>
> 1957—We started *Humbug* magazine and we worked hardest of all and turned out the very best satire of all, which of course now sells the very worst of all.
>
> And now . . . as they throw rocks at Vice President Nixon . . . as space gets cluttered with missiles . . . and as our names are carefully removed from our work in *Mad* pocketbooks—a feeling of beatness creeps through our satirical veins and capillaries and we think how George S. Kaufman once said, "Satire is something that closes Saturday night," and we wonder what day it is.

Later, he faced facts. "I designed a format that would be incredibly cheap to reproduce, so we turned out this incredible magazine which had the most beautiful artwork we'd ever done, the most carefully crafted stories and layouts, and we printed the whole thing on toilet paper! A terrible mistake! The format was a disaster."[29] He further maintained that the fifteen-cent price hurt them, too:

> It was a disaster on the display racks. They didn't know where to put it. They didn't particularly want to handle it, because we had a cover price that was too cheap to bother with. We priced the thing for 15 cents. The wholesaler [has] got his men on a truck and when they hoist a pound of paper, they want to get the maximum buck for hoisting that pound, and

therefore he'd rather handle an expensive magazine with a hefty cover price than a cheap magazine. We thought we were doing the readers a great service by giving them such a cheap cover price. Wrong. We should have charged what we *had* to charge, which was double the fifteen-cent price. If the readers had wanted that artwork, they would have paid for it.[30]

Since Kurtzman alone determined the format and price of *Humbug*, the two things that more than anything doomed the magazine, its failure hit him especially hard. They had worked so hard, produced such fine work and it had all been for nothing. Adele recalled, "At the end, [Harvey] sat on the stairs . . . and cried. It was so terrible because I'd never seen him like that. He was always so optimistic and this was so devastating for him."[31]

EC fan Fred von Bernewitz, who had developed a good rapport with Bill Gaines while producing *The Complete EC Index* (an amateur publication), talked to Gaines about the demise of *Humbug*. "I asked Bill how he felt about the *Humbug* situation. 'As a businessman, I'm delighted,' he said, hastily adding, 'As a friend of those involved, though, I'm sorry.' He added that he felt Kurtzman had continually tried the wrong things with *Humbug*, including distributor, format and price, and that with no real businessman connected to the venture, the whole operation remained loose. Gaines himself would use no text [pieces] as Kurtzman did."[32] When Gaines was describing himself as "a friend of those involved," he was referring to the artists who he hoped to lure back to *Mad*. Kurtzman no longer fell into that category.

Some balm on the emotional wounds arrived in the form of an avalanche of letters from disappointed readers. There were so many that the only way Kurtzman could respond was to mail out a form letter of thanks, which read, in part:

A pleasant, yet distressing circumstance has come about in that the mail continues to arrive and accumulate in a large pile; mail full of friendliness and warmth from all over the hemisphere and Europe. Our writing subscribers have, almost to a man, told us not to worry about their money. Many readers have mailed us cash contributions. We can't remember any experience like this before.

Apart from the letters, condolences have come to us from all sorts of remarkable people—many of them professional humorists who, like we did, felt our magazine was a little something extra-special.

All of this has given us a certain degree of comfort. Unhappily, it has become literally impossible for us to answer the letters individually, so we've decided to use the contributions towards printing and mailing out this note.

After back-and-forth correspondence with Capital, Kurtzman managed to obtain a release from the debt incurred by distributor advances. The owners of *Humbug* weren't saddled with debt upon the magazine's demise.

Looking back on the experience in a 1975 interview, Kurtzman admitted, "Artists should *never* put out their own magazine. Temperamentally, they're not qualified. We stayed with that magazine for a year and a half I think . . . because we believed, we believed, but believing wasn't enough."[33]

Despite the fact that the stockholders lost their investments in the magazine, all felt that producing *Humbug* was one of the happiest creative experiences of their lives. Kurtzman said, "When I talk to the guys about *Humbug*, they get that starry look in their eyes. We'd have our editorial meetings and we'd really operate on a very happy artistic plane where we would choose our targets and discuss the topics that we felt should be talked about and satirized. We really felt we had a place in the world."[34] Or, as Arnold Roth put it, "It was a great romance. It was our romance."[35]

Not long after *Humbug*, Roth created *Poor Arnold's Almanac*, which ran in newspaper syndication from 1959 to 1961. His artwork appeared in *Playboy*, *TV Guide*, the *New Yorker*, *Esquire* and many other magazines over the next few years. Of all the *Humbug* alumni, the upward trajectory of Roth's career was least affected.

Al Jaffee also broke into the syndicated strip field with his unique, wordless *Tall Tales* strip, and quickly began writing and drawing for *Mad*. Once he had shown Gaines the specific items he'd done for *Trump* and *Humbug*, the publisher instantly perceived his value, and they began a long and fruitful association.

Though Jack Davis worked a bit more for *Playboy*, he struggled to find his financial footing, doing comics work for Atlas (Westerns and war stories) to get through the rough patches. He drew bubble gum cards for Topps. In 1961, he wrote, drew and edited *Yak Yak*, his own humor comic book for Dell. Then he began doing high-paying magazine covers, record jackets and movie posters. His poster for the hit movie *It's a Mad, Mad, Mad, Mad World* in 1963 was a major breakthrough for him.

Larry Siegel went to *Mad*, having his first piece in #43 (December 1958), "Mad's MVTBA (Most Valuable Television Baseball Actors)

Awards." Soon his "take no prisoners" writing style earned him a regular spot in the magazine. Eventually he moved to Los Angeles and wrote for *The Carol Burnett Show* and many other TV programs.

Will Elder didn't return to *Mad*, although Gaines was eager to have him. He continued to collaborate with Kurtzman on future projects, filling in the gaps with whatever assignments he could pick up on his own. Harry Chester opened his own business, Chester Productions, to provide mechanical and layout services to magazines, agencies and newspapers. Of all the stockholders of *Humbug*, Chester remained Kurtzman's closest friend and confidante.

Harvey Kurtzman often had occasions to recall his experience producing magazines in the 1950s. There had been highs and lows, with the lows reaching their nadir with the failure of *Humbug*. "I remember [the] problems . . . with distribution and so on," he said. "Despair! Despair!"[36]

FRANKENSTIEN AND HIS MONSTER

Television is reviving this twenty-five year old thriller which was made when scientific talk centered around simple electricity . . . not atomic energy. As the story opens, scientist Count Henry Von Frankenstien, a young, middle-European schvienhunt, is out on the moor gathering bodies for his work.

Above: The Kurtzman-Elder "Frankenstien!" was one of the funniest movie parodies in *Humbug*. Right: Kurtzman's layouts are quite detailed, indicating such things as facial expressions and shading. Copyright © The Harvey Kurtzman Estate.

FRANKENSTIEN AND HIS MONSTER

TV is reviving this 25 year old thriller which was done when scientific talk centered around simple electricity not atomic energy. As the story opens, scientist Count von Frankenstien, a young, middle-European schnienhunt is out on the fields gathering bodies for his work.

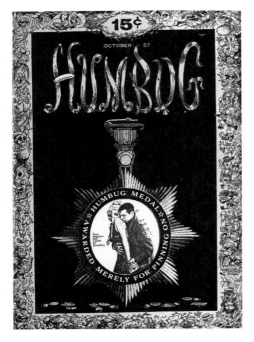

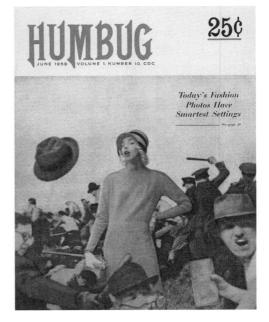

Humbug #3, 6, 7 and 10.

20.

CLIMBING BACK

WHEN HARVEY KURTZMAN found himself back in the freelance market in mid-1958, he was coming off of nine years of groundbreaking work. Even after the stumbles of *Trump* and *Humbug*, his credential as creator of *Mad* would seem to ensure a healthy demand for his talents. But he soon discovered that media venues for iconoclastic satire were few.

Of course, knockoffs of *Mad* surfaced from time to time, including a new one from Bob Sproul and Bernie Brill. Set free by Stan Lee during a major retrenchment at Atlas (formerly Timely Comics) the prior year, Sol Brodsky now edited their *Cracked* magazine, which carried work by John Severin and other comic book veterans. Even Jack Davis, Will Elder and Al Jaffee would appear in its pages, starting with its fifth issue (October 1958)—but not Harvey Kurtzman. The rates were abysmal and Kurtzman may have felt working for a former staff artist for Stan Lee beneath him. The "toilet paper" package of *Humbug* had been a practical necessity. Now he was determined to find a place in honest-to-goodness slick magazines.

To a seriously demoralized Kurtzman, returning to freelancing brought back memories of that difficult summer of 1949, after being fired from *Rusty*. He was in a financial hole and sinking deeper every day. Kurtzman later made a comment that seemed inspired by this period. "I see life," he said, "as the scene out of *The African Queen* when Humphrey Bogart's pulling the boat through the reeds, and he climbs out of the water and he's [covered with] leeches. And then after he's got all the leeches off, he slides back into the water and starts pulling the boat again. Always climbing back."[1] Before the embers of the dying *Humbug* had cooled, Kurtzman rolled up his sleeves and got to work. He dug through his files, made lists of contacts and began jotting down ideas for features and stories. He made phone calls and fired off letters to anyone and everyone who might offer work or provide possible leads.

At first, Kurtzman put most of his energy into three markets: television, magazines (mainly *Playboy*) and paperback books. Of the three, he felt television had the most potential and spent a great deal of his time trying to break into the burgeoning medium. "You've got to follow the trends," he said when interviewed in June 1958. "TV is the big trend today. Everyone is watching it nowadays and not reading magazines. Even *Mad* may sponsor a program soon. I'm trying to do scripts, although I'd like to have a personal hand in the direction. You know, I've always liked to show action in my stories. The right people in the industry seem to like my work."[2]

One of them was Dave Garroway, the first host of the *Today Show*, who also had his own program. Kurtzman and Davis satirized "The Dave Garrowunway Show" in *Mad* #26. An amused Garroway had plugged each of Kurtzman's magazines on the air, so he seemed a logical point of entry. Kurtzman's letter to Garroway in early May began, "In the past, you have been very friendly to my projects, and right now, I need friends." After briefly summing up his history as the creator of *Mad*, *Trump* and *Humbug*, he explained, "Now I am faced with the problem of relocating myself, and I am anxious to find out how my talents might relate to TV. Towards this end, I suspect you could do more to steer me in the right direction than any twenty friends . . . if you had the time." Garroway offered more than advice. He gave Kurtzman a job on his writing staff at NBC. Kurtzman never specified the exact nature of the position.

> Garroway was known for having kind of a wild sense of humor. He appeared in one of his programs with a knife sticking out of his back. I came into the job, the RCA Radio City building, and as I came in the elevator, he came out on a stretcher. He had a heart attack or something.[3] At the time, there was a big union mess and I didn't do much but sit behind a desk. Dave Garroway was the one who hired me, and the people immediately over me didn't really understand the situation. He was out the whole time I worked there. I was supposed to think up ideas, but because of the union I wasn't allowed to type them up.[4] I never saw him again, and they got rid of me pretty quick.[5]

KURTZMAN ALSO THOUGHT he had a pretty good shot at writing for *The Steve Allen Show*. He had appeared on an earlier Allen program with the

Mad crew, and was confident Allen was a kindred soul. (In the three-year interim, Allen had hosted the *Tonight* show, then moved to the eponymous Sunday evening variety hour.) He made his approach through Harold Hayes, the writer for *Pageant* who had praised *Mad* in 1954. Hayes had moved up from *Pageant* to *Esquire* as an assistant to publisher and managing editor Arnold Gingrich. Since Hayes had recently worked with Allen on a humor panel for the magazine, it seemed more likely the comedian would read a letter from him than Kurtzman. Hayes recommended that Allen give the creator of *Mad* a chance to write for his NBC show. He wrote, "In my experience in the magazine business, I have never encountered anyone with such a uniquely original mind and the scrupulous attention he is willing to give an idea in order to bring it off."[6] Allen responded favorably, putting Kurtzman in touch with Leonard Stern, his head writer. Kurtzman submitted some ideas for comedy sketches for the program, which Stern apparently felt were promising enough to pass along to Allen. It came to nothing, possibly due to bad timing. The television star was in the midst of a ratings war with two other popular shows, *The Ed Sullivan Show* and *Maverick*, and may not have had time to look at Kurtzman's material. Or, maybe he didn't like what he saw.

In June, Kurtzman went so far as to hammer out a proposal for an original television series. Each weekly episode of *The Fantastic Adventures of Col. Seymour Mednick* would begin with the aged Colonel telling a tall tale about his life to his young grandson. Then it would flash back to Mednick's days as a swashbuckling soldier of fortune for a wide range of Walter Mitty-esque adventures. "One week, there might be a jungle tale," Kurtzman wrote. "The next week might be a Western. Then a detective story and perhaps a love story. It would be a wonderful way to satirize entertainment itself. You could satirize just about everything in such a format."[7] Kurtzman wrote a script and outlines for possible episodes, but was unable to interest a literary agent in representing the property. On July 17, 1958, William Cooper of Frank Cooper Associates, Inc., wrote, "I regret that after a consideration and evaluation by the various brains in the organization we have decided that this would be too hard a concept to sell and to execute in television. If you get any other genius ideas I would love to hear from you." Kurtzman would attempt to revive the Seymour Mednick script years later, but was never to find a taker.

KURTZMAN CONSIDERED *Playboy* his most promising port of call. As Denis Kitchen related in a 2005 article in *Comic Art* titled "Man, I'm Beat!," Kurtzman pitched ideas for satiric pieces to Hugh Hefner in April or early May. Hefner didn't like them. A follow-up phone call to discuss the ideas in a bit more detail failed to move the editor. In a note to Hefner on May 24, Kurtzman wrote, "My obligations to you are so numerous that I feel the least I can offer is my loyalty. But there are some ugly facts of life facing me . . . mainly, my bank balance is about to run out."[8] The obligations Kurtzman referred to included monies still owed Hefner for back rent and the use of *Trump* material in *Humbug*, which Hefner had allowed him to defer.

He also wrote, "Regarding our last conversation, after I hung up, I got to thinking maybe I didn't fight hard enough for my ideas. A man's got to have pride in his ideas." Then, "I don't think there was ever a publisher I dug so much (beside myself) as you. And yet, I think when it comes to satire, we pass each other by."[9] Hefner responded with general reassurances, leaving the door open for more proposals. A subsequent idea (sexy parodies of famous paintings) was firmly rejected, this time by Hefner's associate Ray Russell. In explaining the piece's rejection by Hefner, Russell wrote that it lacked "the inextricable flash of genius, eruption of joy, effervescent nutsiness that has always been in your work and that has always reduced us to helpless quivering blobs of laughing protoplasm. Everything is too logical, sensible and meticulously planned."[10]

Next, Kurtzman jumped on two subjects suggested by Hefner. The first was motivational research, a hot topic in the wake of Vance Packard's book *The Hidden Persuaders* (1957), which dealt with advertisers' use of consumer motivational research and other psychological and subliminal techniques to sell products. He spent a great deal of time doing drawings of cars inspired by Freudian-based motivational research gone amuck. The other topic was the Beat Generation, a social and literary phenomenon that had received widespread attention after Jack Kerouac's novel *On the Road* was published in 1957. Kurtzman's springboard was that the Beat Generation was nothing new. It had existed in past eras, back all the way to cave paintings. Hefner liked the Beat proposal best. In July, he wrote, "I'm afraid it's going to be a couple more days before I can get a full reaction to your Beat idea. I think we're on the right track here."[11]

Months later, Russell wrote, saying they felt Kurtzman's Beat outline was promising but they would need to see more fully developed roughs before they could commit to it. They weren't prepared to give him the go-ahead based "on faith." When Kurtzman mailed four Beat Generation roughs to *Playboy* on November 30, 1958, Russell responded that Hefner didn't think Kurtzman really understood *Beat*, and that they only wanted the work "if they can make real sense and, most important of all, if they are very, very funny. In some ways, it may sound like a tall order. But when you come right down to it, all we are asking for is the first rate Kurtzman of yore."[12] A discouraged Kurtzman wrote to Hefner, "I'm sorry I've disappointed you again. And I'm sorry at what I sense to be the final flicker of our association, which has existed, like all associations, on the basis of some mutual activity. Trying to create for *Playboy*, I've a blind spot that I don't think I can ever overcome."[13] Hefner's response was frank yet encouraging.

> I don't believe the problem we've been faced with is really a blind spot where *Playboy* is concerned, Harv. You went through a pretty low period near the end with *Humbug* and after it died, and I think that very much influenced your sense of humor and your ability to be critical about it. The only real problem with the work you've submitted to us is that it hasn't been funny. It really hasn't. And in a more critical time, you would have recognized that yourself, I'm sure.
>
> I feel certain, too, that with things moving ahead now for you, the old sharpness will return. There is really no great gap in our senses of humor—I think I have proven that I dig your work by investing $100,000 in it and by running a nine-page portfolio on it in *Playboy*. I bow to no one in my appreciation for H. Kurtzman.[14]

Adele recalled, "Hefner was always very nice. He was always patient with Harvey, who kind of sat around with his head in his hands a lot."[15]

KURTZMAN WAS FASCINATED with the rapidly expanding paperback book displays in stores, which, he wrote, "cover a wall as far as the eye can see out to the horizon."[16] He had convinced Bill Gaines of the softcover books' potential. Now he wanted to create new work especially for that format, and the prospect excited him.

Ballantine Books had published *The Humbug Digest*. A contract was drawn up for a sequel in December 1957. However, perhaps because the magazine had been canceled, plans for a second *Humbug* book were scuttled. On the origins of his proposal for an all-new paperback, Kurtzman later wrote, "*Jungle Book* came about because Ian Ballantine wanted a *Mad* type of thing. After [*Humbug*] went under, he approached me about an all-original art paperback."[17] Kurtzman followed up an initial discussion with Ballantine with a letter on May 20, 1958:

Dear Ian,

Here is the letter you suggested I write.

Whatever follows naturally requires your faith, and I hope that you will really talk this over with Bernie [Shir-Cliff] since I think he extra-specially digs my satirical approach, and between the two of us, I am hoping we can intimidate you into having faith.

Let me repeat, the subjects I talked about doing . . . let's say a Western, a science-fiction story, and a big business story might purely furnish vehicles for [satires of] television today, the science race, and hidden persuaders.

Now because of the money problem, the only practical way I can figure to do this is with the usual contract providing for payments in return for a book (roughly, six stories and two texts). I don't think I could get too deep into the actual material in advance short of discussing an outline since the speculation would make me into a hardship case.

I'd have to get a complimentary arrangement from a magazine publisher so that one or the other party couldn't let me down in the middle of the project. (This would mean disaster.)

Let us start the count-down so's we can put this thing into orbit.

Sincerely, Flash Kurtzman[18]

Kurtzman's paperback "original" would offer his first solo graphic story work, both story and art, since "The Big 'If'!" He asked for an advance based on this rather vague proposal, since he needed the money to survive while working on it. The potential of the project was enormous. If publishing new comics in paperback form worked, and the book was a breakout hit, he could be at the forefront of "the next big thing."

Apparently, Ballantine wasn't convinced. The publisher genuinely admired Kurtzman's writing, but a great deal of the appeal of the *Mad* paperbacks was the stellar artwork by Wallace Wood, Will Elder, Jack Davis and others, the best in the business. Would Kurtzman's own finished artwork have similar appeal? While it's not definitively known, the time that elapsed between Kurtzman's proposal and the execution of the contract—eight months—strongly suggests Ballantine wasn't ready to go ahead on faith. That may be why Kurtzman prepared rough versions of some of the stories, which were probably shown to the publisher for his appraisal.

HAVING STRUCK OUT with his initial three-pronged plan, at least in the short term, Kurtzman fell back to his "Plan B." He would approach three other magazines run by men who admired his work. The first was

Pageant. Harris Shevelson was no longer working there, but publisher Alex L. Hillman remained a Kurtzman fan and encouraged him to submit ideas. Kurtzman began by creating an outer space rumination with Will Elder. "Conquest of the Moon," a visually spectacular ten-page piece, appeared in the December issue. Reminiscent of "Is a Trip to the Moon Possible?" in *Mad* #24, Kurtzman worked satirical riffs on what a trip to the lunar surface would entail, its potential pitfalls and the fallout if the moon mission failed. "The only cheer is in the newspaper comic section, where science-fiction cartoon characters rejoice," Kurtzman wrote. Under images of Flash Gordon and Buck Rogers smiling at the news, it said, "In the great race for space, they are still ahead." This was his first post-*Humbug* item to see print.

Harris Shevelson had become editorial director of *Madison Avenue* magazine, a slick trade journal with the tagline "The magazine of New York advertising." The man who offered Kurtzman a job in 1954 welcomed him with open arms. Shevelson liked Kurtzman's idea of doing humorous continuities pertaining to advertising and media topics. They would be stories between one and three pages long, told with minimal dialogue and captions, something like those of Kurtzman's favorite, H. M. Bateman. The first was "Courage" in the January 1959 issue, followed in succeeding issues with episodes titled "Security," "All-Purpose Cleanser," and "Videoland." Kurtzman was paid $75 a page.

On January 20, 1959, Shevelson wrote a note that conveyed his continuing appreciation of Kurtzman's work: "I guess I like your touch. I'm very glad that you re-edited my editing because I thought the Polaroid piece came off nicely. I was further delighted to see the new contribution which is just fine and which I will use in the February issue. Let's have lunch next week and talk about more. If you can't reach me here, call me at [home] in Westport."[19] Presumably, their meeting at the end of the month was the last time they saw each other. Harris Shevelson and his wife were killed on February 3, 1959, when their American Airlines flight from Chicago plunged into the East River. He was forty-two years old. Kurtzman wrote Carl Rogers, Shevelson's editorial successor, "The shock of Harris's death will be a long time getting out of my system. He was directly and indirectly responsible for many good things that happened to me over the past ten years and he was a nice guy."[20] Kurtzman's work continued to appear in *Madison Avenue* throughout 1959.

WHEN HEFNER REJECTED his proposals, Kurtzman felt free to offer his services to *Esquire, Playboy*'s chief competitor. *Esquire* was more respected than *Playboy* (having largely shed its reputation as a "girlie magazine") though no longer better-selling, after Hefner's magazine surged to a print run of 1.1 million at the end of 1956. Harold Hayes offered Kurtzman a plum project. For "Assignment: James Cagney in Ireland," Kurtzman's debut in *Esquire*, he became a globetrotting graphic journalist as he followed the popular actor to Dublin to watch him on the set of the film *Shake Hands with the Devil*. It was Kurtzman's first trip outside the continental United States. Adele recalled, "Those were the days when Harold Hayes would call up and say, 'tell Harvey to polish up the passport!'"[21] Distributor United Artists apparently subsidized the trip in order to get the movie covered in a splashy *Esquire* feature. It appeared in the April 1959 issue. Kurtzman didn't disappoint.

P. 1 is an impressive, detailed, full-page drawing of Dublin with sun breaking through the clouds, as a cartoon version of Kurtzman follows Cagney through the city streets. The rest of the pages consist of a full-color comic strip following Kurtzman as he journeys to Ireland, meets Cagney, spends time with him on the set and at a sports event and finally returns to discover that all his "great sketches of Cagney with his new moustache" need to be fixed because Cagney shaved it off. Privately, Kurtzman had mixed feelings about the result. He was still smarting over the loss of *Humbug*. "It was okay, but I feel I could have done better," he said at the time. "I think I reached my highest level when I did *Humbug*."[22] Hayes was happy with the piece. It began a long relationship between Kurtzman and *Esquire*.

Kurtzman's paychecks from *Pageant*, *Madison Avenue Magazine* and *Esquire* represented his first income (other than unemployment insurance) in almost two years. They didn't add up to much. It appears he made no more than $2,000 in 1958, forcing him to borrow money from a friend to make ends meet.[23]

Breaking into the pages of a magazine for the first time—especially one that didn't normally carry cartooning other than gag panels—took a great deal of patience and energy. Entreaties to *Horizon* magazine and *Sports Illustrated* yielded nothing, but he got a bite on one sent to *TV Guide*. It yielded an assignment for a single, brief story, small reward for multiple meetings and back-and-forth correspondence with editor Merrill Panitt. The magazine's April 11, 1959 issue carried his three-page "I Went to a Perry Como Commercial," a portrait of the highly successful recording artist on the set of an upcoming television show. The treatment was similar to the Cagney vignette, except the pages in the digest-sized *TV Guide* gave him about a third of the area of an *Esquire* page. Such was the life of a freelancer. Even when one managed to pry a door open and make a sale, there was no guarantee of more work.

AS 1959 ARRIVED, things began looking up. After hemming and hawing for months, Ian Ballantine finally agreed to publish Kurtzman's proposed paperback original, although he seems to have been uncertain about its commercial potential. He had offered an advance of $2,500 for the *Humbug Digest*, essentially based on expected sales, at a royalty rate of 4 percent of the retail price (thirty-five cents). For *The Kurtzman Pleasure Book* (eventually retitled *Harvey Kurtzman's Jungle Book*), he offered an advance of only $1,500. It was payable in twelve equal installments of $125 per week, the first payment commencing upon signing the contract, which was dated January 20, 1959. It called for the book to be completed and delivered by May 1.[24]

Cognizant that Ian Ballantine was looking for something similar to the *Mad* paperbacks, Kurtzman could have created a package that looked as much like them as possible. Again, Kurtzman avoided imitating himself or *Mad*. First of all, the panels wouldn't be printed sideways, as had been necessary with the *Mad* reprints. Far better to design the pages so the book could be held and read like any other book. Because the dimensions of the mass market paperback were about 4" by 7", the pages' horizontal-to-vertical proportions were about 1:1.75, as opposed to the 1:1.45 proportions of the typical comic book page, creating a "narrower" area for the art. Also, since the printed size was so much smaller than the size of a comic book (then about 6.75" by 10.25"), fewer panels would fit on a page if they were to be readable. Hence, the page length of the individual stories would need to be increased if a substantial narrative was to be told. The "narrower" page shape led Kurtzman to use tall, thin word balloons, something he quite liked. To make up for the lack of color, and partly to achieve subtle shadings and depth in the panels, he decided to paint gray tones over the basic inked artwork. Given the thirty-five cent price point, it was determined that he needed to produce about 150 pages. (The finished book has 134 story pages plus a bit of additional matter. A proposed SF story was scrapped.)

Harvey Kurtzman's Jungle Book consists of two TV program satires (a Western and a detective show), the story of a small-town lynching and a look into the world of publishing. Though the *Jungle Book* title might seem to refer to Rudyard Kipling's book with the same name, Kurtzman was really using "jungle" as a metaphor (like W. R. Burnett's *The Asphalt*

Jungle), which gave it the quasi-anthropological angle suggested on the title page:

Harvey Kurtzman's
Jungle Book
-or-
Up From the Apes!
(and right back down)
In Which Are Described
In Words and Pictures
Businessmen, Private Eyes, Cowboys,
And Other Heroes
all exhibiting
The Progress of Man
From the Darkness of the Cave
into the Light of Civilization

Given that there were a staggering twenty Western programs in the 1958–1959 television season, seven in the top ten, it was logical—almost inescapable—that Kurtzman would satirize the genre. He had always had affection for it, going back to *Pot-Shot Pete* for Toby Press. He was inspired by *The Fastest Gun Alive*—the Glenn Ford Western that he'd satirized in *Trump*. The film turned on the lead character's compulsion to be a gunfighter. Kurtzman's abiding fascination with psychological matters had drawn him to the movie; now it would be expressed in a new Western story, which, for commercial reasons, was cloaked as a parody of *Gunsmoke* (the number-one show on television). "Compulsion on the Range" was one of the "test" stories Kurtzman worked up for the new project.

Its introduction states, "In the Nebraska territories a man riding herd months on end in the saddle can get a powerful yearning ta t'ar loose when he gits ta taown." Thus, "Marshall Matt Dollin faces Johnny Ringding . . . gunfighter, horse-thief, fastest draw and worst schizoid in the territory. Of course, Dollin himself, with all his traumatic experiences, was not 100% adjusted either . . . but then again . . . Who is?" In the course of the story, after losing a series of gun duels, Doc Adams psychoanalyzes Dollin until he gives up his gun, having been cured of his father fixation (just as Glenn Ford was in *The Fastest Gun Alive*).

A comparison of the second version of the story compared to the "test" is revealing. The initial attempt at "Compulsion on the Range" employed a simpler, more exaggerated style of art. When he worked on the final version, Kurtzman followed his original layouts closely, but rendered the artwork more carefully and with a slightly more naturalistic style, improving his likeness of actor James Arness as "Dollin." He was never satisfied with it. "This was the first story I did for the book, and I don't really like it," he said. "I hadn't developed the style I was using. It developed as I went along. I don't think I got good until I finished this story. The watercolor wash is lacking. The hard part for me in anything I do is gaining control of what I'm doing. The story doesn't compare with 'Thelonius Violence.'"[25]

Kurtzman put "Thelonius Violence," a stronger story, first in the book. Ostensibly a parody of the *Peter Gunn* television program, it's really a canvas for

Harvey Kurtzman's Jungle Book (1959) was originally a mass market paperback, measuring about 4" by 7".

Kurtzman's experiment with adapting jazz music to sound effects on the printed page. "The Peter Gunn character was the only one I used from the show. What I was trying to get was that Henry Mancini feel to the story. The jazz background gave me the rhythm of the piece. I like the rhythm and movement, especially the karate scenes. Motion and movement within the panels was and is extremely important to me. I had control of this story. It took me time and practice to get it, but it's there."[26]

The story begins, "Va voodle-de blah-da daaa dee ddn-dee raaan. Yeah . . . that's a sad trumpet blowing in the darkness back there. . . . That's the new sound—The new sound of jazz, you say? Oh no, man. That's the new sound of the private eye." It's an interesting experiment, only really effective as a counterpoint to the karate fight between Thelonius Violence (the "cool private eye") and the villain of the tale. What really works is the way the five-page action sequence is choreographed panel-to-panel in a series of sharp, staccato actions and reactions. However, anyone who wanted a *Mad*-style satire of *Peter Gunn* would likely have been disappointed.

Although it runs thirty-two pages, it only evinces a passing interest in the show itself.

Kurtzman had a personal connection with the milieu of the story "Decadence Degenerated." The town of Rottenville was based on Kurtzman's memories of Paris, Texas, the small town near Camp Maxey where he was stationed for much of his time in the service. His closest interaction with the townsfolk back then was at USO dances held on the base, but when he did get to town he noticed some of the local layabouts sitting around the town square trading gossip and tall tales. That's how he began "Decadence," a story of the lynching of an innocent man who turns out to be not so innocent after all.

One two-page sequence in this story stands out. As the men in the town square watch the sensuous Honey Lou slink by, each of their spoken comments is accompanied by their fantasy image of her naked body. In his introduction to a reprinted edition of *Jungle Book*, cartoonist Art Spiegelman wrote that this sequence "burned itself into my impressionable eleven year old brain when I first saw it. No, not just for the—hoo hah!—obvious reasons, though this was hot stuff in 1959, but because something was happening here with the pictures-as-words that could happen in no other medium."[27]

Kurtzman set the best story in the book in the world of magazine publishing. He based his Lucifer Schlock of Schlock Publications on Martin Goodman of Timely Comics. The name of his young, starry-eyed protagonist—Goodman Beaver—makes that clear.

Page from "Decadence Degenerated."

Kurtzman's cynical view of the publishing world (and by extension, all business) became a more important theme in his work from this point forward. The title and possibly some elements of "The Organization Man in the Grey Flannel Executive Suite" came from the 1956 film *The Man in the Gray Flannel Suit*, a movie about a corporate executive (played by Gregory Peck) who must deal with various ethical business dilemmas. Kurtzman used the basic structure of Rod Serling's *Patterns*, an acclaimed television drama in 1955 that was made into a film the following year. Stories of upwardly mobile office workers and executives, usually set in New York City, were in vogue, culminating in Billy Wilder's Academy Award-winning film *The Apartment* in 1960. Kurtzman later discussed the story's theme this way: "When you go into a business, you can either have the attitude of doing something with it, or draining it. It's an eternal conflict, an old story."[28]

The introductory page reads, "Here is a story of the human side of big business. Its message . . . though the business world may look cold and rotten on the surface, underneath . . . well underneath it's much rottener." Goodman Beaver's Candide-like optimism and naiveté is gradually corrupted as he adapts to the duplicitous, Scrooge-like business practices of Lucifer Schlock, whose dictum of magazine publishing is, "We keep our investment low, our income high and our margin of profit wide." Finally, Beaver takes this philosophy to its ultimate extreme by stealing the firm's payroll at gunpoint, leaving an admiring Schlock to muse, "All the time I thought he had a lousy business head. Now I know different. Goodman Beaver's gonna be all right."

Kurtzman's personal connection to the theme of "The Organization Man" inspired him to produce a dark, scathing work that is sharp, smart and genuinely funny. The Goodman Beaver character is to a great degree based on himself as an idealistic young man after World War II. The horror he felt when confronted with the venal side of publishing is captured with an impact and immediacy that isn't found in the other stories in the book.

Harvey Kurtzman's Jungle Book was innovative but imperfect. *Mad* magazine had been the first step in bringing cartoon stories out of the comic book ghetto. This was another step, one that, with its four-story composition, warrants some of the same accolades showered on Will Eisner's *A Contract With God* sixteen years later. As with any experiment, there are aspects that don't work well. The tall, skinny word balloons are difficult to scan. The eye isn't used to reading words arranged vertically, especially when some of them are hyphenated. Kurtzman's use of dialect is also a problem. He had a good ear for it, but sometimes tended to push it a step too far. In "Compulsion on the Range," his first draft "Ah'm makin' muh play" morphed into "Om makin' mop play" in the final version, which stops the reader in his tracks until he works out what's being said. Lettering that borders on sloppy compounds legibility problems, betraying the speed Kurtzman was working to turn out so many pages of new artwork. Normally he wouldn't press himself to work faster, but these weren't normal times. Such problems would detract from his other work in this period.

Kurtzman had his own complaints about *Jungle Book*. "The package itself was rinky-dink. It was small and printed on bad paper and the printing itself was two cuts under the pulps. On top of that, I did the art on sheets of blue-lined paper. It was an experiment. The printer assured me that the lines wouldn't show up, but of course, they did. Still do. The gray wash reinforced the blue and so the thing is noticeable. It was a case of experimenting with a form before all the bugs were out."[29] *Harvey Kurtzman's Jungle Book* was published in mid-September. Of the 150,380 copies printed, royalty reports show that only 78,103 were sold.[30] In other words, it performed about half as well as Ballantine's modest expectations, and earned back enough to cover only two-thirds of Kurtzman's $1,500 advance. One can speculate on the reasons for its commercial failure. Certainly, it was ahead of its time. The size and cheap printing didn't help. Or, it may have been due to Kurtzman's artwork.

Comparing "Big 'If'!" next to "Thelonius Violence," the difference in the overall look is dramatic. His finished art at EC was solid and told the story in the boldest of terms. The brush strokes are thick and alive, and the story flows with exceptional clarity. A different man, almost, could have done *Jungle Book*'s art. Many of Kurtzman's virtues remain, especially his ability to deftly show physical action and the way he underscores dramatic points. He chose to rely more on the pen than the brush, using his Winsor-Newton mainly for emphasis. It's an equally valid technique, yet one that didn't "read" as clearly and make its points as strongly as his former approach. On the other hand, the art in *Jungle Book* sets it apart in his oeuvre, and as an experiment it succeeds more often than it fails. Kurtzman's subsequent work would in large part pick up where *Jungle Book* left off. There would be no attempt to recapture past glories or past artistic approaches.

Whatever the reason, the sales of *Jungle Book* were disappointing, ending any talk of a sequel. Ballantine would never again publish Kurtzman.

Of all the disappointments in 1958–1959, the rejections by Hefner were the hardest for Kurtzman. Had things worked out with his proposed pieces for *Playboy*, his financial picture would have looked distinctly better. Hefner had been confident enough in his talent to spend a fortune to woo him away from *Mad*, but was unwilling to trust him to produce a few pages of satire for *Playboy*. Were Hefner and Russell right? Had Kurtzman's hard times affected his ability to make people laugh? The truth was, his ability to be funny flowered when he could let his creativity flow, as he had been able to do with *Mad* and *Humbug*. Now Kurtzman fully understood that Hefner could offer everything but creative freedom, a conundrum for an artist who needed it to be at his best. With *Jungle Book*, Kurtzman had the freedom that he needed, and it resulted in the extraordinary "The Organization Man" with Goodman Beaver. Though more disturbing than any of his satire work since "Bringing Back Father!" in *Mad* #17, this new story and much of the rest of the book was satirically effective. His creative juices were flowing again.

In turn, Kurtzman created two notable stories in the second half of 1959, one for *Pageant* and the other for *Esquire*. Both reflected his interest in the Beat generation, possibly instigated by the aborted work he'd done for Hefner when prompted with the topic. Aspects of Beat culture strongly appealed to him. He was two years younger than Jack Kerouac. Once he started reading *On the Road*, he told Hefner, he couldn't stop. Although Kurtzman had been against horror comics, he was all for freedom of speech in works for adults. While his drive for respectability and status could not be gainsaid, and he was far too committed to the choices he'd made up till this point in his life to radically alter his lifestyle, Kurtzman's work shared with the Beats a questioning of contemporary American life and values, and a rejection of corporate greed and right-wing militarism. He was no stranger to the jazz and comedy clubs in Greenwich Village, and his ear for dialect and slang enabled him to pick up the lingo, much of it originated by jazz musicians. Beat ideas, as interpreted by Kurtzman, filtered into the versions of two popular children's tales that came off his drawing board in 1959.

The first was "Pinocchio Retold," a clever twelve-page Beat interpretation of Carlo Collodi's story of a puppet who yearns to become a real boy, for *Pageant* (February 1960). Pinocchio tells his beatnik friend Candlewick that the transformation is imminent. But Candlewick moans, "An ordinary flesh-and-blood boy? Ohhh no man. Don'—don' tell me you're goin' conformist!"

While "Pinocchio Retold" deals with the Beat movement from the standpoint of the conformity-nonconformity conundrum, Kurtzman's "The Grasshopper and the Ant" provides a framework to examine aspects of the Beats that appealed to him personally versus his increasingly desperate push for financial security. Aesop's fable of an improvident grasshopper and a hard-working ant who never has time to play dramatizes his own difficulty in reconciling the arts-vs.-commerce conflict in his life. It also expresses a dawning sense of futility, that fate (which he once referred to as "the great system in the sky that I don't quite understand") was working against him.[31]

The "Adult Fable" (as it was billed in the May 1960 *Esquire*) begins in the spring with the beatnik grasshopper asking the worker ant, "Is gathering grain . . . all there is? Must we plod the frightening stretches of the vast back-lot without meditating on the meaning of life?" By summer, the grasshopper plays bongos in a jazz combo, and rants,

> That's the trouble with the back-lot! Everybody walks around in their grey-flannel button-down thoraxes—the same way day after day. Wise up, dad. It's all very sick! The acquisitive society—everyone grabbing grabbing grabbing! Gotta eat a bigger leaf—gotta dig a better nest—gotta keep up with the Jones . . . No individuality! Meanwhile the whole back-lot is going lickety-split to Hell!

But when the grasshopper finally recognizes the value of "doing" rather than merely "talking," he discovers that even the ant has "gone beatnik," and is willing to share his mountain of grain. They attempt to eat the grain, but it turns out the ant had mistaken little pieces of gravel for grain. In the last panel, the two of them lie dead, with snowflakes falling on their corpses. "The End."

Unlike the two-color "Pinocchio Retold," "The Grasshopper and the Ant" was given lavish four-color treatment. Kurtzman's highly expressive illustrations for this story are perfectly complemented by his painted colors, with the overall hues changing for each season: greens for spring, yellow-orange for summer, browns for fall and only gray and white for the final panel representing the bitter cold of winter.

Roger Price wrote Kurtzman a letter that said, in part, "Liked the Grasshopper bit very much. Thought the use of color with seasonal change very original and effective. Also your drawing is just great. I still am bothered a bit by plain old simple legibility. I have to concentrate pretty carefully to get everything . . . I don't mean legibility of ideas but actual legibility of printing. Would like to see it clearer, as what you are saying is too good to be missed because the words sometimes run too close together. This, of course, is really a problem of space which you cannot help."³² But space hadn't really been a problem. While twelve panels had appeared on each page, *Esquire*'s oversized format (10" by 13") meant the 3" by 3.25" panels were plenty large. Also, the magazine printed on slick paper with full-process color, achieving better visual clarity than printing on comic book pulp. There was no excuse, but the fumetti is the only flaw in this otherwise superb story. With "The Grasshopper and the Ant," he achieved what he had hoped to with *Jungle Book*: a work that was artistically mature and masterful from start to finish. He had used his personal adversity—including that increasing sense of futility—to produce brilliant work. It was the creative peak of his post-*Humbug* period, and demonstrated that his talent as a writer and artist burned as bright as ever. Unfortunately, there weren't enough opportunities to do things as personal and expressive as "Pinocchio" and "Grasshhopper."

Kurtzman sometimes found himself putting a great deal of effort into projects that didn't produce a cent, such as another attempt to sell a newspaper comic strip. Elliott Caplin, his old champion, invited him to collaborate on a strip called *Kermit the Hermit*. Toby Press had been a victim of the comics industry shakeout, but Kurtzman knew that Elliott was doing very well writing two syndicated strips. In 1950, he had co-created *Big Ben Bolt* with John Cullen Murphy, and three years later, co-created *The Heart of Juliet Jones* with Stan Drake, both for the King Features Syndicate. When Kurtzman got in touch with Caplin in 1959, both strips were going strong.

Perhaps sensing that the best days for the story/adventure strips were in the past, Caplin wanted to try a funny strip, and Kurtzman seemed the perfect artist for it. Kurtzman was enthusiastic, though he probably wouldn't have worked "on spec" if Caplin wasn't already successful in the syndicated strip arena. *Kermit the Hermit* starred a protagonist who refuses to emerge from his cave, and is represented only by two expressive eyeballs surrounded by darkness. It revolved around Kermit's rejection of society-at-large despite all its inducements, including an entreaty by a pretty young woman named Barbara. The concept was cute but limited, which may be why the presentation (consisting of thirteen sample dailies) went nowhere. Kurtzman was philosophical: "The syndicates are a real rat race. I wouldn't recommend that to anyone. In one of my skirmishes with them, they called me and asked me to do some samples for a strip. I took them in and the fellow who had called me thought that they were great. Then he took them to the higher-ups and . . . that was that."[33] Caplin tried *Kermit the Hermit* again in collaboration with another artist. That version managed to get published, but quickly died.

E*squire* came through with another assignment, "Marlon Brando Sketched," a four-pager for its November 1959 issue. This time, Kurtzman traveled just seventy miles to Milton, New York, where the film version of Tennessee Williams's play *Orpheus Descending*, retitled *The Fugitive Kind*, was being filmed. Adele remembered, "He met Tennessee and [director] Sidney Lumet, but Harvey was terrified of Brando and never spoke to him. He said, 'When you looked at Marlon Brando, you knew that you didn't go up to him and ask questions.'"[34] He also did a little work for the aging *Saturday Evening Post*, doing a couple of illustrations for its "You Be the Judge" page. He might have gotten the idea of approaching the magazine from Will Elder, who had already placed a half-dozen illustrations in its pages in 1959 and early 1960. Like *TV Guide* and other connections Kurtzman made at this time, it didn't turn into a regular market.

IN TWO YEARS OF FREELANCING, Kurtzman produced some fine features, comic strips and continuities for slick magazines and the ambitious and sometimes inspired *Jungle Book*, among a smattering of other jobs. *Pageant* and *Esquire* were his best clients in the 1958 to 1960 period, yet he had done just twenty-eight and sixteen pages for them, respectively. Indeed, he produced less than seventy magazine pages in total (some in collaboration with Elder) during these years. Although information on how much he was paid for these jobs isn't generally available, it's clear that Kurtzman was coming up financially short. True, *Esquire* had sent him to Ireland and also to Austria (which resulted in the four-page "Vienna: Three Views" in their June 1960 issue)—a nice perk, no doubt—but that didn't pay many bills at home. Making $3,000 to $4,000 a year was a far cry from the five-figure salary of yore.

The constant cycle of proposals, meetings and rejections (amid a few approvals) was wearing Kurtzman down. Unless one's work catches on with publishers and the public enough to garner special notice, freelancing can become an exercise in running to stay in the same place. Or, worse, running only to find that one is gradually losing ground. While his assignments had met with approval from editors at *Esquire* and *Pageant*, readers apparently didn't demand more, nor had any of his other efforts scored in a big way. In that situation, the freelancer finds it more difficult to get the editor on the phone, or that letters aren't promptly answered, because new, hotter talents take precedence. Kurtzman may have sensed he was on the edge of that sort of situation, because his solo artwork—exquisite as it was on "The Grasshopper and the Ant"—didn't provide the kind of eye-pleasing results that were easy on the casual reader. Kurtzman's work was "art with a capital *a*" when what was really wanted was well crafted, slickly rendered images.

Working solo had the virtue of being able to bank the whole paycheck, but was offset by Kurtzman's working methods. Although he could draw a quick sketch, when it came to his published work, he had to labor twice as hard as other artists to come up with a finished piece. He was no longer the twenty-five-year-old who could burn the midnight oil night after night, and who was just discovering who he was as a craftsman, as he had been in his early days at EC. Kurtzman was now ten years older, a family man with responsibilities, who had been an editor-writer first and an artist second for half that time. On his own, he was barely able to keep his boat moving through the reeds (to return to the *African Queen* analogy). But there was nothing to do but keep climbing back, keep slogging forward, while staying alert to all opportunities.

Such was Harvey Kurtzman's situation at the decade's end when he was presented with an offer from a young publisher who styled himself after Hugh Hefner, but was producing a magazine that Kurtzman disdained. His name was James Warren, and the magazine was *Famous Monsters of Filmland.*

The complete title "The Organization Man in the Grey Flannel Executive Suite" was derived from William H. Whyte's *The Organization Man*, a best-seller in 1956, and two films: *The Man in the Gray Flannel Suit* (1956) and *Executive Suite* (1954).

21.

HELP!

EACH OF THE TITLES of Harvey Kurtzman's magazines say something about his state of mind at the time. *Mad* suggested creative anarchy, *Trump* signified arrogant dominance, *Humbug* expressed bitterness and *Help!* shouted his career anxieties to the skies.

Harvey Kurtzman and James Warren Taubman had little in common. Both were sons of Russian Jewish parents, both made their living in the magazine trade and both had great admiration for Will Eisner and Hugh Hefner. But there, it seems, their similarities ended. Warren, who dropped his last name when he entered publishing, grew up in Philadelphia, and was six years Kurtzman's junior. Whereas Kurtzman was a creative individual with a soft-spoken manner, Warren was an entrepreneurial type who was brash, pugnacious and confrontational. He was the kind of person Harvey Kurtzman normally avoided, but in 1959, they came together on a small, forgettable one-shot project, and found each could help serve the other's interests, as publisher and editor of a new magazine.

Jim Warren demonstrated an aptitude for art as a youth, and studied architecture at the University of Pennsylvania. After a brief military stint during the Korean War (when his hearing was permanently damaged by getting too close to a .50 caliber heavy machine gun during training), he entered the advertising field. Noting the success of Hugh Hefner's men's magazine, Warren became a publisher with what he later called "an inexpensive replica of *Playboy*" called *After Hours*. The magazine lasted four issues in 1957, brought down by his arrest for publishing obscene material. The sensational headline read, "Porn Merchant Arrested with Million Dollar Business." It was wrong on both counts. The most pornographic item in the magazine was a mild, topless shot of Bettie Page, and Warren had less than $100 in the bank.

Following the *After Hours* debacle, Warren's next publishing endeavor caught a popular culture wave and became an instant hit. It arose from a meeting with Forrest J. Ackerman, a contributor to *After Hours* who was a fantasy film fan and a prominent member of science fiction fandom. When Ackerman showed Warren a copy of a European film magazine called *Cinema 57*, which devoted a whole issue to photos of classic horror films, Warren realized that an American version had commercial potential because such films were experiencing a major revival on television. The magazine would be written by Ackerman and designed by Warren, who named it *Famous Monsters of Filmland*. It was published in January 1958, with Warren under the Frankenstein mask on the cover. Its pages were filled with pun-laden articles by Ackerman accompanied by pages of stills from the movies, many of them featuring monsters played by Boris Karloff, Bela Lugosi and Lon Chaney.

Jim Warren had admired Harvey Kurtzman's work, both in the EC war comics and in *Mad*. A Hefner acolyte, Warren read *Trump* from its inception and discovered *Humbug* with its third issue.[1] Arnold Roth, a high school friend of Jim Warren in Philadelphia, introduced him to Kurtzman. When asked about his earliest memory of Warren, Kurtzman said it was when the younger man visited the *Humbug* office at 598 Madison Ave. with enough hamburgers for everyone's lunch, something Warren later denied doing.[2] The earliest documented point of contact is a letter from Jim Warren to Harry Chester dated September 19, 1957, reminding Chester to send gratis copies of *Humbug* #1 and #2, which had apparently been promised by Kurtzman. (Warren wrote, "Keep putting me off and I shall address a nasty letter to the Managing Editor of this rag, which will no doubt cost you your job.") This was within days of his meeting with Ackerman in New York City, when he saw *Cinema 57*. Several weeks later, Warren obtained permission from Kurtzman to reprint a couple of pages of the "Frankenstien" story by Kurtzman-Elder (which had just been completed for *Humbug* #7) in *Famous Monsters of Filmland* #1, under the title, "Top humor magazine takes a hilarious look at the Frankenstein legend . . . Franky and *Humbug*."

Warren recognized that Kurtzman was a talent of the first magnitude and wanted to work with him. In 1959, after the enormous success of *Famous Monsters*, Warren met with Kurtzman to float an idea.

I said, "All your life from *Mad* on down, you've worked with artists. And artists have to get paid for drawing. But I have a way of utilizing photos, eight by ten inch still photos, and making them commercially saleable if you pick the right subject, and you put the right spin on it, and you make it attractive enough editorially. We can produce a [humor] magazine using photos with funny captions."

Harvey says, "Maybe." And I said, "No maybe. Let's sit down and do it." Those days, Westerns were very popular on television. I said, "Let's take advantage of this. I want to put out a magazine called *Favorite Westerns of Filmland*, in which we're going to use photos but with funny captions. I want you to see how this can be done."[3]

Warren sensed that Kurtzman had few offers coming his way, and needed money. Kurtzman agreed to write it for a substantial flat fee. Given his painful experiences with publishers, Kurtzman approached *Favorite Westerns of Filmland* with caution. Since he was still working on projects for *Esquire* and other slicks, he didn't want to be associated with the publisher of *Famous Monsters of Filmland*, a magazine he considered lowclass. He used the pseudonym "Remuda Charlie Stringer" in *Favorite Westerns*. Warren provided the stills. Harry Chester did the production work.

Kurtzman discovered that putting a magazine full of stills together was quick, easy and even fun. Warren: "[Kurtzman] produced one of the funniest magazines in the world." Reportedly, Richard Boone (*Have Gun Will Travel*) wasn't happy that Kurtzman painted a bullet hole on his forehead on the photo cover. Its semi-serious, jokey approach was similar to *Famous Monsters*. According to Warren, it "sold like crazy." Kurtzman agreed to do another issue. Then Warren had an idea for a different magazine, a general satire magazine that used the photo technique that had been so successful with *Favorite Westerns*. "When I told Harvey this, I could almost see the wheels turning in his head, as he considered it. He was thinking, and trying to envision it and then it finally clicked. Once he could see it in his mind, he realized it could work, and he agreed to do it. Then it was a matter of working out the specifics."[4] At first, Kurtzman told Warren that they should make it a slick magazine like *Trump*. While Warren couldn't afford to publish that sort of lavish magazine, he had other reasons for rejecting the idea. "I loved *Trump*," he said, "but there was nothing in *Trump* that wouldn't work if it had been printed in black and white on regular—not slick—paper." He told Kurtzman that a humor magazine would be successful if it sold for thirty-five cents. Fifty cents was just too much. Finally, Kurtzman agreed to edit the new magazine if he had full editorial control and a substantial percentage of the profits, which had to be spelled out in a legal document. He could see that Warren was confident and aggressive and, therefore, wanted a watertight agreement.

In the contract, Warren said, "Harvey had 50 percent of it. I said, 'I will give you 50 percent of the voting stock, which means that you, in effect, have control. In other words, no decisions can be made unless we both agree. As far as the dividend stock, you only get 25 percent . . . because I'm putting up the $150,000.'"[5] If the profits for an issue were $10,000, Warren would get $7,500 and Kurtzman would get $2,500. Kurtzman would also receive a base salary. A second agreement was drawn up to establish Kurtzman's ownership of anything he wrote or drew for the magazine. The two of them would own the rest of the material equally.[6] Kurtzman ran both of the agreements by his attorney. The title *Help!* was apparently lifted from the cover of *Trump* #1, where it appeared in bright red letters three times as high as the magazine's own title. Kurtzman added the subtitle *For Tired Minds,* a play on the ubiquitous Geritol ads that offered "help for tired blood." High on his editor's talent, Warren believed the magazine was going to be a hit. Again, Kurtzman found that writing funny captions and word balloons for movie stills was easy and fun.

The low editorial budget led to Kurtzman's constant search for material that cost little or nothing: "*Help!* was a trick magazine. We tried to do [it] for nothing. We would get old drawings and old photographs . . . and we would try to enhance them with captions."[7] Some public domain material was used, as well as reprints that could be gotten for a pittance. They used "freebies" wherever they could get them. The "Public Gallery" filled several pages an issue with cartoons sent in by talented neophytes, or reprints from college humor magazines, at $5 per cartoon. Ultimately, the letter column proved to be as entertaining as many other items in the magazine, and helped fill pages.

Beyond Kurtzman's salary, the budget allowed payment for three key functions: production (physically putting the magazine together for the printer), a part-time assistant to Kurtzman and a photographer for the covers and certain interior items. It was a foregone conclusion that Harry Chester would handle the paste-ups and other production tasks. But how to find an editorial assistant? Harold Hayes mentioned that a friend of his wife would be an excellent choice. She was a young woman who was trying to break into magazines. Her name was Gloria Steinem.

In 1960, Gloria Steinem, then twenty-six years old, moved to New York City from Cambridge, after doing some public relations work for an international student conference in Vienna. Through a friend she was introduced to Hayes and his wife Susan. Steinem was willing to accept a part-time position with Warren Publishing. Kurtzman interviewed her at her apartment in a brownstone across West 81st Street from the Museum of Natural History. "I was Harvey's first assistant on *Help!* magazine," Steinem said. "I don't think I had ever read *Mad*. I had been off to India for a couple of years and was really involved in student politics. I was probably the least likely person to be his assistant. Harvey came over to interview me . . . in the midst of my packing cases in my brand new one bedroom apartment."[8] It was immediately obvious to her that Kurtzman was uncomfortable during the interview. Steinem was an attractive young woman. "It was clear that he didn't think that a family man should be sitting in this one room studio . . . with this single woman, and by the end of the interview I was incredibly uncomfortable too. Somehow he hired me anyway, and he had enormous faith in the fact that I was not shy. In fact I was very shy [but] I was typecast as the 'not-shy' person, so I was always sent out to get the celebrities for the [covers, although] I didn't have the foggiest idea of how to get them. It was a challenge. Harvey expected me to do it so I was going to do it!"[9]

Regarding Steinem, Kurtzman said, "She didn't know people in [show] business, but she went and buttonholed people in the business when we had a celebrity problem. Gloria was quick and effective."[10] A key aspect of *Help!* in the beginning was its covers featuring popular comedians of the day: Sid Caesar, Ernie Kovacs, Jerry Lewis, Mort Sahl, Jonathan Winters and others. All of them did it for free. "Movie people are hungry for publicity, and they were willing to do all kinds of favors," Kurtzman said. "We also got a lot of turndowns when we were using celebs."[11] One was Gene Wilder.

Warren paid for space in a building at 545 Fifth Ave., a tiny office it shared with Chester Productions. Chester explained, "I started freelancing. I was doing *Cracked* magazine. I was doing a lot of *Mad* imitations. So I had enough business to get an office. We shared the rent."[12] It consisted of just two rooms and a "microscopic" anteroom.

Steinem was often on the phone. "She had a marvelous telephone voice," Kurtzman said. "Everybody loved Gloria. I was convinced . . . she could get anybody to do anything."[13] Steinem was delegated the job of finding a photographer for the magazine. Someone recommended Ron Harris, a twenty-seven-year-old Brooklyn native who got his start as an "assistant to the assistant" to well-known fashion photographer Francesco Scavullo. Harris remembered, "I'd just opened my first studio. I got a call from a woman who said someone had recommended me to be a photographer. She came over, and I thought she was very hot. Her name was Gloria Steinem. I was showing her my black and white pictures. I said, 'You have beautiful eyes,' and we talked about my motorcycle, which was just downstairs. She said, 'Would you give me a ride home?' So I gave her a ride home to her place on 81st Street . . . and went upstairs and we had sex."[14]

That was the *Help!* staff: Kurtzman, Steinem and Chester, along with Harris on a freelance basis. A monthly schedule was declared. The first issue was to have sixty pages, so there was a lot of work to be done quickly. Warren provided stills, Steinem began lining up celebrities for the covers and Kurtzman began contacting all his "usual suspects," some who quickly offered their services at cut-rate prices: Ed Fisher, Roger Price, Bernard Shir-Cliff and others. It was understood that his artist friends such as Al Jaffee, Will Elder, Jack Davis and Arnold Roth couldn't afford to work for next to nothing, but Roth and Davis sent minor items along for the first issue, and each of them tossed pieces Kurtzman's way as the magazine progressed. Eventually, Elder did much more than that.

Kurtzman decided to expand on something he'd tried in *Favorite Westerns*. Instead of photos with captions, he used funny word and thought balloons pasted onto the photos. He said,

Caption photos were nothing new. College magazines had been doing them for years. I was casting about for a way to do political commentary, and I went to the wire services which would have these news photos. Now, news photos are totally dull and uninteresting by themselves. A movie still has a lot going for it, in that the people in it are acting out some kind of fantasy. But in a news photo, you've got a slice of realism. It doesn't look like anything by itself, but it has personalities. I would take these things [and add] a form of floating [word] balloon . . . which hadn't been done. We really started something.[15]

The balloons were mostly written by Kurtzman and Steinem but Warren, Chester and others also contributed ideas.

Warren lined up a distributor. "You start at the top, and then work your way down. Independent News had *Mad*, *Playboy* and DC comics, and they said no. But Hearst's International Circulation Distributors, or ICD, said yes. They were a better distributor than Kable News, where I had *Famous Monsters*. They had very successful magazines like *Cosmopolitan* and

Good Housekeeping and got great newsstand coverage. When Kable found out I'd taken the 'new *Mad*' to ICD, they were furious. They punished me for it, very definitely, because they wanted *Help!*"[16] The first issue had a print run of 200,000.

A photograph of Sid Caesar in a toga with a word balloon saying, "I am not a candidate!" made up the cover of *Help!* #1 (August 1960). Its editorial page, headlined "THIS

Typical political humor in *Help!*: Soviet leader Nikita Khrushchev job hunting after backing down in the Cuban missile crisis.

IS *HELP!*," introduced itself to readers as "a picture-humor magazine designed to frequently titillate the senses and occasionally tickle the mind. In an age when the mind needs tickling, stimulating, prodding, joggling and kicking—you need *HELP!*" The message was signed, "Harvey Kurtzman, editor." The issue included reprint pieces by Robert Sheckley and Rod Serling, surrounded by many pages of photos and a few items by Jack Davis, Arnold Roth and Will Elder. "The Public Gallery," which encouraged readers to send in cartoons, reprinted a couple of pages from the *Yale Record*.

While waiting for sales results, Kurtzman came up with an idea that became another of the magazine's signature items, and a way to fill pages without having to pay artists: the fumetti. In Italian, the word *fumetti* refers to hand-drawn comics, and the word means "little puffs of smoke," referring to the word and thought balloons. Italians call stories that are acted out by actors in a series of photographs with word and thought balloons "fotoromanzi," but in America, the word fumetti stuck. They hadn't made an impact in North America until they appeared in *Help!*

The first fumetti appeared in *Help!* #3 (October 1960). "On the Coney" bragged that it had "a daring screenplay by Ed Fisher," establishing the conceit that this was a real movie. ("Alfred Hitchhike" supposedly directed it.) It tells the story of a man and woman who meet on a strangely deserted Coney Island beach. Even though they appear to be the last man and woman on earth, the female refuses to cooperate with the man's desire to start a new human race. In the end, her real reason for refusal is revealed, off camera: she's a man who, like Christine Jorgensen, had surgery to reassign her sex. All the reader sees is her hand holding a dangling bikini top before the horrified face of her beau.

The fumettis were produced for a relatively small sum, no more than $1,000 from start to finish. For the same money, a hand-drawn comic strip could have been produced, but it wouldn't spread out over so many pages. The format was popular with readers and worked surprisingly well. Clever scripts were concocted by Ed Fisher, Bernard Shir-Cliff, Algis Butrys, Willard Manus, David Shaber, Chuck Alverson and others, generally after the photos had been shot. In the course of the magazine's run, they starred recognizable actors or comedians such as Henry Jaglom, Jessica Walters, Tom Poston, Orson Bean, Woody Allen, Henny Youngman and Jack Carter. It's unclear how many were plotted by Kurtzman himself, but he storyboarded all of them, and attended the photoshoots to make sure the photographer, often Ron Harris, was clear on what he wanted. "We would have to shoot them in a day," Kurtzman recalled. "If we went beyond a day, we were in trouble, so we would put these enormous days of work into those things, sometimes from 6 a.m. until 10 p.m. to get the whole thing to fit. It was grueling."[17] Ron Harris remembered, "[Fumettis] were fun to shoot. Harvey worked on the storyboards till the last minute, sometimes even while we were shooting. They were very rough, showing a lot of emotion and movement, so they were really easy for me to interpret. There was a certain amount of improvisation. Harvey didn't say much. I would move people around till it worked, and I would start shooting. I would always over-shoot it, probably a thousand pictures or more in a day."[18]

Kurtzman received a telegram from Lenny Bruce in January 1961 stating that he "would love to do a feature photo for *Help!*" Unfortunately, it never came to pass. Later, Kurtzman said, "[Warren] always admired Lenny Bruce. Apparently he had heard that Lenny Bruce ran around his apartment naked. So whenever I'd come to his apartment he'd be naked, except he'd wear a pair of sweat socks. The effect just wasn't the same. I mean you can't run around naked in your apartment and be afraid of athlete's foot. It's just not Lenny Bruce."[19]

Help! was a hit-and-miss affair. Some of the material worked. Some fell flat. Not all of the word balloons added to photos and stills were funny. Kurtzman soon realized that he had to cut down on the number of photo gags and put more energy and thought into other types of editorial matter. The introduction of fumettis in the third issue was a step in the right direction. He allocated a greater portion of the budget for new material from friends and contacts. The magazine improved as he got a fix on what did and didn't work. Warren was around a lot in the beginning, and continued to be impressed by Kurtzman. "Watching Harvey work was fascinating. He did brilliant things that no one else would have been able to do. I don't know how to explain it. He was a unique, one of a kind genius, when he was 'on.' Of course he wasn't always 'on.' Some of the things he did weren't that great. Sometimes he was distracted. But when he was 'on,' what an amazing talent."[20] Warren's regard for Kurtzman led to the adding of his name on the cover. It became *Harvey Kurtzman's Help!* with the fourth issue. When deadline crunch time came, Kurtzman, Warren, Steinem and Chester worked late into the night. Warren ordered sandwiches from the Stage Delicatessen, and the cups of coffee kept coming until the issue was ready for the printer. There was considerable *esprit de corps*. Steinem called her boss "Harvella" (accent on the first syllable), a Yiddish expression of endearment.

Warren asked wholesalers to display *Help!* on newsstands next to *Playboy*, but didn't have any real control over its placement (and later claimed they never got it right). The first sales reports were troubling. The first issue lost money. Everyone expected the magazine's sales to grow, but over time, the magazine was generally in the red, some issues more than others. (Kurtzman later stated that *Help!* never sold 65 percent of the copies printed, as *Trump* #1 had.[21] Sales hovered around 50 percent.)

The same month as *Help!*'s debut, another new humor magazine hit newsstands and sold very well. It was Crestwood Publications' *Sick*, edited by Joe Simon. He described sales of its first issue as "spectacular," which indicates sales north of 70 percent. Both magazines were distributed by Hearst's ICD.[22] Was the different result because *Help!* was placed with *Playboy* while *Sick* was displayed next to *Mad*? Or because *Sick* more closely resembled *Mad*? (Its cover was by Simon. The insides were largely written by Dee Caruso, and drawn by Bob Powell and Angelo Torres.) Or was it because Warren and Kurtzman miscalculated the appeal of the photo-gag format? As always, there were plenty of questions but no definite answers.

Lack of expected profits left Kurtzman in a financial squeeze. It led to an incident that angered Warren, and struck a sour note fairy early in their relationship. According to Warren in an interview given in 1998, the incident began with a phone call from Kurtzman on a Saturday or Sunday, telling him there was something "very serious" he wanted to discuss. Could he meet with him right away to talk about it in person? Since it wasn't a work day, and Kurtzman was coming in from Mount Vernon just for the meeting, Warren knew something was up. They agreed to meet in a luncheonette. When Warren entered, he discovered that Kurtzman had brought his son Pete with him, explaining that he had his son for the day. He then told Warren the reason for the urgent meeting: "I need more money." He was speaking of money for himself, not for editorial purposes. "I have to have it," Kurtzman reportedly said.[23]

Warren recalled, "I said, 'Harv, you can't do that. You made an agreement with me.' Meanwhile, his son is there. And I said to myself, he's using his son against me. I [thought] this is despicable. Now, maybe he's not aware of what he's doing, because he has to have the boy for the day, but why couldn't he wait to have this discussion with me on Monday?" Warren thought Kurtzman brought his autistic son as a bid for sympathy, and was asking for charity in a business situation. Kurtzman often took charge of Pete on weekends, but Warren's interpretation of the situation might have been correct. If so, Kurtzman found this tactic didn't work with Warren. The magazine was operating in the red. Kurtzman's participation in the enterprise was predicated on the expectation that the magazine would be profitable. His regular salary was never intended to be a living wage. Warren said, "He went into this [magazine] knowing what the budget was going to be, because all of those figures were agreed upon on paper first. If Harvey felt that he was going to be screwed, why did he enter into any relationship with me?" Warren flatly refused Kurtzman's request.

Both men had been wary of each other from the beginning. Kurtzman had his usual suspicion of publishers. He had managed to put those feelings aside when it came to Hefner, perhaps because he considered him a classy individual. He didn't have that impression of Warren. Bill Gaines had warned Warren about Kurtzman shortly after *Help!* commenced. (Warren had already met Gaines.) "Gaines congratulated me on the magazine, but warned me that sooner or later, Harvey would turn on me. 'He'll accuse you of being a liar, a cheat,' he purportedly said. 'Just wait, it'll happen.' At the time, Harvey and I were getting along well, so I figured it was sour grapes."[24]

Another disagreement between Kurtzman and Warren, one that nearly led to the cancellation of the magazine, took place toward the end of 1960. When he was reviewing the proofs of *Help!* #8, Warren discovered that it had a full-page photograph of Adolph Eichmann, one of the chief architects of the Holocaust, who had been apprehended in Argentina on May 11, 1960, and put on trial in Israel. The word balloon had him saying,

"Ever get the feeling that the whole world's against you?" Warren told Kurtzman they couldn't run it: that it was outrageous, and showed terrible insensitivity to the survivors of the Holocaust. According to Warren, Kurtzman said, "Jim, you agreed that I have full editorial control. You can't go back on your word."[25] Warren tried to appeal to Kurtzman on the basis that it would be upsetting to Jews and was in poor taste. Kurtzman argued that anything can be satirized, and, "It's handled in good taste." When he told Warren there was nothing he could do to stop him from running it, Warren said he responded: "Yes I can, Harvey. As of issue #7, I'm $80,000 in the hole. I'm pulling out. I'm canceling the magazine. It's all over, Harvey."[26] A day or two later, Kurtzman and Warren met, each accompanied by his attorney. When Warren's attorney explained to the publisher that closing down the magazine would give up any hope of recouping its losses, Warren acquiesced. The Eichmann photo and caption could run as is.

Kurtzman never publicly discussed this disagreement, except to say, "Warren didn't get into the act. As a matter of fact, as we worked, Warren became more and more remote. We just didn't see eye to eye with the format at all, but I don't remember exactly what our differences were."[27] Kurtzman was hyper-sensitive on the matter of editorial control, and probably feared "giving an inch" would open the door to more interference. Along the line, there were other instances when Warren was dissatisfied with certain items in the magazine. Kurtzman wouldn't budge. Due to the terms in his contract, he always prevailed.

For Warren, the Eichmann incident was a turning point in his relationship with Kurtzman. "As we looked at each other, we realized that things could never be the same anymore," he said. "We continued to work together, but there was no more palling around, no more informality, no more fun. I didn't like Harvey Kurtzman as a person."[28] The feeling was mutual.

HELP! INVADED THE LIVES of the Kurtzman family in various ways. "I would hear hysterical laughter coming from Mom's bedroom early in the morning," recalled Meredith, who was eleven years old in 1961. "When my father did *Help!*, [Mom] would proofread things. I think she was reading fumettis, and when she would get going laughing, that would be it."[29]

Gloria Steinem sometimes visited. "She was one of my favorite people," Liz, then four years old, remembered. "My father was very strict with us about bedtimes, and when Gloria was there, I would say 'Oh, please Gloria, read me a story.' So she would read me a story. I just loved her."[30]

Christopher Lee as Dracula in *Help!* #11.

So did Adele, who recalled, "She made me feel I was just as tall and as good-looking as she was. She knew how to make people feel good."[31]

"[Dad] worked a lot at night when it was quiet," Meredith said. "If he was home during the daytime, we'd have lunch together. He always believed in families having meals together. He was very good to his family. Very responsible. He believed in children behaving and in discipline, but at the same time he was consciously or unconsciously very much a part of the loosening up that was beginning in the 1960s." Meredith read copies of *Two-Fisted Tales* that were around the house, and loved them. "He showed war in a different way, didn't glorify it, and I was very impressed by them."[32] Her favorites were the ones with her father's finished artwork. Sometimes the children would go up to his studio to see him. "He never turned us away or got angry," Liz recalled. "But if the door was shut and he really needed to work, he'd say, 'Not now. Another time would be good.'"[33]

The Kurtzmans always got the *New York Times*. On lazy Sundays, everyone took a section, then traded them around. The kids played in the street, perfectly safe because Audrey Avenue was a dead end. In their backyard, which was not large, they had a sandbox and a set of swings. At one point, the big maple tree in the back seemed to be dying. When Kurtzman noticed its trunk had split, he did some research on how to save trees. He saved the maple by filling the split area with concrete. While the mortar was still wet, he wrote the names of all three of the children in it. The Kurtzmans didn't have much money to go on vacations, but often spent a day at the beach. Kurtzman loved Jones Beach on Long Island.

He could be handy around the house. When the time came when he and Adele felt the kids should each have their own room, he figured out how to make a small space usable. "My room was the size of a half of a postage stamp," Liz recalled. "It had been a bathroom that was turned into a bedroom. My father found a bed that could be folded up—otherwise you couldn't walk into the room. It was very funny. It was like a Rube Goldberg type of thing. The desk was hinged to the wall. There were shelves above my head." At four and five years old, she didn't need a lot of space and liked her tiny room. It was reminiscent of some of the creative uses of space Kurtzman had come up with when he and Adele were living in their first one-room apartment. "I adored my father," Liz said. "He was funny and kind. He was the guy that all the neighborhood kids would sort of gravitate to. There's always one person in your life, I think, that knows you the best and I think he was that person for me. He wasn't a man of many words, but used his words wisely. He knew when you were having a problem, when you were happy or sad. He had this great sense of making it all okay, even when it wasn't."[34]

Having an autistic member of the family presented difficulties. Meredith said, "[Pete] couldn't talk. We would give him things we knew he liked, and knew how to make him laugh, but autistic kids aren't that interested in interpersonal relationships. He got quieter when he got to be a teenager, but in those ages from five to eleven, a lot of those kids are continually active and needy in a lot of ways. They need a lot of attention, and they have tantrums about things out of the blue."[35]

"It *was* difficult," Adele remembered. "Like the advertising slogan, you have to own one to know what it's like. I look back and ask myself, 'how did we survive?,' but we did. Harvey was terrific. I couldn't have done it without him. He was extremely good at handling Pete."[36] But he wasn't always home. Adele recalled, "I used to say, 'This is the end.' In fact, he was [away] once and this child, I said I was going to kill him. I really felt that he had to die. My sister called Harvey in Chicago and he came back immediately. He said, 'Look, we'll do what we have to do, but meanwhile I'm here.' He was encouraging that way."[37] They looked in vain for a school for their son, a place where he could learn and maximize his potential. They began meeting with other parents of children with severe mental conditions, and decided they needed to establish a program in Westchester. In 1963, after much effort, an existing school for what were then called "retarded" children in Westchester was given a broader mandate, and then could take children like Pete. Harvey and Adele were involved in the entire process, including fundraising.

JIM WARREN DISCOVERED that while ICD did a great job distributing the Hearst magazines, they didn't do so well with those from other publishers. He tinkered with the *Help!* package to see if he could generate better sales. With *Help!* #9, the magazine sported a less idiosyncratic cover logo, and experimented with using slick paper on 3,500 copies of that issue distributed in seven or eight cities in Ohio. "We are testing . . . the salability of slick stock," he told an interviewer, "and we're going to test this for three consecutive issues and see what it does to sales. You can see that it is a more quality package."[38] The copies printed on slick paper were still priced thirty-five cents. Nothing came of it.

Warren moved the *Help!* operation into new, somewhat larger offices at 501 Madison Ave. on March 1, 1961, but within a few months, work on the magazine was temporarily halted. Sales hadn't improved. To his credit, Warren had kept the magazine going long after others would have scuttled it. Now it seems he was experiencing a cash flow crunch. He had already reduced the magazine's page count from sixty-four to forty-eight. *Help!* #11 (June 1961) turned out to be the last monthly issue. The next edition was dated September, and then there was a five-month wait for the February 1962 issue. When the magazine returned, it was on a quarterly, not monthly, schedule, and no regular issues had more than forty-eight pages.

When asked if he had less interest in *Help!* than in his other magazines, Kurtzman responded, "Not really. Whenever I do something, I really believe in it. But I will admit that I . . . never put out anything else in as short a time, page for page."[39] He wasn't exercising his drawing muscles much, but the editor in him was fully engaged. Once he bowed to necessity and entered into the agreement with Warren, he became convinced that what he was doing was worthwhile, but that didn't mean he didn't recognize that it was a seriously compromised enterprise.

Between *Help!* #12 and #13, another dustup between Warren and Kurtzman occurred. Kurtzman and Steinem thought they should do what *Playboy* did: throw a lavish party and invite the movers and shakers in the city, as a way of raising the profile of *Help!* and getting coverage in other magazines. Kurtzman recalled, "Our . . . Christmas party at the Algonquin [was] a very memorable event. We invited everybody."[40] It was an invitation-only affair. Colleagues Arnold Roth, Roger Price, Ed Fisher, Larry Siegel and Burt Bernstein (Leonard Berstein's younger brother), who was an editor the *New Yorker* (and a *Help!* contributor), were in attendance. Among the guests was young Robert Grossman, a cartoonist who had been in a Yale group who invited Kurtzman to the campus to give him the *Yale Record*'s "Humorist of the Year" Award some months before. Grossman graduated in June and was looking for work. At the party, Kurtzman introduced him to Tom Meehan of the *New Yorker*, who got him an interview shortly thereafter with Jim Geraghty, the legendary editor of the magazine. Geraghty immediately hired Grossman as an assistant cartoon editor, the first step in his career as a prominent cartoonist, painter, filmmaker and author. Unlike Jim Warren, Grossman would always remember the event fondly.

From Warren's point of view, the Christmas party was a fiasco. He didn't buy Kurtzman's contention that the party was an inexpensive way to generate publicity, and had only grudgingly agreed to pay for it. Since he was bankrolling the affair, he saw no reason why he shouldn't invite certain people who had helped provide material for his magazines. One was Sam Sherman, a twenty-two-year-old film fan with a large collection of movie stills that he made available to Warren gratis for *Famous Monsters* and *Help!* According to Warren, Kurtzman, who was trying to recreate the famous Algonquin round table of literary wits in an attempt to impress the cognoscenti of Manhattan, wondered what a "nothing" like Sherman was doing there. "I invited him," Warren snapped. "He contributes to my magazines. You invited your brother-in-law who hasn't contributed a thing to *Help!* and he never will."[41] Warren was incensed, and later recalled, "I walked out of the party with Sam, and we went to see a movie. Sam was a . . . kid and I mentored him. He became a successful Hollywood film producer and distributor."[42] (As Samuel L. Sherman, he teamed up with low-budget horror director Al Adamson in 1971 to produce *Brain of Blood* and a string of exploitation films for drive-ins in the 1970s and 1980s.) Kurtzman never told his side of the contretemps. However, the party didn't produce any notable publicity for the magazine, and that in itself was enough to rankle Warren.

Gloria Steinem left *Help!* shortly after the Algonquin affair. Kurtzman continued to hold her in awe, describing Steinem as "the most potent female that I've ever met. I've never seen guys fall in love with a woman so rapidly . . . in such a rapid succession. She would be knocking them over like in a bowling alley." Kurtzman became convinced she was a female doppelganger of Hugh Hefner and jokingly suggested that the former and the latter should get together. He said, "To me the fascinating similarity was that they both had everything to do with the opposite sex. They are totally dependent in their careers on men and women. Gloria climbed up a beanstalk of men. And of course, Hefner sold females. A mountain of bosoms. So to me they were both extremely talented people who had this great affinity for the opposite sex, and yet this great independence of the opposite sex. So I figured it must come from the same machinery. I figured they've either got to hate each other or love each other. I tried to fix her up with Hefner."[43] Hugh Hefner recently confirmed, "Harvey raved to me about this remarkable woman that he had working for him, because she was second to none in getting male celebrities to appear on his covers. Harvey was convinced that she was the female equivalent of me, that my 'magic way' with women was the equivalent of what Gloria was, in his opinion, with men. He thought we were made for each other. As a result of that, we actually exchanged phone calls, and letters and talked about going out."[44]

Ron Harris volunteered to throw a party at his studio as an excuse to bring them together. When the evening came, the place was filled with models, as well as Kurtzman and friends such as Arnold Roth. Hefner did indeed show up, but Steinem did not. Kurtzman phoned her, and, much to his dismay, she begged off. The truth was that she was working under-cover as a bunny in the New York Playboy Club, and writing an exposé of her experience for *Show* magazine. She was afraid of being recognized by Hefner or an associate. "I was a Playboy Bunny" was her first big ar-ticle, gaining her national attention and setting off her career. Therefore, Kurtzman's attempt to bring them together failed, though they would have encounters in the future. Besides, Steinem was dating Robert Benton, an editor at *Esquire*. For his part, Hefner said, "Gloria has always been an enigma to me."[45]

HELP! BECAME A BETTER MAGAZINE in its next phase. Kurtzman com-mitted to write and lay-out new sequential art stories if there was enough money in the budget to pay him a little extra, and to bring in Will Elder to draw and ink them. Warren went along with it, realizing there was no hope of recouping his mounting losses unless the product was upgraded. Kurtzman revived Goodman Beaver from *Jungle Book* for the only con-tinuing series he wrote for the magazine.[46] The first story was "Goodman Meets T*rz*n," with the vowels in the name of Edgar Rice Burroughs's jun-gle hero obfuscated as a semi-serious way of forestalling legal action. (ERB Inc. was known for its zealous protection of its most valuable character.)

This was a new Goodman Beaver, different in important respects from the character in "The Organization Man." This Goodman still had the round "Little Orphan Annie" eyes and blond hair, but he was more naïve than before, and the events he encountered rolled right off him, leaving him tempted but unchanged. This was necessary if he was to become an ongoing character. The Kurtzman-Elder partnership worked as well as ever. Of all the features in *Help!* magazine, the five Goodman Beaver sto-ries (in as many issues) stand out as the most inspired and memorable.

"Goodman Meets T*rz*n" is set in the aftermath of the bloody Mau Mau uprisings of the 1950s, a period of violent transition in Africa. The story centers on Tarzan himself, leaving Beaver little to say. He mainly observes the jungle king in his native habitat. "Everything pure nature here," Tarzan tells Goodman as they enter his hut, finding Jane bare-breasted. "We no need machines. No need electricity. No need clothes. No need nuttin'!" The natives are less subservient than before. "Listen, T*rz*n . . . just cause you and him white, it don't mean you superior.

Goodman Beaver

Africa is awakening!" In the end, Tarzan and Jane flee to America where she will work as a TV weather forecaster, and he will open a Vic Tanny-type gym. "Goodman Meets T*rz*n" was a fine introduction to the new Goodman Beaver, and subsequent chapters would be even better.

Help! #13 (February 1962) printed the second new Goodman Beaver, "Goodman Goes Playboy." Goodman returns to small town America five years after high school graduation expecting it to be unchanged. Instead, he finds his high school chums—parodies of Archie, Jughead and Veronica—are jaded, pseudo-sophisticated wastrels. When Archer tells him that he and Veromica are living together without being married, Goodman can't believe it. "You don't dig, Goodman. Veromica is sort of . . . my playmate." Archer takes Goodman home to his penthouse, which is revealed to be

Panels from "Goodman Goes Playboy" by Kurtzman and Elder: from *Help!* #13 (February 1962).

the site of a wild Roman-like orgy (shown in a large, elaborate panel with topless women running around, etc.). When a dismayed Goodman asks where the money came from for the penthouse (with its basement full of sex dolls and Nazi Party stag films), Archer exults, "I've signed a pact with the Devil. That's where it comes from! Haaahaha! In exchange for my soul!" In the end, when the Devil announces that he owns Archer's soul, the townspeople line up to sign away theirs in exchange for similar benefits. Standing aside, Goodman muses, "I think it's time for me to leave . . . to find a place where the dark forces aren't closing in . . . where honor is still sacred and where virtue triumphs. Then again . . . maybe I should sign up."

This story is considered the best—certainly the most outrageous—in the series. Kurtzman: "I had a lot to say about *Playboy*, and so it was kind of like shooting fish in a barrel. But I started off with a premise as always, which was: you've got to pay for the life of pleasure, and the life of pleasure can exact a terrible penalty."[47] Hugh Hefner's reaction revealed a lot about the man. "He enjoyed it very much," Kurtzman said. "And whenever he wants to explain me to anybody, he tells them to go read that story. He equates me with Goodman Beaver in the story, and rightly so."[48] It remained Kurtzman's favorite of the run.

John Goldwater of Archie Comics was not amused. Days after *Help!* #13 appeared, an attorney for the publisher sent a letter to Warren asserting that the use of Archie's characters in the story constituted copyright infringement. Furthermore, the story line amounted to "trade libel, and undermines the valuable property my client has developed in these wholesome characters."[49] Kurtzman felt he had the right to parody such characters, as he had with Superman and so many other fictional characters in the past. Goldwater had done nothing when *Mad* published "Starchie!," which Kurtzman thought was because Goldwater and M.C. Gaines had been friends. (This was unlikely, considering how much Goldwater disliked the EC horror comics of the day and that he became a foe of Bill Gaines over the adoption of the Comics Code. Possibly Goldwater felt Bill Gaines had the wherewithal to fight a legal action in court, since *Mad* was so successful.) According to Adele, her husband referred to Goldwater as "another jackass."[50]

A settlement was reached in March 1962. Warren paid $1,000 and agreed to publish an apology in the magazine. Kurtzman said, "We paid off, we settled out of court. I thought it was terrible. I thought . . . it was a wrong thing [Goldwater] was doing. I wasn't able to fight him because I didn't have any money to fight, and my lawyer said I could fight, and I could win, and it would be a Pyrrhic victory. It's very sad."⁵¹ (The issue with the apology states that Kurtzman was editor of everything except the apology. Though he bowed to the inevitable, he insisted on registering his objection in print.)

The dust had hardly settled from the threatened lawsuit when the matter was revisited. Kurtzman and Elder contracted with MacFadden Publishing to put out a paperback book reprinting Goodman Beaver stories. They were reprinted one panel per page. Because of the book's different shape, Elder had to laboriously extend the panels to fill each page. The book included a revised version of "Goodman Goes Playboy" with the names and faces of the Archie characters altered. When John Goldwater saw the *Executive's Comic Book* (1962), he again threatened legal action, and Kurtzman and Elder were forced to pay a $1,000 settlement to Archie Comics out of their own pockets. (They also assigned ownership and copyrights of the work to Archie.) Although this case was even weaker, Archie prevailed because, as with *Help!*, MacFadden didn't want to spend money fighting in court over a publication that made little money. None of this in any way obviates the fact that "Goodman Goes Playboy" was as good as anything Kurtzman and Elder did for *Mad*, *Trump* or *Humbug*.

Goodman Beaver marched on. "Goodman, Underwater" in #14 parodied the *Seahunt* TV show, and in #15, Kurtzman again parodied the Man of Steel with "Goodman Meets S*perm*n." In this tale, Superman has given up his hero role because he's sick of getting nothing in return. It occurred to Kurtzman that the idea of the Good Samaritan hero made no sense. "Superman is still carrying on his work with a martyr's zeal, with absolutely no recompense, and life just isn't that way," he said. "I mean, we have to give and receive, or else we don't hold up. The superhero who gives without compensation distorts reality."⁵²

At one point in the story, when Goodman Beaver is talking to an old lady on the street, a madman runs toward them brandishing a straight razor. "This is the classic test," Goodman thinks. "If I stay to protect the old lady, he'll cut me up! If I run, he'll cut up the old lady. What shall I do?" Then, "there's no question! I know what I have to do . . . RUN! After all . . . when he's finished with me, he'll cut up the old lady anyhow . . . HELP! MANIAC!" The old lady is actually S*perm*n in disguise, testing Goodman. The Man of Steel leaves in disgust, muttering, "Everybody's rotten. And you know why? Because to be 100%, you've got to be a S*perm*n." *Goodman Beaver*'s writing was thematically some of the most ambitious of Kurtzman's career. The feature (consisting of a total of thirty-one pages) was successful on all levels, and lacks only the ideal reprinting (including

"Goodman Goes Playboy") to be rediscovered and given a place of greater prominence in discussions of Kurtzman's work and career.

SALES FOR *HELP!* continued to seesaw. Sometimes encouraging reports arrived, and Warren took the staff to lunch. Kurtzman wracked his brains trying to think of new ways to raise the magazine's profile. On March 23, 1962, he appeared on Vern Greene's FM radio show, *The Cartoonist's Art*. Greene was a cartoonist himself, successor to George McManus on the newspaper strip *Bringing up Father*. Paul Terry and Al Capp had already warmed the seats in Greene's studio. When asked if there was any difference in theme of the old *Mad* comics and *Help!*, Kurtzman responded, "The theme remains the same. I try to do satire and thoughtful humor. We were very heavy on drawings in *Mad*. Now we're very heavy on photographs."[53]

Warren engaged Gerald Gardner as a freelance idea man and huckster. In a single ten-page document, Gardner compiled a list of suggested promotions for *Help!*, reminiscent of movie press books: tie-ins, publicity ideas, moneymaking schemes and so on. One was a *Help!* syndicated comic strip. Another was a *Help!* bumper sticker. Another was a mail order section in the magazine. Some were tried. Others were deemed too expensive, time-consuming or impractical. One successful tie-in and moneymaker in itself was a *Help!* paperback book. Fawcett Books perceived enough of a market for the magazine's material that they contracted to publish a reprint book under their Gold Medal label. It was called *Harvey Kurtzman's Fast-Acting Help!,* and went on sale in January 1962. Kurtzman received a $2,800.00 advance (which was presumably shared with Warren) and the entire print run of 198,024 copies sold. A follow-up book was immediately scheduled.

Help! #16 was a standout issue in several respects. It carried the last Goodman Beaver story ("Goodman Gets a Gun"), an above-average fumetti ("The Company Plane" starring Russ Heath) and Kurtzman's own "Inside *Requiem for a Heavyweight*," in which he combined photographs with his own artwork to convey what it was like when he visited the film set. Not the least of all, the issue presented the first appearance of Gilbert Shelton's "Wonder Wart-Hog" in a national magazine.

Shelton was attending college in Texas. "*Mad* was a great influence," he said. "The drawing was too good for me to attempt to copy, though. Virgil Partch was my favorite gag artist. Harvey Kurtzman's *Hey Look!* strips, which were reprinted once or twice in *Mad*, impressed me with their apparent simplicity and their spontaneous look, although I later realized that it was laboriously constructed."[54] When he was in college, Shelton contributed to the college humor magazines such as *Bacchanal* and the *Texas Ranger*, where his Wonder Wart-Hog ("the Hog of Steel") originally appeared. Pathetic reporter Philbert Desenex, the Hog's secret identity, paralleled the way Clark Bent was portrayed in Kurtzman's "Superduperman!" Shelton said, "I don't know how Kurtzman found this material, but he paid us . . . and I was pleased to see my work published in *Help!*" Shelton's cartoons appeared in the Public Gallery in #14 and #15, and then, in #16, "Wonder Wart-Hog Meets Super Fool" was reprinted from an issue of *Bacchanal* published earlier that year. Kurtzman ran more reprints of the Hog of Steel, and then Shelton produced new Wart-Hog stories for him at $35 a page. Wonder Wart-Hog, essentially a burlesque of Superman, was immensely popular with readers.

After losing assistant editor Gloria Steinem (who went on to do fumetti strips for *Glamour* magazine and other magazine assignments), Kurtzman hired a succession of editorial assistants whose responsibilites were assigned according to their abilities. The first was already in place, suggesting that Steinem had given Kurtzman advance warning. Chuck Alverson was a Los Angeles native who attended the University of California at Berkeley and San Francisco State College. The aspiring writer contributed to the University of California *Pelican*, and founded his own humor magazine at San Francisco State College. One of his first tasks was putting together the material for a second *Help!* paperback, which was called *Second Help-ing* (published in late 1962). Alverson also assisted Kurtzman on a Fawcett book called *Who Said That?*, which consisted solely of photos with funny word balloons. (The material hadn't appeared in *Help!* first, so Kurtzman could keep all royalties.) The book sold only moderately well. This galled Kurtzman, because Gerald Gardner had earlier taken the photo-with-word balloon idea and used it for a book called *Who's in Charge Here?*, which purportedly sold a million copies, and so delighted President Kennedy that Gardner was invited to the White House. Nevertheless, the $2,000 advanced by Fawcett for *Who Said That?* helped Kurtzman get through the lean times when there were few, if any, profits coming in from the magazine itself. It also gave him the cash to pay several people who helped write the captions, among them Larry Siegel and Gloria Steinem. A final accounting in 1965 showed royalties for the book totaled $4,864.00 from a sale of 224,000 copies.[55]

Chuck Alverson, in turn, left for other opportunities. As Adele put it, "Chuck . . . detested Jim [Warren] and wrote a letter to *Time* magazine saying what a horrible person he was. Of course, he was immediately fired."[56]

Terry Gilliam filled the post, starting with *Help!* #17 (February 1963). The twenty-two-year-old former class president of Birmingham High School in Panorama City, California, had been a rabid *Mad* fan. "In college, I managed to turn a genuinely artistic and poetic literary magazine into a cheap, nasty comic book, thanks to Harvey and trying to impress [him]. He opened my eyes [and] changed my way of looking at the world, of not accepting things the way they appear to be. So there I was in college trying to impress him from a distance in Los Angeles, and I was sending him copies of these magazines. We were doing fumettis just like they were doing in *Help!*"[57]

Kurtzman responded with a letter of encouragement in July 1962. "He must have been sending hundreds of people letters of encouragement," Gilliam said. "I didn't realize that. I thought I got the only letter of encouragement from Harvey."[58] Kurtzman had been impressed with a fumetti parody of *West Side Story* that Gilliam and friends had done, and asked if they could create a new fumetti for *Help!* Gilliam immediately wrote back: "I just got your letter concerning the possibility of our doing a 'fumetti' for *Help!* It sounds tremendous. We're ready to roll any time you wish, even if one or two of us have to come to New York."[59] Gilliam recalled, "At that point, [Harvey] realized he'd made one of the biggest mistakes of his life, and he sent a letter trying to stop me. 'Don't come to New York, kid—It's a big town . . . !' Which made me more determined to come. So I rushed to New York."[60] He arrived at the end of August.

When Gilliam phoned after hitting town, Kurtzman agreed to see him. "Meet me at the Algonquin Hotel," he said. Gilliam complied. "The door opens," he recounted, "and it's Arnold Roth, and inside there was Will [Elder] and Al [Jaffee], these absolute *gods* to me. And then, in comes Harvey, the *god of gods*. There they all were, and I was in heaven."[61] After being invited inside and meeting everyone, Gilliam discovered the reason they were all gathered in the room. They were rushing to complete an elaborate, fully painted comic strip, the first time anything like that had ever been attempted. He arrived just as the first installment of a new feature Kurtzman was writing and producing for *Playboy* was being completed.[62]

Celebrities, mostly comedians, appeared on the covers of the first dozen issues of Kurtzman's humor magazine from Warren Publishing. Above: *Help!* #1 had Sid Caesar and #3 featured Jerry Lewis. Below: #5 with Dave Garroway and #12 had Will Jordan.

CLASS OF SERVICE
This is a fast message unless its deferred character is indicated by the proper symbol.

WESTERN UNION
TELEGRAM
W. P. MARSHALL, PRESIDENT

SF-1201

SYMBOLS
DL=Day Letter
NL=Night Letter
LT=International Letter Telegram

The filing time shown in the date line on domestic telegrams is STANDARD TIME at point of origin. Time of receipt is STANDARD TIME at point of destination.

NJ037 PA041

AA021 A MZA032 NL PD TDMZ MIAMI BEACH FLO 5

1961 JAN 6 AM 1 55

HARVEY KURTSMAN

HELP MAGAZINE 545 5 AVE NYK

BE IN NEW YORK FEBRUARY 4TH CARNEGIE HALL ONE DAY WOULD LOVE
TO DO FEATURE PHOTO FOR HELP CALL ME MIAMI TIME JE 17481 MOST
NIGHTS BETWEEN 730 830 KURTSMAN JUNGLE WAS SO VERY GOOD

LENNY BRUCE.

Benjamin Winston
475 Fifth Avenue
New York, 17, N.Y.

COPY

LE 26600

Help! Magazine Inc.
422 Madison Avenue
New York, New York

Gentlemen:

My client, Archie Comic Publications, Inc.,of New York
, N.Y. , theb cpoyright owner of Archie Comics, has consulted
me regarding what it considers a flagrant violation of client's
copyright based on a feature published in the February 1962
issue of HELP! magazine, commencing on page 23 thriugh page 30

In thisfeature you have appropriated a client's characters in
every detail, to a degree that the person reading the
feature would asssume that it is a product emanating from
my client's copy, except for the script which, in my opinion,
constitutes a rtrade libel, and undermines the vakuable property that my client has developed in these wholesome characters.
          been
I have instructed to proceed with suit to recover damages
resulting from your act of copyright infringement and libel
and request that you recall from sale all copies of the issue
referred to.

I request a prompt reply as to your position inthe matter.

Very truly yours,

Benjamin E. Winston

B W:sd
Certified Mail R R R

cc: International Circulation Distributors--Hearst Magazines

Above: Telegram from Lenny Bruce, dated January 6, 1961. Bottom: Letter from Archie Publications' attorney re: "Goodman Goes Playboy" in *Help!* #13.

This photograph from *Help!* #9 (April 1961) shows each member of the staff with a symbol of his or her role. Warren (a cash register, for finance), Kurtzman (a telephoto camera lens, for vision), Steinem (a life preserver, for general assistance) and Chester (a drawing board, for doing the paste-ups).

First page of the "Office Party" fumetti in *Help!* #5, with Gloria Steinem featured. Note Will Elder in the bottom corner.

22.

A LIFELINE

"AT A CERTAIN POINT, *Help!* started crumbling, falling apart," Harvey Kurtzman said. "I started looking for other things."[1]

Playboy was never far from Kurtzman's mind. Indeed, he'd even sold Hugh Hefner a prose piece for its February 1960 issue called "The Real Lady Chatterley," a satire of the then-notorious book by D. H. Lawrence. The two-page item, a "fraudulent chapter" of the racy book, satirized Lawrence's back-to-nature themes and florid writing style. Like Hemingway, Lawrence was an easy target.

On September 9, 1961, Kurtzman wrote Hefner that he "might be looking for work soon." *Help!* was on hiatus while Warren determined if it would continue. Once the magazine was up and running again, Kurtzman sent Hefner the first couple of Goodman Beaver strips (including "Goodman Goes Playboy") and offered him the subsequent stories in the series. Hefner liked them, but didn't feel Goodman Beaver was exactly right for *Playboy*. He wrote, "Maybe there is a way of launching a similar series on a guy that can somehow be related to *Playboy*, and who has all manner of misadventures related to various subjects."[2] Kurtzman proposed a sexy female version of Goodman Beaver, who he described as "a lovable, good-natured idiot" who wandered through the world in various states of undress. "What would you think," Kurtzman wrote, "of a girl character, roughly modeled along the lines of Belle Poitrine . . . very, very roughly, who I could apply to my kind of situations?"[3] Belle Poitrine was the often-underdressed, clueless heroine of the faux autobiography *Little Me* (1961) by Patrick Dennis. (He also wrote the book *Auntie Mame*.)

Hefner responded: "I think your notion of doing a Goodman Beaver strip of two, three or four pages, but using a sexy girl . . . is a bull's eye. We can run it every issue."[4] Kurtzman relayed the news to Elder, and the two of them began sketching.

For the character's basic look, Elder recalled, "I suggested Marilyn Monroe and Brigitte Bardot. They both were cutie pies and very sensuous. Monroe had that sensual innocence. She was like a sexy child. I would make a few sketches in color and show them to Harvey. We went over it about three or four times before we got what we liked. Or rather, I should say what Hefner liked. He was footing the bill."[5]

According to Denis Kitchen's account of the evolution of this strip in *Playboy's Little Annie Fanny* (2000), name suggestions included "The Perils of Zelda," "The Perils of Irma," "The Perils of Shiela," and even "Little Mary Mixup," before Kurtzman and Hefner agreed on "Little Annie Fanny." It would be a humorous twist on Harold Gray's *Little Orphan Annie*, the popular newspaper strip about the adventures of an eleven-year-old orphan. Gray's strip made its debut in 1924, and, while its greatest popularity was behind it, was still running in hundreds of papers. The name *Little Annie Fanny* was chosen for the recognition it evoked, and because Kurtzman intended to offer satirical commentary on political and societal trends, which Gray did to some extent in his comic strip.[6]

In a way, a semi-satire of "Little Orphan Annie" with nudity and a heavy emphasis on sexual misadventures made it a kind of high-class Tijuana bible, the pornographic publications of the 1930s and 1940s that showed such characters as Blondie and Popeye in sexual situations. Kurtzman had no qualms about the sexual content of the strip: "I never saw myself relating to *Playboy* without the sex theme. I've slowly been coming out of the Puritanism that I really was very hot on in my earlier years."[7]

With the basic premise and the protagonist's appearance established, the next key decision to be made involved the type of rendering technique to be used on the art. Kurtzman offered Hefner a couple of options: an India inked version, something like Goodman Beaver, with flat comic book color, or a fully painted version similar to the technique Elder used in his color work for *Trump*. Kurtzman and Elder preferred the former; Hefner opted for the latter. This meant that the work would take much more time, but Hefner was willing to pay a higher rate to make it happen. *Playboy* was one of the last magazines to use high quality rotogravure printing, which was superior to the color printing achievable on photo offset presses in 1962. Hefner knew that a fully painted Annie would look stunning in the expensive printing process.

Kurtzman began making lists of story ideas. Hefner made it clear at the outset that he intended to supervise the work closely, and would continue to do so even after it was established. Once the two men agreed on the concept and illustration media, however, their thinking ran parallel and the creative process went forward without impediments. Kurtzman met with Hefner in Chicago in the first week of May to negotiate the terms of an agreement to produce *Little Annie Fanny*. Hefner outlined them in his letter of May 10, 1962. Kurtzman and Elder were each to receive $400 a page for the first three pages of each story, and $200 each for every succeeding page. They would receive 50 percent of all royalties for reprints, books, movie rights or *Annie Fanny* byproducts, the remainder going to Hefner's company. Monthly advances on their payments were to begin immediately.[8]

Early sketch of Little Annie Fanny, drawn in the style of Goodman Beaver in *Help!* magazine. From *The Mad Playboy of Art*: courtesy of the Will Elder Estate.

The letter also established that all rights to the character would reside with HMH Publishing Co., Inc. In another example of Kurtzman's business naiveté, he had assumed that, as creator and writer of *Little Annie Fanny*, he would be the copyright owner. It's not clear whether Hef explained it to him in Chicago or blindsided him in the ensuing letter, but once again (as with *Mad*), Kurtzman watched as his own creation slipped out of his hands. All he could do was voice his objection, easily batted down by Hefner, though probably with a fair amount of diplomacy. *Playboy* would, after all, pay well for the work, and both Kurtzman and Elder would receive royalties for uses beyond the first printing, and monies from merchandising, et al.

Whatever Kurtzman's feelings about this, he ultimately realized that ownership wasn't something Hefner would concede. Without it, the publisher wouldn't have entertained the project at all. Therefore, if Kurtzman wanted to work for *Playboy* at the time—and he did, desperately—then he would have to yield on the point. His disappointment was overcome by his desire to get started and get those advance payments rolling in.

SECURING A REGULAR PLACE in *Playboy* was the most important turning point in Harvey Kurtzman's career since leaving *Mad* for *Trump*. *Little Annie Fanny* was a lifeline from Hefner, and this time it would not be sundered by a financial earthquake. Now Kurtzman would be well paid working for a highly popular—even prestigious—gorgeously printed, slick magazine, for an editor who was a fan of his work, with Will Elder at his side. It was a lifeline that he would grasp tightly with both hands, having seen how difficult it was find his niche as a freelance cartoonist, and having left *Mad*. This new chapter in his career seemed to offer both creative challenges and a modicum of financial security.

The first *Little Annie Fanny*, the one Terry Gilliam found Kurtzman and cohorts finishing at the Algonquin Hotel, appeared in the October 1962 issue of *Playboy*. Work on the six-page story, unofficially titled "Madison Avenue" (no actual titles appear on the strip itself, but the stories were given working titles for ease of reference), began, as all Annie stories did, with a short, written "pitch" to be approved by Hefner. Then Kurtzman's creative process proceeded along similar lines as his EC work, albeit with more interim steps. The writing began with small thumbnail pages where the basic action of the story was established, and then to letter-sized grid paper with a complete pencil layout, and the script written in the captions and word balloons. On a sheet of vellum over that, Kurtzman created a basic color guide for Elder. Then he enlarged his layouts to the size the original art would be painted (10 ½" by 15"), creating and refining them in successive, color-coded versions, done with fine or medium tip color markers. When the figures, backgrounds and composition were completed to Kurtzman's satisfaction, Elder transferred this detailed blueprint to the large Strathmore art board. After the word balloons were masked, the painting began. (Along the way, Hefner's approval of the script and aspects of the art was required.)

Little Annie Fanny was painted using Grumbacher watercolors, with parts of the board left unpainted to create the white areas. Kurtzman developed a system of applying colors in translucent layers for Annie, generally having Elder begin with light yellow to evoke a feeling of warmth. Other colors were built up over that, ultimately creating a near-iridescent effect. The laborious process was finished with white highlights done with either an ink eraser or opaque tempera paint. Then came some back-

and-forth between Kurtzman and Elder, as Kurtzman indicated changes that were to be made to the painted version. When asked why he made so many fussy little changes, he said, "If I don't ask for them, Hefner will."[9] Then Bob Price lettered the story, the last stage—other than obtaining final approval from *Playboy*.

This time-consuming process was the most elaborate ever used on a comic strip or story. Kurtzman's layouts were nearly as detailed as finished pencil art that was ready to ink, as in a normal four-color comic book. The goal was to produce a strip that could be enjoyed on two levels. "I get satisfaction [in creating] what I call a slow cartoon," Kurtzman said. "That is, a cartoon with a technique where you put so much time into the rendering that your audience will enjoy [it] as much for the drawing itself as they will for the idea."[10]

"Madison Avenue" spoofs television commercials of the day that had a female model address the viewer from her bubble bath.[11] The reader first meets Annie in a tub, trying to cover her nudity while a leering film crew looks on.

> Director: Let's take the shot over again a couple more times, Miss Fanny.
> Annie: But, Mr. Battbarton, all the soapsuds have dissolved!

The episode introduces Annie Fanny's roommate, Ruthie, and her original beau, ad executive Benton Battbarton. It echoes ideas about Madison Avenue advertising that ran through Kurtzman's magazines. One aspect of the first episode is unique from a historical standpoint. It's the only one in which Annie doesn't appear fully, exuberantly topless. (Her nipples are coyly covered.) That wouldn't occur until "Playing Doctor," the second story.

The sex change that turned Goodman Beaver into Little Annie Fanny was more than cosmetic. It allowed for its central conceit. Annie doesn't realize that all the men around her are lusting after her, and willing to do almost anything to bed her. Goodman is a lovable, good-natured, philosophical idiot, a character who can be appreciated on an adult level. Annie is all those things except philosophical, whose sexual appeal is geared toward the adolescent and the arrested adolescent inside the adult readers of *Playboy*. She has the enormous breasts central to the masturbatory fantasies of the teenage male, and is like a walking, talking love doll who offers the promise of guiltless, easy sex. Annie is deliberately vacuous, even more clueless than her predecessor.

Playboy readers loved her. "The readers immediately embraced the feature," Hefner recently recalled. "It was a very big hit from the beginning. Somebody did a profile on Harvey—I can't remember who it was—but he talked about *Little Annie Fanny* as if it was a lesser accomplishment in his career. From my point of view, it was a high point. The two high points of his life were the creation of *Mad* magazine and the creation of *Little Annie Fanny.*'"[12]

For its first year, producing *Little Annie Fanny* was nothing short of frenzied. Nine stories were created in that time, totaling thirty-five pages. Sugardaddy Bigbucks, Annie's benefactor, was introduced, as was Ralphie Towser, another boyfriend. The look of the strip evolved, as Annie became even more "full figured," and the creators gained confidence. Elder said his painting technique "hadn't fully blossomed yet. It developed. It grew, and you can see the development, the change of technique—for the better."[13] Topics satirized in the first year were medical TV shows (*Ben Casey, Dr. Kildare*), the commercialization of Christmas, neorealism in Italian cinema, the "new" comedians (Mort Sahl, Jonathan Winters, Lenny Bruce, etc.), the Kennedys and physical fitness. There are multiple gags per panel, some in the background, though Elder's penchant for "chicken fat"—especially funny signs—was held in check. Per Hefner, "I felt they distracted from getting involved with the characters themselves and making them credible."[14] Elder paraphrased Hefner's dictum as, "We want your talent but not your *Mad* talent."[15]

In order to accelerate the art production and meet deadlines, Kurtzman called upon friends to help. One was Jack Davis. Another was Russ Heath. The fill-ins by Davis and others with distinctive, recognizable art styles (Arnold Roth, Al Jaffee, Paul Coker) came and went, after Hefner asked for a more consistent Elder look. Heath stayed, because he was especially good at replicating Elder's style and painting technique (and had no objection to doing so). He came to be considered the regular "on call" second artist, a role he fulfilled through the decade's end. Heath built a house in Livingston, New Jersey, within reasonable distance of Elder's Englewood home. "I worked on many more *Annie Fanny*s than I signed," he recalled. "People ask me, 'did you pencil or did you ink?' It wasn't like that. More accurately, it was like we all did all of them. Many times we had to actually physically cut the pages apart so Willy could take half and work on it while I was working on the other half. I spent an awful lot of time fixing stuff that we got from the other guys. I retouched all over the place."[16] *Little Annie Fanny* was, to a great degree, a corporate product. Once it was established, there wasn't much leeway allowed in the look of the strip.

WHILE *LITTLE ANNIE FANNY* consumed much of Kurtzman's creative energy, he continued to edit *Help!*, although it took less time due to the

Warren magazine's quarterly schedule. Will Elder worked at home in New Jersey, visiting Audrey Avenue about once a month to review the work and discuss the next story. Often it was easier to mail pages and revisions back and forth.

To keep *Help!* on track, Kurtzman relied more heavily on his new editorial assistant. Terry Gilliam recalled how he got the job, when he arrived in New York. "Luckily, Charles Alverson, who was the assistant editor of *Help!* at that time, was moving on, and Harvey was looking for a new assistant, and bingo! Yours truly got the job. And it was the most wonderful thing. There I was in New York getting paid fifty dollars a week with Harvey."[17] Terry Gilliam proved to be a talented, capable associate editor. "There was always the pressure of trying to get other people to do things that I was doing," Kurtzman admitted. "And, yes, I . . . did get Terry into the areas that I would normally handle."[18] Of course, Goodman Beaver vanished from the magazine.

Gilliam and Kurtzman spent more time together than any of the other assistant editors because Gilliam ended up living with his family. Kurtzman said, "Terry was starving. He needed a place to live and we had a really dirty old attic, so we gave Terry permission to move in. He hung drapes all around and turned it into a palace. I could never get over the little work space he set up for himself." Adele liked Gilliam: "He lived with us for a couple of months. He was fun to have around. We'd watch Soupy Sales together."[19] Gilliam and Kurtzman connected. Gilliam boarded with Kurtzman again in 1968, and their friendship lasted all Kurtzman's life.

Gilliam was astonished by the size of *Help!*'s operation: "This magazine was really being done by a very small handful of people." But it attracted letters, cartoons, phone calls and visits from a wide variety of talented people. Some of them, like Gilliam, were in New York for the first time, trying to break into the magazines. "It was an amazing time," he remembered. "Everybody was pouring in this Mecca . . . and there was Harvey Kurtzman."[20] Gilliam handled the responsibilities and stayed with the magazine until its demise. "I think the thing that still amazes me about Harvey is that, on the one hand, he was the wisest person I ever knew, and he was also the most naive person I ever knew. And I think that's what made him magical, because he never took for granted his talent, his skills. He was always discovering something new. New people, new ideas, it was always a fresh look at things."[21] Gillam appeared on the masthead for the first time on #17, the last issue published in 1962.

Like Kurtzman, Warren became less involved in the later issues of *Help!* He argued that some of Kurtzman's cover ideas were too obscure to catch the eye of newsstand browsers, but his objections fell on deaf ears. "My feelings about Harvey deteriorated to the point where I put less energy into the magazine," he said. "I stopped caring."[22] Yet he kept *Help!* going even though its losses drained profits from *Famous Monsters of Filmland*. Why? "A little thing called hope. I kept hoping that it would gradually improve and become a success, and then, I would have told Harvey to go find someone to buy me out."[23]

AS WITH *LITTLE ANNIE FANNY*, Kurtzman's partners on *Humbug* all came to his aid, providing material for *Help!*, even if, as in Al Jaffee's case, it was merely a reprint from their defunct magazine. Will Elder's primary contribution was his inspired artwork on Goodman Beaver, and there were a few other items. Jack Davis's art appears in nine issues. Arnold Roth's contributions appear in eleven in all, some of them substantial pieces. "Arnold Roth at Cape Canaveral" appeared in #17, and the following edition had his three-page "The Last Days of Burlesque," both very funny. He gave Kurtzman a bunch of his *Poor Arnold's Almanac* syndicated strips to reprint in #25, and did a "Beauty Contest" sketch report in the next.

The biggest flap in *Help!* history occurred in reaction to a piece in *Help!* #20 called "My First Golden Book of God," which began:

> In the beginning there was nothing.
> Nothing, nothing, nothing.
> And then God said, "Let there be light!"
> And there was still nothing.
> And then God took two sticks and
> rubbed them together.
> Look at God rub.
> Rub God, rub.
> And God made light and he looked at it and said,
> "This is good."
> God was conceited.
> Conceited, conceited, conceited.

The article worked its way through Adam and Eve, the Noah's Ark story, and Revelations. It generated a firestorm. The author of the controversial piece was a twenty-year-old UCLA student named Joel Siegel, the same person who ended up becoming the innocuous film critic for *Good Morning America* on ABC-TV for more than twenty-five years.

In the next issue, which was a seventy-five cent "Fifth Anniversary" special consisting entirely of fumetti reprints, editor Kurtzman wrote, "In our last issue we ran a piece called 'The Golden Book of God' in our Cartoon Gallery out of a west coast college magazine. So violent and overwhelming was the mail response, we are devoting three times the space we usually do for letters." Every letter condemned it in strong terms. Typical reactions were, "I hope you will ask God for forgiveness," and, "Whoever wrote this article was obviously mentally unbalanced." The strongest attack was a virtual call to action by a group called "Phoenix Citizens Against *Help!*" They wrote, "We hold our God sacred, and will allow no one to do such as you have done. The distributors of *Help!* here in our area, (Strong News) have taken the magazine off the racks, and Hearst is being notified of your sick story. Letters have been sent to Congressmen and Senators, protesting publications such as yours, and Simon and Schuster, publishers of the beautiful 'Golden Books,' have been notified of your abuse of their book title on your trash. Be very careful in the future." One wrote, "Your 'My First Golden Book of God' was disgusting. You have marred your interesting magazine and the integrity of Wonder Wart-Hog by its presence." It was the only humorous letter of the bunch. One wonders what might have happened had one of the highly disgruntled readers realized the "Statement of Ownership," printed adjacent to the letters, had the home addresses of both Warren and Kurtzman. The next issue's column began with a letter from university student Bill Sommer: "Gentlemen, that letters department was one of the funniest articles you have ever printed. All but two of the 'anti-'letters were a scream."

A startling photo of the Beatles retouched to show them with bald heads appeared on the cover of *Help!* #22. Just as the magazine was published, the British musical group was searching for a title for their second movie, which was to begin shooting in late February 1965. It's worth considering whether the film title *Help!* came after producer Walter Shenson, director Richard Lester, or the Beatles themselves, saw *Help!* #22. It seems likely someone showed the "bald Beatles" cover to members of the group itself. Beatles authority Mark Lewisohn has stated it was probably Shenson or Lester who came up with the new title after filming commenced. Once everyone agreed to call the movie *Help!*, a song by that title was needed. "Help!"—a John Lennon solo composition—was written on April 4, 1965. Lewisohn recently said, "I've not heard of any connection between *Help!* magazine and the film title, but Shenson probably knew it, and Lester, and maybe one or all of the Beatles. I've a feeling it was more than coincidence, but have no proof either way."[24] Kurtzman's view inclined the other way: "It was just a strange coincidence, but those coincidences happen constantly. I like to *think* that they stole the title."[25] It's possible, even probable.

The *Help!* letter department was generally entertaining even when there wasn't a flap. It included missives from a number of people who became notable cartoonists in the coming years. One was Jay Lynch, whose letters were printed in numerous issues, and whose contributions to the "Public Gallery" appeared in many issues too, even filling a full page in #22. The New

Help! #22 (January 1965).

Jersey–born cartoonist, who wrote from addresses in Florida and Illinois, would soon become one of the earliest members of the underground comix movement, along with another young cartoonist named Robert Crumb. In *Help!* #17, Crumb wrote:

> I have searched high and low, far and wide for the latest issue of *Help!* I know it has come out because a friend of mine in Ohio has one. I guess this means that another Kurtzman publication is doomed. I feel bad, I really do! If I were a millionaire I'd send you a few hundred-thousand dollars to keep *Help!* going.
> Don't give up Mr. Kurtzman, someday you'll go over big. It's only a matter of time. Till then, don't do anything rash or foolish, for god's sake!
> R. Crumb
> Dover, Delaware

Crumb had been a Kurtzman follower for a decade, and was already a fine cartoonist. "I was a teenage reject when, at fourteen, I discovered *Mad* and Kurtzman's work," he recalled. "[I] became . . . very devoted to the portrayal of America through Kurtzman's satire and the artwork of Elder, Wood, Davis and those guys. It's my biggest fanaticism about comics in my life. When I look at those old *Mad* magazines now, I still see them as the strongest visual statement about America that was made at that time."[26] On another occasion, he put it more succinctly: "The covers of *Mad* #11 and *Humbug* #2 changed the way I saw the world forever!"[27] He had been doing commercial art for American Greetings after leaving home. Crumb sent a two-page "Fritz the Cat" strip for the *Help!* Public Gallery—which was wordless and didn't reveal its protagonist's name.

"Crumb's work knocked me out," Kurtzman said.[28] He scheduled it for publication and requested more. Like Terry Gilliam before him, Crumb became so excited by this encouragement that he moved to New York and showed up at Kurtzman's door. Warren was also impressed by Crumb's work, and agreed to offer him money to go to Harlem and come back with enough sketches and cartoons to make up a multipage portfolio. Both "Fritz the Cat" and "Harlem" appeared in *Help!* #22 (January 1965) with a brief introduction by Kurtzman: "Our cartoon report has an interesting author. Out of the west has come a fast pen who goes by the unlikely name of Robert Crumb. This child of twenty-one, come east to seek his fortune, is a terror with an ink-loading Rapidograph." As impressive as Crumb's six-page "sketchbook" was in terms of the way it captured details of Harlem life, it was his unique point of view and the way it was expressed in humorous terms that put him in a category all his own.

Over a period of a month, Kurtzman and Crumb bonded on two levels: as cartoonists, and as mentor-student. In 1972, looking back, Crumb said, "Kurtzman's pretty perceptive. He's given me a lot of advice and told me a lot of predictions that later came true. Sometimes he'd tell me things that I would be surprised or offended by, but later I found them to be true."[29] On another occasion, he said, "[Kurtzman] really helped me and taught me a lot. I'd say he was the closest thing I had to a teacher and mentor in

R. Crumb's *Fritz the Cat* made an early appearance in *Help!* #22 (January 1965). Crumb shown "on assignment" in Sofia, Bulgaria, in *Help!* #25 (July 1965).

my life. In the middle '60s when I was in New York he was very helpful. He recognized my talent and gave me a lot of advice that was valuable, about the business as well as artistic techniques, and even about life and love."[30] The Kurtzmans invited Crumb over for dinner, but Robert and his wife Dana were soon off to Europe, financed by checks from American Greetings and Warren Publishing. Kurtzman wanted a sketchbook feature on Bulgaria. The Crumbs spent eight months there, with Dana holed up in their hotel room while Robert prowled the snowy streets of Sofia making sketches. He produced many more drawings than were needed. Kurtzman was impressed with his output, but wondered how they would fit into a humor magazine. He asked Crumb to add some jokes. The "Bulgaria" sketchbook saw print in *Help!* #25.

While Crumb was out of the country, Kurtzman storyboarded what turned out to be the best and funniest fumetti in *Help!* It was "Christopher's Punctured Romance," the title inspired by two famous silent films named *Tillie's Punctured Romance.* In this fumetti, a father becomes sexually obsessed with his daughter's Barbie doll. The dialogue by Dave Crossley was perfect, and it helped that a real comic-actor played the infatuated father. His name was John Cleese.

Cleese was a twenty-six-year-old British writer and actor-comedian who was performing on and off Broadway in New York. He appeared in his self-written *Cambridge Circus* in the city, and some of the sketches were performed on *The Ed Sullivan Show* in 1964. After *Cambridge Circus*, Cleese stayed in New York and became friends with Terry Gilliam. That led to his starring role in "Christopher's Punctured Romance." Cleese and Gilliam would become famous as members of Monty Python's Flying Circus, the British comedy troupe that became enormously popular in the early 1970s, which in turn propelled Gilliam to a career as a film director.[31]

"I think the thing that was maybe frustrating for Harvey, and the thing that I was able to do that he didn't do, was make movies," Gilliam later observed, "because his cartoons were really storyboards for movies. They were moving the camera, doing all the things, using sound effects, using all the skills of movie making. I think they taught me as much as anything about how to make movies. Another thing they taught me was the ability to go for perfection, go all the way, never stop, don't cut corners. If you're making a joke, if you're doing a parody, it's got to be perfect. It can't be 99 percent, it's got to be 100 percent there."[32] Gilliam went to Europe, jokingly announcing in the last issue that he was "being transferred to the European branch" of the magazine.

Robert and Dana were living in Cleveland after their return to America. Kurtzman contacted Crumb. Terry Gilliam was leaving, he said. Could Robert come back to New York and become the new associate editor of *Help!*? Crumb headed east, only to find when he arrived that *Help!* was closing its doors. According to Crumb, when he walked into the *Help!* office, he found Kurtzman looking forlorn as workmen were taking out file cabinets and desks. "What's happening?" Crumb asked. "Warren decided to fold the magazine," Kurtzman replied. "It wasn't making enough money. I'm sorry, I feel really bad about it." To try to compensate, he found Crumb jobs in New York in commercial art.[33]

Sales of *Help!* had never taken off. Warren discontinued it in order to concentrate on new magazines that were deliberately based on EC comics. *Creepy* and *Eerie* published horror stories with art by many of the EC artists (Wood, Williamson, Craig, Orlando and others), though the horror elements were toned down. Warren also added a magazine of war stories in the *Creepy* format, which, according to its editor and chief writer, was inspired by Harvey Kurtzman's *Two-Fisted Tales* and *Frontline Combat*. They also used some veteran artists from those comics, such as John Severin, Wallace Wood, Russ Heath and Reed Crandall.

The editor of Warren's *Blazing Combat* was Archie Goodwin, former fan artist (for Ron Parker's EC fanzine *Hoohah!* and others). Goodwin came up with the title, "just an exciting variation on *Frontline Combat*." While they didn't have the kind of rigorous research behind them, nor attempt to emulate Kurtzman storytelling techniques, the stories in *Blazing Combat* did have an antiwar point of view ("war is hell") that was the essence of the Kurtzman message at EC. Goodwin said, "If there'd never been a *Frontline Combat* or *Two-Fisted Tales* by Kurtzman, there's no way there could ever have been a *Blazing Combat*. His influence can't really be underestimated."[34]

Years later, Jim Warren maintained that Harvey Kurtzman had done "a magnificent job" editing *Help!* but added, philosophically, "We should never get too close to certain things that we love. We should view them from a distance. You view them from afar and you worship them and idolize them. But don't get close, because then you see the warts, and you see the seams that are bad. Suddenly your idol has feet of clay. And that happened with Harvey and me. He's still a genius and I respect him, but I didn't like Harvey Kurtzman as a person. He couldn't reconcile the fact that he had a deal with the guy who publishes *Famous Monsters*, and has people around him like Forry Ackerman. Harvey liked to associate with top talents, like Jack Davis, Arnold Roth and so on, and looked down on anyone who was less talented than he. He was a snob that way. *Help!* was never a 'class' magazine, and 'high class' was very important to Harvey."[35]

This time, Kurtzman wasn't in a funk over a magazine's demise. "We just couldn't make the thing . . . grow," he said, adding, "We didn't have much business success but we had a grand time making acquaintances and meeting people."[36] *Help!* gave Kurtzman a base of operations that was an intersection point for dozens, perhaps hundreds, of talented people. If military strategist Clausewitz's first principle was "have a secure base," then Kurtzman might have appended, "even an insecure base is better than none." While Kurtzman seldom said anything positive about Warren in succeeding years, he never disparaged *Help!* itself, at least not for the record. If he felt the early issues were disappointing, and that too much of it—especially the jokey photos—had little creative value, he had good reason to feel the later issues, the ones with Goodman Beaver and early work by Crumb, Shelton, Lynch and others, were much better. *Help!* had been an effective way of recharging his creative batteries, had a respectable five-year run, and brought him together with people who would be in and out of his life for decades. It demonstrated, once again, his uncanny ability to attract highly talented people to a project, some who went on to become major figures, such as Gloria Steinem, Terry Gilliam and Robert Crumb. Whether Kurtzman would ever edit a magazine that was both creatively and commercially successful (after *Mad*) remained an open question.

JOHN BENSON AND HIS FRIEND Bhob Stewart had done an in-depth interview with Bernard Krigstein, the first of its kind. *Talk with B. Krigstein* was published in a limited edition in 1963. It was only logical for Benson, a Kurtzman fan, to do the same with the creator of *Mad*. On August 20, 1965, Benson met with Harvey Kurtzman in his home on Audrey Avenue to interview him at length.

Despite his status at *Playboy*, Kurtzman had not been the subject of one of the magazine's lengthy interviews, nor would he ever be. Benson's interview was a sort of erudite equivalent, asking all the pertinent questions, and delving into the details of the work itself: *Hey Look!*," the EC war comics, *Mad* and the magazines that followed. Kurtzman was relaxed and forthcoming. The last issue of *Help!* had been published just a month earlier. When asked about its status, Kurtzman responded, "I'm not preparing any issues now. I feel certain that *Help!* is dead, but let's say that it's been temporarily suspended."[37]

Some of Kurtzman's most interesting responses pertain to his approach to his work in the 1960s, after he had moved past the material built up in his youth that he'd used instinctively in *Mad*. "When I started, I was loaded with all kinds of favorite notions which I, frankly, have used up. Now I turn to current experiences rather than history. I now try to work with the current scene, because that's all I have at this point. To me, it's fairly legitimate and fairy important. And sometimes it works out very well, and sometimes it works badly." He found creating humor in a more deliberate way challenging.

> It's very frustrating to me because I'm constantly trying to find the secret of how to hit it off every time. It would make life very easy for me if I could make a "Goodman Goes Playboy" every time. Humor is treacherous that way. You try to do whatever magic it is that knocks your reader out and you discover that the process that makes for humorous stuff is so complex that you don't even know what the hell it is you're doing when you're doing a good job. But if you start questioning and analyzing yourself too much, it can destroy you.

Despite this, he said, "The deeper I get into the business of whatever the hell it is I'm doing, the more I enjoy it. I enjoy my work very much, more than ever."

Benson asked his view of the efforts of Bernard Krigstein and others in 1952 to unionize comic book artists. Kurtzman said, "unionizing cartoonists . . . would have been great for cartoonists" if it could have gotten them better rates. But when Benson suggested that better rates "could have done a lot for the art" because it would give artists the freedom to spend more time on their work, Kurtzman disagreed.

> I think the rates that the artists get are terrible, and I'm all for the union in that respect. But saying that it would improve the comics is like saying that unionizing the coal miners would have improved coal. Can you tell me of one medium where the art has been improved by unionization? A workman's standards of living and workman's income are improved by unionization. But art? Unionization never affects art. How could it improve art?

Giving actors union scale doesn't make for better movies, he said. "What improves the art in mass media is if the masses want the art of the media improved. If they don't want it improved, it's not going to improve." *A Talk with Harvey Kurtzman* ran twenty-four mimeographed pages. Kurtzman wrote to Benson, "The thing reads great! But you must realize that for certain obvious reasons, I take more than a casual passing interest in this thing."[38] Benson also published a portfolio of ten of the best *Hey Look!* pages via photo offset, sold as a set.

Shortly after talking with Benson, Kurtzman was also interviewed by J. P. C. James for Chicago-based *Rogue* magazine for its December 1965 issue. A longform interview in a national magazine (with a circulation in hundreds of thousands) was something accorded few—if any—of Kurtzman's peers, although Al Capp was interviewed the same month in *Playboy*. To provide visuals to go along with the piece, he posed for a session with Ray Komorski, who did much of the photography for the publication. One shot has him sitting on the ground in front of copies of *Two-Fisted Tales, Frontline Combat, Mad, Trump, Humbug* and *Help!* fanned out on the carpet before him. At forty, Kurtzman had lost all his hair but the fringes around the edges, and shaved that off for these shots. He's wearing a dark sweater over a white shirt and is barefooted. He's thin and his skin tone looks dark against the white shirt and pants. Terry Gilliam wrote of his *Mad* mentor, "He was like a beautifully polished acorn, slightly brown and hard and nice."[39]

In another shot from this session, Kurtzman has shed the sweater. He's sitting in a chair with one knee up, hands together with fingers intertwined. His eyes are cast downward. His nephew Adam later said that Kurtzman had beautiful hands and feet. They are on full display here. He looks ascetic, monk-like, yet he's smiling as if a new creative idea has just come to him. The caption under the photo reads, "I sit around and I wait for inspiration. When it comes, I get going. That feels very good."

KURTZMAN'S FRIENDS SOMETIMES brought him lucrative work. Jack Davis was involved with the Rankin/Bass film and animation studio in 1965 on the movie *Willy McBean and His Magic Machine*. Then he was hired to do character designs for the studio's new stop-motion animated movie based on the concept of Universal's *House of Frankenstein*, where all the classic monsters got together for a grand monster-fest. Davis's job was to design the puppet versions of the Frankenstein monster, Dracula, the Wolfman, the Mummy and others. It was to be distributed by Joseph E. Levine. Len Korobkin wrote a screenplay called *The Monster Movie*, and when it was felt that more comic touches were needed, Jack Davis suggested Kurtzman. The idea of hiring the creator of *Mad* appealed to Arthur Rankin. Davis may have shown him the parodies of Frankenstein that Kurtzman had written for *Mad* and *Humbug*.

Photographs taken by Ray Komorski to accompany the
Kurtzman interview in *Rogue* magazine (December 1965).

It's unknown whether Kurtzman had seen earlier Rankin/Bass productions such as *The Daydreamer*, but if he did, he wasn't impressed. "I wrote for them like one evening and made about $3,000, and then they threw it all out the window and they put my name on it. It's totally irrelevant to anything I do or did."[40] The Rankin/Bass film has several comic touches that obviously came from Kurtzman, most notably a reference to *veeblefetzers* which was a Yiddish slang term he used in *Mad* ("Gasoline Valley" and elsewhere). Notwithstanding his statement, his contributions to the screenplay were sufficient to entitle him to credit as its cowriter. One change came from Rankin rather than Kurtzman: retitling the movie *Mad Monster Party.*

The quick $3,000 helped pay for a European vacation taken by the Kurtzmans and the Davises in July 1966. Adele and Dena went over by boat. "I wouldn't fly at the time, and neither would Dena," Adele remembered. "So we went over on the boat, and we had a great time. Jack and Harvey flew over and met us in London. We took a train to Paris because we were meeting René Goscinny."[41]

Unbeknownst to Kurtzman, Goscinny had become an immensely successful editor and writer of comics. "I kept a running conversation with him when he was in France [but] I never had any idea of what René was doing," Kurtzman said, "or maybe I chose never to listen."[42] Goscinny met the foursome at the train station and treated them to famous and expensive restaurants in Paris such as La Tour d'Argent. Kurtzman didn't understand Goscinny's largesse until René showed him the piles of Astérix albums in bookshops. Adele recalled, "We drove to Paris, stayed there for a while, and then drove to Frankfurt. Harvey had an old friend from the army in Frankfurt. His name was Harlin Althen. He and his wife, a former opera singer, took us up and down the Rhine, and we just had a marvelous time."[43]

WORK CONTINUED on *Little Annie Fanny*, Kurtzman's creative priority, but he needed another income stream to replace his *Help!* salary. He let Harold Hayes, now editor of *Esquire*, know that he was available to do more work for the magazine. Since Hayes was looking for someone to produce photo spreads on men's fashion and drinks, he gave Kurtzman the job. Walter Bernard, a young assistant art editor, remembered those projects. "What Harvey did was create scenarios to showcase fashions in an entertaining way. He would do all sorts of wacky things. Harold gave him pretty much free reign."[44] Kurtzman would work up some storyboards or layouts, hire a photographer and the people to appear in it, and then produce it on his own.

Barbara Nessim, a young New York artist who had starred in a fumetti for *Help!*, assisted Kurtzman with at least one of them. "It was some sort of 'Drinking Man's Guide to the South,'" she recalled. "It was shot at locations that I found in the Florida Keys, the Plantation House in New Orleans, and the Camelback Mountain in Arizona. Harvey directed and Harry Stevenson was the photographer. We traveled and shot over a two-week period. It was so much fun to be with Harvey. We had such a good time and became good friends. I stayed in touch with him after that."[45] Nessim became an important artist in the city, an instructor at The School of Visual Arts (Meredith Kurtzman was one of her students) and eventually an administrator at Parsons School of Design for many years.

In the mid-1960s, Kurtzman was trekking to Chicago once a month, sometimes staying several days as he, Elder and others artists (Roth, Jaffee, Heath) finished up an episode of *Little Annie Fanny*, and needed the benefit of Hefner's immediate input and approvals in order to meet a deadline. Hefner confirmed, "There were occasions in which Harv and Will came to Chicago and worked around the clock at the mansion against deadlines. It would sometimes be the last thing in an issue to close. Harv was a perfectionist, and his attention to detail was remarkable. The amount of time and attention that he gave to the feature is probably greater than he gave to anything else he ever did in his career."[46]

The Playboy Mansion was a cavernous, four-story, brick and limestone house built in 1899. It sat behind an ornate iron fence at 1340 North State Parkway just two blocks from Lake Michigan. A brass plaque on the front door read in Latin, "Si Non Oscillas, Noli Tintinnare," which means, "If You Don't Swing, Don't Ring." The mansion's showpiece was its indoor swimming pool and grotto. Many of the bedrooms had marble fireplaces. Kurtzman was both attracted to and repulsed by the place. "Harvey could see all the humor and the decadence," Arnold Roth recalled. "He was against the overdone hedonism involved, I guess is the fairest way to describe it. But here he was in the throes of it. Yet he was like the moth with the flame. It was the huge attraction of . . . that exact stuff that went with *Playboy*: the glamour, the wealth, all the things that he was a great satirist about. And yet he had an attraction to it."[47] Though Kurtzman believed in morality and moral behavior, he also admitted that, like Goodman Beaver at the end of "Goodman Goes Playboy," he was tempted by the devil. Roth recounted a conversation he had with Kurtzman when they were in Chicago at the mansion:

We were sharing a room, and Harvey said to me, "I don't understand it. I come out here every month. I never get laid. Herb Roth"—I think was his name, a novelist from San Francisco—he said, "He came out here for three days, and he got laid four times." I said, "Harvey, he *wanted* to get laid." We had these two big beds and I said, "If Miss January fell through the ceiling and landed on your face you wouldn't get laid. You'd go down and complain, 'What kind of place is this?'" He said, "Well, I was just thinking."[48]

Hearing Roth tell this story, Jaffee—who was aware of the same conflict in Kurtzman—added, "Later on I have a feeling that he did get involved. He was a complicated guy."[49]

Little Annie Fanny stories dealt with all manner of topics and trends of the day: the Ku Klux Klan, gun collectors, space exploration, the James Bond craze (one of the most striking episodes), popular music, surfing (with some panels remarkably rendered by Frank Frazetta), television executives, pop art, high camp and more. One Annie episode promised to be special. Hefner rallied his troops to produce an entire issue of *Playboy* that parodied itself. Kurtzman and Elder duly created an episode of *Little Annie Fanny* that followed Annie on a tour of Hefner's mansion. The entire issue was reportedly completed. Then Hefner had second thoughts and scrapped it all.[50]

In 1966, Playboy Press issued *Playboy's Little Annie Fanny*, the first collected edition of the stories. It was an oversized paperback, 10 ½" by 14," with 128 pages plus covers. It used high quality color printing on pages that were substantially larger than those of the magazine, showing off the artwork to maximum advantage. It was a boon to Kurtzman and Elder, who split 50 percent of the book's substantial royalties.

Kurtzman turned forty-two in 1966. Without *Help!* as a business and social nexus, he might have drifted entirely out of touch with youth culture if it hadn't been for a group of up-and-coming cartoonists for whom he was an icon. Just as he had made a number of them welcome in *Help!*, they gave him entrée to their world.

Above: Little Annie Fanny made her debut in *Playboy* (October 1961). Below: James Bond encounters Annie in a story published at the height of Bond-mania, in the January 1965 issue.

Climactic page from "Christopher's Punctured Romance," perhaps the funniest fumetti to appear in *Help!* magazine. John Cleese played a father whose lust for his daughter's Barbie doll overcomes him. (*Help!* #24, May 1965.)

Gilbert Shelton's Wonder Wart-Hog in *Help!* #26 (September 1961), the magazine's last issue.

PART THREE:

"Kurtzman was (and is) the closest thing to a hero I'll ever have. Had he not existed, I'd be a dull, humorless lout working in a muffler shop somewhere, and so would practically everyone I know. I shudder to think how horrible the world would be today without that which Harvey Kurtzman begat!"[1]

—*Daniel Clowes*

23.

CHILDREN OF *MAD*

THE REBEL COMEDIANS OF THE 1950s such as Mort Sahl and Lenny Bruce satirized societal oppression and injustice for an adult audience. In *Mad*, Harvey Kurtzman did his comedic truthtelling in a medium read largely by youth. Popular culture historian M. Thomas Inge wrote, "Comic books were our special province, and while moral guardians and political leaders wanted to take them away from us, Kurtzman gave them back in ways we would not forget. He made them a part of our intellectual development and imparted a satiric sense of justice and reality that would not allow us to accept the truisms of the world without questioning them and their validity for us and for society."[1] By the mid-1960s, most of the readers of the Kurtzman-edited issues of *Mad* had reached their majority. They were in college, the job market, the Peace Corps or the armed forces.

Many of them participated in the antiwar demonstrations that became larger and more frequent as the US escalated its military involvement in Vietnam. R. C. Harvey wrote, "Through all the years of *Mad*, Kurtzman's influence on the American public was incalculable. Who can say but what the Vietnam War protest among American youth was not in some way inspired by the satire in *Mad*?"[2] As cartoonist Art Spiegelman put it, "*Mad* had at least as great an impact as pot and LSD on the shape of the Sixties."[3] That influence can't be objectively quantified, but the rise of the counterculture was predicated on questioning the status quo, something promulgated by *Mad*. (The term "counterculture" itself wasn't in wide usage until 1969, with the publication of Theodore Roszak's best-selling book, *The Making of a Counter Culture*.)

As *Help!* breathed its last, two underground newspapers provided new outlets for young, idiosyncratic cartoonists who had no desire to work in mainstream comics. They were the *Los Angeles Free Press* and the *East Village Other* (*EVO*) out of New York City. The underground press grew rapidly after 1965, as did other venues of self-expression (such as psychedelic rock concert posters) that led to a whole new category of publication: underground comix. Many of the talented men and women who created the comix, mostly in their early to mid-twenties, were *Mad* and Kurtzman fans, or more accurately, fanatics. Indeed, *Help!* had been a kind of incubator for several founders of this independent publishing movement. Kurtzman responded to their work, and by publishing them, gave some of them their first professional credit. He later acknowledged, "[*Help!*] came slightly ahead of the underground press, but we printed many of the underground press heroes. That is, we printed Shelton and Crumb, and . . . Skip Williamson and a whole group of people."[4] Their appreciation for Kurtzman's work and *Mad* was emphatic.

"The core of what I like in comic art is *Mad* comics," Jay Lynch said.[5] "When we were kids, we thought we'd grow up to work for Kurtzman's *Mad*. Underground comix was just kind of an extension of *Mad*, or what *Mad* would have been if Kurtzman came around initially in 1968 rather than 1952."[6] He added, "In a sense, *Help!* was probably the first underground comic."[7]

Skip Williamson recalled, "I followed Kurtzman assiduously. I stalked him from my little perch in Canton, Missouri. I knew exactly what he was up to. I was one of the Kurtzmaniacs. It was an obsession with a bunch of us. Kurtzman was my hero, the guy that made me want to be a cartoonist and informed the kind of cartoons I would do."[8] Having a cartoon printed in *Help!* #8 when he was just sixteen years old was a formative event in Williamson's life.

Art Spiegelman said, "The first *Mad* comic books by Harvey Kurtzman . . . changed my life. That's what made me become a cartoonist."[9] Cartoonist Wendel Allan Pugh said, "[Kurtzman] deserves credit for the comic book revolution. Everyone working seems to have used his inspiration as a jumping-off place. I personally feel he, more than anyone else, started the whole thing."[10] Lee Marrs put it, "If all the influences on comix could be distilled into one delicious drop, its name would be Harvey Kurtzman."[11]

Kurtzman was both pleased and puzzled by these reactions. Mark James Estren quoted Kurtzman in *A History of Underground Comics*:

Fifteen years later you start running into these people who read your stuff, and you find they have been deeply affected by your stuff, they *have* been. But in what way you don't know. They haven't run out and hung Richard Nixon as a result. But I think that's the way art—if I can put that designation of my stuff—that's the way art will affect people. It will open up new attitudes which don't necessarily do anything specific, but nevertheless make for a more sensitive or sensitized world. I was very serious and very worried about living and life and politics, very involved in "reality" humor in my work and in the material of others. I think all of us collectively helped to sensitize the young people. I still don't know whether it's good or bad. I like to think it's for the eventual good: a sensitive society is capable of so much more.[12]

This statement, which refers to opening up new attitudes through art, acknowledged—tentatively—that *Mad* and his other magazines contributed to a zeitgeist that manifested as the counterculture movement. One thing is certain: *Mad*, more than any other publication, inspired the birth of underground comix.

In 1967, Robert Crumb's work appeared in Brian Zahn's tabloid *Yarrowstalks* in Philadelphia. Skip Williamson moved to Chicago and teamed up with Jay Lynch to publish an underground tabloid, the *Chicago Mirror*. Gilbert Shelton was art director for the Vulcan,

Zap Comix #1

the first psychedelic rock venue in Austin, Texas, producing psychedelic posters in the style of those coming out of San Francisco. *Zap Comix* #1 (February 1968) by Crumb was sold out of a baby carriage in the Haight-Ashbury district. It had the wonderful "Mr. Natural 'Visits the City'" and "Whiteman." Lynch and Williamson decided to convert *The Chicago Mirror* into an underground comic book, and invited Crumb to work on it with them. Before long, Lynch, Williamson, Crumb and a handful of others—Kurtzmaniacs, all—produced *Bijou Funnies* #1 (October 1968), more or less Chicago's "answer" to *Zap Comix*.

Kurtzman's fans and former protégés sent their publications to him. He found them fascinating, and, as usual, responded with comments and encouragement. When Art Spiegelman later referred to him as "the Godfather of underground comix," Kurtzman said, in his typically self-effacing manner, "well . . . maybe the brother-in-law."[13] He was never sure of the connection between *Help!* and the undergrounds. In 1974, he speculated, "Probably the kind of thing *Help!* did that underground comix continue to do was 'reality stuff.' We were really into reality stuff when nobody else was doing reality. I guess that was the bond."[14] The cover of *Mad* #16 did carry the caption "Comics go Underground," but the *underground* in underground comix was doubtless a carryover from underground newspapers.

MEANWHILE, KURTZMAN became more firmly captive of what was then being pejoratively referred to as the Establishment. He bought a larger home in Mount Vernon, having heard that the owners were in a hurry to move and willing to sell low. The "bargain" cost $45,000, an upscale price at the time. The Kurtzman family moved in mid-December, 1966. His rationale was that by establishing the lifestyle, he would "think bigger" and be able to bring in more money.

"When I bought the house I was conscious of a new attitude. I decided to be reckless in another way. I decided to throw myself into debt. The theory being that I would then have to hustle myself . . . out of it. It didn't work that way. The theory sounded neat on the surface, but it got me deeper into the trap."[15] Moving out of the Audrey Avenue house was necessary. Liz had outgrown her "postage stamp" bedroom. Sharing with Meredith wasn't practical, not only because of the seven-year age difference, but because the regular-sized bedrooms were so small. Still, Kurtzman might have found something larger that wasn't as expensive. Taking on hefty mortgage payments by buying the new house tied him more tightly to Hefner, and there was no looking back.

"I used to kid him about that stuff," Crumb said. "He was just part of that World War II generation. Those guys didn't see materialism as being artificial. They saw it as enjoying the fruits of your labor. There was no hypocrisy about it."[16] But there was a motivation apart from practical considerations. To him, a bigger home in a more affluent neighborhood symbolized success.

While not in any way ostentatious, the Kurtzmans' new brick and stucco home, with its distinctive curved turret in front, gave an impression of financial stability and achievement. The neighborhood, the northern part of Mount Vernon known as Fleetwood, was classier and more sequestered than were the working-class environs of Audrey Avenue. The house sat back from the street, had a substantial front lawn, and was ensconced amid tall trees and lush shrubbery. The living room was spacious enough that one could forget there was a piano at one end. From there you stepped out into a covered porch on the side of the house. The backyard with its big elm shade tree and fishpond was ringed with azaleas, rhododendrons and forsythia. There were more and bigger bedrooms, and the third floor attic had room for a substantially larger studio-office. In general, the layout was more commodious and better for entertaining. Kurtzman wrote Gahan Wilson, only partly tongue in cheek, in May 1967:

> Listen, on one of your sojourns to the Big Apple, why don't you come by with the wife, on the way back to the bird farm and have din-din in exurbia with drinkypoos and mean kids running around. I live in a real swell house now. I mean it's really swell. I look out at my manicured lawn through my picture window and I see the neatly clipped azalea bushes blooming and the neighbor's cocker spaniel romping on the front brick path and I get a rich feeling of wanting to commit suicide. Ooh, have I got overhead.[17]

The move didn't involve a change in schools for Meredith, although she would have welcomed one. She hated Mount Vernon High School, as did Liz when she was old enough to attend. "I was in fourth grade," Liz recalled. "I remember saying to my father, 'If we get that house, I'll be like a princess living in a castle,' because of the round turret on the front."[18]

Pete was thirteen. He had been attending the ARC School and Day Training Center in Westchester for four years. In 1967, the Association of Retarded Citizens pulled out of its agreement to teach students like Pete, leaving the Association for Mentally Ill Children of Westchester, Inc. (AMIC) to sponsor its own separate school. New York educator Bill Barnes recalled, "Adele was the editor of an AMIC newsletter that we put out for a while, and Harvey designed the logo, an image of a child sitting with his hands around his knees inside a pentagon, with a helping hand reaching toward him. Adele gave a spectacular interview to the *New York Times* in 1967, during the fight to make sure the new school would receive funding, and it really helped attract attention to our cause." After much fundraising and searching for a new location, the newly named Clearview School was established and began functioning in January 1968. Barnes, who became the school's director, said, "Harvey and Adele were very involved in making this happen."[19]

The same year, another issue in Kurtzman's life was resolved. After ten years, his lawsuit against EC Publications was settled. A seemingly unrelated act by Kurtzman brought about its conclusion.

Kurtzman was always considering ideas for new projects. One of them was a visual history of the comic strips and comic books, which evolved out of discussions with Woody Gelman, editor and art director at Topps Chewing Gum. They'd known each other for some time. Gelman had contributed to *Help!* in 1964. Not much later, they began planning a book about the history of comics, possibly inspired by the publication of Jules Feiffer's book *The Great Comic Book Heroes* in 1965. Gelman, co-creator of *Bazooka Joe* and the *Mars Attacks* cards, was setting up his own side venture called Nostalgia Press to publish books on popular culture favorites of the past. Kurtzman began gathering data and making lists of projected contents. He envisioned it not so much as an all-inclusive history, but a tribute to comics that he personally enjoyed and admired.

Toward that end, Kurtzman sought permission from National Periodical Publications to reprint parts of their Golden Age comics in the book. National refused because they had acquired *Mad*, and weren't about to help someone who was suing them. Frank Jacobs wrote, "National felt the case should be settled out of court. Gaines and Martin Scheiman did not agree, but in late 1966 Scheiman died and Gaines lost his main pillar of support. Eventually, he settled, mostly because he no longer owned *Mad* and felt that it wasn't right to involve National in a fight that wasn't theirs."[20] According to the settlement agreement dated April 25, 1968, Kurtzman would receive a total of $8,500.00, and in exchange would cede any and all rights to his work for EC Publications. The sum, like most settlements, was for much less than the true amount owing. After ten years, Kurtzman was happy to get anything, even just half of that amount, since the other half went to his attorneys.

EVEN THOUGH *LITTLE ANNIE FANNY* was hardly a revolutionary strip (like some of those in underground comix), it came to the attention of J. Edgar Hoover and precipitated another entry into Harvey Kurtzman's file at the Federal Bureau of Investigation. An internal memo by agent M. A. Jones, dated April 24, 1967, reported:

The current issue of *Playboy* magazine includes a comic strip entitled *Little Annie Fanny* written by Harvey Kurtzman and Will Elder. A squad of FBI agents led by "the Chief" (obviously referring to the Director) investigates the kidnapping with the help of Little Annie Fanny. This highly satirical strip attempts to poke fun at the Director and the Bureau's well-established reputation for loyalty, patriotism and high moral behavior. Its ridiculous exaggerations indirectly compliment the character and ideals of the FBI. Typical of the "college humor" tone of irreverence so flagrant in this article is the gross disrespect shown for the American flag.

The flag isn't depicted in the story, but at one point "the chief" (Hoover) barks, "Agent Trueblue, have room service send up a small flag to my room. If anyone wants me, I'll be upstairs, pledging allegiance." The memo continued in the same sycophantic vein: "Recognizing the notoriously low caliber of the whole *Playboy* publication and its staff, this attempt to belittle the Bureau can in effect be considered an unintended compliment. In view of the known hostility and well-established low character of this publication, there would appear to be no advantage to the Bureau in protesting the *Little Annie Fanny* [story], any acknowledgment from the Bureau merely conveying an air of dignity which is completely nonexistent with this publication." The interoffice memo also references the earlier investigation of Kurtzman's EC war comics, noting that they weren't found to urge insubordination, disloyalty, mutiny or refusal of duty by any member of the military or naval forces of the US. Director Hoover's policy of investigating alleged anti-American activity (with the threat of governmental retaliation) had, by the '60s, expanded to encompass any less-than-flattering media portrayal of Hoover himself.

KURTZMAN WAS ATTRACTED to underground comix by the cartoonists themselves and the unfettered nature of their work. He encountered many of them when Crumb opened up the pages of *Zap Comix* to artists such as S. Clay Wilson, Robert Williams, Spain Rodriguez and two artists with reputations as psychedelic poster designers, Victor Moscoso and Rick Griffin. At first, some of it, such as S. Clay Wilson's grotesque images of depraved sex, initially repulsed him. Yet he found himself returning to Wilson's work, eventually realizing that he was a deceptively talented writer. "I think [Wilson] works like Crumb," he said. "They're both guided by the gut rather than by their conscious calculations. And they practically record their dreams. That's all daydream stuff that Wilson does."[21]

In the 1950s, Kurtzman felt an affinity for the Beat writers. Now he felt a similar kinship with the underground cartoonists: "I'm tortured by the same devils. I can talk about them [the cartoonists] to a certain extent because I identify with them. By profession I regard myself as a professional [nudge], a troublemaker. I'm sure I'm driven by my own internal acids and frustrations, and . . . I think that troublemakers are necessary. You have to keep pointing out the bad things. Although I don't believe in the violence that I think is so fashionable today, I certainly subscribe to change and to serious thinking."[22]

He participated in a "jam" project (a collaboration of several artists on a single piece or story) in 1969. Gilbert Shelton was visiting New York and staying with Kim Deitch in his Second Avenue storefront, a stone's throw from the *East Village Other* office. Calls started coming in for Shelton from Kurtzman. He was planning a *Little Annie Fanny* about the underground press, so an invitation to contribute to a jam comic strip at the *EVO* was the perfect opportunity to research the subject.

Robert Crumb was also in town, and was invited to participate. The artists in the order of their appearance (in their own individual panels) were Gilbert Shelton, Simon Deitch, Kim Deitch, Roger Brand, Spain Rodriguez, Ralph Reese, an English *EVO* staff artist named Hetty, Alan Shenker, Robert Crumb and Harvey Kurtzman. Then most of them contributed something to the final, large panel. The title of the piece was "Come the Revolution." Kim Deitch said, "It was a hodgepodge, all held together by a poem mostly written by Gilbert. I say mostly because I was there while he wrote the thing, and I wrote my own hunk of it. 'Come the Revolution' is a historical curio at most."[23] Deitch remembered that Kurtzman was in high spirits, even though he didn't smoke the joints that were being passed around. Skip Williamson later said of Kurtzman, "He'd already established what he was and didn't need to be what we were."[24] (Actually, Kurtzman had tried marijuana, but said it never got him high.) Deitch recalled, "Kurtzman was an excellent guest. He was definitely 'on' that night, a good-natured raconteur."[25] Kurtzman obtained the necessary background material for the *Little Annie Fanny* episode, and "Come the Revolution" ran as a centerfold in the *East Village Other* that fall.

Kurtzman couldn't afford to work for the kind of pay (often very little) available in underground comix. In a panel discussion around this time, he acknowledged that he received offers from the underground press and wished that he could accept them. "I can't," he said, "because I've got my own problems, but it seems like it's wide open for something very exciting to happen. See, there's something that happened to me and I suspect it happens to a lot of people as you travel on through life. I've collected a large family, and . . . I find I'm more restricted than when I was single and had no family."[26]

A new member of the Kurtzman clan was born on April 15, 1969. Harvey and Adele named their third daughter Cornelia, who they nicknamed Nellie, after Little Nell in Charles Dickens' *The Old Curiosity Shop.* Among other family developments that year was the return of Edith Perkes from Florida, after the passing of Abraham Perkes in October. Dan Perkes, Kurtzman's brother, also returned to the New York area. Perkes, who worked for the Associated Press, had been stationed for years in South Dakota. Now he was able to move his family (a wife and two sons) east. Kurtzman saw them from time to time, such as at his annual Fourth of July barbecues.

The Kurtzmans threw a holiday party on Independence Day each year, a tradition that originated when they were still on Audrey Avenue. In addition to their relatives, Harvey and Adele invited many colleagues from the comics and magazine fields, such as Elder, Jaffee, Davis, Roth, Heath and their families, and there were also neighbors, their daughters' friends and others. Kurtzman knew a lot of people, and each year there were new faces in evidence. The raucous gatherings were a way for the Kurtzmans to annually celebrate not only the holiday, but another year of camaraderie with the people in their world. Adele arranged the food on tables in the covered porch. Once one emerged from the porch, Harvey was on the right tending the barbecue, serving hamburgers and hotdogs. The backyard was fairly level, perfect for badminton. The elm tree provided shade for those who wanted it. Food and drink was consumed, and as it got dark, backyard sparklers and fireworks capped the day. Those parties continued for the rest of Kurtzman's life, rain or shine.

WILL ELDER OFTEN VISITED the Kurtzman home for *Little Annie Fanny* script conferences. The two of them liked to lounge on the porch, where Kurtzman acted out the story for Elder, just as he had with *Mad* and Goodman Beaver.

From late 1962 through 1970, Harvey Kurtzman and Will Elder (and collaborators) produced a total of 217 pages of *Little Annie Fanny.* Their production slowed considerably in the latter part of the decade, with only eighty-four pages turned out from 1967 through 1970. Working with the hands-on Hefner, even more of a perfectionist than Kurtzman, proved to be difficult. Knowing that the editor would review every joke and visual gag had Kurtzman second- and third-guessing himself. Even so, when the scripted roughs came back from Chicago, there were endless corrections. It was a laborious process, and there was many a deadline crisis along the way. The feature was still reasonably inventive and visually vibrant, but Kurtzman was tiring of the character and running out of ideas. It became more difficult to come up with a story that fulfilled the "Annie-must-be-nude" requirement, while satirizing the latest trends in popular culture and American society. Adele recalled, "There were times when he would finish a story and say, 'This is the last idea I'm ever going to have. This is the end.'"27

He reached out to Larry Siegel, who had by that time become a linch-pin writer at *Mad*, and also wrote for *Playboy*. Siegel was willing to help for a comparatively small sum. "At a certain point, Harvey had that *Little Annie Fanny* thing going in *Playboy*, which I always hated. I don't like to hurt Harvey; I loved him. But let's face facts, *Little Annie Fanny* really was very childish in a way." Siegel described how the collaboration worked in an interview by Grant Geissman in *Squa Tront* magazine. "[Harvey would] give me a script and he'd tell me to punch it up. So I would go over it and I'd try to throw jokes at it. Then we'd get together up at his house and we'd discuss it, rework it, and then we'd just kind of put it over. I think I was getting $150 a page, which wasn't too bad in the 1960s. Just like found money. And I really didn't have to do very much. Put maybe a half hour or an hour in the script. A joke is a joke, what the hell."28

Hefner was concerned about the slowing production rate of Kurtzman's feature. As early as July 1968, he asked A. C. Spectorsky (then Senior Vice President of Hefner's HMH Publishing, Inc.) to see what he could do to correct the problem. Spectorsky wrote Kurtzman a four-page letter iden-tifying what he thought were the reasons why production of *Annie Fanny* had slowed, and strongly recommending what to do about it. "As you know, I am appalled at the committee nature of your efforts," he wrote. "It seems to me an adequate way to go about planning a new Talmud, but it seems almost designed on purpose to preclude delightful, sharp, topical, satirical humor."29 He felt the chief problem was the writing, and said he thought Larry Siegel's work seemed to be going in the opposite direction of Kurtzman's. He also decried Kurtzman's habit of wanting approvals and input virtually every step of the way, which was taking an inordinate amount of time going back and forth. Then he made his main point:

Perhaps the centrally operative [insight] is that you are suppressing your own creativity, consciously or not, and are trying to be an entrepreneur of creativity. You hire and wheel and deal in concepts, storyboards, art work, scripts, etc., and consume so much time and energy in so doing that you have little of either left for your true *métier*, which is as a creative man, not a business man. I suggest you are not a natural businessman . . . and that even if you were a good one, it would be a bad scene to sacrifice your talent to business.[30]

His solutions were that Kurtzman needed to do more creative work himself, stating, "You're unsurpassed at it." Second, acknowledging that it was necessary to have another writer along with Kurtzman, Spectorsky wanted to help find that writer. (He suggested Mel Brooks and Woody Allen, among others.) Finally, he wanted Kurtzman to allow the editorial staff of *Playboy* to make suggestions for story ideas: "Even if no ideas from editorial prove useful, one or more of them may lead you to a concept you might not have had before."[31] He added that the visual side of the strip was in fine shape, and that there was no danger of *Annie* being dropped.

Kurtzman wrote back indicating he didn't disagree with Spectorsky's points, and that he would act on the suggestions. "I must admit that you have surprising insight into the problems of [*Little Annie Fanny*]. Your unusual understanding gives me much comfort, and I mean this sincerely. I'd like to move ahead with plans as rapidly as possible."[32] Spectorsky's criticism of Kurtzman wanting approvals along the way doesn't acknowledge the chief reason for it: to avoid putting a lot of work into something only to have an avalanche of alterations required by Hefner. Ultimately, Ray Russell was invited to assist with the writing, with Brooks and Allen too busy with their own burgeoning careers.

Some have speculated that Kurtzman unconsciously complicated the process and created problems when things were going smoothly because he was afraid of success. Larry Siegel said, "He [was] self-destructive, sort of like a masochistic streak, the 'death wish' kind of thing. There's confidence, ego, but there's also a little self-loathing there somewhere—the 'I don't deserve to succeed.' We all have that sort of thing going, all mixed up with everything else, and I think Harvey had a certain amount of it."[33] Perhaps his upbringing in the sway of Communist parents created an inner conflict between wanting to get rich and feeling that if he did get rich, he must have been cheating. Thus, he spent more time on projects as they started to pay more.

Kurtzman also storyboarded and directed two new fumetti strips for *Playboy*. The first was a parody of Michelangelo Antonioni's movie *Blow-Up* titled "Blowout," starring Michael J. Pollard, who had received an Academy Award nomination for his role in *Bonnie and Clyde* (1967). It appeared in the magazine's August 1968 issue. The second was "The Good, the Bad, and the Garlic," a Western starring Tony Randall. Kurtzman had to cancel an advertised appearance as guest of honor at the 1969 New York comic con because it conflicted with the only days Randall could participate in the project. Unlike the fumettis in *Help!*, these were in color. In making them, Kurtzman was able to indulge his fantasy of directing a motion picture.

> Maybe the height of fumetti-making came when I did them for *Playboy*. We did this one cowboy story. I had Tony Randall and a cast of thousands, costumes and a storyboarded script. Up to that point, I was doing everything Hitchcock did. Then we would shoot the still pictures, and that was fun. And I think the reason directing is fun for me and anybody else is, you create a fantasy on paper, your own fantasy, and then you live it. It's like playing cops and robbers when you were a kid. You're living your imaginings, and that's why directing is so fascinating.[34]

Of all the projects he had ever done, Kurtzman said the *Playboy* fumettis were "the most fun." The first one was good and the second one was even better. Reader reaction was positive. Unfortunately, they were expensive to produce. The idea that Kurtzman would do fumettis on a regular basis for the magazine, along with *Annie Fanny*, was dropped.

"UNDERGROUND PRESS," THE *ANNIE* STORY that used his experience in the *East Village Other* office as background, appeared in early 1970. The opening splash panel shows Ralphie Towzer holding a copy of the *East Village Mother*, which has Gilbert Shelton's *The Fabulous Furry Freak Brothers* on one side and Robert Crumb's *Angelfood McSpade* on the other. Shelton and Crumb created original one-page sequences with slightly skewed artwork to match the tilt of the newspaper pages.

The emergence of the underground press was just one aspect of the turbulent 1960s that became grist for the *Little Annie Fanny* mill. Another was Feminism, or as it was generally called at the time, Women's Liberation. As early as 1963, the unexpected popularity of Betty Friedan's book *The Feminine Mystique* was indicative of the dissatisfaction felt by many women in terms of career opportunities, equal pay for equal work, reproductive rights and so on. Friedan blamed "the problem with no name" on the oppressive, restrictive role women were allowed in American society. In the following years, other voices—some from the mainstream—joined hers, and *Playboy* found itself under fire for promulgating the objectification of women.

Hefner felt *Playboy* had been a progressive force in the battle for civil rights, sexual liberation and abortion rights, and attributed the strident criticism to leftwing extremists. In 1970, more than one campus demonstration against the magazine took place. At the University of Southern California in April, activists heckled a representative of *Playboy*, finally rushing the stage to try to wrest the microphone from him. Other militant actions and demonstrations took place outside Playboy Clubs. Gloria Steinem and Hugh Hefner finally met when she interviewed him at the Playboy Mansion for *McCall's* magazine. Her article was titled, "What *Playboy* Doesn't Know about Women Could Fill a Book."[35] *Playboy* was being bombarded by criticism from both the political left and right (who considered it pornographic).

While Hugh Hefner was planning a response to the criticism, Harvey Kurtzman experienced some Feminists' reactions to *Little Annie Fanny* firsthand. On a weekend in June 1970, a group called the Alternative Media Project put on a conference at Goddard College in Plainfield, Vermont, to discuss the future of underground media and how to increase its influence. It was a colorful gathering of more than a thousand "media freaks" and students, as well as a number of special guests. Kurtzman was a panelist for a seminar on June 20 called "Comics and Mass Consciousness." The other panelist was Gilbert Shelton.

Isabella Fiske McFarlin, then known as Ladybelle, described the proceedings. "It was a very hectic summer, very hippie-ish," she recalled. "The guys were very happy to have Harvey Kurtzman join them in their world, and there was a sense of showing him off." Ladybelle was there with her then-boyfriend Art Spiegelman, and had the opportunity to meet Kurtzman. "I thought he was a nice, soft-spoken person," she said. "He seemed amused by the whole wild hippie 'jam' and seemed to like summer in Vermont."[36] Kurtzman, in turn, must have been impressed with Ladybelle, because he named a character after her in an upcoming *Little Annie Fanny*.

The informal seminar was held in the well of the basement of the Goddard College Library, with the 200 or so attendees watching from the floor and the balcony above. The panel began with a discussion about the influence of comix on underground culture, but soon zeroed in on why Kurtzman was doing the sexist *Little Annie Fanny* strip for *Playboy*. "It brings in the loot," he said. "It's a job, and I enjoy it. If it is offensive to women, they don't tell us about it, particularly. I don't hear that it's offensive." A woman in the audience responded, "You're hearing it now." Another said, "Mr. Kurtzman, why don't you have Annie Fanny and her friends take over the offices of *Playboy* and show them where it's at?"[37]

Kurtzman admitted, "It's sexist all right, sure. And it intends to be." He said that he didn't have a quarrel with the point of view of either the Feminists or *Playboy*. "To me, they're both extreme, and I like to feel I can tolerate them both." Someone asked whether appearing in a sexist publication like *Playboy* was a good thing for an underground cartoonist. Shelton responded by asking, "What about the idea of the Freak Brothers in *Playboy*? Is there anything wrong with that? Does that mean I'm supporting *Playboy*'s policies, or does that mean I'm slipping a revolutionary message into *Playboy*?"

At a certain point, Kurtzman asked if anyone wanted to talk about cartooning itself. Someone asked him to "tell us how you draw." Kurtzman described how he started with something to say, but that one couldn't create a humorous comic strip if one had to conform to some political agenda. He received applause for this view. A woman shouted, "We're in a revolutionary struggle, and when it happens, when the revolution comes, you're going to be crushed!" Kurtzman responded by saying that he had already gone through a period of working for employers whose morality differed from his own. (He was referring to his quarrel with Gaines about the EC horror comics.)

> I had a very strong feeling about going through life squeaky clean, with my hands unsullied by dealing with people who I considered immoral. I used to talk to people about it, question people, and I slowly began to realize that my position was absolutely ridiculous, for two reasons. First of all, my assessment of what was moral and what wasn't moral was very biased. It was my own point of view. That's number one. Number two, I found that if I wanted to go through life without dealing with what I considered immorality, I couldn't work with anybody. I'd have to become an outcast on a desert island.

The discussion shifted from the panelists to contentious interchanges between members of the audience. "The whole thing was getting pretty furious and I was thinking of slipping out the side door," Ladybelle remembered, "when suddenly a group of [people] took off all their clothes! They stood there and, with smiles on their faces, ignoring the tense atmosphere, said something like 'You guys don't know anything about love and sex! That's where it's at! Love is all there is' and so on. Then several of them broke into couples and lay down right on the library floor. I remember thinking it must be very uncomfortable. They began to make love, ignoring the whole group of people around them, all of whom had reactions according to their beliefs."[38] The resulting chaos ended the panel discussion. When asked if the "fuck-in" was purely theater, and the sex was merely simulated, Gilbert Shelton recently said, "We could probably see it better from the stage than the people in the audience could. It appeared not to be acted. When they were finished, the girl came up and sat on the edge of the stage, and she left a wet spot."[39]

When asked about the Goddard College event, Kurtzman admitted that he had become less judgmental of people with different ideas of morality than his own. His views had evolved. By 1970, he was a family man who could tolerate the values and lifestyle promoted by *Playboy*, and a man with many traditional values who could respect and socialize with the counterculture creators of the underground press.

Kurtzman never publicly spoke about his view on Feminism, or even at home. He was basically a postwar liberal Democrat, hardly a radical, and a traditionalist in certain ways. "He never made any bold statements in front of me," his daughter Liz recalled. "But with all the strong women around him . . . I can't imagine he was anything but supportive of Feminism. He certainly made clear that his daughters should be independent, something I am ever grateful for."[40] However, when Little Annie Fanny encountered Feminists, Kurtzman had no choice but to toe the *Playboy* party line. "Women's Lib" (in the September 1970 *Playboy*) was created in the spring, when the rash of criticism and demonstrations against the magazine broke out, but hadn't seen print by the time of the Alternative Media festival in Vermont. The shrill opening caption, which rings of Hefner rather than Kurtzman, reads, "Our little friend is swept up by the women's liberation movement, which (and let us be fair and objective) should not be taken lightly. Their objections to the abortion laws bear careful study. Their objections to male-biased employment practices merit respect. But where they begin to sound like a ridiculous bunch of effete, blabber-mouthed, radical snobs is when they object to men's magazines!" The story focuses mainly on the "ritual bra burning," and the sisters marveling that Annie Fanny has no need for the "device invented purely for the pleasure of man." When Annie reveals her impossibly perky breasts, one of the women, initially skeptical of Annie's claim that she isn't wearing a brassiere, says "By Wonder Woman's lasso, she's right!"

Kurtzman was tethered to a feature increasingly out of touch with the changing times, even as it tried to examine the latest trends. Yet it remained popular with the readers of a slick magazine with an enormous circulation, a circulation that was still climbing and would reach its highest point in the coming decade. "I don't tend to be . . . hard on Hefner," he said in 1981. "I think that *Playboy* has a lot to do with the male fantasy just as *Cosmopolitan* has to do with female fantasies, and I don't deny people their fantasies. I think we need them. At what point does make-believe become destructive? The point undoubtedly lies somewhere between the Ku Klux Klan fantasy and *The Wizard of Oz*. I don't know where *Playboy* fits, but *Playboy* is a male fantasy and knowing Hefner as I do, I have a great respect for the man. He's not a dummy. He's a thinking, intelligent, progressive man."[41]

Still, it was clear by this time that the *Little Annie Fanny* experience was challenging in ways Kurtzman hadn't anticipated. Going into it, he thought he would be doing a satire strip like Goodman Beaver, albeit with a sexual slant. In practice, he discovered that with Annie, true satire was impossible. She couldn't really engage with anyone or any subject. Instead, the combination of satirical elements and sexual farce resulted in an unsatisfying mix. Hefner's insistence that Annie be frequently nude probably accurately reflected most readers' desire to ogle the expertly crafted images of Annie's unclothed body, just as they would Vargas Girls or other artists' visions. This became monotonous, not as much for the readers—who would get a brief episode every second or third issue—but for Kurtzman, who had to think up new ways to display Annie's body, and for Will Elder, who labored untold hours on every episode. If Annie became numbing to read, one can easily imagine how much more numbing it was to create over the years.

This page from the *Little Annie Fanny* "Women's Lib" story ran in *Playboy* (September 1970).

24.

KURTZMAN IN THE 1970s

IN THE EARLY 1970s, after one of Adele Kurtzman's dinners, Harvey Kurtzman and Gil Kane had a conversation about their experiences in comics, which was tape-recorded. Among many topics, Kane talked about cartoonists who made it big with a popular syndicated strip, and then had to deal with waning success down the road. When the strip's momentum slowed and it lost newspapers as the years went by, many of them struggled. Kane contrasted this with Kurtzman who had always had to work hard, and was now better able to succeed in mid-life. "The guys like you who've been jogging along while [those syndicated cartoonists] have been riding all this time have finally built up the endurance of a Spartan. [You] can overcome anything."[1]

Kurtzman acknowledged the truth in this. "For me it seems to get easier and easier. I've been working and running so hard all these years, and it's all been building up and building up. And it seems to get easier and easier to make it."[2] When the new decade arrived, the financial worry that had descended in his post-*Trump* period began to lift. He still had to work hard, and keep a lot of plates spinning, but the contacts he made over the years gave him enough markets to get him through.

In retrospect, Kurtzman's peak creative years began with *Hey Look!* in 1946 and ended with the last Goodman Beaver story in 1962. One might stretch the seventeen years to twenty, to include the later issues of *Help!* and the early *Little Annie Fanny* episodes, when the strip was at its freshest. Then, as he said in *A Talk with Harvey Kurtzman*, he began working in a more deliberate fashion. His ideas arose from the assignment at hand, often a job doing magazine spreads, special features or one-off art projects. They were the kind of jobs he could handle as a change of pace from his Annie strips, and called more upon his editorial and design abilities than his satirical writing and drawing. When Kurtzman was asked if he thought his "most original contribution" was the twenty-three issues of the *Mad* comic book, he said yes, but added, "On the other hand, I [find] that graphic invention is something that there is no end to, because invention is quite different from an expression or a recording of experiences that writing often is."[3] While there wouldn't be more major innovations in Kurtzman's future, his nature was to "think outside the box," and he would continue to restlessly experiment in the coming years. Still, it's undeniable that Kurtzman's best years as a comics creator—in light of the limitations of *Little Annie Fanny*—were behind him. For the most part, the story of his career going forward was one of finding sufficiently re-munerative work appropriate to his talents. That he was working almost exclusively for slick magazines gave him a great deal of satisfaction.

Woody Gelman told anyone who would listen that he thought Harvey Kurtzman was a genius. As creative director of product development for Topps Chewing Gum (along with Len Brown), Gelman produced nu-merous non-sports trading cards in the 1960s, such as the popular *Mars Attacks* series. In January 1970, he put Kurtzman under contract as a con-sultant. The contract called for him to meet once a month at the Topps of-fice in Brooklyn with Gelman and his staff, when he would give his input on their latest product designs, and help brainstorm and problem solve, as the need arose. (The actual wording in the contract stated it was "to utilize the services of Contributor in conceiving, devising and improving products in the confectionary field.") His first meeting took place in the last week of February. In that capacity, he worked with Art Spiegelman, who had been with Topps since 1966.

Spiegelman would have had his work published in *Help!*, except for bad timing: "[Kurtzman] got my cartoons just as *Help!* magazine was go-ing out of business. He sent me a letter back, which was more than I could have hoped for, telling me he really liked my stuff and that he was going to work for *Playboy*. When [*Help!*] went under, I think he just sort of threw up the white flag and grabbed for safety with *Playboy*."[4] Spiegelman was as impressed by Kurtzman's serious work at EC as he was by the *Mad* comic books, and was thrilled to be able to work with him, even if only once a month. Though they had met before, they would get to know each other better at Topps and on other occasions, and become friends.

Kurtzman continued to take on assignments for mainstream mag-azines such as *Look* (illustrating "How to Win at Basketball: Cheat" by

Bill Cosby in the January 27, 1970, issue), and also expended a significant amount of energy working as a bridge between some of those magazines and the underground comix artists. The comix were at their peak,
and Kurtzman's rapport with some of their creators put him in a special
position.

Even before *Zap Comix* appeared, Kurtzman brought Robert Crumb's
work to Byron Dobell, managing editor of *Esquire*. Dobell recalled, "I
looked at a book Crumb had filled with drawings and thought they were
absolutely marvelous. I went into Harold Hayes's office, which was next
to mine, and told him, 'Harvey has brought in this cartoonist who is out
of this world.' Harold looked at it and became very excited."[5] Over the
next couple of years, Kurtzman began considering various ways to bring
Crumb into the pages of *Esquire*. Not long after the jam session in the offices of *The East Village Other* in the fall of 1969, he came up with an idea.

Like a lot of people, Kurtzman had lost interest in the *Saturday
Evening Post*, the venerable "gray lady" of the magazine trade, which
had been published weekly since 1897. Its conservative editorial policy
made it increasingly irrelevant as the 1960s progressed, and its circulation plummeted. On February 8, 1969, Martin Ackerman, the president of
Curtis Publishing, had announced the magazine was shutting down. This
wasn't a seismic event in Kurtzman's life like the failure of *Collier's* in
1957 (which indirectly brought about the end of *Trump*), but it was still a
major event in magazine history, and he took notice.

While reading post mortems on its demise, and speculation that the
magazine might be brought back by another publisher, Kurtzman found
himself wondering, "What if the hippies and underground artists took
over the *Post*?" This led to a proposal for an ambitious *Esquire* piece along
the lines of the *Sports Illustrated* satire ("Sporty Illustrations") in *Trump*
#2—except, it wouldn't satirize the *Post* as it had been. It would provide
a humorous look at what the magazine might be like if taken over by denizens of the counterculture. Harold Hayes bought the idea, predicated on
the participation of Crumb and other underground cartoonists. *Esquire*
would pay to fly Crumb from San Francisco to New York to work on it
with Kurtzman.

Kurtzman knew that eliciting Crumb's participation would best be
done in person. He accomplished this during a *Playboy*-financed jaunt to
California to do research for *Little Annie Fanny*. Young people were moving out of San Francisco to form communes, where they could "get back
to the land" and work together to live a freer, alternative lifestyle. Hefner
okayed an *Annie* episode on hippie communes for the January 1971 issue,

Harvey Kurtzman and Art Spiegelman in Kurtzman's backyard. Photograph courtesy of Jay Lynch.

which required that Kurtzman fly west and visit a commune or two. In the Bay Area, Kurtzman met more underground comix people.

At Victor Moscoso's house, he took part in jam poster with Moscoso, Robert Crumb, Gilbert Shelton, Robert Williams and Spain Rodriguez. Kurtzman sounded out Crumb about the *Esquire* piece, and asked others to participate. Then Crumb, Spain and Kurtzman visited communes in Marin County. One was on a farm, which eventually became the setting for the *Annie* episode, but a visit to another led to a disturbing incident. Crumb's later description was vague: "It was a screwy scene. It wasn't really a commune. It was just this house that somebody managed to get, and all these people were drifting in and out. There were some really freaky people there and Kurtzman got real freaked out by it."[6] Kurtzman later confided to a friend that he saw a man fondling a young girl at the place, and no one seemed to care. It made him so uncomfortable ("I've got daughters!") that he had to get away as quickly as possible, and caught an earlier flight to New York than had been planned.

Ultimately Robert Crumb, S. Clay Wilson and Victor Moscoso collaborated with Kurtzman on the nine-page parody called "The Great Speckled
Post," which appeared in *Esquire*'s December 1970 issue. The title came
from an old Roy Acuff hit song, "The Great Speckled Bird," a defense of
fundamentalist religion from the attacks of other sects. Crumb did virtually all the artwork, including a cover in the *Post* style (signed "Norman
Stonewell"), as well as a full-page faux advertisement, a caricature of David
Eisenhower and the lettering throughout. Curiously, Harvey Kurtzman's
name appears nowhere on the piece or even on the contents page, which
subtitles it, "After the fall, a thunderbolt of good vibes." Maybe it was
because "Leon Feather," "the Big Banger," "Suzie Woozie" and others supposedly wrote the text. He doesn't have the right feel for the subject, and
it was probably too early for members of the counterculture to laugh at
themselves, but the main problem is that it isn't funny. That may be the
reason it's buried deep in the magazine's back pages. In an interview in
1972, a mortified Crumb recalled the situation.

> That was another big mistake I made, doing that thing for *Esquire*. That
> was another deal where I got my way paid to New York. I could never resist
> guys paying my way to go somewhere back then. So I went to New York
> and Kurtzman showed me the stuff he wanted me to do, and oh God, it was
> like, "Jesus, what have I got myself into?" I told him I didn't want to do it.
> I hung around his house for a couple of days and finally just gave in. He
> kept urging me to do it, and I kind of respected Kurtzman. It was terrible.[7]

Crumb's signature appears only on two cartoons on the last of the
nine pages, in unreadable scribbles (nothing like his usual, clear signature). Someone at *Esquire* changed the punch line of a gag cartoon by S.
Clay Wilson, rendering it nonsensical. "The Great Speckled *Post*" angered
rather than attracted the magazine's younger readers, who felt it was a put-
down of youth culture. It was anything but "a thunderbolt of good vibes."

Another Kurtzman effort for *Esquire* was much more effective. A stick-
er affixed to the cover of the June 1971 issue listed some of the contents,
including "Harvey Kurtzman's History of the Funnies—9 Pages of Color
Comics." The article inside is titled "@&%$#!! or Takin' the Lid off the Id."
Although Kurtzman uses visual material from the collection of Woody
Gelman (who was credited), it isn't a preview of the projected Nostalgia
Press book. The examples of vintage comic strips and comic books are
shown to point out the psychological and social dynamics in American
society that were reflected in the comics from the 1920s (*Bringing Up*

Father) to the present day (Robert Crumb's one-shot *Despair* in the undergrounds). It was the first time Kurtzman looked "between the lines" of comics' history or ventured any kind of serious analysis. "America's psychic past is in these sketches," Kurtzman states on the first page. Under a large reproduction of Crumb's *Despair*, he writes, "The future is on the drawing boards today." His text, parsed in captions among the reprinted comics, has these insights: "Popeye's character corresponded to the years when a culturally inferior America was becoming the world's most powerful nation; he was ugly, ungrammatical and low-life, but in the end always mastered every situation by overwhelming strength. His polarities—innocence and muscle—were later on to be separated out into Clark Kent and Superman." Kurtzman ran examples of his own "Corpse on the Imjin!" ("an imaginative variation on adventure"), George Herriman's *Krazy Kat* and Walt Kelly's *Pogo* ("comics of the intellectuals") and numerous others. "Where does it all lead?," he asks on the final page. "Absolute freedom (or total license, depending on your point of view) is where. Skip the headlines and turn straight to the funnies, where the whole truth is still out front."

His enthusiasm for underground comix remained high. In an appearance at the 1971 New York comic con, Kurtzman confessed, "I don't read newspaper comics anymore because they are totally dead, but underground comix are really exciting. And I tend to think they're exciting because they are related to what's happening today. They're new, and fresh, and they're a frontier. And a frontier is always exciting."

ZAP COMIX #1 ENERGIZED and inspired underground cartoonists across the country. One of them was Denis Kitchen of Milwaukee, Wisconsin. Kitchen's first publication was the underground comic *Mom's Homemade Comics* #1 in late 1968. He was a talented cartoonist who had high hopes for the alternative medium. As he wrote in Michael Barrier's fanzine *Funnyworld*, "By ridiculing the outmoded social system we live in, we are quickening its demise. And in its place, hopefully, will be established a society in which no 'underground' is necessary."[8]

Born in 1946, Kitchen was a bit young to buy *Mad* comic books off the stands, but he saw them as back issues. "The first Kurtzman thing that made a real impact on me was *Humbug* #1," he later recalled. "For some reason, it hit me even more than *Mad*. As I got older, and started collecting more assiduously, the stuff that Harvey did was clearer to me. I was paying close attention by the time *Help!* came out, and I bought them new off the racks."[9] He wanted to send a copy of *Mom's Homemade Comics* to Kurtzman, and got the address from Jay Lynch. Kurtzman responded to

Kitchen with a typically encouraging letter. It was an unremarkable beginning to what became an important relationship for both of them.

Kitchen graduated from the University of Wisconsin-Milwaukee in 1968, then taught a summer class for the Free University. In the spring of 1971, he got the idea of flying Kurtzman to the campus to give a talk. "I had a budget of five hundred bucks to teach a class, and I could do whatever I wanted with it. That was a lot of dough in those days."[10] Kurtzman had never spoken on a campus, but he was up for something new. Kitchen got to work drumming up publicity. Because he had been a journalism student, he had contacts at the local papers and TV stations. He sent out a press release and made a big deal about the creator of *Mad* coming to Milwaukee.

When Kurtzman arrived and was shown the cavernous auditorium where he would speak, he blanched. He thought there would be thirty people in the front rows. As it turned out, Kitchen's publicity worked, and the auditorium was filled with several hundred people. The local television station sent a crew, and there were reporters on hand from the *Milwaukee Journal* and the *Milwaukee Sentinel*. Kurtzman's talk was titled, "Why Flash Gordon Uses a Sword Instead of a Zap Gun." It gave him a chance to revisit his long-held views about Alex Raymond's strip, just as he did at that year's New York Comic Art Convention in July: "*Flash Gordon* is an interesting point, because people say it's science fiction, but he's up there fighting Ming with a sword [when] he's got a perfectly good ray gun on his side. Why are they fencing in jock straps? *Flash Gordon* is just so totally devoted to Freudian symbolism! As opposed to an H. G. Wells story or a good solid science fiction piece which has to do with the truth of science." Kitchen said, "[Kurtzman] was happy to appear in front of a big, enthusiastic crowd. He talked about old comics, his own career, about *Mad, Humbug, Trump, Help!, Little Annie Fanny* and comics in general. He was funny and the crowd loved him."[11] He gave another talk in the Midwest that summer, this time to an art class Jay Lynch was teaching at the Art Institute of Chicago. While he was in town, Kurtzman met with Hefner to discuss a couple of things. One was requesting a raise on *Little Annie Fanny*, and the other was getting Robert Crumb's work into *Playboy*.

DESPITE THEIR FRIENDLY RELATIONSHIP, tension had built up between Kurtzman and Hefner over time. Even though *Annie* had been going for eight years and was well established in *Playboy*, Hefner continued to micromanage Kurtzman and Elder to a degree that passed perfectionism to approach the pathological. Hefner's long critiques of Kurtzman's finished layouts and scripts were amplified by his habitual use of Dexedrine, the appetite suppressant that allowed him to work without sleep for extended periods of time. As it had with Bill Gaines, the drug had a number of deleterious effects, including impaired judgment. This made dealing with Hefner difficult. Kurtzman and Elder had asked for and received raises in the course of the 1960s, but those occasions have been characterized as a "tug of war." Therefore, asking Hefner for another raise had Kurtzman on edge.

It's not clear whether Hefner knew he was coming, but Kurtzman had a standing invitation to drop by the mansion any time he was in Chicago. He showed up on Hefner's doorstep with Robert Crumb, Jay Lynch, Jane Lynch (Jay's wife) and Skip Williamson in tow. Hefner was unavailable (reportedly playing backgammon). The guests were told they could order whatever they wanted while they waited for him. Crumb recalled, "The atmosphere at the mansion, in spite of the libertine, hedonistic impression given by *Playboy* magazine, was rather stuffy, stiff, [and] stilted. Everyone hanging around there—famous comedians, journalists, or whoever—behaved in a very inhibited manner. I believe that Hefner himself set the tone. His own manner seemed to me very held in, stiff, not at all loose or spontaneous."[12] Kurtzman was agitated when Skip Williamson began assaulting the liquor supply. According to Crumb, Kurtzman said, "Please you guys, don't do anything outrageous, okay? I don't want to offend Mr. Hefner."[13]

Williamson said, "I got very drunk, and told Jay that I was going to go to the grotto pool and let loose a floater. It was just an off-hand, drunken comment, but Jay knew that I was kind of a crazy person and there was a possibility that this could happen. Jay told Kurtzman about [it] and Kurtzman thought this would diminish his ability to get a raise, if I did that. I'd completely forgotten that I'd said I'd do that, when I stripped down naked and jumped into the pool." Apparently, a concerned Kurtzman, who felt responsible for getting Williamson into the mansion that day, notified Hefner's security staff. Williamson said, "The security came, closed down the pool, and hustled me out. So I got dressed, kicked a suit of armor in the shins, and stormed out, before Hef even showed up."[14] Jay Lynch related what happened after the publishing mogul joined them. "Harvey had taken off his shoes and was walking around making himself at home. Crumb and I were in the kitchen talking with Hefner. Harvey came in, and Hef asked him what he was doing in town. Harvey told him that the Art Institute flew him out and paid his plane fare. Hef said something like 'Well that's good. Harvey needs the dough. He can't even afford shoes.' At that point Harvey went into another room and returned in a few minutes. Crumb noticed that Harvey was now wearing shoes."[15] This event would haunt Crumb, Lynch said, because it demonstrated "the evils being forced on Harvey because economic circumstances caused him to have to work for The Man."[16]

Crumb later said, "Harvey's obsequious behavior in front of Hefner was a sad thing for me to behold, as I had such great reverence for Kurtzman's accomplishments, while to me Hefner was far below Kurtzman in that regard. I considered *Playboy* a cornball, ridiculous, asinine publication, successful as it was."[17] Nothing came of Crumb's interchange with Hefner, probably because Crumb didn't want or need to work for *Playboy*. He gained insight into the Hefner-Kurtzman relationship during one of his subsequent visits with Kurtzman in Mount Vernon.

> I would have dinner with his family and talk about the profession and all. It was so demoralizing for Kurtzman to work for Hefner. Kurtzman showed me these [critiques] he'd gotten back from Hefner, because he had to send, with every strip, these roughs of [*Little Annie Fanny*] for Hefner's approval. Hefner would send back the roughs with a piece of tracing paper over each of the roughs with these little nit-picky blue pencil changes he wanted made. Kurtzman showed me these, and he'd been drinking a little, and he just started weeping with vexation, literally weeping. He said, "Look at this. Okay, I'm grateful to the man, he rescued me from poverty. [But] look at what I have to endure with Hefner."[18]

Later, Crumb observed, "He was stuck, and the commercial magazine culture he worked in was brutal, showed him no mercy, as portrayed in the story 'The Organization Man in the Grey Flannel Executive Suite' in *Jungle Book*. They just put him through the meat grinder, the poor bastard. I vowed then and there: 'Never allow what happened to Kurtzman happen to you.'"[19] Kurtzman wasn't in the position he had been in 1956 when he escaped the tension and frustration at EC by leaving. Now he had a larger mortgage payment and two more children, and there was no opportunity with another employer beckoning. As he put it, "Unless we're prepared to wipe the slate clean, or wipe it three-quarters clean, you get trapped by this organism you've built."[20] Kurtzman had little choice but to endure Hefner's treatment, although he didn't just lay down and surrender to the editor's every point. He pushed back where he could, but lost more battles than he won.

He seems to have won a key battle that day at the Playboy Mansion in 1971. It was probably the occasion that yielded a raise to $3,000 a page for *Annie Fanny.* (Kurtzman and Elder began receiving that rate in the first year or two of the decade.)[21] This was a seemingly incredible sum, roughly twenty times what top comic book artists were being paid to pencil and ink a page of artwork. But regular comic book artists weren't producing material as elaborate and time-consuming as *Annie Fanny.* Of course, the $3,000 was split with Elder, and the cost of collaborators and taxes had to come out of it. Still, it covered the lion's share of their bills, as long as they kept churning out pages and *Playboy* kept running them. (Twenty pages were published in 1971.)

KURTZMAN AND ELDER needed an assistant to do some of the mundane work on *Annie.* It wasn't easy finding the right person. They needed someone who had art talent yet was willing and able to sublimate his or her own style in a way that Jack Davis and others couldn't. In the spring of 1972, Kurtzman hired a twenty-two-year-old artist named Bill Stout for the job. Stout was living in Hollywood and working for *Cycletoons,* a black and white magazine that ran comics about motorcycles. Having just discovered the original *Mad* comics, he did a story that was a tribute to Wallace Wood, Harvey Kurtzman and Will Elder called "Motorpsycho," and sent copies to all three. Stout got a letter back from Kurtzman, asking if he would like to become his assistant on *Little Annie Fanny.* He accepted, and subsequently received a plane ticket to fly to New Jersey.

Stout's job began with transferring Kurtzman's detailed layouts to the illustration boards. "First I did a mechanical transfer of every single little line," he recalled. "Then I pencilled the entire page, correcting any anatomical errors I might find and stuff like that."[22] Next, Stout took Kurtzman's color guide and filled in the color on the illustration board using watercolors, until it was about 75 percent finished. Then Elder completed the page. "The idea was that by sandwiching me in between the two guys, the strips would come out to look as if there was no assistant, that it was pure Kurtzman and Elder. But I was an ambitious guy and a very creative guy. I wanted to make my mark on the strip, and occasionally I would do stuff that was a little more finished, or add gags and things. And I would often hear the whir of Willy's electric eraser. [Harvey] took me aside after a few stories, and said, 'Bill, you're too creative for us.' So we agreed to part as friends, and Harvey remained one of the best friends of my life." Stout worked on a couple of stories, one of them being "Ralph Nader" in the November 1972 issue.

He recalled, "Early on, Harvey said to me, 'You're going to learn a lot of stuff. You might not realize it at the time, but eventually, you will realize how much you are learning by working with us.' He was absolutely right." Once he was looking at some beautiful artwork produced by artists who wanted to assist on *Annie Fanny*. "I commented on those," Stout said, "and Harvey said, 'Look, see the hands? The guy draws the same hands all the time.' Every time Harvey drew a hand, he would pose it, usually pose his own hand and look at it or pose it in the mirror. Even if he had drawn that same hand position 200 times, he would try to look at it fresh, as if he'd never drawn that hand before or never seen it before. That helped keep the story really fresh. Another time, I had to draw a fire hydrant. I started to draw one from memory. Harvey looked at it, and said, 'Come on, let's go outside.' We went outside, and we found a fire hydrant, and we sketched it from life. It was totally different. The lesson was that 'if the reader buys non-fantasy elements as being real, they'll buy the fantasy as being real.' I learned from Harvey that drawing a real fire hydrant—not just a cartoon fire hydrant that I'd made up or attempted to remember—gave a greater gravity to the strip."

IN 1958, AFTER THE DEMISE of *Humbug*, Kurtzman unsuccessfully tried to work for television. Fourteen years later, he finally made it to the small screen.

First, he appeared in a Scripto pen commercial. It begins with a close-up of his face, as he examines a new nineteen-cent Scripto fiber tip pen. While the voiceover announcer talks about how it compares favorably to a forty-nine cent competitor, the camera pulls back to show Kurtzman finishing a drawing of a shapely young woman in a bathing suit on a wall. The announcer intones, "It's good to know that the Scripto nineteen-center writes just as long as the leading forty-nine cent fiber tip. And that's a long . . . long . . . time," as the camera pulled farther back to reveal that Kurtzman has been drawing on the wall of his prison cell. "You forty-nine cent fiber tips, the handwriting is on the wall." According to a trade ad for the 1972 commercial, more than 142,000,000 people saw it. However, Kurtzman was never identified by name.

The same year, he was invited by Phil Kimmelman & Associates to create some short animated films for *Sesame Street*, the popular TV show for children. Kimmelman and his associate Bill Peckmann had already done animated commercials based on storyboards and designs by such artists as Mort Drucker, Gahan Wilson and Jack Davis. They were Kurtzman fans and felt he would be perfect for the new project. Kurtzman worked up eight ideas in rough form, and the producers of *Sesame Street* selected three of them. Then he prepared the complete storyboards, created detailed character designs and even painted some of the color backgrounds. The animators were impressed by Kurtzman's feel for a new medium and his innate understanding of how to sketch the right moments in the action to guide the animators. The three films were co-directed by Kimmelman and Kurtzman. The working titles were "Nellie" (a number sequence with children's voices chanting along, and objecting when a picture rather than a number appears), "Count Off" (a zero with a sergeant's voice requires numbers to stand at attention and count off), and "Boat" (an old sea dog fills his boat with numbers until it sinks). Kurtzman brought his daughter Nellie along to the sound recording sessions to participate. The Association of International Film Animation East (ASIFA) ultimately gave "Count-off" and "Boat" awards at their 1973 ceremony, both for Kurtzman's conceptualization and for the way they were executed by Kimmelman & Associates. Despite the awards, these short films remained his only work in the animation field.

Kurtzman began working at *Esquire* as a sort of cartoon consultant, which sometimes gave him the chance to work with an old friend. Al Jaffee explained, "[Harold] Hayes paid him to supervise getting some [cartoon] material into the magazine. Harvey hired me for a few assignments, because we worked well together. He knew I wouldn't get upset over his making changes."[23] Both Kurtzman and Jaffee put a lot of work into a full-page cartoon-illustration for a piece in 1972 called "Dinner at Elaine's." The cartoon was to show the patrons of the trendy New York eatery that became known for its celebrity clientele. After examining Jaffee's first drawing, Kurtzman suggested turning all the people into penguins with human heads, a twist that made it special. Much of Kurtzman's time in the 1970s, apart from *Annie Fanny*, was spent as an ad hoc member of *Esquire*'s editorial staff.

Working on "Dinner at Elaine's" gave the two old collaborators a chance to get together and catch up on much that had happened since the days of *Humbug*. By this time, Jaffee was well known for originating and producing the *Mad* Fold-in, as well as the magazine's "Snappy Answers to Stupid Questions" series. That same year, a sequence of events led to an unexpected rapprochement with another past colleague: William M. Gaines.

LIKE ITS CORPSES THAT ROSE from the dead, EC was the comic book company that wouldn't die. The early 1970s saw a virtual explosion of interest in the late, lamented firm and its extraordinary comic books. Jerry Weist's and Roger Hill's professionally printed fanzine *Squa Tront* was the initial catalyst of the resurgence, which was further fueled in the spring of 1971 by the publication of *The EC Horror Library of the 1950's* by Nostalgia Press. It was a deluxe 10" by 14" hardcover book with twenty-three stories reprinted in full color. It sold well, and a year later, the movie *Tales from the Crypt* was playing on movie screens across America. Based on specific EC stories, the film raised the profile of the firm's comics to a higher level.

According to Frank Jacobs, "Gaines divvied up his [movie] proceeds with his editors and artists of the horror days. Although the film wasn't based on anything by Kurtzman, Gaines paid him the second highest amount (after Feldstein)." He quoted Bill Gaines as saying, "I can't exactly explain my actions. Harvey didn't work much in horror. He hated horror. But he was the second most important man at EC during the horror days. Maybe it's because of my compulsion to be fair. Maybe I've mellowed. But I still wouldn't pay him a dime on *Mad* if I could help it."[24] Whatever the reason, Kurtzman adopted a conciliatory attitude toward Gaines in the early 1970s. "We were both operating with a certain degree of misunderstanding," he told an interviewer. "There was a lot of emotion between us at the time."[25]

The EC Fan-Addict Convention organized by Ron Barlow and Bruce Hershenson was held in Manhattan May 26–29, 1972. The highlights were panel discussions on EC's horror, science fiction and war comics, with the creators answering questions from the floor. Bill Gaines was in the audience for the war comics panel, a fact that Harvey Kurtzman acknowledged within the first five minutes by asking him to confirm a point. Those were the first words Kurtzman said to Gaines in seventeen years. (Their legal wrangles had been fought through letters, depositions and affidavits.) The war panel included Harvey Kurtzman, Will Elder, Jack Davis, Wallace Wood, George Evans and Jerry De Fuccio.

Among the artists from the EC war comics, Jack Davis had become the most financially successful. He was one of the highest paid illustrators of the late 1960s and 1970s, having his hands full with as many movie posters and *TV Guide* covers as he could handle. His career reached a higher plateau the year of the convention, when his first cover for *Time* magazine appeared. The Joe Namath cover turned out to be the first of thirty-six covers Davis would do for *Time*. Wallace Wood had been busy in the 1960s working for *Mad*, Marvel and Tower Comics, but the many hours at the drawing board, coupled with the effects of cigarettes and alcohol, had taken a toll on his health. In 1972, he was doing less pencilling and more inking. George Evans was getting by with assignments at DC and Marvel,

after assisting George Wunder on *Terry and the Pirates* in the 1960s. Jerry
De Fuccio worked as an editor at *Mad*, which was selling better than ever.
Its circulation reportedly topped 2,000,000 in the early 1970s.

The members of the panel addressed the antiwar element of the EC
war comics and their emphasis on accuracy with the weapons and uniforms. De Fuccio spoke about going on research trips for Kurtzman, how
stories were assigned to various artists and so on. Evans complained about
having to follow Kurtzman's layouts. Kurtzman acknowledged that there
were some conflicts—"The skeletons in the closet are all coming out"—
but maintained that they mainly got along well: "I don't think we had
that much friction, and that's a tribute to the particular guys here." Wood
chain-smoked and said little. By the end, many of the basic questions fans
had about the EC war comics were answered.

Elder goofed around on the panel, but was a bit more serious for the
convention's program book. "Harvey's always been a great part of my life,"
he wrote. "If I had a brother, Harvey would be him. He's been a tremendous
influence on me. He's made me work very hard which I'm not inclined to
do. That's the tremendous power Harvey has over me."[26] Toward the end of
the discussion, Kurtzman was asked about his book on the history of comics. "We're scheduled to publish this year, but the publishing date seems
to be elusive," he responded. "It advances in front of me."[27]

The new era of good relations between Gaines and Kurtzman took a
step further a year later, when John Benson interviewed them together
for a projected book. Benson was impressed by Peter Bogdanovich's book-
length interviews with John Ford, Fritz Lang and Allan Dwan, and felt
there should be a similar book about a comics person. Kurtzman came
to mind as the most likely candidate. When he approached him in the
summer of 1972 Kurtzman agreed to do it, but felt it would be monotonous
with just him throughout the whole book. He suggested that each chapter
should be with a different person associated with his career. Once this
decision was made, it was obvious that one of the other people had to be
Gaines. "I think that it was Kurtzman alone who decided who each of
the 'other people' would be for each chapter," Benson recalled. "My recollection is that Kurtzman contacted all the other people himself. I feel
sure I didn't contact Gaines."[28] The other interviews for the book paired
Kurtzman with Gil Kane, Will Elder, and Harry Chester as well as a three-
way discussion with both Arnold Roth and Al Jaffee.

In a sense, *The Mad World of William M. Gaines* contributed to the
thaw between Gaines and Kurtzman. Jacobs interviewed Kurtzman for
the book, a sign that Gaines was willing to let him tell his side of the *Mad*

Jack Davis, Will Elder, Harvey Kurtzman, George Evans, Wallace Wood and Jerry De Fuccio, on "The War Panel" at the 1972 EC Fan-Addict Convention. Photo courtesy of Fred von Bernewitz.

story. The account in Jacobs's book was relatively accurate.[29] Meanwhile, Benson taped the interview with Kurtzman and Kane on August 11, 1972. Kane was his usual loquacious self, and held forth after dinner for some four hours, though Kurtzman stayed right with him.

Due to one thing or another, the Gaines-Kurtzman meeting was delayed, and in the interim, Frank Jacobs's book was published. It quoted Kurtzman accurately, which calmed Kurtzman's nerves about the reunion. The interview took place on May 9, 1973, at the Kurtzmans' home, after dinner. When Bill and Annie Gaines arrived, there were a few awkward moments as the two men tried to find a way to reconnect. Soon, however, with the help of a bottle of wine (doubtless supplied by Gaines), the tension eased. John Benson and his wife Friedel were also there, helping to smooth things over. Adele made Chateaubriand. It was a social evening as well as an interview taping. When the time came to turn on the recorder, both men were on their best behavior. While they occasionally differed on this or that, they avoided sore points like the lawsuit. (Excerpts from this interview appear throughout this book.)

Afterward, contact between the two men was sporadic. Kurtzman invited Gaines to a showing of his old movies with the EC gang, but Gaines couldn't make it. Another time, Gaines invited Adele to his home for a winetasting, something that he didn't think Harvey would enjoy. Bill and Annie did show up for a birthday party for the Kurtzmans (Harvey's sixtieth, Adele's fifty-ninth) some years hence. Gaines and Kurtzman were cordial, but they didn't resume their friendship.

WAS THERE ANOTHER MAGAZINE in Kurtzman's future? It was a question that he was often asked. Some were no doubt hoping that he would find the right backing and creative environment to do something as superlative as *Mad*. But even if the right backing was found, Kurtzman's current situation was quite different than in the 1950s. Cartoonist Dave Sim interviewed him on the subject around this time, starting off by asking "Do you ever regret having left *Mad*?" Kurtzman's one-word answer was "No." As to whether he would ever start a new magazine, he responded, "Starting magazines is a rough business, and I'm very comfortable now. I'd like to start a magazine, but it would take a good kick in the rear end for me to want to go into that again. You have to be prepared to . . . sacrifice and sacrifice and sacrifice to start a magazine. When you are relatively unencumbered . . . it is a lot easier to start magazines. When the rent comes due and baby needs new shoes, it becomes a lot more difficult."[30] However, he did have at least one opportunity to edit a new magazine at this time. In 1972, Marvel Comics wanted to publish a humor magazine which at first had the working title *Bedlam*. After Will Eisner declined Stan Lee's offer to edit it, Lee turned to Harvey Kurtzman. On the day Kurtzman came in to meet with Lee, Gil Kane was in the Marvel offices. He later recalled, "Harvey was just standing there at the door, looking around at the office, as if thinking to himself, 'My God, am I back to this?'"[31]

Kurtzman described the meeting. "I had an experience with Stan Lee recently where I was actually considering doing a magazine with him. And the old thing came back to me—pow! He said, 'Harvey, we'll do a magazine. You do whatever you want, anything you want. I want you to do a magazine with me, I want you to do what you want, and I want the title to be so-and-so!' And what was worse was the title was an imitation of *Mad*."[32] As important as making a dollar was to Kurtzman, there were plenty of things he turned down, and this was one of the easiest. A year later, Marvel launched the magazine *Crazy*, with Marv Wolfman as editor. Kurtzman's only contribution was a couple of *Hey Look!* episodes in its second issue. He wouldn't be published by Marvel again for almost two decades.

During their meeting, Lee also offered Kurtzman a job working at Marvel as his right-hand man. When an interviewer asked him why he didn't want to take that kind of position, Kurtzman said he didn't know if it was a serious offer. "I've never really considered myself a comic book man. I felt that I'd left the comics with the old EC, and I didn't see myself going back."[33] His explanation to his friends in private was doubtless more colorful.

About this time, Kurtzman received a proposition from the folks at *National Lampoon* that would have paid well. The magazine was started by Harvard graduates and *Harvard Lampoon* alumni Robert Hoffman, Doug Kenney and Henry Beard, in 1970. It rapidly gained popularity, carrying over the policy of *Harvard Lampoon*, which had an individual theme for each issue. *National Lampoon* had issues that explored such topics as "The Future," "Back to School," "Death" and "Self-Indulgence." The August 1971 issue featured a cover with court-martialed Vietnam War mass-murderer William Calley sporting the idiotic grin of Alfred E. Neuman, with the catchphrase, "What, My Lai?"

In its October 1971 issue, *Lampoon* did an extended *Mad* magazine parody including the strip "Citizen Gaines," with Ernie Colon imitating the style of Mort Drucker. Like Charles Foster Kane in Orson Welles's *Citizen Kane*, Gaines had a sled, but the word that haunted him on the sled wasn't "rosebud." It was "satire." More than once, it mentioned that *Mad* had lost the satirical brilliance of its founder, Harvey Kurtzman, and Kurtzman himself, as caricatured by Colon, appeared in the strip.

Editor Michael C. Gross, a fan of *Mad* as a kid, got the idea to offer Kurtzman space in *Lampoon*. "I was already editing the 'Funny Pages' and most of the cartoons," Gross recalled. "I told Henry Beard that we ought to offer Kurtzman four or eight pages to do what he wanted, not every month but whenever he felt like it. Henry agreed and we had lunch with Harvey. We made our offer, and he said, 'I'd love to, but there's one problem. I don't understand what you guys are doing. I'm out of touch with you completely. I'm a different generation, and I wouldn't know what to do for *Lampoon*.'"[34] Gross said, "That really struck me. He just felt that his time was then, our time was now, and he didn't know how to contribute to it. We said, 'Harvey, do something, and when you're done, we'll write you a check when you come in the door.' It was the loosest situation he could have without publishing his own thing. We paid $400 a page for writing and art, or something close to that. We were revering him, and maybe he was afraid of disappointing us."[35] They continued to woo him in subsequent lunches, but it never happened. As Kurtzman said in an interview in 1976, "*National Lampoon* . . . is a little too rough for me. They feel that everything is fair game for criticism. They set my teeth on edge. I couldn't be that way. I'm embarrassed to hit certain areas."[36] He had once said that anything could be satirized if it was done in good taste (such as the Eichmann gag in *Help!*). Apparently, he wasn't comfortable with the taste level of *Lampoon*. Gross did ask Kurtzman what he thought of "Citizen Gaines." Kurtzman replied, "What's not to like?"[37]

At a comics convention panel with Bill Gaines, Al Feldstein and Nick Meglin, they were also asked what they thought of "Citizen Gaines." Gaines and Feldstein were silent, but Meglin answered, saying he thought it was "too inside" to be funny to the general public, but added, "We have to expect people to satirize us, after all, that's what we do. Maybe someday there'll be a really good one."[38]

René Goscinny also approached Harvey Kurtzman with an offer that could have been lucrative. After their reunion in 1966, they had stayed in touch. Kurtzman consulted the successful cartoonist about possible opportunities in Europe. His first work translated into French was the "Outer Sanctum" strip from *Mad*, which appeared in the monthly comic *Charlie Mensuel* #21 (October 1970). Kurtzman was part of the first American International Congress of Comics, a gathering of professional comics writers and artists in New York City in the spring of 1972 that attracted about 700 attendees, including a sizable European contingent. Awareness of Kurtzman's work was high among the cognoscenti on the Continent. He was awarded the 1972 Lifetime Achievement Award by the European Academy of Comic Book Art on May 29, 1973. Thinking in terms of helping Kurtzman, Goscinny offered his friend a job as the agent of *Pilote* in the United States. Kurtzman declined.

Harvey Kurtzman's romance with the world of French and European comics kicked into high gear when he was invited as a special guest to the first Festival International de la Bande Dessinée d'Angoulême. (*Bande dessinée*, literally "drawn strips," is French for comics.) Like the underground comix people, the European cartoonists held Kurtzman in great esteem.

In January 1974, he flew to Paris where he met Georges Wolinski (publisher of *Charlie Mensuel*), and Marcel Gotlib, Claire Bretécher and Nikita Mandryka, the founding trio of the then comic quarterly for adults *L'Echo des Savanes*. On the eve of the convention, they took Kurtzman to dinner, where he ate a French delicacy called *andouillette*. Andouillette looks like a sausage, but consists of veal or pork entrails cut in ribbons and wrapped in the large intestine of a pig. They are considered a treat in France. The next morning, Kurtzman became ill, and it took him a couple of days to fully recover. His memory of the incident was still vivid at a convention in Grenoble fifteen years later, when he joked about it on a panel. "Many years ago, I took a trip to Paris, and a gentleman by the name of Wolinski took me to dinner, and he fed me andouillettes and it was my earliest impression of Paris. Poisoned by one of your Frenchmen. Don't eat it. It's very bad."[39]

Kurtzman was wined and dined at the salon's expense, and was happy that Arnold Roth was already there. Roth had been in England working for *Punch* magazine, and spent a week before the event sampling Cognac, Pineau, Armagnac and other local spirits. "It was great to see how venerated [Harvey] was," Roth recalled, "and that he was deservedly being celebrated for what he had started and accomplished. It didn't go to his head. He had a natural modesty. He always remained himself, which was his appeal. He was genuine, he knew who he was, he knew what he thought, and could express it."[40] The veneration came from European comics insiders; Kurtzman wasn't well known among the rank-and-file readers of comics on the continent.[41] Before the con was over, he was given a mock prize at a tongue-in-cheek ceremony held by a brand new fanzine association called L'Amicale Laïque Des Petits Merdeux (A.L.D.P.M.). He got the "Harvey Kurtzman Award" for lifetime achievement, a prize consisting of a packet of chewing gum. He was just one of a number of guests who received such humorous awards, amid much laughter.

While in Europe, Kurtzman was exposed to the work of more French cartoonists, and he was impressed by what he saw. He later told his French correspondent Jacques Dutrey, "The cartoon scene in Paris is much more vigorous and fertile than it is in New York, or anywhere, for that matter. In the 1970s, the French are the cartoon leaders." He later named Moebius, Gotlib, Nikita Mandryka and Claire Bretécher as some of his favorite European artists.[42] From this point forward, he frequently found complimentary copies of European comics in his mailbox. Right then and there, Kurtzman was invited to submit work to *L'Echo des Savanes*. He got to work as soon as he returned home, producing three short Dracula parodies (a total of four pages) for the magazine's fall issue. Seemingly out of nowhere, he invented a new black and white graphic style that resulted in some of his most striking finished artwork since the EC days. The editors were delighted.

Harold Hayes (who had left *Esquire*) interviewed Kurtzman on his stateside WNET-TV program *Roundtable* in February 1975. When the discussion turned to European comics, Kurtzman said, "The difference between the cartoon market in France and here, is you can walk into a French bookshop and find dozens and hundreds of hardcover cartoon books like this. There seems to be a very large awareness on the part of the readers and the artists, and there's a market there that doesn't exist here. I think the reasons for it are complicated. They have everything to do with the economy, the background, the printing presses they have, the distribution system . . . but that's the way it's turned out. They're very active in

Harvey Kurtzman was interviewed by Harold Hayes on his WNET-TV program *Roundtable* (February 1975): courtesy of Thirteen Productions, LLC, and the Harold Hayes Collection/Z. Smith Reynolds Library/Wake Forest University.

this business of cartooning." He went on to say that he found the cartoon scene in England worse than in America. When he met with the cartoon editor of *Punch* in London, he learned that he had no interest whatsoever in new forms of comics or what the French cartoonists were doing.

IN ANGOULÊME, KURTZMAN discovered that European cartoonists were inspired by the American underground comix (which, in turn, had been partly inspired by *Mad*). Unfortunately, by the mid-1970s, it was clear that the heyday of the underground comix in America was over. In the 1975 television appearance with Hayes, Kurtzman described the undergrounds as "barely alive." Conservative citizens' groups claimed underground comix, with their glorification of sex and drugs, were socially irresponsible. In 1973, the US Supreme Court ruled that communities could decide what constituted obscenity in their locality, a major blow to the undergrounds. An even more fatal blow was administered when the sale of drug paraphernalia was widely outlawed. The head shops, the main distribution outlet for comix, began closing their doors. Kurtzman couldn't help but hear echoes of the anti-comic book campaigns of the early 1950s, though in this case, the comix weren't sold alongside mainstream comic books (and many were labeled "adults only").

Kurtzman drew an occasional cover for an underground comic such as Kitchen Sink's *Snarf* in 1974, and the all-reprint *Kurtzman Komix*

#1 two years later, which included twelve superb *Hey Look!* pages, but there wasn't much money involved. He attended the 1976 Berkeley Con, where he met with longtime admirer Glenn Bray. Bray was about to publish a Kurtzman index, the first serious attempt to document all his work. Kurtzman gave his blessing to the project, and even drew the cover and some sketches for the interior. *The Illustrated Harvey Kurtzman Index* became an invaluable resource for comics historians and Kurtzman aficionados, not only because it listed virtually everything he'd done through 1975, but because it printed some rare and even unpublished items (such as examples of the *Kermit the Hermit* comic strip). It also printed a photograph of Kurtzman taken by E. B. Boatner, a fan-journalist who visited Kurtzman in his studio in February 1976.

Boatner's exceptional photographs are the best ever taken of Kurtzman in his attic studio. The new studio, unlike the tiny one at the Audrey Avenue house, was a sizable space that had room for many shelves, storage cabinets and more than one desk. Accoutrements included a telephone, a typewriter, an adding machine and an intercom. The intercom allowed him to buzz Adele if an incoming phone call was for her. There were two phone lines, one for business and one for the family, but his calls could come on either one. The intercom also went to the front door, so he didn't have to run downstairs if the doorbell rang when Adele was out. If it was a package, he could just use the intercom to ask the postal worker to leave it on the front stoop. (Packages, special delivery letters, etc. arrived virtually every day. Kurtzman received an enormous amount of mail.) He could hear Adele in the kitchen, and all she had to do was say, "Harvey! Lunch!" or "Harvey! Take out the garbage!"

To add to his *Little Annie Fanny* income, he relied largely on his consultant position at *Esquire*. Editor Bryon Dobell recalled, "Harvey was our cartoon editor. He came in every week with a batch of cartoons that we were to choose from, and he was terrific. He would go through the submissions and pick out the ones he thought were the best. He was always right." Bill Basso, who went on to a notable career as an illustrator of childrens' books, was one of the cartoonists submitting gags. He had been sending his ideas to the *New Yorker* over a period of time, only to have them soundly rejected. Then he tried *Esquire* on a lark. "One memorable day, I got a phone call from none other than the great Harvey Kurtzman. Harvey liked one of my sketches and wanted me to do the finish over the weekend and deliver it to him at his home. Holy smokes! I did it. I was nervous as hell. Harvey put me at ease as Adele brought us some refreshments. What an experience!"[43] Kurtzman was never credited as cartoon editor at the magazine, although he performed the function for a number of years. He also came up with special material, such as a piece on famous cartoonists' favorite pieces among their own work ("What's Your Favorite Cartoon?," August 1979).

Because he worked for *Esquire*, Kurtzman received invitations to promotional and social events. He knew many of the local literati, and enjoyed meeting Tom Wolfe, Norman Mailer, Truman Capote, Gay Talese and others. Adele, on the other hand—despite her wit—found those occasions uncomfortable.

> The worst experience I ever had was when Nora Ephron gave a party for Lee Eisenberg, the editor of *Esquire*. It was a birthday party and Harvey and I went. I wore a dress that can only be described as "cheap renaissance." All these smart, young things were there. You have to realize that I was not working. Ephron was still married to Carl Bernstein, the Watergate guy . . . and I come in ill dressed and not working.
>
> These women turned to me and said, "What do you do?" So, I said, "Well, I stay home." Big mistake. I should have lied. You know when somebody says, "What do *you* do?" then you're in bad trouble. That was one of the worst evenings of my life. Harvey, of course, didn't have that problem. He knew people there and they knew him. He didn't [realize] what was going on [with me]. I wanted to kill.[44]

Adele also felt out of place when she accompanied her husband to functions at the Playboy Mansion. Hefner would try to make her feel comfortable, but it didn't help. "My sister would say, 'Adele, it's *you*. You're allowing yourself to feel that way,' but I just felt like nobody. You know, like what was my talent?"[45]

Adele wasn't as impressed as Harvey was with Hefner. Kurtzman never lost his admiration of the success and glitz of *Playboy*. In 1974, Hugh Hefner had completed his move to the Playboy Mansion West in Los Angeles, a transition that had been ongoing since he purchased it three years earlier. On one occasion, Kurtzman was on his way home in the Playboy jet (known as the Big Bunny) when he realized it had its own telephone. That kind of luxury tickled him so much that he called Adele at home, just to show off. She said, "I'm up to my elbows in diapers, and Harvey calls and he says, 'Guess where I am? I'm flying over the Grand Canyon and talking to you on the phone!' And I said, 'So, Harvey, what do you want?,' or something very cruel, because he was there and I was here.

I said something mean and cutting. He was trying to impress me and I was not ready to be impressed.'"[46]

On October 3, 1975, Kurtzman drove to Boston to appear at a New England comics convention known as Newcon. The list of special guests included Gil Kane, Dick Giordano, Mort Walker, John Cullen Murphy and Archie Goodwin. During the con, the pro artists and some fans collaborated on a giant mural. According to Bob Cosgrove, one of the fans, Kurtzman was the great motivator for the project. The idea was that their sketched characters were supposed to respond to each other. Kurtzman told the participants that he based the idea on a French TV program *Tac Au Tac*, which had artists reacting to each other's drawings. (The program was named for a fencing term involving thrusting and parrying.)[47]

A week after Newcon, a comedy program called *NBC's Saturday Night* made its debut. (It wasn't *Saturday Night Live* at first.) The show was created by Toronto-born Lorne Michaels and developed by Dick Ebersol, and quickly became a ratings hit. When Kurtzman saw its parodies of TV commercials, comic book characters and so on, he couldn't help but feel that it was a sort of descendent of *Mad*. Lorne Michaels was born in 1944, the perfect age to discover the comic book and magazine versions of *Mad*, and his cast of comedic actors (Dan Aykroyd, John Belushi, Chevy Chase, Gilda Radner) had grown up at a time when it seemed like every kid owned at least one *Mad* paperback. Harry Shearer, a member of the *Saturday Night* cast, wrote, "Without Harvey Kurtzman, there would have been no *Saturday Night Live*. I still remember the first edition of *Mad* being passed furtively along the rows of desks in school. Harvey and his crew lit a fire of subversive laughter. They taught us to pay attention to

Kurtzman's attic studio, 1976: courtesy of E. B. Boatner.

sloppiness of thought and execution in our politics and culture, and they taught us that 'popular' need not, for a magical moment at least, be synonymous with 'lower common denominator.'"[48]

By the mid-1970s, it was clear that *Mad* had virtually revolutionized humor in America. Magazines, books, television and even movies satirized popular culture, politics and consumerism in the *Mad* manner. Many of the successful writers and artists whose careers he fostered showed Kurtzman-esque flashes of humor in their work. The poster for the comedy *Airplane!*—famously showing the airplane fuselage tied in a knot—was created by Bob Grossman, the Yale student who got his first job as a result of an introduction at the *Help!* Christmas party at the Algonquin.

AFTER HIS TRIP TO FRANCE in 1974, Kurtzman consistently championed European comics in America. He was in a feisty mood when he joined a panel at the Chicago Comicon on August 8, 1976, along with Stan Lee and Jenette Kahn, who served as publishers of Marvel and DC Comics, respectively. When Stan Lee was in the midst of some opening comments, Kurtzman interrupted and said, "To play devil's advocate for a minute, Stan, I'd like to ask a question. Why is it that comics have such a low grade of integrity? By contrast with the so-called slick magazines . . . and by contrast with the European comics, which we all know are drawn and printed beautifully?"

Harvey Kurtzman at work: courtesy of E. B. Boatner.

Lee sputtered a response, and Kurtzman clarified, "By low I mean . . . low pay, low printing [quality]. I'm not trying to say evil, or bad, just low grade." After Lee and Kahn attempted to explain the economics of a mass market media, Kurtzman again pointed to "the existence of good comic book publishing in certain portions of the globe. And these magazines are being put out by inspired publishers."[49] Lee became angry.

> Yes, I guess you're right, Harvey. It's only the people who are away from the norm, who are doing things on their own who are doing any good.

> *Annie Fanny* is no good because it's part of the Hefner empire and you've
> done nothing new for the last fifteen years and why the hell don't you go
> out and break the mold. Harvey, that's the biggest crock I've ever heard in
> my life! There are inspired comic books [in America]. Read some some-
> times. If people didn't enjoy today's comic books, we wouldn't have these
> conventions.[50]

Kurtzman allowed that there were some inspired creators in American
comics. What he was talking about, he said, was the lack of publishers in
the States who were pushing to try new things. He seemed to get a kick
out of baiting Lee.

Kurtzman and Elder broke into a new type of work in 1976, one that
augmented their income for the next ten years: creating posters and advertisements for TV shows and movies. Advertisements featuring their
artwork appeared in *TV Guide* touting such television series as *The Love
Boat* and *Nine to Five*, as well as some forgettable TV movies including
Three on a Date, For the Love of It and *Make Me an Offer*. They did movie
posters for the theatrical films *Harper Valley PTA* (1978) and *Chattanooga
Choo Choo* (1984).

1977 was a year of highs and lows for Kurtzman. He was a guest of
honor at the San Diego Comic Con (now Comic-Con International: San
Diego) in late July, which meant the convention paid for his transportation
and meals. He took eight-year-old Nellie with him. It showed her that her
father had fans. "I remember that was fun, because I was an outgoing kid,"
Nellie said. "There's something about being the kid of a famous person,
whatever the level of that fame, and people are lining up to get an autograph but you can climb up on his lap. It was a great feeling."[51] He received
the convention's Inkpot Award, and signed many autographs.

Adele recalled, "When people would line up for autographs, it was
very surprising. It was a very positive affirmation for him. People would
come to him about all kinds of his work, not just comic books."[52] Comic
conventions brought a richness and variety to Kurtzman's life that his
work in the 1970s and 1980s often did not. Back in the EC and *Humbug*
days, he answered many of the letters from fans. At the comic cons, which
had sprung up in many cities in the country besides New York and San
Diego, he had the opportunity to meet many of them in person and genuinely enjoyed it. When he signed an autograph, he sometimes added a
small sketch.

Another high that summer (especially since Kurtzman was a lifelong
New Yorker) came with the publication of a major article in the *New York*

Times magazine to coincide with the twenty-fifth birthday of *Mad*. "The 'Mad' Generation" by Tony Hiss and Jeff Lewis appeared on July 31, 1977, and was one of the first mainstream articles to discuss the cultural impact of the comic book and magazine *Mad*. It was accompanied by a new painting of Alfred E. Neuman by Norman Mingo. The authors unequivocally stated, "Those first twenty-eight issues of Kurtzman's *Mad* . . . contain some of the deepest, most probing and hysterical humor in American history." They grappled, however, when attempting to define the magazine's impact. "Parents argued that *Mad* was inculcating destructive attitudes, that it taught teen-agers cynicism and, ultimately, disengagement. Even after twenty-five years, it is difficult to assess *Mad*'s cultural impact. *Mad*, by itself, did not shape a generation. Yet it reflected a social fact and gave expression to feelings shared by young people at a great turning point in American life." The article is a celebration of *Mad* with a strong emphasis on Kurtzman's creation of the magazine. He is identified as its "founding editor" in the first paragraph, and his name appears twenty-five more times, whereas Gaines's name appears three times and Feldstein's just twice. Kurtzman is quoted; they are not. Gaines is identified as *"Mad*'s publisher" and described as "a happy-go-lucky millionaire," while Kurtzman is "a living legend." Predictably, Gaines and Feldstein (and the staff of *Mad*) were upset by the piece's pro-Kurtzman slant. It was another case, like "Citizen Gaines" in *National Lampoon*, where the man whose name Bill Gaines erased from the *Mad* paperbacks was finally getting his due. Kurtzman was pleased.

On the downside, 1977 ended with the sudden death of a dear friend. René Goscinny died of cardiac arrest at fifty-one, while he was in Paris on November 5 having a stress test in his doctor's office. He was buried in the Jewish Cemetery of Nice. In accordance with his will, most of his money was transferred to the chief rabbinate of France. After Goscinny's untimely death, his collaborator Uderzo took over the writing of the Astérix series, although production slowed to one book every three to five years. The critical reception of the books written without Goscinny were mixed to poor. Kurtzman was deeply saddened by the loss of the gifted writer who built a bridge for him to the world of European comics.

APART FROM HIS EDITORIAL WORK at *Esquire*, *Little Annie Fanny* consumed the majority of Harvey Kurtzman's creative energies. The higher page rates were shared with fewer partners for significant stretches of time, which meant more went to Kurtzman and Elder. They both received additional royalties from the 1972 *Little Annie Fanny* reprint book. Kurtzman was finally putting money regularly into savings.

Back in the EC days, Kurtzman's research helped him give the war comic books authenticity, and turned up new ideas for stories. Now he plunged into research for *Annie Fanny* for similar reasons. It wasn't the kind of research that could be done in the New York Public Library. With the help of a generous expense account, Kurtzman became a sort of pop culture investigator who traveled the country (and even Europe) to get a firsthand look at the latest trends in lifestyles, entertainment and fashion. In an interview with Jacques Dutrey, he explained,

> Now when I do my *Little Annie Fanny*s, I have to research my stories, because, like the writer who has to live his next book or have an experience, I go about looking for experiences that will give me new material. So, as a writer works, or as an artist works, everything changes. I mean, it's life itself. Nothing remains the same. You constantly have a new set of circumstances. You don't go back. You don't ever go back. There's really no place to go back to: and to go back to the old *Mad*, I couldn't do it. It's not there anymore. There's nothing left. It's all on paper now.[53]

Some research could be done locally because New York City had so much to offer. Bill Stout saw how Kurtzman operated. "Harvey took me to a party . . . at a kind of warehouse club-type situation. I met all different kinds of people from all different professions and stuff. And then about a day or two later, I got the pencils for the Annie story that we were working on, and there was every single person that was at that party. Harvey went there to observe current fashions, to see what the hairstyles were. It was all homework for him."[54]

Most of Kurtzman's research jaunts were great fun. Denis Kitchen recalled, "There was one time where he pitched an idea on mud wrestling. Hefner said okay so Harvey looked up the schedule of the mud wrestlers. He called me and said: 'They're going to be in Green Bay, Wisconsin, next week. Can you meet me there?' I actually watched him doing his research, getting to go backstage with the mud wrestlers and hang out and so on. Those paid trips were probably the best perk about working for *Playboy*, besides going to the mansion periodically."[55] Kurtzman sojourned to ski lodges, bodybuilding contests, swingers' clubs, the French Riviera (a nude beach in St. Tropez), a Western bar with a mechanical bull, and the redwood forests in California. It meant a lot to him, he said, because he was experiencing a whole world that was beyond the reach of the average man.

Usually he traveled alone—they were business trips, after all—while Adele stayed home with Pete and Nellie. For a man with a modest income, these *Playboy*-funded expeditions were like little no-cost vacations.

Harvey Kurtzman's love-hate attitude about *Little Annie Fanny* became known by the mid-1970s. In 1965, after three years on it, he said, "I may be kidding myself, but I like to have this illusion of a grand *raison d'être*. I have to feel that I'm not hacking for money."[56] He initially resisted thinking negatively about the bawdy comic strip, because that would be counter-productive, considering the degree of his commitment to the feature. Eventually his frustrations with its creative limitations grew until he began expressing such thoughts publicly. When asked in 1976 what his intention was when he originally approached *Little Annie Fanny*, he responded,

> She was supposed to be a sexy vehicle for a satirical story, and that was a difficult format as it turned out, lo, many years later. The sexuality of Fanny tends to conflict with the satire of *Fanny*, because we're always obligated to give the feature that dollop of sex and very often it gets in the way. There's a confusion of purpose. Is it a sex cartoon? Is it a satire? What is it? The satire really is overwhelmed by the sex. Because you never see it as satirical stories. They're jerk-off stories. There are a lot of guys who, I'm sure, do get the details. But that's not what people go to it for. Although I wish they would, because it's there! I think the sex does violence to the satire.[57]

He admitted that, for him, "the best part of the format was and is the research."[58] But there was a consequence to all the detail put into the strip: its pages became overcrowded. "We do try to squeeze as much into a story as we can without graphic clutter," he admitted. "That's something that Hefner really leaned on us for. And I'm not saying he was wrong. Because I think graphically we do good-looking pages. But we do, in another more subtle way, try to squeeze as much into a page as we possibly can. We try to squeeze in a lot of dialogue, a lot of gags per square inch."[59] The density of the panels was partly a result of the short length of each episode. In the plus column, the composition and design on *Annie* was always very good, and the gags were generally amusing, if not fall-down funny. Kurtzman wasn't blind to its lesser status with comics fans, even in the feature's better days. "It's fascinating to me the way *Annie Fanny* doesn't affect people the way the old *Mad* did. But it doesn't. We probably get more integrity in the eyes of Mr. Man-in-the-street through *Annie Fanny*."[60]

Annie has her share of admirers. In 1995, popular culture historian R. C. Harvey wrote, "With his old classmate Will Elder at his elbow, he settled in at *Playboy* to produce the most lavish color comic strip of all time, *Little Annie Fanny*, a satire of hip society and sexual mores. It, like almost all of Kurtzman's endeavors, was a masterpiece."[61] Skip Williamson recently said, "*Goodman Beaver* was better, but I love *Annie Fanny* because Kurtzman did it, and because of the detail. I think it's masterful cartooning and writing." To those who said it got out of touch with what was really new and fresh in American society, Williamson said, "Remember, the stories had to be approved by Hefner, and Hefner really was out of touch."[62]

Working for *Playboy* was never less than challenging. As Will Elder pointed out, *Mad* was a much freer creative situation than *Little Annie Fanny*. "This is a much tighter controlled medium we're working with now," he said. "Not only that, but we have about fifty million editors overseeing everything that's done, and corrections."[63] As time went on, new staffers arrived who had no stake in Annie's ongoing presence in the magazine. Hefner's support was never in doubt, but he had less direct contact with Kurtzman in the later 1970s. One of the intermediaries proved to be a problem.

Michelle Urry was an attractive twenty-six-year-old brunette hired by *Playboy* as a typist in 1965. She had read and collected comic books in her youth, giving her a familiarity with the cartoon medium that helped her gain Hefner's confidence. By the end of the decade, she had been promoted to assistant cartoon editor. (There was no named cartoon editor. Hefner performed that function himself.) According to Skip Williamson, who worked for *Playboy*, "I don't think Michelle Urry did much editing. Her job every month was to gather all the cartoon submissions together, throw out the obvious dead wood, and give them to Hefner. He would make the picks. She was essentially a filter rather than an editor." With regard to her personality and working methods, he said, "Urry was horrible to work with. Many people lived inside of her. She could be sweet and deferring, and two minutes later, snarling and wanting to rip your throat out. You were always unnerved around her because you never knew what was coming."[64]

Urry became a problem for Kurtzman because she was trying to expand her role at *Playboy* and gain editorial control over all the cartoons in the magazine, including the "*Playboy* Funnies" section (created by Williamson) and *Little Annie Fanny*. That meant Kurtzman's story ideas had to be submitted to her for approval first, and then to Chicago where editor Dave Stevens also had to sign off. She would condescend to Kurtzman, and was at various turns aggressive and non-responsive. Her behavior interfered with his production of the strip. In one instance, *Playboy* killed a story that Kurtzman and Elder had already begun. Kurtzman came to loathe her. [65]

Despite these difficulties, the possibility of a *Little Annie Fanny* movie adaptation gained steam in the late 1970s. Back in 1971, a pirate company produced a crude, hardcore Annie cartoon (titled *Little Annie Franny*) that played at the 50th Street Cinema, an adult movie house in New York City. It ran seven minutes, and was quite well animated when compared to the Saturday morning cartoons of the day. When Benson told Kurtzman about it, the cartoonist came back with, "Thank you . . . . *Playboy* has indeed taken action and we're going to get their ass." [66] Hugh Hefner was bullish on the potentialities of an Annie movie and by 1978, the project seemed about to become a reality.

In the *Los Angeles Herald Examiner* on July 27, 1978, *Playboy* executive Edward Russien announced a nationwide search for an actress ("another Marilyn Monroe") to play Little Annie Fanny in a film to be produced by Sidney Beckerman (*Marathon Man*) with Hugh Hefner as Executive Producer. The article stated, "*Little Annie Fanny* would be a $10 million production from Playboy Productions, who were also producing *Saint Jack* to be directed by Peter Bogdanovich." In a brief note to Kurtzman the day after the story broke, Hefner wrote, "We are finally off and running on the *Little Annie Fanny* film, in a manner that promises a first rate, quality production. I will be sending you more information on the project as it develops." The possibility of a movie deal guaranteed that new executives at *Playboy* wouldn't try to kill the strip. It also helped Kurtzman maintain his interest in it, as getting paid to write a screenplay (and even to direct the film) seemed possible.

In an interview in 1978, he said, "*Annie Fanny* takes all of my time . . . days . . . nights. If I'm not writing and drawing, I'm traveling for *Annie Fanny* research. I've begun to notice there's a large pair of tits growing out of my forehead." [67]

He was exaggerating a bit. While *Annie* did take the largest part of his time in the 1970s, Harvey Kurtzman lived a full life and was involved in many other things. He was a loving father who was there for his daughters as Nellie moved through grade school, Liz attended Parsons School of Design and Meredith began a career as a textile designer. He and Adele continued to support Pete and others like him by participating in the annual fundraisers for the Crestview School, the institution they helped found. From a creative standpoint, Kurtzman's association with *Esquire* continued throughout the decade, as both contributor and cartoon editor. His work appeared in *Time*, *Look*, *TV Guide*, *Chicago Midwest* and the *New York Times* magazine. He dabbled in television animation, underground comix and Eurocomics. His love of airports and airplanes was fully indulged not just by his travels on behalf of *Little Annie Fanny*, but by a growing number of appearances on the comics convention circuit. At his annual Fourth of July parties, he welcomed people from an ever-widening group of friends and colleagues.

Nevertheless, everything else was subordinate to *Little Annie Fanny*. *Playboy* provided the bulk of his income, although *Esquire* and Topps nicely supplemented it. Kurtzman further augmented his earnings with a new endeavor in the "me decade," one that contributed to the future of cartooning and comic art in America. Kurtzman became a teacher.

L'Echo des Savanes #8 (Fall 1974).

Kurtzman at home in 1971, in his living room, and in front of his "picture wall." Photographs courtesy of Al Hewetson.

Above: Art Spiegelman, Michelle Brand and Harvey Kurtzman. Photograph courtesy of Jay Lynch. Below: Lynch and Kurtzman are "flipping the bird" at photographer Art Spiegelman.

From a Kurtzman Christmas card, ca. 1973. © the Harvey Kurtzman Estate.

Above: Gil Kane and Harvey Kurtzman working on the giant mural at Newcon 1975. Below: Nellie Kurtzman and her father at the 1977 San Diego Comic-Con. Photographs courtesy of E. B. Boatner.

25.

TUESDAY AFTERNOONS WITH HARVEY

ON TUESDAY, SEPTEMBER 11, 1973, just before 1:00 p.m., an overburdened Harvey Kurtzman entered the building at 209 E. 23rd St. in midtown Manhattan. He held a shopping bag full of magazines and comics with one hand, a six-pack of Pepsi-Cola with the other, and had folders, books and legal pads tucked under his arms. It was his first day of teaching at The School of Visual Arts. He entered a classroom full of students and immediately dropped everything but the soda—not the most auspicious beginning to his new part-time career.

Kurtzman was well aware of The School of Visual Arts (SVA), because his daughter Meredith went there to study textile design. It was established as the Cartoonists and Illustrators School in 1947 to provide training to aspiring artists, many of them fresh out of the military. As time went on, the school expanded its scope beyond cartoon and commercial art to offer courses in film, animation, sculpture and photography, necessitating the name change in 1956. The original focus waned as the markets for gag cartoonists, comic strip and comic book artists contracted. By the early 1970s, the comics-oriented classes were gone. Co-founder Burne Hogarth left to teach elsewhere, leaving Silas Rhodes to run the place. SVA wasn't yet an accredited four-year institution, though it was working toward that goal. The school offered classes taught by working professionals who educated students not only in their craft but in the realities of the marketplace. It was the least expensive art school in the city, making it attractive to those from working- and middle-class backgrounds.

A new crop of freshmen cartoonists arrived in the fall of 1972, weaned on the comic strips and books of the 1960s and the underground comix of more recent years. They discovered that they not only had to take a full year of foundation classes (life drawing, painting, design, art history) before they could get to elective courses, but that among the electives in the curriculum, none taught cartooning or comic art. The closest were illustration classes taught by Edward Sorel and others. Two factions of students decided to do something about it.

One group started a comics club, and asked SVA's alumni director Tom Gill to give informal lectures. Gill was a veteran cartoonist whose best-known work was an eleven-year run on *The Lone Ranger* comic book. "Tom Gill was a very nice man, very convivial and very helpful," student David Pomerantz recalled. "He would give little chalk talks in an area adjacent to his office."[1] Another faction centered on John Holmstrom and Batton Lash. The groups independently asked Silas Rhodes to add a class in cartooning to the curriculum.

"Brian Hall and I stormed into the president's office and asked, 'Why aren't there any cartooning classes?,'" Pomerantz said. Holmstrom and Lash accosted Rhodes in the hallway, asking the same question. Rhodes told them to make a list of potential teachers for such a course, and if they could get ten students (at least) to commit to taking a class taught by anyone on the list, he would pursue the idea. Encouraged by Gill, who took himself out of the running, the students created a list of working professionals, and signed their names to indicate their definite interest. Will Eisner and Harvey Kurtzman topped the list, which also included Gil Kane, Neal Adams, Mort Drucker and possibly Robert Crumb (though everyone knew that was a long shot). True to his word, Rhodes contacted Eisner and Kurtzman. Eisner accepted at once. Kurtzman hesitated.

He had no teaching experience. He hadn't even considered the idea before. While Kurtzman felt art talent was innate, he knew that he had learned useful things in classes at M&A and Cooper Union. He knew a lot about the business of humorous cartooning, and had been willing and able to communicate that knowledge to young practitioners in the field. The more he thought about it, the more the idea appealed to him, especially when it became clear that the position would pay reasonably well. (SVA paid roughly $100 an hour for a weekly, three-hour session.) The extra money would be welcome, especially if the class didn't require a great deal of preparation.

Informed that Eisner had already accepted and would be teaching a class called "Sequential Art," Kurtzman contacted him to discuss the offer. Eisner reportedly once said, "I give Harvey advice. He never takes it!"[2] In this case, Kurtzman listened. One thing Eisner shared helped immensely. "[Will] had an army manual which [said] that the teacher should assume that no one subject will maintain interest for more than half an hour," Kurtzman recalled. "Therefore, since I was to have a three-hour class, I'd need to have six possible subjects in mind, with an additional couple for [an] emergency. This turned out to be a magic system for me."[3] As always, structure was Kurtzman's way of getting a handle on a new endeavor. Kurtzman respected Eisner, so the older cartoonist's acceptance of the offer was reassuring. After getting clearance from Rhodes to have guest lecturers from time to time, he said "yes."

Eisner's "Sequential Art" class would focus primarily on comic book storytelling. It was only logical that Kurtzman, best known for *Mad* and *Little Annie Fanny*, chose to handle the humorous side of the craft. He called his class "Satirical Cartooning." In May, Rhodes told the students that Eisner and Kurtzman would begin teaching in the fall. Kurtzman's class would run from 1:00 to 4:00 p.m. each Tuesday. Pomerantz said, "I have this great memory of phoning my friend Brian [Hall] who was living out on Long Island, saying 'We got Kurtzman!' We were so excited." Holmstrom and Lash, who considered Kurtzman a satiric genius, were also jubilant. Will Eisner met with students during the summer to help formulate his teaching plans. Kurtzman did not. He had no idea what to expect when he entered the classroom on his first day.

WHEN KURTZMAN DROPPED HIS MATERIALS, David Pomerantz and another student rushed to help pick them up. Kurtzman, who was wearing a sport coat and tie, muttered, "I just came in off the street," apparently meaning there was no orientation, no faculty meeting beforehand. He offered a soda to anyone interested, then began class by having the eighteen to twenty students identify themselves, say why they had signed up and what they hoped to learn.

It became obvious that the class members had widely disparate interests. A few wanted to draw super heroes for Marvel or DC. Others wanted to break into the underground newspapers and comix. Some had no idea what they hoped to gain from the class. Many of them didn't know who he was, and Kurtzman didn't enlighten them. (The course description in the catalog stated that he had worked for *Mad*, not that he had created it.) In addition to Pomerantz, Hall, Lash and Holmstrom, others in the first year class were Ken Laager, Ken Landgraf, John Laney, Paul Maringelli, Robert Romagnoli, Allen Schwartz and Bob Wiacek, all who went on to careers in art. "It was a little scattershot at first," Pomerantz recounted. "I think Harvey wasn't quite sure how to approach this. So we took a little break and he took off his tie and jacket. That was the only time we saw him dressed that way. After that, he came in dressed casually." Kurtzman showed the class some of the magazines and comics he brought as give-aways (he always received a lot of freebies in the mail), then consulted a yellow pad where he had the day's activities outlined.

The main subject of the class was the gag cartoon, the kind of single-panel humorous cartoons that appeared in the *New Yorker*, *Esquire*, *Playboy* and dozens of other magazines. This took some, who were familiar with Kurtzman's work, by surprise. While such cartoons weren't Kurtzman's creative specialty, he had given them a lot of thought in his editorial capacity at *Esquire*. For one exercise, he gave the students a caption from a published cartoon from *Playboy*, such as one done by Jack Davis, and they were expected to come up with a cartoon image to match. At the end, the published version was revealed. Other times, he asked everybody to do a cartoon at home during the week, and then Kurtzman would have a one-on-one session with each student the following week to discuss the result.

In contrast to Eisner, Kurtzman was gentle with his criticism. Eisner's class was more like a workshop, with the teacher-as-manager presiding as he had in his own shop operations. Eisner didn't pull his punches. He would say, "Your drawing is weak," in contrast to Kurtzman, who would say, "You're having trouble with your rendering. Maybe you should try this."[4]

Sometimes the students would crowd around Kurtzman to watch him demonstrate something on a drawing board. In one lesson, he drew a circle on the board, and said that cartoon gags could be divided into basic themes. "What are the themes?" he asked. Students made suggestions, and Kurtzman showed how they essentially boiled down to three. He divided the circle three ways like a pie chart, and wrote "life/death," "power," and "sex/love" into the sections. Then he said, "Now let's take different cartoons and see where they fit."[5] A man going into his boss's office would be "power," a husband walking in on his wife and another man would be "sex/love," and two people stranded on a desert island would be "life/death." He started off with the clear-cut categories, then showed how sometimes a cartoon theme could be two of them, or even all three.

On another occasion, Kurtzman did a painting demonstration. The students watched as he created a one-panel *Annie Fanny* layout, layering the watercolors to build up the desired color effects. Most of the students liked the demo, but one female student was so offended by the sexism of *Annie Fanny* that she left the room and dropped out of the class. (There were never more than a few women in Kurtzman's class.) When he was giving this same demonstration in a later year, one of the students asked Kurtzman in all earnestness, "Who invented watercolor?" Kurtzman was completely taken aback. Was it a serious question or a put-on? He wound up responding with a long pause, a double take and ultimately silence.[6]

Kurtzman in the classroom. Photograph courtesy of J. Michael Catron.

Knowing that Elder did the actual painting on *Little Annie Fanny*, someone asked if Kurtzman had ever wanted to paint, either as a hobby or professionally. "No way!," he said. "I never wanted to paint. I've done watercolors, bad ones, on the beach to while away the long vacation days. I'm a much better cartoonist than I am a painter and I'm convinced that my cartoon work will leave a much stronger mark on the world than any kind of painting I'm capable of doing."[7] Naturally, there were lessons in pen and ink. Kurtzman demonstrated several different ways of doing crosshatching, and then had the students practice on their own, while he walked around and saw how they were doing. Kurtzman helped them, stressing, "Don't let the tools get in the way." Holmstrom recalled, "The way he discussed drawing with different techniques—crosshatching, stippling, line-drawing—was short, sweet and to the point. He described black as 'the ultimate weapon.'"[8]

From the start, Kurtzman had trouble with classroom discipline. "He was a very accommodating person and not one to raise his voice or be very assertive," Lash remembered. "The first few weeks of the class, Harvey seemed to have a difficult time keeping order. [Some of us] were pretty much in awe of Kurtzman, so we behaved ourselves. Others . . . were loud, and came and went without permission as if they were in the student lounge rather than a classroom."[9] A longtime SVA instructor teaching across the hall took Kurtzman out for a drink after class one day and gave him a crash course in handling college-age art school students. "It helped," Lash said. "Harvey was a little firmer and regained control of the class. As the school year progressed, it was clear that even the most apathetic student had a great deal of respect for Harvey." There continued to be occasions when the class got out of control. It was a mix of hippies, punks and relatively straightlaced students, most still teenagers or in their early twenties. There were factions, and sometimes insults would fly. Then Kurtzman would have to play babysitter or peacemaker, and his temper would flare. At one point the first year, he interrupted a conflict, and said, "C'mon, it's your money! Make this of value to yourself!"[10]

After the first few weeks, Kurtzman began having guest teachers, all professional artists with some stature. There were three in October alone, on the first, third and fifth Tuesdays of the month: Neal Adams (who demonstrated doing layouts for a Conan the Barbarian story), Gil Kane (who took questions from the students, and impressed them with his articulate answers), and Robert Grossman (who held the class in his studio, one of a few field trips). Periodically, students clamored for a visit from Will Elder. It became something of a running joke. Kurtzman finally explained, "I think something terrible happened to Willy in New York, and he never comes into the city any more." Jack Davis came in and drew a caricature of every student in the class. Other guest teachers later in the school year included David Levine, who was best known for his caricatures in the *New York Review of Books*. (He and Kurtzman had collaborated on a piece for *Esquire* in 1961.)[11] According to one student, Levine did a caricature of Nixon, and "it was as if it flowed out of his pen." Once, when Kurtzman missed a class, his substitute was up-and-coming artist Howard Chaykin.[12]

One of the chief projects in the second semester of both Eisner's and Kurtzman's class was the creation and publication of a magazine. *Will Eisner's Gallery of New Comics* was relatively slick and upscale. The stapled booklet from Kurtzman's class (later a saddle-stitched magazine called *Kar-tünz*), was funkier. *Gallery* may have received some funding from SVA, but *Kar-tünz* was entirely on its own. Marshall Arisman, then chair of the Illustration Department, recalled, "I remember the first year Harvey brought me cartoons from the students in his class. Many of them were scatological. The humor was based in a preoccupation with obscenity, particularly excrement. Harvey . . . requested that SVA print [them in] a book. When I refused, Harvey went back to his class, explained that the chair would not approve it and sent the students out into the neighbor-

Kurtzman cover to his first SVA class's publication, with various class members caricatured in the background (Spring 1974). Copyright © The Harvey Kurtzman Estate.

hood to get local merchants to buy an ad. The students loved his class and his support for their artistic freedom."[13]

   When the students had sold enough ads, the magazine was printed. Kurtzman's first year class's magazine was simply titled *Souvenir*, with the subtitle *Harvey Kurtzman's class of 73–74, School of Visual Arts*. The cover by Kurtzman showed him standing in a crowd of the students in the class. Inside there was a disclaimer that it was "an off campus unofficial publication." Producing the magazine was a practical lesson for the students in publishing, editing, layout, advertising and printing. Each student submitted his or her best cartoons. One served as editor, another did the lettering, others worked on the paste-ups. Then, Kurtzman took the class on a field trip to the printer, familiarizing them with a photo off-set press and the nature of the printing process. At the end of the school year, Kurtzman invited the entire class to his home for a backyard picnic.

David Pomerantz related better to Kurtzman than to Eisner. "Harvey was very in touch with the underground crowd, and I think that's what kept Harvey young in many ways, because he was always picking up on what was going on. He got me interested in all forms of cartooning like the underground comix, particularly Crumb's work. He tried to steer us away from the big mainstream companies, because he knew what that was like. Even though there wasn't a big age difference between the two men, like seven years, Eisner seemed like the older authority figure, whereas Kurtzman was like this perpetually young guy in my eyes."

John Holmstrom's enthusiasm for the class and Kurtzman increased as the year progressed. "Harvey's class was the greatest educational experience of my life. Meeting people like Jack Davis, David Levine, Arnold Roth, Bill Griffith and so many other artists, watching them create work in front of us, while talking about everything that had to do with their work, was a revelation." He was in the group invited to Robert Grossman's studio, and to see Arnold Roth's jazz band at The Player's Club, a private club in the city. "It wasn't your usual education, that's for sure," he said. The class was also a valuable networking experience. "I began a correspondence with Bill Griffith (who had created the comic strip *Zippy*) about self-publishing that encouraged me to start *Punk* magazine."

Kurtzman decided to return in the fall for a second year, and reflected on the experience in an interview with Judd Hurd for *Cartoonist PROfiles*.

> I try to tell the students everything I know. As you're aware I write a little, I draw a little, edit a little, and I've published a little. So I teach a little bit of everything, and I assume that the students are best advanced by learning about all of my professional activities. When you get a bunch of students in a room, you discover that they've come for fifty different reasons. So I don't have a plan, except to make these people take what they've got and make the most of it, relative to the areas I know about.[14]

With regard to disruptive students, he added, "I haven't been looking at portfolios of students who've applied in the past but I'm going to start doing this because some kids shouldn't be in a class of this kind and only distract other students. I won't be hunting for previous art training but rather will try to assess what their talent is before they come into class."[15] Kurtzman didn't follow through with this plan. Sarah Downs, who took Kurtzman's class in 1975 and later assisted Kurtzman with it, recently recalled, "He didn't have portfolio reviews for my classes or for any subsequent classes. He never turned anyone down. SVA capped his classes at about twenty-five students, but often additional students would ask if they could take it. As I recall, he always said yes. I remember some of the first days of his classes where he'd have students scrambling around other classrooms to find chairs for the extra students." As a result, the issue of students who didn't belong in the class, and various degrees of classroom disruption, recurred throughout his years at the school.

The guest visits and lectures were always an important part of the class. In the second year of "Satirical Cartooning," Al Jaffee was a guest. Robert Crumb dropped by in December. Batton Lash recalled, "I had been out of his class for six months by that time. But when Harvey ran into me in the student lounge, he was kind enough to tell me about Crumb and invited me to join in. Of course, I went, and Harvey introduced me to him." Crumb recalled, "I would just stand in front of the class and wing it, improvise, talk at them, make them laugh. It was easy, as they were mostly ready to love me. At that time I was the cartoonist hero of the day. I believe I made two appearances, at least, at his School of Visual Arts classes, maybe three."[16]

Although Kurtzman's class was constructed to run just two semesters, the school permitted students to take it more than one year because he varied the mix of lessons and demonstrations from year to year. Sarah Downs and Phil Felix took it for two years. Drew Friedman joined in 1978 and stayed for three.

The son of the novelist and playwright Bruce Jay Friedman, Drew Friedman was born in 1958 and grew up on *Mad* magazines and paperbacks. Friedman remembered, "I figured out that the early stuff was from the comic books, and I started buying the original *Mad* comic books. I became a Kurtzman addict pretty early on. My childhood goals were to be a contributor to *Mad*—one of the 'Usual Gang of Idiots'—and do cards for Topps Bubble Gum."[17] As he looked through art school catalogs, one item jumped out at him: a class taught by Kurtzman. "I thought I was imagining it, but there it was! You had to plow through the first year courses before you could get to Kurtzman, so that's what I did." He also signed up for Eisner's class in his second year at SVA.

He recounted how the class began: "On the first day, Harvey had a thing where he handed out balloons. You couldn't stop blowing it up until it popped. The theory was that's the way you build up a cartoon or comic strip, and then there's a big *bam* at the end, a big surprise finish. That was his analogy, which was kind of clever." Kurtzman explained the lesson this way:

> I've always likened short-story structure to the blowing up of a balloon. I do this with my class. I bring them a bunch of balloons and say, "OK, blow 'em up 'til they burst." Then, bang, bang, bang and everybody goes "Yaah! Eeeeh! Ooooh!" and then I point out that it's just like the telling of a joke. You invest a balloon/joke with energy—the buildup—and your listener doesn't know where it's going and then it ends very quickly, very unexpectedly. Bang! You never know how or when it's going to end. If you knew, you wouldn't laugh. And there's that rush.[18]

Friedman felt the raucous exercise established the tone of the class. "Right from the get-go, he seemed to encourage chaos in the class, which I liked. It was sort of like a party atmosphere. He loved it too. He'd bring in piles of stuff [to show us], he'd have guests; it was a fun class. I looked forward to it every Tuesday. It was the class I really looked forward to the most."

Once he became comfortable being in the same room with his idol, Friedman began asking joke questions to get a rise out of Kurtzman, drawing caricatures of other students in the class and making sarcastic comments during the portion of the class when everyone put their assignment up on "the Crit Wall" to be evaluated by their peers. Friedman became a ringleader, and was selected by Kurtzman to be an editor of *Kar-tünz*. He had already developed his stipple technique, which he applied to comic strips and cartoons featuring pseudo-realistic caricatures of celebrities such as Andy Griffith, Huntz Hall, Larry Fine of the Three Stooges and the former Mickey Mouse Club Mouseketeers, generally with a morbid twist. Kurtzman recognized Friedman's talent, and liked the energy that he injected into the class, though he would intercede if he thought the student critiques by Friedman and others became too personal or insensitive. "Kurtzman didn't really instruct or teach lessons," Friedman said. "You'd bring in the cartoons you'd do at home, and he'd have the class comment on them. Everything was being graded, in preparation for what would wind up in the magazine at the end of the year."

Nando Pelusi, a member of the class who was taking an eclectic mix of courses at the school, recalled, "I had gone to SVA partly because I wanted to be around artistic types, but I found that the other classes that I took were a little too serious. There were crazy people, but the classes were very rigid in terms of what they expected you to do. Except for Harvey's class. His class was its own universe in some ways, very different from the other SVA classes. Some of the people in the class, like Drew Friedman, were very passionate about their work. It was a fun class. I got the impression that Kurtzman had no agenda other than stimulating us with some challenges."[19] According to Pelusi, sometimes Kurtzman was almost a non-presence. Rather than lecture, he "mused." It wasn't about reaching the class. It was more like, "If anyone's interested, I'll be speaking up here. If you want to draw, or walk around, that's fine with me as well."

Pelusi became interested in psychology and went on to earn a doctorate in the field. When asked if there were any behaviors exhibited by Kurtzman that he could comment on, the psychologist responded, "My recollection is that from his body language, he wasn't particularly interested in being there. He had virtually no interest in getting anyone's approval. Whatever people found useful, he'd talk about . . . but if they didn't, he would move on, or there would be another assignment or some kind of task. I saw Harvey as a gentle person and a very likable person, but somewhat detached. He never got angry at the things students said. He'd ask, 'Any questions?' and someone would say, 'What color is your underwear?' He'd just sort of shrug. He'd have sort of a weary smile."[20]

Not everyone thought highly of Kurtzman's class. Mark Newgarden, one of the class's successful alums and later a teacher at SVA, has been one of the bluntest critics. He took "Satirical Cartooning" in the 1980–1981 school year. Newgarden was a fan of the *Mad* comic book, citing "Mickey Rodent!" as his favorite Kurtzman story. He was curious about the man, and had high expectations when he signed up. "I was extremely disappointed in the class. He never really addressed all of the things he knew better than just about anyone. Most of what he got from the students, and ultimately encouraged, were lame sex jokes. The whole tenor of the class seemed pretty regressive, and, to my thinking, beneath Harvey Kurtzman. It wasn't a serious class."[21] Newgarden was ready to quit after a few weeks. Then he established a rapport with David Dubnanski, Drew Friedman and a few others, and decided to stay. He enjoyed some of the guest lecturers, and also liked the occasions when Kurtzman would open up a bit. Some of the students would go out for drinks with Kurtzman on occasion at the Glocca Morra Pub on Third Ave., generally on special occasions such as after the last class of the semester, or a class trip or a class with a guest speaker. He recalled, "Harvey would let his guard down somewhat and talk about some of the stuff we wanted to hear, like *Mad*, Gaines, *Humbug*, whatever. It felt like more of a meaningful connection there than in the classroom proper."[22]

Kazimieras G. Prapuolenis, the cartoonist known as Kaz, has been another critic of the class. In an interview years later, Kaz pulled no punches: "[Kurtzman's class] was a complete waste of time. He would come in and he'd say, 'Okay, today we are going to practice . . . sound effects.' So we'd sit there going KARANG and BADOOM and POW. It was really stupid. Here's this master who created *Mad* and *Two-Fisted Tales* completely wasting his and our time."[23]

At one point, the classroom chaos got to be too much for Kurtzman. Kaz recalled the incident this way: "Kurtzman was showing some slide and Friedman and some clowns were in the back making Three Stooges noises. Making wisecracks at everything he said. He looked tired. Real tired. He finally bowed his head and turned on the lights and walked out of the classroom. Leaving us there in stunned silence. Then he comes back in and goes into a sad speech about how he doesn't have to do this to make a living blah, blah, blah. It was sad and pathetic. Everyone was nice to him after that, but it was too late."[24] Drew Friedman related his version of events.

Occasionally, Harvey would come in and you could see he was having a bad day. You know, like having to make a million changes on a *Little Annie Fanny*. You could see he just wasn't in the mood to be there, but he was there. Occasionally, the class would get out of hand. Usually, he loved it. One particular time, he had to leave the room and compose himself. He was a very sensitive guy. When he came back in the room, you could see he had been crying out in the hall. Over the years, somebody said, "Drew Friedman made Harvey cry," which was not the case at all. It was just that the class was getting out of hand, as it usually did, but this particular time, he wasn't in the mood for it.

Whatever their opinion of Kurtzman as a teacher, everyone agrees that his approach was as different as night and day from that of Eisner. Nando Pelusi observed, "Comparing Eisner's class with Kurtzman's class, it was like the old world and new world. Eisner was a very stately gentleman who wore a tie, and he would have a lecture prepared about some experience. Harvey seemed like a Beat poet who would sit in a corner with his legs crossed, hunched and kind of muttering to himself more than to us. And we could eavesdrop on his talk if we tried."[25]

If, as more than one of his former students indicated, Kurtzman didn't always seem to want to be there, why did he continue to teach at SVA for seventeen years? The answer is that a time never came when he was earning so much from his other work that he could walk away from the extra income. As a result, dozens of young artists and cartoonists who went on to become working professionals were able to benefit, to one degree or another, from his knowledge and his contacts. Among his first-year students, John Holmstrom became a cartoonist and founder of *Punk* magazine, Ken Laager painted covers for many Western novels, John Laney went on to work with Will Eisner, Batton Lash created the long-running comic book *Supernatural Law* and Bob Wiacek became an inker for Marvel and DC. Drew Friedman reached his twin goals of working for *Mad* and Topps. "With the guests, and the field trips, we learned what life as a cartoonist was like in the real world," Friedman said. "That's what Harvey did and I think he did it well." Also, Kurtzman ended up giving work to several of his students, as assistants on *Little Annie Fanny* and other projects.

Sarah Downs was the first. In 1975, she was a twenty-one-year-old Detroit native whose father was an attorney for the AFL-CIO. She attended Cass Technical High School where she got a regular high school education and also took commercial art classes. After attending Dennison University in Grand, Ohio, for two years, she worked in a couple of art galleries in New York's SoHo neighborhood as part of a work study program. Downs didn't want to go back to Dennison, because she wasn't sure what she wanted to do. Alanna Heiss of the Clocktower Gallery suggested she look into The School of Visual Arts. "We had Harvey's book *Who Said That?* at our house when I was growing up, but I never connected that with him when I signed up for his class," she recalled. "He happened to be a really good teacher. He taught himself how to become a very good teacher, so I really got the benefit of it. He always had a full class, because everybody wanted to take the class with Harvey Kurtzman." Her years in Kurtzman's class ended in the spring of 1977.

IN THE MID-1970S, when *Little Annie Fanny* was done with little or no assistance, Kurtzman was happier with the result. "The product is now much more satisfying, for me, artistically. I think we did some godawful stuff working with a team, which really sets my teeth on edge."[26] However, when working alone, Elder was only able to produce three or four short episodes a year. In 1977, *Playboy* wanted more, so Kurtzman hired Sarah

Downs to help. "[Harvey] was looking to increase his production of *Little Annie Fanny*," Downs said. "He said, 'you have a nice color sense,' and asked if I would be interested in helping with the color work on the strip." Downs wasn't bothered by the sexism or the rampant sexuality of the feature. "I started off by doing the color sketches. Each story was three pages long. He'd get to the point where he'd finished the writing of the story and sketching it out on 8 ½" by 11" pieces of paper. I would trace over his drawings of the three pages and do a preliminary color design. Harvey would've already figured it out in terms of the values [light and dark] just by shading it with a pencil. It would be a color guide for Willy to follow." Then, like Bill Stout before her, she would help transfer the pencils to the big drawing boards, and do the underpainting of the watercolors. "Harvey had a very specific way, a formula, of going about building up the color. With the sexy stuff, it would always go from yellow to orange to hot red. Then the cool stuff, obviously, would be more blues and greens."

Kurtzman paid Downs a weekly salary to take the train from her downtown apartment (and later from Brooklyn) to Mount Vernon and work side by side with him in his studio. On a typical day, she would arrive at about 9:00 a.m. Kurtzman might or might not be up at that point, because he often worked late into the night. She would start, because there were always corrections there to do. Then, mid-morning, Harvey would come up with his tea and start working. Around 12:30 p.m., they went downstairs and had a lunch prepared by Adele. The work continued until about 5:00 p.m. Then Downs would leave to catch the train back to the city. They only worked late if they were rushing to meet a deadline.

Phil Felix was the second SVA student who became a regular assistant on the *Playboy* strip. He was born in 1954, son of a mill worker in Milford, New Jersey. "I was the paperboy in Milford, and I spent all my paper money on comics and *Mad* magazine. I was a fan of Harvey and Willy even then, although I didn't realize it at the time, because I loved the *Mad* paperbacks. I thought 'Superduperman!' and 'Ping Pong!' were the greatest comics ever. I traced that stuff to try to draw like Bill Elder. When I met [Harvey] at The School of Visual Arts, I didn't realize he was the guy who created those favorites of mine. At first, I only knew he was the writer of *Little Annie Fanny*."[27] Felix liked Kurtzman's class, and took it for two years starting in the fall of 1977. In the second year, *Kar-tünz* ran more of Felix's work than any other student besides Friedman. "He asked to see some of my other stuff one day," Felix remembered. "I had done a full-color cartoon for some class—maybe a design class—that he really liked, and he said, 'I want to talk to you. I might have some work for you.' Sarah was already working for him." Felix was hired to transfer Kurtzman's drawings to the heavy art board. On his first day of work, Felix found a note taped to his drawing board that read:

> Felix:
> When you sharpen the drawings, try to improve them—especially where the proportions are wrong. Very often, a head is too big or too small. Be critical when you do the "final" pencilling. And don't worry—I'll go over everything and make it all right.
> H

Felix also blocked out the balloons and captions with Mask-away (a substance that could be peeled off once the painting was done), helped with the underpainting and then assisted Elder on the backgrounds.

Kurtzman, Downs and Felix developed camaraderie in the years they worked in close quarters. The younger two heard about Kurtzman's life in bits and pieces over time, often when a current work problem related to a situation in his past. When Elder dropped by, they sometimes heard anecdotes about his outrageous behavior as a youth. With two assistants, the number of Annie episodes went from three in 1976, to four in 1977 and five in 1978 and 1979.

Often they listened to music as they worked. Felix recalled, "Harvey liked music, and let me bring music in to work. I don't think he had a collection [except for] some jazz records downstairs. I had a little Hitachi cassette player, and I would play compilation tapes of stuff that I thought he would like." Sometimes the sounds of the Grateful Dead could be heard coming from the studio, since Felix was a confirmed Deadhead. Other times, he was a little more adventurous in his selections. "I kind of thought Harvey was an old fogey, you know, a guy from the 1950s, but one day I remember him asking, 'what is this music?' and I told him it was a Frank Zappa instrumental. He goes, 'God, this is great!' and I asked him, 'you're into Zappa?' He said, 'Yeah, I think he's a genius,' and I thought, 'all right, really cool.'"

When Downs and Felix began working on *Annie Fanny*, Annette Kawecki was lettering the feature. She was a Marvel letterer who was working in comics to earn money for medical school. When she dropped out in 1979, Kurtzman invited John Workman out to his place to talk to him about it. Workman, who was then art director for *Heavy Metal*, was also one of the finest letterers in the business, and did freelance work on the side. Workman recently recalled, "Harvey had me sit down at one of the tables and do him up an alphabet. I'd brought along a set of my pens, so I pulled them out and started lettering on a sheet of paper that Harvey provided. When I finished, he looked over the letters and offered me the job. I was ecstatic! The money he offered—$50 a page—was great. I was being paid either $6 or $7 a page by DC. The problem was my preference for working on my own, rather than in a studio situation."[28] Kurtzman was unwilling to let him take the pages home, or to letter on separate paper. He insisted that Workman letter on the original art boards in his studio, which left them at an impasse.

Kurtzman prepared to take Workman to the train station. Downstairs, they found Adele laughing uproariously at something on television. They sat down, wondering what she found so funny. Workman said, "I had never heard of *The 700 Club* or Pat Robertson, but that's what the three of us watched and laughed at that night. I thought Harvey would fall off the couch when Robertson began the 'laying on of hands.' I can still hear him laughing."[29]

Kurtzman then convinced Phil Felix to learn how to letter. "I had this beautiful sample by John Workman that was sort of like the Sword of Damocles hanging over my head," Felix said. "And I didn't know anything about lettering. Harvey said, 'Felix, you can do this.'" Kurtzman arranged for him to have a tutoring session with Ben Oda in the DC offices, and after practicing a bit, he became the *Annie Fanny* letterer. Later, Felix was grateful that Kurtzman had pushed him to learn a new skill. A few years later, when the *Annie Fanny* work was winding down, Kurtzman set up a meeting for him with Joe Orlando at DC. Felix ended up working there as a letterer for years. Kurtzman remembered that a teacher at Cooper Union gave him a tip that led to his first break in comics, and tried to do the same for other fledgling artists who needed a hand.

26.

BEING HARVEY KURTZMAN

"HARVEY, THESE TOUCH-UPS are driving me nuts!"

Some time in 1979, Sarah Downs had reached her wits' end with all the corrections and touch-ups on *Little Annie Fanny*.

Kurtzman thought for a moment, and said, "Okay. Why don't we work on a new strip together?" Downs liked the idea of co-creating something with him. He handed her one of his yellow legal pads, and told her, "Write down what you know."[1]

Kurtzman himself was thoroughly bored with *Annie Fanny*. He admitted to Jacques Dutrey in 1980, "Yes, I get tired of it. But I get tired of a lot of things: paying the bills, taking out the garbage, shaving. But we press on."[2]

Playboy was trying to get the female point of view into the magazine. Downs and Kurtzman chose to do a satirical strip about the life of a sexually active, liberated young woman. They named it *Betsy's Buddies*.

Their collaboration had a teacher-student dynamic. "Harvey said it was kind of like a Ping-Pong thing," Downs said. "There was a lot of back and forth between us. As usual, his process was very structured." It began with her making a list of ideas for episodes, sometimes things she got from talking with her friends. Harvey picked a promising one, and asked her, "What's the conflict going to be?" After that was established, he said, "Okay, now just start writing."

"I wrote like three pages on one little story idea," Downs recalled. "He read through it, and just start crossing things out until there were about ten sentences left."

The next step was determining the episode's ending, so they knew where they were heading. "Then," she said, "he did this amazing thing while I watched. He said, 'Here we have this idea, and this is going to go here, so that'll probably be ten panels,' and I'm thinking, how did he know that? He had a white piece of paper, and he drew some squares, and said, 'It'd kind of go like this,' and I'm watching, thinking yeah, yeah, I can see that." Kurtzman loosely sketched some basic layouts, and Downs drew it up, leaving room for the lettering. Then he put a piece of tracing paper over it and started tweaking it. In time, Downs completed the finishes. After corrections to the page or pages were done, it was ready to be sent to *Playboy*.

The first episode is told in twenty equal-sized panels, ten per page. Betsy and a boyfriend are having sex in bed, shown in profile. (They are naked.) As things are heating up, the phone rings. She answers it, which leads to a tiff. Is that another boyfriend calling? On p. 2, the tiff is smoothed out. They return to making love. Just as they reach the height of excitement again, the phone rings. The End.

The loose artwork is executed by Downs but clearly reflects Kurtzman's storytelling in its rhythms, structure and symmetry. It's sexy and funny, but with an edge, and the expressions on their faces in the last panel manage to convey several emotions at once.

The artwork was finished in India ink then painted with watercolors. (A black and white copy was made before the paint was applied, in case there was ever a need for it. There was.) Having the protagonist act something like a real human being was a great relief after Annie Fanny, and their decision to do the episodes as one or two pagers presented fresh structural challenges as well. In certain respects, *Betsy's Buddies* was a return to the type of continuities Kurtzman had done for *Madison Avenue* magazine in the late 1950s, and before that, *Hey Look!*

"We finished three of them and submitted them to Michelle Urry," Downs said. "She called Harvey soon after that and said, 'Okay,' and we were off and running." Kurtzman took first billing on the basis of his experience and reputation, but Downs was a more than equal partner in the venture. Unlike with *Annie*, he and Sarah were able to retain ownership of the feature. *Playboy* had been forced to make exceptions to its normal ownership policy in order to attract cartoonists to its "Playboy Funnies" section.

Betsy's Buddies made its debut the January 1980 issue of *Playboy*, in the two-page spread titled "Phonus Interruptus." It was sandwiched between *Acid Fun!* by Christopher Browne and *Neon Vincent's Massage Parlor* by Skip Williamson. Five more episodes appeared that year, sometimes in issues that also had *Little Annie Fanny*. Over a period of three or four years, Kurtzman and Downs turned out fifty episodes. Only twenty-eight of them ran in Hefner's magazine, but most if not all of the others were bought for inventory. In 1981, *Betsy* also appeared in *Pilote* with French dialogue. While it reads less like Kurtzman's work than any of his earlier collaborations, one feels his hand at the rudder. (His name appeared at the top of the page, but hers was the only signature in the body of the strips.) Episodes range from genuinely funny to mildly amusing. At a certain point, it seems Urry (or perhaps Hefner) felt it had run its course. It had a more than respectable run.

ALONG WITH MARTIN GOODMAN, Bill Gaines and Hugh Hefner, Russ Cochran became one of the most important publishers of Harvey Kurtzman's comic art. That's because he reprinted virtually every EC story in a series of books called The Complete EC Library, beginning in 1978.

As a boy in the early 1950s, Cochran and his brothers started a chapter of the EC Fan-Addict Club in West Plains, Missouri. Cochran kept his EC comic books when he went to college. He eventually became a physics professor at Drake University in Des Moines, Iowa. In the mid-1960s, he wrote a letter to Bill Gaines that led to a friendship. By the end of the decade, Gaines gave Cochran permission to reprint EC stories and artwork in a series of six classy portfolios, which were published from 1971 to 1977. They sold so well that Cochran planned to reprint every EC comic book in

L. B. Cole and Harvey Kurtzman "reunited" during the 1979 Comic Art Convention, held at the Statler Hilton Hotel in New York City, June 30–July 1, 1979. Photograph courtesy of E. B. Boatner.

deluxe, large-sized hardcover books. Each book would contain six issues, including letter columns, text stories and special editorials.

The Complete EC Library was made possible because Bill Gaines had kept and carefully stored nearly all of the original art to the comic books. Cochran was able to reproduce the pages from the original boards created by Kurtzman, Wood, Davis, Williamson and the rest, an incredible boon to those who appreciated the artistry of the material. The covers were printed in color, and the interiors in black and white, not only to keep the price reasonable but to better display the images in all their virtuosity and detail. Cochran started with *Weird Science* and *Tales from the Crypt* sets, judged to be the most popular titles. The project required negatives, created by photographing the original artwork. By retaining the negatives, Gaines no longer had to store the artwork for future reprints, and could put it up for auction. Apart from the profit motive, the auctions allowed the artwork to be dispersed to collectors while Gaines was alive and able to supervise the process.

Six stories drawn by Kurtzman appeared in the first volume of *The Complete Weird Science Library*. Two more appeared in the first *The Complete Tales from the Crypt Library*. Not long after the artwork in those twelve issues was auctioned, Kurtzman received a check for part of the proceeds. Russ Cochran explained, "To Bill's credit, even though he owned this art himself, and he had paid the storage bill over the last thirty or forty years, to keep it in the condition it was in, when the money started coming in from the sales of the art, he gave the artists a large share of it."[3] Although Kurtzman never specified how much he was paid after this or subsequent auctions, he did confirm that he received money from the auctions (which he deemed "largesse") from Gaines. Kurtzman and the others were also paid an unknown amount from the royalties of the reprint books. He supported the series by commenting on individual stories for the books' annotations.[4]

The Complete Two-Fisted Tales Library and *The Complete Frontline Combat Library* series followed from 1979–1982, putting all of Kurtzman's war comics back into print. According to Cochran, five thousand sets of each of those two libraries were printed.[5] By bringing so much of his work back into print, they created a new wave of interest in Kurtzman. Those who already venerated his humor work in *Mad* discovered a whole new dimension of his talent. They had the opportunity to pore over them in great detail and were spellbound by their power, ambition and artistry. Classics such as "Ambush!," "Enemy Assault!," "Rubble!," and "The Big 'If'!" were just as impressive in the 1980s as they had been in the 1950s, perhaps more so revealed in black and white with pristine printing. Coming after years of comic book mediocrity, their excellence was all the more remarkable. Indeed, Kurtzman looked like a visionary, since much of the work in modern comics fell far short of the Platonic ideal he had achieved twenty-five years earlier. These reprints extended Kurtzman's influence to new generations of artistically ambitious, thoughtful creators of comic books and graphic novels.

Typically, Kurtzman was modest, claiming he didn't quite understand why he was held in such high regard. He marveled when people came up to him at conventions and told him that his work had changed their lives. "I can only ascribe the admiration to the fact that they read my work when they were very young," he said. He had the opportunity to meet many of them in the coming years. At a New York convention, when cartoonist Jay Kinney told him, "You've been one of my biggest influences," Kurtzman replied with mock concern, "Oh, I'm sorry. That's too bad."[6]

It didn't matter to such fans that Kurtzman had limited his comic art mostly to *Annie Fanny* since 1965. He didn't have to prove himself to them because his work at EC was a more than sufficient basis for respect. Just as Mark Twain produced work of lesser consequence in the twenty-five years after *Huckleberry Finn*, Harvey Kurtzman never did anything as brilliant as *Mad* and his other EC stories in the years that followed (other than *Humbug*, which wasn't as well known). Twain spent the latter part of his life simply "being Mark Twain" and was celebrated as such. In the 1980s, all Harvey Kurtzman had to do was show up at a convention to receive fans' admiration. No longer at his creative peak, the achievements of his younger years had grown in stature, and his acclaim had grown accordingly. Now, "being Harvey Kurtzman" was enough.

SOMETIMES KURTZMAN'S comic book past would come back to him in a less welcome way. One such occasion was his reunion with Leonard Cole, who he'd worked with in the Louis Ferstadt shop before World War II.

L. B. Cole was a guest of honor at the 1979 New York Comic Convention, where Bob Overstreet and E. B. Boatner met him in anticipation of preparing an article about his work for the upcoming *Comic Book Price Guide*, the annual book listing the current values of all comic books. Kurtzman wanted to avoid Cole. He had no wish to be reunited with the man who he considered "an absolute snake." However, when he found Cole at his hotel door, Kurtzman let him in and played along. Cole greeted Kurtzman like a long lost friend, and puffed on a cigar as he brought Kurtzman up to date.

In photographs of the meeting, the two-shots of Cole and Kurtzman show Cole pontificating and Kurtzman looking a bit like a trapped animal.[7]

More recognition came Kurtzman's way when a sequel to *A Smithsonian Book of Newspaper Comics* was published in 1981: *A Smithsonian Book of Comic-Book Comics*, edited by Michael Barrier and Martin Williams. In the section on EC, four of the five stories chosen to represent EC were written by Kurtzman: "Air Burst!," "Corpse on the Imjin!," "Superduperman" and "Howdy Dooit." (The fifth was "Master Race" by Feldstein and Krigstein.)

In 1981, Gary Groth, Kim Thompson and Mike Catron of *The Comics Journal* interviewed Kurtzman at great length. It was the most extensive interview since Kurtzman's talks with John Benson and J. P. C. James in 1965. When it saw print, its introduction made clear the regard in which he was now held, at least by some. Kim Thompson wrote, "There are, to my mind, four great American comic book artists who tower above all the others: Carl Barks, Will Eisner, Jack Kirby and Harvey Kurtzman. Each is so outstanding in his own way it would be fatuous to rank them, so let me put it this way: Kurtzman is my favorite."[8] Kurtzman found invitations to comic book conventions and requests for interviews coming with greater frequency. He had attended a substantial number of fan gatherings in the 1970s. In the 1980s, he would appear at many more.

Those convention trips took on an added dimension when he began participating in a series of onsite seminars masterminded by Gil Kane. Initially, the art instruction classes were to be taught by Burne Hogarth, Will Eisner and Kane himself. When Eisner dropped out before they began, Kurtzman was recruited as his replacement. The Master Class seminars (as they were billed) were held several times in 1981 and 1982. Registrants would rotate from Hogarth to Kane to Kurtzman in the course of one day. The conventions supplied rooms for the classes. Kurtzman taught color application and color theory. Gary Groth administered them after Phil Seuling pulled out, and they were successful wherever they were offered.

What with *Little Annie Fanny*, *Betsy's Buddies* (appearing in both America and Europe), teaching at SVA, editing for *Esquire*, an occasional advertisement in *TV Guide* or movie poster, Master Class seminars and checks from Gaines, 1982 represented the financial zenith of Harvey Kurtzman's career. Not, certainly, the creative summit that his talent might have reached had things worked out differently, but he took fierce pride in never having to work outside his field, apart from teaching others how to enter it. From a financial perspective, life was as good as it got for the Kurtzmans.

Nellie entered junior high school in 1982. She was very close to her dad. "I could wrap him around any one of my fingers when I wanted to. I guess that comes with being the youngest. I don't remember a whole lot of discipline, maybe because I was one of those kids who came along later in life. I would go up to his studio, and even when he'd say, 'You've got to let me work,' I'd stick around anyway."⁹

Nellie realized that her father's talent made him special. "He did amazing Christmas cards every year, and things like his Fourth of July cards. I would torture him and say, 'I need a card for my friend so-and-so' and he would do that for me. That stuff, for me, is the most amazing of his work. Not everyone can go to their father and say 'listen, I need a card' and have something really clever and meaningful drummed up." She was able to spend more time with him than a lot of children have with their fathers. "Because he worked at home, he was always there except when he'd be gone for a research trip. But for the most part I had access to my dad, always. I have some friends who have issues with their parents. Either their parents were too controlling or their parents were not controlling and abandoned them. I have to say that my dad was pretty much a fairy tale dad except that he went and got sick."

ONE DAY IN THE AUTUMN of 1982, Harvey remarked to Adele that he felt "strange" and "jittery inside." She recalled, "It was something he felt that was hard to pinpoint. I never really noticed anything." He made an appointment with the family doctor who suggested he should possibly see a psychiatrist. "Eventually he went to a man—a neurologist—in New York. That doctor did some tests and diagnosed it as the early stages of Parkinson's disease."¹⁰ Harvey was stoic. "He didn't say much," Adele said.

Little is known about what he was thinking or feeling at this time because Kurtzman rarely brought the subject up (and then only privately), but such a diagnosis is traumatic for anyone. Robert Crumb said, "I remember, when he was first diagnosed with [Parkinson's], him telling me how scared he was about it."¹¹ Just as he researched his creative projects, he researched Parkinson's (PD) and discovered it was incurable, it would progress and that he would eventually lose control of his physical mobility. It was particularly tragic that he fell victim to a disease that targeted his motor skills such as hand coordination.

At first, it had little effect on his drawing ability. Sarah Downs didn't notice anything different about him. "But even when I had a little party before I was married [in 1982], one of my friends who had met Harvey but hadn't seen him in a while said, 'Oooh, Harvey's looking so old.' I didn't notice it because I saw him every day. He was stooped over a bit, and someone said, 'Hey, Harv. What's wrong? Does your back hurt? Stand up straight.' Then Harvey said, 'Oh, okay, I'll stand up straight now, ha ha.'" Downs found out about the diagnosis when she arrived in the studio one morning. "Harvey wasn't up yet. I don't think I was being nosey, but I just kind of looked at his drawing table and saw something scribbled there. He'd written the word 'Parkinson's.' It looked like something you would write when you're on the phone. When he came up, I asked him about it. He said that he'd been to a doctor and the doctor had told him he had Parkinson's. He was kind of matter-of-fact about it."

Kurtzman was emotional when it came to how the illness would affect his family, especially his youngest daughter. Adele remembered, "The most dramatic thing about his illness was when he was sitting with Nellie, who was about thirteen at the time. They were playing music from *Fiddler on the Roof*, and they both began to cry. It was the first time I'd seen any signs of emotion over it."[12] Kurtzman told Sarah that he and Nellie listened to "Sunrise, Sunset" together not long after the diagnosis. He apologized to Nellie for being sick.

Liz Kurtzman, then twenty-five years old, recalled, "I remember where I was sitting when my mother called and told me he had Parkinson's. I was at work at Perry Ellis and I just flipped. You know, I didn't really know what it was. I went a little bit crazy when I found out. And it was pretty debilitating, pretty fast."[13] Meredith, then thirty-two, said, "I don't remember the specific moment when I got the news, just generally being aware and horrified."[14]

Parkinson's disease is a degenerative disorder of the central nervous system, caused by the death of dopamine-generating cells in the midbrain. The cause is unknown. About three in a thousand people get the disease. Early symptoms are movement related: shaking, rigidity, slowness of movement and difficulty with walking. As PD becomes more advanced, dementia commonly occurs. Mortality statistics showed that Kurtzman's remaining years would likely be reduced in half. The medication Levidopa (L-DOPA) helps minimize the symptoms in the beginning, but is less effective over time.

Adele said, "He always—as opposed to his wife—took very good care of himself. He exercised, he ate well and he was very conscious of his weight. When he found out he had Parkinson's, he got a rowing machine, a bicycle, he ran up and down the stairs, he kept busy. He did gardening, all kinds of things." She described the effect of L-DOPA. "We have a living room that has a step-down. He would take one pill, and he'd kind of tap dance up and down, and say, 'See? I can dance! It's working!'"[15]

With the onset of Kurtzman's illness, the couple decided that it was time to find a group home for Pete. Adele needed to accompany her husband to his doctor appointments, and Nellie was too young to stay home alone and be in charge of Pete. It was a complicated issue, and they acted with careful consideration and the consultation of professionals. Peter Kurtzman, then twenty-eight years old, moved into his new home shortly after the dimensions of his father's illness became clear.

In the first two or three years of PD, Kurtzman was more or less "himself." Initially, he didn't have the shaking symptoms so common to the disease. Instead, he experienced a rigidity of movement. He developed a shuffling gait, something first noticed by Hefner on one of Kurtzman's visits to the mansion. His facial expressions became noticeably less mobile as time went on. "He drove for a while," Adele said. "When he became hesitant about that, I said, 'It's not a good idea' and then I would drive. But we still did a lot. We went to Italy afterwards."[16]

The Kurtzmans were invited to the International Salon of Comics, Animation, and Illustration in Lucca, in Naples, where they feared they would never make it to the hotel during a wild taxi ride through the city. Jay Lynch, who was also in the cab, remembered telling the terrified Kurtzmans in the back seat, "We're all going to die!"[17] Bill Griffith was also there, and found Kurtzman's sense of humor was unimpeded by the onset of PD. They were on a local TV show together. While waiting for their turn to speak, Kurtzman began drawing a caricature of Griffith in a large notepad. The cameraman noticed and zoomed in on the sketch. Griffith recalled, "It was a show stopper and all eyes shifted our way. Harvey had done a great little drawing but he'd added something to the portrait I don't own: a moustache. As he "noticed" this "mistake" for the camera, he did what only a truly great artist does when the real world doesn't match his vision—he changed the real world. With a flourish, Harvey smeared a quick moustache on my upper lip and looked very pleased."[18]

Kitchen Sink Press in Princeton, Wisconsin, had grown into a substantial publishing business. It survived the collapse of the underground market while continuing to keep its spirit alive through reprints, publishing work in other forms by the underground stars, and occasionally putting out a comic book as before. Since 1978, Denis Kitchen had published Will Eisner's work, starting with *The Spirit* magazine (taking over from Warren Publishing). In 1981, Kitchen enlisted some fifty artists and writers to collaborate on the *The Spirit Jam*, an extra-long Spirit story published as a comics album, similar to the European format. Kurtzman contributed to it, alongside work by Milton Caniff, Eisner himself, Frank Miller, Trina Robbins, Michael T. Gilbert and Richard Corben.

Kitchen met with Kurtzman to discuss reprinting some of his non-EC comics in book form. A collection of *Goodman Beaver* stories was planned for early 1984. Kitchen wrote Robin Snyder of Archie Comics to see if the company would allow "Goodman Goes Playboy" to appear in the book. Archie publisher Michael I. Silberkleit refused. When Kitchen announced in *Comics Buyer's Guide* that the story would be printed in reduced size with the faces of the Archie characters blacked out, Silberkleit threatened to sue. Finally, Kitchen dealt with it by writing a foreword for the book detailing the legal history of "Goodman Goes Playboy." To accompany the piece, he reproduced three panels from the story (including the large "orgy" scene), as well as an example from "Starchie" in *Mad* #12. Excerpting a panel or panels was legal when done for educational or historical purposes. Silberkleit may have been gnashing his teeth, but no legal action ensued. Then, out of left field, came another obstacle. Diamond Comic Distributors, then a rapidly growing distributor, refused to list the Goodman Beaver book in its catalog because "beaver" was in the title.[19] An exasperated Kitchen had Capital City and other distributors to handle the book, but Diamond's decision didn't help.[20]

Denis Kitchen was an able, energetic publisher but, by 1984, was questioning his priorities. He felt he had become mired in the noncreative end of the business, and wanted to get back to the drawing board as a full-time cartoonist. On a trip to New York, Kitchen announced his intention to give up publishing for cartooning to Will Eisner and Harvey Kurtzman, who he considered mentors. He assumed Eisner, the businessman, would oppose the idea. "I knew that Will Eisner, who was an experienced businessman, would be my toughest challenge. He would do his best to convince me not to abandon the publishing company I had invested several years building. So I hoped my well-prepared arguments could overcome his anticipated objections. Harvey, on the other hand, had experienced only failure as a publisher and reached his heights as an artist, so I knew he would applaud my decision."[21]

Kitchen was surprised on both counts. Eisner told him he "should follow his heart," whereas Kurtzman "looked at me solemnly and intoned, 'You can't do that.'" Kurtzman reportedly said, "Denis, you're a pretty good cartoonist. But the comics field has many, many good artists. What we need is good publishers. You have a proclivity for this. You must keep doing what you are doing."[22] Kitchen returned to Wisconsin to think it over. Ultimately, he continued as a publisher. For many reasons, it would have been hard for him to give it up. While he acknowledged that he might have stayed with it whether or not he talked to Kurtzman, he would never forget the dual surprise he got from his mentors.

AFTER THE INITIAL ANNOUNCEMENT in 1978, progress on the *Little Annie Fanny* motion picture stalled, started and stalled again. Kurtzman still hoped to write and direct. Kitchen described how *Playboy* dangled this before him whenever he became "difficult" in their eyes. "Because Harvey was promised this was his baby, any time he got a little too uppity for *Playboy*, he would get a letter from Richard Rosenzsweig, who was basically Hefner's ax-man, and he would say something like, 'Now Harvey, if you're going to be demanding a raise, or making other demands, we might have to forget about that movie.' They would use that to beat him into submission."[23]

When plans for the theatrical film fell through, Kurtzman picked up some extra money writing a script for an Annie Fanny movie for the Playboy Channel, a cable station launched in 1982. Larry Siegel, who had moved to Los Angeles to write for television comedy shows, recalled, "Harvey came to me and asked me if I'd [cowrite] it with him and I said, 'Sure, why not?' We got almost nothing for it. I think they paid $20,000 total. But it was an interesting opportunity, so I jumped at it."[24] They didn't work on it together. Siegel did the first draft. Then Kurtzman made some suggestions. They passed it back and forth until they were both satisfied. "All they wanted," Siegel said, "was just the mindless stuff they have on the Playboy Channel. And this was really good satire. The only criticism Harvey got back . . . was 'more Annie, more Annie, where's Annie?' Nude, nude, more, more. They never filmed it [because] there wasn't enough Annie in it. They didn't want anything good, they really didn't."[25] Kurtzman was less certain why the project was scuttled. "I don't know why. The deals that we've gotten have stopped at Hefner's door. I know that Hefner has a very bad track record with movies. I don't know why that is, but it's been very frustrating."[26] That spelled the end of a dozen years of various schemes to exploit Annie in films, and of Kurtzman's dream of directing a movie. His screenplay monies were most welcome, since harder times were just around the corner.

Once the movie was derailed, the handwriting was on the wall: the end was near for *Little Annie Fanny*. Five episodes appeared in 1982, but then there were just three in 1983, only one in 1984 and two in 1985. Kurtzman found it harder and harder to get Michelle Urry or Dave Stevens (much less Hugh Hefner) to respond to his story ideas, letters and phone calls. Fully painted stories were completed, paid for and then sat on a shelf. Approvals for new episodes slowed to a crawl. Relations with Michelle Urry worsened. She also had plenty of unpublished episodes of *Betsy's Buddies* and needed no more.

Kurtzman and Elder had stayed with it for the security, and because Kurtzman hoped he would get to direct an Annie Fanny film. Now, ill with Parkinson's, Kurtzman's main source of income was drying up, and he didn't know what to do about it. "There's no place to go, really. *Little Annie Fanny* is a four-color process that I don't want to let go, because I can't imagine anything beyond. There could be, but there isn't, or at least not at this particular juncture in my life. I can't seem to find it, or get up the energy to make it happen."[27] The winding down of the Annie strip can also be partly attributed to internal power struggles and a changing of the guard at the magazine. The *Playboy* empire was in trouble, having been targeted by Attorney General Ed Meese's commission on pornography, and was rocked by bad publicity that arose after the murder of Playmate Dorothy Stratten. Then, in the early spring of 1985, Hugh Hefner had a stroke. He was forced to work less, pull back from his hands-on approach to editing and delegate more. In August 1986, Hefner appeared on the cover of *Newsweek* next to the caption, "The Party's Over." Playboy Clubs were closing and the magazine business was changing. According to the article, "the publisher and America gradually drifted apart." With *Playboy* scrambling to become relevant again, *Annie Fanny* was an unwelcome remnant of the past.

About this time, Kurtzman's editorial work for *Esquire* also tapered off. The magazine was going through its own changes, which had begun when Clay Felker, who bought the magazine in 1977, sold it not long after. Then it was sold again in the mid-1980s. All that upheaval led to editorial changes. Kurtzman's champions at the magazine were gone. His only steady job was teaching at The School of Visual Arts. To the anxiety over his illness was added the burden of finding new sources of income, and quick.

WHEN KURTZMAN NEEDED to unburden himself, he often got together with his friend Harry Matetsky. Jerry De Fuccio introduced them in the 1970s. Matetsky, who was ten years younger than Kurtzman, worked as an art editor for Sterling Publications. The firm churned out dozens of movie, soap opera, teen and rock 'n' roll magazines. "We drank together, socialized a lot," Matetsky said. "Adele came to our place, and we went to quite a few of their Fourth of July parties. We had some great times."[28] Sometimes Matetsky phoned Kurtzman after midnight to gab, knowing that he was often at his drawing board late at night when all was quiet. Their favorite hangout was the Scoop, an upscale restaurant on East Forty-Third Street between Second and Third Avenue. (It no longer exists.)

In the 1980s, Harry and his wife Mandy started their own publishing company, producing magazines along the same lines as Sterling. For about a year, he owned and operated the Puck

Mad #259 (December 1985). Cover by Kurtzman and Elder.

Gallery on Sixty-Seventh Street in Manhattan, which presented original comic art shows. "The gallery was fun. We gave parties for *Rolling Stone* and Gahan Wilson which were exciting, but we never made any money, so I got back into publishing. Harvey and I talked about a lot of things, as friends do. One of them was starting a humor magazine." Despite all the work involved in producing a new magazine, Kurtzman began considering it. He had given up on his dream of doing a slick, full-color humor magazine. As he told a colleague around this time, "There's no one who will finance the kind of magazine I would want to do. Absolutely no one."[29] His focus at this stage of his life was on earning as much money as possible, in order to provide for his and Adele's future. Behind it all was the realization that Parkinson's would eventually debilitate him completely.

Harry Matetsky's magazines had little interior color and were produced on shoestring budgets. Without money to pay competitive rates, they would find themselves in the same dilemma as *Help!* magazine. But this time, Kurtzman had a pool of talented, young cartoonists who wouldn't demand top dollar: his former SVA students. He had always had an unerring eye for talent, and liked the idea of helping fledgling cartoonists get into print, or even assist him with the editing itself. Drew Friedman recalled, "[Kurtzman] contacted me and asked if I was interested in editing a humor magazine. I said, 'I would love to. You kidding?' He said, 'Okay, Friedman, just keep it under your hat for now.' I was all geared up to edit a humor magazine for Harvey Kurtzman. Of course, you know, the famous Harvey the Vague. I never heard another thing about it."[30] The project Kurtzman was contemplating with Matetsky never materialized. "The numbers didn't add up," Matetsky said. "I believe we would have lost money." As far as is known, this was the last time Kurtzman considered starting a new magazine.

In September 1984, Al Feldstein retired as editor of *Mad* after almost thirty years at the helm. He had steered the magazine to its greatest financial success. By this time, he was bored, and had made more than enough money to retire comfortably. After Feldstein's departure, Gaines named Nick Meglin and John Ficarra co-editors of the magazine. Suddenly there were Kurtzman sightings at EC's Madison Avenue office.

In an interview with Lee Wochner at this time, Kurtzman said he might be doing some work for *Mad* again. "Because Feldstein's leaving?" Wochner asked. Kurtzman replied, "No, it was just a set of coincidences."[31] However, Kurtzman didn't ask for a meeting until Feldstein was gone. He resented Feldstein, principally for becoming wealthy by exploiting a Kurtzman creation, and wouldn't have worked under Feldstein as editor. "Harvey leaving was the best [thing] that ever happened to Al," Adele stated, but added, "Harvey was what he was, and he never could have lasted that long [at *Mad*], or made the money. Because he made everybody erase everything! I never had any bad feelings about Al."[32] The idea of approaching Gaines for work in *Mad* caused Kurtzman a great deal of trepidation. He had made peace with himself about leaving *Mad* because he knew that Gaines would never have published a true slick magazine at that time. But no matter how one looked at it, coming back after the way he had left amounted to eating crow.

"I'm not a hundred percent certain," Matetsky said, "but I believe I was the one who first suggested to Harvey that he work for Bill again. I knew Bill Gaines. My only motive was to reconnect Harvey with Bill so that some good would come out of it for Harvey. It wasn't only about doing work again for *Mad*. I figured it would lead to some other opportunities as well. I was hoping it would get Harvey a lot of ink." The last thing Kurtzman wanted was to publicize his return to *Mad*, but his need for income, and his desire not to deplete his savings, trumped personal pride. He called Gaines.

John Ficarra remembered, "Harvey contacted Bill [Gaines] and came in almost immediately after Feldstein left. He was the only one who came into the office, though he made it clear we would be getting both he and Willy [Elder]."[33] When the pieces—all written by others—began appearing with *Mad* #258 (October 1985), the work by Kurtzman and Elder was signed "WEHK." They did the Caspar Weinberger "Where's the Beef?" back cover, from an idea by Al Jaffee. *Mad* #259 had their Rambo-Reagan front cover. The following issue carried their first interior piece, "Traveler's Blues," a parody of a Glenn Frey song written by Frank Jacobs. Kurtzman and Elder appeared in most issues over the next three years, totaling more than forty pages. Elder's painting ability on the covers was as good as ever, but the interior art, with Elder working over Kurtzman's layouts, lacked the sparkle of their earlier work. It was good, but not great.

"It was nice to be asked," Elder said. "Harvey and I . . . worked together because we took the pressure off each other. But even that became less lucrative and interesting."[34] After a few initial cover assignments, which paid very well, they were mainly relegated to the interior pages that didn't pay as much (though the rates were far above regular comic book work). Kurtzman's return to *Mad* didn't, as Matetsky hoped, generate publicity for him or lead to anything else.

Phil Felix asked Kurtzman about his return to *Mad*. "What's going back to *Mad* like, Harvey?"

"It was like eating shit," Kurtzman replied.[35]

RENÉ GOSCINNY'S WIDOW Gilberte invited Kurtzman to the opening of the Goscinny exhibit on the second floor of the Eiffel Tower in September 1985. All his expenses were paid, and he was delighted to be there. The luxurious show was called "L'Univers de René Goscinny." Kurtzman was able to see most of his European friends at the event, which always boosted his spirits. He also attended the San Diego Comic-Con that year. Jack Davis was a guest of honor, and Kurtzman appeared on a panel with him. On videotapes of the panel, one can detect evidence of Parkinson's, even though he would have timed his medication so that he could be at his best at the event. He had always been a thoughtful speaker, but now he spoke a bit more slowly, with little facial expression. "I used to get mad at him," Adele recalled. "You think he could move his face if he tried, and I'd ask him to try, but it wasn't his fault. It was the illness."[36] *Hypomimia* is the medical term for a reduced degree of facial expression. PD still hadn't affected his drawing ability (at least, when he was on medication), and he did sketches for fans who requested them.

As Denis Kitchen and his staff were working on the reprint of *Jungle Book*, another person entered Harvey Kurtzman's life who would become a major force from 1985 forward. Byron Preiss produced ready-to-print books for various publishers. He was a *wunderkind* who got started in the business with Jim Steranko's Supergraphics. A Jewish native of Brooklyn like Kurtzman, Preiss was an honors graduate of the University of Pennsylvania in 1972 and earned a master's degree in communications from Stanford University. In many ways, he was the canny, resourceful person Kurtzman needed if he was to find work as he moved into the advanced stages of his illness.

Byron Preiss and Harvey Kurtzman met in 1975 or 1976, when Preiss was twenty years old. Kurtzman wrote an introduction to Preiss's project *Fiction Illustrated*. They remained in touch over the years. According to Howard Zimmerman, the former editor-in-chief of *Starlog* magazine who began working with Preiss in 1985, "Kurtzman took Byron under his wing. They got along famously. Byron treated Harvey like a beloved, crazy uncle, and Harvey responded in kind. Byron was extraordinarily familiar with almost everything Harvey had done, and Harvey liked the graphic experiments Byron was doing."[37] Sarah Downs recalled, "Harvey had this collection of little wind-up toys and I remember Byron and Harvey playing with them together. It was very cute. Harvey didn't do that kind of goofy stuff with many people. I think they had a very good relationship." Now Kurtzman contracted with Preiss to produce a number of works. It was Preiss who suggested doing something like a humor magazine but in paperback book form. It would be aimed at the same age group as the current *Mad*, kids from ten to fourteen. Kurtzman would act primarily as editor, and draw on the talents of his former SVA pupils. They decided to call it *Nuts!*

Kurtzman recalled, "We kind of fell into [*Nuts!*] and did it. We didn't know where we were going with it. Maybe that's why we did good work, we didn't get uptight about it, we just did it and it came out pretty good."[38] Like a lot of the projects Kurtzman would do with Preiss, *Nuts!* had a low quotient of Kurtzman material. He collaborated with Sarah Downs on the charming "Laurie and Versella," a humorous look at the daily lives of two pubescent girls. Laurie was partly based on Nellie Kurtzman, and Versella was inspired by Downs' black childhood friend. Laurie's parents are caricatures of Harvey and Adele. It was even more a Downs project than *Betsy's Buddies*. (She is credited as associate editor of the book.)

Nuts! also ran work by Kevin Sacco, Bob Fingerman, Ralph Reese and Rick Geary. Sacco remembered, "Harvey metaphorically adopted a lot of cartoonists and I was lucky to be in the brood. I completely bombed when he invited me to assist on *Annie Fanny*, but Harvey, bless him, still invited me to contribute a couple of stories to *Nuts!* He picked out some drawings of breakdancers from my sketchbook and showed me how to develop them into a story." He added, "After Harvey told me of his diagnosis, he never mentioned it again. He didn't seem to manifest any symptoms when I saw him and watched him draw."[39] *Nuts!* was conceived as an ongoing series, but sales didn't warrant more than two, both published by Bantam Books in 1985.

Another way Kurtzman generated a little extra income during this period was editing cartoons for *American Health Magazine*, one of the fastest growing magazines of the 1980s. According to Downs, this went on for several years, ending shortly before she stopped working with Kurtzman.

In 1986, after a great deal of work, Kitchen Sink reprinted *Harvey Kurtzman's Jungle Book*. The book had a hand-lettered introduction by Art Spiegelman, which said, in part, "The drawing alone would make this book worth reprinting. Nowhere else is there such a large body of Kurtzman's own drawing. All too often his drawings have functioned as guides for his collaborators. Even with the most inspired of these, the lunatic Will Elder, the densely packed eyeball kicks are gotten at the expense of the verve and apparently immediacy of Kurtzman's own drawings. He always makes his drawing look effortless."[40] Although Kurtzman was able to provide the original art for most of it, some of the book had to be shot from the paperback itself, because originals could not be located. Nevertheless, having its pages reproduced significantly larger than a mass market paperback was a big improvement. According to Dave Schreiner of Kitchen Sink, "Lovingly reproduced as a deluxe hardcover, the book was not a phenomenal seller at first, but as it got out in the market and word of mouth spread about its quality, it became a steady, perennial seller."[41] A softcover edition was published two years later.

That same year, volume one of Russ Cochran's *The Complete* Mad *Library* was published. The other three volumes followed in 1987. Although a large portion of the *Mad* comics had been reprinted in not only the paperbacks but color "Nostalgic *Mad*" inserts in the magazine's newsstand specials, these editions were the first time all the *Mad* material was reissued. The Complete Mad Library volumes came out in both black and white and color editions, the only time this was done in Cochran's book series. Suddenly, the crown jewel of Kurtzman's career was back in print, and looking better than ever.

BY THIS TIME, PARKINSON'S began to affect Kurtzman's drawing ability. Sarah Downs attended a comic con with him and recounted a minor, if telling, incident. "He was doing little drawings and autographs. Sometimes he would draw a large breast shape, and write, 'Hi, I'm Annie

Fanny.' It was funny. He normally drew with a very quick movement. He did it this time, and there was a little glitch, so it wasn't a completely smooth arc. He pointed to it, and said, 'That's the Parkinson's.'" When interviewed on a panel at the Dallas Fantasy Fair in 1987, he referred to "how terrific I was," perhaps unconsciously acknowledging that his best work was now behind him.[42]

Two important passages occurred in the Kurtzman family that year. Harvey's mother died on October 23. After residing with Zachary and Sunny in New Jersey, where they had lived since 1967, Edith spent her last years in an assisted living facility. Kurtzman dutifully called her every two weeks, but they never became closer. She lived to be ninety-one. The person who taught him to look "between the lines" outlived Abe by eighteen years.

Also in 1987, Nellie Kurtzman graduated from high school and began attending Kenyon College in Ohio. She was a theater major. "My sisters are both incredibly gifted in terms of drawing and painting and design," Nellie said. "I always drew as a kid, but don't have the talent they have in that way. I was much more of an academic kid than they were. I'm the only one that went to a standard liberal arts college. They both went to art school." Before she left for college, Nellie accompanied her father on a research trip. "It seemed like the research was so fun. I can see why he got into that. Even though *Annie Fanny* wasn't necessarily his chosen platform, he made it the best it could be by doing all that thorough research." Nellie recalled their trip:

> He was about to do a story on the now defunct Jim and Tammy Faye Bakker theme park, which was a Jesus-themed amusement park. At that point he was too sick to go on his own so I guess my parents asked if I could go. We spent a week in Tammy Faye Land [Heritage USA].
>
> The minute we got there, we were consumed by an irrational fear that everyone's going to know we were infiltrators. He was sick a lot of the time, but he sketched, and took a lot of notes. I took some notes for him. I didn't realize the significance, how lucky I was to go on that trip with him, which is just such a shame.

That turned out to be the penultimate *Little Annie Fanny* story. Tired of the mixed signals they were getting from Urry and others, and fed up with being left hanging so often, Kurtzman and Elder informed *Playboy* they were done with the feature. In the opening caption to that story, Kurtzman wrote, "We'd like to make an important announcement. Unless you, the readers, buy 10,000,000 copies of the next Annie Fanny issue, the good lord is going to summon Harvey Kurtzman and Willy Elder home." Elder said, "The strange thing is, they accepted us quitting. Maybe they were getting tired, too. I just think it died. It dried up and died. We made this decision. We just saw it right in front of us. We saw there was no enthusiasm any longer. I don't think we like to say, 'This is the end,' because that means finally, the finish of everything. We didn't want to do that. [It was] like giving up a member of the family. The worst part about it is that it happened slowly, which was upsetting."[43]

The final episode of *Little Annie Fanny* appeared in the September 1988 issue of *Playboy*. Their last piece for *Mad*, "The *Mad* People Watcher's Guide to a Political Convention," appeared the same month. It was the last work produced by the Kurtzman-Elder team, the creative partnership that had largely been responsible for the meteoric success of *Mad* in the early 1950s. After forty years, the collaboration of Harvey Kurtzman and Will Elder ended, with the expected feelings of sadness. (Elder intended to retire.) That it was "not with a bang, but with a whimper" made the occasion even sadder.

WHILE WORKING ON MORE PROJECTS with Byron Preiss, Harvey Kurtzman was contacted by Gary Groth, publisher of Fantagraphics Books, who had gotten to know him quite well over several years of appearing on panels with him at various comic book conventions, administering the master classes and having dinner with him. Groth's phone call concerned a situation that had arisen with the fan awards that were handed out at the San Diego Comic-Con starting in 1985. The Jack Kirby Awards for achievement in comic books were administered by Fantagraphics, and managed by the publisher's employee Dave Olbrich. A dispute arose in 1987 when Olbrich attempted to trademark the Kirby Awards

Harvey Kurtzman and Will Elder ended their forty-year collaboration in 1988. Will Elder art.

in his own name. When Kirby heard about this from Groth, he wanted nothing to do with the controversy, and asked that his name be taken off the awards. Then Olbrich obtained Will Eisner's permission to name new awards after him, with Olbrich managing (but not trademarking) them. They would be given out at the San Diego Comic Con like the Kirby Awards. Therefore, Groth needed to rename the Kirby Awards and arrange to have them awarded at another convention. He was contacting Kurtzman to ask him if he would like to have a comics award named after him.

The primary difference between the two sets of awards, other than differing categories, is that the Harvey Awards are nominated by an open vote among comic book professionals, whereas a select committee does the nominations for the Eisner Awards. Also, comics retailers can vote in the Eisners, whereas the Harveys are strictly for creative people in the business. The first Harvey Awards were handed out in 1988 at the Chicago Comicon. Among the winners were Alan Moore ("Best Writer") and Dave Gibbons ("Best Artist") for *Watchmen*. The following year, they moved to the Dallas Fantasy Fair, where they stayed until the last show in 1995, and then passed to other conventions. Kurtzman had already been a guest of the con the four prior years, and appeared at the awards banquet twice, the first time in 1990. Paul McSpadden, who became the new adminis-trator of the Harveys, recalled, "We always enjoyed having Harvey, and he attracted underground comix artists like Robert Crumb and Gilbert Shelton as guests, because they wanted to see him."[44] At one of his Dallas appearances, Kurtzman showed his *Sesame Street* cartoons, which were well received. At a later Harvey Awards ceremony, writer Neil Gaiman recalled meeting Kurtzman at the Dallas show in 1990.

> He told me how much he appreciated what I was doing, which I took, not as any indication that he had read anything I had written, but as him ex-pressing his pride in a younger generation of comics writers and artists. That there were bright young creators out there who cared about comics as an artform mattered to Harvey Kurtzman. He'd invested his life in the crazy belief that comics were art, and not anything to apologize for, and that investment reaped its dividends in the lives it influenced, in those of us who believed it too, and acted accordingly.[45]

NEXT IN LINE from Kitchen Sink Press was a *Betsy's Buddies* book, which appeared in a bare-bones hardcover edition in 1988, made up of all but six of the fifty installments, both in color and in black and white. The same year, Kitchen also published *Flash Gordon*, a book reprinting the daily strips written by Kurtzman and drawn by Dan Barry. Going forward, Kitchen had ambitious plans for *Hey Look!*, *Trump*, *Humbug* and *Help!* collections. Since Kurtzman only had copies of some of the original *Hey Look!* pages, Kitchen began asking around for other copies or originals, and investigating the best process to drop the color when comic book pages had to be used. (The book would be printed in black and white.)

Kurtzman's next project with Byron Preiss was *My Life as a Cartoonist*. *Nuts!* was aimed at the youth market, readers from ten to fourteen. This autobiography skewed even younger, going for readers from eight to ten. It was part of a multivolume "My Life" series done for Minstrel Books, an imprint of Simon & Schuster. Howard Zimmerman recalled, "It was decided that I would write Harvey's autobiography by doing a series of interviews, which I did mostly at his house [in 1987]. Adele and his kids were quite wonderful in making me feel comfortable, and in helping Harvey remember stuff from time to time." The L-DOPA dulled his mind and often left him confused.

Zimmerman wrote a draft and sent it to Kurtzman for his input and approval. The book only went through a couple of drafts. The photos and artwork were chosen mainly by Kurtzman and Preiss. "It was Byron's idea to do the flip series that runs for more than sixty pages at the bottom right corners of the pages," Zimmerman said. "Harvey chose the sequence from an animated piece ["The Boat"] he had done for *Sesame Street*. It came out well. Harvey Kurtzman was one of my boyhood idols. It was a thrill and an honor to meet him, much less to work with him."

My Life as a Cartoonist, which ran just 108 pages of large type, with numerous illustrations, was lightweight and inconsequential in most respects. It didn't do justice to Harvey Kurtzman's life and work—as a young adult book, it wasn't intended as definitive—but it did contribute to the knowledge we have of Kurtzman's early life, something he seldom talked about beyond a few well-worn stories. In the back, Kurtzman provided a step-by-step guide to the development of one of his *Hey Look!* pages (with the artwork in progressive stages of completion, recreated by Downs). Zimmerman said, "Everyone liked the book when it was published, but I have no idea of how it might have done saleswise. Kurtzman was pleased to have a book that would appeal to an entirely new generation of school-age kids, and certainly the book did sell to schools and libraries." According to Preiss, "the book received good reviews and was named one of the best books of the year for young readers by the New York Public Library."[46] Kurtzman himself never publicly gave his opinion of it. A comparison of the original interview transcripts and the final text shows that the words in the books were Kurtzman's own, although it was shaped by Zimmerman to make it read smoothly.

Meanwhile, after *Nuts!* went nowhere, Preiss and Kurtzman planned two more ambitious projects designed to allow Kurtzman to work on the types of stories he had done for EC. One was a revival of *Two-Fisted Tales* and the other was nothing less than what amounted to a new, extra-long issue of the comic book *Mad*. Using the *Two-Fisted* title would require the approval of Bill Gaines, but, since there was no possibility of using the *Mad* title, Kurtzman got started right away on what would be called *Harvey Kurtzman's Strange Adventures*.

Strange Adventures was envisioned as a one-shot publication consisting of short satirical stories written and laid out by Kurtzman just like he did with *Mad*. Artists came forward for very little money, just for the opportunity to collaborate. The list of artists included Bill Stout, Sergio Aragonés, Tom Bunk, Rick Geary, Dave Gibbons and Sarah Downs. Kurtzman himself would do a Western story from start to finish, his first all-Kurtzman comic story since the black and white Dracula strips (and others done at the same time) for Eurocomics in the 1970s. Stout was lined up to create the book's cover. Moebius contributed a page of art, and, a year or two later, Art Spiegelman agreed to write an introduction that recounted his experience as a guest-lecturer at Kurtzman's SVA class.

Instead of offering a lesson in cartooning, Spiegelman—who had taught comics history at SVA—gave Kurtzman's students a slide presentation on Kurtzman's contributions to comic art. Even Sarah Downs, who had worked at Kurtzman's side for years, learned things about him that she never knew. As Spiegelman wrote in the book's introduction, "Harvey Kurtzman has been the single most significant influence on a couple of

Panels from "A Furshlugginer Genius!" by Art Spiegelman, published in the *New Yorker* (March 29, 1993).

generations of comics artists . . . and I wanted to make sure his students knew that the friendly, unassuming guy they called 'Hey, Teach!' was actually a goddamn National Treasure."[47] Kurtzman was visibly moved by the tribute, and afterward, when parting for the evening, the two men hugged.

First things first: Kurtzman had to script and lay out seven stories for *Harvey Kurtzman's Strange Adventures*, and that was going to take time. With Kurtzman's periods of physical steadiness occurring only after the L-DOPA kicked in, his "drawing window" each day was limited. He approached it methodically, knowing that eventually the work would get done. He had no deadline.

Sarah Downs continued working with Kurtzman through 1988, when *Little Annie Fanny* burst her last blouse. Then Sarah helped him with his SVA class. She would start the class if Kurtzman wasn't feeling up to it. He would be there, waiting for his medication to kick in. In 1989, Downs moved to Pittsburgh because her husband got a job with Westinghouse. At that point, she essentially abandoned her art career. "I think, really, in part I was doing it because I liked Harvey," she said. "I think that the relationship was important. I mean, he could've been a plumber and then I would've become a plumber. And I think Harvey and Adele were like life mentors to me. In many situations later, I'd think, 'how would Adele handle this? How would Harvey handle this?'" In Pittsburgh, Sarah had nightmares of being back in Mount Vernon, going, "'Oh my God, I've got to work on this *Annie Fanny* because Harvey can't and if I don't finish it he won't get paid!' Sort of 'was I supposed to work on *Annie Fanny* and I didn't and I left him hanging there and moved to Pittsburgh?'" Downs stayed in touch, and did a bit of coloring work on a subsequent Kurtzman project via the mail.

SEVEN YEARS INTO KURTZMAN'S illness, he and Adele were guests of the first Salon Européen de la Bande Dessinée in Grenoble, France. It took place March 16–19, 1989. Pierre Pascal organized the Grenoble event as a premier French comics festival to vie with the massive annual convention in Angoulême. Jacques Dutrey personally saw to it that all the Kurtzmans'expenses were covered, even their phone bills. Adele looked after Harvey continuously. They spent most afternoons resting in their hotel room. He had to take a pill every other hour to fight off some of the effects of his illness. "He lost part of his memory in the second hour, which is why Adele had to be constantly with him," Dutrey recalled. "He was invited to long dinners every night, which were exhausting."[48]

It was worth it for Kurtzman, just for the opportunity to reunite with old friends. One of the moving moments of the salon took place just after the gala dinner on opening night, when Kurtzman and Morris (Maurice de Bevere) literally fell into each other's arms. They hadn't seen each other since Morris left America in 1954.[49] The Kurtzmans had lunch with Marcel Gotlib, ran into Gilbert Shelton and shared a table at the gala dinner with Will and Ann Eisner. The *Sesame Street* shorts were shown at his panel. He jokingly remarked that they were "just a little tease to get people in here."[50]

In Grenoble, Harvey Kurtzman met Alan Moore for the second time. Their first encounter had been at the 1985 San Diego Comic Con, the only US convention ever attended by the acclaimed writer of *Swamp Thing* and *Watchmen*. DC editor Julius Schwartz had dragged Moore over to Kurtzman's lunch table to make the introduction, an awkward moment for Moore. This time, the meeting was to be a more meaningful experience for the British author.

Moore was depressed because he was "in the middle of a complex and painful relationship-breakdown," yet he was in Grenoble at the convention with his daughters. There he ran into Adele, Harvey and Liz Kurtzman at the ski resort Alpe d'Huez. (The salon set up and paid for the excursion for its special guests.) Liz was there because she was traveling for work in Europe. Moore recalled the meeting a few years later:

It's strange . . . that this singularly lousy week should also contain a few of the most golden and idyllic hours that I can ever remember spending. Halfway up a mountain, in blazing sunlight above the snowline, I sat at a café table with Harvey Kurtzman, drinking beer while Harvey, suffering from the debilitating effects of Parkinson's disease and bundled up warm on an already warm day, drank cocoa. We both had our families with us, and Harvey's daughter took my daughters up for a trip in a light aeroplane while we talked with Harvey and his wife Adele.

I don't remember every word we said. I wish I did. I remember that he said *Watchmen* was "a damn fine piece o' work," and I know that it's one of those memories that I'll still be clutching at pathetically when I'm old and spent. I remember that he seemed surprised when I told him that *Watchmen* wouldn't exist if he hadn't skewed my perception of the super hero genre with works like "Superduperman." He looked amazed, almost bashful, unbelievably enough, and said, "Well, how about that?"[51]

The convention drew some fifty thousand fans and was judged a great success. Other British and American creators in attendance were Sergio Aragonés, Dave Gibbons, Brian Bolland, John Bolton, David Lloyd, David Mazzucchelli, Bill Sienkiewicz and Mike Zeck.

Not long after they returned home, the Kurtzmans were saddened to hear of the death of Harold Hayes. After leaving *Esquire* in 1973, he worked as a magazine consultant and, toward the end, edited *California* magazine. He was also a producer of *20/20* at ABC News, and wrote two books on ecological subjects. He died of a brain tumor in at the Cedars-Sinai Medical Center in Los Angeles in the first week of April. The man who praised the comic book *Mad* at the height of the anti-comics hysteria, and made a place for Kurtzman in *Esquire*, was gone. He was sixty-two years old.

In July, Kurtzman was inducted into the Will Eisner Hall of Fame. He was selected out of a group that, oddly, was entirely made up of people associated with him save one. (They were Jean "Moebius" Giraud, Stan Lee, Wallace Wood, Alex Toth and Steve Ditko. Only Ditko hadn't been professionally linked with Kurtzman at some point in his career. All five were selected for the Hall of Fame in subsequent years.)

As autumn 1989 approached, Kurtzman had to decide whether he would continue to teach. During his last few years, as his illness worsened, he needed someone to open doors, carry materials and "do" for him. Retiring from teaching meant forgoing a substantial portion of his income, and he wanted to continue as long as possible. He contacted another former student, Eric Palma, who he had gotten to know when Palma and a friend painted the Kurtzmans' kitchen some months earlier. Palma recently recounted their typical preparation ritual, beginning on the morning of each class day: "We'd go up to his studio, chit-chat a while, then prepare for class. Harvey always had the day's lesson planned out on yellow legal paper, divided into time segments. We'd go over each segment and discuss the minutiae of how the class would proceed. Harvey took his teaching duties seriously. It was not in his nature to be unprepared or to 'wing it.' A car [service] would come and take us to SVA. After class, a car would drive Harvey back home, and I would go my own way."[52] Palma went on to become an editorial illustrator whose work has appeared in a broad range of publications, including the *New Yorker*, the *New York Times*, the *Wall Street Journal* and *Fortune* magazine.

Kurtzman penciled a cover for the second issue of James Vance's *Kings in Disguise*, an award-winning graphic story set in the Great Depression. Soon after that, because Kitchen Sink published both of them, the artist and writer ended up appearing at a number of conventions together, giving Vance the opportunity to get to know both Harvey and Adele Kurtzman. He recounted an incident that probably occurred when they were in Rye Brook, New York, at the Museum of Cartoon Art, where Kurtzman was given a special award.

> I remember . . . a moment at a convention when I ran into Harvey and Adele while I was carrying my daughter Brigid through the hotel. She was only a few years past the toddler stage then, and a little overtired and overwhelmed by all these people who were a little more, ah, interesting than she was accustomed to. I stopped to say hello to the Kurtzmans, hoping that Brigid wouldn't dissolve into tears over yet another delay on the way to our room. And the damnedest thing happened.
>
> Harvey completely ignored me and simply inclined his body forward, fixing Brigid with a deadpan stare over that prodigious nose of his. Within seconds, she'd turned bright red . . . oh, shit, I thought, please don't scream . . . and she began to giggle uncontrollably. He took my daughter's hand and glanced at Adele with a little self-satisfied shrug. Adele shook her head in her familiar wry manner and said, "Oh, the children always love Harvey."
>
> I liked Harvey personally, I respected him tremendously, I was in awe of him professionally; but that was the first time I'd seen him become magic. His public persona was largely constructed of cynical wit, but I felt privileged to have gotten a brief glimpse of the lovely human being that lay beneath.[53]

The pencils Kurtzman did for *Kings in Disguise* showed that his drawing skills, still pretty good when he was working up the layouts for *Harvey Kurtzman's Strange Adventures*, had diminished, although the overall design was adequate. Pete Poplaski, who had worked with Kurtzman on other projects, inked it carefully so as to honor the pencilled drawing yet enhance it enough to make it look as impressive as possible.

The Kurtzmans took the train to a comic con organized by Jim Amash in Greensboro, North Carolina, in November. Harvey continued to make appearances at conventions and other events as the 1990s arrived, but it was getting harder to simply "be Harvey Kurtzman." Like Mark Twain in his final years, as illness encroached, he saw fewer people and traveled less, especially after his doctor gave him more bad news about his health.

Kurtzman and Elder returned to *Mad*, providing the art for features such as this satire of *Wheel of Fortune* in #266 (October 1986). They signed their work "WEHK."

Top: Panel at the Dallas Fantasy Fair, 1986. Coutesy of Gary Groth. L-R: Burne Hogarth, Harvey Kurtzman, Kenneth Smith, Moebius (Jean Giraud). Bottom: Elder and Kurtzman ca. 1980. Photograph courtesy of E. B. Boatner.

Playboy (January 1984). An example of *Little Annie Fanny* toward the end of its run.

27.

"IT BURNS ME UP!"

"I REGARD MY TIME AS VALUABLE, and I use my time to my best advantage because God knows I'm running out of it," Kurtzman said, during a panel appearance at the Dallas Fantasy Fair in 1987. Couched in the middle of a discussion of the current state of comics in France and America, the comment engendered little notice. It was a rare reference to his illness in a public forum.[1] He may have had the endurance of a Spartan, and had overcome normal obstacles in life, but the progression of Parkinson's could not be stopped.

Kurtzman was luckier than some. Adele recalled, "When we would go to the Parkinson's doctor, we would see people who shook a lot, and they couldn't even feed themselves. It was so dreadful. Harvey could feed and he could eat."[2] The L-DOPA kept the symptoms at bay for two or three hour stretches, but as the disease advanced, the medication gradually produced a complication called *dyskinesia*, marked by involuntary writhing movements. Nevertheless, Kurtzman wasn't depressed, the most common psychiatric symptom among PD sufferers. He still had the desire to work, though the illness slowed him down a great deal.

Kurtzman held onto his teaching career as long as possible. However, completing the 1989–1990 school year had been a strain, even with assistance. After seventeen years at The School of Visual Arts, Kurtzman retired. Now he would put his diminishing energy into his family life, such creative projects as Byron Preiss was able to arrange for him and occasional trips.

One project that had been on his "to do" list for years was the book on the history of comics. Woody Gelman had passed away in 1978 due to complications from a stroke, so Nostalgia Press was out. He once said he was convinced the project had a curse on it. Byron Preiss thought such a book had good commercial potential and was able to interest Prentice Hall Press in publishing it. The problem was that Kurtzman was too ill to research and write it himself, as originally intended. Fantagraphics Books had been trying to pull the book together for several years, and sent Preiss all they had (not much). Preiss's editor Howard Zimmerman contacted Michael Barrier to see if he was interested in working with Kurtzman to produce the manuscript.

"I don't recall the basis on which I was chosen, if anyone ever told me," Barrier recently said.[3] Perhaps it was because of his introduction to the EC section in *A Smithsonian Book of Comic-Book Comics*. He had written about Kurtzman as early as the late 1960s in Bill Spicer's *Graphic Story Magazine*, and had established a reputation as one of the most intelligent, thoughtful and capable writers on the subject of animation and comic art. Rather than receiving royalties, Barrier would be paid a flat $3,000 for the job. He met with Kurtzman in his home in Mount Vernon on March 31, 1990, to tape-record Kurtzman's thoughts for the book. That, added to whatever material came from Fantagraphics, were well short of what was required. Kurtzman's past interviews were tapped. "I had to work all of the sources very hard, because so much of the material was thin," Barrier said. He penned Chapter Six, "The Super Hero Revival," virtually on his own. It was felt Marvel Comics and other comic book highlights of the 1960s, which Kurtzman had seldom investigated or addressed, had to be represented for commercial reasons.

The manuscript was short, but Kurtzman had always envisioned a book tilted more toward artwork than text. *From Aargh! to Zap!* was subtitled *Harvey Kurtzman's Visual History of the Comics*. About 75 percent of its ninety-six large-sized pages (11" by 15") were filled with reproductions of covers and panels from the comic books under discussion. Kurtzman himself selected the images and wrote the captions for the illustrations. "All of the comics choices were his, except for a few of the more recent titles in the back," Howard Zimmerman said. "More than half of the covers and pages reproduced in the book came from my personal collection. I ended up doing major work on the book, doing edits and a rewrite based on my prior conversations with Harvey for the autobiography. Harvey reviewed and approved the manuscript. He made a number of changes and deletions. I remember his deleting some critical remarks about super hero comics of the '80s."[4] Byron Preiss's public comments made it clear just how ill Kurtzman was by this time: "This was a difficult time for

Harvey medically. It was an unsung and particularly heroic commitment [on Kurtzman's part] to complete the book."[5]

In September 1990, *From Aargh! to Zap!* was published. Preiss reported, "It came out to critical acclaim, and Harvey appeared on *Good Morning America*. The first printing sold out, and the book went back to press."[6] Compromised though it is, the book successfully puts forward the comic book work Kurtzman thought was the best and most significant. It emphasizes Eisner's *The Spirit*, the work of the Simon and Kirby team, and Biro's *Crime Does Not Pay*. There's a thirty-page section on EC and Kurtzman's own work (*Mad, Trump, Humbug, Help!* and *Little Annie Fanny*). The latter part of the book devotes considerable attention to underground comix, European comics and Art Spiegelman's *Maus*.

Of *Maus*, he wrote, "Grown-ups can read *Maus* and feel a respect for Spiegelman's writing; they can read *Maus* as if they were reading a novel. Spiegelman has opened an avenue of interest that's a real service to the medium."[7] Those were Kurtzman's words, not those of Barrier or Zimmerman.

In a review for *Library Journal*, Keith R. A. DeCandido seemed to miss the premise of the book, and was off-base in other respects. He wrote,

> That this is Kurtzman's history is significant; the entire book is colored by his tastes and perceptions. Kurtzman spends an inordinate amount of time on his own work. His look at contemporary comics tilts a bit too often toward the commercial. The illustrations are uneven—some are reproduced beautifully, others are almost illegibly fuzzy. Despite the book's size (11" x 15"), many reproductions are very small . . . and hence difficult to read. Recommended only as a supplement to other comics histories; this work is neither objective, nor academic, nor complete.

The book was never intended to be a balanced, complete history, only a history of comics Kurtzman felt were important and worthy. Images aren't "fuzzy," but a number of them are rather dark, which bespeaks inadequate attention by Preiss and his staff. Contrary to what Preiss said for public consumption, the book wasn't acclaimed by critics.

Apart from the inclusion of super hero material and other comics added at the behest of Preiss (or Prentice-Hall), its flaws primarily had to do with compromises made to accommodate Kurtzman's illness. The book's "voice" shifts back and forth between what sounds like Kurtzman and a scholarly tone more in keeping with Barrier's writing style. Although Kurtzman approved the text, he was obviously unable to proofread it carefully, or he would have caught a major error. On p. 88, René Goscinny is described as "the Astérix artist," when he knew very well that Goscinny was the writer, and Albert Uderzo was the artist. Years later, Adele said, "*From Aargh! to Zap!* was okay, but it could have been better. Harvey liked it, but I think he wouldn't say out loud that it could have been better. I just wanted something more. It felt incomplete. I was a little disappointed, but I would never say it to him."[8]

IN EARLY 1991, a division of Marvel published *Harvey Kurtzman's Strange Adventures*, four years in the making, in hardcover. It was his first new work published by the company since 1951. (Martin Goodman, though still alive at this time, no longer had any connection to the firm.) The book was much anticipated by Kurtzman fans. Given the range of talents, and the prospect of *Mad*-style parodies from Kurtzman, this was understandable. It was also exciting that Kurtzman himself had done the finished art for one of the stories. That story, "Drums Along the Shmohawk," was originally supposed to be finished by Robert Crumb.

Crumb recently explained, "I did try to work from Kurtzman's layouts, but it just didn't work for me. I got about a half a page into it and gave up on it. I couldn't do it. Part of the problem for me was that, frankly, I didn't think the story was very good, or that any of the stories for that book were very good. To me it looked like Kurtzman had lost it, lost his comic genius, his sharp satirical edge."[9] Instead, Crumb opted to create a two-page strip about his friendship with Kurtzman called, "Ode to Harvey Kurtzman."

"[The book] didn't sell spectacularly in the US," Preiss admitted, though he added, "Foreign rights sales were exceptional. France, Spain, Scandanavia, Germany and Italy all committed."[10] An indicator of poor sales was the scuttling

Panel from R. Crumb's "Ode to Harvey Kurtzman" in *Harvey Kurtzman's Strange Adventures* (1991).

of an already planned limited edition, even though Bill Stout had completed a new wraparound cover and the contributing artists had done a special "jam" two-page spread. As for its critical reception, Preiss said, "The French review of the American edition was a rave, but critical response here [in the US] was mixed."[11] Tom De Haven of *Entertainment Weekly* gave it a grade "B," and wrote, "Although *Strange Adventures* contains seven full-color *Mad*-silly stories scripted by Kurtzman, all

of them (except one) are illustrated by others. Professional as these artists are, none can match Kurtzman as a stylist. Fortunately, editor Byron Preiss has had the good sense to include an appendix with the master's complete black-and-white pencil breakdowns for each of the stories. A rare glimpse of the complete cartoonist at his purest."[12]

The book's problems can partly be attributed to Kurtzman's Parkinson's. His layouts, printed in the back of the book, reveal that he was still in control of his pencil, but the illness was affecting him in other ways. By the late 1980s, his world was slowly closing down. He engaged with fewer and fewer new developments in popular culture, so he mostly fell back on satirizing old movies and TV shows. The more serious problem is that his heart doesn't seem to be in it. Without real enthusiasm behind it, the work definitely lacks (as Crumb put it) "his sharp satirical edge." The best thing in the book is Robert Crumb's two-page "Ode," which was wisely placed first in the book. It dramatized the impact of young Crumb's discovery of *Humbug* #2 on a spinner rack in 1957—a moment that changed his life— and captured the essence of their mentor-student relationship with brilliance and economy. The Kurtzman-Stout "Shmegeggi of the Cave Men," with the protagonist looking much like Goodman Beaver, is the best of the other stories.

It's hard to argue with *The Comics Journal* review by Darcy Sullivan, who wrote, "Kurtzman, one of comics' most admired innovators, may have indirectly or directly influenced most of today's comics art greats, but this volume is stale work indeed, and passé to a frightening degree. Its stunning artwork notwithstanding, the book fails at every level, being both superficially hackneyed and resoundingly irrelevant to modern times."[13] Had the opportunity to do something like *Strange Adventures* come in the 1970s, it would have better shown whether Kurtzman was capable of recapturing the *Mad* comic book magic at a later stage of his life. By the end of the 1980s, it was too late. The book added nothing of importance to his legacy, other than Crumb's piece and Spiegelman's introduction. Such would be the case for the subsequent projects that Kurtzman completed in the remaining years of his life. He was trying to build up a nest egg for Adele.

"I never made any money in this damn business," he once said. "It's my own fault."[14] When Michael Barrier was interviewing him for *From Aargh! to Zap*, Kurtzman expounded on the subject at greater length. "I saw Mort Walker the other day. Mort and I started in the business at exactly the same moment. We had the same customers. There's just one minor difference between us, besides the talent: he never lost the priority of making a buck. Now he's a millionaire. He was telling me how he used the three- or four-fingered device on *Beetle Bailey* to cut corners. He took out all the blacks, so that the flow of the ink is faster. He's got all kinds of gimmicks to make the feature bleed money. I've never been able to do that. Don't get me wrong. I would love to make money. But I don't know how to keep that priority. My focus was on the fun of the art, and not on the buck. To this very day, I still fall into that trap. I can only seem to work when it gives me pleasure."[15] At the end of his life, he had just $35,000 in the bank.[16]

Unlike others with serious illnesses, he didn't huddle at home and block out the world. He was generally upbeat, even as his mobility was much reduced: "Aside from taking out the garbage, I have little need to leave the house, which sometimes is good and sometimes bad. When I want isolation, it's splendid. When I want company, it can be grim."[17] He got out of the house when he could, and saw friends as much as possible. Sometime in late 1990, Kurtzman had dinner with Terry Gilliam and Joel Siegel at Liz Kurtzman's downtown apartment on Crosby Street. Gilliam, whose first feature film as a director was *Monty Python and the Holy Grail* in 1975, was helming big productions. In *Brazil* (1985), he named key characters Mr. Kurtzmann, Mr. Warrenn and Mr. Helpmann.

Bill Stout recalled, "The last dinner with Harvey in New York, he arranged it so that we were having dinner at his daughter's SoHo loft. It was me, Harvey, Joel, Terry and Liz. Terry had just finished directing *The Fisher King* and so I asked him how that went, because that was a hired gun film. That wasn't a project that he originated." Gilliam replied, "I had such a reputation for being so difficult, everybody walked on eggshells around me and did everything I wanted . . . immediately!' It was fantastic."[18]

Early in 1991, Arizona-based publisher Bruce Hamilton arranged for Kurtzman to produce lithographs of the original draft cover of *Mad* #1. They were to be signed and numbered by Kurtzman, so Liz accompanied him to Prescott City for this to be done. A respite from the winter cold of New York was not unwelcome. She said, "We went to Arizona . . . and Dad was really not well. I kept frantically calling my mother and saying, 'This is not Parkinson's. Something is very wrong,' and I knew. You know, you get that gut feeling. Everybody kept saying, 'Oh, you're being paranoid. It's the Parkinson's.'"[19]

Adele recalled, "My daughter said, 'he keeps falling asleep.' That hadn't been happening with the Parkinson's. Then when he came home, he looked pretty bad. He went to see doctors, and they discovered colon cancer." Kurtzman underwent exploratory surgery. When he got home from the hospital, he wrote in his daily diary just one large word: "CANCER."[20]

Once Kurtzman was sufficiently recovered from the surgery, he began a regime of chemotherapy. "He was the star of the chemotherapy unit," Adele said. "He'd make people laugh. In that sense, there were good times. The people who worked there said it was always a pleasure to see him come into the room."[21] Then it was discovered that his colon cancer had spread to his liver. Kurtzman wrote Jacques Dutrey in February of 1991, "My afflictions go on and on. Parkinson's led to an operation. My red blood count wasn't right and I was bleeding internally. That led to the dreaded cancer, which I am now being treated for (liver cancer). I go for chemotherapy treatments and I'm like a juggler, trying to keep all the pins moving. It's not as horrible as one might think. The chemotherapy is a scene where pleasant-looking people sit around getting their IV injections every other week. It almost looks like fun. But, I'm not getting any work done."

Barbara Nessim, roommate of Gloria Steinem in the early 1960s, called Kurtzman one day. "He told me on the phone that he had cancer. I had no idea. I was just calling to say hello, when he told me. He said, 'Adele, can I tell her?' I said 'Tell me what?' He said, 'I'm sick, I have cancer.' He was kind of cheerful, probably resigned. He wasn't 'Oh, woe is me!' He was Harvey. He always had a sense of humor. And that was what was so great about it. There was a realization that no one lives forever. 'Okay, this is my time.' He seemed like he was living in the moment."[22] Then the cancer went into remission. The family's spirits rallied. As is common with cancer, treatment seemed to be working for a time. Then the cancer would return, and more treatments would be tried. This was the scenario playing out in Kurtzman's life through 1991 and 1992.

Though Harvey Kurtzman was no longer working for *Playboy*, Hugh Hefner kept Kurtzman on the magazine's insurance plan, which paid his medical bills. Hefner acknowledged this, adding, "I always felt he was part of the extended *Playboy* family."[23]

The Parkinson's continued to progress. "I'd visit with him occasionally," Robert Crumb recalled. "It was terrible to watch the progression of Parkinson's disease on him. He became steadily more debilitated. The last time I saw him was at a dinner, I think, at his daughter Meredith's place in New York City. I think Adele was there. Harvey just sat there and barely said a word. He was far gone. I think he barely understood what was going on around him by then. He just sat there staring into space." His lucidity fluctuated depending on where he was in the L-DOPA drug cycle.

In the spring of 1991, Nellie received her college degree as a theater major. "When I first got out of college, I was running a theater company with some fellow graduates. I was also working in theater on Broadway doing marketing." In addition, Nellie worked for Byron Preiss, as did some of her friends. Of Preiss, she said, "He was nothing but a total mensch with me and my friends. He was a little nuts, in that I think he had so many ideas going on all the time [and was] trying to manage them all. I really adored him."[24]

Liz married Marc Hirschfeld on June 15. He was a young casting director in the city who she had been with for some time. "Part of the reason why we chose that time to get married is because my dad was ill," she said. "We wanted him to see us make that step. My father had a good time and walked me across the yard. Earlier, he tried to move the piano in the living room and I got so freaked out that I moved it, and spent my wedding day in horrible pain. We all had a good laugh about it later."

At the 1991 San Diego Comic Con, its first year at the new San Diego Convention Center, Byron Preiss talked to artists who were interested in collaborating on a new Kurtzman project. Preiss later said, "I was hoping, having known Bill Gaines in a business context for twenty years, that he would give some consideration to allowing Harvey, at this stage in his career, to return to *Two-Fisted* and do one of the things he does best. I think that in working on *From Aargh! to Zap!*, Harvey thought a lot more about his work on *Two-Fisted*. And I think Bill Gaines, towards the end of his life, had a very big soft spot for Harvey, and as a result of this and conversations with Dorothy Crouch who represents EC Publications, Bill agreed to let us do this in collaboration with Harvey. It really took shape at the 1991 San Diego con."[25]

Preiss visited Kurtzman in Mount Vernon to show him the work of artists who wanted to work with him on the *New Two-Fisted Tales*. Kurtzman was to act mainly as editor, though he would do layouts for the covers, and if he felt up to it, write and lay out one story per issue. Others would submit scripts for his approval, and finished pencils as well, which he would go over. Preiss publicly claimed, "[Kurtzman's] intellectual sharpness, his sense of humor and his determination are unabated."[26] It's not possible to know how much Preiss believed in the artistic potential of the project, and how much he was doing it to help his friend. (Preiss died in an auto accident in 2005.) What is known is that he expended a great deal of energy on keeping *The New Two-Fisted Tales* going forward.

SOME YEARS EARLIER, a neighbor in her late twenties named Alison Porter had become friendly with the Kurtzmans. "I would see [Harvey] taking out the garbage, looking a little frail. He would wave once in a while, and I gradually got to know him. Adele was such a warm and lovely person."[27] She sometimes kept Kurtzman company when Adele went shopping or did fundraising for the Clearview School. "I got to spend a lot of time with Harvey because I was unemployed," she said. "Generally, he would work for a bit in the morning, and then he'd have to take a break from 11:00 a.m. to 1:00 p.m. because his pill would be wearing off. He would eat lunch, and have coffee, while he was waiting until he could take his next pill. He would get very shaky, and it was kind of excruciating. During that time in the day when he couldn't work, we would talk and hang out." Kurtzman showed her his work, and she discovered just how talented he was. Once, Porter asked Kurtzman to draw a Christmas card for her. "When I think about it, I cringe," she said recently. "He took twenty minutes out of his precious two-and-a-half-hour window when he could work to do something for me. I just didn't understand the big picture, especially not at first."

Porter remembered a time, shortly after meeting Kurtzman, when she found out how well regarded he was by other cartoonists. At one of the Fourth of July parties, she wandered inside and was talking to Art Spiegelman in the living room. When she said something like, "Oh, that's just Harvey," Spiegelman got excited and, looking her in the eye, stated emphatically, "HARVEY—IS—GOD!" Porter said, "He was mad I wasn't in awe of Harvey. I said, kind of meekly, 'Uh, okay!'"

Not all of Kurtzman's friends saw him after his cancer diagnosis. Some didn't want to intrude. Others didn't realize how ill he was. The exact nature and seriousness of his afflictions weren't widely known. Some were no longer living in New York. But many did see him, and found him in good spirits.

Kurtzman was able to get together with Jack Davis and other old friends when he was asked to participate in the taping of a series called *Comic Book Greats* in early 1992. The documentary series was produced by Starbur Home Video and hosted by Stan Lee. It had begun shooting in late 1991 with some of the "hot" creators working for Image comics such as Rob Liefeld and Todd McFarlane, and now was bringing in some older veterans in the field. Kurtzman accepted an invitation to appear as long as the producers would pay for Adele to accompany him to Los Angeles. The plan was that Kurtzman would appear alongside Jack Davis in a "dual interview."

On the day of the shoot, despite having taken a pill so that he could be at his best, Kurtzman managed to say very little during the filming. Lee would ask a question, but Kurtzman was so slow on the uptake that Davis would jump in with an answer. To keep things rolling, Davis did a number of sketches (including one of Kurtzman) while he and Stan talked. Kurtzman would have been a better interviewee if his pauses could be edited out, but that wasn't possible with the way things were set up. "It was awful," Adele said.[28] However, he appeared front and center in a memorable group photo taken that day. Kurtzman, clad in his favorite bright red sweater, was flanked by Stan Lee, Jack Davis, Bob Kane, John Romita and Michael Reilly, producer of the interview series.

Kurtzman told what happened later that day in a letter to a friend. "That evening, I was invited to the Hugh Hefner mansion (always a shattering experience)," he wrote. "Hef was surrounded at the buffet by a coterie of aging actors and who did he choose to talk to . . . Yes! You guessed right—Adele! Will wonders never cease? So life goes on."[29]

More family illness cropped up. Adele's brother-in-law was diagnosed with cancer, as was the father of Liz's husband. This caused Kurtzman to muse, "Do you think the planet is rotting away?"[30]

Kurtzman's illness didn't cause him to rethink his atheism. Harry Chester's wife Irene recalled, "He would sometimes talk about death, what it meant, and he'd say the reason for religion is that no one can understand what happens to you after you die. He said, 'picture nothingness. Nobody can picture nothingness. That's why people have decided that there's got to be a God, there's got to be a Hereafter, because it's impossible to think that there is nothing.'"[31] In offhand remarks, he sometimes wryly referred to "that great system in the sky that I don't quite understand."[32]

On June 3, 1992, Bill Gaines passed away in his sleep. He wasn't especially ill, though he was vaguely complaining of not feeling quite right. Other than his phone calls to Adele relating to health insurance, the Kurtzmans hadn't heard much from him in recent years. They were both shaken by this unexpected loss.

That same month, Kurtzman went back on chemotherapy while trying to work on projects with Preiss. One was *The New Two-Fisted Tales*. The cover of the first issue was a collaboration between Harvey Kurtzman and Will Eisner, with Eisner working from Kurtzman's layout. It was the only time the signatures of the two giants of comics appeared together on a single piece of art.

The Fourth of July picnic at the Kurtzmans' house was only slightly muted by the tacit understanding held by most that it could be Kurtzman's last. Adele phoned Batton Lash and said, "He wants to see some of his students again."[33] Lash invited several former members of Kurtzman's "Satirical Cartooning" classes. His chief memory of the party was of

During the filming of *The Comic Book Greats*, some of the participants gathered for this photograph. L-R: Bob Kane (co-creator of *Batman*), Stan Lee (co-creator of many Marvel Comics characters), Bill Liebowitz (owner of the Golden Apple stores), Harvey Kurtzman, Jack Davis, Michael R. Reilly (Executive Producer of *The Comic Book Greats*) and John Romita (*Spider-Man* artist and Marvel art director). Courtesy of Paul Burke for Stabur Corp./Stabur Home Video.

Harvey, ensconced in a lawn chair, signing numerous comics, books and other items. Someone else manned the barbecue. The group was large and spirited. Sarah Downs was there. Kurtzman interacted with his guests as much as he could in his condition.

Denis Kitchen officially became Harvey Kurtzman's art agent (and, later, literary agent). Kurtzman felt Kitchen was "a first rate human being" and trusted him implicitly.[34] This was done to assure Kurtzman that someone he trusted would help leverage his work to maximum advantage, both in the short term and for Adele when he was gone. She later wrote, "Others talked about publishing Harvey's work. Denis did—and does."[35] Meredith helped her father sort through his papers in the studio, in preparation for allowing Denis to take custody of them. Kitchen spent a week in that attic going through the material.[36]

In July, Kitchen Sink published the *Hey Look!* reprint book. It collected all of the pages from that early, inspired cartoon series. It also reprinted all of *Pot-Shot Pete*, *Genius* and *Egghead Doodle*. John Benson wrote the introduction. At the end of his creative life, Kurtzman was glad that *Hey Look!*, which gave him the chance to find himself as a writer and artist in comics, was back in print.

As illness further reduced his activities, going through the daily mail became the big event in his day. Kurtzman got more mail than ever in his last years. Some of it was letters and packages from fans who sent him their publications, or artwork hoping for a critique or just to tell him what his work had meant to them. There were a fair amount of packages with work he had to edit. His outgoing letters to people in his personal life were where the supposed introvert let his emotions spill across the page, as in his 1940s letters to Jo Ann and Adele. He was a man of unexpected emotion and wistful yearning, always expressed with humor and charm. One of his principal joys was receiving letters from friends. A diary entry reads, "Heard from Jacques D. today—He always makes me feel good."[37]

Meanwhile, Byron Preiss was publicizing *The New Two-Fisted Tales*. In "Kurtzman Today," an article and interview with Preiss in *The Comics Journal* #153 (October 1992), he gave some background on how the project came to be. "It was strictly defined by Gaines . . . that this would only be done if it was Harvey's project. Not some *Two-Fisted* celebration or homage. This really had to be an extension of the old *Two-Fisted Tales*. Harvey has . . . laid out all the covers. But Harvey, by virtue of his medical concerns, has only done some writing on the book. The hat that he wears—and which he wore on all of *Two-Fisted* and *Frontline*—is that of editor. Every inch of the book is gone over by Harvey."

Preiss added, "One of the reasons that Harvey started *Mad* was his complete exhaustion at writing every *Two-Fisted Tales* story. And I don't think that was something he really wanted to do again. Dark Horse will be the distributor of the book, and it will be the first book in thirty years to carry the EC logo. This will be the first new EC comic in a long time."[38]

IN SPITE OF BYRON PREISS'S announcement, Harvey Kurtzman was entering the final stage of his life. He had been in the grip of a progressive illness for ten years, and suffering from cancer for almost two.

On October 3, 1992, Kurtzman asked his neighbor Alison Porter if she would walk with him into Bronxville. "He didn't tell me why. When we got there, we had lunch, because he had to eat something, and then he bought a rose. He and Adele had the same birthday, and he wanted to get her something for her birthday. That walk took a monumental effort for him. He had to take extra pills, which meant a lot of discomfort later, and on the way back, he started to falter so I had to help him. But I thought it was so romantic of him to make that effort just to buy a rose for Adele, who is such a lovely person." Adele turned sixty-seven that day. Harvey turned sixty-eight.

Somehow Kurtzman managed to complete his part of the *New Two-Fisted Tales* #2, which involved writing and doing the layouts for what would be his last self-written new story, "War." (It was capably finished by Brian Franczak and Chuck Majewski, and colored by Sarah Downs.) The story showed the evolution of life on earth to the point that mankind has the weapons to destroy itself, and does so in a nuclear holocaust. But "in the aftermath, a survivor emerges." It is a cockroach, of which Kurtzman

Panel from "It Burns Me Up!," adapted from a Ray Bradbury story by Harvey Kurtzman and Matt Wagner: *Ray Bradbury Comics* #2 (April 1993).

wrote, "With the passage of time, it may evolve into a sentient species. But it, too, is a predator." Though the story is overly ambitious and doesn't quite come off, it's significant that Kurtzman ended it—after all the death and destruction in the story—with a ray of hope. But then, he had always characterized himself as essentially an optimist. He didn't live to see "War" published. (Dark Horse had contracted for six issues, but there were only two.)

Kurtzman tried his best to adapt the Ray Bradbury story "A Memory of Murder," which originally saw print in the pulp magazine *Dime Mystery* in November 1944. Kurtzman's version was prepared for a new Topps comic book series adapting Bradbury's work. He tackled the story his usual way, breaking it down into rough layouts. Matt Wagner, well known for his comics *Mage* and *Grendel*, agreed to do the pencils and inks just for the opportunity to collaborate with Kurtzman. (They had met briefly years before.) When he received the layouts, he was shocked. Wagner recounted, "It was with nervous exaltation that I ripped open the envelope and pulled out what I was sure were the foundations for a masterpiece that I merrily would get to decorate. I can't even begin to describe the sinking feeling that overtook me as I gazed at the layouts and realized that I was not only working with a sick but, indeed, a dying man."[39] The Xeroxes of Kurtzman's work on the eleven-page story were incomplete, and weighed down by his apparent desire to include as many of Bradbury's words as possible. The layouts for the action itself (in a very talky story) consisted of what Wagner called "blurry depictions." The last three pages had no drawing at all, just the six-panel grid and scribbled lettering. Obviously, Kurtzman tried, but now both his mind and body were failing him. As Preiss recalled, "There was Harvey, very ill, apologizing for not working enough."[40] Per Wagner,

One can quite literally feel him slipping away as the story progresses [but] I found myself able to see past the surface infirmities and gaze into the heart of the genius at work here. Suddenly, something clicked and I realized why Harvey had been so insistent about the choice of [that story] to adapt. It's a story about a pissed-off dead guy! This was Harvey saying to the world, "I'm not ready to die yet, and I think the whole situation really sucks."

I was . . . determined that I was gonna do Harvey proud. So . . . I rolled up my sleeves and went to work. Like some artistic Frankenstein, I set about rearranging a mass of incomplete pieces into a living, breathing creation. I excitedly set about painting [and] was quite happy with the

Euro-Harvey-Disney that I was achieving and even more so with my decision to have the murder victim bear a likeness to Harvey himself.

Kurtzman's name appeared first in the credits, though the finished story (which Kurtzman had retitled "It Burns Me Up!") was mostly Wagner's
work. He did an extraordinarily fine job, honoring Kurtzman's contribution
while making use of his own strong, well-honed visual style and painting
ability. Unfortunately, when it was published in April 1993, *Ray Bradbury
Comics* #2 was packaged in a sealed poly-bag with trading cards, which
meant many of the copies would never be opened and read, since they were
purchased for their supposed "investment value." This was one of the un-
fortunate marketing ploys endemic in comics in the 1990s. It upset Wagner,
who naturally wanted people to see what he had done.

AS 1993 ARRIVED, Adele encouraged Harvey to keep trying, to keep fighting, but began calling some of his friends and colleagues to let them know
that they should visit if they wanted to see him again. Phil Felix remembered, "I went to see him a few times. It was rough. Once when I went to
see him, he said, 'You should've been here last week. Jerry Garcia sent
a limousine and backstage passes to a Grateful Dead show at Madison
Square Garden.' I was like, *'Argh!* You're lucky you're sick because if you
weren't I would kill you!' We both laughed."[41]

"A while later, Adele called and said, 'you'd better come see him because he'd like to see you one more time,'" Felix said. His last visit was
several weeks into the New Year. "That time he was really bad. He could
barely respond. He had all these bound volumes of *Playboy*, and he told
me he wanted me to have them. I wouldn't take them, because they were
worth money and I told him he should keep them for his family."[42]

Sarah Downs visited sometime in early February. "He had lost so much
weight," she said. "His fingers looked longer because he didn't really have
any body fat left. He knew who I was. We talked and . . . I remember coming
down the stairs, and crying because Harvey was going to die soon."[43]

Underweight and weak but still walking, Kurtzman was able to spend
his last days in his home, which held so many memories: the living room,
with its wall of photographs of Will Eisner, Gloria Steinem, Harry Chester
and others, along with pieces of his favorite artwork (including Severin's
"A 'Normal' Day at the Chas-Wm-Harvey Studio!!!" cartoon); the dining
room, where he reconciled with Bill Gaines over wine and Chateaubriand;
the porch where he acted out *Annie Fanny* stories for Will Elder. Although
bereft of many of its treasures, his attic studio still displayed artifacts

on its walls, reminders of thousands of days spent at his drawing board. The house itself was a monument to his determination to rise up from the working class and have a place where he could entertain his extraordinarily large number of friends, family, colleagues, students, collaborators, neighbors and fans.

The end drew near. Liz recalled, "Joel [Siegel] and Terry [Gilliam] came to see my father right before he died, and we drove back to the city together. Two incredibly kind people, so passionate about their work."

One of the last things Kurtzman found in his mail was a package from Byron Preiss. It contained a copy of the artwork for "It Burns Me Up!" for *Ray Bradbury Comics*. Later, Adele told Matt Wagner that "Harvey had seen the story, shortly before the end," and "he had gotten quite a lingering smile from the final product."[44] Given that Kurtzman had chosen to be cremated, one might find the words of the dead narrator at the story's end quite eerie:

> And a week from now a man who is worrying about his income tax will turn a handle and flames will burn me. I will rush up the flue of the crematory in so many gray flecks.

Adele's account of his "lingering smile" bespoke her husband's appreciation both Wagner's work and Bradbury's ending. A faltering collaboration with one of the great writers of his time, and a prominent, young comics creator, was the last known creative act of Harvey Kurtzman.

Denis Kitchen was one of the last people outside the family to see him. By that time, the doctor had taken Kurtzman off the L-DOPA, which had slowed his speech and clouded his mind. Kitchen was amazed at the difference. "The last conversation I had with him, he spoke in a normal voice. He had complete clarity. It was like talking to the old Harvey. He couldn't control the palsy any more, but when he was dying, it didn't matter that he had herky-jerky movements, I guess. He was too weak and it didn't matter."[45] That day, they touched on a number of things. Kurtzman encouraged Kitchen to go ahead with various projects they had planned.

> He was mostly talking about taking care of Adele and selling the art and making sure she would be all right. I kept assuring him there was plenty of stuff to sell and I would do my best. It was that kind of a conversation. He was just making sure people were taken care of because really at the end, all he had was a house and his art. He didn't have any stock, he didn't have any annuities, he didn't have, really, ownership in anything,

and I think it was sad that he didn't end up with more in that sense. At the same time, I remember telling him that he had a legacy that would live on and I don't think he quite believed it. He wanted to, because on the one hand, he was definitely proud of the work he did, but with him there was always the doubt.

Kitchen had already organized Kurtzman art and ephemera for Sotheby's Comic Book and Comic Art auction several months earlier. Among the auctioned items was the original art of a *Little Annie Fanny* story that Hefner finally gave him, and a printer's proof of the rejected first cover of *Humbug* #1.

In his last visit with Denis Kitchen, Kurtzman reminisced about the earliest days of his career.

> Harvey told me about when he was working for Louis Ferstadt back in the '40s. He told me in great detail—I can only paraphrase because I didn't have a tape recorder—how he could smell the turpentine when he walked in to get that job. Ferstadt had been a painter and only turned to comic books because he couldn't make a living with his oil painting. So he very reluctantly set up these drawing boards and hired these artists to do what he probably considered schlock material until he could get on his feet and do murals again. Harvey described this room that was quite large with high ceilings, and there were canvasses around the edge of it, and the smell of turpentine. I think he was just reminiscing in a way because he could see his life was ebbing.

Kurtzman had endured a lot with little complaint, but now he wanted it to be over. Adele said, "He would ask people, 'how can I end this?' And I would say, 'I'll tell you when it's time.'"[46]

When creating a story, he always planned the ending early so that he knew where he was heading. Now he did his best to write the ending of his own life, by hastening its coming. He stopped eating. All Adele could do was make sure the children were there as it became obvious that their father's last moments approached. Liz quietly told him, "It's okay if you have to go. You've done enough."

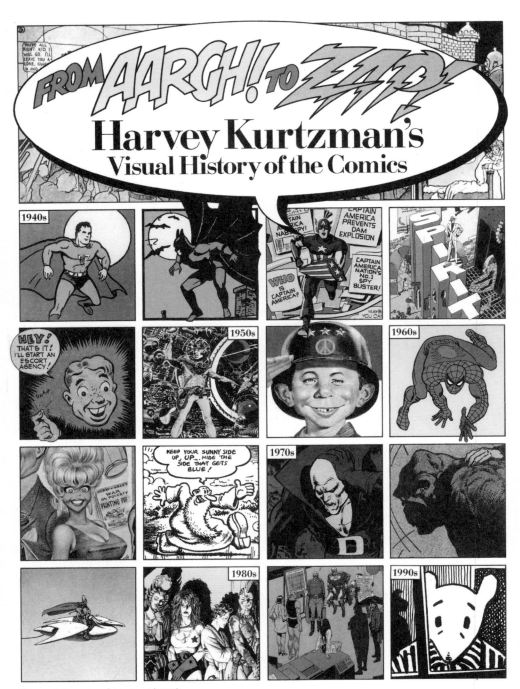

Cover of *From Aargh! to Zap!* (1990).

The cover to *The New Two-Fisted Tales* #1 (1993) is the only piece of comic art signed by both Will Eisner and Harvey Kurtzman.

28.

IN MEMORIAM

ON SUNDAY, FEBRUARY 21, 1993, at 8:00 p.m., Harvey Kurtzman died. News of his passing became public knowledge the next day when the *New York Times* ran his obituary.

Even in death, it seemed Kurtzman would be denied the credit for his greatest achievement. The obituary in the *Times* stated that Kurtzman had merely "helped found *Mad* magazine." As Art Spiegelman later recounted in the pages of the *New Yorker*, "I called to tell them it was like saying Michelangelo helped paint the Sistine Chapel just because some pope owned the ceiling." Spiegelman had sufficient heft that the paper substituted a corrected obit the following day. It read, in part,

> Harvey Kurtzman Is Dead at 68;
> Cartoonist Was Creator of *Mad*
>
> Harvey Kurtzman, a cartoonist and pop-culture historian who founded and created *Mad* magazine and was a guiding force in several other satirical magazines, died on Sunday at his home in Mount Vernon, N.Y. He was 68.
>
> Byron Preiss, his publisher at Visual Publications Inc., in New York, said the cause was complications of liver cancer. Mr. Preiss described Mr. Kurtzman as "one of the greatest cartoonists of the twentieth century." Art Spiegelman, a friend who created the Pulitzer Prize-winning *Maus* books, said Mr. Kurtzman had developed a new kind of humor that changed the way America saw itself. "Kurtzman's *Mad* held a mirror up

to American society, exposing the hypocrisies and distortions of mass media with jazzy grace and elegance," he said. "He's our first post-modern humorist."

Since Kurtzman was cremated and there was no burial service, Spiegelman organized a memorial gathering, which was held on March 26. Joe Orlando, then vice president of DC Comics, provided a room in the Time-Life Building in Manhattan for the informal gathering of family, friends, students, coworkers and luminaries from all areas of popular culture, Kurtzman's latter-day community in chalk.

It began with Spiegelman describing Kurtzman as "a quiet, middle-class anarchist" who was a kind of "D. W. Griffith of comics." He presented a short slideshow, with examples of Kurtzman's work through all the major phases of his career. He got a laugh when he said, "All of Harvey's financial advisors, please leave the room." His talk made clear how much Kurtzman had given to his work, and to the world of comics and publishing.

After Spiegelman, some eighteen speakers took the podium to share their thoughts, among them Byron Preiss, Jules Feiffer, Zachary Kurtzman, Terry Gilliam, Gloria Steinem, Al Jaffee and Will Elder. Liz read selections from several of the cards that had arrived from friends who couldn't make it to the memorial. *The Okeh Laughing Record* was played, and while some laughed, others felt it had a special kind of poignancy.

IN ONE OF THE RARE OCCASIONS when Kurtzman assessed his art, he said (in reference to his EC war comics, but it applied to all his best work):

> I'm very proud of the stuff I did, and I'm happy I did it, and I wouldn't have done it any other way. I feel that where I didn't sell anybody short, was in the stories where I was trying to get a little bit of truth to them. The reader was getting a little experience that's for real, and he's learning a little bit about real life. To me, the biggest reason for living is to be able to contribute. And that was my contribution.[1]

Later, when asked to sum up her life with Harvey, Adele responded, "It was a very exciting life. We met incredible people that came through the doors. It would never have happened otherwise. He was very quiet, but people loved his advice. He was an incredible father. I couldn't have asked for a better husband or a better father. He was here all the time. You have to think of the life as opposed to the death."[2]

There is no grave for Harvey Kurtzman. In the spring, his ashes were spread without ceremony in the backyard of the Mount Vernon home, amid the blooming rhododendrons and forsythia. Adele remained in the house, and continued to celebrate the Fourth of July there with the usual assortment of family, friends, students and colleagues. She lives there still.

Harvey Kurtzman in 1973: courtesy of Jay Lynch.

ACKNOWLEDGMENTS

HARVEY KURTZMAN'S WORK has been widely discussed and dissected in print, beginning in the 1950s, and with increasing frequency in subsequent years as his importance to American popular culture became clearer. He was always amenable to giving interviews, often by people knowledgeable about his work. *The Comics Journal Library* Volume 7, collects several of the most extensive, cogent Kurtzman interviews. It includes John Benson's seminal interview, "A Talk with Harvey Kurtzman," and J. P. C. James's "Hey Look! An Interview with Harvey Kurtzman" from *Rogue* magazine, both conducted in 1965. It also has the extensive interview titled "The Man Who Brought Truth to Comics," conducted by Gary Groth, Kim Thompson and Mike Catron. Those interviews provide his point of view, and have been sourced by many who have written about EC comics and/or Kurtzman's own oeuvre, including this writer.

I have also relied on important Kurtzman interviews conducted by Paul Buhle (*Shmate* #6), T. Durwood (*Crimmer's* #3), Judd Hurd (*Cartoonist PROfiles* #26), S. C. Ringgenberg (*Comics Scene* #47) and Jeffrey K. Wasserman (*Inside Comics* #2). John Benson's interviews with Harvey-plus-colleague(s) that appeared in *Squa Tront* magazine were also invaluable: Harvey with Bill Gaines (#9), Harvey with Will Elder (also in #9), Harvey with Arnold Roth and Al Jaffee (#10), and Harvey with Harry Chester (#12). Although I interviewed Roth and Jaffee, I also frequently referenced Benson's superb interview with them in the deluxe *Humbug* reprint book(s). Some of Adele Kurtzman's words in the manuscript came from interviews conducted by Grant Geissman (*Tales of Terror!*), and Blake Bell (*I Have to Live with This Guy*). Geissman's interview with Larry Siegel in *Squa Tront* #12 was also helpful.

The Kurtzman and Kurtzman-related interviews amount to an embarrassment of riches. Harvey Kurtzman was deposed on most of the important aspects of his life and career. Any biographer stands on the shoulders of the writers and researchers who came before. Even so, a good biography must do more than simply regurgitate and rearrange material that has already been published elsewhere (though ignoring it would be foolhardy). I wanted to offer a healthy quotient of fresh, unfamiliar material, and in so doing, hoped to find answers to questions that lingered about Kurtzman's life and career. While dead writers' and artists' interviews continue to speak for them, further utterances would seem unavailable. Fortunately, that did not prove to be the case. I received a number of unpublished interviews, not only with Harvey Kurtzman himself but with his colleagues and friends. The greatest "find" was a transcript of a fascinating, lengthy after-dinner conversation between Kurtzman and Gil Kane, which revealed a great deal about their early days in the comics industry, including a brief period when they worked shoulder-to-shoulder in the Louis Ferstadt comics shop before World War II. I thank Gary Groth and John Benson for making this available, as well as allowing me to use a bit of Benson's unpublished Gene Colan interview.

In addition, I was given translations of Kurtzman's panel discussions at European comic conventions, thanks to the late Jacques Dutrey, who worked prodigiously to help with this biography before his untimely passing in 2013. Michael Barrier generously shared the notes from his interview with Kurtzman for *From Aargh! to Zap*. Special thanks to Howard Zimmerman, Kurtzman's collaborator on the autobiographical book *My Life as a Cartoonist*, who provided the unedited transcripts of his interviews with Kurtzman for that book, with Harvey's corrections, interlineations and comments. The additional bits of information about his birth family and early life that were gleaned from this material are like gold nuggets, especially since Kurtzman spoke so seldom about his youth.

John Benson's name has cropped up several times in these acknowledgments already. He is perhaps the world's preeminent Kurtzman scholar, especially with regard to *Mad*, *Trump* and *Humbug*, as well as the EC war comics. He was both a fan and friend of Kurtzman, beginning with correspondence and visits in the late 1950s. Therefore, it's appropriate that Benson is a character in the book, especially when he brought Kurtzman and Gaines together for a dual interview, an event of great personal importance to both men. John has also been my friend for many years. When I first considered writing a Kurtzman biography, I immediately called and asked if he intended to write such a book himself. If he did, I would bow out. When he said "no," I asked for his support—which I knew would be no small thing—and he came through, magnificently. Benson not only provided a tidal wave of information, images and insights, but he reviewed two drafts of the manuscript, appending his comments and suggestions. In addition, he visited Denis Kitchen, curator of Kurtzman's archival papers, and provided hundreds of digital photographs of those documents. Kurtzman saved carbon copies of many of his outgoing letters and memoranda starting in 1956, providing more "new words" from him. Also in those archives were royalty statements, letters from Hugh Hefner, Bill Gaines, Harold Hayes, Harris Shevelson and other colleagues, and a great deal of other fascinating ephemera. In sum, the debt this book owes to John Benson is incalculable. It isn't the book he would have written, because John and I have our fair share of disagreements on matters of opinion and interpretation, but it would have been the poorer without his help.

The quest for fresh material led to new interviews with dozens of people. Most important, of course, was my series of interviews with Adele Kurtzman, who was friendly and tremendously forthcoming (that rapier wit fully intact), as were her daughters Meredith, Liz and Nellie. While I didn't intend to spend a great deal of time on family matters, they painted a vivid picture of life with their father. Often one hears that highly creative individuals were distant or event neglectful parents. It was a pleasure to learn that this was not true in Kurtzman's case. I also interviewed Harvey's nephew (Zachary Kurtzman's son) Adam Kurtzman, who lived with his grandmother Edith Perkes when he was a teenager, and was able to relate some important facts about her early years in America that helped fill in some of the blanks. I also had access to Zachary Kurtzman's comments about Harvey, taped in 1993.

Interviewing as many of Kurtzman's publishers as possible was high on my priority list. I had a lively, fascinating talk with Hugh Hefner, and an equally interesting conversation with Jim Warren. I spoke with Tom Hayes, son of editor Harold Hayes, Kurtzman's champion at *Esquire*, as well as Walter Bernard and Byron Dobell, also of that estimable magazine. Thanks to John Ficarra for describing Kurtzman's return to *Mad* in 1984. I'm also indebted to Denis Kitchen, publisher of Kurtzman's work in reprints of *Hey Look!*, *Harvey Kurtzman's Jungle Book* and others. Kitchen is the literary agent of the Harvey Kurtzman Estate. He was also Harvey's friend, knew him better than most, and generously shared his insights into Kurtzman's personality and career in a substantial interview. He also helped with photos and artwork, providing scans of the photograph of Adele in 1948 and the "Lost Battalion!" rough layouts, which originally appeared in his book with Paul Buhle, *The Art of Harvey Kurtzman.* In addition, certain details about Kurtzman's postwar studios were derived from that book.

Unfortunately, Bill Gaines is no longer with us. I consider myself lucky to have met him at the 1973 Comic Art Convention in New York City. I also bought a copy of Frank Jacobs's invaluable book *The Mad World of William M. Gaines* on that occasion (and had Gaines sign it). Jacobs's account of the

Gaines-Kurtzman relationship provided important information available nowhere else. Another key source was the lengthy Bill Gaines interview in *The Comics Journal* (#81). Interviewers Gary Groth and Dwight Decker asked all the right questions, and because they are Kurtzman fans, especially concentrated their questions on Gaines's dealings and friendship with Harvey. For fresh accounts of the EC New Trend of 1950–1955, I got in touch with Al Feldstein, who had been helpful to me on my Otto Binder biography. With little prompting, Al talked about EC, Gaines and Harvey Kurtzman at length. I am also grateful to Jack Davis for adding to my understanding about working with Harvey on the war comics and *Mad*.

Humbug magazine was owned equally by five men. I was able to speak with three of them: Jack Davis, Al Jaffee and Arnold Roth. They all shared their memories and insights into Harvey Kurtzman as a person, artist and editor. They are his friends. Having them (and also Arnold's wife Caroline) contribute to this project has been a joy. One of the benefits of doing this kind of book is getting to talk to my personal idols, such as these three gentlemen. They made the *Trump* and *Humbug* days come alive as no others could.

Help! magazine may not have been Kurtzman's greatest magazine, but its story is colorful and interesting. To my interview with Jim Warren, and my talk with *Help!* photographer Ron Harris, I was able to add interviews with a number of cartoonists whose early work was published by Kurtzman in *Help!*, and went on to become important artists in underground comix and beyond: Robert Crumb, Jay Lynch, Gilbert Shelton and Skip Williamson. I was also able to include previously unpublished comments by Gloria Steinem about her time with Harvey. I am particularly grateful to Terry Gilliam for his introduction to this book, and his memories of working with Kurtzman. Kim Deitch provided the description of the *East Village Other* jam session. Gilbert Shelton added to Mark James Estren's account of the "Fuck-In" on Goddard campus in 1970, as did Isabella (Ladybelle) Fiske McFarlin. I also thank Art Spiegelman, a valued friend of Kurtzman, whose words about Harvey appear in various places in the book.

Having access to in-depth interviews in *The Comics Journal*—especially with Will Elder and John Severin, but also David Levine, Arnold Roth and Jules Feiffer—was a great boon. Bill Spicer's interviews with Alex Toth in *Graphic Story Magazine* and Lyle Stuart in *Squa Tront* provided a great deal of the perspective of those two colleagues. I was also fortunate to be able to interview the following people, for which I offer my sincere thanks: Jesse Drew (for providing a tape recording of his mother,

Jo Ann Bergtold Drew, reminiscing about her romance with Harvey in the 1940s), Barbara Nessim (on working with Harvey for *Esquire*), William T. Barnes (on the history of the Clearview School), Mark Lewisohn (on the possible Kurtzman-Beatles connection), and Alison Porter (on her friendship with Kurtzman in his last years). I'm grateful to Todd Hignite (for permission to use images from the Heritage Auctions webpage) and James Vadeboncoeur Jr. (for providing scans of rare Kurtzman art). Also thanks to Bill Basso, Mitch Berger, Michael Gross, Robert Grossman, Paul McSpadden, Harry Matetsky, Jack Mendelsohn, Eric Palma and Kevin Sacco. For their memories of assisting Kurtzman on *Little Annie Fanny*, special thanks to Russ Heath, Bill Stout, Sarah Downs and Phil Felix. Also, I was fortunate to have been able to interview Irene Chester, widow of Harry, Kurtzman's closest friend, who filled in much information about their relationship.

For fleshing out the chapter on Kurtzman's class at The School of Visual Arts, I thank Drew Friedman, Sam Henderson, John Holmstrom, Batton Lash, Mark Newgarden, Dr. Nando Pelusi, David Pomerantz and "Kaz" Prapuolenis for their accounts and evaluations of the class at various times during its eighteen years. Sarah Downs and Phil Felix also helped illuminate the discussion of the "Satirical Cartooning" class, as did SVA administrator Marshall Arisman. Thanks also to Michael Grant of SVA.

For early family photographs, I am indebted to Adam Kurtzman. Having David Douglas Duncan's image of the crying soldier in Korea accompany the discussion of "Big 'If'!," was a great privilege, and I'll never forget my conversation with the eminent, ninety-eight-year-old photographer. I was fortunate to be able to use a number of E. B. Boatner's fine photographs of Kurtzman in the mid- to late 1970s. I also thank Ben Asen for contributing his superb photos of Kurtzman in 1987, David Bentley for his permission to use the photos of Ray Komorksi and Paul Burke for further help with photographs.

For other valuable assistance, I thank Jim Amash, Bob Andelman, Ger Apeldoorn, Mark Arnold, Alberto Becattini, Al Bradford, Glenn Bray, Gary Brown, Aaron Caplan, Mike Carlin, Sig Case, Dewey Cassell, Shaun Clancy, Russ Cochran, Jon B. Cooke, Tom Conroy, Bob Cosgrove, Jean Davenport, Gary Delain, Mark Evanier, Ron Franz, John Garcia, Michael T. Gilbert, Rick Goldschmidt, Tom Hegeman, Wendy Hewetson, Roger Hill, Allan Holtz, Alan Hutchinson, Anne Hutchinson, Bob Ingersoll, Diane Karaca, Bill Kieffer, Jim Korkis, Paul Krasner, Larry Lankford, Mell Lazarus, Nick Meglin, Cathy Gaines Mifsud, John Morrow, Michelle

Nolan, Bob Overstreet, Bill Pearson, Bud Plant, Ken Quattro, Arthur Rankin Jr., Trina Robbins, Patrick Rosenkranz, Greg Sadowski, the Seattle Public Library, Marie Severin, Scott Shaw, Steve Starger, Roy Thomas, Maggie Thompson, Anthony Tollin, James Vance, Dr. Michael J. Vassallo, Matt Wagner, Don Watson, John Wells and Bill Wormstedt. For transcribing the many hours of recorded interviews, thanks go to the indefatigable Brian K. Morris and the unflappable Carl Gafford.

Posthumous thanks to Harry Chester, L. B. Cole, Jerry De Fuccio, Will Eisner, Will Elder, William M. Gaines, Harold Hayes, Al Hewetson, Larry Ivie, Gil Kane, Joe Pilati, John Severin, Harris Shevelson, A. C. Spectorsky, Bhob Stewart, Lyle Stuart, Al Williamson and Wallace Wood.

You would not be holding this book in your hands without the efforts of the folks at Fantagraphics Books. In particular, I extend profound thanks to Gary Groth for committing to this project when it was just an idea, and providing his guidance and editorial support all along the way. Groth is an unsung hero for his efforts to not only keep many of the great talents of comics and graphic arts in print, but for conducting in-depth interviews with a great number of them over the years. His late partner Kim Thompson, deserves equal accolades for his efforts as a comics historian, and for his bringing European comics (and those from other regions around the world) to American readers, a cause dear to Harvey Kurtzman's heart. I'm also grateful to Mike Catron, Jacq Cohen, Keeli McCarthy, Eric Reynolds, Kristy Valenti, and Preston White, as well as the rest of the smart, hard-working people at Fantagraphics who produce many of the finest books in their field. Thanks for making me feel a part of your mission.

For their unstinting support and encouragement, I'm grateful to Nancy Balin, Tina Bradley, Jules Jones, Maureen Jones, Jeffrey Kipper, Judd Lawson, Terry Martell, Dale Nash, Nils Osmar, Steve Peters, Steve Schelly, Andrea Schock, Terry Schock, Stephanie Seymour, Tara Seymour, John Teegarden and Rita Wentlandt. No writer works in a vacuum, nor is a book "out of mind" when he or she isn't at the keyboard working. I appreciate your patience and forbearance over the past four years. Also, I want to express my thanks to the person who acted as a sounding board and kept me on course during the sometimes-difficult process of making this book a reality. His name is Jeff Gelb. I couldn't have done it without his sage advice and unflagging support.

Comments, corrections for Bill Schelly can be sent to: hamstrpres@aol.com.

HARVEY KURTZMAN CHRONOLOGY

Note: Periodical publications (comic books, magazines) are noted when they appeared on newsstands, not by the cover date, which can be anywhere from one to three months after they go on sale.

1924

October 3: Harvey Kurtzman is born in a Manhattan hospital.

1928

November 29: David Kurtzman, Harvey's father, dies.

1929

Harvey's mother Edith marries Abraham Perkes.

1935

Approx. date the Perkes family moves from Brooklyn to the Bronx.

1937

September: Twelve-year-old Kurtzman enters the High School of Music and Art as a freshman. (He turns thirteen weeks later.) He admires future colleagues Al Jaffee and Will Elder from afar, and meets Harry Chester, who becomes his best friend. Also meets Charles Stern.

1938

April: *Action Comics* #1 introducing Superman is published, giving the new comic book medium a shot in the arm. Soon many more publishers enter the field, and super heroes abound.

1939

February: Approx. date Harvey's first published cartoon appears in *Tip Top Comics* Vol. 3 #12, the April 1939 issue.
Kurtzman befriends John Severin at M&A.

1940

June 2: Will Eisner's *The Spirit* newspaper insert makes its debut and becomes a favorite of Kurtzman's.

1941

June: Kurtzman graduates from high school. Begins a series of noncreative jobs.
September: Approx. date he starts night classes at Cooper Union, which he does for one school year.

1942

June 11: Abraham Perkes, convicted of federal crimes, is sentenced to ten years in Allenwood Federal Prison in Montgomery, Pennsylvania.
June: Kurtzman begins assisting Louis Ferstadt on comic book work for Gilberton and Ace Publications.

Visits Alfred Andriola, artist of *Charlie Chan* comic strip (and later *Kerry Drake*), and is told he should give up cartooning.

September–October: Approx. date Kurtzman's first comic book story ("Murphy's Mess Boy") in *Four Favorites* #8 (cover dated December 1942). Signed "Kurtzman with Looey."

November: Approx. date Ace's *Super-Mystery Comics* Vol. 3 #3 (cover date 1943) is published. His first comic book cover, signed H. Kurtzman. Inside, he draws Mr. Risk.

Works briefly alongside Gil Kane (b. Eli Katz) and L. B. Cole.

1943

Continues in Ferstadt shop, drawing stories featuring Mr. Risk, Buckskin, Lightning, Magno and Davey, and others. He draws (and probably writes) *Flatfoot Burns*, his first ongoing humor feature, in *Police Comics*. Draws *Bill the Magnificent* in *Hit Comics*, among his last work before entering the military.

June 23: Enters US Army, basic training at Fort Dix, New Jersey. He spends twenty-eight months in uniform, serving in the Morale Services Branch of the Information-Education Division at Camp Sutton, North Carolina, and other military bases. Contributes artwork and comic strip (*Private Brown Knows*) for *Carry All*, the base newspaper.

1944

May: Approx. date his last prewar work was published, the cover of *Four Favorites* #15.

June: Transfers from Camp Sutton to base in Louisiana.

Christmas: On furlough in New York, Kurtzman draws *Black Venus* for *Contact Comics* #6 (May 1945). L. B. Cole is the editor.

1945

January: Transferred with the Twenty-Fifth Infantry Regiment at Camp Maxey, Texas. Works in Special Services on various art projects, including the *Maxey Times*, the base newspaper.

August (after V-J Day): Transferred to Fort Bragg, South Carolina.

November: Discharged from military service. Draws another *Black Venus* story for *Contact Comics* #11 (dated March 1946), his first postwar work.

November 23: Cartoon is published in *Yank* Vol. 4 #23.

1946

February–March: Begins work for Stan Lee at Timely Comics: the first *Hey Look!* ran in *Joker* #23 (dated June 1946) and *Pigtales* made its debut in *Kid Movie Komics* #11 (summer 1946). Timely staffers Al Jaffee and Adele Hasan become fans of *Hey Look!*

Mid-1946: Adele is introduced to Harvey, when she is on a date with Will Elder. Harvey begins dating Adele, and becomes friends with Will Elder.

September: Approx. date Adele leaves for State Teachers College in Cortland, New York.

1947

Kurtzman continues doing *Hey Look!* throughout the year, a little over one per week.

January: Charles William Harvey Studio is formed.

Spring: Harvey meets Jo Ann Bergtold, a young model and aspiring actress. Visits Will Eisner's studio and meets Eisner for the first time.

August 20: Maxwell Gaines, of EC comics, is killed in a boating accident on Lake Placid. Responsibility for the publishing company falls to his son, William M. Gaines.

November: Charles William Harvey Studio moves to its "permanent" location at 1151 Broadway, in the Chelsea-Flatiron neighborhood.

December: Kurtzman's letters to Jo Ann—when she temporarily returns to Wisconsin—represent the end of their romantic relationship.

1948

Adele returns to New York City early in the year and resumes dating Harvey.
February: Approx. date *Margie* #40 (April 1948) is published, introducing the new *Hey Look!* logo.
March 7: First of nine *Silver Lining* newspaper strips appears in the *New York Herald Tribune*. (Last one appears in June.)
Spring: John Severin joins the Charles William Harvey Studio, begins a seven-year association with Kurtzman.
September 7: Harvey and Adele are wed in Connecticut, and honeymoon at Cape Cod.
Fall: Kurtzman does his last *Hey Look!* Wallace Wood drops by the studio, and is referred to the Will Eisner studio. Kurtzman meets French writer-artist René Goscinny.
October 25: Stepfather Abraham Perkes is paroled.
November: Approx. date when Kurtzman meets Elliott Caplin, who is setting up Toby Press for his brother, Al Capp. Caplin helps him get work at the Parents Magazine Institute in *Varsity* magazine.

1949

January: Approx. date Kurtzman begins *Rusty* for Timely, a *Blondie* imitation.
Spring: Designs jigsaw puzzle children's books for Kunen Publishing.
Summer: Martin Goodman doesn't like Kurtzman's work on *Rusty*, so feature is dropped. Kurtzman meets Dr. Harvey Zorbaugh at New York University to discuss educational comics. Zorbaugh refers him to EC Comics.
Fall: Kurtzman inks two Severin stories in *Prize Comics Western* and completes "Lucky Fights it Through" for David Gaines. Bill Gaines and Al Feldstein are impressed with Kurtzman's "serious" comic art on the story, and give him the script for "House of Horror" for their upcoming New Trend horror comics.
Kurtzman creates *Pot-Shot Pete*, and sells two pages to National/DC comics. Not long after, he creates longer Pete stories for Toby Press, and toys with the idea of submitting it to the newspaper syndicates. He also creates *Genius* for Toby Press.
Teams up with Goscinny on four more children's books for Kunen Publishing, for which he is never paid.

1950

Begins working mainly for EC as a freelance artist.
February: Approx. date (early-to-mid month) *Vault of Horror* #12, the first New Trend comic book, appears; it includes the Kurtzman-drawn story "Horror in the Night."
April: "Madness at Manderville" and "Island of Death" appear—the second and third strips drawn by Kurtzman for the EC horror books to be published. "Island of Death" in *Vault of Horror* #13 was his first as both a writer and artist.
May: "House of Horror," the EC story Kurtzman drew first, is published in *Haunt of Fear* #15 (cover dated May–June 1950).
Kurtzman conceives *Two-Fisted Tales* and work begins. He is not yet editor.
June 25, 1950: Korean War begins. Decision is made to convert *Two-Fisted Tales* into an all-war title.
July 28: Meredith Kurtzman, daughter of Harvey and Adele, is born.
July: Ben Oda is hired to letter Kurtzman's EC stories, eliminating the Leroy lettering. The film *All Quiet on the Western Front* is rereleased.
September: Approx. date *Two-Fisted Tales* #18 appears (first issue), with Kurtzman's first EC cover.
November: Approx. date *Two-Fisted Tales* #19 appears, with "War Story!," cowritten by Kurtzman and Severin. Brings Severin-Elder team to EC.

1951

January: Approx. date of *Two-Fisted Tales* #20, the first EC book to list Kurtzman as editor. Includes first story drawn by Jack Davis for Kurtzman. Marie Severin is hired as a colorist and to help with research.

March: Approx. date *Weird Science* #7 (May–June 1951) appears, with " . . . Gregory Had a Model-T!," Kurtzman's last SF story for EC.

May: Announcement of new EC title *Frontline Combat*, conceived and edited by Kurtzman. First issue contains classic story "Enemy Assault!," which acknowledges the humanity of an enemy soldier. Kurtzman stories rated "objectionable" in *Parents* magazine.

July: Approx. date the Kurtzmans buy their house at 11 Audrey Avenue in Mount Vernon, New York.

September: Gaines gives key players movie cameras.

December: Begins ghostwriting the *Flash Gordon* daily strip for Dan Barry.

1952

January: Approx. date *Frontline Combat* #5 is released, with "Big 'If'!," the last new interior story at EC with Kurtzman's finished artwork.

April 7: Kurtzman-scripted *Flash Gordon* daily newspaper strips begin appearing. He scripts the dailies for a little over a year.

April: Gaines and Kurtzman have a discussion that leads to *Mad*.

April 20: FBI director J. Edgar Hoover authorizes an investigation of the war comics edited by Kurtzman for EC.

June–July: Kurtzman begins work on his all-Civil War issues of *Two-Fisted Tales* and *Frontline Combat*; meets with historian Fletcher Pratt, who helps with research.

August: Approx. date (late July, early August) *Mad* #1 is published.

1953

February: *Mad* #4, with lead feature "Superduperman!," appears on newsstands.

February–March: Kurtzman is ill from hepatitis.

April: *Mad* #5 with spurious Gaines biography creates a furor at BIPAD wholesaler convention, necessitating a quick apology from EC.

July 27: Korean War armistice. Sales of EC war books begin slipping.

October 31: Kurtzmans hold their "great Halloween party" with many EC staffers present. The mood is festive because sales reports show *Mad* sales passing 750,000 copies per issue.

November–December: First issue of *Playboy* (published by Hugh Hefner) appears on newsstands and quickly sells out.

December–January 1954: Approx. date decision is made to up *Mad*'s publishing frequency to monthly.

1954

January: Approx. date *Mad* #10 appears, first appearance of Basil Wolverton's work in the comic book. Polish word "potrzebie" is used for first time in the letter column.

March: Wolverton cover appears on *Mad* #11, a satire of the cover of *Life*.

April 19: Dr. Fredric Wertham's *Seduction of the Innocent* is published.

April 21: William M. Gaines appears before the Senate Subcommittee to Investigate Juvenile Delinquency.

Spring: Kurtzman draws cover of *Three Dimensional EC Classics* #1 and re-does "V-Vampires!" (with Wallace Wood) and "Frank Luke!" (with George Evans) to take advantage of the 3-D process.

May: "Starchie!" appears in *Mad* #12, Kurtzman's first Archie satire.

May–June: "Now Comics Have Gone Mad" in June *Pageant* sets events in motion that lead to *Mad* becoming a magazine. Kurtzman meets Harold Hayes, who would be an important professional contact for him in future years.

June 29: Peter Kurtzman, the Kurtzmans' second child, is born.

August 14: John Severin informs Gaines that he will no longer work on any book edited by Kurtzman.

Fall: Kurtzman receives offer to become an assistant editor of *Pageant*. Gaines counter-offers a small raise and commits to converting *Mad* into magazine form. Kurtzman accepts Gaines offer.

October 3: Kurtzman celebrates thirtieth birthday.

October 26: The Comics Magazine Association of America adopts the Comics Code.

November: Ballantine publishes *The Mad Reader*, the first paperback reprint. Kurtzman's first use of the "What, Me Worry?" face is on the cover of the paper-back.

December: Approx. date Kurtzman launches into work on *Mad* #24, the first magazine issue.

1955

January: First appearance of the "What, Me Worry?" face in *Mad*, on the cover of #21.

March: *Mad* #23, last comic book issue, appears. Though EC has joined the CMAA and submitted its New Direction titles to the CCA at this time, the last four-color *Mad* slips by without the Seal of Approval.

May 12: First magazine issue of *Mad* is published. (Date varies across the US.)

July: "What, Me Worry?" boy is called Alfred E. Neuman for the first time in *Mad* #25.

November: Approx. date EC publishes its last comic book, *Incredible Science Fiction* #33.

December: Kurtzman pressures Gaines into terminating Lyle Stuart's employment as EC business manager.

1956

January: Gaines and Kurtzman meet with Jessie Gaines to convince her to invest more money in *Mad* to keep it going. She agrees.

February: Approx. date Leader News declares bankruptcy.

March: Approx. date Kurtzman meets with Hugh Hefner.

April: Kurtzman leaves (technically fired by Gaines) to work on a new satire magazine for Hugh Hefner.

July: Approx. date *Mad* #28 is published, Kurtzman's last issue as editor.

September: Approx. date *Mad* #29 is published, Feldstein's first issue as editor.

September 24: New satire magazine from Hefner is announced in *Time* magazine.

December: Approx. date *Trump* #1 is published (cover date January 1957).

1957

January 21: Hefner informs Kurtzman publication of *Trump* is being suspended after #2. Kurtzman's daughter Elizabeth ("Liz") is born.

January: Kurtzman and core *Trump* contributors meet to discuss the end of the maga-zine, in the days after Hefner's announcement. *Humbug*, a new satire magazine, is conceived.

February: Approx. date *Trump* #2 (the last issue) is published (cover dated March 1957).

April: Approx. date work on *Humbug* begins in earnest, after Kurtzman arranges for printing and distribution through Charlton Publications, Inc.

July: Approx. date *Humbug* #1 (dated August 1957) appears.

September 19: Letter from Jim Warren to Harry Chester at *Humbug* is Warren's first documented point of contact with Kurtzman.

October 17: Approx. date final sales report on *Humbug* #1 reveals poor sales (35 percent of print run).

November: Approx. date article "The Little World of Harvey Kurtzman" appears in *Playboy*.

December: Charlton indicates it wants to take over *Humbug* and employ Kurtzman and collaborators as freelancers. They decline. Kurtzman begins looking for outside investors.

1958

February: *Cracked* #1 is published.

April: Approx. date *Mad for Keeps* (hardback) is published; it's made up entirely of uncredited reprints of Kurtzman-written material.

May 14: Kurtzman initiates lawsuit for unpaid royalties from *Mad* paperbacks.

May: Approx. date *Humbug* is discontinued. Gaines is "delighted."

June: *Humbug* #10, first full-size issue, appears.

June: Approx. date Kurtzman is hired to "think up ideas" for Dave Garroway at NBC.

August: Approx. date *Humbug* #11 appears. Last issue. (States October on cover.)

September: Approx. date Kurtzman flies to Ireland on assignment from *Esquire*.

November 30: Kurtzman's "Beat Generation" piece for *Playboy* is rejected. He doesn't work for Hefner again until May 1962, with exception of his prose satire "The Real Lady Chatterley" in late 1959.

December: "Conquest of the Moon" appears in *Pageant*, Kurtzman's first published work (with Will Elder) after demise of *Humbug*.

1959

January: "Courage," Kurtzman's first continuity for *Madison Avenue* magazine is published.

January 20: Kurtzman signs contract for *Harvey Kurtzman's Jungle Book* with Ballantine.

February 3: Harris Shevelson, editor and Kurtzman benefactor, is killed in plane crash.

April: Approx. date "Assignment: James Cagney" in *Esquire* appears, Kurtzman's first work for the magazine.

April 11: "I Went to a Perry Como Rehearsal" appears in *TV Guide*.

September: Approx. date *Jungle Book* is published. Includes first Goodman Beaver story, "The Organization Man."

November: Approx. date "Marlon Brando Sketched," *Esquire*.

1960

January: Approx. date Jim Warren proposes *Favorite Westerns of Filmland*.

April: Approx. date Warren and Kurtzman agree to terms for *Help!*

May: "The Grasshopper and the Ant," *Esquire*.

May: *Favorite Westerns of Filmland* #1, Kurtzman's first magazine for Warren, is published. Kurtzman uses pseudonym Remuda Charlie Stringer.

July: *Help* #1 is published. *Sick* #1 appears at almost the same time.

September: "On the Coney," first fumetti in *Help!* (#3).

1961

March 1: *Help!* moves to bigger offices at 501 Madison Ave..

May: *Help!* #11 is last monthly issue. Chuck Alverson is hired as new assistant editor.

August: *Help!* #12 introduces "new" Goodman Beaver.

December: *Help!* Christmas Party at the Algonquin.

1962

January: Approx. date paperback reprint *Harvey Kurtzman's Fast-Acting Help!* is published.

January: *Help!* returns (#13) after a five-month hiatus, now on a quarterly schedule. Includes reprint of *The Spirit*, as well as "Goodman Goes Playboy." Archie Comics threatens lawsuit.

March: Approx. date Warren settles lawsuit with Archie Comics for $1,000 and promise not to reprint the story.

March 23: Kurtzman appears on Vern Greene's FM radio show, *The Cartoonist's Art*.

May 10: Hefner and Kurtzman agree to terms for *Little Annie Fanny*, work commences immediately.

August: Approx. date Terry Gilliam is hired as new assistant editor of *Help!*.

September: *Little Annie Fanny* makes its debut in *Playboy*.

October: Gilbert Shelton's Wonder Wart-Hog makes his national magazine debut in *Help!* #16.

October: Second appearance of *Little Annie Fanny*.

November 11: On sale date for Kurtzman's *Who Said That*.

November: Third appearance of *Little Annie Fanny*.

1963

Little Annie Fanny appears in January, March, April, May, July, September, November, December issues of *Playboy*. Feature continues for twenty-six years.

Help! #17–19 are published.

1964

Help! #20–22 are published.

February: Flap over "My First Golden Book of God" in *Help!* #20.

September: *Help!* #21 ("Anniversary Issue") is an extra-thick, all-fumetti reprint issue.

October 3: Kurtzman celebrates fortieth birthday.

December: Robert Crumb published in *Help!* #22 (January 1965), with "Fritz the Cat" and "Harlem."

1965

Help! #23–26 are published.

August 20: Kurtzman sits for in-depth interview with John Benson. Publication of *A Talk with Harvey Kurtzman* is delayed until 1966.

August: *Help!* #26, last issue, is published.

October: *Blazing Combat* #1 from Warren Publishing is published, inspired by Kurtzman's EC war comics.

November: *Rogue* magazine publishes interview with Kurtzman, conducted by J. P. C. James.

1966

Hefner publishes *Playboy's Little Annie Fanny*, the first book collection of the strip, in an oversized edition.

Kurtzman begins working for *Esquire*, creating scenarios to showcase fashions and other products.

July: The Kurtzmans and Davises vacation in Europe. Kurtzman sees Goscinny for the first time in more than a decade.

July 4: The Kurtzmans throw an Independence Day party, possibly for the first time. It becomes an annual tradition.

December 17: Kurtzman family moves to a larger home in Mount Vernon, New York.

1967

March: *Mad Monster Party* is released, with screenplay cowritten by Kurtzman.

April 24: FBI adds a memorandum to Kurtzman's file re: the *Little Annie Fanny* story in the May 1967 issue of *Playboy*, which parodies Director J. Edgar Hoover.

July 4: First Independence Day party in the Kurtzmans' new home, with a larger back-yard that accommodates more guests.

1968

January: Crestview School is established. Peter Kurtzman attends.
February: Robert Crumb's *Zap Comix* #1 is published.
April 25: Kurtzman's lawsuit against EC (for unpaid royalties from *Mad* paperbacks reprinting his work) is settled. To get the check, Kurtzman is required to relinquish all rights to his EC work.
July: "Blowout," Kurtzman's first fumetti for *Playboy* (August), is published.
Fall: Approx. date Kurtzman participates in "jam" strip "Come the Revolution" for the *East Village Other*, along with Robert Crumb, Gilbert Shelton, Kim Deitch, Spain Rodriguez and others.
October: *Bijou Comics* #1 is published.

1969

April 15: Cornelia Kurtzman is born to Adele and Harvey. They nickname her Nellie.
October: Abraham Perkes (stepfather) dies.
December: "The Good, the Bad, and the Garlic," Kurtzman's second and last fumetti for *Playboy* (January 1970), is published.

1970

January: Kurtzman signs contract to work for Topps Chewing Gum, Inc. on "products in the confectionary field," i.e. trading cards.
May: *Little Annie Fanny* "Underground Press" story appears in *Playboy*, with art by Crumb and Shelton on its first page.
June 20: Kurtzman's panel at the Alternative Media Festival on the Goddard College campus in Vermont.
August: *Little Annie Fanny* "Women's Lib" story appears in *Playboy*.

1971

Spring: Kurtzman gives talk on the University of Wisconsin Milwaukee campus, titled "Why Flash Gordon Uses a Sword Instead of a Zap Gun." Denis Kitchen organizes the event.
May: "@&%$#!! or Takin' the Lid off the Id," Kurtzman's piece on how comics reflect their times for *Esquire* (June), is published.
September: *National Lampoon* (October) publishes "Citizen Gaines" as part of *Mad* parody.

1972

Kurtzman creates and codirects three short animated films for *Sesame Street*, with Phil Kimmelman & Associates.
Gains work as a cartoon consultant/editor for *Esquire*.
May 27: Kurtzman appears on EC war comics panel at the EC Fan-Addict Convention in New York City. Speaks briefly to Bill Gaines for the first time since 1956.

1973

May 9: John Benson conducts a duel interview with Bill Gaines and Harvey Kurtzman at the latter's home.
September 11: Kurtzman begins teaching "Satirical Cartooning" at The School of Visual Arts in Manhattan. First year "guest cartoonists" are Neal Adams, Gil Kane, Robert Grossman, Jack Davis, David Levine and Arnold Roth. He teaches at SVA until 1990.

1974

Hefner moves to Playboy Mansion West in Los Angeles.

January: Kurtzman is guest of honor at the first Festival International de la Bande Dessinée d'Angoulême.

September: Robert Crumb is "guest cartoonist" in Kurtzman's SVA class this year.

October 3: Kurtzman celebrates fiftieth birthday.

1975

February: Appears on Harold Hayes's WNET-TV program *Roundtable* and extolls the merits of French comics.

September: Meets Sarah Downs in his SVA class.

1976

The Illustrated Harvey Kurtzman Index by Glenn Bray is published.

1977

Sarah Downs begins assisting Kurtzman on *Little Annie Fanny*. She becomes his longest-running assistant, from 1977 to 1989.

July 31: "The 'Mad' Generation" by Tony Hiss and Jeff Lewis appears in the *New York Times* magazine to coincide with the twenty-fifth anniversary of *Mad*. Article is heavily pro-Kurtzman.

November 5: René Goscinny dies of cardiac arrest during a routine stress test, at fifty-one years old.

1978

The Complete EC Library book series begins from publisher Russ Cochran. The first volumes are *The Complete Weird Science Library* and *The Complete Tales from the Crypt Library*. They include eight stories drawn by Kurtzman. Gaines begins auctioning the EC original art, once the pages have been photographed for this series.

1979

Russ Cochran publishes *The Complete Two-Fisted Tales*.

July: Approx. date Kurtzman "reunites" with L. B. Cole in a hotel room during the New York Comic Convention.

December: Kurtzman's and Downs's *Betsy's Buddies* makes its debut in *Playboy* (January 1980). Twenty-eight episodes appear from 1980 to 1985. (Others are published in the French magazine *Pilote* beginning in 1981.)

1981

A Smithsonian Book of Comic-Book Comics is published: Kurtzman wrote four of the five stories chosen for the EC section.

"Master Class" seminars begin, with Kurtzman teaching seminars in color theory to registrants at various comic book conventions. Other teachers are Burne Hogarth and Gil Kane.

1982

Fall: Kurtzman is diagnosed with Parkinson's disease.

Russ Cochran publishes *The Complete Frontline Combat*: all of the EC war comics edited by Kurtzman are back in print.

1984

January 3: The first draft of a screenplay for a *Little Annie Fanny* television movie is completed, a collaboration between Larry Siegel and Harvey Kurtzman, and is intended for The Playboy Channel.

Kitchen Sink Press publishes *Goodman Beaver*, reprinting all the stories from *Help!* magazine except "Goodman Goes Playboy."

September 7: Gaines announces Feldstein's retirement from *Mad* in a letter to his staff. He names Nick Meglin and John Ficarra co-editors. Shortly thereafter, Kurtzman meets with Gaines seeking work for himself and Will Elder in the magazine.

October 3: Kurtzman celebrates his sixtieth birthday, at a party for him and Adele (who turns fifty-nine) given by Arnold and Caroline Roth.

1985

Early spring: Approx. date Hugh Hefner has a stroke. He recovers quickly but begins delegating editorial functions at *Playboy*.

July: *Nuts!* #1 and #2 are published, the first project produced in association with Byron Preiss.

September: Kurtzman-Elder work appears in *Mad* for the first time in thirty years, the back cover of #258, signed WEHK.

Kurtzman attends an exhibit of René Goscinny's work in France.

1986

Harvey Kurtzman's Jungle Book is reprinted by Kitchen Sink Press.

1987

The Complete Mad Library is published by Russ Cochran in both black and white and color editions.

October 23: Edith Kurtzman Perkes, Kurtzman's mother, passes away.

1988

The Harvey Awards (formerly known as the Jack Kirby Awards) begin and are held at the Chicago Comic-Con. *Betsy's Buddies* is reprinted in a hardcover book, collecting forty-four episodes.

My Life as a Cartoonist, Kurtzman's autobiography for young adult readers, is published.

August: Last *Little Annie Fanny* episode sees print in *Playboy*. Last piece for *Mad* appears the same month, the end of the Kurtzman-Elder collaboration.

1989

The Harvey Awards move to the Dallas Fantasy Fair, where they continue until the fair's last year, 1995.

March 16–19, 1989: Adele and Harvey attend the first Salon Européen de la Bande Dessinée in Grenoble, France.

April 5: Harold Hayes, formerly of *Esquire*, dies.

1990

March 31: Michael Barrier interviews Kurtzman, in preparation for ghostwriting the text of *From Aargh! to Zap!*

June: Kurtzman completes his last year of teaching at SVA.

September: Approx. date *From Aargh! To Zap!* is published.

1991

January: Approx. date Kurtzman is diagnosed with colon cancer.

March: Approx. date *Harvey Kurtzman's Strange Adventures* is published.

June 15: Liz Kurtzman marries Marc Hirschfeld in the backyard of her parents' Mount Vernon home.

July: Preiss enlists artists and writers for the *New Two-Fisted Tales* at the San Diego Comic Con.

1992

February: Approx. date Kurtzman flies to Los Angeles, films an interview for Starbur's *Comic Book Greats* video series (with Jack Davis and Stan Lee), and has dinner at the Playboy Mansion for the last time.

June 3: Bill Gaines dies in his sleep.

July: Kitchen Sink Press publishes *Hey Look!* reprint book.

July 4: Kurtzman throws his last Fourth of July party.

1993

February 21: Harvey Kurtzman dies at sixty-eight years old.

February 22: Kurtzman obituary appears in the *New York Times*. When its inaccurate statement that Kurtzman "helped found *Mad* magazine" is protested by Art Spiegelman, a corrected obituary appears the next day.

March 26: Kurtzman memorial is held in a room of the Time-Life Building in Manhattan. About 150 attend.

March 29: Adam Gopnik's "Kurtzman's Mad World" appears in the *New Yorker*, along with a comic strip honoring Kurtzman by Art Spiegelman.

New Two-Fisted Tales #1 is published, with a cover by Kurtzman and Eisner.

April: Approx. date: *Ray Bradbury Comics* #2 (with "It Burns Me Up!," apparently the last story Kurtzman worked on, finished by Matt Wagner) is published.

1994

New Two-Fisted Tales #2 is published, with Kurtzman's last self-written story ("War!").

ENDNOTES

All of the author's interviews were conducted from 2011 to 2014. Likewise, all the emails to the author cited below are from that four-year period.

Part One: Cartoonist

1   Gary Groth and Kim Thompson: with Mike Catron. "Harvey Kurtzman: The Man Who Brought Truth to Comics" Interview. *The Comics Journal Library* Vol. 7: *Harvey Kurtzman* (Washington: Fantagraphics Books, Inc., 2006), 84.

Chapter 1

1   Harvey Kurtzman rarely spoke of his childhood. The material in this chapter is based on the few things he revealed, augmented by interviews by the author with Adele Kurtzman (Harvey's wife), his eldest daughter Meredith and his nephew (Zachary's son) Adam Kurtzman.
2   David Kurtzman was born circa 1892, and Edith Sherman December 10, 1896.
3   Denis Kitchen and Paul Buhle, *The Art of Harvey Kurtzman* (New York: Abrams, 2009), 4.
4   Harvey Kurtzman with Howard Zimmerman, *My Life as a Cartoonist* (New York: Minstrel Books/Simon & Shuster, Inc., 1988), 6. Zimmerman adapted Kurtzman interviews into the final text (which is relatively short). The words are Kurtzman's, though phrases have been rearranged and edited. This was verified by a comparison of the original interview transcripts (conducted by Zimmerman and Byron Preiss) with the book's text. Therefore, quotations from it can be reliably attributed to Kurtzman himself.
5   Adele Kurtzman, interviews by author.
6   Abraham Perkes was born on May 2, 1894.
7   Paul Buhle. "Harvey Kurtzman," *Shmate* #6 (Summer 1983), 24.
8   Kurtzman, *My Life as a Cartoonist*, 13.
9   Ibid, 4.
10   Ibid, 4.
11   Ibid, 5, 6.
12   "Why I drew" from *My Life as a Cartoonist*, 6. "We never had . . . appreciated a buck" from Shel Dorf, "The 'Mad' Man Interviewed," *Overstreet's Advanced Collector* (Summer 1993), 116.
13   Groth and Thompson, "The Man who Brought Truth to Comics," 84.
14   Dorf, "The 'Mad' Man Interviewed," 116.
15   Kurtzman, *My Life as a Cartoonist*, 9.
16   Ibid, 9.
17   Groth and Thompson, "The Man who Brought Truth to Comics," 84.
18   "I loved 'em all," Ibid, 84. "I had . . . preference," S. C. Ringgenberg, "Memories Most Mad," *Comics Scene* #47 (November 1994), 14.
19   Kurtzman, *My Life as a Cartoonist*, 7, 8.
20   From interview transcript for *My Life as a Cartoonist*.
21   Buhle, "Harvey Kurtzman," 24.
22   Adele Kurtzman, interviews by author.
23   Gary Groth. Jules Feiffer Interview. "Memories of a Pro Bono Cartoonist." *The Comics Journal Library* Vol. 4: *Drawing the Line* (Seattle: Fantagraphics, 2004), 3.
24   Buhle, "Harvey Kurtzman," 24.
25   Kurtzman never pinpointed the date when his family moved to the Bronx. On the radio show *The Cartoonist's Art*, hosted by Vern Greene, on March 23, 1962, he referred to drawing "in the gutter" in front of his home in the Bronx at the age of ten. He turned ten years old on October 3, 1934. Joe Pilati took notes while listening to the program that were the basis of the article "Afterthoughts on a man and a program," published in the fanzine *Smudge* #3 (May 1962), 11.
26   Groth and Thompson, "The Man Who Brought Truth to Comics," 111.
27   Letter to Dorothy Thompson of the *Ladies' Home Journal*, August 28, 1954.

28   From the interview transcript for *My Life as a Cartoonist*.

29   Kurtzman, *My Life as a Cartoonist*, 13.

30   "When I was . . . weren't acceptable," from interview transcript for *My Life as a Cartoonist*. Rest of paragraph from J. P. C. James's *"The Comics Journal Library* Vol. 7: *Harvey Kurtzman*, "Hey Look! An Interview with Harvey Kurtzman," 39.

31   "I found . . . had ever seen" from Jacques Dutrey's unpublished Harvey Kurtzman interview, conducted by mail, in two parts in 1978 and 1980. "It was . . . approach to humor" from *The Complete* Mad *Library*. *The Complete* Mad *Library* reprints in its entirety Kurtzman's run on the comic book version of *Mad*. Benson interviewed Kurtzman for the book and edited the contextual notes and comments, which he, Bill Mason, and Bhob Stewart wrote. (West Plains: Russ Cochran Publishing, 1986). "It was that quality of parody . . . influenced me enormously," from unpublished Jacques Dutrey interview.

32   Kurtzman, *My Life as a Cartoonist*, 14.

33   Harvey Kurtzman, "Introduction," *Smokey Stover Book 1*, 2.

34   Harvey Kurtzman with Michael Barrier, *From Aargh! to Zap*, (New York: Prentice Hall Press, 1991), 24. One must exercise great care in attributing quotations from this book, since Michael Barrier ghosted it and wrote whole sections with little or no input from Kurtzman. However, this passage is quoted virtually word for word from Barrier's notes.

35   James, "Hey Look! An Interview with Harvey Kurtzman," 39.

36   Kurtzman, *My Life as a Cartoonist*, 11.

37   "The cars would . . . down the street," from Gary Delain and Sig Case, "Hello, Harvey Kurtzman," *Shag* #1 (February 1959), 12. "By the next morning . . . my first comic strip," from Kurtzman, *My Life as a Cartoonist*, 11.

38   Joe Pilati, "Afterthoughts on a Man and a Program," *Smudge* #3 (May 1962), 11.

39   Don Markstein, *Don Markstein's Toonopedia*, http://toonopedia.com/mikenike. htm, accessed 4/16/2014.

40   Zachary Kurtzman at memorial for Harvey (1993). Zachary's son Adam described him to the author as "a mean son of a bitch" and said, "a lot of people detested my dad."

41   Kurtzman, *My Life as a Cartoonist*, 10.

42   Ibid, 16.

43   John Benson, "A Conversation with Harvey Kurtzman and . . . Arnold Roth and Al Jaffee," *Squa Tront* #10 (2002), 23.

44   Buhle, "Harvey Kurtzman," 24

45   Al Jaffee, email to author.

46   Zachary Kurtzman at memorial for Harvey, 1993.

47   Roger Ebert, *Back to School* review, http://www.rogerebert.com/reviews/back-to-school-1986, accessed 4/16/2014.

48   Elizabeth McLeod, "Radio's Forgotten Years," www.midcoast.com/~lizmcl/rfy. html, accessed 4/16/2014.

49   Al Jaffee, email to author.

50   Dave Schreiner, "Flash Gordon vs. the Reluctant Collaborators of Manhattan Isle, *Flash Gordon* (Wisconsin: Kitchen Sink, 1988), 121.

51   Ibid, 120–1.

52   Kurtzman, *My Life as a Cartoonist*, 16.

Chapter 2

1   The school abbreviated its name HSMA, but students always called it M&A.

2   Benjamin M. Steigman, *Accent on Talent, New York's High School of Music and Art* (Michigan: Wayne State University Press, 1964), 8.

3   Ibid, ii.

4   Mary-Lou Weisman, *Al Jaffee's Mad Life* (New York: HarperCollins, 2010), 124.

5   Kurtzman, *My Life as a Cartoonist*, 14.

6   Bill Schelly, *Man of Rock* (Washington: Fantagraphics, 2008), 40. Joe Kubert is the "the M&A student."

7   Steigman, *Accent on Talent*, 26.

8   Al Jaffee, interview with author.

9   Kurtzman, *My Life as a Cartoonist*, 15.
10 Gary Groth. John Severin Interview, *The Comics Journal* #215 (August 1999), 55–6.
11 Groth and Thompson, "The Man Who Brought Truth to Comics," 105.
12 Harvey Kurtzman letter to Justin Green, March 28, 1972.
13 Kurtzman, *My Life as a Cartoonist*, 16.
14 "While I was getting educated . . . had a lot to do with it," from *My Life as a Cartoonist*, 15, 12. "My social life . . . high school was rough," from interview transcript for *My Life as a Cartoonist*.
15 Weisman, *Al Jaffee's Mad Life*, 131.
16 Benson, "A Conversation with Harvey Kurtzman and Bill Elder," *Squa Tront* #9 (1983), 67.
17 Gary Groth, "The Will Elder Interview," *The Comics Journal* website (tcj.com), February 8, 2011, http://www.tcj.com/the-will-elder-interview. Originally appeared in *The Comics Journal* #254 (July 2003).
18 Will Elder, *The Mad Playboy of Art* (Washington: Fantagraphics, 2003), 15.
19 Will Elder, interview by Gary Groth.
20 Dorf, "The 'Mad' Man Interviewed," 117.
21 John Benson conducted this Kurtzman interview for annotations in *The Complete* Mad *Library*, 1986–7. (Portions of the interview originally appeared in publisher Russ Cochran's series, The Complete EC Library.)
22 Groth and Thompson, "The Man Who Brought Truth to Comics," 96.
23 James, "Hey Look! An Interview with Harvey Kurtzman," 40.
24 Groth and Thompson, "The Man Who Brought Truth to Comics," 84.
25 Ibid, 84–5.
26 Ibid, 84.
27 Interview transcript for *My Life as a Cartoonist*.
28 Ibid.
29 From *The Complete* Mad *Library* annotations.
30 Groth, Severin Interview, 63.
31 Ibid.
32 Ibid.
33 Kurtzman, *From Aargh! to Zap*, 8. Kurtzman's genuine sentiments are reflected in this quotation from the book.
34 Benson, "A Conversation with Harvey Kurtzman and Bill Gaines," 83.
35 Harvey Kurtzman interview conducted by S. C. Ringgenberg on January 19, 1985. This is from the unedited transcript. The edited interview appeared in *Comics Scene* #47 (November 1985).
36 Kurtzman, *My Life as a Cartoonist*, 16.
37 Buhle, "Harvey Kurtzman," 24. The cartoon was originally for a Parent Teachers Association (PTA) publication.
38 Steigman, *Accent on Talent*, 132.
39 James, "Hey Look! An Interview with Harvey Kurtzman," 39.
40 Harry Chester's M&A yearbook, loaned to the author by Irene Chester.

Chapter 3

1   Kurtzman, *My Life as a Cartoonist*, 17.
2   Ibid.
3   Groth and Thompson, "The Man Who Brought Truth to Comics," 96.
4   Dorf, "The 'Mad' Man Interviewed," 117.
5   Kurtzman-Gil Kane interview conducted by John Benson on August 11, 1972: unpublished.
6   Interview transcript for *My Life as a Cartoonist*.
7   "During this time . . . you were an artist," from Shel Dorf, "The 'Mad' Man Interviewed," 117. "Deep down inside . . . nondescript jobs," from Interview transcript for *My Life as a Cartoonist*.
8   Interview transcript for *My Life as a Cartoonist*.
9   Buhle, "Harvey Kurtzman," 24.
10 John Benson, "A Talk with Harvey Kurtzman," *The Comics Journal Library* Vol. 7: *Harvey Kurtzman* (Seattle: Fantagraphics Books, 2006), 21.

11 Kurtzman, *My Life as a Cartoonist*, 17.

12 Martin Sheridan, editor, *Comics and Their Creators* (Massachusetts: Ralph T. Hale & Company, 1942), 120.

13 *The Art of Harvey Kurtzman*, (New York: Abrams, 2009), 11–2. Andriola's rejection also appears in an early transcript of John Benson's unpublished interview with Gil Kane and Harvey Kurtzman on August 11, 1972. It reads: "When I was thirteen, I went up to see Alfred Andriola, and he told me to get out of the business."

14 Adam Kurtzman (Zachary's son), interview with author.

15 Letter from the US Department of Justice, Federal Bureau of Prisons, dated February 7, 2012. Zachary's son, Adam Kurtzman, told the author about the "horse thief" comment.

16 Kurtzman-Kane interview conducted by John Benson: unpublished. (Adele Kurtzman was also there, and occasionally contributed.)

17 Interview transcript for *My Life as a Cartoonist*.

18 Ibid.

19 Groth and Thompson, "The Man Who Brought Truth to Comics," 96.

20 All quotations in this paragraph are from the unpublished Kurtzman-Kane interview conducted by John Benson in 1972.

21 Barrier notes, March 31, 1990.

22 Kurtzman-Kane interview by John Benson: unpublished.

23 Dorf, "The 'Mad' Man Interviewed," 117.

24 Barrier notes, March 31, 1990.

25 Kurtzman-Kane interview by John Benson: unpublished.

26 Ibid.

27 Ibid.

28 "[My] work . . . bad stuff," from Kurtzman-Kane interview: unpublished. "You'd spit on a page, and they'd publish it," from Dorf, "The 'Mad' Man Interviewed," 117.

29 Unpublished Kurtzman-Kane interview (1972).

30 Benson, "A Talk with Harvey Kurtzman," 21.

31 Kurtzman-Kane interview: unpublished.

32 Scott Moore, "L. B.L. B. Cole . . . Artist, Author, & Publisher!," *Comic Book Marketplace*, Vol. 2, #30, (December 1995), 31.

33 Kurtzman-Kane interview: unpublished.

34 Harvey Kurtzman interview by Jacques Dutrey: unpublished. Kurtzman wrote, "I'm sure I didn't write . . . *Bill the Magnificent*. I think I wrote *Flatfoot Burns*, *Pigtales*, *Muscles Malone*."

35 Kurtzman-Kane interview: unpublished.

Chapter 4

1 Wiseman, *Al Jaffee's Mad Life*, 151.

2 Elder, *The Mad Playboy of Art*, 28.

3 John Benson, "The '72 EC War Panel." *The Comics Journal Library* Vol.7: *Harvey Kurtzman* (Seattle: Fantagraphics Books, 2006), 1978, 68–9.

4 Ibid, 69.

5 Will Eisner interview, by Gary Groth, *The Comics Journal* #46 (May 1979), 45–6.

6 Kitchen and Buhle, *The Art of Harvey Kurtzman*, 14.

7 Mike Benton, *The Comic Book in America* (Texas: Taylor Publishing, 1989), 37–9.

8 Benson, "A Talk with Harvey Kurtzman," 24.

9 Number of weekly episodes of *Private Brown Knows* per Ger Apeldoorn, "'Lost' Kurtzman: The War Years,"*Alter Ego* #86 (June 2008), 74–6. Apeldoorn has found seventeen of these strips, though it's possible there are a few more.

10 Kitchen and Buhle, *The Art of Harvey Kurtzman*, 14.

11 Buhle, "Harvey Kurtzman," 24.

12 William F. Ryan. "H. Kurtzman Still Laughing in the Jungle," *Amazing Heroes* #178 (April 1990), 36.

13 Kurtzman-Kane interview: unpublished.

14 Apeldoorn, "'Lost' Kurtzman: The War Years," 77.

15 Kitchen and Buhle, *The Art of Harvey Kurtzman*, 18.
16 James, "Hey Look! An Interview with Harvey Kurtzman," 40.
17 Zachary Kurtzman at memorial for Harvey, 1993.
18 James, "Hey Look! An Interview with Harvey Kurtzman," 40.

Chapter 5

1 Kurtzman-Kane interview: unpublished.
2 *Contact* #11 had a story drawn by another young artist named Al Feldstein.
3 James, "Hey Look! An Interview with Harvey Kurtzman," 40.
4 Interview transcript for *My Life as a Cartoonist*. "Right vibrations" quotation in the same paragraph is from this source.
5 Kurtzman-Kane interview: unpublished. Kurtzman used "animated cartoons" because Flatfoot Burns wasn't anthropomorphic (i.e. a funny animal), though the art style would be about the same.
6 Kurtzman, *My Life as a Cartoonist*, 16.
7 Wiseman, *Al Jaffee's Mad Life*, 158. The figure in Wiseman's book is $15,000, but in a recent email, Jaffee said he must have been confused because he was sure he never made more than $15,000 in comic books at his peak of production, which was the early 1950s. He said he did reach $10,000 not long after leaving the military. His income figures mentioned here and elsewhere are subject to Jaffee's memory, rather than an examination of old IRS records.
8 Kurtzman-Kane interview: unpublished.
9 Ibid.
10 Kurtzman interview by Jacques Dutrey: upublished.
11 John Benson used voucher numbers on the strips themselves to help determine the order they were done, as he explains in his introduction to *Hey Look!* (Kitchen Sink, 1992).
12 Grant Geissman and Fred von Bernewitz, "A Talk with Adele Kurtzman," *Tales of Terror! The EC Companion* (Maryland: Gemstone Publishing, and Washington: Fantagraphics Books, 2000), 187.
13 Al Jaffee, interview with author.
14 Ibid.
15 Ibid.
16 Kurtzman-Kane interview: unpublished.
17 Al Jaffee, interview with author.
18 Adele Kurtzman, interviews by author.
19 Ibid.
20 Blake Bell, *I Have to Live with This Guy* (North Carolina: Twomorrows Publishing, 2002), 84.
21 Adele Kurtzman, interviews by author.
22 Bell, *I Have to Live with This Guy*, 85.
23 Ibid.
24 Adele Kurtzman, interviews by author.
25 Ibid.
26 Kurtzman-Kane interview: unpublished. Adele was there and participated in the discussion.
27 Bell, *I Have to Live with This Guy*, 86.
28 Ibid, 85.
29 Kurtzman-Kane interview: unpublished.
30 Ibid.
31 Geissman, "A Talk With Adele Kurtzman," 186.
32 Kitchen and Buhle, *The Art of Harvey Kurtzman*, 30.
33 Adele Kurtzman, interviews by author.
34 "My parents . . . now or never," from Geissman, "A Talk with Adele Kurtzman," 186. "In our family . . . was more so," from Bell, *I Have to Live with This Guy*, 86.
35 Bell, *I Have to Live with This Guy*, 86.
36 Will Elder, interview by Gary Groth.
37 Elder, *The Mad Playboy of Art*, 37.
38 Will Elder, interview by Gary Groth.
39 Bell, *I Have to Live with This Guy*, 86.

40   Adele Kurtzman, interview by Blake Bell for *I Have to Live with This Guy*: from the unedited transcript. This quotation was edited out before publication.

Chapter 6

1   Benson, "A Conversation with Harvey Kurtzman and Bill Elder," 70.
2   Ibid.
3   Ibid, 69, 70.
4   Groth and Thompson, "The Man Who Brought Truth to Comics," 87.
5   Benson, "A Conversation with Harvey Kurtzman and Bill Elder," 70.
6   Ibid.
7   Ibid.
8   Harvey Kurtzman, interview by S. C. Ringgenberg, January 19, 1985: from the unedited transcript.
9   Groth and Thompson, "The Man Who Brought Truth to Comics," 87.
10   Kitchen and Buhle, *The Art of Harvey Kurtzman*, 6.
11   Adele Kurtzman, interviews by author.
12   Ibid.
13   Interview with Jo Anne Bergtold conducted by her son Jesse Drew: unpublished.
14   Kitchen and Buhle, *The Art of Harvey Kurtzman*, 21.
15   Benson, "A Conversation with Harvey Kurtzman and Bill Elder," 70.
16   Barrier notes, March 31, 1990.
17   Groth, "Jules Feiffer Memories of a Pro Bono Cartoonist," 7.
18   "Sheer hell" from interview transcript for *My Life as a Cartoonist*: the rest of the quotation from the published book, 28.
19   The page rate information is from Kitchen and Buhle, *The Art of Harvey Kurtzman*, 22.
20   Kurtzman, *My Life as a Cartoonist*, 98–105.
21   Kurtzman, *From Aargh! to Zap*, 27.
22   Walt Kelly letter to Harvey Kurtzman: dated November 2, 1948.
23   Jim Vadeboncoeur Jr. "The Early Years: An Interview with John Severin," *Squa Tront* #11 (2005), 36.
24   Ibid.
25   Groth and Thompson, "The Man Who Brought Truth to Comics," 85.
26   Jo Anne Bergtold Drew Interview: unpublished.
27   *Gay Comics* #37 (April 1949)
28   Harry Wilback, "Recent Crimes and the Veterans," *Journal of Criminal Law and Criminology*, Vol. 38 #5 (1948), 501–8.
29   The school was an expansion of Hogarth's Manhattan Academy of Newspaper Art, and was founded with the support of the Veterans Administration where Rhodes worked.
30   Ron Barlow, "Wallace Wood," *EC Lives!* con program, New York (1972), 27.
31   Kurtzman, *From Aargh! to Zap*, 22. This quotation accurately reflects Kurtzman's view on the arrival of more reality-based comic books.
32   Judd Hurd, *Cartoonist PROfiles* #26 (June 1975), 46–7.
33   Benson, "A Conversation with Harvey Kurtzman and Bill Gaines," 83.
34   Hitchcock quotation from T. Durwood. "Harvey Kurtzman Interviewed by T. Durwood,"*Crimmer's* #3, (Spring 1976). Kurtzman was an admirer of Hitchcock and had paid close attention to his films.
35   Letter from Karl A. Menninger, M.D. to Kurtzman, dated October 5, 1946.
36   Letter from Karl A. Menninger, M.D. to Kurtzman dated November 25, 1946.
37   Fredric Wertham, "The Psychopathology of Comic Books," *American Journal of Psychiatry* #11 (July 1948), 472–90.
38   Bell, *I Have to Live with This Guy*, 87.
39   John Benson, "Hey Look!," introduction, *Hey Look!* (Princeton: Kitchen Sink Press, 1992), 10.
40   Kurtzman, *My Life as a Cartoonist*, 28.
41   Denis Kitchen letter to John Benson, dated November 9, 1987.
42   Adele Kurtzman, interviews by author.

43   Ibid. In his co-interview with Bill Gaines in *Squa Tront* #9, Kurtzman says the apartment was on 116th Street, but his memory for that kind of detail wasn't good, and the buildings on 116th Street are too nice for the kind of apartment that he and Adele described.

44   Bell, *I Have to Live with This Guy*, 87.

45   Adele Kurtzman, interviews by author.

Chapter 7

1   Kurtzman-Kane interview: unpublished.
2   Benson, "A Conversation with Harvey Kurtzman and Bill Elder," 70.
3   Kurtzman-Kane interview: unpublished.
4   Ibid.
5   Elder, *The Mad Playboy of Art*, 39–40.
6   Groth and Thompson, "The Man Who Brought Truth to Comics" 97, 99.
7   From a December 2011 letter from Jacques Dutrey, translating an interview with René Goscinny in a French magazine.
8   Jacques Dutrey, "The EC French Connection," *Squa Tront* #11 (Spring 2005), 27.
9   Adele Kurtzman, interview by Blake Bell for *I Have to Live with This Guy*: from the unedited transcript.
10   Kurtzman-Kane interview: unpublished.
11   Groth and Thompson, "The Man Who Brought Truth to Comics," 99.
12   S. C. Ringgenberg, "Memories Most Mad," 14.
13   Kurtzman-Kane interview: unpublished.
14   Ibid.
15   "It was . . . hustling," ibid. "I was a beggar . . . anything to sell," from Groth and Thompson, "The Man Who Brought Truth to Comics," 87.
16   Benson, "A Conversation with Harvey Kurtzman and Bill Gaines," 83.
17   Harvey Zorbaugh and Mildren Gilman, "What can YOU do about Comic Books?," *Family Circle* (February 1949), 60-3.

Chapter 8

1   How Bill Gaines was abused as a boy is detailed in Frank Jacobs's biography *The Mad World of William M. Gaines*.
2   Bill Gaines's address at unidentified comic book convention in 1975 (possibly in New York on January 3): from a tape recorded by John Benson.
3   Ron Goulart, *The Encyclopedia of American Comics* (New York: Facts on File Inc., 1990), 147.
4   Frank Jacobs, *The Mad World of William M Gaines* (New Jersey: Lyle Stuart, Inc., 1972), 61.
5   Ibid, 63.
6   Kurtzman-Kane interview: unpublished.
7   One extant copy of *Animated Comics* #1 has an arrival date (November 28, 1947) pencilled on the cover.
8   Benson, "A Conversation with Harvey Kurtzman and Bill Gaines," 83.
9   Kurtzman-Kane interview: unpublished.
10   Dorf, "The 'Mad' Man Interviewed," 118. The phrase "a pretty radical thing to do at the time" is from an interview transcript for *My Life as a Cartoonist*.
11   Kitchen and Buhle, *The Art of Harvey Kurtzman*, 47. The exact amount was $161.
12   Kurtzman-Kane interview: unpublished.
13   Groth and Thompson, "The Man Who Brought Truth to Comics," 96.
14   Jim Amash, "Toby Press Was My College," *Alter Ego* #96 (August 2010), 33.
15   Jacques Dutrey, "The EC French Connection," *Squa Tront* #11 (Spring 2005), 24.
16   Kurtzman-Kane interview: unpublished.

Chapter 9

1   The arrival date on EC fan Bill Spicer's copy is February 16, 1950. Since he lived in California, he may have received his copy a week or so after copies appeared on the east coast.

2   Barlow, "William M. Gaines," *EC Lives!*, 5.
3   Harvey Kurtzman interview conducted by S. C. Ringgenberg on January 19, 1985: unedited transcript.
4   From annotations discussing *Weird Science* #7, *The Complete Weird Science Library*, second edition, (West Plains: Russ Cochran Publishing, 1980), no page number.
5   Grant Geissman, *Feldstein: The Mad Life and Fantastic Art of Al Feldstein* (California: IDW Publishing, 2013), 132.
6   Gary Groth and Dwight Decker, "An Interview with William M. Gaines," *The Comics Journal* #181 (May 1983), 60.
7   Interview transcript for *My Life as a Cartoonist.*
8   Groth and Thompson, "The Man Who Brought Truth to Comics," 109.
9   Interview transcript for *My Life as a Cartoonist.*
10 Gary Groth, "Kurtzman at Creation Los Angeles, 1982," *The Comics Journal Library*, Vol. 7: *Harvey Kurtzman* (Washington: Fantagraphics Books, 2006), 126.
11 Will Eisner, "Harvey Kurtzman," *Will Eisner's Shop Talk* (Oregon: Dark Horse Comics, Inc., 2001), 262.
12 Ibid, 276.
13 "Gaines and Feldstein started . . . writing structure," from Michael Barriers notes taken on March 31, 1990, for *From Aargh! to Zap.* "Bill Gaines inspired me with much of my respect for short stories," from "Harvey Kurtzman Interviewed by T. Durwood," *Crimmer's* #3, 29.
14 Barrier's notes on March 31, 1990.
15 Durwood, "Harvey Kurtzman Interviewed by T. Durwood," 27.
16 From annotations discussing *Weird Science* #7, *The Complete* Weird Science *Library.*
17 Durwood, "Harvey Kurtzman Interviewed by T. Durwood," 28.
18 Dorf, "The 'Mad' Man Interviewed," 118.
19 Barrier's notes on March 31, 1990.
20 From annotations by John Benson, *The Complete* Two-Fisted Tales *Library,* (West Plains: Russ Cochran Publishing: 1982), no page number.
21 From annotations by John Benson, *The Complete* Haunt of Fear *Library,* (West Plains: Russ Cochran Publishing).
22 Interview transcript for *My Life as a Cartoonist.*
23 Author's interviews with Adele Kurtzman in which she quoted lines from *The Decay of Living* by George Meredith.
24 Roald Dahl, "The Sound Machine," the *New Yorker*, September 17, 1949.
25 From annotations about *Weird Science* #7 in *The Complete* Weird Science *Library* (1978).
26 From annotations by Max Allan Collins, discussing *Crime SuspenStories* #3, *The Complete* Crime SuspenStories *Library* (West Plains: Russ Cochran Publishing), 1983.
27 Benson, "A Conversation with Harvey Kurtzman and Bill Gaines," 86.
28 Harvey Kurtzman interview conducted on January 19, 1985 by S. C. Ringgenberg: from the unedited transcript.
29 From annotations discussing *Weird Science* #7 in *The Complete* Weird Science *Library* (1978).

Part Two: Editor

1   Gary Groth, "Comics Sans Frontiéres," *The Comics Journal Library*, Vol.7: *Harvey Kurtman* (Seattle: Fantagraphics Books, 2006), 142.

Chapter 10

1   Groth and Decker, "An Interview with William M. Gaines," 56, 76.
2   Ibid, 56.
3   The house ad on the inside front cover of the first *Two-Fisted Tales* listed the EC roster as *Tales from the Crypt*, *Two-Fisted Tales*, *Crime SuspenStories*, *Weird*

Science, *Weird Fantasy* and *Modern Love*. No *Vault of Horror* or *Haunt of Fear* in sight. The annotations in *The Complete* Two-Fisted Tales *Library* Vol.1 state: "Wholesaler reluctance to handle horror titles caused EC to change *Haunt of Fear* to *Two-Fisted Tales* with issue #18. Later, the wholesaler problem was resolved, and *Haunt of Fear* was revived." *Vault of Horror* continued, and *Crime SuspenStories* was launched as a new title. Note that the ad with the cover of the first *Crime SuspenStories* in *Two-Fisted Tales* #18 gives the issue number as "#15." This was changed to "#1" once it was decided to continue *Vault of Horrors*.

4   "A slam bang high adventure book" is from Benson, "A Conversation with Harvey Kurtzman and Bill Gaines," 85. "Blood and thunder . . . adventure" is from Benson, "The '72 EC War Panel," 68.

5   Benson, "A Conversation with Harvey Kurtzman and Bill Gaines, *Squa Tront* #9, 83.

6   Ibid.

7   Ibid.

8   Groth and Decker, "An Interview with William M. Gaines," 83.

9   Benson, "A Talk with Harvey Kurtzman," 24.

10   Kurtzman quote from John Benson's *The Complete* Two-Fisted Tales *Library* annotations.

11   Benson, "A Talk with Harvey Kurtzman," 24.

12   Groth and Thompson, "The Man Who Brought Truth to Comics," 104.

13   Ibid.

14   Interview transcript for *My Life as a Cartoonist*.

15   Jeffrey Wasserman, "Conversations with the Brother-in-Law of Underground Comix," *Inside Comics* #2 (Summer 1974), 20.

16   Hurd, Harvey Kurtzman Interview, 467.

17   Benson, "A Talk with Harvey Kurtzman," 24.

18   Benson, "The '72 EC War Panel," 69.

19   Durwood, "Harvey Kurtzman Interviewed by T. Durwood," 25.

20   Barlow, "John Severin," *EC Lives!*, 27.

21   The Davis cartoon appeared in *Tip Top Comics* #9 (December 1936).

22   Bruce Bennett, "Jack Davis—A Really Quick Draw on Pop Culture," *The Wall Street Journal*, December 3, 2011.

23   Barlow, "Jack Davis," *EC Lives!*, 23.

24   Groth and Decker, "An Interview with William M. Gaines," 69.

25   Groth and Thompson, "The Man Who Brought Truth to Comics," 105.

26   Monte Wolverton, "Basil Wolverton and *Mad*," *Comic Art* #4 (Fall 2003), 63.

27   Kurtzman quote from John Benson's *The Complete* Two-Fisted Tales *EC Library* annotations (1979).

28   Benson, "A Talk with Harvey Kurtzman," 25.

29   Kurtzman quote from John Benson's *The Complete* Two-Fisted Tales *EC Library* annotations (1979).

30   Katherine Keller, "The Chromatic Queen Marie Severin," http://www.sequentialtart.com/archive/may02/severin.shtml.

31   Marie Severin panel at a comic con (probably in New York), January 3, 1975.

32   Chip Selby, director, *Tales from the Crypt: From Comic Books to Television* [video], 2004.

33   Groth and Thompson, "The Man Who Brought Truth to Comics," 99, 100.

34   Ibid, 103.

35   Barlow, "Wallace Wood," *EC Lives!*, 37.

36   Ibid.

37   Barlow, "Harvey Kurtzman," *EC Lives!*, 10.

38   Selby, *Tales from the Crypt: From Comic Books to Television* [video], 2004.

39   Jacobs, *The Mad World of William M. Gaines*, 74.

40   Monroe Froelich testimony for the US Senate hearings, April 20, 1954: http://www.thecomicbooks.com/froehlich.html.

41   "NY 14-366," US Federal Bureau of Investigation documents, 1952–3.

42   Kurtzman quote from John Benson's *The Complete* Two-Fisted Tales *EC Library* annotations (1979).

43   Benson, "A Conversation with Harvey Kurtzman and Bill Gaines," 84.

44 Jerry De Fuccio, "Kurtzman," *Squa Tront* #4 (1970), 7.
45 Ibid.
46 Bill Keiffer, "Jerry De Fuccio," *Comics Interview* #120 (1993), 31–2.
47 Ibid.
48 De Fuccio, "Kurtzman," *Squa Tront* #4 (1970), 10.

Chapter 11

1 Durwood, "Harvey Kurtzman Interviewed by T. Durwood," 28.
2 Andrew Kelly, *All Quiet on the Western Front, The Story of a Film* (New York, London: I. B. Tauris, 1998), 154.
3 Erich Maria Remarque, correspondence with General Sir Ian Hamilton, G.C.B., *Life and Letters*, Vol. 3, November 1929, 403.
4 "Comic Book Ratings," *Parents Magazine*, November 1952 and October 1953.
5 From annotations in *The Complete* Frontline Combat *Library* (1981).
6 All quotations about "Rubble!" are from annotations in *The Complete* Two-Fisted Tales *Library* (1979).
7 Ibid.
8 Ibid.
9 Ibid.
10 From Bill Mason's annotations in *The Complete* Frontline Combat *Library*.
11 From annotations in *The Complete* Weird Science *Library*, second edition.
12 Ibid.
13 From annotations in *The Complete* Two-Fisted Tales *Library*.
14 Harvey Kurtzman, interview by Jacques Dutrey: unpublished.
15 Benson, "A Talk with Harvey Kurtzman," 22.
16 David Douglas Duncan is the photographer who took the famous *Life* photo of a crying soldier in the early days of the war. It showed Corporal Leonard Hayworth with tears sliding down his right cheek after losing all but two of his squad at No Name Ridge. It appeared in the September 18, 1950 issue of the magazine.
17 From annotations in *The Complete* Frontline Combat *Library*: the photo originally appeared in an exhibit called *Faces of Korea* at the New York Museum of Modern Art that opened in the spring of 1951. Then it was printed in *This is War!*
18 Ibid.
19 Durwood, "Harvey Kurtzman Interviewed by T. Durwood," 35.
20 From annotations in *The Complete* Two-Fisted Tales *Library*.
21 From annotations in *The Complete* Frontline Combat *Library*.
22 De Fuccio, "Kurtzman," *Squa Tront* #4, 10.
23 Adele Kurtzman, interviews by author.
24 Bell, "*I Have to Live with This Guy*," 91.
25 Barlow, "Harvey Kurtzman," *EC Lives!*, 9.
26 Ibid.
27 Benson, "The '72 EC War Panel," 63.
28 Barlow, "Harvey Kurtzman," *EC Lives!*, 9.
29 Ibid.
30 Ibid.
31 Ibid.
32 Gary Groth, John Severin interview, *The Comics Journal* #215 (August 1999), 68–9.
33 Vince Davis, Richard Kyle and Bill Spicer, "Interview with Alex Toth," *Graphic Story Magazine* #10, 36.
34 John Benson convention tape from January 3, 1975.
35 James, "Hey Look! An Interview with Harvey Kurtzman," 43.
36 Will Eisner, "Harvey Kurtzman," *Will Eisner's Shop Talk*, 261.
37 Adele Kurtzman, interviews by author.
38 Bell, *I Have to Live with This Guy*, 88.
39 Quotations in this paragraph are from Adele Kurtzman, interviews by author.
40 Jacques Dutrey, "The EC French Connection," *Squa Tront* #11, 24, 27.

41   A December 2011 letter from Jacques Dutrey, which translates a French interview with Goscinny.

42   John Benson's telephone conversation with Bill Gaines ca. December 1982. It has previously been stated that Gaines gave the cameras to his key players at the 1951 EC Christmas party. In Benson's 1982 phone call with Gaines, the publisher described it as occurring "mid-year," and internal evidence in the surviving photographs (showing Gaines handing them cameras) indicates it probably took place in late September or early October 1951. This is based on the EC comic books on display in the photos taken at the event (printed in *Tales of Terror!*), which would have come out from August 21 to September 21, 1951. Gaines always kept the latest issues on display.

43   Groth and Thompson, "The Man Who Brought Truth to Comics," 114.

44   Geissman, "A Talk with Adele Kurtzman," 188.

45   Page 81 of *The Art of Harvey Kurtzman*, by Kitchen and Buhle, states Kurtzman made between $445 and $638 pretax dollars for each issue of *Two-Fisted Tales* and *Frontline Combat*, with each issue representing a month's income. Average of $550 x 12 = $6,600 + 990 for 22 pages of SF stories in 1951 + a bit for *Genius* & three assignments for Parents Institute, so round to $8,000.

46   Groth and Decker, "An Interview with William M. Gaines," 62.

47   Both quotations in this paragraph are from Schreiner, "Flash Gordon vs. the Reluctant Collaborators of Manhattan Isle," 121.

48   Ibid.

49   Ibid.

50   "NY 14-366," US Federal Bureau of Investigation documents, 1952–3.

51   Ibid.

52   Ibid.

53   M. A. Jones memo, US Federal Bureau of Investigation documents, April 24, 1967.

54   Harvey and Adele made a trip to Washington, DC about the time they were being investigated by the FBI, which included a visit to the Pentagon. EC was just one of fourteen comic book publishers whose books were examined by the Department of Justice for possible violations at this time.

55   Harold Hayes interviewed Harvey Kurtzman on his WNET-TV show *Roundtable* in 1975.

56   From annotations in *The Complete* Frontline Combat *Library*.

57   From annotations in *The Complete* Two-Fisted Tales *Library*.

58   From annotations in *The Complete* Frontline Combat *Library*.

59   Ibid.

60   Davis, Kyle and Spicer, "Interview with Alex Toth," 14.

61   From annotations in *The Complete* Two-Fisted Tales *Library*.

Chapter 12

1   Groth and Decker, "An Interview with William M. Gaines," 60.

2   From annotations in *The Complete* Frontline Combat *Library*. Last sentence, "I bashed . . . that one," from interview transcript for *My Life as a Cartoonist*.

3   Fred von Bernewitz and Grant Geissman, editors, "Bill Gaines: Vintage 1969," interview by Rich Hauser, *Tales of Terror!*, 182–3.

4   From an email from Al Jaffee: "During a chat with Harvey I asked him why he wanted to connect with fellow Music and Art High School grads which included Will Elder, Charlie Stern, John Severin, myself and others. He told me it was always his lifelong dream to become a publisher and bring in talent he met along the way. When he arrived in M&A high he said he took note of certain students whom he would someday hire for his future publication, whatever that might be. He certainly accomplished his dream in spades." Since Elder, Severin and Jaffee were gifted "funny" cartoonists, as was Kurtzman, and he was ill equipped to edit a general interest or literary magazine, he had almost certainly been thinking in terms of a humor magazine. According to Elder, within minutes of being formally introduced to each other (after the war) by Harry Jaffee, he and Kurtzman talked about collaborating.

5   Geissman, "A Talk with Adele Kurtzman," 188. "I remember what we served" from *I Have to Live with This Guy*, 89.

6   James, "Hey Look! An Interview with Harvey Kurtzman," 43.
7   Both quotations in this paragraph are from Groth and Decker's "An Interview with William M. Gaines," #81, 60.
8   James, "Hey Look! An Interview with Harvey Kurtzman," 43.
9   Groth and Decker, "An Interview with William M. Gaines," 79.
10   Al Feldstein, interview with author.
11   Harvey Kurtzman letter to George Zolotar (his attorney), dated November 3, 1962.
12   Geissman, "A Talk with Adele Kurtzman," 188.
13   Harvey Kurtzman letter to George Zolotar (his attorney), dated November 3, 1962.
14   David B. Guralnik, editor in chief, *Webster New World Dictionary of the American Language*, second college edition (New York, Cleveland: The World Publishing Company, 1972), 849.
15   Gaines and Feldstein did end up writing the fake bio of Bill Gaines in *Mad* #5.
16   Geissman, *Feldstein: The Mad Life and Fantastic Art of Al Feldstein*, 223.
17   Barrier's notes for *From Aargh! to Zap.*
18   From annotations in *The Complete* Mad *Library.*
19   Benson, "A Talk with Harvey Kurtzman," 29.
20   John Benson's September 8, 1961 interview with Kurtzman was published in *Squa Tront* #10 (2002), 42. (It originally appeared in his fanzine *Image* #5.)
21   From annotations in *The Complete* Mad *Library.*
22   Harvey Kurtzman art exhibition, Society of Illustrators, New York (May 2013): *Mad* #1 "thumbnails" for the stories were displayed. The card before the display read, "Virtually none of Kurtzman's large second-stage vellum layouts for *Mad* survive, but many of his much smaller first-stage thumbnail roughs do. Though his initial concept drawings were minuscule, his first impressions in almost every instance translated to the final published compositions."
23   Will Elder, interview by Gary Groth.
24   Benson, "A Conversation with Harvey Kurtzman and Bill Elder," 71.
25   Ibid, 71–2.
26   Will Elder, interview by Gary Groth.
27   From *The Complete* Mad *Library* annotations.
28   Ibid.
29   Based on data from Bill Spicer, this issue appeared about thirty days before *Mad* #1.
30   Bill Spicer wrote on his copy of *Mad* #1 that it arrived on August 6. This meant copies might have appeared as early as the last week of July on the east coast, since it's closer to the printer.
31   John Benson, "Harvey Kurtzman Interview," *Squa Tront* #10, 42.
32   Durwood, "Harvey Kurtzman Interview by T. Durwood," 25.
33   After Kurtzman's death, Al Feldstein said that it was his suggestion to Kurtzman to satirize American popular culture figures in *Mad*. In an interview conducted by Grant Geissman in April 1996 that appeared in *Tales of Terror!*, according to Feldstein "If you examine the first, second and maybe third issue of *Mad*, they were just funny science fiction, funny crime story, funny horror story, funny romance story, whatever had to do with what we were publishing. And I remember walking to the subway with [Harvey] and chastising him and saying, 'This is a cute satire and it's great, but you're limiting your scope. Why don't you go out into Americana, and certainly do comic strips rather than just the comic books. And do supermarkets and movies and television.'" (83) He repeated this story in other places, such as Geissman's *The Mad Life and Fantastic Art of Al Feldstein!* (2013). Since Kurtzman is unable to respond, and the story is unverifiable, the author feels it doesn't warrant inclusion in the body of the main text. That isn't to say that Al Feldstein is being less than truthful, merely that a creative person is exposed to dozens of suggestions and influences, and what's important—beyond his or her own ideas—are the things he or she selects or distills from everything around him or her. Including Feldstein's statement(s) in the main body of the text, even with disclaimers, would give it more weight than is probably justified.

34   From annotations in *The Complete* Mad *Library.*
35   Will Elder, interview by Gary Groth.
36   Gary Groth, editor. Elder interview by Rob Veri, Will Elder Interview, *The Comics Journal* #177 (May 1995), 110.
37   From annotations in *The Complete* Mad *Library.*

Chapter 13

1   Benson, "A Talk with Harvey Kurtzman," 27.
2   From *The Complete* Two-Fisted Tales *Library*'s annotations.
3   Ibid.
4   From annotations in *The Complete* Frontline Combat *Library.*
5   Groth and Thompson, "The Man Who Brought Truth to Comics," 100.
6   Greg Sadowski, *B. Krigstein* (Washington: Fantagraphics Books, Inc., 2002), 160.
7   From annotations in *The Complete* Two-Fisted Tales *Library.*
8   Ibid.
9   Gary Groth, Joe Kubert Interview, *The Comics Journal* #172 (November 1994), 84.
10   From annotations in *The Complete* Two-Fisted Tales *Library.*
11   Gene Colan, interview by John Benson, 1999: unpublished.
12   Ibid.
13   From annotations in *The Complete* Two-Fisted Tales *Library.*
14   Benson, "The '72 EC War Panel," 67.
15   George Evans, interview by John Garcia, July 1, 1979: unpublished.
16   Benson, "The '72 EC War Panel," 67.
17   Groth and Decker, "An Interview with William M. Gaines," 60.
18   Davis, Kyle and Spicer, "Interview with Alex Toth," 16.
19   These thumbnails are printed in *The Art of Harvey Kurtzman*, 54–5.
20   George Evans, interview by John Garcia, July 1, 1979: unpublished.
21   Ibid.
22   From annotations in *The Complete* Frontline Combat *Library.*
23   Benson, "The '72 EC War Panel," 67.
24   From annotations in *The Complete* Frontline Combat *Library.*
25   Ibid.
26   Ibid.
27   Ibid.
28   John Benson, "Is War Hell?," *Panels* #2 (Spring 1981), 19.
29   From annotations in *The Complete* Two-Fisted Tales *Library.*
30   Keiffer, "Jerry De Fuccio," *Comics Interview* #120, 31–2.
31   Ibid.
32   Benson,"The '72 EC War Panel," 64.
33   From annotations in *The Complete* Frontline Combat *Library.*
34   Kurtzman was misled by the data available in 1953. It's now known that approximately 74,000 people died at Nagasaki from the blast.
35   John Benson, John Severin Interview, *Graphic Story Magazine* #13 (Spring 1971), 49.
36   Ibid.
37   Benson, "A Talk with Harvey Kurtzman," 27–8.
38   Ibid, 27.

Chapter 14

1   Groth and Decker, "An Interview with William M. Gaines," 72.
2   Groth and Thompson, "The Man Who Brought Truth to Comics," 114.
3   Kurtzman, *My Life as a Cartoonist*, 47. It wasn't true that no one had made fun of comic books before. They had been parodied here and there in various media, including college humor magazines, years before *Mad*. A prominent example is the February 1949 issue of the *Yale Record,* titled *Record Comics* on its cover. It's a full-color magazine dedicated exclusively to satires of Superman ("Supergoon"), *Dick Tracy* ("Hotshot Stacy"), *Blondie* ("Bleachie") and several more, drawn to approximate the styles of Joe Schuster, Chester Gould, Chic Young, etc. It's unlikely (though not impossible) that Kurtzman saw *Record Comics* or others like

it, given the limited circulations of college humor magazines. (When he mentioned such magazines, it was always in reference to the college magazines he found as a boy.)

4   In 1952, the Superman versus Captain Marvel lawsuit was in the news. National sued Fawcett in 1941; it alleged that Captain Marvel was an illegal copy of Superman. The case finally went to trial in 1948, and the verdict, delivered in 1951, was decided in Fawcett's favor over an apparent lapse in the Superman copyright. However, the court reversed this decision in 1952, and the case was sent back to a lower court for further adjudication. When Kurtzman was preparing the next *Mad*, Fawcett's management was considering the wisdom of continuing to fight while sales of its Captain Marvel comic books were slipping. This legal wrangle was a hot topic in the comics business and inspired the Superman vs. Captain Marvel plot of "Superduperman!," though readers needed no knowledge of it to understand the rivalry between the two characters.

5   Benson, "A Conversation with Harvey Kurtzman and Bill Gaines," 89.

6   Ibid, 89–90.

7   Ibid, 88.

8   Groth and Decker, "An Interview with William M. Gaines," 75.

9   From annotations in *The Complete* Mad *Library.*

10   Elder, *The Mad Playboy of Art*, 48.

11   Will Elder, interview by Gary Groth.

12   "Harvey Kurtzman" *Knight Owl*, Vol. 1 #2, Fairleigh Dickinson University, 6, 8.

13   Adele Kurtzman, interviews by author.

14   Groth and Decker, "An Interview with William M. Gaines," 75–6.

15   Ibid.

16   Benson, "A Conversation with Harvey Kurtzman and Bill Gaines," 89.

17   Groth and Decker, "An Interview with William M. Gaines," 75–6.

18   William M. Gaines, "An Apology," *Squa Tront* #12, 47.

19   Ibid, 48.

20   There remains a question involving the actual distribution of *Mad* #5. Collectors and historians have deemed it a "low circulation" issue, presuming that the Gaines bio furor caused wholesalers to fail to distribute some of the print run. Its value in the Overstreet *Comic Book Price Guide* (the benchmark of the industry) has been about double that of #4 or #6 in top condition, because supposedly fewer copies sold. Yet, Bill Gaines wrote with certainty about how profitable *Mad* #5 was in the article "Madman Gaines Pleads For Plots," only six months after the fact (*Writer's Digest*, February 1954). If even 10 percent of the copies were returned without being distributed, that would have affected the issue's profitability, especially at that early stage. Therefore, it seems *Mad* #5's distribution was unhindered.

21   Kurtzman, *My Life as a Cartoonist*, 28.

22   From annotations in *The Complete* Mad *Library.*

23   Harvey Kurtzman, "Introduction," *Smokey Stover, Book 1*, 2.

24   M. Thomas Inge, "Harvey Kurtzman and Modern American Satire," http://classic.tcj.com/history/m-thomas-inge-harvey-kurtzman-and-modern-american-satire-part-one-of-two/, March 15, 2010.

25   From annotations in *The Complete* Mad *Library.*

26   William M. Gaines, "Madman Gaines Pleads for Plots," *Writer's Digest*, February 1954, 20.

27   Arnold Roth, interview with author, August 2011.

28   Kurtzman consistently heard from adults who bought *Mad* not because they were regular comic book readers, but because a friend introduced it to them, and the humor appealed to their adult sensibilities. Arnold Roth introduced Jim Warren to *Mad* after discovering it himself. Hugh Hefner picked *Mad* off a newsstand and immediately loved it. People in show business—such as Steve Allen, Pat McCormick, Stan Freberg, Ernie Kovacs, Doodles Weaver and others—heard the buzz, bought *Mad*, recommended it to their friends (and wrote fan letters to Kurtzman). *Mad* became popular on college campuses early on, and so forth. There weren't enough EC fans to explain why it sold twice the other EC titles.

29   Wasserman, "Conversations with the Brother-in-Law of Underground Comix," 19.
30   John Benson, "EC Fanzines," *Squa Tront* #5 (1954), 40.
31   Benson, "A Talk with Harvey Kurtzman," 30.
32   From annotations in *The Complete* Mad *Library*.
33   The two panels from the only surviving example of Kurtzman's large layouts for *Mad* are from "Little Orphan Melvin!," found among Wallace Wood's papers. *The Art of Harvey Kurtzman* shows them on p. 85, where Denis Kitchen described them as "the last *Mad* link to the integral middle stage of Kurtzman's story creation technique."
34   Groth, "Kurtzman at Creation Los Angeles, 1982," 127.
35   Geissman, "A Talk with Adele Kurtzman," 190.
36   Benson, "A Conversation with Harvey Kurtzman and Bill Elder," 71.

Chapter 15

1   From annotations in *The Complete* Mad *Library*.
2   Durwood, "Harvey Kurtzman Inteview by T. Durwood," 24–5.
3   From annotations in *The Complete* Mad *Library*.
4   Groth, Severin Interview, 72.
5   Kurtzman, *From Aargh! to Zap*, 24.
6   Adele Kurtzman, interview by Blake Bell for *I Have to Live with This Guy*: from the unedited transcript.
7   Monte Wolverton, "Basil Wolverton and *Mad*," *Comic Art* #4, (Fall 2003), 63. Kurtzman's letter to Wolverton was dated September 16, 1953.
8   Will Elder, interview by Gary Groth. In the interview transcript for *My Life as a Cartoonist*, Kurtzman said, "Parody is mimicry. Satire is criticism."
9   From annotations in *The Complete* Mad *Library*: Russ Heath had drawn the story "O.P.!" in *Frontline Combat* #1.
10   Quotations in this paragraph from Benson, "A Conversation with Harvey Kurtzman and Bill Gaines," 83, 92.
11   Groth and Thompson, "The Man Who Brought Truth to Comics," 114.
12   Adele Kurtzman, interviews by author.
13   Ibid.
14   Irene Chester, interview with author.
15   Meredith Kurtzman, interview with author.
16   John Benson, "A Conversation with Harvey Kurtzman and Harry Chester, *Squa Tront* #12 (Summer 2007), 40.
17   Will Elder, interview by Gary Groth.
18   Davis-Kurtzman panel at the 1985 San Diego Comic-Con [from video courtesy of Rick Goldschmidt].
19   Jacobs, *The Mad World of William M. Gaines*, 100.
20   Benson, "A Conversation with Harvey Kurtzman and Bill Gaines," 88.
21   Carol Polsgrove, *It Wasn't Pretty, Folks, But Didn't We Have Fun?, Surviving the '60s with* Esquire's *Harold Hayes* (New York: W.W. Norton & Company, Inc., 1995), 21.
22   John Benson, commentary on "How Comics Have Gone *Mad*," *Squa Tront* #5, 36.
23   Harold Hayes, "Now Comics Have Gone Mad," *Pageant* (June 1954).
24   Hurd, Harvey Kurtzman Iinterview, 46.
25   From annotations in *The Complete* Mad *Library*.
26   Benson, "A Talk with Harvey Kurtzman," 29.

Chapter 16

1   "I was very fond . . . haunted house," from Ron Barlow, "Harvey Kurtzman," *EC Lives!*, 9. "We'd drink . . . wonderful time," from Groth and Decker, "An Interview with William M. Gaines," 80.
2   Groth and Decker, "An Interview with William M. Gaines," 80.
3   Ibid, 79.
4   John Benson, "Roth & Jaffee," *Humbug, Book One* (Washington: Fantagraphics Books, Inc., 2009), 214.

5   Harvey Kurtzman's letter to George Zolotar, dated September 22, 1966. Magazine Management published Timely Comics.
6   Bill Spicer, Lyle Stuart interview, *Squa Tront* #12, 51.
7   Ibid.
8   Al Feldstein interview with author.
9   Benson, "A Conversation with Harvey Kurtzman and Harry Chester, 39.
10   Geissman, "A Talk with Adele Kurtzman," 189.
11   Geissman, *Feldstein: The Mad Life and Fantastic Art of Al Feldstein*, 239.
12   Spicer, "Interview with Lyle Stuart," #12, 53.
13   James, "Hey Look! An Interview with Harvey Kurtzman," 44.
14   Groth and Decker, "An Interview with William M. Gaines," 79.
15   Benson, "A Conversation with Harvey Kurtzman and Bill Gaines," 86.
16   Ibid, 90.
17   Harvey Kurtzman, interview with John Benson via telephone, October 10, 1985: unpublished.
18   Ibid.
19   Harvey Kurtzman letter to George Zolotar, dated February 20, 1962. Gaines never contested that they had made an arrangement regarding royalties; the exact percentages are per Kurtzman.
20   Ibid.
21   Harvey Kurtzman, "The Face is Familiar. Have We Met?" the *New York Times*, January 10, 1975.
22   Harvey Kurtzman, editor, Introduction by Roger Price, *The Mad Reader* (New York: Ballantine Books, 1954).
23   Jeffrey Wasserman, Harvey Kurtzman Interview (unedited transcript): the final version ran in "Conversations with the Brother-in-Law of Underground Comix," in *Inside Comics* #2 (Summer 1974).
24   Benson, "A Conversation with Harvey Kurtzman and Bill Gaines," 88.
25   Ibid.
26   Ibid, 89.
27   The Comics Magazine Association of America, a new industry trade association, had adopted the Comics Code on October 26, 1954.
28   Benson, "A Conversation with Harvey Kurtzman and Bill Gaines," 88–9.
29   Ibid.
30   Even if Shevelson had given Kurtzman a section of the magazine, *Pageant* wasn't a humor magazine and couldn't have supported a substantial all-humor section. Kurtzman would likely have been expected to perform at least some general editing duties.
31   Ibid, 90.
32   Quatations are from Bhob Stewart's email to the author.

Chapter 17

1   S. C. Ringgenberg, "Memories Most Mad," 25.
2   Jacobs, *The Mad World of William M. Gaines*, 118.
3   Groth and Thompson, "The Man Who Brought Truth to Comics," 117. Actually, Daugherty was Gaines's printing broker.
4   Ibid, 118.
5   Ibid, 117.
6   Ibid.
7   Benson, "A Conversation with Harvey Kurtzman and Harry Chester, 37.
8   Groth and Thompson, "The Man Who Brought Truth to Comics," 117.
9   Kurtzman's "six-fingered hand" continued to appear in *Mad* after Kurtzman left.
10   This author's copy of *Mad* #24 has the retailer display date "5/12" pencilled on the cover.
11   Benson, "A Conversation with Harvey Kurtzman and Bill Gaines," 88.
12   Ringgenberg, "Memories Most Mad," 256.
13   Geissman, "A Talk with Adele Kurtzman," 188.
14   Groth and Decker, "An Interview with William M. Gaines," 78. The publication of the last New Direction comics overlapped with the first Picto-Fiction books.
15   Benton, *The Comic Book in America*, 54–5.

16   "Roth & Jaffee" interview by John Benson, *Humbug, Book One*, 23.
17   Jacobs, *The Mad World of William M. Gaines*, 118.
18   Irene Chester, interview with author.
19   Benson, "A Conversation with Harvey Kurtzman and Harry Chester, 39.
20   Ibid.
21   Ibid.
22   Groth and Decker, "An Interview with William M. Gaines," 81–2.
23   Ibid, 80. Gaines stated that Kurtzman was making a salary of $15,000 at that time. This seems inflated, since he had only been getting $10,000 when *Mad* became a magazine.
24   Jacobs, *The Mad World of William M. Gaines*, 119–20.
25   Ibid, 119.
26   Kurtzman letter to Zolotar, dated November 3, 1962.
27   It doesn't make sense that Gaines thought he would have to suspend publication of *Mad*, since the magazine was so profitable. His printer would logically have been willing to continue printing it, because *Mad* profits would pay the back printing bill. We can presume that Bill and Jessie Gaines wouldn't have injected another $50,000 each into EC unless it was absolutely necessary for the firm to continue to function. Without having more information about EC's finances at the time, and Gaines's relationship with his printer, one must either accept what Gaines told his biographer at face value, or consider that this point may not have been reported or recorded accurately.
28   Kurtzman letter to Zolotar, February 20, 1962.
29   Jacobs, *The Mad World of William M. Gaines*, 118–9, 126. Jacobs's book is the only source that mentions an employment agreement, although it doesn't say whether it was verbal or in writing. Kurtzman read the book, and while he reacted to certain passages, he didn't refute the existence of the agreement.
30   From annotations in *The Complete* Mad *Library*.
31   Gary Groth, editor, "Goodbye, Harvey," *The Comics Journal* #157 (March 1993), 3.
32   From annotations in *The Complete* Mad *Library*.
33   John Redmond Kelly, "The Fall of a Distributor," *Quest*, March 12, 1956, 3.
34   Groth and Decker, "An Interview with William M. Gaines," 60.
35   Benson, "A Conversation with Harvey Kurtzman and Bill Gaines," 88.
36   Harvey Kurtzman and Will Elder, *Playboy's Little Annie Fanny*, "Introduction" by Hugh Hefner (Illinois: Playboy Press, 1966), 5.
37   Hugh Hefner interview with author.
38   Ibid.
39   James, "Hey Look! An Interview with Harvey Kurtzman," 46.
40   There are three different versions of the cover of *Mad* #28. Each version can be identified by the verbiage in the yellow band on the lower right-hand corner of each version. The first version reads, "Spring Issue with very useful Income Tax Guide deductions, cheating, etc." The second reads, "Spring issue with a late and utterly useless Income Tax Guide deductions, cheating, etc. you should have tried." The third, "Spring Issue with enjoyable article on Guided Missiles and how they can blow up earth." The first also includes the initials "ACE," which stand for Ace Distributors. The second and third have the initials "ANC," which stand for American News. (Periodicals carried distributor initials so wholesalers could easily tell where they got them from, thus facilitating the return process.) Gaines initially made a distribution deal with Ace, but switched to American News in the middle of the press run. When the cover was altered to include the initials of American (ANC), it was decided that touting the Income Tax Guide was no longer timely (since the deadline for filing taxes at that time was March 15th) and the wording was changed. The reason for the switch from ACE to ANC: in the "Surprise" panel at the EC Convention (May 29, 1972), Gaines explained that he signed a contract with Ace, then found that wholesalers wouldn't handle *Mad* unless Gaines personally guaranteed responsibility for Leader News's debts. Since that was impossible, he scrambled and signed a deal with ANC, who was the owner and sole distributor to Union News, a company that had some 1,500 newsstands in premier display locations across the country. ANC/Union News didn't require Gaines to take responsibility for Leader News's debts. The third version of the cover of *Mad* #28 remains a mystery. Possibly American News

requested a second printing of the entire issue, since they had more outlets than Ace. This is pure supposition on the part of this author. Such are the confusing vagaries of the publishing business.

41 Jacobs, *The Mad World of William M. Gaines*, 120.

42 Kurtzman letter to Zolotar, February 20, 1962.

43 Adele Kurtzman, interview by Blake Bell for *I Have to Live with This Guy*: from the unedited transcript.

44 Jacobs, *The Mad World of William M. Gaines*, 120–1.

45 Steve Starger and J. David Spurlock, *Wally's World* (New Jersey: Vanguard Productions, 2006), 129. Gaines's willingness to offer 49 percent to Kurtzman is also related in Benson's "Roth & Jaffee" interview in *Humbug, Book One*, 214.

46 Kurtzman letter to Zolotar, November 3, 1962.

47 Hugh Hefner, interview with the author.

48 Jacobs, *The Mad World of William M. Gaines*, 121. While this seems to be a conversation that would logically occur before Gaines said "Goodbye, Harvey," Jacobs places it afterward. The story seems to have come from Stuart (whose company published Jacobs's book).

49 Ibid.

50 "Sassy Newcomer," *Time*, September 24, 1956.

51 Kurtzman letter to Zolotar, dated November 3, 1962.

52 Gaines continued the New Direction and started the Picto-Fiction books partly to give his staff work. Kurtzman had no patience with that thinking, which offended Gaines.

53 Wasserman, "Conversations with the Brother-in-Law of Underground Comix," 19.

54 Will Elder, interview by Gary Groth.

55 Bell, *I Have to Live with This Guy*, 90.

56 Groth and Thompson, "The Man Who Brought Truth to Comics," 117.

57 Larry Ivie, "Return to EC," *Hoohah!* #5 (September 1956), 33.

Chapter 18

1 Steven Watts, *Mr. Playboy, Hugh Hefner and the American Dream* (New Jersey: John Wiley & Sons, Inc., 2008), 71.

2 Harvey Kurtzman, interview by Hurd, 49.

3 Hugh Hefner, interview with author.

4 Ibid.

5 James, "Hey Look! An Interview with Harvey Kurtzman," 47. The exact amount of Kurtzman's stake in *Trump* is unknown, but has generally been thought to be a small or token amount, suggesting 5 percent or less.

6 Benson, "A Talk with Harvey Kurtzman," 31.

7 Benson, "A Conversation with Harvey Kurtzman, and . . . Arnold Roth and Al Jaffee," *Squa Tront* #10, 23. Recently, Jaffee wrote, in an email to the author, that he never made $22,000 or $24,000 a year at Timely, as he said in *Squa Tront* #10. He now says he's certain his maximum was around $15,000 a year at Timely Comics.

8 Will Elder, interview by Gary Groth.

9 Jacobs, *The Mad World of William M. Gaines*, 122.

10 Starger and Spurlock, *Wally's World*, 129.

11 Jacobs, *The Mad World of William M. Gaines*, 123.

12 Ibid, 123–4.

13 "Roth & Jaffee" interview by John Benson, *Humbug, Book One*, 196.

14 James, "Hey Look! An Interview with Harvey Kurtzman," 46.

15 Groth and Thompson, "The Man Who Brought Truth to Comics," 117.

16 Benson, "A Conversation with Harvey Kurtzman and Harry Chester, 44.

17 Jacobs, "*The Mad World of William M. Gaines*, 123.

18 Gaines letter to Kurtzman. From Kurtzman archives.

19 Arnold Roth, interview with author.

20 "Death to a Salesman" by Mel Brooks reused material from the movie *New Faces* (1954), which originated in the Broadway show.

21 Benson, "A Conversation with Harvey Kurtzman and Harry Chester, 42.
22 James, "Hey Look! An Interview with Harvey Kurtzman," 46.
23 Benson, "A Talk with Harvey Kurtzman," 31–2.
24 Barbara Nachman, "What, Him Worry?," *Suburban People*, Vol. 4 #22, July 9, 1989.
25 Watts, *Mr. Playboy*, 132.
26 Kurtzman and Elder, *Playboy's Little Annie Fanny*, Volume 1 (Oregon: Dark Horse Comics, 2000), 204. From annotations by Denis Kitchen: the Lyle Stuart quotation in *The Mad World of William M. Gaines*—that $250,000 was lost—was incorrect.
27 "Roth & Jaffee" interview by John Benson, *Humbug, Book One*, 185.
28 Jacobs, *The Mad World of William M. Gaines*, 126.
29 Kitchen and Buhle, *The Art of Harvey Kurtzman*, 123.
30 Hefner's interview with the author.
31 Groth and Thompson, "The Man Who Brought Truth to Comics," 117–8.
32 Ibid, 118.
33 Will Elder, interview by Gary Groth.
34 Benson, "A Conversation with Harvey Kurtzman and Harry Chester, 42.

Chapter 19

1 James, "Hey Look! An Interview with Harvey Kurtzman," 47.
2 Ibid.
3 Benson, "Roth & Jaffee," *Humbug, Book One*, 190.
4 Hefner letter to Kurtzman, April 17, 1957. All *Humbug* correspondence is from the Kurtzman archives.
5 Al Jaffee, interview with author.
6 Benson, "Roth & Jaffee," *Humbug, Book One*, 198.
7 Ibid, 190.
8 Ibid, 199–200.
9 John Benson, editor, "Larry Siegel Talks about Harvey Kurtzman," by Grant Geissman, *Squa Tront* #12, 24.
10 Adele Kurtzman, interviews by author.
11 Adele Kurtzman at memorial for Harvey, 1993.
12 Arnold Roth, interview with author, 2011.
13 Benson, "Roth & Jaffee," *Humbug, Book One*, 203-4.
14 According to a note written ca. 1958 by Kurtzman among legal papers pertaining to the EC/Gaines lawsuit.
15 Benson, "Roth & Jaffee," *Humbug, Book One*, 211.
16 Benson, "A Conversation with Harvey Kurtzman and Harry Chester," 42.
17 Gary Groth, "Take Five" interview with Arnold Roth, *The Comics Journal* #142 (June 1991), 70.
18 Kurtzman letter to Doodles Weaver, October 31, 1957.
19 Kurtzman letter to Ed Fisher, October 31, 1957.
20 Kurtzman letter to Ed Fisher, November 22, 1957.
21 Some suspect that "Rolf Malcolm" was a pen name for Ray Russell, who was a knowledgeable Kurtzman enthusiast who would have been the logical person to handle the article.
22 Al Jaffee described the trip in a December 2013 email. Other quotes in this account are derived from the "Introduction" in *Humbug, Book One*, xii-xiii; "A Conversation with Harvey Kurtzman and Harry Chester," *Squa Tront* #12, 42; "A Conversation with Harvey Kurtzman, and . . . Arnold Roth and Al Jaffee," *Squa Tront* #10, 28. Based on this interview, it's unclear how much money was in contention, or whether Jaffee and Roth put in another $3,000 to match the same amount from Santangelo.
23 Benson, "Roth & Jaffee," *Humbug, Book One*, 203.
24 Al Feldstein, interview with author.
25 Al Jaffee, interview with author.
26 Arnold Roth, interview with author.
27 Allan Adams letter to Kurtzman, March 10, 1958.
28 John Benson, "A Visit with Kurtzman," *Spoof* #4 (August 1958), 7, 8.

29   Groth and Thompson, "The Man Who Brought Truth to Comics," 118.
30   Ibid, 120.
31   Bell, *I Have to Live with This Guy*, 92.
32   Fred von Bernewitz, "Maddiction and Humbugging," *Spoof* #4, 13.
33   Harold Hayes's interview with Kurtzman on *Roundtable*, 1975.
34   James, "Hey Look! An Interview with Harvey Kurtzman," 47.
35   Benson, "Roth & Jaffee," *Humbug Book One*, 192.
36   Benson, "A Conversation with Harvey Kurtzman and Bill Gaines," 92.

Chapter 20

1   Kurtzman-Kane interview by John Benson: unpublished.
2   John Benson, "A Visit with . . . Kurtzman," *Spoof* #4 (August 1958), 6, *7*.
3   Ringgenberg, "Memories Most Mad," 19.
4   John Benson and Larry Ivie, "Another Visit with . . . Kurtzman," *Squa Tront* #10, 40.
5   Ringgenberg, "Memories Most Mad," 19.
6   Harold Hayes letter to Steve Allen, May 9, 1958. From the Kurtzman archives.
7   Proposal for Seymour Mednick TV show: from Kurtzman archives.
8   Denis Kitchen, "Man, I'm Beat!," *Comic Art* #7 (Winter 2005), 3.
9   Ibid.
10   Ibid, 7.
11   Ibid.
12   Ray Russell letter to Kurtzman, December 23, 1958; From Kurtzman archives.
13   Denis Kitchen, "Man, I'm Beat!," *Comic Art* #7, 8.
14   Kitchen, Playboy's *Little Annie Fanny*, Volume 1, 204.
15   Geissman, "A Talk with Adele Kurtzman," 188.
16   Kurtzman's notes for a proposed article, titled "Designing Covers for Paper-Backs, or You Can't Tell a Cover by its Book."
17   Dave Schreiner, "Outro," *Harvey Kurtzman's Jungle Book* (Wisconsin: Kitchen Sink Press, 1986), xi.
18   Kurtzman letter to Ian Ballantine, May 20, 1958. From the Kurtzman archives.
19   Harris Shevelson letter to Kurtzman, January 20, 1959. From the Kurtzman archives.
20   Kurtzman letter to Carl Rogers, February 11, 1959: from the Kurtzman archives.
21   Adele Kurtzman, interview by Blake Bell for *I Have to Live with This Guy*: from the unedited transcript.
22   David Kravitz, "Calling . . . . Kurtzman," *Squatront* #2 (Fall 1959), 12.
23   Adele Kurtzman can no longer remember the name of the friend.
24   In *The Art of Harvey Kurtzman*, Kitchen and Buhle state that *Harvey Kurtzman's Pleasure Book* would have been the title of the aborted follow-up to *Harvey Kurtzman's Jungle Book*, but the date of the *Pleasure Book* contract, over six months *before* Kurtzman finished *Jungle Book*, seems to more likely indicate that *Pleasure Book* was a working title for the first (and, as it turned out, only) Ballantine original paperback by Kurtzman.
25   "Outro," *Harvey Kurtzman's Jungle Book*, xii.
26   Ibid, xi.
27   Art Spiegelman, "Intro," *Harvey Kurtzman's Jungle Book* (Wisconsin: Kitchen Sink Press, 1986), vii, viii. *Kitchen Sink Press, The First 25 Years*, viii.
28   "Outro," *Harvey Kurtzman's Jungle Book*, xii.
29   Ibid, xi.
30   Ballantine sales report, 1963.
31   "The great system in the sky" quotation from James, "Hey Look! An Interview with Harvey Kurtzman," 51.
32   Price letter undated: from the Kurtzman archives.
33   John Benson and Larry Ivie, "Another Visit with . . . Kurtzman," *Squa Tront* #10, 40.
34   Adele Kurtzman, interview by Blake Bell for *I Have to Live with This Guy*: from the unedited transcript.

Chapter 21

1   James Warren's interview with the author (January 2014), informs much of this chapter.
2   Benson, "A Conversation with Harvey Kurtzman and Harry Chester," 44. Warren denied ever bringing hamburgers up to the office in the unpublished interview conducted by Gary Groth and Mike Catron. *Humbug* moved its offices from the *Trump* brownstone to 598 Madison Ave. circa July 1957, so Warren must have met Kurtzman in July or August 1957, even if there were no hamburgers involved.
3   James Warren, interview by Gary Groth and Mike Catron: unpublished.
4   Both quotations in this paragraph from Jim Warren, interview with author.
5   James Warren, interview by Gary Groth and Mike Catron: unpublished. The $150,000 figure seems questionable, and Warren could no longer remember how he got that figure when asked about it by the author.
6   Denis Kitchen, interview with the author, November 2011.
7   Harold Hayes's interview with Kurtzman on *Roundtable*, 1975.
8   Gloria Steinem at memorial for Kurtzman, 1993.
9   Ibid.
10 S. C. Ringgenberg, "Memories Most Mad," 18.
11 Ibid, 18–9.
12 Benson, "A Conversation with Harvey Kurtzman and Harry Chester," *Squa Tront* #12, 44.
13 Ibid.
14 Ron Harris, interview with August 2012.
15 James, "Hey Look! An Interview with Harvey Kurtzman," 48.
16 Jim Warren, interview with author.
17 S. C. Ringgenberg, "Memories Most Mad," 19.
18 Ron Harris, interview with author.
19 Dave Sim, Kurtzman interview, *Comic Art News and Reviews (CANAR)* Vol. 3 #25, September 1974, 3.
20 Jim Warren, interview with author.
21 Benson, "A Talk with Harvey Kurtzman," 31.
22 *Sick* left ICD and went with PDC in order to get a larger cash advance, beginning with its fourth issue.
23 Unpublished Warren interview by Groth and Catron. All quotes and description of this incident are from this interview.
24 Jim Warren, interview with author, 2014.
25 Unpublished Warren interview by Groth and Catron.
26 Ibid.
27 S. C. Ringgenberg, "Memories Most Mad," 19.
28 Unpublished Warren interview by Groth and Catron.
29 Meredith Kurtzman, interview with author.
30 Liz Kurtzman, interview with author.
31 Bell, *I Have to Live with This Guy*, 97.
32 Meredith Kurtzman, interview with author.
33 Liz Kurtzman, interview with author.
34 Ibid.
35 Meredith Kurtzman, interview with author.
36 Adele Kurtzman, interviews by author.
37 Geissman, "A Talk with Adele Kurtzman," 190.
38 John Benson, "An Interview with Jim Warren," *Squa Tront* #10, 46.
39 Benson, "A Talk with Harvey Kurtzman," 17.
40 Groth and Thompson, "The Man Who Brought Truth to Comics," 122.
41 Unpublished Warren interview by Groth and Catron.
42 Ibid.
43 Benson, "A Conversation with Harvey Kurtzman and Harry Chester," *Squa Tront* #12, 46.
44 Hefner's interview with the author.
45 Ibid.

46   "Goodman Meets T*rz*n" is labeled "Chapter II" because "The Organization Man" in *Harvey Kurtzman's Jungle Book* was Beaver's first appearance.
47   Benson, "A Talk with Harvey Kurtzman," 34.
48   Ibid, 32.
49   Letter from Archie attorney Benjamin E. Winston to *Help!* Magazine, Inc., December 6, 1961.
50   From the unedited transcript of his interview with Adele Kurtzman that appeared in *I Have to Live with This Guy.*
51   Benson, "A Talk with Harvey Kurtzman," 34.
52   Harvey Kurtzman and Will Elder, *Goodman Beaver* (Wisconsin: Kitchen Sink Press, 1984), 92.
53   Joe Pilati, "Afterthoughts on a man and a program," *Smudge* #3, May 1962, 10.
54   Quotations in this chapter from author's interview with Gilbert Shelton.
55   Gardner went on to cowrite scripts with writer Dee Caruso for *The Monkees*, *Get Smart* and other television shows.
56   From the unedited transcript of his interview with Adele Kurtzman that appeared in *I Have to Live with This Guy.*
57   Terry Gilliam at memorial for Kurtzman, 1993.
58   Ibid.
59   Gilliam letter to Kurtzman, July 25, 1962.
60   Terry Gilliam at memorial for Kurtzman, 1993.
61   Ibid.
62   Ibid.

Chapter 22

1   S. C. Ringgenberg, "Memories Most Mad," 19.
2   Kitchen, *Playboy's Little Annie Fanny,* Vol. 1, 2000), 208.
3   Ibid, 209.
4   Ibid.
5   Groth, "The Will Elder Interview," *The Comics Journal* website.
6   Though the *Playboy* strip would bear a resemblance to the racy novel *Candy* by Terry Southern and Mason Hoffenberg—also a modern version of *Candide*—there's no evidence that it influenced Kurtzman's thinking, or even that he read it.
7   "I never saw . . . sex theme," from Wasserman, "Conversations with the Brother-in-Law of Underground Comix," 23. "I've slowly been coming . . . earliest years," from Benson, "A Talk with Harvey Kurtzman," 34.
8   Hefner letter to Kurtzman, May 10, 1962. From the Kurtzman archives.
9   Bill Stout, interview with author, 2012.
10   Harvey Kurtzman, interview by Jacques Dutrey: unpublished.
11   Marilyn Monroe's character in *The Seven Year Itch* worked as a model in toothpaste ads for television.
12   Hefner's interview with the author.
13   Will Elder, interview by Gary Groth, tcj.com.
14   Hefner's interview with the author.
15   Benson, "A Conversation with Harvey Kurtzman and Bill Elder," 76.
16   Russ Heath, interview with author, 2011.
17   Terry Gilliam at memorial for Kurtzman, 1993. Others who assisted editorially on *Help!* were George Kirgo and Myrna Dressler.
18   Ringgenberg, "Memories Most Mad," 19.
19   Bell, *I Have to Live with This Guy,* 95-7.
20   Terry Gilliam at memorial for Kurtzman, 1993.
21   Ibid.
22   Jim Warren, interview with author.
23   Ibid.
24   Mark Lewisohn, email to author.
25   Wasserman, "Conversations with the Brother-in-Law of Underground Comix," 19.
26   Jean-Pierre Mercier, *R. Crumb Conversations* (Mississippi: University Press of Mississippi, 2004), 205.

27   Kitchen and Buhle, *The Art of Harvey Kurtzman*, iii.
28   Ringgenberg, "Memories Most Mad," 19.
29   Al Davoren, *R. Crumb Conversations* (Mississippi: University Press of Mississippi, 2004), 44.
30   Ibid, 205–6.
31   Kurtzman later said that while *Monty Python's Flying Circus* amused him, he couldn't relate to much of the humor because "it was very literate." He liked the work of Gilliam and Cleese, but not so much Eric Idle, Graham Chapman and Terry Jones. "Jones's humor wasn't my kind of humor." From *Comics Scene* #47, 58.
32   Terry Gilliam at memorial for Kurtzman, 1993.
33   Gary Groth, "One of My Main Reasons to go on Living is I Still Think I Haven't Done My Best Work," Robert Crumb Interview, *The Comics Journal Library*, Vol. 3 (Washington: Fantagraphics Books, Inc., 2004), 24.
34   J. Michael Catron, "An Interview with Archie Goodwin," *Blazing Combat* (Washington: Fantagraphics Books, Inc., 2009), 207.
35   Jim Warren, interview with author.
36   Harvey Kurtzman, interview with Harold Hayes on *Roundtable*, 1975.
37   All quotes in the section from Benson, "A Talk with Harvey Kurtzman," 21-37.
38   Kurtzman note to John Benson, June 13, 1967. From the Kurtzman archives.
39   Terry Gilliam, "My Mad Mentor: Terry Gilliam on Harvey Kurtzman," www. telegraph.co.uk, July 10, 2009.
40   Benson, "The '72 EC War Panel," 71.
41   Adele Kurtzman, interviews by author.
42   Harvey Kurtzman, interview by Jacques Dutrey: unpublished.
43   Adele Kurtzman, interviews by author.
44   Walter Bernard, interview with author, 2012.
45   Barbara Nessim, interview with author, 2012.
46   Hefner, interview with author.
47   Benson, "Roth & Jaffee," *Humbug, Book One*, 207.
48   Ibid.
49   Ibid, 207–8.
50   The story reportedly showed Hefner as a hero who ripped off his clothes to reveal himself as Super-Bunny: from Skip Williamson's interview with author.

Part Three: Icon

1   Gary Groth, editor, "Harvey Kurtzman," *The Comics Journal* #157, 12.

Chapter 23

1   M. Thomas Inge, "Harvey Kurtzman and Modern American Satire," .http://classic.tcj.com/history/m-thomas-inge-harvey-kurtzman-and-modern-american-satire-part-one-of-two/, March 15, 2010.
2   R. C. Harvey, *Art of the Comic Book* (Mississippi: University of Mississippi Press, 1996), 140.
3   Harvey Kurtzman, et al, *Harvey Kurtzman's Strange Adventures* (New York: Epic Comics, 1990), 4.
4   Harold Hayes's interview with Kurtzman on *Roundtable*, 1975.
5   Mark James Estren, *A History of Underground Comics* (California: Ronin Publishing, Inc., 1993), 41.
6   Jay Lynch, interview with the author.
7   Patrick Rosencrantz, *Rebel Visions* (Washington: Fantagraphics Books, Inc., 2008), 34.
8   Skip Williamson, interview with author.
9   Art Spiegelman, "Harvey Kurtzman par Art Spiegelman" video, at www.youtube.com/watch?v=whi0Fcjs820.
10   *A History of Underground Comics*, 41–2.
11   Dez Skinn, *Comix The Underground Revolution* (New York: Thunder's Mouth Press, 2004), 220.

12   Ibid, 42.
13   Wasserman, "Conversations with the Brother-in-Law of Underground Comix,"
     22.
14   Ibid.
15   Ibid.
16   Groth, "One of My Main Reasons to go on Living is I Still Think I Haven't Done
     My Best Work," Robert Crumb Interview, 26–7.
17   Kurtzman letter to Gahan Wilson, May 16, 1967. From the Kurtzman archives.
18   Liz Kurtzman, interview with author.
19   Bill Barnes, interview with author, 2011.
20   Jacobs, *The Mad World of William M. Gaines*, 126-7.
21   Estren, *A History of Underground Comics*, 67.
22   Ibid, 39.
23   Kim Deitch, email to author, 2012.
24   Skip Willimason, interview with author.
25   Kim Deitch, email to author.
26   Estren, *A History of Underground Comics*, 295.
27   Bell, *I Have to Live with This Guy*, 95.
28   Quotations in this paragraph from Geissman, "Larry Siegel Talks about Harvey
     Kurtzman," 23.
29   Spectorsky letter to Kurtzman, July 16, 1968. From the Kurtzman archives.
30   Ibid.
31   Ibid.
32   Kurtzman letter to Spectorsky, July 21, 1968. From the Kurtzman archives.
33   Geissman, "Larry Siegel Talks about Harvey Kurtzman," 27.
34   S. C. Ringgenberg, "The Kurtzman Cometh," *Heavy Metal* (November 1985), 10.
35   Gloria Steinem, "What *Playboy* Doesn't Know about Women Could Fill a Book,"
     McCall's (October 1970).
36   Ladybelle McFarlin interview, 2011.
37   Quotations from the panel at Goddard College are from Estren, *A History of
     Underground Comics*, 294–300.
38   Ladybelle McFarlin, interview with author.
39   Gilbert Shelton, interview with author.
40   Liz Kurtzman, interview with author.
41   Groth and Thompson, "The Man Who Brought Truth to Comics," 123.

Chapter 24

1   Kurtzman-Kane interview by Benson: unpublished.
2   Ibid.
3   Harvey Kurtzman, interview by Jacques Dutrey: unpublished.
4   Roger Sabin, *Art Spiegelman Conversations* (Mississippi: University Press of
     Mississippi, 2007), 96.
5   Byron Dobell, interview with author, 2012.
6   Al Davoren, "What I Think of All the Foolish Nonsense I've Been Involved In," *R.
     Crumb Conversations* (Mississippi: University Press of Mississippi, 2004), 64–5.
7   Ibid, 67.
8   Denis Kitchen, "Confessions of an Underground Comics Publisher," *Funnyworld*
     #13, (Spring 1971), 295.
9   Denis Kitchen, interview with the author.
10   Ibid.
11   Dave Schreiner, *Kitchen Sink Press The First 25 Years* (Wisconsin: Kitchen Sink
     Press, 1994), 21–2.
12   Robert Crumb, interview with the author, 2014.
13   Robert Crumb, "Crumb on Hefner and Harvey Kurtzman," www.crumbproducts.
     com.
14   Quotations from Skip Williamson in this paragraph are from "Interview [with
     Skip Williamson," www.thedailycrosshatch.com, March 1, 2007.
15   Jay Lynch, interview with author.
16   Ibid.
17   Robert Crumb, interview with author.

18   Crumb, "Crumb on Hefner and Harvey Kurtzman," www.crumbproducts.com.
19   Robert Crumb, interview with author.
20   Benson, "A Conversation with Harvey Kurtzman and Harry Chester," *Squa Tront* #12, 43.
21   Kitchen and Buhle, *The Art of Harvey Kurtzman*, 212.
22   Quotations in this section are from Bill Stout's interview with author.
23   Al Jaffee, "Dinner at Elaine's," *The Comics Journal Library*, Vol.7: *Harvey Kurtman*, 54.
24   Jacobs, *The Mad World of William M. Gaines*, 127.
25   Wasserman, Conversations with the Brother-in-Law of Underground Comix," 19.
26   Barlow, "Harvey Kurtzman," *EC Lives!*, 9.
27   Benson, "The '72 EC War Panel," 71.
28   John Benson, email to the author.
29   Kurtzman was angry when he read that Lyle Stuart had recommended that Gaines fire Kurtzman: Stuart told Gaines to "throw him out the window." But Kurtzman's anger didn't extend to Gaines or *The Mad World of William M. Gaines*.
30   Dave Sim, Kurtzman interview, *Comic Art News and Review*, Vol. 3 #1 (September 1974), 3. Sim interviewed Kurtzman at York University.
31   Roy Thomas wrote about the incident in an email to the author.
32   Kurtzman-Kane interview by Benson: unpublished.
33   Lee Wochner, "Catching Up With Kurtzman," *The Comic Journal Library*, Vol. 7: *Harvey Kurtzman*, 130.
34   Michael C. Gross, interview with the author, 2012.
35   Ibid.
36   Durwood, "Harvey Kurtzman interviewed by T. Durwood," 26.
37   Michael C. Gross, interview with the author.
38   John Benson's "January 3, 1975," comic con tape, probably in New York.
39   Kurtzman panel in Grenoble, 1989, translated by Jacques Dutrey.
40   Arnold Roth, interview with author.
41   *Jungle Book* was reprinted in 1978 in Europe with disappointing sales, per Jacques Dutrey.
42   Harvey Kurtzman, interview by Jacques Dutrey: unpublished.
43   Bill Basso, email to author.
44   Adele Kurtzman, interview by Blake Bell for *I Have to Live with This Guy*: from the unedited transcript.
45   Bell, *I Have to Live with This Guy*, 97.
46   Geissman, "A Talk with Adele Kurtzman," 189.
47   Gary Brown, "The 1975 Newcon Mural," *Ibid* #277, *CAPA-alpha* #535, April 2009, 4–7.
48   Kitchen and Buhle, *The Art of Harvey Kurtzman*, xi.
49   Mike Gold, "Jenette Kahn, Stan Lee, and Harvey Kurtzman Discuss Comics," *Stan Lee Conversations* (Mississippi: University Press of Mississippi, 2007), 41.
50   Ibid, 43–4.
51   Nellie Kurtzman, interview with the author, 2011.
52   Unedited manuscript of Blake Bell's interview with Adele Kurtzman for *I Have to Live with This Guy*.
53   Harvey Kurtzman, interview by Jacques Dutrey: unpublished.
54   Bill Stout, interview with author.
55   Denis Kitchen, interview with author.
56   James, "Hey Look! An Interview with Harvey Kurtzman," 43.
57   Benson, "A Conversation with Harvey Kurtzman and Bill Elder," 79.
58   Groth and Thompson, "The Man Who Brought Truth to Comics," 123.
59   Benson, "A Conversation with Harvey Kurtzman and Bill Elder," 77.
60   Ibid, 78.
61   Harvey, *Art of the Comic Book*, 140.
62   Skip Williamson, interview with author.
63   Benson, "A Conversation with Harvey Kurtzman and Bill Elder," 73.
64   All quotations in this paragraph are from Skip Williamson, interview with author.
65   Phil Felix, Denis Kitchen, interview with author.

66   Note from Kurtzman to Benson, November 8, 1971.
67   Harvey Kurtzman, interview by Jacques Dutrey: unpublished.

Chapter 25

1   David Pomerantz, interview with author. All quotations in this chapter from Pomerantz are derived from this interview.
2   Adele Kurtzman, interview by Shaun Clancy: unpublished.
3   Hurd, "Kurtzman" interview, 46.
4   David Pomerantz, interview with author.
5   Sarah Downs, interview with author. All quotations in this chapter from Downs derived from this interview.
6   Mark Newgarden, email to author, 2011.
7   Harvey Kurtzman, interview by Jacques Dutrey: unpublished.
8   John Holmstrom, interview with author, 2013.
9   Batton Lash emails to author. All quotations from Lash in this chapter derived from this series of emails.
10   From Pomerantz.
11   It was "The Return of a Christmas Carol," *Esquire* (December 1961).
12   Pomerantz provided material in this paragraph.
13   Marshall Arisman, email to author.
14   Hurd, "Kurtzman" interview, 46.
15   Ibid.
16   Robert Crumb, interview with author.
17   Drew Friedman, interview with author. All quotations in this chapter from Friedman derived from this interview.
18   Groth and Thompson, "The Man Who Brought Truth to Comics," 107.
19   Dr. Nando Pelusi, interview with author.
20   Ibid.
21   Mark Newgarden, email to author.
22   Ibid.
23   John Kelly, "Kaz" interview, *The Comics Journal* #186 (April 1996), 118.
24   Ibid.
25   Pelusi, interview with author.
26   Benson, "A Conversation with Harvey Kurtzman and Bill Elder," 76.
27   Phil Felix, email to author. All quotations in this chapter from Felix are from this interview.
28   John Workman, email to author.
29   Ibid.

Chapter 26

1   Sarah Downs, interview with author. All quotations from Downs in this chapter are from that interview. It's her description of how *Betsy's Buddies* was created.
2   Harvey Kurtzman, interview by Jacques Dutrey: unpublished.
3   Chip Selby, *Tales from the Crypt: From Comic Books to Television* [video], 2004.
4   Gary Groth, "Kurtzman, Kane, and a Career in Comics," Kurtzman and Kane interviewed at the Dallas Fantasy Fair in 1988, *The Comics Journal* #157 (March 1993), 16.
5   Russ Cochran email. He wrote, "The print runs on titles in the Complete EC Library varied quite a bit, reflecting the fact that EC's horror comics were always the most popular, followed by science fiction and then followed by war comics. On some of the horror titles, there were 10,000 sets printed and sold."
6   Quotes from unedited transcript of John Benson's interview for *The Complete Two-Fisted Tales Library*.
7   Story from John Benson.
8   Groth and Thompson, "The Man Who Brought Truth to Comics," 83.
9   Nellie Kurtzman, interview with author. All quotations from her in this chapter are from that interview.
10   Adele Kurtzman, interviews by author.
11   Robert Crumb, interview with author.

12   Adele Kurtzman, interviews by author.
13   Liz Kurtzman, interview with author.
14   Meredith Kurtzman, interview with author.
15   Adele Kurtzman, interviews by author.
16   Ibid.
17   Jay Lynch, interview with author.
18   Groth, "Harvey Kurtzman" tribute, *The Comics Journal* #157 (March 1993), 7.
19   "Goodman Goes Playboy" was eventually reprinted in full in *The Comics Journal* #262 (August–September 2004), with no legal repercussions.
20   Cooke, Jon B., "The Comix Book Life of Denis Kitchen," *Comic Book Creator* #5, Bonus PDF edition, Spring 2014, www.twomorrows.com/freestuff, 6.
21   Don Thompson and Maggie Thompson, "Harvey Kurtzman The Modest Genius" tribute, *Comics Buyer's Guide* #1011, April 2, 1993, 36.
22   Ibid.
23   Denis Kitchen, interview with author.
24   Geissman, "Larry Siegel Talks about Harvey Kurtzman," 24–5.
25   Ibid.
26   S. C. Ringgenberg, "The Kurtzman Cometh," *Heavy Metal* (November 1985), 10.
27   Wochner, "Catching up with Kurtzman," 133.
28   Harry Matetsky, interview with author, 2014. All quotations from Matetsky in this chapter are from that interview.
29   Kurtzman circa the 1980s, according to Gary Groth in 2014.
30   Drew Friedman, interview with author.
31   "Catching up with Kurtzman," 131.
32   Adele Kurtzman, interview by John Benson, 2002.
33   John Ficarra, email to author.
34   Will Elder, interview by Gary Groth.
35   Phil Felix, interview with author.
36   Adele Kurtzman, interviews with author.
37   Howard Zimmerman, interview with author. All quotations from Zimmerman in this chapter are from that interview.
38   From Jack Davis-Harvey Kurtzman panel at the 1985 San Diego Comic-Con.
39   Kevin Sacco, email to author.
40   Art Spiegelman, "Intro," *Harvey Kurtzman's Jungle Book* (Wisconsin: Kitchen Sink Press, 1986, vii, viii.
41   Schreiner, *Kitchen Sink Press The First 25 Years*, 78–9.
42   Groth, "Comics Sans Frontiéres," 148.
43   Will Elder, interview by Gary Groth.
44   Paul McSpadden, interview with author.
45   From Neil Gaiman's speech at the 2004 Harvey Awards ceremony.
46   Byron Preiss, "Harvey Kurtzman Today," *The Comics Journal* #153 (October 1992), 57.
47   Art Spiegelman, "Introduction," *Harvey Kurtzman's Strange Adventures* (New York: Epic Comic, 1990), 4.
48   Email from Jacques Dutrey.
49   Jacques Dutrey, "Grenoble Spotlights Kurtzman, Calvo," *The Comics Journal* #130 (July 1989), 44.
50   Kurtzman and European cartoonists panel, Grenoble, March 17, 1989: from unpublished transcript translated by Dutrey.
51   Alan Moore, "Harvey Kurtzman" tribute, *The Comics Journal* #157 (March 1993), 11.
52   Eric Palma, email to author.
53   Michael Vance, email to author.

Chapter 27

1   Groth, "Comics Sans Frontiéres," 149.
2   Adele Kurtzman, interviews by author.
3   Michael Barrier, interview by author, as is the other quotation in this paragraph.
4   Howard Zimmerman, interview with author.
5   Preiss, "Harvey Kurtzman Today," 58.

6   Ibid.
7   Kurtzman, *From Aargh! to Zap*, 93–4. The author compared this text with the material in Barrier's notes from his interview with Kurtzman, and it matches word for word.
8   Bell, *I Have to Live with This Guy*, 99.
9   Robert Crumb, interview with author. All quotations by Crumb in this chapter are from this interview.
10   Preiss, "Harvey Kurtzman Today," 57.
11   Ibid.
12   Tom DeHaven, Entertainmentweekly.com, March 29, 1991.
13   Darcy Sullivan, "The Hoo Hah is Gone," *The Comics Journal* #141 (April 1991), 65.
14   Benson, "A Talk with Harvey Kurtzman," 27–8.
15   Barrier's notes for *From Aargh! to Zap*.
16   Bell, *I Have to Live with This Guy*, 100–1.
17   Interview transcript for *My Life as a Cartoonist*.
18   All quotations from Bill Stout, interview with author.
19   Liz Kurtzman, interview with author. All quotes by Liz in this chapter are from this interview.
20   Adele Kurtzman, interviews with author.
21   Ibid.
22   Barbara Nessim, interview with author.
23   Hugh Hefner, interview with author.
24   Nellie Kurtzman, interview with author.
25   Preiss, "Harvey Kurtzman Today," 58–9.
26   Ibid.
27   Alison Porter, interview by author. All quotationses by Porter in this chapter are from this interview.
28   Adele Kurtzman, interview by Shaun Clancy: unpublished.
29   Kurtzman letter to Jacques Dutrey.
30   Ibid.
31   Irene Chester, interview with author.
32   James, "Hey Look! An Interview with Harvey Kurtzman," 51.
33   Batton Lash, emails to author.
34   Kurtzman letter to Dutrey.
35   Schreiner, *Kitchen Sink Press The First 25 Years*, 78.
36   Efforts to organize Kurtzman's papers and artwork began as early as 1986.
37   Adele Kurtzman, letter to Jacques Dutrey.
38   Preiss, "Harvey Kurtzman Today," 58–9. Dark Horse is listed as the publisher in the comic book.
39   Matt Wagner, "It Burns Him Up," *The Comics Journal* #179 (August 1995), 1, 2. All Wagner quotes are from this article.
40   Byron Preiss at Kurtzman Memorial service.
41   Phil Felix, interview with the author.
42   Ibid.
43   Sarah Downs, interview with the author.
44   "It Burns Him Up," 2.
45   Denis Kitchen, interview with the author. All quotes by Kitchen in this chapter are from this interview.
46   Adele Kurtzman, interviews by author.

Chapter 28

1   Benson, "A Talk with Harvey Kurtzman," 2–8.
2   Geissman, "A Talk with Adele Kurtzman," 189.

INDEX